This book is Kerry V. Donnelly's updated version of William A. Bruette's classic first published in 1921. It should not be confused with any official publication of the American Kennel Club.

ONLY
$6.95

The Original
Complete Dog Book

Dr. William A. Bruette
and
Kerry V. Donnelly

Photo credits: frontispiece by Sally Anne Thompson; photos pages 33, 79, 91, 98, 101, 111, 119, 152 (below), 157, 160, 162, 174, 299, 396, 411, 416, 420, 453, 461, 495 by Anne Roslin-Williams; page 545 courtesy of Mrs. Betty Hyslop.

ISBN 0-87666-667-5

© 1979 by T.F.H. Publications, Inc. Ltd.

Distributed in the U.S. by T.F.H. Publications, Inc., 211 West Sylvania Avenue, P.O. Box 427, Neptune, N.J. 07753; in England by T.F.H. (Gt. Britain) Ltd., 13 Nutley Lane, Reigate, Surrey; in Canada to the book store and library trade by Clarke, Irwin & Company, Clarwin House, 791 St. Clair Avenue West, Toronto 10, Ontario; in Canada to the pet trade by Rolf C. Hagen Ltd., 3225 Sartelon Street, Montreal 382, Quebec; in Southeast Asia by Y.W. Ong, 9 Lorong 36 Geylang, Singapore 14; in Australia and the South Pacific by Pet Imports Pty. Ltd., P.O. Box 149, Brookvale 2100, N.S.W., Australia; in South Africa by Valiant Publishers (Pty.) Ltd., P.O. Box 78236, Sandton City, 2146, South Africa; Published by T.F.H. Publications, Inc., Ltd., The British Crown Colony of Hong Kong.

Contents

NOTE: Included in the contents listing for each breed are the current retail prices in effect in the greater New York area. Of course, these prices will vary depending on area, season, popularity trends, and the individual breeders.

Foreword...7
Introduction: The Origin of the Dog..............................9

THE BREEDS

GROUP 1: SPORTING DOGS............................... 15-113

Pointer, $325	15	Spaniel, Brittany, $275	66
Pointer, German Shorthaired, $300	19	Spaniel, Clumber, $395	71
Pointer, German Wirehaired, $350	24	Spaniel, Cocker, $250	74
Retriever, Chesapeake Bay, $450	28	Spaniel, English Cocker, $300	79
Retriever, Curly-Coated, $480	33	Spaniel, English Springer, $325	84
Retriever, Flat-Coated, $425	36	Spaniel, Field, $350	91
Retriever, Golden, $350	39	Spaniel, Irish Water, $580	94
Retriever, Labrador, $325	43	Spaniel, Sussex, $375	98
Setter, English, $300	47	Spaniel, Welsh Springer, $425	101
Setter, Gordon, $375	51	Vizsla, $375	104
Setter, Irish, $300	57	Weimaraner, $385	107
Spaniel Family	61	Wirehaired	
Spaniel, American Water, $350	63	Pointing Griffon, $425	111

GROUP 2: HOUNDS....................................... 114-190

Afghan Hound, $375	114	Greyhound, $425	157
Basenji, $325	119	Harrier, $365	160
Basset Hound, $250	122	Ibizan Hound, $500	162
Beagle, $175	127	Irish Wolfhound, $600	166
Black and Tan Coonhound, $450	132	Norwegian Elkhound, $325	170
Bloodhound, $500	135	Otter Hound, $450	174
Borzoi, $425	139	Rhodesian Ridgeback, $325	177
Dachshund, $245	143	Saluki, $425	180
Foxhound, American, $300	151	Scottish Deerhound, $475	183
Foxhound, English, $325	151	Whippet, $380	187

GROUP 3: WORKING DOGS...191-347

Akita, $450	191	Great Pyrenees, $485	278
Alaskan Malamute, $425	195	Komondor, $590	282
Bearded Collie, $385	200	Kuvasz, $475	286
Belgian Malinois, $375	205	Mastiff, $450	290
Belgian Sheepdog, $350	209	Newfoundland, $500	294
Belgian Tervuren, $425	214	Old English Sheepdog, $395	299
Bernese Mountain Dog, $400	220	Puli, $425	302
Bouvier des Flandres, $375	223	Rottweiler, $550	306
Boxer, $325	228	Saint Bernard, $475	310
Briard, $375	235	Samoyed, $375	316
Bullmastiff, $425	241	Shetland Sheepdog, $325	322
Collie, $300	244	Siberian Husky, $450	328
Doberman Pinscher, $475	251	Standard Schnauzer, $350	334
German Shepherd Dog, $425	256	Welsh Corgi, Cardigan, $320	339
Giant Schnauzer, $475	264	Welsh Corgi, Pembroke, $300	343
Great Dane, $425	269		

GROUP 4: TERRIERS..348-441

Airedale Terrier, $365	348	Manchester Terrier, $300	401
American Staffordshire Terrier, $285	352	Miniature Schnauzer, $325	405
Australian Terrier, $300	355	Norfolk Terrier, $280	410
Bedlington Terrier, $345	358	Norwich Terrier, $280	410
Border Terrier, $265	362	Scottish Terrier, $300	416
Bull Terrier, $250	367	Sealyham Terrier, $400	420
Cairn Terrier, $250	371	Skye Terrier, $375	423
Dandie Dinmont Terrier, $300	375	Soft-Coated Wheaten Terrier, $310	428
Fox Terrier, $225	380	Staffordshire Bull Terrier, $275	432
Irish Terrier, $325	387	Welsh Terrier, $250	435
Kerry Blue Terrier, $350	392	West Highland White Terrier, $310	438
Lakeland Terrier, $280	396		

GROUP 5: TOY DOGS..442-497

Affenpinscher, $325	442	Papillon, $275	474
Brussels Griffon, $380	445	Pekingese, $290	478
Chihuahua, $270	449	Pomeranian, $345	481
English Toy Spaniel, $375	453	Poodle (Toy), $350	485
Italian Greyhound, $400	458	Pug, $325	486
Japanese Chin, $325	461	Shih Tzu, $375	489
Maltese, $375	464	Silky Terrier, $300	492
Manchester Terrier (Toy), $300	467	Yorkshire Terrier, $400	495
Miniature Pinscher, $310	469		

GROUP 6: NON-SPORTING DOGS............................498-543

Bichon Frise, $320	498	Keeshond, $300	523
Boston Terrier, $270	502	Lhasa Apso, $400	528
Bulldog, $380	506	Poodle, $400	531
Chow Chow, $400	512	Schipperke, $325	537
Dalmatian, $325	515	Tibetan Terrier, $410	540
French Bulldog, $275	519		

DOG CARE

A guide to health care, training, breeding and showing............545-601

The New Puppy...546
    Preparing for puppy's arrival . . . Male or female? . . . Show dog or pet? . . . Where to buy your puppy . . . Signs of good health . . . Papers . . . Registering . . . Puppy's first night with you . . . Puppy's bed . . . Feeding . . . Transitional diet . . . Breaking to collar and leash . . . Disciplining . . . Housebreaking . . . All dogs need to chew

Training..556
    When to start . . . Your part in training . . . Training voice . . . Lessons . . . Equipment . . . "Heel" . . . "Sit" . . . "Lie down" . . . "Stay" . . . "Come" . . . "Stand" . . . Training schools . . . Classes . . . Advanced training and obedience trials

Breeding..564
    Spaying . . . Sexual physiology . . . The female in estrus . . . Should you breed your male? (female?) . . . When to breed . . . Selection of stud . . . Preparing to breed . . . Genetics . . . Dominance and recessiveness

Care of the Mother and Family......................................578
    Prenatal care of the female . . . Preparing whelping quarters . . . Supplies to have on hand . . . Whelping . . . Caesarean section . . . Eclampsia . . . A large litter . . . Raising and airing the puppies . . . Worming . . . Puppy socialization

Health...586
    Watching your puppy's health . . . The thermometer . . . Emergency first aid . . . Inoculations . . . Hip Dysplasia . . . Coughs and colds . . . Diabetes Mellitus . . . Parasites . . . Skin ailments . . . Eyes, ears, teeth and nails . . . The aged dog . . . Tattooing

Showing...598
    How to select a show dog . . . Types of dog shows . . . How to enter . . . Junior showmanship . . . Advanced preparation . . . The day of the show

Index...603
Suggested bibliography..608

Acknowledgments

Many thanks to Diane McCarty for supplying words when they would not come, and to Beverly Pisano for her proofreading expertise. I would like to thank those national specialty clubs that took the time to submit photos to serve as representatives of their breed, thereby ensuring that a top quality specimen illustrates the breed standard. Above all, Franny gets the credit for providing the love and inspiration that keeps me going. And—thanks Mom.

Included in this book are numerous photos of excellent dogs that have been sent to T.F.H. over the years. Since they were not solicited especially for use in this text, captioning is not given for the photo in the appropriate breed section. Included here are the names of those dogs whose photos I have taken from the historical files to use as representatives of their breeds. My apologies to those owners and dogs that could not be identified due to insufficient information.

English Setter: Ch. Frenchtown Calico Flower, owned by J. Brady.
Basset Hound: Ch. Lyn-Mar's Clown, owned by J. Stuart Walton.
Beagle: Ch. Sogo Masterpiece, owned by Clint Callahan.
Irish Wolfhound: Fleetwood Rury Shaun.
Norwegian Elkhound: Ch. Carro of Ardmere.
Great Dane: Guerin's Shawn of Brookdane, owned by J. Nester.
Newfoundland: Ch. Dryad's Coastwise Show Boat.
Siberian Husky: Ch. Snow Ridge Czar, owned by R. Anderson.
Wire Fox Terrier: Ch. Copper Beech Storm.
Manchester Terrier: Ch. Grenadier Kettledrum, owned by Mr. and Mrs. C. Tehman. Toy: Ch. Shir-Lee's Joker, bred and owned by Shirley Swanstrom.
Skye Terrier: Ch. Cimarron Sara Lone Wolfe, owned by E. Weehunt.
Welsh Terrier: Ch. Syl-Von Personal Appearance.
Brussels Griffon: Ch. Buka Proctor, owned by N. Aubrey-Jones.
Italian Greyhound: Ch. Bennato.
Pomeranian: Ch. Mickey Joe, owned by M.F. Chambers
Toy Poodle: Ch. Ro-Mary's Silver Rhythm, owned by R. Bosso.
Boston Terrier: Ch. Torch's Pilot.
Bulldog: Ch. Maxmal Surprise, owned by the Maxmal Kennels.

Foreword

The dog fancy has undergone tremendous growth during the fifty years since the original publication of this volume. Many of today's most popular breeds were only rarely seen in the 1920's, and the number of AKC recognized breeds was only slightly more than sixty. This number has doubled since that time, due for the most part to the technical advances that have made world travel and importation easily accessible to the interested fancier. There continues to be an ever-growing interest in breeding purebred dogs for their distinct breed characteristics, and this trend can only enhance and strengthen the dog sport for future generations.

The most remarkable growth shown in the half century since Dr. Bruette's writing has been in the Working Group, which has swelled from eleven recognized breeds to thirty-one strong. These newly admitted dogs are not new breeds, but rather, most are breeds that had not reached our shores even though they flourished in other lands.

The breed standards and scales of points presented in this book have been drawn up by the individual specialty clubs in America and approved by the American Kennel Club. They are used in judging the most important shows in this and other countries and will serve as an informative guide for the uninitiated, yet will enable the expert judge and fancier to refresh their memory whenever necessary. Changes occur in these standards from time to time, and it is the intention of the publisher to incorporate them in successive editions, corrected and revised to include the latest mandates of the breed clubs.

K.V.D.

Introduction

THE ORIGIN OF THE DOG

Although the exact origin of the dog is shrouded in that old and familiar refuge of the scientists, "the mists of antiquity," their family history is easily traced back through the bronze age and the stone age to the geological drift that first evidenced the use of fire, which is ordinarily accepted as indicating the advent of man upon earth. Further than this science sayeth not. Statues and carvings exist which show there were dogs in the most ancient times resembling in important particulars the breeds of the present, but it has never been decided whether these dogs or those of today were descended from some dog-like ancestor or were relatives of the fox, the jackal or the wolf. On this subject it may be said that there is a resemblance in appearance between some breeds of dogs and foxes. They are unlike, however, in character and habits, for the fox is not a social animal and does not hunt in packs, and foxes also have a peculiar odor that dogs do not. It may also be stated that despite the many cases referred to of crosses between foxes and dogs, there is not on record a duly authentic case of such a cross ever having occurred.

What has been said about the lack of relationship between dogs and foxes does not hold good in reference to wolves and jackals, for the latter so closely resemble many breeds of dogs in general appearance, structure, habits, instincts and mental qualities that they may be regarded as of one stock. It is impossible to formulate a definition that will include all the varieties of the domestic dog and exclude all of the wild species. In addition to their marked similarity in size, appearance and anatomical structure, both wolves and jackals can be and frequently are trained, while domesticated dogs frequently become wild, consorting and interbreeding with the former, assuming their habits and changing their characteristics back to a wolf-like hound. The wolf and jackal when trained will wag their tails, lick their masters' hands, crouch or throw themselves on their back in submission, come when called, jump about when caressed, and in high spirits run around in circles or in figure eights, their plaintive howl changing to a businesslike bark.

There are so many breeds of dogs so unlike in size and appearance that it is difficult to reconcile their being derived from a common ancestry. The marked disparity in size, however, between the tiny Pomeranian and the St. Bernard is no greater than the disparity between the Percheron horse and the Shetland pony, the Patagonian and the pygmy.

In the *Origin of Species,* Darwin reports several interesting experiments, one being the breeding together promiscuously of a large number of fancy pigeons of totally different sizes, varieties and types. The result was one uniform type, the common wild wood pigeon. In the face of these experiments it is probable that the breeding together of several varieties of horses would revert back to one uniform type, the wild horse, and the mating of all the different varieties of dogs would result in an animal in all respects

An ancestor of several mammalian species including the bear and dog, the *Miacis* was a small carnivore that inhabited prehistoric forests, living and stalking prey in the tree tops.

Tomarctus, considered the ancestor of all canine-type creatures, lived fifteen million years ago in a manner not unlike that of today's wolf and species of wild dog. It was a stealthy predator, with short prick ears and a long tail used to maintain balance.

similar to the wild dogs which are to be found in different parts of the world, particularly in Africa.

There is conclusive evidence to prove that the people who lived in the monolithic age, in both the Eastern and Western hemispheres, possessed dogs, living with them on the same terms of intimacy as exist today. Later, the Chaldeans, the Assyrians, the Greeks and the Romans owned dogs that were the progenitors of those of the present time.

In fact, the prehistoric drifts (the ashes of fires and mold in caves revealing man's first presence on the globe) also reveal the presence of the dog. The history of the dog is the history of man; their origin is coexistent, their lives have been lived together, and the extinction of the human race would likely be punctuated by the extinction of the dog.

In the last century great care has been given to the breeding of dogs. Thanks to dog shows and the rigid rules of registration demanded by the American Kennel Club, the various canine types have been brought to a high state of perfection and kept uncompromisingly distinct. The elimination of the nondescript cur is steadily progressing, and the meeting on the streets of dogs that do

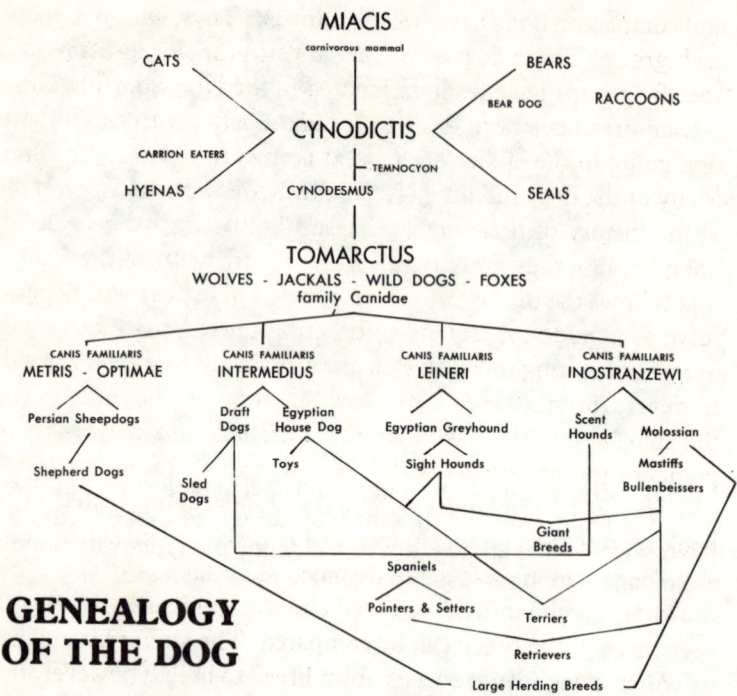

GENEALOGY OF THE DOG

The line of descent of *Miacis,* common ancestor of many distinct species including cat and dog, extended to *Tomarctus,* believed to be the prototype of canines. Evolving from Tomarctus were four more highly individualized canine prototypes, each of which figured in the eventual rise of one or more of the modern day breed groups including the herding breeds, hunting and toy breeds, sight hounds and terriers, and mastiff-types and water dogs.

not bear resemblance to some recognized breed is becoming more and more uncommon, for even the amateur dog owner is alive to the importance of keeping breeds distinct.

This volume will be devoted to the purebred dogs that are currently officially recognized by the American Kennel Club. They have been broken down breed by breed into six groups (Sporting, Hound, Working, Terrier, Toy and Non-Sporting), with each breed assigned to a group depending on their intended usage. Dogs that were originally bred to guard the home, herd the cattle or pull carts were naturally classified in the Working Group. Hunting and gun dogs are found in the Sporting Group; small lap and companion dogs have been grouped as Toys, and so it goes for each group. Those dogs which do not fit properly into any of the specific groups have been designated to the Non-Sporting Group.

Each breed has been dealt with individually, with careful attention going to the choice of dog that is used to illustrate the breed. Many of the dogs pictured are Best In Show winners and top dogs in the history of their breed. These fine specimens were decided upon because they aptly typified the requirements of the standard that follows the discussion of the breed. These dogs will hopefully serve as a guide for anyone considering purchasing a quality dog or just aquainting themselves with the breed. They are just guides, however, for most standards allow for variations not only in color but some also in size, coat length, ear carriage and many other fine points of the breed standard.

It should be remembered that the standards presented in this book represent the *ideal* concept of the breed; an ideal that few, if any, dogs can be expected to meet. The standards have been drawn up by the individual breed clubs as guidelines by which all specimens of the breed can be compared. The strengths and faults by which a dog is judged vary from breed to breed; however, there are numerous faults which are deemed very undesirable, and therefore disqualifying, *for every breed*. Any dog possessing any of these traits is disqualified from show ring competition: a dog which is spayed or castrated, blind, lame at the time of the show, altered or changed in appearance by the use of any cleaning or modifying substance, a cryptorchid or monorchid male. Although disqualified from show competition, many dogs are still eligible to compete in obedience trials, and can advance the good name of their breeds if not by their excellence of structure, then by their aptitude for performing these events requiring skill and intelligence.

Group 1: Sporting Dogs

POINTER

The Pointer deservedly occupies a high place in the esteem of American sportsmen, for he is attractive in form and possesses fine field qualities. The pointing dogs, from which they are descended, originated in Spain during the Middle Ages, later crossing the mountains into France, and eventually finding their way over to England. These early Spanish dogs were so heavy, coarse, and cumbersome that English sportsmen, with the object of lightening up their heavy frames and gaining more speed, crossed them with the Foxhound. In the colonial days of this country there were many enthusiastic sportsmen, particularly in Maryland and the Carolinas, who imported Pointers from abroad. These were judiciously mated, new dogs brought over from time to time, and eventually their progeny became scattered throughout the country, making warm friends and admirers, so that today they are one of the most popular of America's sporting breeds.

The Pointer as a rule does not make up to strangers as readily as a setter, but to his owner he is an affectionate and loyal companion. Pointer admirers claim that as a class their short-haired favorites are more naturally inclined to point than setters, that they are more easily broken, retain their training longer, and are more obedient in the field. No question will be raised over the fact that their shortness of coat constitutes a strong recommendation for warm climate or for summer shooting on the prairies or in sections of the country where cockle burrs, sand fleas, nettles, and other pests abound and annoy long-haired dogs to distraction.

There are no accurate records of the Pointers brought to this country previous to 1870. At that time the magazine *Forest and Stream* was founded, and it soon attained a wide circulation among sportsmen and fanciers, who began recording in its columns the descriptions and pedigrees of various celebrated dogs as well as the pedigrees, records and appearance of the Pointers that were being brought to this country from abroad.

Buyer's guide: This speedy, muscular dog is a superb hunting dog and should be used as such. Their gun dog instincts are very keen and should be fostered by routine training in the field. Pointers are good natured and will adapt to being housepets, but will require a large yard or kennel run to exercise in. They are quick to respond to sudden noises and often bolt off in search of them, so small children should not be allowed to walk this breed until they are old enough to restrain and discipline them. Pointers make enthusiastic show dogs and are keen competitors. Their instinctive ability to freeze and hold their position for extended periods of time aids them in the judging procedure where they must submit to the touch of handling of the judge. Pointers are easily kept in good tone and their short, smooth coat requires little more than a going over with a hound glove to look its best.

STANDARD FOR THE POINTER

General Appearance: The Pointer is bred primarily for sport afield; he should unmistakably look and act the part. The ideal specimen gives the immediate impression of compact power and agile grace; the head noble, proudly carried; the expression intelligent and alert; the muscular body bespeaking both staying power and dash. Here is an animal whose very movement shows him to be a wide-awake, hard-driving hunting dog possessing stamina, courage, and the desire to go. And in his expression are the loyalty and devotion of a true friend of man.

Temperament: The Pointer's even temperament and alert good sense make him a congenial companion both in the field and in the home. He should be dignified and should never show timidity toward man or dog.

Head: The skull of medium width, approximately as wide as the length of the muzzle, resulting in an impression of length rather than width. Slight furrow between the eyes, cheeks cleanly chiseled. There should be a pronounced stop. From this point forward the muzzle is of good length, with the nasal bone so formed that the nose is slightly higher at the tip than the muzzle at the stop. Parallel planes of the skull and muzzle are equally acceptable. The muzzle should be deep without pendulous flews. Jaws ending square and level, should bite evenly or as scissors. Nostrils well developed and wide open. **Ears:** Set on at eye level. When hanging naturally, they should reach just below the lower jaw, close to the head, with little or no folding. They should be somewhat pointed at the tip—never round—and soft and thin in leather. **Eyes:** Of ample size, rounded and intense. The eye color should be dark in contrast with the color of the markings, the darker the better.

Neck: Long, dry, muscular and slightly arched, springing cleanly from the shoulders.

Shoulders: Long, thin, and sloping. The top of blades close together.

Front: Elbows well let down, directly under the withers and truly parallel so as to work just clear of the body. Forelegs straight and with oval bone. Knee joint never to knuckle over. Pasterns of moderate length, perceptibly finer in bone than the leg, and slightly slanting. Chest, deep rather than wide, must not hinder free action of forelegs. The breastbone bold, without being unduly prominent. The ribs well sprung, descending as low as the elbow-point.

Back: Strong and solid with only a slight rise from croup to top of shoulders. Loin of moderate length, powerful and slightly arched. Croup falling only slightly to base of tail. Tuck-up should be apparent, but not exaggerated.

Tail: Heavier at the root, tapering to a fine point. Length no greater than to hock. A tail longer than this or docked must be penalized. Carried without curl, and not more than 20 degrees above the line of the back; never carried between the legs.

Hindquarters: Muscular and powerful with great propelling leverage. Thighs long and well developed. Stifles well bent. The hocks clean; the legs straight as viewed from behind. Decided angulation is the mark of power and endurance.

Feet: Oval, with long, closely-set, arched toes, well-padded, and deep. Cat-foot is a fault. Dewclaws on the forelegs may be removed.

Coat: Short, dense, smooth with a sheen.

Color: Liver, lemon, black, orange; either in combination with white or solid-colored. A good Pointer cannot be a bad color. In the darker colors, the nose should be black or brown; in the lighter shades it may be lighter or flesh-colored.

Gait: Smooth, frictionless, with a powerful hindquarter's drive. The head should be carried high, the nostrils wide, the tail moving from side to side rhythmically with the pace, giving the impression of a well-balanced, strongly-built hunting dog capable of top speed combined with great stamina. Hackney gait must be faulted.

Balance and Size: Balance and over-all symmetry are more important in the Pointer than size. A smooth, balanced dog is to be more desired than a dog with strongly contrasting good points and faults. Hound or terrier characteristics are most undesirable. Because a sporting dog must have both endurance and power, great variations in size are undesirable, the desirable height and weight being within the following limits:

Dogs: Height—25-28 inches
        Weight—55-75 pounds
Bitches: Height—23-26 inches
        Weight—45-65 pounds

APPROVED NOVEMBER 12, 1968

GERMAN SHORTHAIRED POINTER

This hardy sporting breed combines all the ability of a staunch pointing and scenting dog with the temperament of a favorite companion and guard dog. The breed stems from judicious crossings of the Spanish Pointer, English Foxhound and Bloodhound with the old German hound base stock to produce the "all purpose" breed, as they were originally referred to by German sportsmen. Their versatility makes them easily and eagerly suited for work on feather or fur, night trailing or day stalking. German Shorthairs also retrieve with natural grace and style whether in the water or field. Their movement is smooth and free flowing.

The original German Shorthaired Pointer was a rather heavily constructed dog, very staunch on the point, although somewhat slow in the field. Through some select outcrosses with English Pointer stock, European sportsmen were able to retain the remarkable scenting and pointing power of the GSP and infuse some speed and agility. The result was a smaller, faster dog which still maintained the beauty, intelligence, character and hunting know-how of the earlier breed. They have particularly keen noses and will maintain and follow a scent over long distances.

Breeders and GSP fanciers have strived to maintain the versatility of the breed. While good conformation specimens frequently place high in the Sporting Group, the same dogs retain their instinct for the hunt. The German Shorthaired generally works close to the gun and is not as lightning quick as the setters nor as ranging as the English Pointer. These traits make him a favorite with American hunters where conditions of the terrain favor a close-ranging gun dog.

After the hunt, the German Shorthaired Pointer is satisfied with being a house dog, leaving the excitement of the hunt for another day and exhibiting little of the high-strung nature common to many sporting dogs. They are cooperative and unassuming animals that train easily to the rules of the house. The GSP has a high degree of intelligence which they use to their best advantage.

Buyer's guide: Their excellent temperament has led to this breed's rise in popularity as a housepet. They require no extensive grooming or bathing and are not voracious eaters. Of the larger sporting breeds, German Shorthaired Pointers adapt better than most to the indoor life; however, they should be allowed frequent access to the outdoors to keep in top shape. If not properly exercised, they may become overactive or possibly destructive in the house.

STANDARD FOR THE GERMAN SHORTHAIRED POINTER

The Shorthair is a versatile hunter, an all-purpose gun dog capable of high performance in field and water. The judgment of Shorthairs in the show ring should reflect this basic characteristic.

General Appearance: The overall picture which is created in the observer's eyes is that of an aristocratic, well-balanced, symmetrical animal with conformation indicating power, endurance and agility and a look of intelligence and animation. The dog is neither unduly small nor conspicuously large. It gives the impression of medium size, but is like the proper hunter, "with a short back, but standing over plenty of ground."

Tall leggy dogs, or dogs which are ponderous or unbalanced because of excess substance should be definitely rejected. The first impression is that of a keenness which denotes full enthusiasm for work without indication of nervous or flighty character. Movements are alertly coordinated without waste motion. Grace of outline, clean-cut head, sloping shoulders, deep chest, powerful back, strong quarters, good bone composition, adequate muscle, well-carried tail and taut coat, all combine to produce a look of nobility and an indication of anatomical structure essential to correct gait which must indicate a heritage of purposefully conducted breeding. Doggy bitches and bitchy dogs are to be faulted. A judge must excuse a dog from the ring if it displays extreme shyness or viciousness toward its handler or the judge. Aggressiveness or belligerence toward another dog is not to be considered viciousness.

Symmetry: Symmetry and field quality are most essential. A dog in hard and lean field condition is not to be penalized; however, overly fat or poorly muscled dogs are to be penalized. A dog well-balanced in all points is preferable to one with outstanding good qualities and defects.

Head: Clean-cut, neither too light nor too heavy, in proper proportion to the body. Skull is reasonably broad, arched on side and slightly round on top. Scissura (median line between the eyes at the forehead) not too deep, occipital bone not as conspicuous as in the case of the Pointer. The foreface rises gradually from nose to forehead. The rise is more strongly pronounced in the dog than in the bitch as befitting his sex. The chops fall away from the somewhat projecting nose. Lips are full and deep, never flewy. The chops do not fall over too much, but form a proper fold in the angle. The jaw is powerful and the muscles well developed. The line to the forehead rises gradually and never has a definite stop as that of the Pointer, but rather a stop-effect when viewed from the side, due to the position of the eyebrows. The muzzle is sufficiently long to enable the dog to seize properly and to facilitate his carrying game a long time. A pointed muzzle is not desirable. The entire head never gives the impression of tapering to a point. The depth is in the right proportion to the length, both in the muzzle and in the skull proper. The length of the muzzle should equal the length of skull. A pointed muzzle is a fault. A dish-faced muzzle is a fault. A definite Pointer stop is a serious fault. Too many wrinkles in forehead is a fault.

Ears: Ears are broad and set fairly high, lie flat and never hang away from the head. Placement is just above eye level. The ears, when laid in front without being pulled, meet the lip angle. In the case of heavier dogs, the ears are correspondingly longer. Ears too long or fleshy are to be faulted.

Eyes: The eyes are of medium size, full of intelligence and expression, good humored and yet radiating energy, neither protruding nor sunken. The eye is almond shaped, not circular. The eyelids close well. The best color is dark brown. Light yellow (Bird of Prey) eyes are not desirable and are a fault. Closely set eyes are to be faulted. China or wall eyes are to be disqualified.

Nose: Brown, the larger the better, nostrils well-opened and broad. Spotted nose not desirable. Flesh colored nose disqualifies.

Teeth: The teeth are strong and healthy. The molars intermesh properly. The bite is a true scissors bite. A perfect level bite (without overlapping) is not desirable and must be penalized. Extreme overshot or undershot bite disqualifies.

Neck: Of proper length to permit the jaws reaching game to be retrieved, sloping downwards on beautifully curving lines. The nape is rather muscular, becoming gradually larger towards the shoulders. Moderate houndlike throatiness permitted.

Chest: The chest in general gives the impression of depth rather than breadth; for all that, it should be in correct proportion to the other parts of the body with a fair depth. The chest reaches down to the elbows, the ribs forming the thorax show a rib spring and are not flat or slabsided; they are not perfectly round or barrel-shaped. Ribs that are entirely round prevent the necessary expansion of the chest when taking breath. The back ribs reach well down. The circumference of the thorax immediately behind the elbows is smaller than that of the thorax about a hands-breadth behind elbows, so that the upper arm has room for movement.

Back, Loins and Croup: Back is short, strong and straight with slight rise from root of tail to withers. Loin strong, of moderate length and slightly arched. Tuck-up is apparent. Excessively long, roached or swayed back must be penalized.

Forequarters: The shoulders are sloping movable, well-covered with muscle. The shoulder blades lie flat and are well laid back nearing a 45° angle. The upper arm (the bones between the shoulder and elbow joints) is as long as possible, standing away somewhat from the trunk so that the straight and closely muscled legs, when viewed from the front appear to be parallel. Elbows which stand away from the body or are too close indicate toes turning inwards, which must be regarded as faults. Pasterns are strong, short and nearly vertical with a slight spring. Loose, short-bladed or straight shoulders must be faulted. Knuckling over is to be faulted. Down in the pasterns is to be faulted.

Hindquarters: The hips are broad with hip sockets wide apart and fall slightly towards the tail in a graceful curve. Thighs are strong and well-muscled. Stifles well bent. Hock joints are well angulated and strong, straight bone structure from hock to pad. Angulation of both stifle and hock joint is such as to combine maximum combination of both drive and traction. Hocks turn neither in nor out. A steep croup is a fault. Cowhocked legs are a serious fault.

Feet: Are compact, close-knit and round to spoon-shaped. The toes sufficiently arched and heavily nailed. The pads are strong, hard and thick. Dewclaws on the forelegs may be removed. Feet pointing in or out is a fault.

APPROVED MAY 7, 1946

Representing the breed: Fld. Ch. Kerlacres Dek's Birdie, owned and bred by Dean M. Kerl.

GERMAN WIREHAIRED POINTER

The ruggedness, intelligence and hunting ability of the German Wirehaired Pointer make this breed a preferred hunting partner. They are a well-rounded dog, equally capable of finding game or tracking and trailing in both coarse underbrush and marshes. They respond quickly to training and are good natural retrievers.

The German Wirehaired Pointer hails from Germany and the breed later spread throughout Northern Europe. They stem from crossings of Griffons, Stichelhaars, and Pudel Pointers. In Germany, the breed is known as *Drahthaar*, which translates to *wirehaired* in English.

Wirehaired Pointers were specifically developed by sportsmen who were seeking an all-around sporting dog. This dog had to combine the already available qualities of speed, staunch pointing and scenting, with the desired traits of liking water and having trailing skills, retrieving abilities, intelligence, ease and eagerness for training. The German Wirehaired was bred to be especially hardy and persevering. Because of this last requirement, a protective coat suitable for work in harsh underbrush and varying climates was needed. The coarse coat of the Wirehaired Pointer shields him against inclement weather and the cuts and scrapes that shorthaired breeds would experience in hunting in rough terrain.

American sportsmen enjoy a wide range of hunting interests and travel to many locales in search of their sport. Today's versatile GWP is adept at numerous types of hunting, being able to flush the fields for birds and rabbits, work the woods for birds and fur-bearing animals, or retrieve in the open water and marshy areas for waterfowl. They have proven time and time again that they are willing and proficient enough for any task that the hunter may ask of them.

Buyer's guide: These dogs excel in sporting and field trial competition, but are not commonly kept as house dogs. They seem more at home in a comfortable kennel with other dogs than in a living room. If you care to keep them as housepets, remember that they require considerable exercise to work off their extensive energy.

STANDARD FOR THE
GERMAN WIREHAIRED POINTER

The German Wirehaired Pointer is a dog that is essentially Pointer in type, of sturdy build, lively manner, and an intelligent, determined expression. In disposition the dog has been described as energetic, rather aloof but not unfriendly.

Head: **The head** is moderately long, **the skull** broad, the occipital bone not too prominent. **The stop** is medium, **the muzzle** fairly long with nasal bone straight and broad, **the lips** a trifle pendulous but close and bearded. **The nose** is dark brown with nostrils wide open, and **the teeth** are strong with scissors bite. **The ears,** rounded but not too broad, hang close to the sides of the head. **Eyes** are brown, medium in size, oval in contour, bright and clear and overhung with bushy eyebrows. Yellow eyes are not desirable. **The neck** is of medium length, slightly arched and devoid of dewlap; in fact, the skin throughout is notably tight to the body.

Body and Tail: The body is a little longer than it is high, as ten is to nine, with the back short, straight and strong, the entire back line showing a perceptible slope down from withers to croup. The chest is deep and capacious, the ribs well sprung, loins taut and slender, the tuck-up apparent. Hips are broad, with croup nicely rounded and the tail docked, approximately two-fifths of original length.

Legs and Feet: Forelegs are straight, with shoulders obliquely set and elbows close. The thighs are strong and muscular. The hind legs are moderately angulated at stifle and hock and as viewed from behind, parallel to each other. Round in outline, the feet are webbed, high arched with toes close, their pads thick and hard, and their nails strong and quite heavy. Leg bones are flat rather than round, and strong, but not so heavy or coarse as to militate against the dog's natural agility.

Coat: The coat is weather-resisting and to some extent water-repellent. The undercoat is dense enough in winter to insulate against the cold but so thin in summer as to be almost invisible. The distinctive outer coat is straight, harsh, wiry and rather flat-lying, from one and one-half to two inches in length; it is long enough to protect against the punishment of rough cover but not so long as to hide the outline. On the lower legs it is shorter and between the toes of softer texture. On the skull it is naturally short and close fitting, while over the shoulders and around the tail it is very dense and heavy. The tail is nicely coated, particularly on the underside, but devoid of feather. These dogs have bushy eyebrows of strong, straight hair and beards and whiskers of medium length.

A short smooth coat, a soft woolly coat, or an excessively long coat is to be severely penalized.

Color: The coat is liver and white, usually either liver and white spotted, liver roan, liver and white spotted with ticking and roaning or sometimes solid liver. The nose is dark brown. The head is brown, sometimes with a white blaze, the ears brown. Any black in the coat is to be severely penalized. Spotted and flesh-colored noses are undesirable and are to be penalized.

Size: Height of males should be from 24 to 26 inches at the withers, bitches smaller but not under 22 inches.

APPROVED FEBRUARY 7, 1959

Representing the breed: Dual Ch. Lutz Zur Codenburg, owned by Ms. Silke Alberts.

CHESAPEAKE BAY RETRIEVER

These splendid retrievers have a claim to the distinction of being absolutely American. They are native to the shores of the historic Chesapeake Bay, and have a history that considerably antedates the period of dog shows.

There are a number of stories in regard to their origin. Among them are two recorded in *Forest and Stream* nearly a century ago. One is that a vessel from Newfoundland ran aground near an estate called Walnut Grove, on the shores of the Chesapeake. On board the ship were two Newfoundland dogs which were given by the captain to Mr. Law, the owner of the estate, in return for the kindness and hopitality shown him and his crew. It is claimed that a cross between these two Newfoundlands and the common yellow-and-tan hound of that part of the country was the origin of the Chesapeake Bay Dog. Another story is that about the year 1807 the good ship *Canton*, of Baltimore, fell in at sea with an

English brig bound from Newfoundland to England that had met disaster and was in a sinking condition. The crew were taken aboard the *Canton*, along with a pair of puppies that eventually became the property of the captain of the *Canton*, and were taken by him to Baltimore. The dog puppy, a dingy red in color, was named Sailor, and the bitch, black in color, was called Canton. Both of these dogs eventually attained great reputations as duck retrievers, and Sailor and Canton are said to be the foundation of the breed. This all may be so, for there is no doubt that as a retriever of dead and wounded ducks no dog equals the Chesapeake. His brave heart, unlimited powers of endurance, and dense coat fit him eminently for braving the roughest weather. Nothing daunts him, and a good specimen of the breed will swim for miles in a rough sea covered with broken ice after a wounded bird. It is one of the few breeds that has always been kept pure, and although at one time it was confined largely to the duck marshes on the Maryland coast, today there are good specimens in all parts of the country.

Buyer's guide: The Chesapeake is a powerfully built, strong dog that is long on hunting instinct. Considerable time should be paid to training these dogs because they are among the smartest of the sporters and make excellent field and obedience competitors. Chesapeakes are not satisfied to remain inactive for long, and should be used on frequent duck hunts. Those people who are not active outdoors should not choose a Chesapeake.

STANDARD FOR THE
CHESAPEAKE BAY RETRIEVER

Head: Skull broad and round with medium stop, nose medium short-muzzle, pointed but not sharp. Lips thin, not pendulous. Ear small, set well up on head, hanging loosely and of medium leather. Eyes medium large, very clear, of yellowish or amber color and wide apart.

Neck: Of medium length with a strong muscular appearance, tapering to shoulders.

Shoulder, Chest and Body: Shoulders, sloping and should have full liberty of action with plenty of power without any restrictions of movement. Chest strong, deep and wide. Barrel round and deep. Body of medium length, neither cobby nor roached, but rather approaching hollowness, flanks well tucked up.

Hindquarters and Stifles: Hindquarters should be as high or a trifle higher than the shoulders. They should show fully as much power as the forequarters. There should be no tendency to weakness in either fore or hindquarters. Hindquarters should be especially powerful to supply the driving power for swimming. Back should be short, well-coupled and powerful. Good hindquarters are essential. Stifles should be well angulated.

Legs, Elbows, Hocks and Feet: Legs should be medium length and straight, showing good bone and muscle, with well-webbed hare feet of good size. The toes well rounded and close, pasterns slightly bent and both pasterns and hocks medium length—the straighter the legs the better when viewed from front or rear. Dewclaws, if any, must be removed from the hind legs. Dewclaws on the forelegs may be removed. A dog with dewclaws on the hind legs must be disqualified.

Stern: Tail should extend to hock. It should be medium heavy at base. Moderate feathering on stern and tail is permissible. Tail should be straight or slightly curved. Tails should not curl over back or side kink.

Coat and Texture: Coat should be thick and short, nowhere over 1½ inches long, with a dense fine woolly undercoat. Hair on face and legs should be very short and straight with tendency to wave on the shoulders, neck, back and loins only. The curly coat or coat with a tendency to curl not permissible.

The texture of the dog's coat is very important, as the dog is used for hunting under all sorts of adverse weather conditions, often working in ice and snow. The oil in the harsh outer coat and woolly undercoat is of extreme value in preventing the cold water from reaching the dog's skin and aids in quick drying. A Chesapeake's coat should resist the water in the same way that a duck's feathers do. When he leaves the water and shakes himself, his coat should not hold the water at all, being merely moist. Color and coat are extremely important, as the dog is used for duck hunting. The color must be as nearly that of his surroundings as possible and with the fact that dogs are exposed to all kinds of adverse weather conditions, often working in ice and snow, the color of coat and its texture must be given every consideration when judging on the bench or in the ring.

Tail should be medium length—varying from: males, 12 inches to 15 inches, and females from 11 inches to 14 inches; medium heavy at base, moderate feathering on stern and tail permissible.

Color: Any color varying from a dark brown to a faded tan or deadgrass. Deadgrass takes in any shade of deadgrass, varying from a tan to a dull straw color. White spot on breast, toes and belly permissible, but the smaller the spot the better. Solid and self-colored dogs are preferred.

Weight: Males, 65 to 80 pounds; females 55 to 70 pounds. **Height:** Males, 23 inches to 26 inches; females, 21 inches to 24 inches. Oversized or undersized does are to be severely penalized.

Courage, willingness to work, alertness, nose, intelligence, love of water, general quality, and, most of all, disposition, should be given primary consideration in the selection and breeding of the Chesapeake Bay dog.

POSITIVE SCALE OF POINTS

Head, incl. lips, ears & eyes....16	Color........................4
Neck......................4	Stern and tail................10
Shoulders and body..........12	Coat and texture.............18
Hindquarters and stifles.......12	General conformation........12
Elbows, legs and feet.........12	TOTAL................100

Note:—The question of coat and general type of balance takes precedence over any scoring table which could be drawn up.

APPROXIMATE MEASUREMENTS

Length head, nose to occiput............................9½ to 10
Girth at ears..20 to 21
Muzzle below eyes..................................10 to 10½
Length of ears.......................................4½ to 5
Width between eyes..................................2½ to 2¾
Girth neck close to shoulder...........................20 to 22
Girth at flank......................................24 to 25
Length from occiput to tail base.......................34 to 35
Girth forearms at shoulders..........................10 to 10½

GROUP I: SPORTING DOGS

Girth upper thigh....................................19 to 20
From root to root of ear, over skull.....................5 to 6
Occiput to top shoulder blades.........................9 to 9½
From elbow to over the shoulders.....................25 to 26

DISQUALIFICATIONS

Black colored.
Dewclaws on hind legs.
White on any part of body, except breast, belly or spots on feet.
Feathering on tail or legs over 1¾ inches long.
Undershot, overshot or any deformity.
Coat curly or tendency to curl all over body.
Specimens unworthy or lacking in breed characteristics.

APPROVED JULY 9, 1963

Representing the breed: Ch. Alnwick Castle King, C.D., W.D., owned by Susan and Michael LaMielle.

CURLY-COATED RETRIEVER

The Curly-Coated Retriever is a much older breed than the Flat-Coat, which has to a great extent displaced him in the affections of the public. The Flat-Coat has a setter or spaniel ancestry, while the progenitor of the Curly-Coat was undoubtedly the Poodle and the Irish Water Spaniel, breeds plentiful in England in the 18th and 19th centuries which were used for sporting purposes.

The Curly-Coated Retriever is a beautiful dog, and many of them are the equal of the Flat-Coats as workmen. They are just as intelligent, but are believed to be slightly inferior in nose and naturally harder mouthed. They are exceptional swimmers and perform well despite thick and punishing underbrush.

The only physical difference of importance between the two breeds lies in the character of their coats, that of the typical Curly-

Coat being a close fitting, inseparable curl, each knot being solid, and the small locks and curls so close together as to be impervious to water. All parts of the body should be covered from the occiput to the tip of the tail. The curls on the head should finish in a straight line across the occiput, the hair on the face being short and smooth.

The coat requires a good deal of attention. It should never be combed or brushed. If the old coat does not shed it should be carefully pulled out, and open-coated dogs, which do not grow the short, crisp curl, should be clipped all over, as that usually induces the new coat to come out stronger and more tightly curled. A brisk swim serves best for setting the natural curl.

In selecting Curly-Coated Retrievers look for the conformation and points that distinguish the short, crisp coat typical of this breed.

Buyer's guide: This breed is still quite rare in the United States, even though they make good gun dogs. Do not choose a Curly unless you are interested in a show career for the dog or to use them under the gun for retrieves. They do best in rural settings where they can run freely and perform the tasks they were bred for.

STANDARD FOR THE CURLY-COATED RETRIEVER

Head: Long and well proportioned, skull not too flat, jaws long and strong but not inclined to snipiness, nose black, in the black coated variety, with wide nostrils. Teeth strong and level. **Eyes:** Black or brown, but not yellow, rather large but not too prominent. **Ears:** Rather small, set on low, lying close to the head, and covered with short curls.

Coat: Should be one mass of crisp curls all over. A slightly more open coat not to be severely penalized, but a saddle back or patch of uncurled hair behind the shoulder should be penalized, and a prominent white patch on breast is undesirable, but a few white hairs allowed in an otherwise good dog. Color, black or liver.

Shoulders, Chest, Body and Loins: Shoulders should be very deep, muscular and obliquely placed. Chest, not too wide, but decidedly deep.

Body, rather short, muscular and well ribbed up. Loin, powerful, deep and firm to the grasp.

Legs and Feet: Legs should be of moderate length, forelegs straight and set well under the body. Quarters strong and muscular, hocks low to the ground with moderate bend to stifle and hock. Feet round and compact with well-arched toes.

Tail: Should be moderately short, carried fairly straight and covered with curls, slightly tapering towards the point.

General Appearance: A strong smart upstanding dog, showing activity, endurance and intelligence.

FLAT-COATED RETRIEVER

The Flat-Coated Retriever is a product of modern manufacture—in all likelihood the product of the Labrador and Curly-Coated Retriever, with a splash of spaniel, Newfoundland or setter.

In size, head, and general conformation, the Flat-Coated Retriever differs but little from the Curly-Coat. The points and features are all practically the same, the only real difference being in coat. This, as stated in the name, should be flat, the outer coat rather harsh to the touch. The undercoat is for warmth; the outer one serves for weather resistance. The legs, both before and aft, and the tail should be feathered, and the feet protected by well-feathered pads.

In breeding Flat-Coated Retrievers the object is to produce a strong, well-made, useful dog, showing quality—a workman in architecture, with the finish of a gentleman. Length of head, good shoulders, a strong loin and quarters, straight forelegs, and a flat coat are the chief points to aim at and preserve. The Flat-Coats rarely have the same spring of rib as the Curly-Coats, in which they reveal their unmistakable setter ancestry; but this should be cultivated. Light eyes have been a prevailing defect in the Flat-Coats, and should be avoided as much as possible, as it is invariably an indication of uncertain temper or a headstrong disposition.

The chief points to look for in the selection of Flat-Coated Retriever puppies at from two to four months old and after are: a long, level head, free from lippiness; dark eye; nicely balanced skull; small ears set close to side of head; short back; short straight tail; deep chest; well sprung ribs; straight forelegs; well boned; and a flat, close, dense coat.

Buyer's guide: The Flat-Coat is a naturally active dog and therefore requires less formal exercising than other dogs of their size; however, they should not be kept strictly indoors. They are good retrievers and will have a happier disposition if they are allowed to perform certain tasks around the house, or better still, if they are used regularly on hunts. If chosen as a house dog, they should be given plenty of attention as they tend to become bored easily. Obedience work is recommended.

STANDARD FOR THE
FLAT-COATED RETRIEVER

General Appearance: A bright, active dog of medium size (weighing from 60 pounds to 70 pounds) with an intelligent expression, showing power without lumber and raciness without weediness.

Head: This should be long and nicely molded. The skull flat and moderately broad. There should be a depression or stop between the eyes, slight and in no way accentuated, so as to avoid giving either a down or a dish-faced appearance. The nose of good size with open nostrils. The eyes, of medium size, should be dark brown or hazel, with a very intelligent expression (a round prominent eye is a disfigurement), and they should not be obliquely placed. The jaws should be long and strong, with a capacity of carrying a hare or pheasant. The ears small and well set on close to the side of the head.

Neck, Shoulders and Chest: The head should be well set in the neck, which latter should be long and free from throatiness, symmetrically set and obliquely placed in shoulders, running well into the back to allow of easily seeking for the trail. The chest should be deep and fairly broad, with a well-defined brisket, on which the elbows should work cleanly and evenly. The fore ribs should be fairly flat showing a gradual spring and well arched in the center of the body but rather lighter towards the quarters. Open couplings are to be ruthlessly condemned.

Back and Quarters: The back should be short, square and well ribbed up, with muscular quarters. The stern short, straight and well set on, carried gaily but never much above the level of the back.

Legs and Feet: These are of the greatest importance. The forelegs should be perfectly straight, with bone of good quality carried right down to the feet which should be round and strong. The stifle should not be too straight or too bent and the dog must neither be cowhocked nor move too wide behind; in fact, he must stand and move true all round on legs and feet, with toes close and well arched, the soles being thick and strong. When the dog is in full coat the limbs should be well feathered.

Coat: Should be dense, of fine quality and texture, flat as possible.

Color: Black or liver.

Representing the breed: Am., Bda., Can. Ch. Mantayo Bo James Bolingbroke, Am. C.D.X., Bda. C.D., Can. C.D.X., owned by Vernon W. Vogel.

GOLDEN RETRIEVER

This beautifully coated and colored breed has won the hearts of American fanciers, not only for their hardy dedication to the sport of the hunt, but also for their keen intelligence, loyalty, and gentleness. The Golden Retriever is a multi-faceted dog. They are exceptionally eager to learn and this trainability has made them top obedience trial performers. Their size, beautiful appearance and ease of care, combined with an uncanny intelligence and level disposition, have made this breed one of the most popular today.

A medium-sized retrieving dog, the Golden traces his ancestry (as do numerous other retrieving breeds), to early water spaniels, setters (especially the Gordon), other hunting and water breeds, and the St. John's Newfoundland (an early breed found in the ancestry of the Flat-Coated, Labrador, and Curly-Coated Retrievers). As sporting dogs they have proven themselves as being unrelenting and thoroughly dependable. Because their mouth is soft and their disposition gentle, they have been successfully used on all types of waterfowl. The Golden is dedicated to the retrieve and has a thick, water repellent undercoat that enables him to work in all types of weather.

In the show ring the Golden is a constant competitor for top honors. Their overall handsomeness and alert, eager disposition make them a great crowd pleaser. Golden Retrievers have one of the nicest temperaments of all the breeds and serve well as companion and friend. They excel as field and obedience trial workmen, yet they are gentle and sensitive housepets with mellow mannerisms.

Buyer's guide: They make great all-around pets. Golden Retrievers require some grooming to keep their coat tangle-free, but they are basically weather-resistant. They are well-built and active and blend well into a family situation. Goldens are attentive and protective of children and are not quarrelsome. They can be kept inside or out, but are most happy around people.

STANDARD FOR THE GOLDEN RETRIEVER

A symmetrical, powerful, active dog, sound and well put together, not clumsy or long in the leg, displaying a kindly expression and possessing a personality that is eager, alert and self-confident. Primarily a hunting dog, he should be shown in hard working condition. Over-all appearance, balance, gait and purpose to be given more emphasis than any of his component parts.

Size: Males 23-24 inches in height at withers; females 21½-22½. Length from breastbone to buttocks slightly greater than height at withers in ratio of 12-11. Weight for dogs 65-75 pounds; bitches 60-70 pounds.

Head: Broad in skull, slightly arched laterally and longitudinally without prominence of frontal or occipital bones. Good stop. Foreface deep and wide, nearly as long as skull. Muzzle, when viewed in profile, slightly deeper at stop than at tip; when viewed from above, slightly wider at stop than at tip. No heaviness in flews. Removal of whiskers for show purposes optional. **Eyes:** Friendly and intelligent, medium large with dark rims, set well apart and reasonably deep in sockets. Color preferably dark brown, never lighter than color of coat. No white or haw visible when looking straight ahead. **Teeth:** Scissors bite with lower incisors touching inside of upper incisors. **Nose:** Black or dark brown, though lighter shade in cold weather not serious. Dudley nose (pink without pigmentation) to be faulted. **Ears:** Rather short, hanging flat against head with rounded tips slightly below jaw. Forward edge attached well behind and just above eye with rear edge slightly below eye. Low, houndlike ear-set to be faulted.

Neck: Medium long, sloping well back into shoulders, giving sturdy muscular appearance with untrimmed natural ruff. No throatiness.

Body: Well-balanced, short-coupled, deep through the heart. Chest at least as wide as a man's hand, including thumb. Brisket extends to elbows. Ribs long and well sprung but not barrel shaped, extending well to rear of body. Loin short, muscular, wide and deep, with very little tuck-up. Topline level from withers to croup, whether standing or moving. Croup slopes gently. Slabsidedness, narrow chest, lack of depth in brisket, excessive tuck-up, roach or sway back to be faulted.

Forequarters: Forequarters well co-ordinated with hindquarters and capable of free movement. Shoulder blades wide, long and muscular, showing angulation with upper arm of approximately 90 degrees. Legs straight with good bone. Pastern short and strong, sloping slightly forward with no suggestion of weakness.

Hindquarters: Well-bent stifles (angulation between femur and pelvis approximately 90 degrees) with hocks well let down. Legs straight when viewed from rear. Cowhocks and sickle hocks to be faulted.

Feet: Medium size, round and compact with thick pads. Excess hair may be trimmed to show natural size and contour. Open or splayed feet to be faulted.

Tail: Well set on, neither too high nor too low, following natural line of croup. Length extends to hock. Carried with merry action with some upward curve but never curled over back nor between legs.

Coat and Color: Dense and water-repellent with good undercoat. Texture not as hard as that of a shorthaired dog, nor silky as that of a setter. Lies flat against body and may be straight or wavy. Moderate feathering on back of forelegs and heavier feathering on front of neck, back of thighs and underside of tail. Feathering may be lighter than rest of coat. Color lustrous golden of various shades. A few white hairs on chest permissible but not desirable. Further white markings to be faulted.

Gait: When trotting, gait is free, smooth, powerful and well co-ordinated. Viewed from front or rear, legs turn neither in nor out, nor do feet cross or interfere with each other. Increased speed causes tendency of feet to converge toward center line of gravity.

DISQUALIFICATIONS

Deviation in height of more than one inch from standard either way.
Undershot or overshot bite. This condition not to be confused with misalignment of teeth.
Trichiasis (abnormal position or direction of the eyelashes).

APPROVED SEPTEMBER 10, 1963

Representing the breed: Ch. Ranchero Gold Rush Sundancer, owned by Dick Marks and Kate King.

LABRADOR RETRIEVER

This breed of dogs is a compatriot of the Newfoundland, and although they have played an important part in the evolution of the Flat-Coated Retriever, one of the most important sporting dogs in Britain, they never succeeded in attracting much attention to themselves until recently.

The Labrador is a sort of smooth-coated Newfoundland in disposition and character, and a Flat-Coated Retriever in appearance. Their names indicate their origin. The breed first made its appearance at those maritime towns in England that were engaged in the fishing industry with Newfoundland. There is no question about this breed being one of the most intelligent of all dogs, lending themselves promptly to all useful purposes. They are extremely courageous and industrious, and are unsurpassed for amiability and faithfulness. Their rough-and-ready appearance is indicative of endurance, and their keen powers of scent were at once recognized and utilized by sportsmen.

In the early years of the breed, only the black Labrador Retrievers were considered true-to-type; the puppies of other colors were often mistakenly classed as Golden Retrievers or other breeds. Since that time the yellow and chocolate Labs (their color being a genetic recessive to the dominant black coloring) have become very popular and their numbers are on the rise.

The desire to work is inherent in the Lab, and they love most the person who trains them. They thrive on affection and are acutely sensitive and perceptive of the moods and actions of those around them. Labs learn quickly and do not forget what they have been taught, which makes them a most obedient and pleasant housepet.

Buyer's guide: Labs are very personable and love the indoor family life. They are obedient to commands and require little grooming or extensive exercising. If properly trained they will get along with other animals peaceably, although they prefer to be one-man dogs. They are very tolerant and protective of children.

STANDARD FOR THE LABRADOR RETRIEVER

General Appearance: The general appearance of the Labrador should be that of a strongly built, short-coupled, very active dog. He should be fairly wide over the loins, and strong and muscular in the hindquarters. The coat should be close, short, dense and free from feather.

Head: The skull should be wide, giving brain room; there should be a slight stop, i.e. the brow should be slightly pronounced, so that the skull is not absolutely in a straight line with the nose. The head should be clean-cut and free from fleshy cheeks. The jaws should be long and powerful and free from snipiness; the nose should be wide and the nostrils well developed. Teeth should be strong and regular, with a level mouth. The ears should hang moderately close to the head, rather far back, should be set somewhat low and not be large and heavy. The eyes should be of a medium size, expressing great intelligence and good temper, and can be brown, yellow or black, but brown or black is preferred.

Neck and Chest: The neck should be medium length, powerful and not throaty. The shoulders should be long and sloping. The chest must be of good width and depth, the ribs well sprung and the loins wide and strong, stifles well turned, and the hindquarters well developed and of great power.

Legs and Feet: The legs must be straight from the shoulder to ground, and the feet compact with toes well arched, and pads well developed; the hocks should be well bent, and the dog must neither be cowhocked nor be too wide behind; in fact, he must stand and move true all round on legs and feet. Legs should be of medium length, showing good bone and muscle, but not so short as to be out of balance with rest of body. In fact, a dog well balanced in all points is preferable to one with outstanding good qualities and defects.

Tail: The tail is a distinctive feature of the breed; it should be very thick towards the base, gradually tapering towards the tip, of medium length, should be free from any feathering, and should be clothed thickly all round with the Labrador's short, thick, dense coat, thus giving the peculiar "rounded" appearance which has been described as the "otter" tail. The tail may be carried gaily but should not curl over the back.

Coat: The coat is another very distinctive feature; it should be short, very dense and without wave, and should give a fairly hard feeling to the hand.

Color: The colors are black, yellow, or chocolate and are evaluated as follows:

(a) **Blacks:** All black, with a small white spot on chest permissible. Eyes to be of medium size, expressing intelligence and good temper, preferably brown or hazel, although black or yellow is permissible.

(b) **Yellows:** Yellows may vary in color from fox-red to light cream with variations in the shading of the coat on ears, the underparts of the dog, or beneath the tail. A small white spot on chest is permissible. Eye coloring and expression should be the same as that of the blacks, with black or dark brown eye rims. The nose should also be black or dark brown, although "fading" to pink in winter weather is not serious. A "Dudley" nose, (pink without pigmentation) should be penalized.

(c) **Chocolates:** Shades ranging from light sedge to chocolate. A small white spot on chest is permissible. Eyes to be light brown to clear yellow. Nose and eye-rim pigmentation dark brown or liver colored. "Fading" to pink in winter weather not serious. "Dudley" nose should be penalized.

Movement: Movement should be free and effortless. The forelegs should be strong and true, and correctly placed. Watching a dog move towards one, there should be no signs of elbows being out in front, but neatly held to the body with legs not too close together, and moving straight forward without pacing or weaving. Upon viewing the dog from the rear, one should get the impression that the hind legs, which should be well muscled and not cowhocked, move as nearly parallel as possible, with hocks doing their full share of work and flexing well, thus giving the appearance of power and strength.

Approximate Weights of Dogs and Bitches in Working Condition: Dogs—60 to 75 pounds; bitches—55 to 70 pounds.

Height at Shoulders: Dogs—22½ inches to 24½ inches; bitches—21½ inches to 23½ inches.

APPROVED APRIL 9, 1957

ENGLISH SETTER

The English Setter is one of the handsomest of all sporting dogs. Their abundant coat gives them an advantage over the Pointer in facing cold, wet, windy weather. Their admirers also claim they possess more dash and vim, do not thicken up so quickly with age as the Pointer, and that they improve in their work from year to year. The picture presented by a well-bred setter with soft, expressive eye, low-set ear, head chiseled on classic lines, clean-cut neck, graceful outline, and attractive coat and coloring, leaves nothing to be desired in point of beauty. In addition, they possess the sweetest and most companionable of dispositions.

The modern setter is said to be descended from spaniels which had been trained to stop and set the birds instead of flushing them.

The time and place, however, where this first occurred is shrouded in obscurity. The excellences of our present-day setters can be attributed largely to Edward Laverack. This gentleman, in about 1825, secured a brace of setters, Ponto and Old Moll, from the Rev. Mr. Harrison, of Carlisle. These dogs he mated, their progeny in turn were interbred, and this formula of breeding was continued for upward of fifty years, in the course of which time Mr. Laverack created a strain of setters bearing his name, which were as famous for their field qualities as for their beauty.

The conclusions that men arrive at in writing a bench-show standard as to how a practical working dog should be built and how his head should be supported on his neck or his shoulders placed in relationship to his body, is more or less whimsical and subject to change. There is no way of determining that which is right and that which is wrong. There is always danger of overemphasizing the importance of some point at the expense of others and losing sight of the fact that under the laws of correlation it is impossible to change one point without changing all others to a greater or less degree.

The field-trial men have never permitted details of conformation to detract from their single object of practical performance. The bench-show winning setter today is a very elegant animal, but no more so than the field trial dog, with every element of utility expressed in his countenance, written in his frame, and recorded in his pedigree.

Buyer's guide: Lively and outgoing in temperament, the English Setter adapts quickly to a family situation, but be careful to select a puppy with a stable disposition and no signs of nervousness. Their coat should be brushed daily to prevent matting, but on the whole they do not make big grooming demands on their owners. The breed is at their best when not pampered.

STANDARD FOR THE ENGLISH SETTER

Head: Long and lean, with a well-defined stop. The skull oval from ear to ear, of medium width, giving brain room but with no suggestion of coarseness, with but little difference between the width at base of skull and at brows and with a moderately defined occipital protuberance. Brows should be at a sharp angle from the muzzle. Muzzle should be long and square, of width in harmony with the skull, without any fullness under the eyes and straight from eyes to tip of the nose. A dish-face or Roman nose objectionable. The lips square and fairly pendant. Nose should be black or dark liver in color, except in white, lemon and white, orange and white dogs, when it may be of lighter color. Nostrils should be wide apart and large in the openings. Jaws should be of equal length. Overshot or undershot jaw objectionable. Ears should be carried close to the head, well back and set low, of moderate length, slightly rounded at the ends, and covered with silky hair. Eyes should be bright, mild, intelligent and dark brown in color.

Neck: The neck should be long and lean, arched at the crest, and not too throaty.

Shoulders: Shoulders should be formed to permit perfect freedom of action to the forelegs. Shoulder blades should be long, wide, sloping moderately well back and standing fairly close together at the top.

Chest: Chest between shoulder blades should be of good depth but not of excessive width.

Ribs: Ribs, back of the shoulders, should spring gradually to the middle of the body and then taper to the back ribs, which should be of good depth.

Back: Back should be strong at its junction with the loin and should be straight or sloping upward very slightly to the top of the shoulder, the whole forming a graceful outline of medium length, without sway or drop. Loins should be strong, moderate in length, slightly arched, but not to the extent of being roached or wheel-backed. Hipbones should be wide apart without too sudden drop to the root of the tail.

Forelegs: The arms should be flat and muscular, with bone fully developed and muscles hard and devoid of flabbiness; of good length from the point of the shoulder to the elbow, and set at such an angle as will bring the legs fairly under the dog. Elbows should have no tendency to turn either in or out. The pastern should be short, strong and nearly round with the slope from the pastern joint to the foot deviating very slightly forward from the perpendicular.

Hind Legs: The hind legs should have wide, muscular thighs with well developed lower thighs. Stifles should be well bent and strong. Hocks should be wide and flat. The hind pastern or metatarsus should be short, strong and nearly round.

Feet: Feet should be closely set and strong, pads well developed and tough, toes well arched and protected with short, thick hair.

Tail: Tail should be straight and taper to a fine point, with only sufficient length to reach the hocks, or less. The feather must be straight and silky, falling loosely in a fringe and tapering to the point when the tail is raised. There must be no bushiness. The tail should not curl sideways or above the level of the back.

Coat: Coat should be flat and of good length, without curl; nor soft or woolly. The feather on the legs should be moderately thin and regular.

Height: Dogs about 25 inches; bitches about 24 inches.

Colors: Black, white and tan; black and white; blue belton; lemon and white; lemon belton; orange and white; orange belton; liver and white; liver belton; and solid white. **Markings:** Dogs without heavy patches of color on the body, but flecked all over preferred.

Symmetry: The harmony of all parts to be considered. Symmetrical dogs will have level backs or be very slightly higher at the shoulders than at the hips. Balance, harmony of proportion, and an appearance of breeding and quality to be looked for, and coarseness avoided.

Movement and Carriage: An easy, free and graceful movement, suggesting rapidity and endurance. A lively tail and a high carriage of head. Stiltiness, clumsiness or a lumbering gait are objectionable.

SCALE OF POINTS

Head
  Skull 5
  Ears 5
  Eyes 5
  Muzzle 5   20
Body
  Neck 5
  Chest and shoulders 12
  Back, loin and ribs 10   27
Running Gear
  Forelegs 5
  Hips, thighs
    and hind legs 12
  Feet 6   23
Coat
  Length and texture 5
  Color and marking 3   8
Tail
  Length and carriage 5   5
General Appearance and Action
  Symmetry, style and
    movement 12
  Size 5   17

TOTAL 100

APPROVED MAY 8, 1951

GORDON SETTER

This handsome breed of setters derives its name from the Dukes of Gordon, who owned a most important kennel of black-and-tan and black-white-and-tan setters at a period considerably in advance of dog shows. The early history of the Gordon Setter is wrapped in much mystery, considering the fact that they are of comparatively recent origin. A great many writers have stated that in the early days of the breed the Duke crossed one of his best dogs with a black-and-tan Collie named Maddy which lived on the estate and was remarkably clever in finding grouse. It is said that she did not point them, her habit being to stop and watch the birds as soon as she had them located. It is conceded, even by those who deny the authenticity of this story, that occasionally one sees the tail of the Collie in strains that trace back to the Duke's kennel, and it is also notable that many Gordon Setters display in working birds a desire to go round their game, just as a Collie goes round a flock of sheep.

Another theory is that the breed is the result of crossing the ordinary setter with the leggy, black Springing Spaniel. There is similarity in the physiognomy of the Gordon Setter and the Field Spaniel, and the latter in early days was a leggy dog of setter-like type, so that this cross could have been made without affecting the working characteristics of the setter. This is a plausible explanation of the dog's origin.

Still another theory provides that the black-and-tan setter has been produced by a cross with the Irish Setter and the black Pointer. All of these explanations are, however, mere conjecture, and there exists no definite or conclusive information on the subject.

Today's Gordon Setters make steady, reliable shooting dogs, as they have splendid noses and biddable dispositions. Their strikingly handsome coloring and intelligence commend them to many people.

In selecting Gordon Setter puppies the usual setter points should be looked for, such as long head; square muzzle; well-developed occipital bone; short body; deep chest; straight forelegs; short, straight tail; and the typical black-and-tan markings, the tan of rich, dark mahogany.

Buyer's guide: Breeders have worked hard to retain the "bird sense" that this breed is noted for, so it is hoped that the Gordon will be used in the field. They can become fairly high-strung if kept confined to the house, so apartment dwelling is not recommended. They are intelligent and clean in their mannerisms, and develop stable, gentle dispositions when given plenty of personal attention.

STANDARD FOR THE GORDON SETTER

General Impression: The Gordon Setter is a good-sized, sturdily built, black and tan dog, well muscled, with plenty of bone and substance, but active, upstanding, and stylish, appearing capable of doing a full day's work in the field. He has a strong, rather short back, with well-sprung ribs and a short tail. The head is fairly heavy and finely chiseled. His bearing is intelligent, noble, and dignified, showing no signs of shyness or viciousness. Clear colors and straight or slightly waved coat are correct. He suggests strength and stamina rather than extreme speed. Symmetry and quality are most essential. A dog well-balanced in all points is preferable to one with outstanding good qualities and defects. A smooth, free movement, with high head carriage, is typical.

Size: Shoulder height for males, 24 to 27 inches. For females, 23 to 26 inches.

Weight: Males, 55 to 80 pounds; females, 45 to 70 pounds. Animals that appear to be over or under the prescribed weight limits are to be judged on the basis of conformation and condition. Extremely thin or fat dogs should be discouraged on the basis that under- or overweight hampers the true working ability of the Gordon Setter. The weight-to-height ratio makes him heavier than other setters.

Head: The head is deep, rather than broad, with plenty of brain room; a nicely rounded, good-sized skull, broadest between the ears. The head should have a clearly indicated stop. Below and above the eyes should be lean, and the cheek as narrow as the leanness of the head allows. The muzzle is fairly long and not pointed, either as seen from above or from the side. The flews should not be pendulous. The nose should be broad, with open nostrils and black in color. The muzzle is the same length as the skull from occiput to stop, and the top of the muzzle is parallel to the line of the skull extended. The lip line from the nose to the flews shows a sharp, well-defined, square contour.

Eyes: Of fair size, neither too deep-set, nor too bulging, dark brown, bright, and wise. The shape is oval rather than round. The lids should be tight. *Ears:* Set low on the head approximately on line with the eye, fairly large and thin, well folded and carried close to the head. *Teeth:* The teeth should be strong and white, and preferably should meet in front in a scissors bite, with the upper incisors slightly forward of the lower incisors. A level bite is not to be considered a fault. Pitted teeth from distemper or allied infections should not be penalized.

Neck: Long, lean, arched to the head, and without throatiness.

Shoulders: Should be fine at the points, and lying well back, giving a moderately sloping topline. The tops of the shoulder blades should be close together. When viewed from behind, the neck appears to fit into the shoulders in smooth, flat, lines that gradually widen from neck to shoulder.

Chest: Deep and not too broad in front; the ribs well sprung, leaving plenty of lung room. The chest should reach to the elbows. A pronounced forechest should be in evidence.

Body: The body should be short from shoulder to hips, and the distance from the forechest to the back of the thigh should approximately equal the height from the ground to the withers. The loins should be short and broad and not arched. The croup is nearly flat, with only a slight slope to the tailhead.

Forequarters: The legs should be big-boned, straight, and not bowed, with elbows free and not turned in or out. The angle formed by the shoulder blade and upper arm bone should be approximately 90° when the dog is standing so that the foreleg is perpendicular to the ground. The pasterns should be straight.

Hindquarters: The hind legs from hip to hock should be long, flat, and muscular; from hock to heel, short and strong. The stifle and hock joints are well bent and not turned either in or out. When the dog is standing with the hock perpendicular to the ground, the thigh bone should hang downward parallel to an imaginary line drawn upward from the hock.

Feet: The feet should be formed by close-knit, well-arched toes with plenty of hair between; with full toe pads and deep heel cushions. Feet should not be turned in or out. Feet should be catlike in shape.

Tail: Short and should not reach below the hocks, carried horizontal or nearly so; thick at the root and finishing in a fine point. The feather which starts near the root of the tail should be slightly waved or straight, having triangular appearance, growing shorter uniformly toward the end. The placement of the tail is important for correct carriage. If the croup is nearly flat, the tail must emerge nearly on the same plane as the croup to allow for horizontal carriage. When the angle of the tail bends too sharply at the first coccygeal bone, the tail will be carried too gaily or will droop. The tail placement should be judged in its relationship to the structure of the croup.

Temperament: The Gordon Setter should be alert, gay, interested, and aggressive. He should be fearless and willing, intelligent and capable. He should be loyal and affectionate, and strong-minded enough to stand the rigors of training.

Gait: The action of the Gordon Setter is a bold, strong, driving, free swinging gait. The head is carried up and the tail "flags" constantly while the dog is in motion. When viewed from the front, the forefeet move up and down in straight lines so that the shoulder, elbow, and pastern joints are approximately in line with each other. When viewed from the rear, the hock, stifle, and hip joints are approximately in line.

Thus the dog moves in a straight pattern forward without throwing the feet in or out. When viewed from the side, the forefeet are seen to lift up and reach forward to compensate for the driving hindquarters. The hindquarters reach well forward and stretch far back, enabling the stride to be long and the drive powerful. The over-all appearance of the moving dog is one of smooth-flowing, well-balanced rhythm, in which the action is pleasing to the eye, effortless, economical and harmonious.

Coat: Should be soft and shining, straight or slightly waved, but not curly, with long hair on ears, under stomach and on chest, on back of the fore- and hind legs, and on the tail.

Color and Markings: Black with tan markings, either of rich chestnut or mahogany color. Black penciling is allowed on the toes. The borderline between black and tan colors should be clearly defined. There should not be any tan hairs mixed in the black. The tan markings should be located as follows: (1) Two clear spots over the eyes and not over three quarters of an inch in diameter; (2) On the sides of the muzzle. The tan should not reach to the top of the muzzle, but resembles a stripe around the end of the muzzle from one side to the other; (3) On the throat; (4) Two large clear spots on the chest; (5) On the inside of the hind legs showing down the front of the stifle and broadening out to the outside of the hind legs from the hock to the toes. It must not completely eliminate the black on the back of the hind legs; (6) On the forelegs from the carpus, or a little above, downward to the toes; (7) Around the vent; (8) A white spot on the chest is allowed, but the smaller the better. Predominantly tan, red or buff dogs which do not have the typical pattern of markings of a Gordon Setter are ineligible for showing and undesirable for breeding.

SCALE OF POINTS

While not a part of the official breed standard, may be helpful in placing proper emphasis upon qualities desired in the physical make-up of the breed.

Head and neck (incl. ears and eyes) 10	Coat and markings 5
Body 15	Color and markings 5
Shoulders, forelegs, forefeet 10	Temperament 10
Hind legs and feet 10	Size, general appearance 15
Tail 5	Gait 12
Coat 8	TOTAL 100

DISQUALIFICATIONS

Predominantly tan, red, or buff dogs which do not have the typical pattern of markings of a Gordon Setter.

APPROVED, NOVEMBER 13, 1962

Representing the breed: Am., Can. Ch. Sangerfield Jed, owned by Fred Itzenplitz and bred by Jean Sanger Look.

IRISH SETTER

The Irish Setter is conceded by most authorities to be the purest bred member of the bird dog family. This is singular, in view of the fact that very little is known about his origin, and while he is frequently alluded to by writers of a century or more ago, they have failed to tell what kind of a dog he was either in color or form. In all probability he was a red-and-white dog; a smart, active animal, full of courage, tireless energy, inclined to be headstrong, and with a nose quite as good as any other dog used for a similar purpose.

The American Irish Setter of many years ago was of this stamp, a favorite among sportsmen, and a successful competitor at the early field trials. In those days there was no particular craze for coat or coloring, and no criticism was aimed at dogs of a light red color or those with white markings, so long as they were courageous and capable workmen in the field.

With the advent of dog shows came a demand in the standards for a dark red, mahogany-colored coat. A yellowish coat was not tolerated, and bench-show judges looked with disfavor upon dogs with white markings. As a result fanciers bred largely for color. Workmanlike qualities were all but forgotten, and although they succeeded in getting beautiful dark, rich, solid red dogs, it was at the expense of their utilitarian qualities, and the Irish Setter, once a reckless daredevil, frequently headstrong and a difficult dog to break, became a much more docile dog.

That the Irish Setter is a beautiful dog no one will deny. The chief points to look for in the selection of Irish Setter puppies at from two to four months old and after are almost identical with those of the English Setter, with color added, which should, of course, be a deep red.

Buyer's guide: A level disposition is an essential trait to look for when selecting an Irish Setter puppy. Give them plenty of chance to exercise and work off their energy and they will be fine companions in the home. Confinement does not suit the breed, as they should have plenty of human contact to bring out their sweet nature. Irish Setters are well suited to young owners who enjoy the outdoors and who have the patience to teach this sometimes slow learning breed.

STANDARD FOR THE IRISH SETTER

General Appearance: The Irish Setter is an active, aristocratic birddog, rich red in color, substantial yet elegant in build. Standing over two feet tall at the shoulder, the dog has a straight, fine, glossy coat, longer on ears, chest, tail, and back of legs. Afield he is a swift-moving hunter; at home, a sweet-natured, trainable companion. His is a rollicking personality.

Head: Long and lean, its length at least double the width between the ears. The brow is raised, showing a distinct stop midway between the tip of nose and the well-defined occiput (rear point of skull). Thus the nearly level line from occiput to brow is set a little above, and parallel to, the straight and equal line from eye to nose. The skull is oval when viewed from above or front; very slightly domed when viewed in profile. Beauty of head is emphasized by delicate chiseling along the muzzle, around and below the eyes, and along the cheeks. Muzzle moderately deep, nostrils wide, jaws of nearly equal length. Upper lips fairly square but not pendulous, the underline of the jaws being almost parallel with the top line of the muzzle. The teeth meet in a scissors bite in which the upper incisors fit closely over the lower, or they may meet evenly. **Nose:** Black or chocolate. **Eyes:** Somewhat almond-shaped, of medium size, placed rather well apart; neither deep-set nor bulging. Color, dark to medium brown. Expression soft yet alert. **Ears:** Set well back and low, not above level of eye. Leather thin, hanging in a neat fold close to the head, and nearly long enough to reach the nose.

Neck: Moderately long, strong but not thick, and slightly arched; free from throatiness and fitting smoothly into the shoulders.

Body: Sufficiently long to permit a straight and free stride. Shoulder blades long, wide, sloping well back, fairly close together at the top, and joined in front to long upper arms angled to bring the elbows slightly rearward along the brisket. Chest deep, reaching approximately to the elbows; rather narrow in front. Ribs well sprung. Loins of moderate length, muscular and slightly arched. Top line of body from withers to tail slopes slightly downward without sharp drop at the croup. Hindquarters should be wide and powerful with broad, well-developed thighs.

Legs and Feet: All legs sturdy, with plenty of bone, and strong, nearly straight pastern. Feet rather small, very firm, toes arched and close. Forelegs straight and sinewy, the elbows moving freely. Hind legs long and muscular from hip to hock, short and nearly perpendicular from hock to ground; well angulated at stifle and hock joints, which, like the elbows, inclined neither in nor out.

Tail: Strong at root, tapering to fine point, about long enough to reach the hock. Carriage straight or curving slightly upward, nearly level with the back.

Coat: Short and fine on head, forelegs, and tips of ears; on all other parts, of moderate length and flat. Feathering long and silky on ears; on backs of forelegs and thighs long and fine, with a pleasing fringe of hair on belly and brisket extending onto the chest. Feet well feathered between the toes. Fringe on tail moderately long and tapering. All coat and feathering as straight and free as possible from curl or wave.

Color: Mahogany or rich chestnut red, with no trace of black. A small amount of white on chest, throat, or toes, or a narrow centered streak on skull, is not penalized.

Size: There is no disqualification as to size. The make and fit of all parts and their over-all balance in the animal are rated more important. Twenty-seven inches at the withers and a show weight of about 70 pounds is considered ideal for a dog; the bitch 25 inches, 60 pounds. Variance beyond an inch up or down to be discouraged.

Gait: At the trot the gait is big, very lively, graceful, and efficient. The head is held high. The hindquarters drive smoothly and with great power. The forelegs reach well ahead as if to pull in the ground, without giving the appearance of a hackney gait. The dog runs as he stands: straight. Seen from the front or rear, the forelegs, as well as the hind legs below the hock joint, move perpendicularly to the ground, with some tendency towards a single track as speed increases. But a crossing or weaving of the legs, front or back, is objectionable.

Balance: At his best, the lines of the Irish Setter so satisfy in over-all balance that artists have termed him the most beautiful of all dogs. The correct specimen always exhibits balance whether standing or in motion. Each part of the dog flows and fits smoothly into its neighboring parts without calling attention to itself.

APPROVED JUNE 14, 1960

THE SPANIEL FAMILY

The name borne by this family of beautiful dogs indicates that the parent stock came from Spain. In response to special environment or to gratify the fancy of breeders, or bred to serve useful purposes, they have since divided into several important groups.

Just when the spaniel came to England it is impossible to say, for while the early writers refer to Water Dogges and Water Spaniels, their descriptions are so lacking in clarity that it is impossible to form an opinion that is free from reservations.

The fact that many of the older writers refer to the presence among English sportsmen of a dog used for retrieving wild fowl that was known as the Water Dogge, has prompted writers to jump to the conclusion that this dog was the parent spaniel type. This was a great mistake. The Water Dogge was not a true spaniel, but on the contrary was descended from the French Barbet, the ancestor of the Poodle. This early Water Dogge, if old pictures and engravings are to be believed, was quite similar to the modern Irish Water Spaniel and presented the same general conformation, coat, and topknot. It is probable that both are of Barbet ancestry; certainly the Irish Water Spaniel is not of true spaniel type.

The Old English Water Spaniel, the progenitor of the modern family of spaniels, was a distinct breed. Early paintings portray him as being much like the Springer of today, differing principally in the character of his coat, which was curly. The Old English Water Spaniel was crossed occasionally with other breeds and the progeny mated with careful seletion, and from them we have derived the various families of modern Springers, Field Spaniels, Cockers, Sussex, Welch, and diminutive toys. Some of these breeds are useful to the sportsman, others are simply pets; but from the forty-pound Springer to the five-pound toy, they all resemble each other in marked amiability of character and unusual intelligence.

Another important branch of the Old English Water Spaniel

breed is the setter family. All setters are of spaniel origin, and early writers refer to the Setting Spaniel in contradistinction to those that sprang in and flushed the game, which were known as Springers. There is also another breed of dogs mentioned by Cuvier and other authorities as the Alpine Spaniel. This dog is said to have been the progenitor of the St. Bernard and the Clumber. However this may be, there is no question that there is a similarity in coloration between the Clumber and the St. Bernard, as well as a further resemblance in their massive structure and peculiarities of the head, eyes, and flews.

The Old English Water Spaniel broke up into the several groups of spaniels we have enumerated, but unfortunately while the breeds were being created the parent breed was lost. There have been several attempts to resurrect the parent type without much success, and nothing can be said about them other than that in appearance they probably resembled the modern Springer, the principal difference being a curlier coat. Like him, they were a useful dog that would hunt fur or feather and retrieve from land or water.

AMERICAN WATER SPANIEL

One of the few native American breeds, the American Water Spaniel traces back to the early 19th century when the breed was being developed in the midwestern area of the United States. The Irish Water Spaniel, the Curly-Coated Retriever and the now extinct Old English Water Spaniel figure heavily in the ancestry of this breed. Like these other breeds, the American Water Spaniel is a medium-sized dog. He is equally adept at hunting fur and feathers, and is quite hardy and rugged. Keen to the hunt, the American Water Spaniel can make retrieves in even the most demanding conditions of weather or terrain.

Although the breed is only rarely seen today, they are first-rate hunting dogs. American Water Spaniels are known for having a keen memory which can enable them to unhesitantly locate and recover up to six felled birds on one retrieve. The densest brush is easily accessable because his coat is thick and closely curled to give him protection against weather, water or the undercover. He is an able swimmer and dives eagerly into the water on a retrieve.

Aside from his role as able shooting dog, the American Water Spaniel has been acclaimed as a faithful watchdog and household companion. People who experience the outdoors for recreation should consider the American Water Spaniel—they're always ready for action.

Buyer's guide: Fanciers of this breed are quite adamant that the breed be used as a hunting dog first and foremost. It might be hard to obtain an American Water Spaniel from a breeder without stating that the dog will be actively used in the hunting field. They are a dual dog, however, and are very friendly to their owners. They require little grooming and present no problem with other animals or children. Athletic owners are suggested.

STANDARD FOR THE AMERICAN WATER SPANIEL

General Appearance: Medium in size, of sturdy typical spaniel character, curly coat, an active muscular dog, with emphasis placed on proper size and conformation, correct head properties, texture of coat and color. Of amicable disposition; demeanor indicates intelligence, strength and endurance.

Head: Moderate in length, skull rather broad and full, stop moderately defined, but not too pronounced. Forehead covered with short smooth hair and without tuft or topknot. Muzzle of medium length, square and with no inclination to snipiness, jaws strong and of good length, and neither undershot nor overshot, teeth straight and well shaped. Nose sufficiently wide and with well-developed nostrils to insure good scenting power. **Faults:** Very flat skull, narrow across the top, long, slender or snipy muzzle.

Eyes: Hazel, brown or of dark tone to harmonize with coat; set well apart. Expression alert, attractive, intelligent. **Fault:** Yellow eyes to disqualify.

Ears: Lobular, long and wide, not set too high on head, but slightly above the eyeline. Leather extending to end of nose and well covered with close curls.

Neck: Round and of medium length, strong and muscular, free of throatiness, set to carry head with dignity, but arch not accentuated.

Body Structure: Well developed, sturdily constructed but not too compactly coupled. General outline is a symmetrical relationship of parts. Shoulders sloping, clean and muscular. Strong loins, lightly arched, and well furnished, deep brisket but not excessively broad. Well-sprung ribs. Legs of medium length and well-boned, but not so short as to handicap for field work.

Legs and Feet: Forelegs powerful and reasonably straight. Hind legs firm with suitably bent stifles and strong hocks well let down. Feet to harmonize with size of dog. Toes closely grouped and well padded. **Fault:** Cowhocks.

Tail: Moderate in length, curved in a slightly rocker shape, carried slightly below level of back; tapered and covered with hair to tip, action lively. **Faults:** Rat or shaved tail.

Coat: The coat should be closely curled or have marcel effect and should be of sufficient density to be of protection against weather, water or punishing cover, yet not coarse. Legs should have medium short, curly feather. **Faults:** Coat too straight, soft, fine or tightly kinked.

Color: Solid liver or dark chocolate, a little white on toes or chest permissible.

Height: 15 to 18 inches at the shoulder.

Weight: Males, 28 to 45 pounds; females, 25 to 40 pounds.

DISQUALIFICATION: Yellow eyes.

Representing the breed: Ch. Countryside's Happy Hiram, owned by Barbara Spisak.

BRITTANY SPANIEL

This French sporting dog is a competent, wide-ranging hunting dog that not only retrieves but also points its game. In their homeland they were originally called the Epagneul Breton. They have the agility of a sprinter and are compactly, though not lightly, built. In the field, they are stylish in movement and go to their task with vigor and determination. These characteristics have helped to make the Brittany one of the most popular dogs in America.

The breed stems from ancient lineage, possibly from the stock of early Spanish setters and spaniels. Outcrosses with European pointer strains helped set the colors and type of today's Brittany. Because of their lightness of bone, they are quick and agile runners capable of covering great expanses of ground. They are leggy, but should not be spindly, and should create an overall appearance of ruggedness without bulkiness. Brittanies are noted for their endurance and level-headedness and they will adapt quickly to any environment, provided they are allowed freedom of movement.

The Brittany's coat is dense and wavy and of a lovely dark orange and white or liver and white color. This coat has been lauded for being highly visible to the hunter despite dense underbrush. Their lips are naturally dry so that feathers do not stick during a retrieve. Brittany Spaniels are well adapted to hunting and retrieving game and are well used by sportsmen who find the breed quick in movement and long on interest and energy.

Buyer's guide: Brittany Spaniels are moderately sized and suitable for both home and field. They are at their best when taken hunting regularly and this outlet makes them more amiable in the home. Large city dwellers should not choose a Brittany for this breed will find it hard to relax in an urban setting. Their retrieving instincts should be encouraged as this produces a lively, alert dog.

STANDARD FOR THE BRITTANY SPANIEL

General Description: A compact, closely-knit dog of medium size, a leggy spaniel having the appearance, as well as the agility, of a great ground coverer. Strong, vigorous, energetic and quick of movement. Not too light in bone, yet never heavy-boned and cumbersome. Ruggedness, without clumsiness, is a characteristic of the breed. So leggy is he that his height at the withers is the same as the length of his body. He has no tail, or at most, not more than 4 inches.

Weight: Should weigh between 30 and 40 pounds.

Height: 17½ to 20½ inches--measured from the ground at the highest point of the shoulders. Any Brittany Spaniel measuring under 17½ inches or over 20½ inches shall be disqualified from bench-show competition.

Coat: Dense, flat or wavy, never curly. Texture neither wiry nor silky. The ears should carry little fringe. The front and hind legs should have some feathering but too little is definitely preferable to too much. Dogs with long or profuse feathering or furnishings shall be so severely penalized as to effectively eliminate them from competition.

Skin: Fine and fairly loose. (A loose skin rolls with briars and sticks, thus diminishing punctures or tearing. But a skin so loose as to form pouches is undesirable).

Color: Orange and white or liver and white in either clear or roan patterns. Some ticking is desirable. The orange or liver is found in standard parti-color or piebald patterns. Washed out colors are not desirable. Black is a disqualification.

Skull: Medium length (approximately 4¾ inches). Rounded, very slightly wedge-shaped, but evenly made. Width, not quite as wide as the length (about 4 3/8 inches) and never so broad as to appear coarse, or so narrow as to appear racy. Well-defined, but gently sloping stop effect. Median line rather indistinct. The occipital crest only apparent to the touch. Lateral walls well rounded. The Brittany should never be "apple-headed" and he should never have an indented stop. (All measurements of skull are for a 19½-inch dog).

Muzzle: Medium length, about two thirds the length of the skull, measuring the muzzle from the tip to the stop, and the skull from the occipital crest to the stop between the eyes. Muzzle should taper gradually in both horizontal and vertical dimensions as it approaches the nostrils. Neither a Roman nose nor a concave curve (dish-face) is desirable. Never broad, heavy, or snipy.

Nose: Nostrils well open to permit deep breathing of air and adequate scenting while at top speed. Tight nostrils should be penalized. Never shiny. Color, fawn, tan, light shades of brown or deep pink. A black nose is a disqualification. A two-tone or butterfly nose should be penalized.

Eyes: Well set in head. Well protected from briars by a heavy, expressive eyebrow. A prominent, full or pop eye should be heavily penalized. It is a serious fault in a hunting dog that must face briars. Skull well chiseled under the eyes, so that the lower lid is not pulled back to form a pocket or haw for catching seeds, dirt and weed dust. Judges should check by forcing head down to see if lid falls away from the eye. Preference should be for darker-colored eyes, though lighter shades of amber should not be penalized. Light and mean-looking eyes to be heavily penalized.

Ears: Set high, above the level of the eyes. Short and leafy, rather than pendulous, reaching about half the length of the muzzle. Should lie flat and close to the head, with the tip rounded very slightly. Ears well covered with dense, but relatively short hair, and with little fringe.

Lips: Tight to the muzzle, with the upper lip overlapping the lower jaw only sufficiently to cover under lip. Lips dry so that feathers do not stick. Drooling to receive a heavy penalty. Flews to be penalized.

Teeth: Well-joined incisors. Posterior edge of upper incisors in contact with anterior edge of lower incisors, thus giving a true scissors bite. Overshot or undershot jaw to be penalized heavily.

Neck: Medium length. Not quite permitting the dog to place his nose on the ground without bending his legs. Free from throatiness, though not a serious fault unless accompanied by dewlaps. Strong, without giving the impression of being overmuscled. Well set into sloping shoulders. Never concave or ewe-necked.

Body Length: Approximately the same as the height when measured at the withers. Body length is measured from the point of the forechest to the rear of the haunches. A long body should be heavily penalized.

Withers: Shoulder blades should not protrude much. Not too widely set apart with perhaps two thumbs' width or less between the blades. At the withers, the Brittany is slightly higher than at the rump.

Shoulders: Sloping and muscular. Blade and upper arm should form nearly a 90-degree angle when measured from the posterior point of the blade at the withers to the junction of the blade and upper arm, and thence to the point of the elbow nearest the ribs. Straight shoulders do not permit sufficient reach.

Back: Short and straight. Slight slope from highest point of withers to the root of the tail. Never hollow, saddle, sway, or roach-backed. Slight drop from hips to root of tail. Distance from last rib to upper thigh short, about three to four finger widths.

Chest: Deep, reaching the level of the elbow. Neither so wide nor so rounded as to disturb the placement of the shoulder bones and elbows, which causes a paddling movement, and often causes soreness from elbow striking ribs. Ribs well sprung, but adequate heart room provided by depth as well as width. Narrow or slab-sided chests are a fault.

Flanks: Rounded. Fairly full. Not extremely tucked up, nor yet flabby and falling. Loins short and strong. Narrow and weak loins are a fault. In motion the loin should not sway sideways, giving a zigzag motion to the back, wasting energy.

Hindquarters: Broad, strong and muscular, with powerful thighs and well-bent stifles, giving a hip set well into the loin and the marked angulation necessary for a powerful drive when in motion. Fat and falling hindquarters are a fault.

Tail: Naturally tailless, or not over four inches long. (A tail substantially more than 4 inches in length shall disqualify). Natural or docked. Set on high, actually an extension of the spine at about the same level.

Front Legs: Viewed from the front, perpendicular, but not set too wide as in the case of a dog loaded in shoulder. Elbows and feet turning neither in nor out. Viewed from the side, practically perpendicular to the pastern. Pastern slightly bent to give cushion to stride. Not so straight as in terriers. Falling pasterns, however, are a serious fault. Leg bones clean, graceful, but not too fine. An extremely heavy bone is as much a fault as spindly legs. One must look for substance and suppleness. Height to the elbows should approximately equal distance from elbow to withers.

Hind Legs: Stifles well bent. The stifle generally is the term used for knee joint. If the angle made by the upper and lower leg bones is too straight, the dog quite generally lacks drive, since his hind legs cannot drive as far forward at each stride as is desirable. However, the stifle should not be bent as to throw the hock joint far out behind the dog. Since factors not easily seen by the eye may give the dog his proper drive, a Brittany should not be condemned for straight stifle until the judge has checked the dog in motion from the side. When at a trot, the Brittany's hind foot should step into or beyond the print left by the front foot. The stifle joint should not turn out making a cowhock. The cowhock moves the foot out to the side, thus driving out of line, and losing reach at each stride. Thighs well feathered, but not profusely, halfway to the hock. Hocks, that is, the back pasterns, should be moderately short, pointing neither in nor out; perpendicular when viewed from the side. They should be firm when shaken by the judge.

Feet: Should be strong, proportionately smaller than other spaniels, with close-fitting, well-arched toes and thick pads. The Brittany is not "up on his toes." Toes not heavily feathered. Flat feet, splayed feet, paper feet, etc., are to be heavily penalized. An ideal foot is halfway between the hare-and cat-foot.

A Guide to the Judge: The points below indicate only relative values. To be also taken into consideration are type, gait, soundness, spirit, optimum height, body length and general proportions.

SCALE OF POINTS

Head 25
Body 35
Running gear 40
TOTAL 100

DISQUALIFICATIONS

Any Brittany Spaniel measuring under 17½ inches or over 20½ inches.
Any black in the coat or a nose so dark in color as to appear black.
A tail substantially more than 4 inches in length.

APPROVED SEPTEMBER 13, 1966

Representing the breed: Ch. Jxpection's Ali Baba, owned by Josie Gakenheimer and Judith McGrath.

CLUMBER SPANIEL

This handsome and useful member of the spaniel family is of ancient lineage, and his solemn and majestic aspect mark him as a true aristocrat of long descent. The Clumbers are deserving of their popularity with shooting men, for no dog is a more capable assistant to the gun. They are by inclination the keenest and most persevering of hunters, have the best noses, and, considering their massive build, have remarkable powers of endurance.

The Clumber Spaniel is easily trained, easily controlled and unusually intelligent. They take naturally to retrieving, are good water dogs, and as all-round workmen have no superiors.

There is a good deal of mystery about the origin of this breed, and history carries them back to the middle of the eighteenth century. About that time the French Duc de Noailles presented a kennel of spaniels to the second Duke of Newcastle, whose Nottinghamshire country place is known as Clumber Park. Here the breed is said to have originated; certainly it is here that it received its name.

There is no trace of their origin in France, for there at the present day the Clumber is accepted as a purely English product. It has been suggested that the Duke, finding that the spaniels that had been presented to him were too fast, reduced their pace by crossing them on some heavier breed. What the cross or crosses were will never be known, but the Clumber's general type, his massive frame, powerful limbs, white coat with lemon markings, and his solemn and majestic aspect and demeanor suggest the St. Bernard. There is also a theory that they owe their origin to a cross of Baron Cuvier's Alpine Spaniel, a dog indirectly related to the St. Bernard.

The Clumber Spaniel has been very successful in the English Spaniel Trials, and the most convincing evidence of their worth is the tenacity with which the owners of old strains hang on to them and continue to breed and shoot over them year after year.

In selecting Clumber puppies look for short, massive heads; square muzzles; well marked stop; low-set, massive body of moderate length; big bone; flat, dense coat; down-carried tail and pale orange or lemon markings.

Buyer's guide: The stocky, slow-moving Clumber Spaniel is a great companion for older people who still enjoy the sport of the hunt or anyone who likes to take long, leisurely strolls in the country. Clumbers are a sedate and affectionate breed and will be great partners to those who appreciate the qualities of a fine sporting dog but do not have the time or energy to trail after the speedy flight of the setters or pointers. Clumbers get along well with just about everyone—other animals included. They are not aggressive and can be fine guardians for children.

STANDARD FOR THE CLUMBER SPANIEL

General Appearance and Size: General appearance, a long, low heavy-looking dog, of a very thoughtful expression, betokening great intelligence. Should have the appearance of great power. Sedate in all movements, but not clumsy. Weight of dogs averaging between 55 and 65 pounds; bitches from 35 to 50 pounds.

Head: Head large and massive in all its dimensions; round above eyes, flat on top, with a furrow running from between the eyes upon the center. A marked stop and large occipital protuberance. Jaw long, broad and deep. Lips of upper jaw overhung. Muzzle not square, but at the same time powerful-looking. Nostrils large, open and flesh-colored, sometimes cherry-colored. **Eyes:** Eyes are large, soft, deep-set and showing haw. Hazel in color, not too pale, with digified and intelligent expression. **Ears:** Ears long and broad at the top, turned over on the front edge; vine-shaped: close to the head; set on low and feathered only on the front edge, and there but slightly. Hair short and silky, without the slightest approach to wave or curl.

Neck and Shoulders: Neck long, thick and powerful, free from dewlap, with a large ruff. Shoulders immensely strong and muscular, giving a heavy appearance in front.

Body: Long, low and well ribbed up. The chest is wide and deep, the back long, broad, and level, with very slight arch over the loin.

Legs and Feet: Forelegs short, straight, and very heavy in bone; elbows close. Hind legs only slightly less heavily boned than the forelegs. They are moderately angulated, with hocks well let down. Quarters well developed and muscular. No feather above the hocks, but thick hair on the back of the legs just above the feet. Feet large, compact, and well filled with hair between the toes.

Coat and Feathers: Coat silky and straight, not too long, extremely dense; feather long and abundant.

Color and Markings: Color, lemon and white, and orange and white. Fewer markings on body the better. Perfection of markings, solid lemon or orange ears, evenly marked head and eyes, muzzle and legs ticked.

Stern: Stern set on a level and carried low.

SCALE OF POINTS

General appearance and size....10	Body and quarters............20
Head......................15	Legs and feet................10
Eyes 5	Coat and feather.............10
Ears......................10	Color and marking............5
Neck and shoulders..........10	TOTAL 100

APPROVED FEBRUARY 6, 1960

Representing the breed: Ch. Cypress Woods Dealer's Choice, owned by Betty L. Young. Photo by Michael Allen.

COCKER SPANIEL

The Cocker Spaniel, unlike the field varieties, is free from any abnormalities, being a rationally built and symmetrical little dog, full of buoyancy and beaming with intelligence and tireless energy. These features and characteristics account for his continued popularity.

As to his origin there is some mystery, but little doubt exists that the Cocker is among the most ancient of the spaniel family. He derives the name from the fact that he was first used as an aid to the gun in shooting woodcocks. The Cocker Spaniel is a handy little dog in getting through the dense thickets and bramble, while as a retriever he has probably no equal for nose and cleverness. At all the leading shows in America the Cocker section is a very large one, the classes numerous, and the interest in this merry little sportsman probably keener than it is in England.

The chief points to aim at in breeding Cocker Spaniels are compactness of body, straightness of forelegs, squareness of muzzle, dark eyes and flat coats, with a down-carriage of stern. Common defects in the breed, especially the colored variety, are crooked fronts, light eyes and cock-tails, which are an abomination to sporting men and to good judges alike.

Buyer's guide: The Cocker can fit in with most every lifestyle. They are merry in disposition and pleasant companions for both old and young. They are active and love the excitement of the hunt, yet readily adapt to the more sedate life of housepet. Cockers do not take well to being left alone for any length of time. They are also less tolerant than many dogs of the tail-pulling that can come from some young children, and may react with a warning growl or snap. Occasional trips to the grooming parlor are required to keep the coat neatly clipped and odor-free.

STANDARD FOR THE COCKER SPANIEL

General Appearance: The Cocker Spaniel is the smallest member of the Sporting Group. He has a sturdy, compact body and a cleanly chiseled and refined head, with the overall dog in complete balance and of ideal size. He stands well up at the shoulders on straight forelegs with a topline sloping slightly toward strong, muscular quarters. He is a dog capable of considerable speed, combined with great endurance. Above all he must be free and merry, sound, well balanced throughout, and in action show a keen inclination to work; equable in temperament with no suggestion of timidity.

Head: To attain a well-proportioned head, which must be in balance with the rest of the dog, it embodies the following:

Skull: Rounded but not exaggerated with no tendency to flatness; the eyebrows are clearly defined with a pronounced stop. The bony structure beneath the eyes is well chiseled with no prominence in the cheeks.

Muzzle: Broad and deep, with square, even jaws. The upper lip is full and of sufficient depth to cover the lower jaw. To be in correct balance, the distance from the stop to the tip of the nose is one half the distance from the stop up over the crown to the base of the skull.

Teeth: Strong and sound, not too small, and meet in a scissors bite.

Nose: Of sufficient size to balance the muzzle and foreface, with well-developed nostrils typical of a sporting dog. It is black in color in the blacks and black and tans. In other colors it may be brown, liver or black, the darker the better. The color of the nose harmonizes with the color of the eye rim.

Eyes: Eyeballs are round and full and look directly forward. The shape of the eye rims gives a slightly almond-shaped appearance; the eye is not weak or goggled. The color of the iris is dark brown and in general the darker the better. The expression is intelligent, alert, soft and appealing.

Ears: Lobular, long, of fine leather, well feathered, and placed no higher than a line to the lower part of the eye.

Neck and Shoulders: The neck is sufficiently long to allow the nose to reach the ground easily, muscular and free from pendulous "throatiness." It rises strongly from the shoulders and arches slightly as it tapers to join the head. The shoulders are well laid back forming an angle with the upper arm of approximately 90 degrees which permits the dog to move his forelegs in an easy manner with considerable forward reach. Shoulders are clean-cut and sloping without protrusion and so set that the upper points of the withers are at an angle which permits a wide spring of rib.

Body: The body is short, compact and firmly knit together, giving an impression of strength. The distance from the highest point of the shoulder blades to the ground is fifteen (15%) per cent or approximately two inches more than the length from this point to the set-on of the tail. Back is strong and sloping evenly and slightly downward from the shoulders to the set-on of the docked tail. Hips are wide and quarters well rounded and muscular. The chest is deep, its lowest point no higher than the elbows, its front sufficiently wide for adequate heart and lung space, yet not so wide as to interfere with the straightforward movement of the forelegs. Ribs are deep and well sprung. The Cocker Spaniel never appears long and low.

Tail: The docked tail is set on and carried on a line with the topline of the back, or slightly higher; never straight up like a terrier and never so low as to indicate timidity. When the dog is in motion the tail action is merry.

Legs and Feet: Forelegs are parallel, straight, strongly boned and muscular and set close to the body well under the scapulae. When viewed from the side with the forelegs vertical, the elbow is directly below the highest point of the shoulder blade. The pasterns are short and strong. The hind legs are strongly boned and muscled with good angulation at the stifle and powerful, clearly defined thighs. The stifle joint is strong and there is no slippage of it in motion or when standing. The hocks are strong, well let down, and when viewed from behind, the hind legs are parallel when in motion and at rest.

Feet: Compact, large, round and firm with horny pads; they turn neither in nor out. Dewclaws on hind legs and forelegs may be removed.

Coat: On the head, short and fine; on the body, medium length, with enough undercoating to give protection. The ears, chest, abdomen and legs are well feathered, but not so excessively as to hide the Cocker Spaniel's true lines and movement or affect his appearance and function as a sporting dog. The *texture* is most important. The coat is silky, flat or slightly wavy, and of a texture which permits easy care. Excessive or curly or cottony textured coat is to be penalized.

Color and Markings: *Black Variety* is jet black; shadings of brown or liver in the sheen of the coat is not desirable. A small amount of white on the chest and throat is to be penalized, and white in any other location shall disqualify.

Any Solid Color Other Than Black shall be a uniform shade. Lighter coloring of the feathering is permissible. A small amount of white on the chest and throat is to be penalized, and white in any other location shall disqualify.

Black and Tans, shown under the Variety of Any Solid Color Other than Black, have definite tan markings on a jet black body. The tan markings are distinct and plainly visible and the color of the tan may be from the lightest cream to the darkest red color. The amount of tan markings is restricted to ten (10%) per cent or less of the color of the specimen; tan markings in excess of ten (10%) per cent shall disqualify. Tan markings which are not readily visible in the ring or the absense of tan markings in any of the specified locations shall disqualify. The markings shall be located as follows:

(1) A clear spot over each eye.
(2) On the sides of the muzzle and on the cheeks.
(3) On the undersides of the ears.
(4) On all feet and legs.
(5) Under the tail.
(6) On the chest, optional, presence or absence not penalized.

Tan on the muzzle which extends upward, over and joins, shall be penalized. A small amount of white on the chest and throat is to be penalized, and white in any other location shall disqualify.

Parti-Color Variety—Two or more definite colors appearing in clearly defined markings, distinctly distributed over the body, are essential. Primary color which is ninety (90%) per cent or more shall disqualify;

secondary color or colors which are limited solely to one location shall disqualify. Roans are classified as Parti-colors and may be of any of the usual roaning patterns. Tri-colors are any of the above colors combined with tan markings. It is preferable that the tan markings be located in the same pattern as for Black and Tans.

Movement: The Cocker Spaniel, though the smallest of the sporting dogs, possesses a typical sporting dog gait. Prerequisite to good movement is balance between the front and rear assemblies. He drives with his strong, powerful rear quarters and is properly constructed in the shoulders and forelegs so that he can reach forward without constriction in a full stride to counterbalance the driving force from the rear. Above all, his gait is coordinated, smooth and effortless. The dog must cover ground with his action and excessive animation should never be mistaken for proper gait.

Height: The ideal height at the withers for an adult dog is 15 inches and for an adult bitch 14 inches. Height may vary one-half inch above or below this ideal. A dog whose height exceeds 15½ inches or a bitch whose height exceeds 14½ inches shall be disqualified. An adult dog whose height is less than 14½ inches or an adult bitch whose height is less than 13½ inches shall be penalized.

Note: Height is determined by a line perpendicular to the ground from the top of the shoulder blades, the dog standing naturally with its forelegs and the lower hind legs parallel to the line of measurements.

DISQUALIFICATIONS

Color and Markings—

Blacks—White markings except on chest and throat.

Solid Colors Other Than Black—White markings except on chest and throat.

Black and Tans—Tan markings in excess of ten (10%) per cent; tan markings not readily visible in the ring, or the absence of tan markings in any of the specified locations; white markings except on chest and throat.

Parti-Colors: Ninety (90%) per cent or more of primary color; secondary color or colors limited solely to one location.

Height—Males over 15½ inches; females over 14½ inches.

APPROVED DECEMBER 12, 1972

Representing the breed: Ch. Feinlyne by George, owned by Mr. and Mrs. Al Davies.

ENGLISH COCKER SPANIEL

Although officially recognized as a separate breed, the English Cocker Spaniel is still often confused with the more plentiful Cocker Spaniel. The English Cocker is slightly larger than his cousin, giving an overall leggier appearance, and with this greater size comes greater endurance. They also have a larger, longer muzzle that is well fitted to carrying game. English Cockers make excellent hunting partners, showing not only eagerness but also delight for their task. They are strongly built and their compact body is covered with a silky flat or wavy coat which enables them to withstand the rigors of the hunt, whether it is retrieving in icy water or trailing game through thorny underbrush.

The English Cocker Spaniel is a jolly pet for the home, satisfied with any attention he receives and overflowing with affection for his owner and friends. He is a willing competitor in both show and obedience competition and always appears ready to learn and perform. Although the breed was once quite active in field trial competitions in which man and dog are tested as hunting teams, today English Cockers are rarely seen demonstrating their talents in these trials.

Several hundred years ago when hunting spaniels were first being bred in England, the English Cocker Spaniel, the Cocker Spaniel and the English Springer Spaniel became differentiated strictly on the basis of their size. Each size of dog was valued for a specific type of field behavior and the three breed types slowly became set. Novice or uncaring breeders commonly interbred the cockers, however, and slowed the recognition of the English Cocker as a separate breed. Through careful importations of fine specimens from England and extensive pedigree research sponsored by a dedicated American fancier, Mrs. Geraldine Dodge, the separate strains of cockers have become segregated and enhanced. Due to the confusion over the early interbreedings, official recognition by the AKC was long in coming, but was finally granted in 1946.

As a sporting dog, the English Cocker Spaniel is an eager, competent hunting dog whose enthusiasm is contagious to all who hunt with him. In the home, his high intelligence and merry disposition can always be relied upon. Although they are at their best in country settings where they can take off on the scent of a rabbit or after small game, they adapt well to most any environment. Given proper outlets, the English Cocker Spaniel will prove to be one of the hardiest of the sporting dogs. They are noted primarily for their stamina and zest as workers, rather than for overpowering speed in the field.

Buyer's guide: The fine temperament and compact, yet strong body of the English Cocker make them good additions for both the home and sporting parties. Time outside is necessary to keep them in stable and satisfied disposition, without such releases they tend to be overly active in the house or melancholy. English Cockers make fine pets for older, yet still active people who have the inclination to give them plenty of attention. If in a household with small children, they may exhibit some signs of jealousy.

STANDARD FOR THE
ENGLISH COCKER SPANIEL

General Appearance: The English Cocker Spaniel is an attractive, active, merry sporting dog; with short body and strong limbs, standing well up at the withers. His movements are alive with energy; his gait powerful and frictionless. He is alert at all times, and the carriage of head and incessant action of his tail while at work give the impression that here is a dog that is not only bred for hunting, but really enjoys it. He is well balanced, strongly built, full of quality and is capable of top speed combined with great stamina. His head imparts an individual stamp peculiar to him alone and has that brainy appearance expressive of the highest intelligence; and is in perfect proportion to his body. His muzzle is a most distinctive feature, being of correct conformation and in proportion to his skull.

Character: The character of the English Cocker is of extreme importance. His love and faithfulness to his master and household, his alertness and courage are characteristic. He is noted for his intelligence and merry disposition; not quarrelsome; and is a responsive and willing worker both in the field and as a companion.

Head: The skull and forehead should be well developed with no suggestion of coarseness, arched and slightly flattened on top when viewed both from the stop to the end of the skull as well as from ear to ear, and cleanly chiseled under the eyes. The proportion of the head desirable is approximately one half for the muzzle and one half for the skull. The muzzle should be square with a definite stop where it blends into the skull and in proportion with the width of the skull. As the English Cocker is primarily a sporting dog, the muzzle and jaws must be of sufficient strength and size to carry game; and the length of the muzzle should provide room for the development of the olfactory nerve to insure good scenting qualities, which require that the nose be wide and well developed. Nostrils black in color except in reds, livers, parti-colors and roans of the lighter shades, where brown is permissible, but black preferred. Lips should be square, full and free from flews. Teeth should be even and set squarely. **Faults:** Muzzle too short or snipy. Jaw undershot. Lips snipy or pendulous. Skull too flat or too rounded, cheeky or coarse. Stop insufficient or exaggerated.

Eyes: The eyes should be of medium size, full and slightly oval shaped; set squarely in skull and wide apart. Eyes must be dark brown except in livers and light parti-colors where hazel is permissible, but the darker the better. The general expression should be intelligent, alert, bright and merry. **Faults:** Light, round or protruding eyes. Conspicuous haw.

Ears: Lobular; set low and close to the head; leather fine and extending at least to the nose, well covered with long, silky, straight or slightly wavy hair. **Faults:** Set or carried too high; too wide at the top; insufficient feathering; positive curls or ringlets.

Neck: Long, clean and muscular; arched towards the head; set cleanly into sloping shoulders. **Faults:** Short; thick; with dewlap or excessive throatiness.

Body: Close coupled, compact and firmly knit, giving the impression of great strength without heaviness. Depth of brisket should reach to the elbow, sloping gradually upward to the loin. Ribs should spring gradually to middle of body, tapering to back ribs which should be of good depth and extend well back. **Faults:** Too long and lacking depth; insufficient spring of rib; barrel rib.

Shoulders and Chest: Shoulders sloping and fine; chest deep and well developed but not too wide and round to interfere with the free action of the forelegs. **Faults:** Straight or loaded shoulders.

Back and Loin: Back short and strong. Length of back from withers to tail-set should approximate height from ground to withers. Height of the dog at the withers should be greater than the height at the hip joint, providing a gradual slope between these points. Loin short and powerful, slightly arched. **Faults:** Too low at withers; long, sway-back or roach back; flat or narrow loin; exaggerated tuck-up.

Forelegs: Straight and strong with bone nearly equal in size from elbow to heel; elbows set close to the body with free action from shoulders; pasterns short, straight, and strong. **Faults:** Shoulders loose; elbows turned in or out; legs bowed or set too close or too wide apart; knees knuckled over; light bone.

Feet: Size in proportion to the legs; firm, round and catlike with thick pads and strong toes. **Faults:** Too large, too small; spreading or splayed.

Hindquarters: The hips should be rounded; thighs broad; well developed and muscular, giving abundance of propelling power. Stifles strong and well bent. Hock to pad moderately short, strong and well let down. **Faults:** Excessive angulation; lightness of bone; stifle too short; hocks too long or turned in or out.

Tail: Set on to conform with the topline of the back. Merry in action. **Faults:** Set too low; habitually carried too high; too short or too long.

Color: Various. In self colors a white shirt frill is undesirable. In particolors, the coloring must be broken on the body and be evenly distributed. No large portion of any one color should exist. White should be shown on the saddle. A dog of any solid color with white feet and chest is not a parti-color. In roans it is desirable that the white hair should be distributed over the body, the more evenly the better. Roans come in various colors: blue, liver, red, orange and lemon. In black and tans the coat should be black; tan spots over the eyes, tan on the sides of the muzzle, on the throat and chest, on forelegs from the knees to the toes and on the hind legs on the inside of the legs, also on the stifle and extending from the hock to the toes. **Faults:** White feet are undesirable in any specimen of self color.

Coat: On head, short and fine; on body, flat or slightly wavy and silky in texture. Should be of medium length with enough undercoating to give protection. The English Cocker should be well feathered but not so profusely as to hide the true lines or interfere with his field work. **Faults:** Lack of coat; too soft, curly or wiry. Excessive trimming to change the natural appearance and coat should be discouraged.

Height: Ideal height at withers: Males, 16 to 17 inches; females, 15 to 16 inches. Deviations to be severely penalized but not disqualified.

Weight: The most desirable weights. Males, 28 pounds to 34 pounds; females, 26 pounds to 32 pounds. Proper physical conformation and balance should be considered more important than weight alone.

APPROVED SEPTEMBER 13, 1955

ENGLISH SPRINGER SPANIEL

This is probably the prototype of the whole of the sporting spaniel family. Some of the earliest records speak of the "Springing Spaniel," and he is no doubt a contemporary of the "Setting Spaniel," the two dogs doubtless being the only spaniels in existence at one period. They were probably much the same in type and conformation, the former being taught to "spring" at his quarry in flushing it, and the other to "set" it; hence the distinction. From the latter the setter was doubtless evolved, and from the "Springing Spaniel" the whole of the beautiful varieties we now possess have emanated, leaving the original a derelict on the sands of time.

The English Springer is one of the most rational dogs in point of architecture of all the spaniel varieties, viewed from the vantage point of utility. He may be almost any color, and is a leggy dog in comparison to the Field Spaniels, with a short and more symmetrical body, straight front, flat coat, a long head, a square muzzle, rather narrow skull, and low-set ears. His eyes and expression, gait and feathering are distinctly spaniel. He combines strength with activity, courage with docility, and all the characteristics of a workman. He is a medium-sized dog of from 45 to 55 pounds in weight.

Buyer's guide: The Springer is at its best as a bird dog, and this instinct should be cultivated. They are eager learners, obedient and willing workers. In the home they are warm and compassionate, but must be allowed adequate space to roam and time to themselves. Constant attention by small children may cause them to become somewhat irritable and they much prefer to have only one or two close relationships. The person who takes them hunting is the person they most care to be with.

STANDARD FOR THE ENGLISH SPRINGER SPANIEL

General Appearance and Type: The English Springer Spaniel is a medium-size sporting dog with a neat, compact body, and a docked tail. His coat is moderately long and glossy with feathering on his legs, ears, chest and brisket. His pendulous ears, soft gentle expression, sturdy build and friendly wagging tail proclaim him unmistakably a member of the ancient family of spaniels. He is above all a well proportioned dog, free from exaggeration, nicely balanced in every part. His carriage is proud and upstanding, body deep, legs strong and muscular with enough length to carry him with ease. His short level back, well developed thighs, good shoulders, excellent feet, suggest power, endurance, agility. Taken as a whole he looks the part of a dog that can go and keep going under difficult hunting conditions, and moreover he enjoys what he is doing. At his best he is endowed with style, symmetry, balance, enthusiasm and is every inch a sporting dog of distinct spaniel character, combining beauty and utility. **To be penalized:** Those lacking true English Springer type in conformation, expression, or behavior.

Temperament: The typical Springer is friendly, eager to please, quick to learn, willing to obey. In the show ring he should exhibit poise, attentiveness, tractability, and should permit himself to be examined by the judge without resentment or cringing. **To be penalized:** Excessive timidity, with due allowance for puppies and novice exhibits. But no dog to receive a ribbon if he behaves in vicious manner toward handler or judge. Aggressiveness toward other dogs in the ring not to be construed as viciousness.

Size and Proportion: The Springer is built to cover rough ground with agility and reasonable speed. He should be kept to medium size—neither too small nor too large and heavy to do the work for which he is intended. The ideal shoulder height for dogs is 20 inches; for bitches, 19 inches. Length of topline (the distance from top of the shoulders to the root of the tail) should be approximately equal to the dog's shoulder height—never longer than his height—and not appreciably less. The dog too long in body, especially when long in loin, tires easily and lacks the compact outline characteristic of the breed. Equally undesirable is the dog too short in body for the length of his legs, a condition that destroys his balance and restricts the gait.

Weight is dependent on the dog's other dimensions: a 20-inch dog, well proportioned, in good condition should weigh about 49-55 pounds. The resulting appearance is a well-knit, sturdy dog with good but not too heavy bone, in no way coarse or ponderous. **To be penalized:** Over-heavy specimens, cloddy in build. Leggy individuals, too tall for their length and substance. Oversize or undersize specimens (those more than one inch under or over the breed ideal).

Color: Color may be black or liver with white markings or predominantly white with black or liver markings; tricolor: black and white or liver and white with tan markings (usually found on eyebrows, cheeks, insides of ears and under tail); blue or liver roan. Any white portions of coat may be flecked with ticking. All preceding combinations of colors and markings to be equally acceptable. To be penalized: Off colors such as lemon, red or orange not to place.

Coat: On ears, chest, legs and belly the Springer is nicely funished with a fringe of feathering of moderate length and heaviness. On head, front of forelegs, and below hocks on front of hindlegs the hair is short and fine. The body coat is flat or wavy, of medium length, sufficiently dense to be waterproof, weatherproof and thornproof. The texture fine, and the hair should have the clean, glossy, live appearance indicative of good health. It is legitimate to trim about head, feet, ears; to remove dead hair; to thin and shorten excess feathering particularly from the hocks to the feet and elsewhere as required to give a smart, clean appearance. To be penalized: Rough, curly coat. Over-trimming especially of the body coat. Any chopped, barbered or artificial effect. Excessive feathering that destroys the clean outline desirable in a sporting dog.

Head: The head is impressive without being heavy. Its beauty lies in a combination of strength and refinement. It is important that the size and proportion be in balance with the rest of the dog. Viewed in profile the head should appear approximately the same length as the neck and should blend with the body in substance. The skull (upper head) to be of medium length, fairly broad, flat on top, slightly rounded at the sides and back. The occiput bone inconspicuous, rounded rather than peaked or angular. The foreface (head in front of the eyes) approximately the same length as the skull, and in harmony as to width and general character. Looking down on the head the muzzle to appear to be about one half the width of the skull. As the skull rises from the foreface it makes a brow or "stop," divided by a groove or fluting between the eyes. This groove continues upward and gradually disappears as it reaches the middle of the forehead. The amount of "stop" can best be described as moderate. It must not be a pronounced feature; rather it is a subtle rise where the muzzle blends into the upper head, further emphasized by the groove and by the position and shape of the eyebrows which should be well-developed. The stop, eyebrow and the chiseling of the bony structure around the eye sockets contribute to the Springer's beautiful and characteristic expression.

Viewed in profile the topline of the skull and the muzzle lie in two approximately parallel planes. The nasal bone should be straight, with no inclination downward toward the tip of the nose which gives a downfaced look so undesirable in this breed. Neither should the nasal bone be concave resulting in a "dish-faced" profile; nor convex giving the dog a Roman nose. The jaws to be of sufficient length to allow the dog to carry game easily; fairly square, lean, strong, and even, (neither undershot nor overshot). The upper lip to come down full and rather square to cover the line of the lower jaw, but lips not to be pendulous nor exaggerated. The nostrils, well opened and broad, liver color or black depending on the color of the coat. Flesh-colored ("Dudley noses") or spotted ("butterfly noses") are undesirable. The cheeks to be flat, (not rounded, full or thick) with nice chiseling under the eyes. **To be penalized:** Oval, pointed or heavy skull. Cheeks prominently rounded, thick and protruding. Too much or too little stop. Over heavy muzzle. Muzzle too short, too thick, too narrow. Pendulous slobbery lips. Under- or over-shot jaws—a very serious fault, to be heavily penalized.

Teeth: The teeth should be strong, clean, not too small; and when the mouth is closed the teeth should meet in a close scissors bite (the lower incisors touching the inside of the upper incisors). **To be penalized:** Any deviation from above description. Irregularities due to faulty jaw formation to be severely penalized.

Eyes: More than any other feature the eyes contribute to the

Springer's appeal. Color, placement, size influence expression and attractiveness. The eyes to be of medium size, neither small, round, full and prominent, nor bold and hard in expression. Set rather well apart and fairly deep in their sockets. The color of the iris to harmonize with the color of the coat, preferably a good dark hazel in the liver dogs and black or deep brown in the black and white specimens. The expression to be alert, kindly, trusting. The lids, tight with little or no haw showing. **To be penalized:** Eyes yellow or brassy in color or noticeably lighter than the coat. Sharp expression indicating unfriendly or suspicious nature. Loose droopy lids. Prominent haw (the third eyelid or membrane in the inside corner of the eye).

Ears: The correct ear-set is on a level with the line of the eye; on the side of the skull and not too far back. The flaps to be long and fairly wide, hanging close to the cheeks, with no tendency to stand up or out. The leather, thin, approximately long enough to reach the tip of the nose. **To be penalized:** Short round ears. Ears set too high or too low or too far back on the head.

Neck: The neck to be moderately long, muscular, slightly arched at the crest, gradually blending into sloping shoulders. Not noticeably upright, nor coming into the body at an abrupt angle. **To be penalized:** Short neck, often the sequence to steep shoulders. Concave neck, sometimes called ewe neck or upside down neck (the opposite of arched). Excessive throatiness.

Body: The body to be well coupled, strong, compact; the chest deep but not so wide or round as to interfere with the action of the front legs; the brisket sufficiently to reach to the level of the elbows. The ribs fairly long, springing gradually to the middle of the body then tapering as they approach the end of the ribbed section. The back (section between the withers and loin) to be straight and strong, with no tendency to dip or roach. The loins to be strong, short; a slight arch over loins and hip bones. Hips nicely rounded, blending smoothly into hind legs. The resulting topline slopes *very gently* from withers to tail—the line from withers to back descending without a sharp drop; the back practically level; arch over hips somewhat lower than the withers; croup sloping gently to base of tail; tail carried to follow the natural line of the body. The bottom line, starting on a level with the elbows, to continue backward with almost no up-curve until reaching the end of the ribbed section, then a more noticeable up-curve to the flank, but not enough to make the dog appear small waisted or "tucked up." **To be penalized:** Body too shallow, indicating lack of brisket. Ribs too flat sometimes due to immaturity. Ribs too round (barrel-shaped), hampering the gait. Swayback (dip in back), indicating weakness or lack of muscular development, particularly to be seen when dog is in action and viewed from the side. Roach back (too much arch over loin and extending forward into middle section). Croup falling away too sharply; or croup too high—unsightly faults, detrimental to outline and good movement. Topline sloping sharply, indicating steep withers (straight shoulder placement) and a too low tail-set.

Tail: The Springer's tail is an index both to his temperament and his conformation. Merry tail action is characteristic. The proper set is somewhat low following the natural line of the croup. The carriage should be nearly horizontal, slightly elevated when dog is excited. Carried straight up is untypical of the breed. The tail should not be docked too short and should be well fringed with wavy feather. It is legitimate to shape and shorten the feathering but enough should be left to blend with the dog's other furnishings. **To be penalized:** Tail habitually upright. Tail set too high or too low. Clamped down tail (indicating timidity or undependable temperament, even less to be desired than the tail carried too gaily).

Forequarters: Efficient movement in front calls for proper shoulders, the blades sloping back to form an angle with the upper arm of approximately 90 degrees which permits the dog to swing his forelegs forward in an easy manner. Shoulders (fairly close together at the tips) to lie flat and mold smoothly into the contour of the body. The forelegs to be straight with the same degree of size to the foot. The bone, strong, slightly flattened, not too heavy or round. The knee, straight, almost flat; the pasterns short, strong; elbows close to the body with free action from the shoulders. **To be penalized:** Shoulders set at a steep angle limiting the stride. Loaded shoulders (the blades standing out from the body by overdevelopment of the muscles). Loose elbows, crooked legs. Bone too light or too coarse and heavy. Weak pasterns that let down the feet at a pronounced angle.

Hindquarters: The Springer should be shown in hard muscular condition, well developed in hips and thighs and the whole rear assembly should suggest strength and driving power. The hip joints to be set rather wide apart and the hips nicely rounded. The thighs broad and muscular; the stifle joint strong and moderately bent. The hock joint somewhat rounded, not small and sharp in contour, and moderately angulated. Leg from hock joint to foot pad, short and strong with good bone structure. When viewed from the rear the hocks to be parallel whether the dog is standing or in motion. **To be penalized:** Too little or too much angulation. Narrow, undeveloped thighs. Hocks too short or too long (a proportion of ⅓ the distance from hip joint to foot is ideal). Flabby muscles. Weakness of joints.

Feet: The feet to be round, or slightly oval, compact, well arched, medium size with thick pads, well feathered between the toes. Excess hair to be removed to show the natural shape and size of the foot. **To be penalized:** Thin, open or splayed feet (flat with spreading toes). Hare foot (long, rather narrow foot).

Movement: In judging the Springer there should be emphasis on proper movement, which is the final test of a dog's conformation and soundness. Prerequisite to good movement is balance of the front and rear assemblies. The two must match in angulation and muscular development if the gait is to be smooth and effortless. Good shoulders laid back at an angle that permits a long stride are just as essential as the excellent rear quarters that provide the driving power. When viewed from the front, the dog's legs should appear to swing forward in a free and easy manner, with no tendency for the feet to cross over or interfere with each other. Viewed from the rear, the hocks should drive well under the body following on a line with the forelegs, neither too widely nor too closely spaced. As speed increases there is a natural tendency for the legs to converge toward the center line of gravity or a single line of travel. Seen from the side, the Springer should exhibit a good, long forward stride, without high-stepping or wasted motion. **To be penalized:** Short choppy stride, mincing steps with up and down movement, hopping. Moving with forefeet wide, giving roll or swing to body. Weaving or crossing of fore or hind feet. Cowhocks—hocks turning in toward each other.

In judging the English Springer Spaniel, the over-all picture is a primary consideration. It is urged that the judge look for type which includes general appearance, outline and temperament and also for soundness, especially as seen when the dog is in motion. Inasmuch as the dog with a smooth easy gait must be reasonably sound and well balanced he is to be highly regarded in the show ring; however, not to the extent of forgiving him for not looking like an English Springer Spaniel. A quite untypical dog, leggy, foreign in head and expression, may move well. But he should not be placed over a good all-round specimen that has a minor fault in movement. It should be remembered that the English Springer Spaniel is first and foremost a sporting dog of the spaniel family and he must look and behave and move in character.

Representing the breed: Ch. Salilyn's Aristocrat, owned by the Salilyn Kennels and bred by Mrs. F.H. Gasgow. Photo by Bill Williams Studio.

FIELD SPANIEL

At one time one of the most popular varieties of sporting spaniel, the versatile Field Spaniel is, in its present form, a fairly modern creation, dating from somewhere about the advent of dog shows. The Field Spaniel is lower on leg and longer in body in proportion than any other spaniel. This anatomical formation had its origin in the production of a spaniel better adapted for getting under brushwood than was the Springer and a dog that was less active than the Cocker. It is from these two older varieties, with an admixture of the Sussex, that the beautiful Field Spaniels of today, in all their pretty colors, were first evolved. The colors are black-and-tan, black, liver, liver-and-tan, liver-roan, blue-roan, etc. The blacks at one time were the most popular, but the craze for great length of body and lowness on leg was carried to such extremes that the breed at once degenerated into little less than elongated monstrosities. It lost the beautiful chiseling of head, at least in many of the specimens exhibited, and straightness of forelegs, and the activity which all sporting spaniels should possess more or less. A reaction among sporting men set in, and, owing to their efforts and those of the Sporting Spaniel Club, happily the heavy-headed, crooked-fronted, and sluggish crocodile-like pattern are now happily almost obsolete.

We have today, too, a more rational type of dog, one that possesses all the features of an animal well fitted to perform the work originally prescribed for him, and yet free from the abnormalities which so disfigured the dog at one stage of his career.

Buyer's guide: The Field Spaniel is rarely seen and is owned almost exclusively by sporting men who value the breed's bird sense and perseverance. They are a very docile breed and get along with most every lifestyle, yet they do not protest the life of the kennel.

STANDARD FOR THE FIELD SPANIEL

Head: Should be quite characteristic of this grand sporting dog, as that of the Bulldog, or the Bloodhound; its very stamp and countenance should at once convey the conviction of high breeding, character and nobility; skull well developed, with a distinctly elevated occipital tuberosity, which, above all, gives the character alluded to; not too wide across the muzzle, long and lean, never snipy or squarely cut, and in profile curving gradually from nose to throat; lean beneath the eyes—a thickness here gives coarseness to the whole head. The great length of muzzle gives surface for the free development of the olfactory nerve, and thus secures the highest possible scenting powers.

Nose: Well developed, with good open nostrils.

Eyes: Not too full, but not small, receding or overhung, color dark hazel or brown, or nearly black, according to the color of the dog. Grave in expression and showing no haw.

Ears: Moderately long and wide, sufficiently clad with nice setterlike feather and set low. They should fall in graceful folds, the lower parts curling inwards and backwards.

Neck: Long, strong and muscular, so as to enable the dog to retrieve his game without undue fatigue.

Body: Should be of moderate length, well ribbed up to a good strong loin, straight or slightly arched, never slack.

Shoulders and Chest: Former long, sloping and well set back, thus giving great activity and speed; latter deep and well developed, but not too round and wide.

Back and Loin: Very strong and muscular.

Hindquarters: Strong and muscular. The stifles should be moderately bent, and not twisted either in or out.

Stern: Well set on and carried low, if possible below the level of the back, in a straight line or with a slight downward inclination, never elevated above the back, and in action always kept low, nicely fringed with wavy feather of silky texture.

Forelegs: Should be of fairly good length, with straight, clean, flat bone, and nicely feathered. Immense bone is no longer desirable.

Feet: Not too small; round, with short soft hair between the toes; good, strong pads.

Coat: Flat or slightly waved, and never curled. Sufficiently dense to resist the weather, and not too short. Silky in texture, glossy and refined in nature, with neither duffleness on the one hand, nor curl or wiriness on the other. On the chest, under belly and behind the legs, there should be abundant feather, but never too much, especially below the hocks, and that of the right sort, *viz.* setterlike. The hindquarters should be similarly adorned.

Color: Black, liver, golden liver, mahogany red, or roan; or any one of these colors with tan over the eyes and on the cheeks, feet, and pasterns. Other colors, such as black and white, liver and white, red or orange and white, while not disqualifying, will be considered less desirable since the Field Spaniel should be clearly distinguished from the Springer Spaniel.

Height: About 18 inches to shoulder.

Weight: From about 35 pounds to 50 pounds.

General Appearance: That of a well-balanced, noble, upstanding sporting dog; built for activity and endurance. A grand combination of beauty and utility, and bespeaking of unusual docility and instinct.

SCALE OF POINTS

Head and jaw	15	Hind legs	10
Eyes	5	Feet	10
Ears	5	Stern	10
Neck	5	Coat and feather	10
Body	10	General appearance	10
Forelegs	10	TOTAL	100

APPROVED JULY 14, 1959

IRISH WATER SPANIEL

As to the origin of the Irish Water Spaniel there is very little documented information. Mr. Justin McCarthy, one of first exhibitors and breeders of these dogs, claimed to have created the breed in about 1850. Fanciers, however, state that he did not create the breed, but perfected the strain through careful selection of available specimens. At this time there were two varieties of the breed present in Ireland, the Northern Water Spaniel and the Southern Water Spaniel. From this stock he interbred until the Irish Water Spaniel was stylized to its present type. Historically, the Irish Water Spaniel was kept largely for sporting purposes and as a valued member of "Ireland's Reds"—Red Setter, Red Spaniel, Red Terrier, Red Wolfhound.

The most feasible theory of his origin is a cross between the

Poodle and the old European Water Dog. There is much in common in type and character between the Poodle and Irish Water Spaniel—namely the coat, conformation, head and general character, while in disposition the dog inherits all the dash and determination of the Irish Setter, and partakes of his color. The Irish Water Spaniel partakes, too, of the great intelligence of the Poodle, who will hunt and retrieve on land or water with most spaniels. The breed has never made the progress with the public that it merited by their many good qualities. They are smart and upstanding in appearance, combining intelligence and endurance with a dashing temperament all of which makes them charming companions. They are splendid guards for children, and will play with them by the hour and act as their guards in time of danger.

The chief points to look for in the selection of Water Spaniel puppies at from two to four months old and after, are: a clean head, dark eye, long ears, short back, short whip tail, good size and bone, straight forelegs, and a dark, close coat.

Buyer's guide: These large sporting dogs have remarkably spirited personalities and fit well with outgoing individuals, since they are always ready to play or show how much they care. Irish Water Spaniels require plenty of time outdoors for both temperament and conditioning's sake. They may be a bit too vivacious for infants, but are great companions for growing children. People who live near water are the best suited owners for this breed.

STANDARD FOR THE IRISH WATER SPANIEL

Head: Skull rather large and high in dome with prominent occiput; muzzle square and rather long with deep mouth opening and lips fine in texture. Teeth strong and level. The nose should be large with open nostrils, and liver in color. The head should be cleanly chiseled, not cheeky, and should not present a short wedge-shaped appearance. Hair on face should be short and smooth.

Topknot: Topknot, a characteristic of the true breed, should consist of long loose curls growing down into a well-defined peak between the eyes and should not be in the form of a wig; *i.e.* growing straight across.

Eyes: Medium in size and set almost flush, without eyebrows. Color of eyes hazel, preferably of dark shade. Expression of the eyes should be keenly alert, intelligent, direct and quizzical.

Ears: Long, lobular, set low with leathers reaching to about the end of the nose when extended forward. The ears should be abundantly covered with curls becoming longer toward the tips and extending two or more inches below the ends of the leathers.

Neck: The neck should be long, arching, strong and muscular, smoothly set into sloping shoulders.

Shoulders and Chest: Shoulders should be sloping and clean; chest deep but not too wide between the legs. The entire front should give the impression of strength without heaviness.

Body, Ribs and Loins: Body should be of medium length, with ribs well sprung, pear-shaped at the brisket, and rounder toward the hind quarters. Ribs should be carried well back. Loins should be short, wide and muscular. The body should not present a tucked-up appearance.

Hindquarters: The hindquarters should be as high or a trifle higher than the shoulders and should be very powerful and muscular with well-developed upper and second thighs. Hips should be wide; stifles should not be too straight; and hocks low-set and moderately bent. Tail should be set on low enough to give a rather rounded appearance to the hindquarters and should be carried nearly level with the back. Sound hindquarters are of great importance to provide swimming power and drive.

Forelegs and Feet: Forelegs medium in length, well boned, straight and muscular with elbows close set. Both fore and hind feet should be large, thick and somewhat spreading, well clothed with hair both over and between toes, but free from superfluous feather.

Tail: The so-called "rat tail" is a striking characteristic of the breed. At the root it is thick and covered for 2 or 3 inches with short curls. It tapers to a fine point at the end, and from the root-curls is covered with short, smooth hair so as to look as if the tail had been clipped. The tail should not be long enough to reach the hock joint.

Coat: Proper coat is of vital importance. The neck, back and sides should be densely covered with tight crisp ringlets entirely free from wooliness. Underneath the ribs the hair should be longer. The hair on lower throat should be short. The forelegs should be covered all around with abundant hair falling in curls or waves, but shorter in front than behind. The hind legs should also be abundantly covered by hair falling in curls or waves, but the hair should be short on the front of the legs below the hocks.

Color: Solid liver; white on chest objectionable.

Height and Weight: Dogs, 22 to 24 inches; bitches, 21 to 23 inches. Dogs, 55 to 65 pounds; bitches, 45 to 58 pounds.

General Appearance: That of a smart, upstanding, strongly built but not leggy dog, combining great intelligence and the rugged endurance with a bold, dashing eagerness of temperament.

Gait: Should be square, true, precise and not slurring.

SCALE OF POINTS

Head
- Skull and topknot........6
- Ears....................4
- Eyes 4
- Muzzle and nose........6   20

Body
- Neck..................5
- Chest, shoulders, back, loin and ribs........12   17

Driving Gear
- Feet, hips, thighs, stifles and continuity of hindquarter muscles...14
- Feet, legs, elbows and muscles of forequarters..9   23

Coat
- Tightness, denseness of curl and general texture....16
- Color 4   20

Tail
- General appearance and "set on," length and carriage..............5   5

General Conformation and Action
- Symmetry, style, gait, weight and size.......15   15

TOTAL 100

APPROVED JUNE 11, 1940

Representing the breed: Ch. Oaktree's Irishtocrat, owned by Anne Snelling.

SUSSEX SPANIEL

This handsome breed derives its name from the English county of Sussex, where it originated, or at least has existed for many years. The Sussex is one of the oldest of the spaniel family.

The well-bred Sussex is a beautiful spaniel, for his symmetrical proportions are clothed in a rich red coat that would lend distinction to any dog. In the field they are most reliable workmen, somewhat slower to be sure than the leggier Springer, but surpassing them in patience and perseverance. They will force their way through the thickest cover and allow nothing to escape them. They differ from the rest of the spaniels by giving tongue on scent, and those who are accustomed to them can tell by the difference in their tone whether they are after fur or feather.

The modern Field Spaniel gets his size and weight from the

Sussex Spaniel, and in years gone by they have undoubtedly been resorted to in developing other breeds.

The chief points to look for in the selection of Sussex Spaniel puppies at from two to four months old and after, are: a short, massive head; square muzzle; well-defined stop; lengthy body on short, straight forelegs; great bone; flat coat of a deep golden color; down-carried tail.

Buyer's guide: Older individuals still interested in the leisurely hunt will do well with a Sussex Spaniel, since their movements are slower than most sporters, yet still very efficient. Daily grooming is suggested to avoid matting of the coat, but aside from this they demand very little from their owners. Sussex Spaniels are happy to be in the home and are satisfied with little more than companionship. They are amicable to children, although they may tend to ignore their presence. Without encouraging exercise, they may become lethargic.

STANDARD FOR THE SUSSEX SPANIEL

Head: The skull should be moderately long and also wide, with an indention in the middle and a full stop, brows fairly heavy; occiput full, but not pointed, the whole giving an appearance of heaviness without dullness. **Eyes:** Hazel color, fairly large, soft and languishing, not showing the haw overmuch. **Nose:** The muzzle should be about three inches long, square, and the lips somewhat pendulous. The nostrils well developed and liver color. **Ears:** Thick, fairly large and lobe shaped; set moderately low, but relatively not so low as in the black Field Spaniel; carried close to the head and furnished with soft, wavy hair.

Neck: Is rather short, strong and slightly arched, but not carrying the head much above the level of the back. There should not be much throatiness about the skin, but well-marked frill in the coat.

Chest and Shoulders: The chest is round, especially behind the shoulders, deep and wide giving a good girth. The shoulders should be oblique.

Back and Back Rib: The back and loin is long and should be very muscular, both in width and depth; for this development the back ribs must be deep. The whole body is characterized as low, long and level.

Legs and Feet: The arms and thighs must be bony as well as muscular, knees and hocks large and strong; pasterns very short and bony, feet large and round, and with short hair between the toes. The legs should be very short and strong, with great bone, and may show a slight bend in the forearm, and be moderately well feathered. The hind legs should not appear to be shorter than the forelegs, nor be too much bent at the hocks. They should be well feathered above the hocks but should not have much hair below that point. The hind legs are short from the hock to the ground, and wide apart.

Tail: Should be docked from 5 to 7 inches, set low, and not carried above the level of the back, thickly covered with moderately long feather.

Coat: Body coat abundant, flat or slightly waved, with no tendency to curl, moderately well feathered on legs and stern, but clean below the hocks.

Color: Rich golden liver; this is a certain sign of the purity of the breed, dark liver or puce denoting unmistakably a recent cross with the black or other variety of Field Spaniel.

General Appearance: Rather massive and muscular, but with free movements and nice tail action, denoting a cheerful and tractable disposition.

Weight: From 35 pounds to 45 pounds.

POSITIVE POINTS

Head 10	Legs and feet 10
Eyes 5	Tail 5
Nose 5	Coat 5
Ears 10	Color 15
Neck 5	General appearance 15
Chest and Shoulders 5	TOTAL 100
Back and back ribs 10	

NEGATIVE POINTS

Light eyes 5	White on chest 5
Narrow Head 10	Color, too light or too dark 15
Weak muzzle 10	Legginess or light of bone 5
Curled ears or set on high 5	Shortness of body or flat sided 5
Curled coat 15	
Carriage of stern 5	General appearance—sour or crouching 10
Topknot 10	TOTAL 100

APPROVED JULY 14, 1959

WELSH SPRINGER SPANIEL

The Welsh Springer is a smart, active spaniel, more lightly built and smaller than Field Spaniels, being very little larger than the Cocker. They are invariably white in color, with red markings. They have beautifully chiseled heads, small Clumber-shaped ears, and are generally most attractive.

The Welsh Springer is undoubtedly an old breed that has been used by the sportsmen of Wales, who refer to them not as spaniels, but as starters. They are eminently sportsmanlike in appearance, and have proven themselves to be capital workmen in the field, so that their future popularity is assured. They have made great headway on the show benches, and their classes are well filled with specimens of uniform type.

The Welsh Springer is a dog of from 30 to 40 pounds, proportionate in all his parts, with a well-balanced head, straight front, grand spring of rib, and powerful hindquarters. He may be described as an enlarged Cocker, but shows less feathering than is found in most of the other varieties, and the ears are also shorter. As in all spaniels, snipiness and thick heads are common defects, and the Welsh Springer is no exception. This said, the breed is at once a rational one, and possesses all the traits of his English cousin, while the uniformity of color and its irregular distribution give to a group of Welsh Springers quite a picturesque appearance. In this way the variety has made great headway on the show bench and enlisted a number of enthusiasts within its ranks, who are much devoted to the breed not only for its general beauty, but also for its wonderful prowess in the field.

The chief points to look for in the selection of Welsh Springer puppies from two to four months and after are almost the same as those of the English Springer, the recognized color being, of course, red-and-white.

Buyer's guide: The Welsh Springer is highly adaptable, not only to lifestyles but also to climates and terrains. They make excellent gun dogs and this outlet should be encouraged. They will not actively protest city living, provided they are exercised daily. The breed was originally designed to be a kennel dog, but they will make fine companions if shown plenty of affection from puppyhood.

STANDARD FOR THE WELSH SPRINGER SPANIEL

The "Welsh Spaniel" or "Springer" is also known and referred to in Wales as a "Starter." He is of very ancient and pure origin, and is a distinct variety which has been bred and preserved purely for working purposes.

Head: **Skull:** Proportionate, of moderate length, slightly domed, clearly defined stop, well chiseled below the eyes. **Muzzle:** Medium length, straight, fairly square; the nostrils well developed and flesh colored or dark. **Jaw:** Strong, neither undershot nor overshot. **Eyes:** Hazel or dark, medium size, not prominent, nor sunken, nor showing haw. **Ears:** Set moderately low and hanging close to the cheeks, comparatively small and gradually narrowing towards the tip, covered with nice setterlike feathering. A short chubby head is objectionable.

Neck and Shoulders: **Neck:** Long and muscular, clean in throat, neatly set into long and sloping shoulders. **Forelegs:** Medium length, straight, well boned, moderately feathered.

Body: Not long; strong and muscular with deep brisket, well sprung ribs; length of body should be proportionate to length of leg, and very well balanced; with muscular loin slightly arched and well coupled up. **Quarters:** Strong and muscular, wide and fully developed with deep second thighs. **Hind Legs:** Hocks well let down; stifles moderately bent (neither twisted in nor out), moderately feathered. **Feet:** Round with thick pads. **Stern:** Well set on and low, never carried above the level of the back; lightly feathered and with lively action.

Coat: Straight or flat and thick, of a nice silky texture, never wiry nor wavy. A curly coat is most objectionable. **Color:** Dark rich red and white.

General Appearance: A symmetrical, compact, strong, merry, very active dog; not stilty, obviously built for endurance and activity.

VIZSLA

Although a relatively new member of the American pointing dog team, the Vizsla is quickly gaining popularity both as an intelligent, able pointer and retriever and as show dog and pet. Commonly known as the Hungarian Pointer, the Vizsla is a sleek, handsome breed which sports a rich rusty-gold coat color not found in any other pointing breed.

The Vizsla's innate hunting sense has been carefully fostered over the years by Hungarian hunters. Vizslas exhibit an unyielding drive in the field, are a close-range working dog with superior scenting abilities and a keen sense of the stalk. They are staunch on the point and eager retrievers. This breed developed in an area of Hungary that was heavily covered with grain fields and pockets of water. In this terrain waterfowl and game birds flourished, as did hares and small game. The Vizsla possesses the sense of caution that is necessary for a dog to work without scaring away the prey. They are both swift and fearless, exhibiting all the attributes of a first class hunting dog.

The growth of the breed in its homeland of Hungary reached a near standstill during the war years. At one point, the breed was feared to be heading for extinction. However, several concerned breeders exported their dogs to Austria and other European countries so that the Vizsla would be preserved. Since then the breed has grown continuously in America and the Vizsla received official recognition by the American Kennel Club in 1960.

Buyer's guide: These dogs excel at being both companions in the home and masters of the field. They require no grooming or pampering to speak of, but must be exercised routinely to retain muscle tone and endurance. Vizslas are outwardly affectionate and get along well with children. Training to obedience and the hunt makes these dogs achieve their full potential. A happy disposition reflects their appreciation of a good home. City dwelling is not advised for this breed.

STANDARD FOR THE VIZSLA

General Appearance: That of a medium-sized hunting dog of quite distinguished appearance. Robust but rather lightly built, his short coat is an attractive rusty-gold, and his tail is docked. He is a dog of power and drive in the field, and a tractable and affectionate companion in the home.

Head: Lean but muscular. The skull is moderately wide between the ears, with a median line down the forehead. Stop moderate. The muzzle is a trifle longer than the skull and, although tapering, is well squared at its end. Jaws strong, with well-developed white teeth meeting in a scissors bite. The lips cover the jaws completely but they are neither loose nor pendulous. Nostrils slightly open, the nose brown. A black or slate-gray nose is objectionable.

Ears: Thin, silky, and proportionately long, with rounded-leather ends; set fairly low and hanging close to the cheeks.

Eyes: Medium in size and depth of setting, their surrounding tissue covering the whites, and the iris or color portion harmonizing with the shade of the coat. A yellow eye is objectionable.

Neck: Strong, smooth, and muscular; moderately long, arched, and devoid of dewlap. It broadens nicely into shoulders which are well laid back.

Body: Strong and well proportioned. The back is short, the withers high, and the topline slightly rounded over the loin to the set-on of the tail. Chest moderately broad and deep, and reaching down to the elbows. Ribs well sprung, and underline exhibiting a slight tuck-up beneath the loin.

Legs and Feet: Forelegs straight, strong, and muscular, with elbows close. The hind legs have well-developed thighs, with moderate angulation at stifles and hocks. Too much angulation at the hocks is as faulty as too little. The hocks, which are well let down, are equidistant from each other from the hock joint to the ground. Cowhocks are faulty. Feet are cat-like, round and compact, with toes close. Nails are brown and short; pads thick and tough. Dewclaws, if any, to be removed. Hare feet are objectionable.

Tail: Set just below the level of the back, thicker at the root, and docked one third off.

Coat: Short, smooth, dense, and close-lying, without woolly undercoat.

Color: Solid. Rusty gold or rather dark sandy yellow in different shades, with darker shades preferred. Dark brown and pale yellow are undesirable. Small white spots on chest or feet are not faulted.

Temperament: That of the natural hunter endowed with a good nose and above-average ability to take training. Lively, gentle-mannered, and demonstratively affectionate. Fearless, and with well-developed protective instinct.

Gait: Far-reaching, light-footed, graceful, smooth.

Size: Males, 22 to 24 inches; females, 21 to 23 inches at the highest point of the shoulders. Any dog measuring over or under these limits shall be considered faulty, the seriousness of the fault depending on the extent of the deviation. Any dog that measures more than 2 inches over or under these limits shall be disqualified.

DISQUALIFICATION
Deviation in height of more than 2 inches from standard either way.

APPROVED DECEMBER 10, 1963

WEIMARANER

The origin of the Weimaraner goes back to the 19th century in Germany, where the dog seems to have originally been used in the hunting of large, dangerous prey such as bear, mountain lions, wolves, etc. Sportsmen trailed behind the working Weimaraner as they followed the scent of the game. When they came upon the animal the Weimaraner kept it at bay until the hunters could make the kill.

Today, the dog is more often used as a small game and waterfowl gun dog. They excel as a water retriever because they use a very soft, yet secure mouth on their catch. Weimaraners are excellent companion dogs, both in the field and at home. Because of their friendly disposition, the Weimaraner is not content to be part of a kennel, but rather accepts a place within the family. They are fiercely loyal and of above average trainability. In modern obedience trials the Weimaraner is an avid competitor, as they can master any task they put their mind to.

As for appearance, the Weimaraner is a medium-sized dog of a sound and balanced body. They have a smooth, sleek gray coat that distinguishes the breed from its other sporting dog relatives. Their light amber or gray eyes reflect the Weimaraner's inherent good disposition. Above all they are a well-rounded dog, equally adept on hunting fur or feather and complete with an unerring desire to be a watchdog, companion and friend.

Buyer's guide: These hardy hunters have very malleable personalities. If trained to the field they become efficient and zealous in their work, but if encouraged to be primarily a housepet they take on a much mellower disposition. They are best as dual-dogs. When left alone, Weimaraner housepets have been noted for being quite destructive out of loneliness. Obedience training to one master is suggested.

STANDARD FOR THE WEIMARANER

General Appearance: A medium-sized gray dog, with fine aristocratic features. He should present a picture of grace, speed, stamina, alertness and balance. Above all, the dog's conformation must indicate the ability to work with great speed and endurance in the field.

Height: Height at the withers: dogs, 25 to 27 inches; bitches, 23 to 25 inches. One inch over or under the specified height of each sex is allowable but should be penalized. Dogs measuring less than 24 or more than 28 inches and bitches measuring less than 22 inches or more than 26 inches shall be disqualified.

Head: Moderately long and aristocratic, with moderate stop and slight median line extending back over the forehead. Rather prominent occipital bone and trumpets well set back, beginning at the back of the eye sockets. Measurements from tip of nose to stop equal that from stop to occipital bone. The flews should be straight, delicate at the nostrils. Skin drawn tightly. Neck clean-cut and moderately long. Expression kind, keen and intelligent. **Ears:** Long and lobular, slightly folded and set high. The ear when drawn snugly alongside the jaw should end approximately 2 inches from the point of the nose. **Eyes:** In shades of light amber, gray or blue-gray, set well enough apart to indicate good disposition and intelligence. When dilated under excitement the eyes may appear almost black. **Teeth:** Well set, strong and even; well-developed and proportionate to jaw with correct scissors bite, the upper teeth protruding slightly over the lower teeth but not more than one-sixteenth of an inch. Complete dentition is greatly to be desired. **Nose:** Gray. **Lips and Gums:** Pinkish flesh shades.

Body: The back should be moderate in length, set in a straight line, strong, and should slope slightly from the withers. The chest should be well developed and deep with shoulders well laid back. Ribs well sprung and long. Abdomen firmly held; moderately tucked-up flank. The brisket should extend to the elbow.

Coat and Color: Short, smooth and sleek, solid color, in shades of mouse-gray to silver-gray, usually blending to lighter shades on the head and ears. A small white marking on the chest is permitted, but should be penalized on any other portion of the body. White spots resulting from injury should not be penalized. A distinctively long coat is a disqualification. A distinctly blue or black coat is a disqualification.

Forelegs: Straight and strong, with the measurement from the elbow to the ground approximately equaling the distance from the elbows to the top of the withers.

Hindquarters: Well-angulated stifles and straight hocks. Musculation well developed.

Feet: Firm and compact, webbed, toes well arched, pads closed and thick, nails short and gray or amber in color. **Dewclaws:** Should be removed.

Tail: Docked. At maturity it should measure approximately 6 inches with a tendency to be light rather than heavy and should be carried in a manner expressing confidence and sound temperament. A non-docked tail shall be penalized.

Gait: The gait should be effortless and should indicate smooth coordination. When seen from the rear, the hind feet should be parallel to the front feet. When viewed from the side, the topline should remain strong and level.

Temperament: The temperament should be friendly, fearless, alert and obedient.

FAULTS

Minor Faults—Tail too short or too long. Pink nose.

Major Faults—Doggy bitches. Bitchy dogs. Improper muscular condition. Badly affected teeth. More than four teeth missing. Back too long or too short. Faulty coat. Neck too short, thick or throaty. Low-set tail. Elbows in or out. Feet east and west. Poor gait. Poor feet. Cowhocks. Faulty backs, either roached or sway. Badly overshot, or undershot bite. Snipy muzzle. Short ears.

Very Serious Faults—White, other than a spot on the chest. Eyes other than gray, blue-gray or light amber. Black mottled mouth. Non-docked tail. Dogs exhibiting strong fear, shyness or extreme nervousness.

DISQUALIFICATIONS
Deviation in height of more than one inch from standard either way. A distinctly long coat. A distinctly blue or black coat.

APPROVED DECEMBER 14, 1971

WIREHAIRED POINTING GRIFFON

The Wirehaired Pointing Griffon is mentioned as far back as the 16th century, and paintings and drawings of the 17th and 18th century represent them practically as they are today. German, Belgian and French gundogs of various types are believed to have contributed to the styling of the breed, with the Barbet being thought to figure most highly in the modern conformation.

The Wirehaired Pointing Griffon is highly regarded as a hunting dog, being easily trained and remarkably retentive. They lack the elegance of other popular gundogs, but more than compensate for their harsh appearance by being vigorous, dedicated and obedient by nature.

The celebrated artist, Percival L. Rosseau, who had much to do with the breed's introduction in this country, in discussing them in an article which he wrote for *Forest and Stream* many years ago, said:

"A race of dogs that has survived for four centuries must have remarkable qualities, and the Griffon is par excellence a dog for swamps and rough country. His coat affords protection from cold and dampness, thorns and briars, and as a mixed-game dog for any shooting in rough country he has no superior.

"As a race they are built more for strength and endurance than for speed, although individuals under favorable conditions have shown as good speed and range as any other breed of bird dog. They are at their best, however, in close, careful ranging, covering the roughest ground thoroughly, and in America are especially adapted to grouse, woodcock, and snipe shooting. They are natural retrievers on land and water, easily broken to any kind of game, and their puppies show a higher average of nose and hunting qualities than any other existing breed of dogs. The sportsmen who love rough shooting and derive their greatest pleasure from a mixed bag will find the Griffon admirably adapted to their purpose."

Buyer's guide: True sporting people should be drawn to the Wirehaired Pointing Griffon for they have been bred to see action in the field. They are obedient and teachable and should be actively used in hunting or field trial competition. If being selected as a housepet, take care to fulfill the excercise requirements necessary to retain physical tone and a good temperament. This breed does not do well in cramped quarters over long periods of time.

STANDARD FOR THE WIREHAIRED POINTING GRIFFON

The Wirehaired Griffon is a dog of medium size, fairly short-backed, rather a little low on his legs. He is strongly limbed, everything about him indicating strength and vigor. His coat is harsh like the bristles of a wild boar and his appearance, notwithstanding his short coat, is as unkempt as that of the long-haired Griffon, but on the other hand he has a very intelligent air.

Head: Long, furnished with a harsh coat, forming a mustache and eyebrows, skull long and narrow, muzzle square. **Eyes:** Large, open, full of expression, iris yellow or light brown. **Ears:** Of medium size, flat or sometimes slightly curled, set rather high, very lightly furnished with hair. **Nose:** Always brown.

Neck: Rather long, no dewlap.

Shoulders: Long, sloping.

Ribs: Slightly rounded.

Forelegs: Very straight, muscular, furnished with rather short wire hair.

Hind Legs: Furnished with rather short stiff hair, and thighs long and well developed.

Feet: Round, firm and well formed.

Tail: Carried straight or gaily, furnished with a hard coat without plume, generally cut to a third of its length.

Coat: Hard, dry, stiff, never curly, the undercoat downy.

Color: Steel gray with chestnut splashes, gray white with chestnut splashes, chestnut, dirty white mixed with chestnut, never black.

Height: 21½ to 23½ inches for males, and 19½ to 21½ inches for females.

Group 2: Hounds

AFGHAN HOUND

The Afghan Hound traces its ancestry back to the ancient lands of Egypt where desert sheiks bred these exquisite coursing hounds to hunt in the sandy terrains. The Afghan Hound's presence as a revered pet of royalty has been documented to be found in scrolls dated to 3000 B.C. They have been called the "King of Dogs" and today's specimens still possess the aloof, aristocratic air that has been the breed's trademark through time.

Like other coursing or sight hounds, the Afghan Hound hunts by sight. Their highly developed vision is adept at spotting the movement of prey in the distance, and through their blazing speed of foot they overrun the game or keep it at bay until the kill is made by the hunter. In teams, Afghan Hounds are said to be the match for even large game, for while one dog keeps the animal at bay the other lunges for the neck and can make the kill itself.

The most distinguishing feature of the sleek Afghan Hound is their hipbone assembly. At times they have been referred to as being "pivotal"—seemingly able to completely change direction while in mid-air or on the track of prey. While this claim has never been substantiated, the fact remains that their hipbones are set considerably higher and wider apart than other dogs. This enables them to easily traverse all types of terrain—from the hilly country and mountains to the sands of the desert. The Afghan can turn exceptionally quickly and ably and can get tremendous power in their leaps.

Although the Afghan Hound is slightly slower in racing speed than some other hound breeds, they have great endurance and their turning and leaping ability is unmatched. At recent racing meets held throughout this country, the Afghan Hound's speed has been clocked at surpassing 25 m.p.h. in the heat of the race.

The exquisite coat of the Afghan Hound is not only beautiful but it gives the dog the ability to withstand all types of weather, from extreme desert heat to the cold of high mountain tops. The overall beauty of the Afghan Hound has aided in a great growth of popularity for the breed in America since the first importations of the 1920's. Their striking appearance makes them a standout in the show ring and careful breeding and care has helped to foster what is probably the most lustrous coat in the dog world.

Buyer's guide: These active dogs require a lot of space to run around in and must have considerable attention paid to their coats to avoid severe matting and tangles. They are slow to learn, but are generally valued for their beauty and aloof personalities. Only those people willing to pay a great amount of attention to the care of their dogs should consider the Afghan Hound.

STANDARD FOR THE AFGHAN HOUND

General Appearance: The Afghan Hound is an aristocrat, his whole appearance one of dignity and aloofness with no trace of plainness or coarseness. He has a straight front, proudly carried head, eyes gazing into the distance as if in memory of ages past. The striking characteristics of the breed—exotic, or "Eastern," expression, long silky topknot, peculiar coat pattern, very prominent hipbones, large feet, and the impression of a somewhat exaggerated bend in the stifle due to profuse trouserings—stand out clearly, giving the Afghan Hound the appearance of what he is, a king of dogs, that has held true to tradition throughout the ages.

Head: The head is of good length, showing much refinement, the skull evenly balanced with the foreface. There is a slight prominence of the nasal bone structure causing a slightly Roman appearance, the center line running up over the foreface with little or no stop, falling away in front of the eyes so there is an absolutely clear outlook with no interference; the underjaw showing great strength, the jaws long and punishing; the mouth level, meaning that the teeth from the upper jaw and lower jaw match evenly, neither overshot nor undershot. This is a difficult mouth to breed. A scissors bite is even more punishing and can be more easily bred into a dog than a level mouth, and a dog having a scissors bite, where the lower teeth slip inside and rest against the teeth of the upper jaw, should not be penalized. The occipital bone is very prominent. The head is surmounted by a topknot of long silky hair. *Ears:* The ears are long, set approximately on level with outer corners of the eyes, the leather of the ear reaching nearly to the end of the dog's nose, and covered with long silky hair. *Eyes:* The eyes are almond-shaped (almost triangular), never full or bulgy, and are dark in color. *Nose:* Nose is of good size, black in color. *Faults:* Coarseness; snipiness; overshot or undershot; eyes round or bulgy or light in color; exaggerated Roman nose; head not surmounted with topknot.

Neck: The neck is of good length, strong and arched, running a curve to the shoulders which are long and sloping and well laid back. *Faults:* Neck too short or too thick; a ewe neck; a goose neck; a neck lacking in substance.

Body: The back line appearing practically level from the shoulders to the loin. Strong and powerful loin and slightly arched, falling away toward the stern, with the hipbones very pronounced; well ribbed and tucked up in flanks. The height at the shoulders equals the distance from the chest to the buttocks; the brisket is well let down, and of medium width. **Faults:** Roach back, swayback, goose rump, slack loin; lack of prominence of hipbones; too much width of brisket, causing interference with elbows.

Tail: Tail set not too high on the body, having a ring, or a curve on the end; should never be curled over, or rest on the back, or be carried sideways; and should never be bushy.

Legs: Forelegs are straight and strong with great length between elbows and pastern; elbows well held in; forefeet large in both length and width; toes well arched; feet covered with long thick hair; fine in texture; pasterns long and straight; pads of feet unusually large and well down on the ground. Shoulders have plenty of angulation so that the legs are well set underneath the dog. Too much straightness of shoulder causes the dog to break down in the pasterns, and this is a serious fault. All four feet of the Afghan Hound are in line with the body, turning neither in nor out. The hind feet are broad and of good length; the toes arched, and covered with long thick hair; hindquarters powerful and well muscled, with great length between hip and hock; hocks are well let down; good angulation of both stifle and hock; slightly bowed from hock to crotch. **Faults:** Front or back feet thrown outward or inward; pads of feet not thick enough; or feet too small; or any other evidence of weakness in feet; weak or broken down pasterns; too straight in stifle; too long in hock.

Coat: Hindquarters, flanks, ribs, forequarters, and legs well covered with thick, silky hair, very fine in texture; ears and all four feet well feathered; from in front of the shoulders; and also backwards from the shoulders along the saddle from the flanks and the ribs upwards, the hair is short and close, forming a smooth back in mature dogs—this is a traditional characteristic of the Afghan Hound. The Afghan Hound should be shown in its natural state; the coat is not clipped or trimmed; the head is surmounted (in the full sense of the word) with a topknot of long, silky hair—that is also an outstanding characteristic of the Afghan Hound. Showing of short hair on cuffs on either front or back legs is permissible. **Fault:** Lack of shorthaired saddle in mature dogs.

Height: Dogs, 27 inches, plus or minus one inch; bitches, 25 inches, plus or minus one inch.

Weight: Dogs, about 60 pounds; bitches about 50 pounds.

Color: All colors are permissible, but color or color combinations are pleasing; white markings, especially on the head, are undesirable.

Gait: When running free, the Afghan Hound moves at a gallop, showing great elasticity and spring in his smooth, powerful stride. When on a loose lead, the Afghan can trot at a fast pace; stepping along, he has the appearance of placing the hind feet directly in the foot prints of the front feet, both thrown straight ahead. Moving with head and tail high, the whole appearance of the Afghan Hound is one of great style and beauty.

Temperament: Aloof and dignified, yet gay. **Faults:** Sharpness or shyness.

APPROVED SEPTEMBER 14, 1948

Representing the breed: Ch. Sahadi Shikari, owned by Dr. and Mrs. Earl Winter and bred by Joan Brearley.

BASENJI

In his homeland of Central Africa, the Basenji is acclaimed as a tireless hunter of small game. The breed's moderate size, lack of traceable body odor and good scenting ability were great assets in the wilds where the pygmies of the Ituri Forest used them to track down their food. Basenjis were treated with such high regard that they were typically carried to the hunt around the neck of their owner in a ceremonious parade.

They are unique among dogs, and hounds in particular, in several traits. The Basenji is often referred to as *the barkless dog of Africa*. Although they are not totally mute, the breed emits what is sometimes described as a soft yodeling sound. The Basenji is also the most fastidious of all the breeds and can often be found licking themself clean in much the same manner as a cat. His inherent cleanliness and short coat make him an ideal pet for even the most fastidious housekeeper.

This handsome breed has many notable physical characteristics and identifying traits. The Basenji's coat is uncommonly silky and adds a lustrous shine to their chestnut red or black coloring. The forehead is broad and covered with deep, profuse wrinkles. Basenji ears are prick and stand straight and attentively, while their eyes are notably dark and far-seeing. The tail is tightly curled and lies on one side of the back, and they move with a gazelle-like grace.

Basenjis are quite compact (about the size of a Fox Terrier), but their size in no way detracts from their hunting capabilities. They stand proudly and carry themselves with poise and attentiveness. Character traits, such as intelligence, alertness and a gentle nature, have endeared the Basenji to a growing number of owners. They are steady companions and delight in teasing their friends into play. Basenjis will readily defend their home from any and all intruders should the need arise and will learn quickly to respond to the commands of their master.

Buyer's guide: The perky Basenji is good natured and even-tempered, lending themselves to being excellent pets. They are naturally alert and active and require little formal excercising or grooming. Basenjis are spotless in their habits and serve as loyal companions to adults. They are not rough and tumble enough to enjoy a household full of children, but will be a good pet for moderately active people.

STANDARD FOR THE BASENJI

Characteristics: The Basenji should not bark, but is not mute. The wrinkled forehead and the swift, tireless running gait (resembling a racehorse trotting full out) are typical of the breed.

General Appearance: The Basenji is a small, lightly built, short backed dog, giving the impression of being high on the leg compared to its length. The wrinkled head must be proudly carried, and the whole demeanor should be one of poise and alertness.

Head and Skull: The skull is flat, well chiseled and of medium width, tapering towards the eyes. The foreface should taper from eye to muzzle and should be shorter than the skull. Muzzle, neither coarse, nor snipy but with rounded cushions. Wrinkles should appear upon the forehead, and be fine and profuse. Side wrinkles are desirable, but should never be exaggerated into dewlap. **Nose:** Black greatly desired. A pinkish tinge should not penalize an otherwise first class specimen, but it should be discouraged in breeding. **Eyes:** Dark hazel, almond shaped, obliquely set and far seeing. **Ears:** Small, pointed and erect, of fine texture, set well forward on top of head. **Mouth:** Teeth must be level with scissors bite.

Neck: Of good length, well crested and slightly full at base of throat. It should be well set into flat, laid back shoulders.

Forequarters: The chest should be deep and of medium width. The legs straight with clean fine bone, long forearm and well defined sinews. Pasterns should be of good length, straight and flexible.

Body: The body should be short and the back level. The ribs well sprung, with plenty of heart room, deep brisket, short coupled, and ending in a definite waist.

Hindquarters: Should be strong and muscular, with hocks well let down, turned neither in nor out, with long second thighs.

Feet: Small, narrow and compact, with well-arched toes.

Tail: Should be set on top and curled tightly over to either side.

Coat: Short and silky. Skin very pliant.

Color: Chestnut red (the deeper the better) or pure black, or black and tan, all with white feet, chest and tail tip. White legs, white blaze and white collar optional.

Weight: Bitches 22 pounds approximately. Dogs 24 pounds approximately.

Size: Bitches 16 inches and dogs 17 inches from the ground to the top of the shoulder. Bitches 16 inches and dogs 17 inches from the front of the chest to the farthest point of the hindquarters.

FAULTS

Coarse skull or muzzle. Domed or peaked skull. Round eyes. Low set ears. Overshot or undershot mouths. Wide chest. Wide behind. Heavy bone. Creams, shaded or off colors, other than those defined above, should be heavily penalized.

APPROVED JUNE 8, 1954

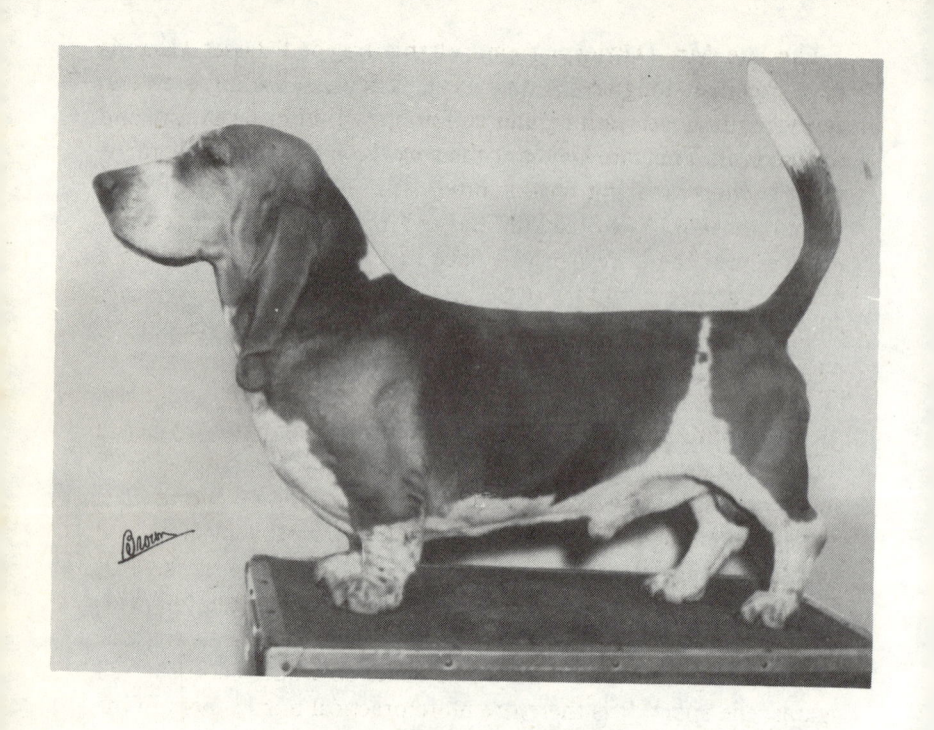

BASSET HOUND

These quaint-appearing dogs are of very ancient descent, and have existed in France for centuries in exactly the same type that they present today. They are essentially hunting dogs, possess marvelous powers of scent and wonderful voices, their clear, bell-like notes surpassing in sweetness those of any other hound, and when once heard are never forgotten.

For hunting on foot they are claimed to be superior to Beagles, their short, crooked legs almost incapable of becoming tired. Their natural pace is about seven miles an hour.

Basset Hounds have the best of tempers. In fact, their dispositions seem to be almost too mild and inoffensive for a sporting dog, although when trained to follow wounded game, for which purpose they are most useful, they take up a trail with the utmost keenness and will never give up until it is brought to bay, when they give tongue fiercely, but show no desire to go into close quarters.

The late Mr. Dalziel has said of this breed: "Basset Hounds have excellent tongues for their size. They are willing workers, and when in good training and condition will hunt every day and thrive on it. They are clever at their work, and when the game is missed when breaking covert, often succeed in 'ringing' it back within gunshot. As a breed the Basset Hound is highly prized, being, perhaps the purest in existence in France. They bring large prices and many could not be bought on any terms. They are employed in hunting roebuck, deer, wild boars, wolves, foxes, hares, and rabbits, but where trained to enter on only one species of game will keep to it exclusively. They move slowly and allow plenty of time for the shooter to take his vantage station, hence their popularity in the estimation of shooters. They work best in small woods, furze fields, and the like, for they do not drive their game fast enough for work in the large forests. The latter are usually cut by streams and deep ravines set with rocks and boulders, which the short, crooked-legged hound surmounts with great difficulty, and while eventually they will bring their game out, the long time which they take to do so would seriously tell against the sport. It is therefore more practical to run them in the smaller coverts, where their voices can readily be heard through the hunt, directing the shooter to the proper posts of vantage."

In build the Basset is long in the barrel and is very low on his pins; so much so that when hunting he literally drags his long ears on the ground. He is the slowest of hounds, and his value as such cannot be overestimated. His style of hunting is peculiar insomuch that he will have his own way. Each hound tries for himself, and if one of them finds and "says" so, the others will not blindly follow him and give tongue simply because he does, as some hounds accustomed to work in packs are apt to do. On the contrary, they are slow to acknowledge the alarm given, and will investigate the matter for themselves. Bassets following a trail go Indian file, and each speaks to the line according to his own sentiments on the point, irrespective of what the others may think about it. In this manner it is not uncommon to see the little hounds when following a mazy track cross each other's route without paying any attention to one another; in short, each of them works as if he were alone. This style is attributed to their slowness, to their extremely delicate powers of scent, and to their innate stubborn confidence in their own powers. Nevertheless, it is a fashion which has its drawbacks, for should the individual hound hit on separate tracks of different animals, unless at once stopped and put together on the same one, each will follow its own find, and let the shooters do their best. That is why a shooter who is fond of that sport rarely owns more than one or two of these hounds. One is enough, two may be handy in difficult cases, but more would certainly entail confusion, precisely because each one of them will rely only on the evidence of his own senses.

In selecting puppies, look for length of head and a narrow skull, with prominent occipital bone; foreface deep and square, ears long and low-set, long body, deep chest, big quarters, and plenty of bone.

Buyer's guide: Although the Basset is somewhat of a stubborn dog by disposition, they are also faithful and devoted to those they love. They do not have the physical prowess of many other hunting hounds, but still retain the desire for the chase and will go about their work with slow, but determined eagerness. If not encouraged, Bassets may take to lying about lazily, content just being in the house. Good companions for all ages.

STANDARD FOR THE BASSET HOUND

General Appearance: The Basset Hound possesses in marked degree those characteristics which equip it admirably to follow a trail over and through difficult terrain. It is a short-legged dog, heavier in bone, size considered, than any other breed of dog, and while its movement is deliberate, it is in no sense clumsy. In temperament it is mild, never sharp or timid. It is capable of great endurance in the field and is extreme in its devotion.

Head: The head is large and well proportioned. Its length from occiput to muzzle is greater than the width at the brow. In over-all appearance the head is of medium length. **The skull** is well domed, showing a pronounced occipital protuberance. A broad flat skull is a fault. The length from nose to stop is approximately the length from stop to occiput. The sides are flat and free from cheek bumps. Viewed in profile the top lines of the muzzle and skull are straight and lie in parallel planes, with a moderately defined stop. The skin over the whole of the head is loose, falling in distinct wrinkles over the brow when the head is lowered. A dry head and tight skin are faults. **The muzzle** is deep, heavy, and free from snipiness. **The nose** is darkly pigmented, preferably black, with large wide-open nostrils. A deep liver-colored nose conforming to the coloring of the head is permissible but not desirable. **The teeth** are large, sound, and regular, meeting in either a scissors or an even bite. A bite either overshot or undershot is a serious fault. **The lips** are darkly pigmented and are pendulous, falling squarely in front and, toward the back, in loose hanging flews. **The dewlap** is very pronounced. **The neck** is powerful, of good length, and well arched. **The eyes** are soft, sad, and slightly sunken, showing a prominent haw, and in color are brown, dark brown preferred. A somewhat lighter-colored eye conforming to the general coloring of the dog is acceptable but not desirable. Very light or protruding eyes are faults. **The ears** are extremely long, low set, and when drawn forward, fold well over the ends of the nose. They are velvety in texture, hanging in loose folds with the ends curling slightly inward. They are set far back on the head at the base of the skull and, in repose, appear to be set on the neck. A high set or flat ear is a serious fault.

Forequarters: **The chest** is deep and full with prominent sternum showing clearly in front of the legs. **The shoulders** and elbows are set close against the sides of the chest. The distance from the deepest point of the chest to the ground, while it must be adquate to allow free movement when working in the field, is not to be more than one-third the total height at the withers of an adult Basset. The shoulders are well laid back and powerful. Steepness in shoulder, fiddle fronts, and elbows that are out, are serious faults. **The forelegs** are short, powerful, heavy in bone, with wrinkled skin. Knuckling over of the front legs is a disqualification. **The paw** is massive, very heavy with tough heavy pads, well rounded and with both feet inclined equally a trifle outward, balancing the width of the shoulders. Feet down at the pastern are a serious fault. **The toes** are neither pinched together nor splayed, with the weight of the forepart of the body borne evenly on each. The dewclaws may be removed.

Body: The rib structure is long, smooth, and extends well back. The ribs are well sprung, allowing adequate room for heart and lungs. Flat-sidedness and flanged ribs are faults. The topline is straight, level, and free from any tendency to sag or roach, which are faults.

Hindquarters: The hindquarters are very full and well rounded, and are approximately equal to the shoulders in width. They must not appear slack or light in relation to the over-all depth of the body. The dog stands firmly on its hind legs showing a well-let-down stifle with no tendency toward a crouching stance. Viewed from behind, the hind legs are parallel, with the hocks turning neither in nor out. Cowhocks or bowed legs are serious faults. The hind feet point straight ahead. Steep, poorly angulated hindquarters are a serious fault. The dewclaws, if any, may be removed.

Tail: The tail is not to be docked, and is set in continuation of the spine with but slight curvature, and carried gaily in hound fashion. The hair on the underside of the tail is coarse.

Size: The height should not exceed 14 inches. Height over 15 inches at the highest point at the shoulder blades is a disqualification.

Gait: The Basset Hound moves in a smooth, powerful, and effortless manner. Being a scenting dog with short legs, it holds its nose low to the ground. Its gait is absolutely true with perfect co-ordination between the front and hind legs, and it moves in a straight line with hind feet following the line with the front feet, the hocks well bent with no stiffness of action. The front legs do not paddle, weave, or overlap, and the elbows must lie close to the body. Going away, the hind legs are parallel.

Coat: The coat is hard, smooth, and short, with sufficient density to be of use in all weather. The skin is loose and elastic. A distinctly long coat is a disqualification.

Color: Any recognized hound color is acceptable and the distribution of color and markings is of no importance.

DISQUALIFICATIONS

Height of more than 15 inches at the highest point of the shoulder blades.
Knuckled over front legs.
Distinctly long coat.

APPROVED JANUARY 14, 1964

BEAGLE

These deservedly popular little dogs are the loveliest of the hound family. They are the merriest little fellows imaginable, shrewd workmen, with the keenest of noses and the most musical of voices. Although pretty and affectionate enough to make the sweetest of pets, they never forget that their true mission in life is to run the rabbit, and never are they more appreciated than when their bell-like melodious voices open up upon the trail.

As the country has settled up and feathered game been exterminated, lovers of field sport who have heretofore devoted their time in the field to bird shooting over setters and pointers, have been obliged to discard their bird dogs in favor of the little hounds, for even in the immediate vicinity of the large cities one can usually find rabbits plentiful enough to furnish good sport.

The origin of the Beagle is lost in obscurity, but it is quite probable that the was evolved from the Foxhound by selecting the smallest specimens and breeding them together until the proper size was arrived at. The typical Beagle is designated in the same standards as a miniature Foxhound. This is a mistake. He is a distinct breed, although having many points in common with all hounds, such as short back, compact body, straight legs, round feet, powerful loins, and nicely-placed shoulders. The true Beagle head has a skull free from coarseness, but with plenty of room; a soft, pleading eye; wide and large nostrils; deep, pendulous lips, and thin, long, low-set ears. It is always difficult to get such a head on a perfect body and legs. In color, the blue mottle is very typical and greatly admired, but black, tan-and-white, black-and-tan, lemon-and-white, or any other hound color is perfectly allowable. In selecting Beagle puppies, look for a compact body, straight forelegs, a roomy head with well-defined stop, and a square muzzle.

Buyer's guide: The lively, eager Beagle was originally meant to be a pack dog hot on the chase of game, but they have become popular pets for their merry temperament. Although many owners have noted some problems in housebreaking the breed, they are affectionate and pleasant with children. Beagle owners should be willing to take their dogs on long runs, preferably with other dogs, to cultivate the true Beagle nature. Once a housepet, they should not be left alone for long lengths of time as they tend to become agitated. Female Beagles are generally easier to train as indoor pets, but training should be done gently yet firmly. If you are too severe in early disciplining, you can damage their spirit and thwart further attempts at making the Beagle obedient while still retaining their merry disposition.

STANDARD FOR THE BEAGLE

Head: The skull should be fairly long, slightly domed at occiput, with cranium broad and full. **Ears:** Ears set on moderately low, long, reaching when drawn out nearly, if not quite, to the end of the nose; fine in texture, fairly broad—with almost entire absence of erectile power—setting close to the head, with the forward edge slightly inturning to the cheek—rounded at tip. **Eyes:** Eyes large, set well apart—soft and houndlike—expression gentle and pleading; of a brown or hazel color. **Muzzle:** Muzzle of medium length—straight and square-cut—the stop moderately defined. **Jaws:** Level. Lips free from flews; nostrils large and open. **Defects:** A very flat skull, narrow across the top; excess of dome, eyes small, sharp and terrierlike, or prominent and protruding; muzzle long, snipy or cut away decidedly below the eyes, or very short. Roman-nosed, or upturned, giving a dish-face expression. Ears short, set on high or with a tendency to rise above the point of origin.

Body: **Neck and Throat:** Neck, rising free and light from the shoulders strong in substance yet not loaded, of medium length. The throat clean and free from folds of skin; a slight wrinkle below the angle of the jaw, however, may be allowable. **Defects:** A thick, short, cloddy neck carried on a line with the top of the shoulders. Throat showing dewlap and folds of skin to a degree termed "throatiness."

Shoulders and Chest: Shoulders sloping—clean, muscular, not heavy or loaded—conveying the idea of freedom of action with activity and strength. Chest deep and broad, but not broad enough to interfere with the free play of the shoulders. **Defects:** Straight, upright shoulders. Chest disproportionately wide or with lack of depth.

Back, Loin and Ribs: Back short, muscular and strong. Loin broad and slightly arched, and the ribs well sprung, giving abundance of lung room. **Defects:** Very long or swayed or roached back. Flat, narrow loin. Flat ribs.

Forelegs and Feet: **Forelegs:** Straight, with plenty of bone in proportion to size of the hound. Pasterns short and straight. **Feet:** Close, round and firm. Pad full and hard. **Defects:** Out at elbows. Knees knuckled over forward, or bent backward. Forelegs crooked or Dachshundlike. Feet long, open or spreading.

Hips, Thighs, Hind Legs and Feet: Hips and thighs strong and well muscled, giving abundance of propelling power. Stifles strong and well let down. Hocks firm, symmetrical and moderately bent. Feet close and firm. **Defects:** Cowhocks, or straight hocks. Lack of muscle and propelling power. Open feet.

Tail: Set moderately high; carried gaily, but not turned forward over the back; with slight curve; short as compared with size of the hound; with brush. **Defects:** A long tail. Teapot curve or inclined forward from the root. Rat tail with absence of brush.

Coat: A close, hard, hound coat of medium length. **Defects:** A short, thin coat, or of a soft quality.

Color: Any true hound color.

General appearance: A miniature Foxhound, solid and big for his inches, with the wear-and-tear look of the hound that can last in the chase and follow his quarry to the death.

SCALE OF POINTS

Head
- Skull 5
- Ears 10
- Eyes 5
- Muzzle 5   25

Body
- Neck 5
- Chest and shoulders 15
- Back, loin and ribs 15   35

Running Gear
- Forelegs 10
- Hips, thighs and hind legs 10
- Feet 10   30
- Coat 5
- Stern 5   10

TOTAL 100

Varieties: There shall be two varieties:

Thirteen Inch—which shall be for hounds not exceeding 13 inches in height.

Fifteen Inch—which shall be for hounds over 13 but not exceeding 15 inches in height.

DISQUALIFICATION

Any hound measuring more than 15 inches shall be disqualified.

Packs of Beagles
Score of Points for Judging

Hounds—General levelness of pack 40%
Individual merit of hounds 30%
                                                                70%
Manners 20%
Appointments 10%
  TOTAL 100%

Levelness of Pack: The first thing in a pack to be considered is that they present a unified appearance. The hounds must be as near to the same height, weight, conformation and color as possible.

Individual Merit of the Hounds: Is the individual bench-show quality of the hounds. A very level and sporty pack can be gotten together and not a single hound be a good beagle. This is to be avoided.

Manners: The hounds must all work gaily and cheerfully, with flags up—obeying all commands cheerfully. They should be broken to heel up, kennel up, follow promptly and stand. Cringing, sulking, lying down to be avoided. Also, a pack must not work as though in terror of master and whips. In Beagle packs it is recommended that the whip be used as little as possible.

Appointments: Master and whips should be dressed alike, the master or huntsman to carry horn—the whips and master to carry light thong whips. One whip should carry extra couplings on shoulder strap.

RECOMMENDATIONS FOR SHOW LIVERY

Black velvet cap, white stock, green coat, white breeches or knickerbockers, green or black stockings, white spats, black or dark brown shoes. Vest and gloves optional. Ladies should turn out exactly the same except for a white skirt instead of white breeches.

APPROVED SEPTEMBER 10, 1957

BLACK AND TAN COONHOUND

Although Black and Tan Coonhounds are generally recognized for their keen ability to tree raccoons, they are further endowed with the ability to hunt a wide variety of larger game. While a Coonhound can be a fierce hunter and fighter on the trail of wild beasts, at home he is affectionate and has a mellow temperament. He responds warmly to kindness and shows a great desire for training and vigorous sport.

The Black and Tan is wonderful company and an alert watchdog, but he is most adept nose to the ground on the scent of the 'coon. He was bred to hunt and his keen nose enables him to track any game which leaves a scent behind. While the Black and Tan is most commonly used in the South for hunting raccoon and possum, with the proper training they will discriminate to any scent that the hunter wants them to track—whether this be minks, cats, people—whatever!

Although there are six Coonhound breeds, only the Black and Tan is officially recognized by the AKC. These Coonhounds have very glossy, smooth, thick coats. They are predominantly black, with tan markings on the face, legs, and chest. At first glance you get an overall impression of strength and power. They sport a friendly, alert expression and their muscular hindquarters reflect the Black and Tan's ability to run through all types of underbrush with long rhythmic strides. This breed is a relatively new addition to the list of AKC approved breeds, having been admitted only in 1945, but they have proven themselves to be great dual purpose dogs that even after active campaigning on the dog show circuits retain their love for the field and the hunt.

Buyer's guide: This breed is primarily a hunter's dog and should be treated as such. They are a strong, rugged breed that needs adequate room and exercise to maintain their qualities. They are generally too big for small children and have not been kept extensively as housepets.

STANDARD FOR THE BLACK AND TAN COONHOUND

The Black and Tan Coonhound is first and fundamentally a working dog, capable of withstanding the rigors of winter, the heat of summer, and the difficult terrain over which he is called upon to work. Judges are asked by the club sponsoring the breed to place great emphasis upon these facts when evaluating the merits of the dog. The general impression should be that of power, agility, and alertness. His expression should be alert, friendly, eager, and aggressive. He should immediately impress one with his ability to cover the ground with powerful rhythmic strides.

Head: The head should be cleanly modeled, with medium stop occurring midway between occiput bone and nose. The head should measure from 9 to 10 inches in males and from 8 to 9 inches in females. Viewed from the profile, the line of the skull is on a practically parallel plane to the foreface or muzzle. **The skin** should be devoid of folds or excess dewlap. **The flews** should be well developed with typical hound appearance. **Nostrils** well open and always black. **Skull** should tend toward oval outline. **Eyes** should be from hazel to dark brown in color, almost round and not deeply set. **The ears** should be low set and well back. They should hang in graceful folds giving the dog a majestic appearance. In length they should extend well beyond the tip of the nose. **Teeth** should fit evenly with slightly scissors bite.

Body: **Neck, Shoulders, and Chest:** The neck should be muscular, sloping, medium length, extending into powerfully constructed shoulders and deep chest. The dog should possess full, round, well-sprung ribs, avoiding flatsidedness. **Back and Tail:** The back should be level, powerful and strong, with a visible slope from withers to rump. Tail should be strong, with base slightly below level of back line, carried free, and when in action at approximately right angle to back.

Legs and Feet: The forelegs should be straight, with elbows well let down, turning neither in nor out; pasterns strong and erect. Feet should be catlike with compact, well-arched toes and thick strong pads. **Hindquarters:** Quarters should be well boned and muscled. From hip to hock long and sinewy, hock to pad short and strong. Stifles and hock well bent and not inclining either in or out. When standing on a level surface the hind feet should set back from under the body, and leg, and leg from pad to hock be at right angles to the ground when viewed both from profile and the rear. The stride of the Black and Tan Coonhounds should be easy and graceful with plenty of reach in front and drive behind.

Coat and Color: The coat should be short but dense to withstand rough going. As the name implies, the color should be coal black, with rich tan markings above eyes, on sides of muzzle, chest, legs and breeching with black pencil markings on toes.

Size: Measured at the shoulder: males, 25 to 27 inches; females, 23 to 25 inches. Height should be in proportion to general conformation so that dog appears neither leggy nor close to the ground. Dogs oversized should not be penalized when general soundness and proportion are in favor.

Judges should penalize the following defects:

Undersize, elbows out at shoulders, lack of angulation in hindquarters. Splay feet, sway- or roach back, flatsidedness, lack of depth in chest, yellow or light eyes, shyness and nervousness.

Faults: Dewclaws; white on chest or other parts of body is highly undesirable and if it exceeds 1½ inches in diameter should be disqualified.

DISQUALIFICATION
White on chest or other parts of the body if it exceeds 1½ inches in diameter.

APPROVED JULY 10, 1945

BLOODHOUND

This is one of the oldest as well as one of the least understood of all breeds of dogs. The most extravagant tales are related and stories written about them. The name suggests a ferocious animal, whereas they are of the most kindly nature, entirely lacking in all of the qualities which their name implies. They are the gentlest of companions, and if of pure breeding far less dangerous than any of the other big breeds. In the days of the bow and arrow the Bloodhound was trained to hunt the stag, and was expected to track the wounded deer by the blood that dropped from the wounds of the arrow, all of which has been done away with for many years.

A great deal has been written about hunting slaves in southern states in pre-war times. As a matter of fact the dogs that were used to trail the runaways were small Foxhounds and not Bloodhounds.

The stories told of Bloodhounds following the scent of a man through the crowded streets are also gross exaggerations. It is impossible for them to do so. Therefore they are of little or no use to the police authorities in detecting criminals in crowded cities. In the country, however, Bloodhounds can be used to capture criminals. They will make out a scent that is several hours old and follow it accurately. Repeated trials, however, indicate that it is impossible for them to carry these trails where they have been crossed by cattle, sheep or horses.

At one time the Bloodhound had been crossed with nearly all of the sporting breeds, and doing so improved their voices as well as their power of scent.

The chief points to look for in the selection of Bloodhound puppies at from two to four months old, and even afterward, are: great length of head; narrowness of skull; great depth and squareness of foreface; big nostrils; long ears set low; great bone; and short back.

Buyer's guide: The big, gentle Bloodhound is a country dog, and should remain so. They enjoy the open fields and the chance to track game with their masters more than anything. They are exceptionally affectionate and are easy to get along with since they require little from their owners. They are well mannered and aren't quarrelsome with anyone or thing that they are introduced to.

STANDARD FOR THE BLOODHOUND

General Character: The Bloodhound possesses, in a most marked degree, every point and characteristic of those dogs which hunt together by scent (Sagaces). He is very powerful, and stands over more ground than is usual with hounds of other breeds. The skin is thin to the touch and extremely loose, this being more especially noticeable about the head and neck, where it hangs in deep folds.

Height: The mean average height of adult dogs is 26 inches, and of adult bitches 24 inches. Dogs usually vary from 25 to 27 inches, and bitches from 23 to 25 inches; but, in either case, the greater height is to be preferred, provided that character and quality are also combined.

Weight: The mean average weight of adult dogs, in fair condition, is 90 pounds, and of adult bitches 80 pounds. Dogs attain the weight of 110 pounds, bitches 100 pounds. The greater weights are to be preferred, provided (as in the case of height) that quality and proportion are also combined.

Expression: The expression is noble and dignified, and characterized by solemnity, wisdom, and power.

Temperament: In temperament he is extremely affectionate, neither quarrelsome with companions nor with other dogs. His nature is somewhat shy, and equally sensitive to kindness or correction by his master.

Head: The head is narrow in proportion to its length, and long in proportion to the body, tapering but slightly from the temples to the end of the muzzle, thus (when viewed from above and in front) having the appearance of being flattened at the sides and of being nearly equal in width throughout its entire length. In profile the upper outline of the skull is nearly in the same plane as that of the foreface. The length from end of nose to stop (midway between the eyes) should be not less than that from stop to back of occipital protuberance (peak). The entire length of head from the posterior part of the occipital protuberance to the end of the muzzle should be 12 inches, or more, in dogs, and 11 inches, or more, in bitches. **Skull:** The skull is long and narrow, with the occipital peak very pronounced. The brows are not prominent, although, owing to the deep-set eyes, they may have that appearance. **Foreface:** The foreface is long, deep, and of even width throughout, with square outline when seen in profile. **Eyes:** The eyes are deeply sunk in the orbits, the lids assuming a lozenge or diamond shape, in consequence of the lower lid being dragged down and everted by the heavy flews. The eyes correspond with the general tone of color of the animal, varying from deep hazel to yellow. The hazel color is, however, to be preferred, although very seldom seen in red-and-tan hounds. **Ears:** The ears are thin and soft to the touch, extremely long, set very low, and fall in graceful folds, the lower parts curling inward and backward.

Wrinkle: The head is furnished with an amount of loose skin, which in nearly every position appears superabundant, but more particularly so when the head is carried low; the skin then falls into loose, pendulous ridge and folds, especially over the forehead and sides of the face. **Nostrils:** The nostrils are large and open. **Lips, Flews and Dewlap:** In front the lips fall squarely, making a right angle with the upper line of the foreface; whilst behind they form deep, hanging flews, and, being continued into the pendant folds of loose skin about the neck, constitute the dewlap, which is very pronounced. These characters are found, though in a less degree, in the bitch.

Neck, Shoulders and Chest: The neck is long, the shoulders muscular and well sloped backwards; the ribs are well sprung; and the chest well let down between the forelegs, forming a deep keel.

Legs and Feet: The forelegs are straight and large in bone, with elbows squarely set; the feet strong and well knuckled up; the thighs and second thighs (gaskins) are very muscular; the hocks well bent and let down and squarely set.

Back and Loin: The back and loins are strong, the latter deep and slightly arched. **Stern:** The stern is long and tapering, and set on rather high, with a moderate amount of hair underneath.

Gait: The gait is elastic, swinging and free, the stern being carried high, but not too much curled over the back.

Color: The colors are black and tan, red and tan, and tawny; the darker colors being sometimes interspersed with lighter or badger-colored hair, and sometimes flecked with white. A small amount of white is permissible on chest, feet, and tip of stern.

Representing the breed: Ch. The Rectory's Limbo, owned by Patricia A. Simancek and Harriet Jack.

BORZOI

In Russia, the land of their birth, these handsome, stately, highbred dogs are known as Borzoi or Psovoi, and are used for coursing and wolf hunting. They are carefully trained to run up alongside of a fleeing wolf, collar him by the neck just under the ear, and never loose their hold, no matter how often they may roll over together, until the hunter comes up and either muzzles the dog or dispatches the victim.

When slipped in pairs, which is the usual procedure, the art comes in having them so evenly matched in speed that they can range up on either side of the wolf simultaneously, pin him by the neck, and hold him safely without injury to themselves.

In the early trials that these dogs were given on western wolves they did not perform as satisfactorily as had been expected of them, probably due to the fact that they lacked experience and training.

Their aristocratic appearance is very much in their favor as companions. Some question has been raised as to their disposition, and there is no disputing that many of them are snappy, quarrelsome, and uncertain, while others are as sweet and lovable as it is only possible for a dog to be. It may be safely said that all depends upon the way they have been raised and bred.

The points to look for in Borzoi puppies at from two to four months old and after, are: a phenomenally long head; rather Roman in shape of muzzle, very well filled up under the eyes; small eyes, set in obliquely; very narrow skull, with occipital bone well developed; powerful neck; very narrow shoulders; long, straight forelegs; very deep chest; loin arched; graceful outline.

Buyer's guide: The Borzoi is not a dog to be kept in small places because they are large and fast and require a good deal of free running and exercise. Owners must be willing to keep their Borzoi's coat properly groomed and brushed and they should be shown great affection to keep their disposition friendly, as they have a tendency to become distant. They are too large to be controlled by small children. Training comes slowly since they are somewhat stubborn.

STANDARD FOR THE BORZOI

General Appearance: The Borzoi was originally bred for the coursing of wild game on more or less open terrain, relying on sight rather than scent. To accomplish this purpose, the Borzoi needed particular structural qualities to chase, catch and hold his quarry. Special emphasis is placed on sound running gear, strong neck and jaws, courage and agility, combined with proper condition. The Borzoi should always possess unmistakable elegance, with flowing lines, graceful in motion or repose. Males, masculine without coarseness; bitches, feminine and refined.

Head: Skull slightly domed, long and narrow, with scarcely any perceptible stop, inclined to be Roman-nosed. Jaws long, powerful and deep, somewhat finer in bitches but not snipy. Teeth strong and clean with either an even or a scissors bite. Missing teeth should be penalized. Nose large and black.

Ears: Small and fine in quality, lying back on the neck when in repose with the tips when thrown back almost touching behind occiput; raised when at attention.

Eyes: Set somewhat obliquely, dark in color, intelligent but rather soft in expression; never round, full nor staring, nor light in color; eye rims dark; inner corner midway between tip of nose and occiput.

Neck: Clean, free from throatiness; slightly arched, very powerful and well set on.

Shoulders: Sloping, fine at the withers and free from coarseness or lumber.

Chest: Rather narrow, with great depth of brisket.

Ribs: Only slightly sprung, but very deep, giving room for heart and lung play.

Back: Rising a little at the loins in a graceful curve.

Loins: Extremely muscular, but rather tucked up, owing to the great depth of chest and comparative shortness of back and ribs.

Forelegs: Bones straight and somewhat flattened like blades, with the narrower edge forward. The elbows have free play and are turned neither in nor out. Pasterns strong.

Feet: Hare-shaped, with well-arched knuckles, toes close and well padded.

Hindquarters: Long, very muscular and powerful with well bent stifles; somewhat wider than the forequarters; strong first and second thighs; hocks clean and well let down; legs parallel when viewed from the rear.

Dewclaws: Dewclaws, if any, on the hind legs are generally removed; dewclaws on the forelegs may be removed.

Tail: Long, set on and carried low in a graceful curve.

Coat: Long, silky (not wooly), either flat, wavy or rather curly. On the head, ears and front of legs it should be short and smooth; on the neck the frill should be profuse and rather curly. Feather on hindquarters and tail, long and profuse, less so on chest and back of forelegs.

Color: Any color, or combination of colors, is acceptable.

Size: Mature males should be at least 28 inches at the withers and mature bitches at least 26 inches at the withers. Dogs and bitches below these respective limits should be severely penalized; dogs and bitches above the respective limits should not be penalized as long as extra size is not acquired at the expense of symmetry, speed and staying quality. Range in weight for males from 75 to 105 pounds and for bitches from 15 to 20 pounds less.

Gait: Front legs must reach well out in front with pasterns strong and springy. Hackneyed motion with mincing gait is not desired nor is weaving and crossing. However, while the hind legs are wider apart than the front, the feet tend to move closer to the center line when the dog moves at a fast trot. When viewed from the side there should be a noticeable drive with a ground-covering stride from well-angulated stifles and hocks. The over-all appearance in motion should be that of effortless power, endurance, speed, agility, smoothness and grace.

FAULTS

The foregoing description is that of the ideal Borzoi. Any deviation from the above described dog must be penalized to the extent of the deviation keeping in mind the importance of the contribution of the various features toward the basic original purpose of the breed.

APPROVED JUNE 13, 1972

DACHSHUND

These long, low, and peculiarly shaped dogs are the national dog of Germany. They are classified with the hounds, but in reality are terriers, as their work is almost entirely underground.

They derive their name from the fact that in their native land they are used to draw the *dachs,* an animal similar to our badger. Their long, low structure, powerful legs, strong claws, sharp teeth, muscular jaws, and fierce fighting spirit admirably adapts them for underground work of this character. They are also used in following the fox, and will track the fox or badger to his haunts and fight him in his burrow. They have fair noses, and are sometimes trained to follow wounded deer. Attempts have been made to use them for rabbit dogs, but they are not such capable workers as either hounds or Beagles, lacking in both nose and intelligence.

Although the Smooth Dachshund is most commonly seen, there are two other varieties for the breed: the Wirehaired and the Longhaired. Miniature versions of these varieties are also accepted and bred for.

Because of the long-bodied structure of the breed, care must be taken to keep these dogs in proper weight. Dachshunds sometimes exhibit greedy tendencies and will often overeat if allowed. The overweight Dachshund is prone to have severe spinal problems, but if these dogs are kept fit they enjoy good health and a long life.

The chief points to look for in the selection of Dachshund puppies at from two to four months old and after, are: a long, level head; small eye; ears set rather low; long body, showing distinct arch in loin; deep chest; great bone; short legs.

Buyer's guide: The Dachshund is kept almost strictly as a housepet these days, and is one of the easiest to get along with. Their small size and even temperament make them suitable for any size house, whether city or country, and they do not constant-

SMOOTH DACHSHUND

WIREHAIRED DACHSHUND

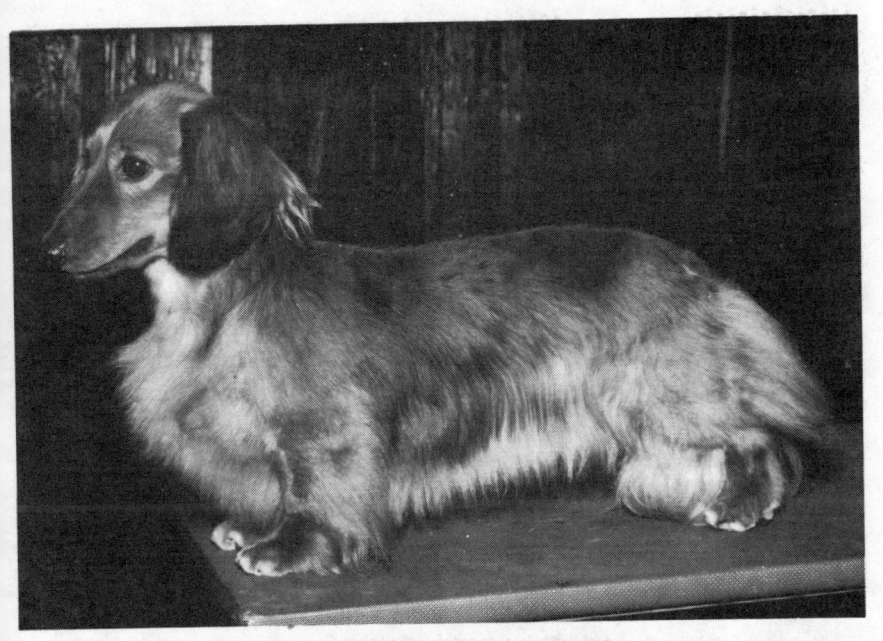

LONGHAIRED DACHSHUND

ly pester their owners to get out. Dachshunds require no grooming to speak of, are small eaters and are well suited to share a home with children. By fact of their size, they should not be expected to be overly athletic, although they are playful.

STANDARD FOR THE DACHSHUND

General Appearance: Low to ground, short-legged, long-bodied, but with compact figure and robust development; with bold and confident carriage of the head and intelligent facial expression. In spite of his shortness of leg, in comparison with his length of trunk, he should appear neither crippled, awkward, cramped in his capacity for movement, nor slim and weasel-like.

Qualities: He should be clever, lively, and courageous to the point of rashness, perserving in his work both above and below ground; with all the senses well developed. His build and disposition qualify him especially for hunting game below ground. Added to this, his hunting spirit, good nose, loud tongue, and small size, render him especially suited for beating the bush. His figure and his fine nose give him an especial advantage over most other breeds of sporting dogs for trailing.

CONFORMATION OF BODY

Head: Viewed from above or from the side, it should taper uniformly to the tip of the nose, and should be clean-cut. The skull is only slightly arched, and should slope gradually without stop (the less stop the more typical) into the finely-formed slightly-arched muzzle (ram's nose). The bridge bones over the eyes should be strongly prominent. The nasal cartilage and tip of the nose are long and narrow; lips tightly stretched, well covering the lower jaw, but neither deep nor pointed; corner of the mouth not very marked. Nostrils well open. Jaws opening wide and hinged well back of the eyes, with strongly developed bones and teeth.

Teeth: Powerful canine teeth should fit closely together, and the outer side of the lower incisors should tightly touch the inner side of the upper. (Scissors bite.)

Eyes: Medium size, oval, situated at the sides, with a clean, energetic, though pleasant expression; not piercing. Color, lustrous dark reddish-brown to brownish-black for all coats and colors. Wall eyes in the case of dapple dogs are not a very bad fault, but are also not desirable.

Ears: Should be set near the top of the head, and not too far forward, long but not too long, beautifully rounded, not narrow, pointed, or folded. Their carriage should be animated, and the forward edge should just touch the cheek.

Neck: Fairly long, muscular, clean-cut, not showing any dewlap on the throat, slightly arched in the nape, extending in a graceful line into the shoulders, carried proudly but not stiffly.

Front: To endure the arduous exertion underground, the front must be correspondingly muscular, compact, deep, long and broad. Forequarters in detail:

Shoulder Blade: Long, broad, obliquely and firmly placed upon the fully developed thorax, furnished with hard and plastic muscles.

Upper Arm: Of the same length as the shoulder blade, and at right angles to the latter, strong of bone and hard of muscle, lying close to the ribs, capable of free movement.

Forearm: This is short in comparison to other breeds, slightly turned inwards; supplied with hard but plastic muscles on the front and outside, with tightly stretched tendons on the inside and at the back.

Joint between forearm and foot (wrists): These are closer together than the shoulder joints, so that the front does not appear absolutely straight.

Paws: Full, broad in front, and a trifle inclined outwards; compact, with well-arched toes and tough pads.

Toes: There are five of these, though only four are in use. They should be close together, with a pronounced arch; provided on top with strong nails, and underneath with tough toe-pads. Dewclaws may be removed.

Trunk: The whole trunk should in general be long and fully muscled. The back, with sloping shoulders, and short, rigid pelvis, should lie in the straightest possible line between the withers and the very slightly arched loins, these latter being short, rigid, and broad.

Chest: The breastbone should be strong, and so prominent in front that on either side a depression (dimple) appears. When viewed from the front, the thorax should appear oval, and should extend downward to the mid-point of the forearm. The enclosing structure of ribs should appear full and oval, and when viewed from above or from the side, full-volumed, so as to allow by its ample capacity, complete development of heart and lungs. Well ribbed up, and gradually merging into the line of the abdomen. If the length is correct, and also the anatomy of the shoulder and upper arm, the front leg when viewed in profile should cover the lowest point of the breast line.

Abdomen: Slightly drawn up.

Hindquarters: The hindquarters viewed from behind should be of completely equal width.

Croup: Long, round, full, robustly muscled, but plastic, only slightly sinking toward the tail.

Pelvic Bones: Not too short, rather strongly developed, and moderately sloping.

Thigh Bone: Robust and of good length, set at right angles to the pelvic bones.

Hind Legs: Robust and well-muscled, with well-rounded buttocks.

Knee Joint: Broad and strong.

Calf Bone: In comparison with other breeds, short; it should be perpendicular to the thigh bone, and firmly muscled.

The bones at the base of the foot (tarsus) should present a flat appearance, with a strongly prominent hock and a broad tendon of Achilles.

The central foot bones (metatarsus) should be long, movable toward the calf bone, slightly bent toward the front, but perpendicular (as viewed from behind).

Hind Paws: Four compactly closed and beautifully arched toes, as in the case of the front paws. The whole foot should be posed equally on the ball and not merely on the toes; nails short.

Tail: Set in continuation of the spine, extending without any pronounced curvature, and should not be carried too gaily.

Note—Inasmuch as the Dachshund is a hunting dog, scars from honorable wounds shall not be considered a fault.

SPECIAL CHARACTERISTICS OF THE THREE COAT-VARIETIES

The Dachshund is bred with three varieties of coat: (1) Shorthaired (or *Smooth)*; (2) Wirehaired; (3) Longhaired. All three varieties should conform to the characteristics already specified. The longhaired and shorthaired are old, well-fixed varieties, but into the wirehaired Dachshund, the blood of other breeds has been purposely introduced; nevertheless, in breeding him, the greatest stress must be placed upon conformity to the general Dachshund type. The following specifications are applicable separately to the three coat-varieties, respectively:

(1) Shorthaired (or Smooth) Dachshund

Hair: Short, thick, smooth and shining; no bald patches. Special faults are: Too fine or thin hair, leathery ears, bald patches, too coarse or too thick hair in general.

Tail: Gradually tapered to a point, well but not too richly haired, long, sleek bristles on the underside are considered a patch of strong-growing hair, not a fault. A brush tail is a fault, as is also a partly or wholly hairless tail.

Color of Hair, Nose and Nails:

One-Colored Dachshund: This group includes red (often called tan), red-yellow, yellow, and brindle, with or without a shading of interspersed black hairs. Nevertheless a clean color is preferable, and red is to be considered more desirable than red-yellow or yellow. Dogs strongly shaded with interspersed black hairs belong to this class, and not to the other color groups. A small white spot is admissable, but not desirable. Nose and Nails—Black; brown is admissible, but not desirable.

Two-Colored Dachshund: These comprise deep black, chocolate, gray (blue), and white; each with tan markings over the eyes, on the sides of the jaw and underlip, on the inner edge of the ear, front, breast, inside and behind the front legs, on the paws and around the anus, and from there to about one-third to one-half of the length of the tail on the under side. The most common two-colored Dachshund is usually called black-and-tan. A small white spot is admissible but not desirable. Absence, undue prominence or extreme lightness of tan markings is undesirable. Nose and Nails—In the case of black dogs, black; for chocolate, brown (the darker the better); for gray (blue) or white dogs, gray or even flesh color, but the last named color is not desirable; in the case of white dogs, black nose and nails are to be preferred.

Dappled Dachshund: The color of the dappled Dachshund is a clear brownish or grayish color, or even a white ground, with dark irregular patches of dark-gray, red-yellow or black (large areas of one color not desirable). It is desirable that neither the light nor the dark color should predominate. Nose and Nails—As for One- and Two-Colored Dachshund.

(2) Wirehaired Dachshund

The general appearance is the same as that of the shorthaired, but without being long in the legs, it is permissible for the body to be somewhat higher off the ground.

Hair: With the exception of jaw, eyebrows, and ears, the whole body is covered with perfectly uniform tight, short, thick, rough, hard coat, but with finer, shorter hairs (undercoat) everywhere distributed between the coarser hairs, resembling the coat of the German Wirehaired Pointer. There should be a beard on the chin. The eyebrows are bushy. On the ears the hair is shorter than on the body; almost smooth, but in any case conforming to the rest of the coat. The general arrangement of the hair should be such that the wirehaired Dachshund, when seen from a distance should resemble the smooth-haired. Any sort of soft hair in the coat is faulty, whether short or long, or wherever found on the body; the same is true of long, curly, or wavy hair, or hair that sticks out irregularly in all directions; a flag tail is also objectionable.

Tail: Robust, as thickly haired as possible, gradually coming to a point, and without a tuft.

Color of Hair, Nose and Nails: All colors are admissible. White patches on the chest, though allowable, are not desirable.

(3) Longhaired Dachshund

The distinctive characteristic differentiating this coat from the shorthaired, or smooth-haired Dachshund is alone the rather long silky hair.

Hair: The soft, sleek, glistening, often slightly wavy hair should be longer under the neck, on the underside of the body, and especially on the ears and behind the legs, becoming there a pronounced feather; the hair should attain its greatest length on the underside of the tail. The hair should fall beyond the lower edge of the ear. Short hair on the ear, so-called "leather" ears, is not desirable. Too luxurious a coat causes the longhaired Dachshund to seem coarse, and masks the type. The coat should remind one of the Irish Setter, and should give the dog an elegant appearance. Too thick hair on the paws, so-called "mops," is inelegant, and renders the animal unfit for use. It is faulty for the dog to have equally long hair over all the body, if the coat is too curly, or too scrubby, or if a flag or overhanging hair on the ears are lacking; or if there is a very pronounced parting on the back, or a vigorous growth between the toes.

Tail: Carried gracefully in prolongation of the spine; the hair attains here its greatest length and forms a veritable flag.

Color of Hair, Nose and Nails: Exactly as for the smooth-haired Dachshund, except that the red-with-black (heavily sabled) color is permissible and is formally classed as a red.

Miniature Dachshunds

Note—*Miniature Dachshunds are bred in all three coats. Within the limits imposed, symmetrical adherence to the general Dachshund conformation, combined with smallness, and mental and physical vitality, should be the outstanding characteristics of Miniature Dachshunds. They have not been given separate classification but are a division of the Open Class for "under 10 pounds, and 12 months old or over."*

General Faults

Serious Faults: Over- or undershot jaws, knuckling over, very loose shoulders.

Secondary Faults: A weak, long-legged, or dragging figure; body hanging between the shoulders; sluggish, clumsy, or waddling gait; toes turned inwards or too obliquely outwards; splayed paws; sunken back, roach (or carp) back; croup higher than withers; short-ribbed or too weak chest; excessively drawn-up flanks like those of a Greyhound; narrow, poorly-muscled hindquarters; weak loins; bad angulation in front or hindquarters; cowhocks; bowed legs; wall eyes, except for dappled dogs; bad coat.

Minor Faults: Ears wrongly set, sticking out, narrow or folded; too marked a stop; too pointed or weak a jaw; pincer teeth; too wide or too short a head; goggle eyes, wall eyes in the case of dappled dogs, insufficiently dark eyes in the case of all other coat-colors; dewlaps; short neck; swan neck; too fine or too thin hair; absence of, or too profuse or too light tan markings in the case of two-colored dogs.

APPROVED JANUARY 12, 1971

Representing the Smooth: Ch. Karlstad's Lionel, owned by Dee Hutchinson and bred by Barbara Murphy. Wirehaired: Ch. Rose Farms Sweet William, M.W., owned by Dee Hutchinson and bred and co-owned by Betty Wilson. Longhaired: Ch. Rose Farms Rip of Low Tor, owned and bred by Dee Hutchinson.

AMERICAN AND ENGLISH FOXHOUND

It has been claimed that the Foxhound is the most perfect member of his race, and that no dog equals him in beauty of conformation, nose and courage. However that may be, more time and money may have been spent on them than on any other breed.

The Foxhound is said to be the result of a cross between the Bloodhound and the Greyhound. They have been recognized as a distinct breed, however, for nearly three centuries. In this country there are two distinct types of Foxhounds—the American and the English. The English hound is larger and heavier-boned than his American cousin. English breeders have established a high standard of excellence as to size, conformation, general symmetry, beauty of form and style, but this has been done at the expense of nose, speed, endurance and fox sense.

The English hound is more satisfactory to hunt clubs in the East, where the majority hunt to ride, for English dogs are better trained and broken, more evenly matched as to speed, and not fast enough to get away from the rider. They also present a more pleasing appearance to the eye.

The American hound is descended from hounds brought to this country in pre-Revolutionary days by the sport-loving gentry of Virginia, Maryland and Carolina, who bred them on purely utilitarian lines, and succeeded in producing a family of dogs which admirably filled the purpose for which they were desired, and which are now scattered all over the United States.

The American hound lacks the uniform size and the regular markings of the English hound. They are lighter in bone and muscle, but far excel them in brains and fox sense. Their noses are keener, and they will strike out boldly and search the likely place for the fox, and will then drive them faster and harder and give tongue with sweeter voices than their English rivals.

Snipiness, coarse skull, cow hocks, flat sides, crooked forelegs, and open feet are unpardonable faults in a Foxhound.

AMERICAN FOXHOUND

ENGLISH FOXHOUND

The chief points to look for in the selection of Foxhound puppies at from two to four months old and after, are: a long, level head; big nostrils; square muzzle; great bone; deep chest; short back.

Buyer's guide: Foxhounds have not been used very extensively as housepets, as they seem to prefer the company of their kennel mates. Although they are reasonably trainable, they do need plenty of room and a substantial amount of exercise daily. Foxhounds are not the most personable dogs and are not recommended for children or aged people. For those who hunt with packs, the Foxhound is a good worker.

STANDARD FOR THE AMERICAN FOXHOUND

Head: **Skull:** Should be fairly long, slightly domed at occiput, with cranium broad and full. **Ears:** Ears set on moderately low, long, reaching when drawn out nearly, if not quite, to the tip of the nose; fine in texture, fairly broad, with almost entire absence of erectile power— setting close to the head with the forward edge slightly inturning to the cheek— round at tip. **Eyes:** Eyes large, set well apart: soft and houndlike— expression gentle and pleading; of a brown or hazel color. **Muzzle:** Muzzle of fair length— straight and square-cut— the stop moderately defined.

Defects: A very flat skull, narrow across the top; excess of dome; eyes small, sharp and terrierlike, or prominent and protruding; muzzle long and snipy, cut away decidedly below the eyes, or very short. Roman-nosed, or upturned, giving a dish-face expression. Ears short, set on high, or with a tendency to rise above the point of origin.

Body: **Neck and Throat:** Neck rising free and light from the shoulders, strong in substance yet not loaded, of medium length. The throat clean and free from folds of skin, a slight wrinkle below the angle of the jaw, however, is allowable.

Defects: A thick, short, cloddy neck carried on a line with the top of the shoulders. Throat showing dewlap and folds of skin to a degree termed "throatiness."

Shoulders, Chest and Ribs: Shoulders sloping: clean, muscular, not heavy or loaded—conveying the idea of freedom of action with activity and strength. Chest should be deep for lung space, narrower in proportion to depth than the English hound—28 inches (*girth*) in a 23-inch hound being good. Well-sprung ribs—back ribs should extend well back—a three-inch flank allowing springiness.

Back and Loins: Back moderately long, muscular and strong. Loins broad and slightly arched.

Defects: Very long or swayed or roached back. Flat, narrow loins.

Forelegs and Feet: Forelegs: Straight, with fair amount of bone. Pasterns short and straight.

Feet: Foxlike. Pad full and hard. Well-arched toes. Strong nails.

Defects: Straight, upright shoulders, chest disproportionately wide or with lack of depth. Flat ribs. Out at elbow. Knees knuckled over forward, or bent backward. Forelegs crooked. Feet long, open or spreading.

Hips, Thighs, Hind Legs and Feet: Hips and thighs, strong and muscled, giving abundance of propelling power. Stifles strong and well let down. Hocks firm, symmetrical and moderately bent. Feet close and firm.

Defects: Cowhocks, or straight hocks. Lack of muscle and propelling power. Open feet.

Tail: Set moderately high; carried gaily, but not turned forward over the back; with slight curve; with very slight brush.

Defects: A long tail. Teapot curve or inclined forward from the root. Rat tail, entire absence of brush.

Coat: A close, hard, hound coat of medium length.

Defects: A short thin coat, or of a soft quality.

Height: Dogs should not be under 22 or over 25 inches. Bitches should not be under 21 or over 24 inches measured across the back at the point of the withers, the hound standing in a natural position with his feet well under him.

Color: Any color.

SCALE OF POINTS

Head
- Skull 5
- Ears 5
- Eyes 5
- Muzzle 5 20

Body
- Neck 5
- Chest and Shoulders 15
- Back, loins and ribs 15 35

Running Gear
- Forelegs 10
- Hips, thighs and hind legs 10
- Feet 15 35

Coat and Tail
- Coat 5
- Tail 5 10
- TOTAL 100

STANDARD FOR THE ENGLISH FOXHOUND

Head: Should be of full size, but by no means heavy. Brow pronounced, but not high or sharp. There should be a good length and breadth, sufficient to give in a dog hound a girth in front of the ears of fully 16 inches. The nose should be long (4½ inches) and wide, with open nostrils. Ears set on low and lying close to the cheeks. Most English hounds are "rounded" which means that about 1½ inches is taken off the end of the ear. The teeth meet squarely, either a *pig-mouth* (overshot) or undershot being a disqualification.

Neck: Must be long and clean, without the slightest throatiness, not less than 10 inches from cranium to shoulder. It should taper nicely from shoulders to head, and the upper outline should be slightly convex.

The Shoulders should be long and well clothed with muscle, without being heavy, especially at the points. They must be well sloped, and the true arm between the front and the elbow must be long and muscular, but free from fat or lumber. **Chest and Back Ribs:** The chest should girth over 31 inches in a 24-inch hound, and the back ribs must be very deep.

Back and Loin: Must both be very muscular, running into each other without any contraction between them. The couples must be wide, even to raggedness, and the topline of the back should be absolutely level, the **Stern** well set on and carried gaily but not in any case curved *over* the back like a squirrel's tail. The end should taper to a point and there should be a fringe of hair below. The **Hindquarters** or propellers are required to be very strong, and as endurance is of even greater consequence than speed, straight stifles are preferred to those much bent as in a Greyhound. **Elbows** set quite straight, and neither turned in nor out are a *sine qua non*. They must be well let down by means of the long true arm above mentioned.

Legs and Feet: Every Master of Foxhounds insists on legs as straight as a post, and as strong; size of bone at the ankle being especially regarded as all important. The desire for straightness had a tendency to produce knuckling-over, which at one time was countenanced, but in recent years this defect has been eradicated by careful breeding and intelligent adjudication, and one sees very little of this trouble in the best modern Foxhounds. The bone cannot be too large, and the feet in all cases should be round and catlike, with well-developed knuckles and strong horn, which last is of the greatest importance.

Color and Coat: Not regarded as very important, so long as the former is a good "hound color," and the latter is short, dense, hard, and glossy. Hound colors are black, tan, and white, or any combinations of these three, also the various "pies" compounded of white and the color of the hare and badger, or yellow, or tan. The **Symmetry** of the Foxhound is of the greatest importance, and what is known as "quality" is highly regarded by all good judges.

SCALE OF POINTS

Head....................5	Elbows...................5
Neck....................10	Legs and feet.............20
Shoulders................10	Color and coat............5
Chest and back ribs........10	Stern....................5
Back and loin.............15	Symmetry................5
Hindquarters.............10	Total................100

DISQUALIFICATION

Pig-mouth (overshot) or undershot.

APPROVED 1935

Representing the American Foxhound: Ch. Brown's Mr. Charge, owned by Ms. Ashlyn Cannon and bred by Dewey H. Brown.

GREYHOUND

The Greyhound is probably the oldest member of his race. From time immemorial they have been popular as companions at home and in the hunting field. As a result of the time and care that have been spent on them, they are the most highly developed domestic animal in existence.

In elegance of form, dignity, and cleanliness, Greyhounds are worthy of their long descent. They are much more affectionate and intelligent than is usually believed, and in point of speed, courage, fortitude, endurance, and sagacity, they are the equals of any dog that lives. Well-bred Greyhounds know no fear, turn from no game animal on which they are sighted, no matter how large or ferocious, pursue with the speed of the wind, seize the instant they come up with the game, and stay in the fight until they or the quarry are dead. The general supposition that Greyhounds are devoid of the power of scent is a mistake, as can be attested by anyone who has ever hunted them in the West on large game. The uses to which they are put do not require keen olfactory organs;

consequently their sense of smell has deteriorated somewhat from lack of use, but it is far from being entirely gone.

Coursers have no regular standard of size and weight, but the medium sized dog of about 60 to 70 pounds in weight is usually the most useful.

With them the head is a part of the dog's anatomy of little or no account, since he has no particular use for it except to kill with his jaws. For this purpose the longer and stronger the jaws are the better. Ears again count for nothing, but a small eye is objectionable, since it is with his eyes that the Greyhound sights the hare, and a rather large eye, set in not too close, enables him the better to see many turns. A long and muscular neck is a great essential, set well into obliquely placed shoulders.

The forelegs should be as straight as gun barrels, but the elbows should not be turned in, which prevents a dog from getting down to his work. Rather they should be turned out a trifle. The chest should be deep, the ribs gradually widening as they reach their terminus. The loins should be slightly arched, very broad and thick, and merging into broad and big hindquarters, the muscles of which should resemble two big, round loaves of bread stuck on the dog. The thighs should be wide and very muscular, both first and second thighs, the stifles well bent and the hocks well let down, being so formed as to appear from behind perfectly parallel and free from the slightest taint of what is called "cow-hocks."

Flat or long loins are very objectionable, by which the dog loses control over his hindquarters. The dog should be well "cut-up" under his loins in order that he may have greater freedom for the working of his hind limbs. Briefly, the dog should be comparatively short-coupled on the top, but should, when standing, cover a lot of ground below, and he should be neither too long on the leg nor too short.

Color is an altogether immaterial point; a good Greyhound, like a good horse, cannot be a bad color. The tail should be long and strong, since it is to the dog what the rudder is to the ship.

Buyer's guide: The Greyhound has very high exercise requirements and should not be kept by anyone who cannot supply them with a large area to run in daily. They are not really suited to be housepets primarily, but ideally should be kept out all day with companions and brought in to socialize with the family at night. Very active owners are most suitable because the Greyhound is always ready for a good spirited round of play or a run in the woods. The quick, sudden moves of children may be very irritating to these dogs, so they are not recommended as companions for the young. Racing and coursing these sighthounds will help them develop very satisfied dispositions.

STANDARD FOR THE GREYHOUND

Head: Long and narrow, fairly wide between the ears, scarcely perceptible stop, little or no development of nasal sinuses, good length of muzzle, which should be powerful without coarseness. Teeth very strong and even in front.

Ears: Small and fine in texture, thrown back and folded, except when excited, when they are semipricked.

Eyes: Dark, bright, intelligent, indicating spirit.

Neck: Long, muscular, without throatiness, slightly arched, and widening gradually into the shoulder.

Shoulders: Placed as obliquely as possible, muscular without being loaded.

Forelegs: Perfectly straight, set well into the shoulders, neither turned in nor out, pasterns strong.

Chest: Deep, and as wide as consistent with speed, fairly well-sprung ribs.

Back: Muscular and broad.

Loins: Good depth of muscle, well arched, well cut up in the flanks.

Hindquarters: Long, very muscular and powerful, wide and well let down, well-bent stifles. Hocks well bent and rather close to ground, wide but straight fore and aft.

Feet: Hard and close, rather more hare than cat-feet, well knuckled up with good strong claws.

Tail: Long, fine and tapering with a slight upward curve.

Coat: Short, smooth and firm in texture.

Color: Immaterial.

Weight: Dogs, 65 to 70 pounds; bitches, 60 to 65 pounds.

SCALE OF POINTS

General symmetry and quality 10	Back 10
Head and neck............ 20	Quarters 20
Chest and shoulders........ 20	Legs and feet............. 20
	TOTAL 100

HARRIER

The Harrier is a distinct breed of dog used primarily in England to hunt the hare, as their name suggests. Harriers were originally large, slow working hounds, but breed size has decreased in the last fifty years. If the pack is to be hunted on foot, Harriers averaging 16 inches at the shoulder do very well. If the hare is to be followed on horseback, the more popular size is 20 to 22 inches at the shoulder. While resembling the Foxhound in many points, Harriers lack the uniformity in size and type that distinguishes that breed. There are packs of Harriers in which some dogs will average in weight as low as 40 or 50 pounds, while others run up to 70 or 75 pounds. Both Foxhound and Bloodhound crosses were turned to in the early days of the breed, and this variation in breed type is attributed to these crosses, even though the practices have long since been stopped.

There are, however, certain leading features common to all Harriers, and these are: long heads, free from "stop;" square muzzles;

sloping shoulders; straight forelegs; round, catlike feet; short backs; well-sprung ribs; strong loins; sound hindquarters, with well-bent stifles. Height about 19 inches, weight 56 pounds, and any hound color.

Buyer's guide: People interested in rabbit hunting should consider the Harrier. They are rarely seen in the United States except in hunt clubs and are not commonly found as housepets. Unless purchased as a young puppy and raised strictly in the home, they are not recommended for an indoor life.

STANDARD FOR THE HARRIER

The points of the modern Harrier are very similar to those of the English Foxhound. The Harrier, however, is smaller than the English Foxhound and the most popular size is 19 to 21 inches. They should be active, well balanced and full of strength and quality, with shoulders sloping into the muscles of the back, clean and not loaded on the withers or point.

The back level and muscular, and not dipping behind the withers or arching over the loin. The elbow's point set well away from the ribs, running parallel with the body and not turning outwards. Deep, well-sprung ribs, running well back, with plenty of heart room, and a deep chest.

Good straight legs with plenty of bone running well down to the toes, but not overburdened, inclined to knuckle over very slightly but not exaggerated in the slightest degree. Round catlike feet, and close toes turning inwards. Hind legs and hocks stand square, with a good sweep and muscular thigh to take the weight off the body.

The head should be of a medium size with good bold forehead, and plenty of expression; head must be well set up on a neck of ample length, and not heavy; stern should be set well up, long and well controlled.

IBIZAN HOUND

Although just recently recognized by the American Kennel Club, the Ibizan Hound breed dates far back into antiquity. The hunting dogs depicted in painting and sculpture from the Egyptian age bear remarkable resemblance to the modern Ibizan Hound and cast considerable weight to the belief that the conformation of this breed has remained true to type throughout time. Historians of the breed cite *Ca Eivissenc* as the Ibizan's original name and believe that the breed originated on the island of Ibiza, a member of the Balearic Islands which lie off the coast of Spain. The breed later came to inhabit the Spanish peninsula, but the best specimens are said to have come from the island of Majorca.

Ibizan Hounds have been bred as hunters, and are equally adept at hunting by sight or sound, although they will also track by scent. Their sleek, long-legged conformation affords them great speed and agility. Owners of Ibizan Hounds during the 19th century called their dogs *Podengos,* and used them for coursing rabbits and partridges. Modern day hunters claim them to be fine gun dogs that can be relied on to point and retrieve their game. Ibizans can be hunted alone, but are usually worked in packs. Many Ibizans have a peculiar pattern of interest: after a very long or intense series of hunts, they lose their gameness and require an extended period of rest to recoup their interest.

As is typical of the running breeds, Ibizan Hounds have long, strong hindquarters and are among the tallest of the hounds. They sport large, erect ears that are unique among the large sighthounds with which they are often compared. They can be found in two coat types—one short and smooth, the other longer and harsh—but the latter type is rarely seen outside of Europe.

Ibizans are generally of a steady temperament, but like most sighthounds, they can become quite excited and restless if not given proper outlets for their energy. They are quick and keen learners and have been shown to top obedience.

Buyer's guide: Ibizans have not been kept extensively as indoor pets due to their large exercise requirements. They do get along quite well as kennel dogs, but can adjust to life with the family if frequently allowed to run outside. Ibizans have an independent nature which borders on the aloof, but once attached to their owner, they can be very affectionate and attentive. Their grooming needs are minimal, needing only routine nail trimming and an occasional brushing. Ibizan Hounds are not recommended for pets in homes with small children or where they are not given plenty of space to relax in.

STANDARD FOR THE IBIZAN HOUND

Head: Long and narrow, in the form of a sharp cone truncated at its base; extremely dry-fleshed. **Skull:** Long and flat, prominent occipital bone, little defined stop; narrow brow. **Ears:** Prominent prick ears, always rigid; erect on alert, but highly mobile and at times pointed forward, sideways, or backward, according to mood. The center of the base is at the level of the eyes, and in the form of an enlarged rhomboid truncated at a third of its longer diagonal. Thin, with texture of fine leather; no hair in interior. **Eyes:** Oblique and small, ranging in color from clear amber to caramel; aspect intelligent and unpredictable. **Muzzle:** Elongated, fine, and slender, sometimes snipy; very light Roman convex. Length from eyes to point of nose equal to distance from eyes to occiput. **Nose:** Prominent, extending beyond lower jaw; flesh color tending to harmonize with that of coat; nostrils open. **Jaws:** Exceptionally strong, lean. **Lips:** Thin and tight. **Teeth:** Level mouth; teeth perfectly opposed in scissor-bite; white and well-set.

Neck: Long, slender, slightly arched; strong, yet flat-muscled. **Withers:** Loose and detached. **Shoulders:** Sloping.

Back: Level and straight; taut yet elastic. **Loins:** Medium breadth, slightly arched. **Rump:** Very slightly sloping. **Tail:** Long, set rather low; highly mobile, and carried in sickle, ring, otter or saber positions according to mood and individual specimen.

Chest: Deep and long; breastbone sharply angled and very prominent; flat ribs, protruding when dog is in top working condition. **Belly:** Underbelly retracted, but not so deeply as Greyhound.

Forequarters: Straight front; forearms very long, strong, straight and close, lying flat on chest and continuing in straight line to ground. Clean fine bone; well-developed sinews; pasterns straight and flexible.

Hindquarters: Relatively vertical; strong but flat-muscled; hocks strong and close to ground.

Feet: Hare-foot; toes long and closed, very strong; interdigital spaces well protected by hair; durable pads.

Coat: Short; shortest on head and ears and longest at back of thighs and under tail. **Wire-Haired;** can be from one to three inches in length with a possible generous moustache, more hair on back, back of thighs and tail. Both types of coat are always hard in texture. Neither coat is preferable to the other.

Color: Red and white, red with white, white with red, lion and white, lion with white, white with lion; solid white, solid red; all other colors excluded. The preponderant pattern is predominantly red, with white feet and "socks", tail tip, chest, and muzzle, with blaze on forehead. The solid colors are desirable but relatively rare.

Height: Height of dogs at withers ranges from 23½ to 27½ inches; height of bitches at withers ranges from 22½ to 26 inches. Sizes somewhat over or under norms not to be regarded as demerits when other qualities are good. **Weight:** Average weight of dogs, 50 pounds; bitches, 42 to 49 pounds.

Gait: A trot in suspension; elegant and graceful in the manner of the Afghan. In speed the Ibizan is in the same class as other coursing breeds, and is without equal in agility and high-jumping ability, being capable of springing to great heights from a standstill.

APPROVED JANUARY 1, 1979

IRISH WOLFHOUND

It is clearly attested both by history and tradition that there existed in Ireland in early times a large, rugged hound of Greyhound form, used to hunt the Irish elk, the wolf, the red deer, and the fox. This dog was known to the Romans, who carried them back after their invasion of the island, and there are records of them being presented to Norwegian kings. In the course of time the wolves disappeared, the elk became extinct, and with them all but passed away a noble breed of dogs. In fact, it has been claimed that the real Irish Wolfhound became extinct about 150 years ago. This was vigorously denied by others who, while they admitted that the breed had deteriorated, asserted that there was still enough of the old blood to restore the breed to a resemblance of its original type. The leader in this movement was Captain Graham, who for a score of years devoted himself to the resuscitation of the breed with conspicuous success.

There have been many theories advanced as to the origin of the Irish Wolfhound, but the opinion of Captain Graham is probably nearest the truth, for it is his belief that the Irish hound that was kept to hunt wolves never became extinct, but is now repeated in the Scottish Deerhound, only altered a little in size and strength to suit the easier work required of it, that of hunting the deer. The old Irish Wolfhound was called upon to hunt the wolf and the Irish elk, an immense animal standing six feet high at the shoulder, with a spread of antlers of ten or twelve feet, and it required a much more powerful hound to cope with these animals than the deer which are now existent.

One thing is certain: the chief factor in the resuscitation of the Irish Wolfhound had been the Scottish Deerhound. In building up the breed Captain Graham secured bitches from three strains, which it was believed were direct and pure descendants of the old line, although they were not nearly as large as those mentioned in early writings. These were crossed on the Scottish Deerhound and the Great Dane. Later on Borzoi blood was introduced through a dog named Koratai. These matings and the mixing of the blood of these breeds resulted in progeny with both size and bone, but unshapely in form. By careful elimination and selection they were eventually graded up to a fixity of type.

There is naturally a great deal of similarity between the Scottish Deerhound and the Irish Wolfhound, for much of the same blood is in their veins. The Irish dog is larger, more powerful, and less elegant in outline. His coat is also harder in texture and his jaw more powerful.

As in the case of the most big dogs, the great difficulty in breeding the Irish Wolfhound is to insure straight forelegs and sound hindquarters. Of course, a great deal depends upon the rearing of the dogs in this particular connection. A puppy may be found sound and straight in limb and become incurably defective by his faulty bringing up. This is the tendency, and such faults as cow hocks (which are very prevalent in the breed), crooked forelegs, or splay feet, once established become hereditary, and should be carefully avoided. A little white on the chest is perfectly immaterial, and color is but of secondary importance, the favorite color being grizzle or wheaten.

Buyer's guide: Once past puppyhood, the Irish Wolfhound is a gentle, affectionate pet. During their first year, however, much time must be devoted to training these dogs to control their natural liveliness and enthusiasm—for an uncontrolled adult the size of an Irish Wolfhound would be intolerable. Give them plenty of room to run and only consider owning one of these dogs if you are in a rural, spacious area.

STANDARD FOR THE IRISH WOLFHOUND

General Appearance: Of great size and commanding appearance, the Irish Wolfhound is remarkable in combining power and swiftness with keen sight. The largest and tallest of the galloping hounds, in general type he is a rough-coated, Greyhoundlike breed; very muscular, strong though gracefully built; movements easy and active; head and neck carried high, the tail carried with an upward sweep with a slight curve towards the extremity. The minimum height and weight of dogs should be 32 inches and 120 pounds; of bitches, 30 inches and 105 pounds; these to apply only to hounds over 18 months of age. Anything below this should be debarred from competition. Great size, including height at shoulder and proportionate length of body, is the desideratum to be aimed at, and it is desired to firmly establish a race that shall average from 32 to 34 inches in dogs, showing the requisite power, activity, courage and symmetry.

Head: Long, the frontal bones of the forehead very slightly raised and very little indentation between the eyes. Skull, not too broad. Muzzle, long and moderately pointed. Ears, small and Greyhoundlike in carriage.

Neck: Rather long, very strong and muscular, well arched, without dewlap or loose skin about the throat.

Chest: Very deep. Breast, wide.

Back: Rather long than short. Loins arched.

Tail: Long and slightly curved, of moderate thickness, and well covered with hair.

Belly: Well drawn up.

Forequarters: Shoulders, muscular, giving breadth of chest, set sloping. Elbows well under, neither turned inwards nor outwards.

Leg: Forearm muscular, and the whole leg strong and quite straight.

Hindquarters: Muscular thighs and second thigh long and strong as in the Greyhound, and hocks well let down and turning neither in nor out.

Feet: Moderately large and round, neither turned inwards nor outwards. Toes, well arched and closed. Nails, very strong and curved.

Hair: Rough and hard on body, legs and head; especially wiry and long over eyes and underjaw.

Color and Markings: The recognized colors are gray, brindle, red, black, pure white, fawn, or any other color that appears in the Deerhound.

FAULTS

Too light or heavy a head, too highly arched frontal bone; large ears and hanging flat to the face; short neck; full dewlap; too narrow or too broad a chest; sunken or hollow or quite straight back; bent forelegs; overbent fetlocks; twisted feet; spreading toes; too curly a tail; weak hindquarters and a general want of muscle; too short in body. Lips or nose liver-colored or lacking pigmentation.

LIST OF POINTS IN ORDER OF MERIT

1. *Typical.* The Irish Wolfhound is a rough-coated Greyhound-like breed, the tallest of the coursing hounds and remarkable in combining power and swiftness.
2. *Great size* and commanding appearance.
3. Movements easy and active.
4. Head, long and level, carried high.
5. Forelegs, heavily boned, quite straight; elbows well set under.
6. Thighs long and muscular; second thighs, well muscled, stifles nicely bent.
7. Coat, rough and hard, specially wiry and long over eyes and under jaw.
8. Body, long, well ribbed up, with ribs well sprung, and great breadth across hips.
9. Loins arched, belly well drawn up.
10. Ears, small, with Greyhoundlike carriage.
11. Feet, moderately large and round; toes, close, well arched.
12. Neck, long, well arched and very strong.
13. Chest, very deep, moderately broad.
14. Shoulders, muscular, set sloping.
15. Tail, long and slightly curved.
16. Eyes, dark.

Note: The above in no way alters the "Standard of Excellence," which must in all cases be rigidly adhered to; they simply give the various points in order of merit. If in any case they appear at variance with Standard of Excellence, it is the latter which is correct.

NORWEGIAN ELKHOUND

This breed of dogs has been developed in Scandinavian countries. Although they are referred to as hounds, properly speaking they are all-purpose dogs used for elk and bear hunting, as well as for black cock shooting. They are remarkable for their scenting powers, and it is said that under favorable conditions they will catch the scent of an elk or a bear three miles away.

The breed is very old, dating back to Viking times, and among their notable characteristics are intelligence, courage and great endurance. In appearance they are rather short in stature, with an average height of about 20 inches. The head, which is carried high, is large and square, broad between the ears; muzzle of good length; stop well defined; eyes dark and full of expression; the ears sharply pointed, erect, and very mobile; the neck short and thick; chest broad and deep; the back straight and not too long. The tail is thick and heavy, and carried over the back. As in most northern dogs, the coat is long and deep on the body, with a dense, woolly undercoat. The hair about the head is short and smooth.

Modern Norwegian Elkhounds differ little from their forebears, retaining their hunting instincts and love for the outdoor life. They are capable of withstanding the coldest weather, yet are not limited to any terrain or environment. Pound for pound they can match stamina with dogs of much larger stature, yet their temperament is mild and poised.

Buyer's guide: These dogs prefer the company of humans over other dogs and are fiercely loyal. They make excellent watchdogs and should not be kept cramped up in small apartments, but they do not need extensive exercise. A moderate amount of grooming is necessary to keep the coat shiny and tangle-free. Not a recommended pet for aged or infirm individuals or families with small infants.

STANDARD FOR THE NORWEGIAN ELKHOUND

General Description: The Norwegian Elkhound is a hardy gray hunting dog. In appearance, a typical northern dog of medium size and substance, square in profile, close coupled and balanced in proportions. The head is broad with prick ears, and the tail is dense and smooth-lying. In temperament, the Norwegian Elkhound is bold and energetic, an effective guardian yet normally friendly, with great dignity and independence of character. As a hunter, the Norwegian Elkhound has the courage, agility and stamina to hold moose and other big game at bay by barking and dodging attack, and the endurance to track for long hours in all weather over rough and varied terrain.

Head: Broad at the ears, wedge-shaped, strong, and dry (without loose skin). Viewed from the side, the forehead and back of the skull are only slightly arched; the stop not large, yet clearly defined. The bridge of the nose is straight, parallel to and about the same length as the skull. The muzzle is thickest at the base and, seen from above or from the side, tapers evenly without being pointed. Lips are tightly closed and teeth meet in a scissors bite.

Ears: Set high, firm and erect, yet very mobile. Comparatively small; slightly taller than their width at the base with pointed (not rounded) tips. When the dog is alert, the orifices turn forward and the outer edges are vertical.

Eyes: Very dark brown, medium in size, not protruding.

Neck: Of medium length, muscular, well set up with a slight arch and with no loose skin on the throat.

Body: Square in profile and close coupled. Distance from brisket to ground appears to be half the height at the withers. Distance from forechest to rump equals the height at the withers. Chest deep and moderately broad; brisket level with points of elbows; and ribs well sprung. Loin short and wide with very little tuck-up. The back is straight and strong from its high point at the withers to the root of the tail.

Forequarters: Shoulders sloping with elbows closely set on. Legs well under body and medium in length; substantial, but not coarse, in bone. Seen from the front, the legs appear straight and parallel. Single dewclaws are normally present.

Hindquarters: Moderate angulation at stifle and hock. Thighs are broad and well-muscled. Seen from behind, legs are straight, strong and without dewclaws.

Feet: Paws comparatively small, slightly oval with tightly-closed toes and thick pads. Pasterns are strong and only slightly bent. Feet turn neither in nor out.

Tail: Set high, tightly curled, and carried over the centerline of the back. It is thickly and closely haired, without brush, natural and untrimmed.

Coat: Thick, hard, weather-resisting and smooth-lying; made up of soft, dense, woolly undercoat and coarse, straight covering hairs. Short and even on head, ears, and front of legs; longest on back of neck, buttocks and underside of tail. The coat is not altered by trimming, clipping or artificial treatment. Trimming of whiskers is optional.

Color: Gray, medium preferred, variations in shade determined by the length of black tips and quantity of guard hairs. Undercoat is clear light silver as are legs, stomach, buttocks, and underside of tail. The gray body color is darkest on the saddle, lighter on the chest, mane and distinctive harness mark (a band of longer guard hairs from shoulder to elbow). The muzzle, ears, and tail tip are black. The black of the muzzle shades to lighter gray over the forehead and skull. Yellow or brown shading, white patches, indistinct or irregular markings, "sooty" coloring on the lower legs and light circles around the eyes are undesirable. Any overall color other than gray as described above, such as red, brown, solid black, white or other solid color, disqualifies.

Gait: Normal for an active dog constructed for agility and endurance. At a trot the stride is even and effortless; the back remains level.

As the speed of the trot increases, front and rear legs converge equally in straight lines toward a center line beneath the body so that the pads appear to follow in the same tracks (single-track). Front and rear quarters are well balanced in angulation and muscular development.

Size: The height at the withers for dogs is 20½ inches, for bitches 19½ inches. Weight for dogs about 55 pounds; for bitches about 48 pounds.

DISQUALIFICATIONS

Any overall color other than gray as described above, such as red, brown, solid black, white or other solid color.

APPROVED FEBRUARY 13, 1973

OTTER HOUND

The Otter Hound is one of the oldest breeds, but little documented information can be found which details the breed's beginnings. In general form they are not unlike a Bloodhound, with something of the shape of the skull and jaw, curve of throat, and texture of the coat that suggests the Dandie Dinmont. They are a rugged breed. Everything about them conveys the impression of usefulness, and they are as capable of coping with as many different conditions and environments as any other breed of dog.

They have been used in the creation of other breeds, and the Airedale in particular undoubtedly owes his water-loving traits to a touch of the Otter Hound. The early Otter Hounds were said to have been much smaller in size than those of the present day. In England otter hunting is termed the queen of summer sports, and is in fact the only form of chase that may be followed during the summer months. It is good sport, for the quarry is a wily, resourceful animal, with haunts of its own choosing, with the odds always in its favor. It is also engaged in during the best days of the year when nature and the weather are to be found at their finest.

The Otter Hound is as talented a hunting dog as can be found, with a remarkably keen nose and persistance on the stalk. Their webbed feet enable them to swim with both power and grace. Otter Hounds are quick thinkers and cautious workers, never giving tongue unless sure of their trail and willing to follow wherever the hunt might take them.

Buyer's guide: This breed is rarely enjoyed as a housepet and is used mainly as a water dog. They are large, requiring considerable space to move about in, and are big eaters. Otter Hounds require good grooming, but they are not argumentative with other animals and children and are very trainable. A strong, authoritative owner is advised.

STANDARD FOR THE OTTER HOUND

General Appearance: The Otter Hound is a large, rough-coated, squarely symmetrical hound. The length of a dog's body from withers to base of tail is approximately equal to its height at the withers. However, a bitch is not to be faulted if her length of body is slightly greater than her height. The Otter Hound is amiable and boisterous. It has an extremely sensitive nose, and is inquisitive and perservering in investigating scents. The Otter Hound should be shown on a loose lead. The Otter Hound hunts its quarry on land and water and requires a combination of characteristics unique among hounds—most notably a rough, double coat and webbed feet.

Head: The head is large, fairly narrow, and well covered with hair. The length from tip of nose to occiput is 11 to 12 inches in a hound 26 inches at the withers. This proportion should be maintained in larger and smaller hounds.

The **skull** (cranium) is long, fairly narrow under the hair, and only slightly domed. The muzzle is long and square in cross-section with powerful jaws and deep flews. The **stop** is not pronounced. The **nose** is large, dark, and completely pigmented. The **ears** are long, pendulous, and folded. They are set low and hang close to the head. They are well covered and fringed with hair. The tips of the **ear** leather reach at least to the tip of the nose. The **eyes** are deeply set. The haw shows only slightly.

The eyes are dark, but may vary with the color of the hound. The **jaws** are powerful and capable of a crushing grip. A scissors bite is preferred. **Faults:** Bite grossly undershot or overshot.

Neck and Body: The **neck** looks shorter than it really is because of the abundance of hair on it. The neck blends smoothly into the trunk. The **chest** is deep; the **ribs** extend well toward the rear of the trunk. The **topline** is level. The **tail** is fairly long, reaching at least to the hock. It is well feathered (covered and fringed with hair). It is carried sickle-fashion (not over the back) when a dog is moving or alert, but may droop when the dog is at rest.

Forequarters: **Shoulders** clean, powerful, and well-sloped. **Legs** heavy-boned and straight.

Hindquarters: Thighs large and well-muscled. **Legs** moderately angulated. Legs parallel when viewed from the rear. **Feet** large, broad, compact, and well padded, with membranes connecting the toes (web-footed). **Dewclaws,** if any, on the hind legs are generally removed; dewclaws on the forelegs may be removed.

Coat: The rough outer coat is three to six inches long on the back, shorter on the extremities. It must be hard (coarse and crisp). A water-resistant inner coat of short woolly hair is an essential feature of the breed. A naturally stripped coat lacking length and fringes is correct for an Otter Hound that is being worked. A proper hunting coat will show the hard outer coat and woolly undercoat. **Faults:** A soft outer coat is a very serious fault as is a woolly-textured top coat. Lack of undercoat is a serious fault. An outer coat much longer than six inches becomes heavy when wet and is a fault.

Color: Any color or combination of colors is acceptable. The nose should be darkly pigmented, black or liver, depending on the color of the hound.

Gait: The Otter Hound moves freely with forward reach and drive. The gait is smooth and effortless and capable of being maintained for many miles. Otter Hounds single-track at slower speed than light-bodied hounds. Because they do not lift their feet high off the ground, Otter Hounds may shuffle when they work or move at a slow trot.

Size: Males range from 24 to 27 inches at the withers, and weigh from 75 to 115 pounds, depending on the height and condition of the hound. Bitches are 22 to 26 inches at the withers and 65 and 100 pounds. A hound in hard working condition may weigh as much as 15 pounds less than one of the same height that is not being worked. Otter Hounds should not be penalized for being shown in working condition (lean, well-muscled, naturally stripped coat).

APPROVED OCTOBER 12, 1971

RHODESIAN RIDGEBACK

The majestic Rhodesian Ridgeback, sometimes referred to as the African Lion Hound, sports a unique ridge along the back which is formed by the hair growing in the opposite direction to the rest of the coat. The Ridgeback is a totally fearless hunter and it has been reported that in the wild a pack of three could attack and subdue a pride of lions. When hunting they work in teams, one as leader and two as flankers. They are classified as sight hunters because they have great distance vision and are adept at keeping their quarry always in their sight.

Rhodesian Ridgebacks present a strong, muscular appearance and embody the stamina necessary to withstand the wilds of the African backlands. The half-wild native hunting dogs of southern Africa were reported to have been crossbred with Mastiffs, Bloodhounds, Danes, Scottish Deerhounds and various terrier breeds to produce the Ridgeback of today. The natives of South Africa found that these "dogs with snakes on their backs" were not only capable hunters of both bird and game, but also loyal companions and watchdogs. Ridgebacks have an innate desire to please their master and are of a quiet, even temperament.

Today's Rhodesian Ridgeback is becoming a more common sight not only on the show circuit, but also in the obedience rings. The breed was first imported to the United States prior to World War II, but admittance into the Hound Group was not given by the American Kennel Club until 1955, when they became the 112th breed to be officially recognized. Rhodesian Ridgebacks are becoming increasingly popular as housepets.

Buyer's guide: Rhodesian Ridgebacks are strong, active dogs that require a considerable amount of house-training to make them good inside pets. They make excellent watchdogs and should be allowed plenty of space to move about in. No special grooming is required. They are moderate eaters and get along rather aloofly with children.

STANDARD FOR THE RHODESIAN RIDGEBACK

The peculiarity of this breed is the **ridge** on the back, which is formed by the hair growing in the opposite direction to the rest of the coat. The ridge must be regarded as the characteristic feature of the breed. The ridge should be clearly defined, tapering and symmetrical. It should start immediately behind the shoulders and continue to a point between the prominence of the hips, and should contain two identical crowns opposite each other. The lower edges of the crown should not extend further down the ridge than one third of the ridge.

General Appearance: The Ridgeback should represent a strong muscular and active dog, symmetrical in outline, and capable of great endurance with a fair amount of speed.

Head: Should be of a fair length, the skull flat and rather broad between the ears and should be free from wrinkles when in repose. The stop should be reasonably well defined. **Muzzle:** Should be long, deep and powerful, jaws level and strong with well-developed teeth, especially the canines or holders. The lips clean, closely fitting the jaws. **Eyes:** Should be moderately well apart, and should be round, bright and sparkling, with intelligent expression, their color harmonizing with the color of the dog. **Ears:** Should be set rather high, of medium size, rather wide at base, and tapering to a rounded point. They should be carried close to the head. **Nose:** Should be black, or brown, in keeping with the color of the dog. No other colored nose is permissible. A black nose should be accompanied by dark eyes, a brown nose by amber eyes.

Neck and Shoulders: The neck should be fairly strong and free from throatiness. The shoulders should be sloping, clean and muscular, denoting speed.

Body, Back, Chest and Loins: The chest should not be too wide, but very deep and capacious; ribs moderately well sprung, never rounded like barrel hoops (which would indicate want of speed), the back powerful, the loins strong, muscular and slightly arched.

Legs and Feet: The forelegs should be perfectly straight, strong and heavy in bone; elbows close to the body. The feet should be compact, with well-arched toes, round, tough, elastic pads, protected by hair between the toes and pads. In the hind legs the muscles should be clean, well defined, and hocks well down.

Tail: Should be strong at the insertion, and generally tapering towards the end, free from coarseness. It should not be inserted too high or too low, and should be carried with a slight curve upwards, never curled.

Coat: Should be short and dense, sleek and glossy in appearance, but neither woolly nor silky.

Color: Light wheaten to red wheaten. A little white on the chest and toes permissible but excessive white there and any white on the belly or above toes is undesirable.

Size: A mature Ridgeback should be a handsome, upstanding dog; dogs should be of a height of 25 to 27 inches, and bitches 24 to 26 inches.

Weight: (Desirable) dogs 75 pounds, bitches 65 pounds.

SCALE OF POINTS

Ridge 20	Coat 5
Head 15	Tail 5
Neck and shoulders 10	Size, symmetry, general
Body, back, chest, loins 10	appearance 20
Legs and feet 15	TOTAL 100

APPROVED NOVEMBER, 1955

Representing the breed: Ch. Blue Chip's Armstrong, owned by Rosemary and Walter Ziegler and bred by Vonnabeth Thompson. Photo by Gilbert.

SALUKI

The Saluki typifies the exotic Eastern beauty that has been revered in sighthounds since antiquity. The question of which breed is the oldest known domestic dog has been a continuing controversy in the dog fancy. The Saluki is certainly among the oldest as the breed can trace its ancestry back to carvings dated 7,000 to 8,000 B.C. in the Sumerian Empire with other carvings of Saluki-like dogs having been found in Egypt that date to before 2,000 B.C. No other breed has proven evidences of earlier existence.

The Saluki is known as the Royal Dog of Egypt, and they must have enjoyed an imperial past as mummified Saluki-type dogs have been found in the ancient tombs of the Pharoahs of the Upper Nile. While the Mohammeden religion normally called the dogs of that time "unclean," the Saluki was viewed as "sacred" and was allowed the privilege of sleeping in the tents of the Sheiks.

Today's Saluki is of medium size, but ample variations in size are acceptable, especially with the bitches. They are essentially smooth coated, with muscles that form a graceful sweeping line from brisket to tuck-up. Their powerful loins are indicators of great running ability, and they move with an elegance that portrays their overall noble stature.

Saluki temperaments are quietly subdued, yet they are keenly alert and affectionate dogs. They are clean and carry themselves with dignity, whether they are on the hunt, racing or giving their all in the show ring. While the Saluki is very loyal, they hold themselves in reserve—but do not mistake this for coolness. Although easy-going, they do not take lightly to sharing the spotlight, or their master, with other dogs and prefer to be the lone dog in the home. The breed is highly intelligent (although sometimes quite reluctant to be formally trained) and delights in the thrill of the chase. This increasingly popular breed has proven to be great coursing and hunting hounds, and as show dogs they often captivate the show spectators with their overall beauty and poise.

Buyer's guide: Only active, outdoors-loving people should own a Saluki because they are a speedy dog that requires extensive outside exercising. Although sometimes slow to warm up to people, once accustomed they are gentle with children and very loyal. Try not to own other small animals in the same house with a Saluki as the sudden movements of these animals may cause the dog to instinctively move in on them.

STANDARD FOR THE SALUKI

Head: Long and narrow, skull moderately wide between the ears, not domed, stop not pronounced, the whole showing great quality. Nose black or liver. **Ears:** long and covered with long silky hair hanging close to the skull and mobile. **Eyes:** Dark to hazel and bright; large and oval, but not prominent. **Teeth:** Strong and level.

Neck: Long, supple and well muscled.

Chest: Deep and moderately narrow. **Forequarters:** Shoulders, sloping and set well back, well muscled without being coarse. **Forelegs:** Straight and long from the elbow to the knee.

Hindquarters: Strong, hipbones set well apart and stifle moderately bent, hocks low to the ground, showing galloping and jumping power.

Loin and Back: Back fairly broad, muscles slightly arched over loin.

Feet: Of moderate length, toes long and well arched, not splayed out, but at the same time not cat-footed; the whole being strong and supple and well feathered between the toes.

Tail: Long, set on low and carried naturally in a curve, well feathered on the underside with long silky hair, not bushy.

Coat: Smooth and of a soft silky texture, slight feather on the legs, feather at the back of the thighs and sometimes with slight woolly feather on the thigh and shoulder.

Colors: White, cream, fawn, golden, red, grizzle and tan, tricolor (white, black and tan) and black and tan.

General Appearance: The whole appearance of this breed should give an impression of grace and symmetry and of great speed and endurance coupled with strength and activity to enable it to kill gazelle or other quarry over deep sand or rocky mountains. The expression should be dignified and gentle with deep, faithful, far-seeing eyes. Dogs should average in height from 23 to 28 inches and bitches may be considerably smaller, this being very typical of the breed.

The Smooth Variety: In this variety the points should be the same with the exception of the coat, which has no feathering.

Representing the breed: Ch. Srinager Megha of Beckonwind, owned by Holly Trello.

SCOTTISH DEERHOUND

This magnificent breed of dogs has occupied a prominent place in the romantic history of Scotland, and well looks the part they have played as companion to Highland Chieftains. They have a most noble presence, and are at once docile, sagacious and undeniably courageous. As companions and guards they are unsurpassed, for they never forget their friends, and their attachment for their owners is a blind devotion that will lead them to fight for their protection with the utmost desperation.

In the field the Deerhound not only has a very keen nose, but can run down the deer, jackrabbit, coyote or wolf, and can kill them alone and unaided. He will tree a mountain lion or a black bear, and would not hesitate to fight a grizzly if in protection of his master. No dog combines more beauty, strength and utility than these aristocrats of the canine world.

Buyer's guide: The Deerhound is very good natured and loves to be around people, so much so that they do not take very well to being a watchdog. They are dignified, not aggressive, and are very friendly towards children. Since they are so large, their space and exercise requirements are also large, so do not choose the Scottish Deerhound unless you have plenty of space and time to work on their training. They are slow to learn and overanxious trainers can do damage to their spirit.

STANDARD FOR THE SCOTTISH DEERHOUND

Head: Should be broadest at the ears, narrowing slightly to the eyes, with the muzzle tapering more decidedly to the nose. The muzzle should be pointed, but the teeth and lips level. The head should be long, the skull flat rather than round with a very slight rise over the eyes but nothing approaching a stop. The hair on the skull should be moderately long and softer than the rest of the coat. The nose should be black (in some blue fawns: blue) and slightly aquiline. In lighter colored dogs the black muzzle is preferable. There should be a good mustache of rather silky hair and a fair beard.

Ears: Should be set on high; in repose, folded back like a Greyhound's, though raised above the head in excitement without losing the fold, and even in some cases semierect. A prick ear is bad. Big thick ears hanging flat to the head or heavily coated with long hair are bad faults. The ears should be soft, glossy, like a mouse's coat to the touch and the smaller the better. There should be no long coat or long fringe, but there is sometimes a silky, silvery coat on the body of the ear and the tip. On all Deerhounds, irrespective of color of coat, the ears should be black or dark colored.

Neck and Shoulders: The neck should be long: of a length befitting the Greyhound character of the dog. Extreme length is neither necessary nor desirable. Deerhounds do not stoop to their work like the Greyhounds. The mane, which every good specimen should have, sometimes detracts from the apparent length of the neck. The neck, however, must be strong as is necessary to hold a stag. The nape of the neck should be very prominent where the head is set on, and the throat clean cut at the angle and prominent. Shoulders should be well sloped; blades well back and not too much width between them. Loaded and straight shoulders are very bad faults.

Tail: Should be tolerably long, tapering and reaching to within 1½ inches of the ground and about 1½ inches below the hocks. Dropped perfectly down or curved when the Deerhound is still, when in motion or excited, curved, but in no instance lifted out of line of the back. It should be well covered with hair, on the inside, thick and wiry, underside longer and towards the end a slight fringe is not objectionable. A curl or ring tail is undesirable.

Eyes: Should be dark: generally dark brown, brown or hazel. A very light eye is not liked. The eye should be moderately full, with a soft look in repose, but a keen, far-away look when the Deerhound is roused. Rims of eyelids should be black.

Body: General information is that of a Greyhound of larger size and bone. Chest deep rather than broad but not too narrow or slab-sided. Good girth of chest is indicative of great lung power. The loin well arched and drooping to the tail. A straight back is not desirable, this formation being unsuited for uphill work, and very unsightly.

Legs and Feet: Legs should be broad and flat, and good broad forearms and elbows are desirable. Forelegs must, of course, be as straight as possible. Feet close and compact, with well-arranged toes. The hindquarters drooping, and as broad as possible, the hips being set wide apart. A narrow rear denotes lack of power. The stifles should be well bent, with great length from hip to hock, which should be broad and flat. Cowhocks, weak pasterns, straight stifles and splay feet are very bad faults.

Coat: The hair on the body, neck and quarters should be harsh and wiry, about 3 or 4 inches long; that on the head, breast and belly much softer. There should be a slight fringe on the inside of the forelegs and hind legs but nothing approaching the "feather" of a Collie. A woolly coat is bad. Some good strains have a mixture of silky coat with the hard which is preferable to a woolly coat. The climate of the United States tends to produce the mixed coat. The ideal coat is a thick, close-lying ragged coat, harsh or crisp to the touch.

Color: is a matter of fancy, but the dark blue-gray is most preferred. Next come the darker and lighter grays or brindles, the darkest being generally preferred. Yellow and sandy red or red fawn, especially with black ears and muzzles, are equally high in estimation. This was the color of the oldest known strains: the McNeil and Chesthill Menzies. White is condemned by all authorities, but a white chest and white toes, occurring as they do in many of the darkest-colored dogs, are not objected to, although the less the better, for the Deerhound is a self-colored dog. A white blaze on the head, or a white collar, should entirely disqualify. The less white the better but a slight white tip to the stern occurs in some of the best strains.

Height: Height of Dogs: From 30 to 32 inches, or even more if there be symmetry without coarseness, which is rare.

Height of Bitches: From 28 inches upwards. There is no objection to a bitch being large, unless to coarse, as even at her greatest height she does not approach that of the dog, and therefore could not be too big for work as overbig dogs are.

Weight: From 85 to 110 pounds in dogs, and from 75 to 95 pounds in bitches.

POINTS OF THE DEERHOUND ARRANGED IN ORDER OF IMPORTANCE

1. *Typical*—A Deerhound should resemble a rough-coated Greyhound of larger size and bone.
2. *Movements*—Easy, active and true.
3. As tall as possible consistent with quality.
4. *Head*—Long, level, well balanced with quality.
5. *Body*—Long, very deep in brisket, well-sprung ribs and great breadth across hips.
7. *Thighs*—Long and muscular, second thighs well muscled, stifles well bent.
8. *Loins*—Well arched, and belly well drawn up.
9. *Coat*—Rough and hard, with softer beard and brow.
10. *Feet*—Close, compact, with well-knuckled toes.
11. *Ears*—Small (dark) with Greyhoundlike carriage.
12. *Eyes*—Dark, moderately full.
13. *Neck*—Long, well arched, very strong with prominent nape.
14. *Shoulders*—Clean, set sloping.
15. *Chest*—Very deep but not too narrow.
16. *Tail*—Long and curved slightly, carried low.
17. *Teeth*—Strong and level.
18. *Nails*—Strong and curved.

DISQUALIFICATION
White blaze on the head, or a white collar.

APPROVED MARCH, 1935

Representing the breed: Ch. Timber of Gayleward, owned by Gayle Bontecou.

WHIPPET

This graceful breed is nothing more or less than a miniature Greyhound, and was originally known as a snap dog by the colliers and working men in the north of England, who originated the breed, and used them for rabbit coursing. In later years these dogs have been taught straight running. In early races they were held on leash at a given mark by an attendant while the owner or some other person standing at the other edge of the track shook a handkerchief at the dogs and encouraged them to race for it. There was an official starter, and the dogs were liberated at the shot of a pistol and immediately made a dash, straining every nerve to get at the handkerchief. The usual course was two hundred yards, and the dogs were handicapped according to weight or previous performances.

The origin of the Whippet was probably obtained by a cross between the small Greyhound and the white English Terrier. They are keen little sportsmen, easily kept in condition, and of a most companionable disposition.

In selecting a Whippet puppy at from two to four months old, the points to look for are almost identical with those of the Greyhound, except that less bone is required and probably a little more arch of loin, both of which variations are calculated to give the Whippet a little more speed.

The points of the Whippet may be briefly summed up by saying he should be a duplicate in miniature of the Greyhound.

Buyer's guide: Given the chance, Whippets will keep themselves in good shape through their normal daily routine, but they do not react well to small, cramped quarters. They are somewhat nervous by nature and will become more so if kept in a city dwelling or in the presence of many or boisterous people. Whippets are good natured and can be fine companions for children, but they must be protected from any possible abuse that might be incurred through childish roughhousing.

STANDARD FOR THE WHIPPET

General Appearance: A moderate size sight hound giving the appearance of elegance and fitness, denoting great speed, power, and balance without coarseness. A true sporting hound that covers a maximum of distance with a minimum of lost motion.

Head: Long and lean, fairly wide between the ears, scarcely perceptible stop, good length of muzzle which should be powerful without being coarse. Nose entirely black.

Ears: Small, fine in texture, thrown back and folded. Semipricked when at attention. Gay ears are incorrect and should be severely penalized.

Eyes: Large, dark, with keen intelligent alert expression. Lack of pigmentation around eyelids is undesirable. Yellow or dilute-colored eyes should be strictly penalized. Blue or china-colored eyes shall disqualify. Both eyes must be of the same color.

Muzzle: Muzzle should be long and powerful denoting great strength of "bite" without coarseness. Teeth should be white and strong. Teeth of upper jaw should fit closely over teeth of lower jaw creating a strong scissors bite. Extremely short muzzle or lack of underjaw should be strictly penalized. An even bite is extremely undesirable. Undershot shall disqualify. Overshot one-quarter inch or more shall disqualify.

Neck: Long, clean and muscular, well arched with no suggestion of throatiness, widening gracefully into the top of the shoulder. A short thick neck, or concave curvature of the top neckline sometimes called ewe (opposite of arched), should be penalized.

Shoulders: Long, well laid back, with flat muscles, allowing for moderate space between shoulder blades at the peak of withers. The length of the shoulder blade equals the length of the upper arm. A straight shoulder blade, short upper arm, a heavily muscled or loaded shoulder, or a very narrow shoulder, all restricting low free movement, should be strictly penalized.

Brisket: Very deep and strong, reaching as nearly as possible to the point of the elbow. Ribs well sprung but with no suggestion of barrel shape. Should fill in the space between the forelegs so that there is no appearance of a hollow between them.

Back and Loin: The back broad, firm and well muscled, having length and a strong natural arch over the loin, creating a definite tuck-up of the underline. A short loin creating a cramped stance should be penalized.

Topline and Croup: The topline runs smoothly from the withers with a graceful and not too accentuated arch beginning over the loin and carrying through over the croup, with the arch being continuous without flatness. A wheelback, flat back, dip behind shoulder blades, or a back that falls away sharply creating a cut-away appearance should be penalized. A steep or flat croup should be penalized.

Hindquarters: Long and powerful, stifles well bent, hocks well let down and close to the ground. Thighs broad and muscular. The muscles are long and flat and carry well down toward the hock. Sickle or cowhocks should be strictly penalized.

Tail: The tail long and tapering, reaching to the hipbone when drawn through between the hind legs. When the dog is in motion, the tail is carried low with a gentle upward curve; tail should not be carried higher than top of back. A curled tail should be penalized.

Coat and Color: Close, smooth and firm in texture. A coarse, or woolly coat should be penalized. Color immaterial.

Gait: Low, free moving and smooth, with reach in the forequarters and strong drive in the hindquarters. The dog has great freedom of action when viewed from the side; the forelegs reach forward close to the ground; the hindlegs have strong propelling power. Lack of front reach or rear drive, a short, mincing gait with high knee action should be strictly penalized. When moving and viewed from front or rear, legs should turn neither in nor out, nor should feet cross or interfere with each other. Crossing in front or moving too closely should be strictly penalized.

N.B.: Old scars and injuries, the result of work or accident should not be allowed to prejudice the dog's chance in the show ring, unless they interfere with its movement or ability to perform.

Size: Ideal height for dogs, 19 to 22 inches; for bitches, 18 to 21 inches; measured across the shoulders at the highest point. One-half inch above or below the above stated measurements will disqualify.

DISQUALIFICATIONS

Blue or china-colored eyes.
Undershot.
Overshot one-quarter inch or more.
A dog one-half inch above or below the measurements specified under "Size."

APPROVED, OCTOBER 12, 1971

Representing the breed: Ch. Gypsy's Chevalier, owned by Karen Johnston.

Group 3: Working Dogs

AKITA

No other breed of dog besides the Akita can claim to be a national monument and treasure! In the early days of the breed in Japan, only members of royalty were allowed to own an Akita, and the special leashes used on these dogs revealed the status of the owner. The breed gets its name from Prefecture of Akita, a section of northern Japan in which the breed was derived through judicious outcrossings of Chow Chows with Japanese Kari and Tosas dogs. Like these ancestors, the Akita was used for a time as a fighting dog. They proved to have unfaltering bravery and great endurance and strength. Moreover, the Akita was originally valued for their hunting prowess, being equally able to hunt anything from bears to ducks!

Today's Akita is a picture of power and strength, and they sport a magnificent plumed tail that is proudly carried curled above their back. They have an unending love for work and exercise and are amazingly trainable. They are still the true working dog and they relish it. Many Akitas are currently being trained for advanced obedience trial competition and are taking their share of the ribbons.

In the home, the owner of an Akita is blessed with a truly loyal watchdog and companion. They adapt well to the presence of small children and will tolerate a reasonable amount of the ear and tail pulling that sometimes results. In fact, they have been called as lovable as a teddy bear—but should the occasion arise, the Akita would fiercely defend his home with unfaltering courage.

The Akita's versatility is making this breed an increasingly popular show dog and pet. They are not given to excessive barking and fit well into most any home. Many northern Akita fanciers are even training their dogs for sled racing—and they are having great success. This combination of intelligence, trainability and gentleness will go far in making the Akita a widely accepted and respected dog.

Buyer's guide: The muscular Akita is not a dog to be taken lightly. Attention must be paid to making them obedient, but this training should be undertaken only in a calm, assertive manner because too-firm handling can lead to a sharp, unreasonable disposition in the dog. They can become somewhat cranky if they are constantly surrounded by children or other pets. Provide Akitas with plenty of room to exercise themselves and they will be more at ease in the home.

STANDARD FOR THE AKITA

General Appearance: Large, powerful, alert, with much substance and heavy bone. The broad head, forming a blunt triangle, with deep muzzle, small eyes and erect ears carried forward in line with back of neck is characteristic of the breed. The large, curled tail, balancing the broad head, is also characteristic of the breed.

Head: Massive but in balance with body; free of wrinkle when at ease. Skull flat between ears and broad; jaws square and powerful with minimal dewlap. Head forms a blunt triangle when viewed from above. ***Fault:*** Narrow or snipy head.

Muzzle: Broad and full. Distance from nose to stop is to distance from stop to occiput as 2 is to 3. **Stop:** Well defined, but not too abrupt. A shallow furrow extends well up forehead.

Nose: Broad and black. Liver permitted on white Akitas, but black always preferred. **Disqualification:** Butterfly nose or total lack of pigmentation on nose.

Ears: The ears of the Akita are characteristic of the breed. They are strongly erect and small in relation to rest of head. If ear is folded forward for measuring length, tip will touch upper eye rim. Ears are triangular, slightly rounded at tip, wide at base, set wide on head but not too low, and carried slightly forward over eyes in line with back of neck. **Disqualification:** Drop or broken ears.

Eyes: Dark brown, small, deep-set and triangular in shape. Eye rims black and tight.

Lips and Tongue: Lips black and not pendulous; tongue pink.

Teeth: Strong with scissors bite preferred, but level bite acceptable. **Disqualification:** Noticeably undershot or overshot.

Neck and Body: **Neck:** Thick and muscular; comparatively short, widening gradually toward shoulders. A pronounced crest blends in with base of skull.

Body: Longer than high, as 10 is to 9 in males; 11 to 9 in bitches. Chest wide and deep; depth of chest is one-half height of dog at shoulder. Ribs well sprung, brisket well developed. Level back with firmly-muscled loin and moderate tuck-up. Skin pliant but not loose. **Serious Faults:** Light bone, rangy body.

Tail: Large and full, set high and carried over back or against flank in a three-quarter, full, or double curl, always dipping to or below level of back. On a three-quarter curl, tip drops well down flank. Root large and strong. Tail bone reaches hock when let down. Hair coarse, straight and full, with no appearance of a plume. **Disqualification:** Sickle or uncurled tail.

Forequarters and Hindquarters: **Forequarters:** Shoulders strong and powerful with moderate layback. Forelegs heavy-boned and straight as viewed from front. Angle of pastern 15 degrees forward from vertical. **Faults:** Elbows in or out, loose shoulders. **Hindquarters:** Width, muscular development and comparable to forequarters. Upper thighs well developed. Stifle moderately bent and hocks well let down, turning neither in nor out. **Dewclaws:** On front legs generally not removed; dewclaws on hind legs generally removed. **Feet:** Cat feet, well knuckled up with thick pads. Feet straight ahead.

Coat: Double-coated. Undercoat thick, soft, dense and shorter than outer coat. Outer coat straight, harsh and standing somewhat off body. Hair on head, legs and ears short. Length of hair at withers and rump approximately two inches, which is slightly longer than on rest of body, except tail, where coat is longest and most profuse. **Fault:** Any indication of ruff or feathering.

Color: Any color including white; brindle; or pinto. Colors are brilliant and clear and markings are well balanced, with or without mask or blaze. White Akitas have no mask. Pinto has a white background with large, evenly placed patches covering head and more than one-third of body. Undercoat may be a different color from outer coat.

Gait: Brisk and powerful with strides of moderate length. Back remains strong, firm and level. Rear legs move in line with front legs.

Size: Males 26 to 28 inches at the withers; bitches 24 to 26 inches. **Disqualification:** Dogs under 25 inches; bitches under 23 inches.

Temperament: Alert and responsive, dignified and courageous. Aggressive toward other dogs.

DISQUALIFICATIONS

Butterfly nose or total lack of pigmentation on nose.
Drop or broken ears.
Noticeably undershot or overshot.
Sickle or uncurled tail.
Dogs under 25 inches; bitches under 23 inches.

APPROVED DECEMBER 12, 1972

Representing the breed: Ch. Akita Tani's Arashi, owned by Don and Twyla Lusk.

ALASKAN MALAMUTE

This powerful breed from the northlands of Alaska is rapidly becoming one of the most popular of all the working breeds. The Malamute was originally bred to serve as a harness dog in the arctic regions, but they have found their way into the homes of fanciers the world over who value them as affectionate housepets and superior watchdogs. This is not to say that the Alaskan Malamute of today enjoys a pampered life around the house—far from it. They still relish racing, pulling and any form of exercise that challenges their natural instinct for hard work!

The Malamute is a *natural* breed, that is, a breed that evolved through selective breeding by the Eskimos and many years of natural culling of the weaker progeny that could not endure the rigors of the northlands. Only those dogs that were strong and resourceful could survive the grueling work and biting cold and snow that is a fact of life in their homeland. The end product is the hardy, densely coated Malamute of today.

Alaskan Malamutes are the largest of the three popular sled dogs, the others being the Samoyed and the Siberian Husky. They are easily differentiated from the pure white Samoyed, but many novice dog fanciers have difficulty telling the Malamutes apart from their smaller, lighter-boned Siberian relatives. Whereas the Siberian is adept at pulling light sleds at great speed for long distances, the Malamute excels in overall strength and is capable of pulling great weights over long distances.

The Malamute is most happy when it is constantly active and the breed requires plenty of exercise to stay in top physical shape. They are strikingly handsome, alert in appearance and a delight for most households. Although many people are taken aback by the Malamute's large size, the sound and pleasant temperament of these dogs has won them a devoted following. While they are certainly large enough to roughhouse with, Malamutes are also friendly and gentle enough to trust around the smallest children. They thrive on affection—and will return kindness threefold.

Buyer's guide: Good tempered and outgoing, the Malamute is a fine housepet. They require a moderate amount of brushing to keep their coat tangle-free and they should be allowed plenty of access to the outdoors. Malamutes have hearty appetites, a by-product of their excessive energy.

STANDARD FOR THE ALASKAN MALAMUTE

General Appearance and Characteristics: The Alaskan Malamute is a powerful and substantially built dog with a deep chest and strong, compact body, not too short coupled, with a thick, coarse guard coat of sufficient length to protect a dense, woolly undercoat, from 1 to 2 inches in depth when dog is in full coat. Stands well over pads, and this stance gives the appearance of much activity, showing interest and curiosity. The head is broad, ears wedge-shaped and erect when alerted. The muzzle is bulky with only slight diminishing in width and depth from root to nose, not pointed or long, but not stubby. The Malamute moves with a proud carriage, head erect and eyes alert. Face markings are a distinguishing feature. These consist of either cap over head and rest of face solid color, usually grayish white, or face marked with the appearance of a mask. Combinations of cap and mask are not unusual. The tail is plumed and carried over the back, not like a fox brush, or tightly curled, more like a plume waving.

Malamutes are of various colors, but are usually wolfish gray or black and white. Their feet are of the "snowshoe" type, tight and deep, with well-cushioned pads, giving a firm and compact appearance. Front legs are straight with big bone. Hind legs are broad and powerful, moderately bent at stifles, and without cowhocks. The back is straight, gently sloping from shoulders to hips. The loin should not be so short or tight as to interfere with easy, tireless movement. Endurance and intelligence are shown in body and expression. The eyes have a "wolf-like" appearance by their position, but the expression is soft and indicates an affectionate disposition.

Temperament: The Alaskan Malamute is an affectionate, friendly dog, not a "one-man" dog. He is a loyal, devoted companion, playful on invitation, but generally impressive by his dignity after maturity.

Head: The head should indicate a high degree of intelligence, and is broad and powerful as compared with other "natural" breeds, but should be in proportion to the size of the dog so as not to make the dog appear clumsy or coarse. **Skull:** The skull should be broad between the ears, gradually narrowing to eyes, moderately rounded between ears, flattening on top as it approaches the eyes, rounding off to cheeks, which should be moderately flat. There should be a slight furrow between the eyes, the topline of skull and topline of the muzzle showing but little breaks downward from a straight line as they join. ***Muzzle:*** The muzzle should be large and bulky in proportion to size of skull, diminishing but little in width and depth from junction with skull to nose; lips close fitting; nose black; upper and lower jaws broad with large teeth, front teeth meeting with a scissors grip but never overshot or undershot.

Eyes: Brown, almond shaped, moderately large for this shape of eye, set obliquely in skull. Dark eyes preferred.

Ears: The ears should be of medium size, but small in proportion to head. The upper halves of the ears are triangular in shape, slightly rounded at tips, set wide apart on outside back edges of the skull with the lower part of the ear joining the skull on a line with the upper corner of the eye, giving the tips of the ears the appearance, when erect, of standing off from the skull. When erect, the ears point slightly forward, but when the dog is at work the ears are sometimes folded against the skull. High-set ears are a fault.

Neck: The neck should be strong and moderately arched.

Body: The chest should be strong and deep; body should be strong and compactly built but not short coupled. The back should be straight and gently sloping to the hips. The loins should be well muscled and not so short as to interfere with easy, rhythmic movement with powerful drive from the hindquarters. A long loin which weakens the back is also a fault. No excess weight.

Shoulders, Legs and Feet: Shoulders should be moderately sloping; forelegs heavily boned and muscled, straight to pasterns, which should be short and strong and almost vertical as viewed from the side. The feet should be large and compact, toes, tight-fitting and well arched, pads thick and tough, toenails short and strong. There should be a protective growth of hair between toes. Hind legs must be broad and powerfully muscled through thighs; stifles moderately bent, hock joints broad and strong, moderately bent and well let down. As viewed from behind, the hind legs should not appear bowed in bone, but stand and move true in line with movement of the front legs, and not too close or too wide. The legs of the Malamute must indicate unusual strength and tremendous propelling power. Any indication of unsoundness in legs or feet, standing or moving, is to be considered a serious fault. Dewclaws on the hind legs are undesirable and should be removed shortly after pups are whelped.

Tail: Moderately set and following the line of the spine at the start, well furred and carried over the back when not working—not tightly curled to rest on back—or short furred and carried like a fox brush, a waving plume appearance instead.

Coat: The Malamute should have a thick, coarse guard coat, not long and soft. The undercoat is dense, from 1 to 2 inches in depth, oily and woolly. The coarse guard coat stands out, and there is thick fur around the neck. The guard coat varies in length, as does the undercoat; however, in general, the coat is moderately short to medium along the sides of the body with the length of the coat increasing somewhat around the shoulders and neck, down the back and over the rump, as well as in the breeching and plume. Malamutes usually have shorter and less dense coats when shed out during the summer months.

Color and Markings: The usual colors range from light gray through the intermediate shadings to black, always with white on underbodies, parts of legs, feet, and part of mask markings. Markings should be either caplike and/or mask-like on face. A white blaze on forehead and/or collar or spot on nape is attractive and acceptable, but broken color extending over the body in spots or uneven splashings is undesirable. One should distinguish between mantled dogs and splash-coated dogs. The only solid color allowable is the all-white.

Size: There is a natural range in size in the breed. The desirable freighting sizes are:

Males: 25 inches at the shoulders—85 pounds.
Females: 23 inches at the shoulders—75 pounds.

However, size consideration should not outweigh that of type, proportion, and functional attributes, such as shoulders, chest, legs, feet, and movement. When dogs are judged equal in type, proportion, and functional attributes, the dog nearest the desirable freighting size is to be preferred.

IMPORTANT: *In judging Alaskan Malamutes their function as a sledge dog for heavy freighting must be given consideration above all else.* The judge must bear in mind that this breed is designed primarily as the working sledge dog of the North for hauling heavy freight, and therefore he should be a heavyboned, powerfully built, compact dog with sound legs, good feet, deep chest, powerful shoulders, steady, balanced, tireless gait, and the other physical equipment necessary for the efficient performance of his job. He isn't intended as a racing sled dog designed to compete in speed trials with the smaller Northern breeds.

The Malamute as a sledge dog for heavy freighting is designed for strength and endurance and any characteristic of the individual specimen, including temperament, which interferes with the accomplishment of this purpose is to be considered the most serious of faults. Faults under this provision would be splayfootedness, any indication of unsoundness or weakness in legs, cowhocks, bad pasterns, straight shoulders, lack of angulation, stilted gait or any gait which isn't balanced, strong, and steady, ranginess, shallowness, ponderousness, lightness of bone, poor over-all proportion, and similar characteristics.

SCALE OF POINTS

General Appearance	20	Feet	10
Head	15	Coat and Color	10
Body	20	Tail	5
Legs and Movement	20	TOTAL	100

APPROVED APRIL 12, 1960

Representing the breed: Am., Can., Ch. Northwood's Lord Kipnuk, owned by Ruth Zimmerman. Photo by Martin Booth.

BEARDED COLLIE

The gregarious Beardie is one of the most recent breeds to gain American Kennel Club recognition, but it is one of Great Britain's oldest breeds. They have a long history of shepherding in the wilds of the Scottish Highlands, and many Beardies can be found moving cattle today just as they did for the herdsmen of the 1700's. Like many of the shaggy coated herding dogs, the Bearded Collie is thought to have descended from the Hungarian Komondor. Their ability to work steadily despite the harsh climate, yet be a gentle companion won them many admirers. By day they maneuvered and drove the cattle on the rocky hillsides, working eagerly and swiftly to contain the wandering herd. After a full day's work they were welcomed back into the home and treated like a returning family member. Beardies have always thrived on the affection of a loving family, returning all personal attention with an abounding loyalty and devotion that is truly characteristic of the breed.

While this breed has also been known as the Highland or Mountain Collie, their distinctive beard and appealing facial expression gave rise to their official name of Bearded Collie. They present an overall shaggy, although not ragged, appearance. The Beardie is a medium-sized dog with a long, double-layered coat that ranges in many shades of color, from a light silver gray to black. The typical Beardie puppy is born with a very dark coat that slowly fades throughout the dog's first year, usually darkening again somewhat and settling into its mature color during the dog's second or third year. The outer coat is quite harsh, the hairs being strong and straight, and serves to protect the robust Beardie from the mist and rain that is typical of their homeland. The soft inner coat provides the all-weather insulation that lets them withstand the extremes of both cold winters and steamy summers.

The Bearded Collie makes a lovable housepet. They are at their best when surrounded by the family, and their fun-loving nature invites a spirited round of play whenever they can find a willing partner. They are not frivolous, however. When given a task or responsibility the Beardie can be relied on to give their all. They are not only affectionate towards children, but they instinctively seem to know what is proper recreation for them to be doing. They have been known to subtly herd home the wandering children much in the same manner that they used to drive home the cattle! The Bearded Collie is easily trained to most any task, a skill made possible by their tremendous desire to please. They have been very successful in obedience competition. Gentleness and affection are the key terms to apply to the Bearded Collie's temperament. If ever there was a dog to be termed man's best friend—this breed qualifies.

Buyer's guide: Beardies are by nature charming and lovable housepets. They are easily trained to the rules of the house and are very protective of their owner's possessions. They are too large for apartment living, but will do fine in the suburbs or country. A large yard or kennel run will allow the Beardie to maintain physical tone and their jovial disposition. A goodly amount of time should be devoted to brushing their coat, but clipping and trimming are unnecessary. Great pets for kids.

STANDARD FOR THE BEARDED COLLIE

Characteristics: The Bearded Collie is hardy and active, with an aura of strength and agility characteristic of a real working dog. Bred for centuries as a companion and servant of man, the Bearded Collie is a devoted and intelligent member of the family. He is stable and self-confident, showing no signs of shyness or aggression. This is a natural and unspoiled breed.

General Appearance: The Bearded Collie is a medium sized dog with a medium length coat that follows the natural lines of the body and allows plenty of daylight under the body. The body is long and lean, and, though strongly made, does not appear heavy. A bright inquiring expression is a distinctive feature of the breed. The Bearded Collie should be shown in a natural stance.

Head: The head is in proportion to the size of the dog. The skull is broad and flat; the stop is moderate; the cheeks are well filled beneath the eyes; the muzzle is strong and full; the foreface is equal in length to the distance between the stop and occiput. The nose is large and squarish. A snipy muzzle is to be penalized. (See Color section for pigmentation.)

Eyes: The eyes are large, expressive, soft and affectionate, but not round nor protruding, and are set widely apart. The eyebrows are arched to the sides to frame the eyes and are long enough to blend smoothly into the coat on the sides of the head. (See Color section for eye color.)

Ears: The ears are medium sized, hanging and covered with long hair. They are set level with the eyes. When the dog is alert, the ears have a slight lift at the base.

Teeth: The teeth are strong and white, meeting in a scissors bite. Full dentition is desirable.

Neck: The neck is in proportion to the length of the body, strong and slightly arched, blending smoothly into the shoulders.

Forequarters: The shoulders are well laid back at an angle of approximately forty-five degrees; a line drawn from the highest point of the shoulder blade to the forward point of articulation to the point of the elbow. The top of the shoulder blades lie in against the withers, but they slope outwards from there sufficiently to accommodate the desired spring of ribs. The legs are straight and vertical with substantial, but not heavy, bone and are covered with shaggy hair all around. The pasterns are flexible without weakness.

Body: The body is longer than it is high in an approximate ratio of five to four, length measured from point of chest to point of buttocks, height measured at the highest point of the withers. The length of the back comes from the length of the ribcage and not that of the loin. The back is level. The ribs are well sprung from the spine but are flat at the sides. The chest is deep, reaching at least to the elbows. The loins are strong. The level back line blends smoothly into the curve of the rump. A flat croup or a steep croup is to be severely penalized.

Hindquarters: The hind legs are powerful and muscular at the thighs with well bent stifles. The hocks are low. In normal stance, the bones below the hocks are perpendicular to the ground and parallel to each other when viewed from the rear; the hind feet fall just behind a perpendicular line from the point of buttocks when viewed from the side. The legs are covered with shaggy hair all around.

Tail: The tail is set low and is long enough for the end of the bone to reach at least the point of the hocks. It is normally carried low with an upward swirl at the tip while the dog is standing. When the dog is excited or in motion, the curve is accentuated and the tail may be raised but is never carried beyond a vertical line. The tail is covered with abundant hair.

Feet: The feet are oval in shape with the soles well padded. The toes are arched and close together, and well covered with hair including between the pads.

Coat: The coat is double with the undercoat soft, furry and close. The outercoat is flat, harsh, strong and shaggy, free from wooliness and curl, although a slight wave is permissable. The coat falls naturally to either side but must never be artifcially parted. The length and density of the hair are sufficient to provide a protective coat and to enhance the shape of the dog, but not so profuse as to obscure the natural lines of the body. The dog should be shown as naturally as is consistent with good grooming but the coat must not be trimmed in any way. On the head, the bridge of the nose is sparsely covered with hair which is slightly longer on the sides to cover the lips. From the cheeks, the lower lips and under the chin, the coat increases in length towards the chest, forming the typical beard. An exceedingly long, silky coat or one which has been trimmed in any way must be severely penalized.

Color: Coat: All Bearded Collies are born either black, blue, brown or fawn, with or without white markings. With maturity, the coat color may lighten, so that a born black may become any shade of gray from black to slate to silver, a born brown from chocolate to sandy. Blues and fawns also show shades from dark to light. Where white occurs, it only appears on the foreface as a blaze, on the skull, on the tip of the tail, on the chest, legs and feet and around the neck. The white hair does not grow on the body behind the shoulder nor on the face to surround the eyes. A predominately white dog (over fifty percent) must be disqualified. Tan markings occasionally appear and are acceptable on the eyebrows, inside the ears, on the cheeks, under the root of the tail, and on the legs where the white joins the main color.

Pigmentation: Pigmentation on the Bearded Collie follows coat color. In a born black, the eye rims, nose and lips are black, whereas in the born blue, the pigmentation is a blue-gray color. A born brown dog has brown pigmentation and born fawns a correspondingly lighter brown. The pigmentation is completely filled in and shows no sign of spots.

Eyes: Eye color will generally tone with the coat color. In a born blue or fawn, the distinctively lighter eyes are correct and must not be penalized.

Size: The ideal height at the withers is 21-22 inches for adult dogs and 20-21 inches for adult bitches. Height over and under the ideal is to be severely penalized. Height more than an inch over the ideal is to be disqualified. The express objective of this criterion is to insure that the Bearded Collie remains a medium sized dog.

Gait: Movement is free, supple and powerful. Balance combines good reach in forequarters with strong drive in hindquarters. The back remains firm and level. The feet are lifted only enough to clear the ground, giving the impression that the dog glides along making minimum contact. Movement is lithe and flexible to enable the dog to make the sharp turns and sudden stops required of the sheepdog. When viewed from the front and rear, the front and rear legs travel in the same plane from shoulder and hip joint to pads at all speeds. Legs remain straight, but feet move inward as speed increases until the edges of the feet converge on a center line at a fast trot.

Serious faults: snipy muzzle, flat croup or steep croup, excessively long, silky croup, trimmed or sculptured coat, height over or under the ideal.

DISQUALIFICATIONS
predominately white dogs (over 50%)
height more than an inch over the ideal

Representing the breed: Am., Can. Ch. Brambledale Blue Bonnet, C.D., owned by Mr. and Mrs. Robert Lachman.

BELGIAN MALINOIS

The short coat of the Belgian Malinois is the trait which separates this breed from two other Belgian sheepherding dogs, the Belgian Tervuren and the Belgian Sheepdog. These three dog breeds all stem from the same original stock and in Belgium and France they are referred to as the *Chien de Berger Belge*. All three are alike in conformation, with the length and color of the hair being the breeds' distinguishing characteristics. The Malinois' coat is straight with a dense undercoat. The hair on the head, ears and lower legs is very short in contrast to the longer growth on the tail, back of the thighs and around the neck where it forms a collarette. In color, the Malinois is similar to the Tervuren since they both have a coat of rich fawn to mahogany with a black overlay on the tips of the hairs.

The Malinois has been recognized as a separate breed by the American Kennel Club since 1965. Although the numbers of

Malinois in the country are still relatively low, the breed is becoming very popular with obedience competition fanciers because they are very quick to learn and perform well under pressure. Malinois are also making their presence known on the show scene where they are noted for their elegant carriage of the head and an overall well-balanced appearance.

Buyer's guide: They are a stable, dependable dog for the household, provided they are supplied with plenty of exercise and affection. Malinois owners should be active outdoors and should enjoy the company of an active, energetic dog. Their short coat seldom needs bathing or grooming, so they are an easy to get along with breed.

STANDARD FOR THE BELGIAN MALINOIS

General Appearance: The Belgian Malinois is a well-balanced, square dog, elegant in appearance, with an exceedingly proud carriage of the head and neck. The dog is strong, agile, well-muscled and full of life. It stands squarely on all fours and viewed from the side, the topline, forelegs and hind legs closely approximate a square. The whole conformation gives the impression of depth and solidity without bulkiness. The expression indicates alertness, attention and readiness for activity, and the gaze is intelligent and questioning. The male is usually somewhat more impressive and grand than its female counterpart, which has a distinctly feminine look.

Size and Substance: Males, 24 to 26 inches in height; females, 22 to 24 inches, measured at the withers. The length, measured from point of breastbone to point of rump, should equal the height, but bitches may be slightly longer. Bone structure is moderately heavy in proportion to height so that the dog is well balanced throughout and neither spindly or leggy nor cumbersome and bulky.

Coat: Comparatively short, straight, with dense undercoat. Very short hair on the head, ears and lower legs. The hair is somewhat longer around the neck where it forms a collarette, and on the tail and the back of the thighs.

Color: Rich fawn to mahogany, with black overlay. Black mask and ears. The upper parts of the body, tail, and breeches are lighter fawn, but washed-out fawn color on the body is a fault. The tips of the toes may be white and a small white spot on the chest is permitted.

Head: Clean-cut and strong, over-all size in proportion to the body. **Skull:** Top flattened rather than rounded, the width approximately the same as the length but no wider. **Stop:** Moderate. **Muzzle, Jaws, Lips:** Muzzle moderately pointed, avoiding any tendency to snipiness, and approximately equal in length to that of the topskull. The jaws are strong and powerful. The lips tight and black, with no pink showing on the outside. **Ears:** Triangular in shape, stiff, erect and in proportion to the head in size. Base of the ear should not come below the center of the eye. **Eyes:** Brown, preferably dark brown, medium size, slightly almond shaped, not protruding. **Nose:** Black, without spots or discolored areas. **Teeth:** A full complement of strong, white teeth, evenly set and meeting in an even bite or a scissors bite, neither overshot nor undershot.

Torso: **Neck:** Round and rather outstretched, tapered from head to body, well muscled with tight skin. **Topline:** The withers are slightly higher and slope into the back, which must be level, straight and firm from withers to hip joints. The loin section, viewed from above, is relatively short, broad and strong, but blending smoothly into the back. The croup is medium long, sloping gradually. **Tail:** Strong at the base, bone to reach hock. At rest it is held low, the tip bent back level with the hock. In action it is raised with a curl, which is strongest toward the tip, without forming a hook. **Chest:** Not broad, but deep. The lowest point reaches the elbow, forming a smooth ascendant curve to the abdomen, which is moderately developed, neither tucked-up nor paunchy.

Forequarters: **Shoulders:** Long and oblique, laid flat against the body, forming a sharp angle (approximately 90°) with the upper arm. **Legs:** Straight, strong and paralleled to each other. Bone oval rather than round. Length and substance well proportioned to the size of the dog. Pastern: Medium length, strong and very slightly sloped. Dewclaws may be removed. **Feet:** Round (cat-footed), toes curved close together, well padded. Nails strong and black except that they may be white to match white toe tips.

Hindquarters: **Thighs:** Broad and heavily muscled. The upper and lower thigh bones approximately parallel the shoulder blade and upper arm respectively, forming a relatively sharp angle at stifle joint. **Legs:** length and substance well proportioned to the size of the dog. Bone oval rather than round. Legs are parallel to each other. The angle at the hock is relatively sharp, although the Belgian Malinois does not have extreme angulation. Metatarsus medium length, strong and slightly sloped. Dewclaws, if any, should be removed. **Feet:** Slightly elongated, toes curved close together, well padded. Nails strong and black except that they may be white to match white toe tips.

Gait: Smooth, free and easy, seemingly never tiring, exhibiting facility of movement rather than a hard driving action. The dog tends to single-track at a fast gait, the legs, both front and rear, converging toward the center line of gravity of the dog, while the backline remains firm and level, parallel to the line of motion with no crabbing. The Belgian Malinois shows a marked tendency to move in a circle rather than a straight line.

FAULTS

Any deviation from these specifications is a fault, the degree to which a dog is penalized depending on the extent to which the dog deviates from the standard and the extent to which the particular fault would actually affect the working ability of the dog.

DISQUALIFICATIONS

Ears hanging, as on a hound.
Tail: cropped or stump.
Males under 22½ or over 27½ inches in height. Females over 20½ or over 25½ inches in height.

APPROVED APRIL 13, 1965

Representing the breed: Ch. Crocs-Blancs Nicole, owned by Daniele Daugherty.

BELGIAN SHEEPDOG

While the physical structure of all three recognized types of Belgian Sheepdogs is remarkably similar (some people say identical), the main difference between these breeds is the texture and color of the dogs' coats. In their native Belgium six different strains of herding dogs were developed, each strain derived and named from the area where they flourished. Although all strains still exist, the American Kennel Club recognizes only three: the Groenendael, known here as the Belgian Sheepdog; the Belgian Tervuren; and the Belgian Malinois. The first two differ only in that the Tervuren is a fawn to mahogany colored dog while the Belgian Sheepdog is black.

The Belgian Sheepdog is a long haired dog with a heavy coat and a dense undercoat. The hair around the neck is very thick and forms a distinctive collarette that frames the typically expressive face. He stands proudly and is squarely built.

The Belgian Sheepdog is a naturally talented herder, but his keen intelligence lends him to many endeavors, including obedience competion, police work and the military service. The Groenendael makes light of even rugged work, is powerfully built and a speedy runner. His zest and desire to learn makes him a joy to train, whether for simple chores or advanced obedience competition.

The even temperament of Belgian Sheepdogs qualifies them as a good choice for a pet. Although they are generally leery of strangers, at home they are very affectionate and faithful. Loyalty and sensitivity to their master are this breed's trademark. The Belgian Sheepdog's delightful humor and ingenuity is refreshing to be around.

Buyer's guide: People interested in large, free-thinking dogs should take a good look at the Belgian Sheepdog, for they are fun-loving company for all ages. They are quite quick-witted and responsible—two perfect qualities for families with several children. A thorough brushing and some regular exercise will keep them in proper condition.

STANDARD FOR THE BELGIAN SHEEPDOG

Personality: The Belgian Sheepdog should reflect the qualities of intelligence, courage, alertness, and devotion to master. To his inherent aptitude as guardian of flocks should be added protectiveness of the person and property of his master. He should be watchful, attentive, and always in motion when not under command. In his relationship with humans he should be observant and vigilant with strangers but not apprehensive. He should not show fear or shyness. He should not show viciousness by unwarranted or unprovoked attack. With those he knows well, he is most affectionate and friendly, zealous of their attention, and very possessive.

General Appearance: The first impression of the Belgian Sheepdog is that of a well-balanced, square dog, elegant in appearance, with an exceedingly proud carriage of the head and neck. He is a strong, agile, well-muscled animal, alert and full of life. His whole conformation gives the impression of depth and solidity without bulkiness. The male dog is usually somewhat more impressive and grand than his female counterpart. The bitch should have a distinctly feminine look.

Size and Substance: Males should be 24-26 inches in height and females 22-24 inches, measured at the withers. The length, measured from point of breast-bone to point of rump, should equal the height. Bitches should be slightly longer. Bone structure should be moderately heavy in proportion to his height so that he is well balanced throughout and neither spindly or leggy nor cumbersome and bulky. **Stance:** The Belgian Sheepdog should stand squarely on all fours. Side view: the topline, front legs, and back legs should closely approximate a square.

Expression: Indicates alertness, attention, readiness for activity. Gaze should be intelligent and questioning.

Coat: The guard hairs of the coat must be long, well-fitting, straight, and abundant. They should not be silky or wiry. The texture should be a medium harshness. The undercoat should be extremely dense, commensurate, however, with climatic conditions. The Belgian Sheepdog is particularly adaptable to extremes of temperature or climate. The hair is shorter on the head, outside of the ears, and lower part of the legs. The opening of the ear is protected by tufts of hair. **Ornamentation:** Especially long and abundant hair, like a collarette, around the neck; fringe of long hair down the back of the forearm; especially long and abundant hair trimming the hindquarters, the breeches; long, heavy, and abundant hair on the tail.

Color: Black. May be completely black or may be black with white, limited as follows: Small to moderate patch or strip on forechest. Between pads of feet. On *tips* of hind toes. On chin and muzzle (frost—may be white or gray). On *tips* of front toes—allowable but a fault.

Head: Clean-cut and strong, over-all size should be in proportion to the body. **Skull:** Top flattened rather than rounded. The width approximately the same, but not wider, than the length. **Stop:** Moderate. **Muzzle, Jaws, Lips:** Muzzle moderately pointed, avoiding any tendency to snipiness, and approximately equal in length to that of the topskull. The jaws should be strong and powerful. The lips should be tight and black, with no pink showing on the outside. **Ears:** Triangular in shape, stiff, erect, and in proportion to the head in size. Base of the ear should not come below the center of the eye. **Eyes:** Brown, preferably dark brown. Medium size, slightly almond shaped, not protruding. **Nose:** Black, without spots or discolored areas. **Teeth:** A full complement of strong, white teeth, evenly set. Should not be overshot or undershot. Should have either an even bite or a scissors bite.

Torso: **Neck:** Round and rather outstretched, tapered from head to body, well muscled, with tight skin. **Topline:** The withers are slightly higher and slope into the back which must be level, straight, and firm from withers to hip joints. The loin section, viewed from above, is relatively short, broad and strong, but blending smoothly into the back. The croup is medium long, sloping gradually. **Tail:** Strong at the base, bone to reach hock. At rest the dog holds it low, the tip bent back level with the hock. When in action he raises it and gives it a curl, which is strongest toward the tip, without forming a hook. **Chest:** Not broad, but deep. The lowest point should reach the elbow, forming a smooth ascendant curve to the abdomen. **Abdomen:** Moderate development. Neither tuck-up nor paunchy.

Forequarters: **Shoulder:** Long and oblique, laid flat against the body, forming a sharp angle (approximately 90°) with the upper arm. **Legs:** Straight, strong, and parallel to each other. Bone oval rather than round. Development (length and substance) should be well proportioned to the size of the dog. Pastern: Medium length, strong, and very slightly sloped. **Feet:** Round (cat-footed), toes curved close together, well padded. Nails strong and black except that they may be white to match white toe tips.

Hindquarters: **(Thighs):** Broad and heavily muscled. The upper and lower thigh bones approximately parallel the shoulder blade and upper arm respectively, forming a relatively sharp angle at stifle joint. **Legs:** Length and substance well proportioned to the size of the dog. Bone oval rather than round. Legs are parallel to each other. The angle at the hock is relatively sharp, although the Belgian Sheepdog does not have extreme angulation. Metatarsus medium length, strong, and slightly sloped. Dewclaws, if any, should be removed. **Feet:** Slightly elongated. Toes curved close together, well padded. Nails strong and black except that they may be white to match white toe tips.

Gait: Motion should be smooth, free and easy, seemingly never tiring, exhibiting facility of movement rather than a hard driving action. He tends to single-track on a fast gait; the legs, both front and rear, converging toward the center line of gravity of the dog. The backline should remain firm and level, parallel to the line of motion with no crabbing. He shows a marked tendency to move in a circle rather than a straight line.

FAULTS

Any deviation from the specifications is a fault. In determining whether a fault is minor, serious, or major, these two factors should be used as a guide: 1. the extent to which it deviates from the Standard. 2. The extent to which such deviation would actually affect the working ability of the dog.

DISQUALIFICATIONS

Viciousness.
Color: any color other than black, except for white in specified areas.
Ears: hanging (as on a hound).
Tail: cropped or stump.
Males under 22½ or over 27½ inches in height.
Females under 20½ or over 25½ inches in height.

APPROVED JUNE 9, 1959

BELGIAN TERVUREN

This hardy sheepherding dog originated in the town of Tervuren, a small border town between Belgium and France. Although common ancestry closely ties the Belgian Tervuren with the other *Chien de Berger Belge* breeds, the Tervuren is most similar to the Groenendael (Belgian Sheepdog) in conformation. The two breeds are separated by color differences. The coat of the Tervuren is long and rather harsh, while not being wiry or silky, and is a rich fawn to mahogany in color with the tips of the hairs being black. The Sheepdog is solid black. As a puppy, the coat is a light fawn color and it reaches its adult coloring at about eighteen months of age. The black tipping of the hairs in effect looks as if the coat was lightly brushed over by a hand covered with soot. The shoulders, face, ears, back and tip of the tail have more pronounced blackenings than do other parts of the double pigmented coat.

The Belgian Tervuren is a handsome dog with a regal bearing. He is exceptionally intelligent and is a zealous worker who delights in a challenge. During the world wars, the Belgian Tervuren served in many military assignments. The Tervuren was used primarily to deliver messages and help wounded soldiers during the day, when his fawn coloring would blend with the ground and surroundings. At night, the dark coloring of the Groenendael made them the likely messengers to the front.

Today, the Belgian Tervuren excels as an obedience contender and watchdog. He is a patient and tireless worker, and has proven himself as being both protective and loving towards children. A Tervuren tends to cast a cautious eye on strangers and will steadfastly defend his master's home in an authoritative, although not viscious, manner. He is a well balanced, strong dog with a proud carriage and overall vitality and alertness. He combines a natural beauty with a natural ability to serve and excels in all aspects of dog training and showing.

Buyer's guide: The Tervuren is quite obedient, easily trained and good company around the house or at play. They need room to roam around (as much as possible), so apartments will generally cramp them. Tervurens thrive in country settings where they are allowed to follow their instincts. They do not roam very far from home, however, as they prefer to be with their owners. They seem to understand kids very intuitively and are dependable watchdogs.

STANDARD FOR THE BELGIAN TERVUREN

General Appearance: The first impression of the Belgian Tervuren is that of a well-balanced medium size dog, elegant in appearance, standing squarely on all fours, with proud carriage of head and neck. He is strong, agile, well muscled, alert and full of life. He gives the impression of depth and solidity without bulkiness. The male should appear unquestionably masculine; the female should have a distinctly feminine look and be judged equally with the male. The Belgian Tervuren is a *natural* dog and there is no need for excessive posing in the show ring.

Personality: The Belgian Tervuren reflects the qualities of intelligence, courage, alertness and devotion to master. In addition to his inherent ability as a herding dog, he protects his master's person and property without being overly aggressive. He is watchful, attentive and usually in motion when not under command.

Temperament: In his relationship with humans he is observant and vigilant with strangers, but not apprehensive. He does not show fear or shyness. He does not show viciousness by unwarranted or unprovoked attack. He must be approachable, standing his ground and showing confidence to meet overtures without himself making them. With those he knows well, he is most affectionate and friendly, zealous for their attention and very possessive.

Head: Well chiseled, skin taut, long without exaggeration. **Skull and Muzzle:** Measuring from the stop are of equal length. Overall size is in proportion to the body, top of skull flattened rather than rounded, the width approximately the same as, but not wider than the length. The topline of the muzzle is parallel to the topline of the skull when viewed from the side. Muzzle moderately pointed, avoiding any tendency toward snipiness or cheekiness.

Stop: Moderate.

Jaws: Strong and powerful.

Lips: Tight and black, no pink showing on the outside when mouth is closed.

Nose: Black without spots or discolored areas.

Nostrils: Well defined.

Teeth: Full complement of strong white teeth, evenly set, meeting in a scissors or a level bite. Overshot and undershot teeth are a fault. Undershot teeth such that contact with the upper incisors is lost by two or more of the lower incisors is a disqualification. Loss of contact caused by short center incisors in an otherwise correct bite shall not be judged undershot. Missing teeth are a fault, but teeth broken by accident or discolored should not be penalized.

Eyes: Dark brown, medium size, slightly almond shape, not protruding. Light, yellow, or round eyes are a fault.

Ears: Triangular in shape, well cupped, stiff, erect, height equal to width at base. Set high, the base of the ear does not come below the center of the eye. Hanging ears, as on a hound, are a disqualification.

Expression: Intelligent and questioning, indicating alertness, attention and readiness for action.

Torso: **Neck:** Round, muscular, rather long and elegant, slightly arched and tapered from head to body. Skin well fitting with no loose folds.

Topline: Horizontal, straight and firm from withers to hip. Withers accentuated.

Chest: Not broad without being narrow, but deep; the lowest point of the brisket reaching the elbow, forming a smooth ascendant curve to the abdomen.

Abdomen: Moderately developed, neither tucked up nor paunchy. Ribs well sprung but flat on the sides.

Loin Section: Viewed from above is relatively short, broad and strong, but blending smoothly into the back.

Croup: Medium long, sloping gradually to the base of the tail.

Tail: Strong at the base, the last vertebra to reach at least to the hock. At rest the dog holds it low, the tip bent back level with the hock. When in action, he may raise it to a point level with the topline giving it a slight curve, but not a hook. Tail is not carried above the backline nor turned to one side. A cropped or stump tail is a disqualification.

Forequarters: **Shoulder:** Long, laid back 45°, flat against the body, forming a right angle with the upper arm. Top of the shoulder blades roughly two thumbs width apart.

Arms: Should move in a direction exactly parallel to the longitudinal axis of the body.

Forearms: Long and well muscled.

Legs: Straight and parallel, perpendicular to the ground. Bone oval rather than round. Dewclaws may be removed.

Pasterns: Short and strong, slightly sloped.

Feet: Rounded, cat footed, turning neither in nor out, toes curved close together, well padded, strong nails.

Hindquarters: **Thighs:** Broad and heavily muscled.

Stifles: Clearly defined, with upper shank at right angles to hip bones.

Hocks: Moderately bent.

Metatarsi: Short, perpendicular to the ground, parallel to each other when viewed from the rear.

Legs: Powerful without heaviness, moving in the same pattern as the limbs of the forequarters. Dewclaws are removed. Bone oval rather than round.

Feet: Slightly elongated, toes curved close together, heavily padded, strong nails.

Coat: The Belgian Tervuren is particularly adaptable to extremes of temperature or climate. The guard hairs of the coat must be long, close fitting, straight and abundant. The texture is of medium harshness, not silky or wiry. Wavy or curly hair is undesirable. The undercoat is very dense, commensurate, however, with climatic conditions. The hair is short on the head, outside the ears, and on the front part of the legs. The opening of the ear is protected by tufts of hair. **Ornamentation:** Consists of especially long and abundant hair, like a collarette around the neck, particularly on the males; fringe of long hair down the back of the forearm; especially long and abundant hair trimming the breeches: long, heavy and abundant hair on the tail.

Color: **Body:** Rich fawn to russet mahogany with black overlay. The coat is characteristically double pigmented, wherein the tip of each fawn hair is blackened. On mature males, this blackening is especially pronounced on the shoulders, back and rib section, but blackening in patches is undesirable. The underparts of the body, tail and breeches are cream, grey, or light beige. Belgian Tervuren characteristically become darker with increasing age. Although allowance should be made for females and young males, absence of blackening in mature dogs is a serious fault. Washed out predominant color, such as cream or grey is to be severely penalized. Solid black, solid liver or any area of white except as specified on the chest, tips of toes, chin and muzzle are disqualifications.

Face: The face has a black mask and the ears are mostly black. A face with a complete absence of black is a serious fault. Frost or white on chin or muzzle is normal.

Chest: The chest is normally black, but may be a mixture of black and grey. A single white patch is permitted on the chest, not to extend to the neck or breast.

Feet: The tips of the toes may be white. Nail color may vary from black to transparent.

Breeches: Cream, grey, or off-white.

Tail: The tail typically has a darker or black tip.

Gait: Lively and graceful, covering the maximum ground with minimum effort. Always in motion, seemingly never tiring, he shows ease of movement rather than hard driving action. He single tracks at a fast gait, the legs both front and rear converging toward the center line of gravity of the dog. The back line should remain firm and level, parallel to the line of motion, viewed from the side he exhibits full extension of both fore and hindquarters. His natural tendency is to move in a circle, rather than a straight line. Padding, hackneying, weaving, crabbing and similar movement faults are to be penalized according to the degree to which they interfere with the ability of the dog to work.

Size and Substance: The ideal male is 24 to 26 inches in height and female 22 to 24 inches in height measured at the withers. Dogs are to be penalized in accordance to the degree they deviate from the ideal. The body is square; the length measured from the point of shoulder to the point of the rump approximates the height. Females may be somewhat longer in body. Bone structure is medium in proportion to height, so that he is well balanced throughout and neither spindly or leggy nor cumbersome and bulky. Males under 23 inches or over 26.5 inches or females under 21 inches or over 24.5 inches are to be disqualified.

Faults: The Belgian Tervuren is a herding dog, and faults which affect his ability to herd under all conditions, such as poor gait, bite, coat or temperament should be particularly penalized.

DISQUALIFICATIONS

Ear hanging as on a hound

Tail cropped or stump

Solid black or solid liver or any area of white except as specified on the chest, tip of toes, chin, or muzzle.

Undershot teeth such that contact with the upper incisors is lost by two or more of the lower incisors.

Males under 23 inches or over 26.5 inches; females under 21 inches or over 24.5 inches in height.

Representing the breed: Ch. D'Jimmy Du Clos Saint Clair, C.D., owned by Dorothy Hollister.

BERNESE MOUNTAIN DOG

Invading Roman soldiers first introduced the prototype of today's Bernese Mountain Dog into Helvetia nearly two thousand years ago. Descended from Mastiff type dogs, Bernese were commonly used as workers around farms, not only as watchdogs but also as droving dogs for herds of cattle. This longhaired worker was exceptionally hardy and showed an affinity for hauling carts. Craftsmen around the town of Berne, Switzerland, began succesfully using these dogs to transport woven baskets and other wares to and from town. Their fame as eager workers requiring little supervision quickly spread, and the breed soon flourished throughout the Alps, where they are known as the Berner Sennenhund.

The approach of the 20th century and the subsequent outmoding of dog carts were disastrous for the breed. The once plentiful Bernese diminished to near extinction. Through the dedication of an avid fancier, Professor Albert Heim of Zurich, a few good specimens of the breed were located and a strict breeding program was designed to maintain and enhance these remaining strains.

Within a few years a sufficient number of quality Bernese Mountain Dogs had been bred by Professor Heim and the breed was once again secure. Today Bernese Mountain Dogs are fairly common on the farms in the Bernese middle and oberland, where they are still kept as farm dogs and workers.

Today the Bernese Mountain Dog is gaining much attention in the United States as both a show dog and pet. They have a delightfully easy-going personality, yet retain the natural courage and strength that is the hallmark of a good working dog. Given plenty of exercise and affection, they prove to be fine and faithful watchdogs and companions.

The Bernese's distinctive colorings and proud carriage make them a most beautiful sight to see in motion. Their jet black coat is soft and silky in texture and has a natural sheen. There are russet-brown or tan markings on the legs and a large white blaze on the chest that meld together to give the Bernese a soft, yet vibrant look about them. They are unassuming by nature and do not complain or pester their owners.

Buyer's guide: People who want to own large working dogs, such as the Bernese Mountain Dog, must have adequate land around them to meet the breed's requirements. They need a proper diet and a substantial amount of exercise daily to keep from going to fat and to retain their physical stature. They are frisky and outgoing with their owners, and alert to most others. Bernese Mountain Dogs are very even tempered and do not get excited to extremes. They enjoy the companionship of an inside life, but still retain the love for the country. Their long coat is remarkably dirt-resistant and is easily maintained with just a daily brushing.

STANDARD FOR THE BERNESE MOUNTAIN DOG

General Appearance: A well-balanced dog, active and alert; a combination of sagacity, fidelity and utility.

Height: Dogs, 23 inches to 27½ inches; bitches, 21 inches to 26 inches at shoulder.

Head: Skull flat, defined stop and strong muzzle. Dewlaps very slightly developed, flews not too pendulous, jaw strong with good, strong teeth. **Eyes:** dark, hazel-brown, full of fire. **Ears:** V-shaped, set on high, not too pointed at tips and rather short. When in repose, hanging close to head; when alert, brought slightly forward and raised at base.

Body: Rather short than too long in back, compact and well ribbed up. Chest broad with good depth of brisket. Loins strong and muscular.

Legs and Feet: Forelegs perfectly straight and muscular, thighs well developed and stifles well bent. Feet round and compact. Dewclaws should be removed.

Tail: Of fair thickness and well covered with long hair, but not to form a flag; moderate length. When in repose, should be carried low, upward swirl permissible; when alert, may be carried gaily, but may never curl or be carried over back.

Coat: Soft and silky with bright, natural sheen; long and slightly wavy but may never curl.

Color and Markings: Jet-black with russet-brown or deep tan markings on all four legs, a spot just above forelegs, each side of white chest markings and spots over eyes, which may never be missing. The brown on the forelegs must always be between the black and white. **Preferable, but not a condition, are:** White feet, tip of tail, pure white blaze up foreface, a few white hairs on back of neck, and white star-shaped markings on chest. When the latter markings are missing, it is not a disqualification.

FAULTS

Too massive in head; light or staring eyes; too heavy or long ears; too narrow or snipy muzzle; undershot or overshot mouth; pendulous dewlaps; too long or Setterlike body; splay or hare feet; tail curled or carried over back; cowhocks; and white legs.

SCALE OF POINTS

General appearance	15	Tail	10
Size and height	5	Coat	10
Head	15	Color and markings	15
Body	15		
Legs and feet	15	TOTAL	100

APPROVED APRIL 13, 1937

Representing the breed: Ch. Tryarr Alphorn Knight Echo, owned by Mrs. Gretchen Johnson.

BOUVIER DES FLANDRES

This rugged worker is a Belgian sheepherding dog that is so efficient at its work that it is oftentimes left alone to control the herds while the farmers attend to other business! They have a rather unusual style of controlling their herds. While most cattle dogs nip at the heels of the unruly cattle, the Bouvier typically throws a body block against the side of the wandering cow and bumps it back into the herd. They also have been used to pull carts, and are effective trackers because they possess a highly developed sense of smell. Few tasks are beyond the capabilities of this tireless worker since they are equipped with massive lungs and chests and they grow to be an average weight of nearly 100 pounds.

The Bouviers' origin traces back to Flanders, Belgium, where they were theorized to have developed through crosses of the native Belgian Martin-type dogs with Scottish Deerhounds or Tibetan Mastiffs. The basic body conformation is attributed to be a natural form that developed in response to the work the dogs were doing in that terrain. Their wiry, tousled coat is waterproof and harsh enough to protect the dog from the elements and possible injury from the bites of attacking animals.

Although the breed is growing in popularity, they are still a newcomer to the American dog scene. The Bouvier des Flandres is a keen and speedy learner and he has proven to be an exceptional obedience competitor. The breed is also finding success in police work as they combine their physical attributes of great size and strength with their superior intelligence and dependability.

Bouviers des Flandres make great pets for the home since they are naturally obedient and well mannered. They are not submissive, however, and still retain a mischievous and playful nature.

Buyer's guide: This rugged worker should not be kept as a pet in anything but a large home where they have plenty of room to move. Bouviers are powerful dogs and have large requirements for outside exercise and food. They are just a little too big to be considered as good companions for kids, but they are of amiable character and trustworthy. Their grooming needs are minimal, and the Bouvier des Flandres will be fit and take care of itself as long as the basics of food, shelter and companionship are there.

STANDARD FOR THE BOUVIER DES FLANDRES

The Bouvier des Flandres is a powerfully built, compact, short-coupled, rough-coated dog of notably rugged appearance. He gives the impression of great strength without any sign of heaviness or clumsiness in his overall makeup. He is agile, spirited and bold, yet his serene, well-behaved disposition denotes his steady, resolute and fearless character. His gaze is alert and brilliant, depicting his intelligence, vigor and daring. By nature he is an equable dog.

His origin is that of a cattle herder and general farmer's helper, including cart pulling. He is an ideal farm dog. His harsh coat protects him in all weather, enabling him to perform the most arduous tasks. The coat may be trimmed slightly only to accent the body line. Overtrimming which alters the natural rugged appearance is to be avoided.

He has been used as an ambulance and messenger dog. Modern times find him as a watch and guard dog as well as a family friend, guardian and protector. His physical and mental characteristics and deportment, coupled with his olfactory abilities, his intelligence and initiative enable him to also perform as a tracking dog and a guide dog for the blind.

Head: The head is impressive in scale, accentuated by beard and mustache. It is in proportion to body and build.

Skull: Well developed and flat, slightly less wide than long. When viewed from the side, the top lines of the skull and the muzzle are parallel. It is wide between the ears, with the frontal groove barely marked. The stop is more apparent than real, due to upstanding eyebrows. The proportions of length of skull to length of muzzle are 3 to 2.

Eyes: The expression is bold and alert. They neither protrude nor are sunken in the sockets. Their shape is oval with the axis on a horizontal plane, when viewed from the front. Their color is a dark nut brown. The eye rims are black without lack of pigment and the haw is barely visible. Yellow or light eyes are to be strongly penalized, along with a walleyed or staring expression.

Ears: Placed high and alert. They are rough-coated. If cropped, they are to be a triangular contour and in proportion to the size of the head. The inner corner of the ear should be in line with the outer corner of the eye. Ears that are too low or too closely set are serious faults.

Muzzle: Broad, strong, well filled out, tapering gradually toward the nose without ever becoming snipy or pointed. The cheeks are flat and lean, with the lips being dry and tight fitting. A narrow, snipy muzzle is faulty.

Nose: Large, black, well developed, round at the edges, with flared nostrils. A brown, pink or spotted nose is a serious fault.

Jaws and Teeth: The jaws are powerful and of equal length. The teeth are strong, white and healthy, with the incisors meeting in a scissors bite. Overshot or undershot bites are to be severely penalized.

Neck: The neck is strong and muscular, widening gradually into the shoulders. When viewed from the side, it is gracefully arched with upright carriage. A short, squatty neck is faulty. No dewlap.

Body or Trunk: Powerful, broad and short. The length from the point of the shoulders to the tip of the buttocks is equal to the height from the ground to the highest point of the withers. The chest is broad, with the brisket extending to the elbow in depth. A long-lined, rangy dog should be faulted.

Ribs: The ribs are deep and well sprung. The first ribs are slightly curved, the others well sprung and very sloped nearing the rear, giving proper depth to the chest. Flat ribs or slabsidedness is to be strongly penalized.

Back: Short, broad, well muscled with firm level topline. It is supple and flexible with no sign of weakness.

Flanks and Loins: Short, wide and well muscled, without weakness. The abdomen is only slightly tucked up.

Croup or Rump: The horizontal line of the back should mold unnoticeably into the curve of the rump, which is characteristically wide. A sunken or slanted croup is a serious fault.

Tail: Is to be docked, leaving 2 or 3 vertebrae. It must be set high and align normally with the spinal column. Preferably carried upright in motion. Dogs born tailless should not be penalized.

Forequarters: Strong boned, well muscled and straight.

Shoulders and Upper Arms: The shoulders are relatively long, muscular but not loaded, with good layback. The shoulder blade and humerus are approximately the same length, forming an angle slightly greater than 90 degrees when standing. Straight shoulders are faulty.

Elbows: Close to the body and parallel. Elbows which are too far out or in are faults.

Forearms: Viewed either in profile or from the front are perfectly straight, parallel to each other and perpendicular to the ground. They are well muscled and strong boned.

Wrists: Exactly in line with the forearms. Strong boned.

Pasterns: Quite short, slightly sloped forward. Dewclaws may be removed.

Feet: Both forefeet and hind feet are rounded and compact turning neither in nor out; the toes close and well arched; strong black nails; thick tough pads.

Hindquarters: Firm, well muscled with large, powerful hams. They should be parallel with the front legs when viewed from either front or rear.

Thighs: Wide and muscular. The upper thigh must be neither too straight nor too sloping. There is moderate angulation at the stifle.

Legs: Moderately long, well muscled, neither too straight nor too inclined.

Hocks: Strong, rather close to the ground. When standing and seen from the rear, they will be straight and perfectly parallel to each other and perpendicular to the ground. In motion, they must turn neither in nor out. There is a slight angulation at the hock joint. Sickle or cowhocks are serious faults.

Metatarsi: Hardy and lean, rather cylindrical and perpendicular to the ground when standing. If born with dewclaws, they are to be removed.

Coat: A tousled, double coat capable of withstanding the hardest work in the most inclement weather. The outer hairs are rough and harsh, with the undercoat being fine, soft and dense.

Topcoat: Must be harsh to the touch, dry, trimmed, if necessary, to a length of approximately 2½ inches. A coat too long or too short is a fault, as is a silky or woolly coat. It is tousled without being curly. On the skull, it is short, and on the upper part of the back, it is particularly close and harsh always, however, remaining rough.

Undercoat: A dense mass of fine, close hair, thicker in winter. Together with the topcoat, it will form a water-resistant covering. A flat coat, denoting lack of undercoat is a serious fault.

Mustache and Beard: Very thick, with the hair being shorter and rougher on the upper side of the muzzle. The upper lip, with its heavy mustache and the chin with its heavy and rough beard gives that gruff expression so characteristic of the breed.

Eyebrows: Erect hairs accentuating the shape of the eyes without ever veiling them.

Color: From fawn to black, passing through salt and pepper; gray and brindle. A small white star on the chest is allowed. Other than chocolate brown, white, or parti-color, which are to be severely penalized, no one color is to be favored.

Height: The height as measured at the withers—Dogs, from 24½ to 27½ inches; bitches, from 23½ to 26½ inches. In each sex, the ideal height is the median of the two limits, i.e., 26 inches for a dog and 25 inches for a bitch. Any dog or bitch deviating from the mimimum or maximum limits mentioned shall be severely penalized.

Gait: The whole of the Bouvier des Flandres must be harmoniously proportioned to allow for a free, bold and proud gait. The reach of the forequarters must compensate for and be in balance with the driving power of the hindquarters. The back, while moving in a trot, will remain firm and flat. In general, the gait is the logical demonstration of the structure and build of the dog. It is to be noted that while moving at a fast trot, the properly built Bouvier will tend to single track.

Temperament: As mentioned under general description and characteristics, the Bouvier is an equable dog, steady, resolute and fearless. Viciousness or shyness is undesirable.

Faults: The foregoing description is that of the ideal Bouvier des Flandres. Any deviation from this is to be penalized to the extent of the deviation.

Representing the breed: Ch. Tacquin Du Posty Arlequin, owned by Chet Collier. Photo by Gilbert.

BOXER

In appearance the Boxer creates an aura of power and ferocity, but the true temperament of the breed is most amiable and affectionate. They are intelligent and easy to train, and add a warm sense of humor to any household. The breed was originally developed as a guard dog and companion and they excel in both areas. Their formidable appearance, backed up by uncompromising strength and courage, is enough to deter any intruder. They adore the company of children and remain good natured and protective of them despite the roughest treatment.

The Boxer breed dates back at least 100 years in their native Germany. Although their exact lineage cannot be accurately determined, the Boxer is thought to have derived mainly from the

Bullenbeissers, or Bull Biters, that were common to the area. These dogs were quite strong, with a short muzzle and a slightly undershot jaw. This last trait was necessary to enable them to grab hold of the bull by the nose and hold on with a grip that was hard to break away from. The Bullenbeisser strain was infused with the lines of some imported Bulldogs and the Boxer type was on the way towards being set. The substance and compact power of the resulting dogs so impressed the breeders that great care was taken to quickly fix the Boxer type and preserve and standardize the breed.

The Boxer has gained much popularity in the United States since the breed's arrival in 1904. Their name stems from the manner in which the dog plays or fights, advancing and sparring with their forepaws. They are not pugnacious by nature, however. The Boxer has been used very successfully as guide dogs for the blind and they are among the top competitors in the obedience rings. Clean by nature, Boxers are reliable and pleasant housepets whose even temper and outgoing personality make them valued additions to any dog-oriented family.

Buyer's guide: The Boxer is one of the best housepets among the larger working breeds since they get along well with everyone, especially children, and they do not require any special attention to keep them at their best. They are willing to cooperate with their owners. An excellent choice for watchdog and companion.

STANDARD FOR THE BOXER

General Appearance: The Boxer is a medium-sized, sturdy dog, of square build, with short back, strong limbs, and short, tight-fitting coat. His musculation, well developed, should be clean, hard and appear smooth (not bulging) under taut skin. His movements should denote energy. The gait is firm yet elastic (springy), the stride free and ground-covering, the carriage proud and noble. Developed to serve the multiple purposes of guard, working and escort-dog, he must combine elegance with substance and ample power, not alone for beauty but to ensure the speed, dexterity and jumping ability essential to arduous hike, riding expedition, police or military duty. Only a body whose individual parts are built to withstand the most strenuous efforts, assembled as a complete and harmonious whole, can respond to these combined demands. Therefore, to be at his highest efficiency he must never be plump or heavy, and, while equipped for great speed, he must never be racy.

The head imparts to the Boxer a unique individual stamp, peculiar to him alone. It must be in perfect proportion to the body, never small in comparison to the over-all picture. The muzzle is his most distinctive feature, and great value is to be placed on its being of correct form and in absolute proper proportion to the skull.

In judging the Boxer, first consideration should be given to general appearance; next, over-all balance, including the desired proportions of the individual parts of the body to each other, as well as the relation of substance to elegance—to which an attractive color or arresting style may contribute. Special attention is to be devoted to the head, after which the dog's individual components are to be examined for their correct construction and function, and efficiency of gait evaluated.

General Faults: Head not typical, plump, bulldoggy appearance, light bone, lack of balance, bad condition, lack of noble bearing.

Head: The beauty of the head depends upon the harmonious proportion of the muzzle to the skull. The muzzle should always appear powerful, never in its relationship to the skull. The head should be clean, not showing deep wrinkles. Folds will normally appear upon the forehead when the ears are erect, and they are always indicated from the lower edge of the stop running downward on both sides of the muzzle. The dark mask is confined to the muzzle and is in distinct contrast to the color of the head. Any extension of the mask to the skull, other than dark shading around the eyes, creates a somber, undesirable expression. When white replaces any of the black mask, the path of any upward extension should be between the eyes. The muzzle is powerfully developed in length, width and depth. It is not pointed, narrow, short or shallow. Its shape is influenced first through the formation of both jawbones, second through the placement of the teeth, and third through the texture of the lips.

The Boxer is normally undershot. Therefore, the lower jaw protrudes beyond the upper and curves slightly upward. The upper jaw is broad where attached to the skull and maintains this breadth except for a very slight tapering to the front. The incisor teeth of the lower jaw are in a straight line, the canines preferably up front in the same line to give the jaw the greatest possible width. The line of incisors in the upper jaw is slightly convex toward the front. The upper corner incisors should fit snugly back of the lower canine teeth on each side, reflecting the symmetry essential to the creation of a sound, non-slip bite.

The lips, which complete the formation of the muzzle, should meet evenly. The upper lip is thick and padded, filling out the frontal space created by the projection of the lower jaw. It rests on the edge of the lower lip and, laterally, is supported by the fangs (canines) of the lower jaw. Therefore, these fangs must stand far apart, and be of good length so that the front surface of the muzzle is broad and squarish and, when viewed from the side, forms an obtuse angle with the topline of the muzzle. Over-protrusion of the overlip or underlip is undesirable. The chin should be perceptible when viewed from the sides as well as from the front without being over-repandous (rising above the bite line) as in the Bulldog. The Boxer must not show teeth or tongue when the mouth is closed. Excessive flews are not desirable.

The top of the skull is slightly arched, not rotund, flat, nor noticeably broad, and the occiput not too pronounced. The forehead forms a distinct stop with the topline of the muzzle, which must not be forced like that of a Bulldog. It should not slant down (down-faced), nor should it be dished, although the tip of the nose should lie somewhat higher than the root of the muzzle. The forehead shows just a slight furrow between the eyes. The cheeks, though covering powerful masseter muscles compatible with the strong set of teeth, should be relatively flat and not bulge, maintaining the clean lines of the skull. They taper into the muzzle in a slight, graceful curve. The ears are set at the highest points of the sides of the skull, cut rather long without too broad a shell, and are carried erect. The dark brown eyes, not too small, protruding or deep-set, are encircled by dark hair, and should impart an alert, intelligent expression. Their mood-mirroring quality combined with the mobile skin furrowing of the forehead gives the Boxer head its unique degree of expressiveness. The nose is broad and black, very slightly turned up; the nostrils broad, with the nasolabial line running between them down through the upper lip, which, however, must not be split.

Faults: Lack of nobility and expression, somber face, unserviceable bite. Pinscher or Bulldog head, sloping topline of muzzle, muzzle too light for skull, too pointed a bite (snipy). Teeth or tongue showing with mouth closed, driveling, split upper lip. Poor ear carriage, light ("Bird of Prey") eyes.

Neck: Round, of ample length, not too short; strong, muscular and clean throughout, without dewlap; distinctly marked nape with an elegant arch running down to the back. **Fault:** Dewlap.

Body: In profile, the build is of square proportions in that a horizontal line from the front of the forechest to the rear projection of the upper thigh should equal a vertical line dropped from the top of the withers to the ground.

Chest and Forequarters: The brisket is deep, reaching down to the elbows; the depth of the body at the lowest point of the brisket equals half the height of the dog at the withers. The ribs, extending far to the rear, are well arched but not barrel-shaped. Chest of fair width and forechest well defined, being easily visible from the side. The loins are short and muscular; the lower stomach line, lightly tucked up, blends into a graceful curve to the rear. The shoulders are long and sloping, close-lying and not excessively covered with muscle. The upper arm is long, closely approaching a right angle to the shoulder-blade. The forelegs, viewed from the front, are straight, stand parallel to each other, and have strong, firmly joined bones. The elbows should not press too closely to the chest wall or stand off visibly from it. The forearm is straight, long and firmly muscled. The pastern joint is clearly defined but not distended. The pastern is strong and distinct, slightly slanting, but standing almost perpendicular to the ground. The dewclaws may be removed as a safety precaution. Feet should be compact, turning neither in nor out, with tightly arched toes (cat feet) and tough pads. **Faults:** Chest too broad, too shallow or too deep in front; loose or overmuscled shoulders; chest hanging between shoulders; tied-in or bowed-out elbows; turned feet; hare feet; hollow flanks; hanging stomach.

Back: The withers should be clearly defined as the highest point of the back; the whole back short, straight and muscular with a firm topline. **Faults:** Roach back, sway back, thin lean back, long narrow loins, weak union with croup.

Hindquarters: Strongly muscled with angulation in balance with that of forequarters. The thighs broad and curved, the breech musculature hard and strongly developed. Croup slightly sloped, flat and broad. Tail attachment high rather than low. Tail clipped, carried upward. Pelvis long and, in females especially, broad. Upper and lower thigh long, leg well angulated with a clearly defined, well-let-down hock joint. In standing position, the leg below the hock joint (metatarsus) should be practically perpendicular to the ground, with a slight rearward slope permissible. Viewed from behind, the hind legs should be straight, with the hock joints leaning neither in nor out. The metatarsus should be short, clean and strong, supported by powerful rear pads. The rear toes just a little longer than the front toes, but similar in all other respects. Dewclaws, if any, may be removed. **Faults:** Too rounded, too narrow, or falling off of croup; low-set tail; higher in back than in front; steep, stiff, or too slightly angulated hindquarters; light thighs; bowed or crooked legs; cowhocks; overangulated hock joints (sickle hocks); long metatarsus (high hocks); hare feet; hindquarters too far under or too far behind.

Gait: Viewed from the side, proper front and rear angulation is manifested in a smoothly efficient, level-backed, ground-covering stride with powerful drive emanating from a freely operating rear. Although the front legs do not contribute impelling power, adequate "reach" should be evident to prevent interference, overlap or "side-winding" (crabbing). Viewed from the front, the shoulders should remain trim and the elbows not flare out. The legs are parallel until gaiting narrows the track in proportion to increasing speed, then the legs come in under the body but should never cross. The line from the shoulder down through the legs should remain straight, although not necessarily perpendicular to the ground. Viewed from the rear, a Boxer's breech should not roll. The hind feet should "dig in" and track relatively true with the front. Again, as speed increases, the normally broad rear track will become narrower.
Faults: Stilted or inefficient gait, pounding, paddling or flailing out of front legs, rolling or waddling gait, tottering hock joints, crossing over or interference—front or rear, lack of smoothness.

Height: Adult males—22½ to 25 inches; females—21 to 23½ inches at the withers. Males should not go under the minimum nor females over the maximum.

Coat: Short, shiny, lying smooth and tight to the body.

Color: The colors are fawn and brindle. Fawn in various shades from light tan to dark deer red or mahogany, the deeper colors preferred. The brindle variety should have clearly defined black stripes on fawn background. White markings on fawn or brindle dogs are not to be rejected and are often very attractive, but must be limited to one third of the ground color and are not desirable on the back of the torso proper. On the face, white may replace a part or all of the otherwise essential black mask. However, these white markings should be of such distribution as to enhance and not detract from true Boxer expression.

Character and Temperament: These are of paramount importance in the Boxer. Instinctively a "hearing" guard dog, his bearing is alert, dignified and self-assured, even at rest. In the show ring, his behavior should exhibit constrained animation. With family and friends, his temperament is fundamentally playful, yet patient and stoical with children. Deliberate and wary with strangers, he will exhibit curiosity, but, most importantly, fearless courage and tenacity if threatened. However, he responds promptly to friendly overtures when honestly rendered. His intelligence, loyal affection and tractability to discipline make him a highly desirable companion. **Faults:** Lack of dignity and alertness, shyness, cowardice, treachery and viciousness (belligerency toward other dogs should not be considered viciousness.)

DISQUALIFICATIONS

Boxers with white or black ground color, or entirely white or black, or any color other than fawn or brindle. (White markings, when present, must not exceed one third of the ground color.)

APPROVED DECEMBER 12, 1967

Representing the breed: Ch. My-R's Wizard, owned by Mrs. Kenneth W. Meyer.

BRIARD

Descended from a very old line of French dogs, the Briard in its earliest traceable lineage was used to safeguard its charges from robbers and predatory animals. Authorities say animals very close in type and appearance to the Briard are evident in native French tapestries and monuments from the 1300's and 1500's. These dogs were supposedly present at the court of Charlemagne, and Napolean was said to have owned one as well.

After the French Revolution when the nobility was on the outs and the land was redivided for farming, the Briard was used primarily as a herder of sheep and cattle and to guard the master's property. Early 19th century writings from that country refer to the dog as the Berger de Brie (Sheepdog of Brie), though they are believed to have originated near Picardy. In later times, the breed distinguished itself in wartimes as a guard dog and carrier of supplies. The Briard's acute sense of hearing made it invaluable at guard posts, where they served as sentries. In present day they are still found all over France herding sheep and cattle and guarding farms.

Briards have gained a strong foothold in Britain and in this country. The Briard Club of America was formed in 1928, adopting the standard established in France in 1900 by a group called Les Amis du Briard.

The Briard is square of build standing between 22 and 27 inches at the withers. Naturally drop-eared, in France the dogs' ears are cropped somewhat to make them stand semi-erect. The Briard's coat is rough textured, comprised of a hard, wavy outer coat that sheds water easily. It may be of any solid color with the exception of white, and in its native country is shown in two classes, black and colored. The Briard must possess two sets of dewclaws on the hindlegs, absence of these being cause for disqualification. Lack of claws is considered to reflect crossbreeding and corruption of the breed.

Briards are not demanding animals and make fine pets. They have a natural preference to stay close to home, confining their wanderings to the boundaries of the master's property. Essentially quiet animals, they will generally bark only when they feel property or master is being threatened.

Buyer's guide: The Briard is a longhaired breed, and therefore requires scheduled brushings. They are large and should not be asked to live in an apartment, but they are good natured enough not to protest their surroundings by barking or whining. Briards like to learn, but do so slowly, so be patient. Once they have mastered the rules of the house, they have good retentive powers and will not purposely violate their owner's wishes. They generally well mannered. Exercise is a must to bring out the their personality.

STANDARD FOR THE BRIARD

General Appearance: Vigorous and alert, powerful without coarseness, strong in bone and muscle, exhibiting the strength and agility required of the herding dog. Dogs lacking these qualities, however concealed by the coat, are to be penalized.

Character: A dog of handsome form. He is a dog at heart, with spirit and initiative, wise and fearless with no trace of timidity. Intelligent, easily trained, faithful, gentle and obedient, the Briard possesses an excellent memory and an ardent desire to please his master. He retains a high degree of his ancestral instinct to guard home and master. Although he is reserved with strangers, he is loving and loyal to those he knows. Some will display a certain independence.

Head: The head of a Briard always gives the impression of length, having sufficient width without being cumbersome. The correct length of a good head, measured from the occiput to the tip of the nose, is about forty (40%) per cent of the height of the dog at the withers. There is not objection to a slightly longer head, especially if the animal tends to a longer body line. The width of the head, as measured across the skull, is slightly less than the length of the skull from the occiput to the stop. Viewed from above, from the front or in profile, the fully-coated silhouette gives the impression of two rectangular forms, equal in length but differing in height and width, blending together rather abruptly. The larger rectangle is the skull and the other forms the muzzle. The topline of the muzzle is parallel to the topline of the skull, and the junction of the two forms a well-marked stop, which is midway between the occiput and the tip of the nose, and on a level with the eyes. The muzzle with mustache and beard is somewhat wide and terminates in a right angle. The muzzle must not be narrow or pointed. Although not clearly visible on the fully-coated head, the occiput is prominent and the forehead is very slightly rounded. The head joins the neck in a right angle and is held proudly alert. The head is sculptured in clean lines, without jowls or excess flesh on the sides, or under the eyes or temples. The lips are of medium thickness, firm of line and fitted neatly, without folds or flews at the corners. The lips are black. The head is well covered with hair which lies down, forming a natural part in the center. The eyebrows do not lie flat but, instead, arch up and out in a curve that lightly veils the eyes. The hair is never so abundant that it masks the form of the head or completely covers the eyes.

Nose: Square rather than round, always black with nostrils well opened. *Disqualification:* Any color other than black.

Teeth: Strong, white and adapting perfectly in a scissors bite.

Eyes: Eyes set well apart with the inner corners and outer corners on the same level. Large, well opened and calm, they must never be narrow or slanted. The gaze is frank, questioning and confident. The color must be black or black-brown with very dark pigmentation of the rim of the eyelids, whatever the color of the coat. *Disqualification:* Yellow eyes or spotted eyes.

Ears: The ears should be attached high, have thick leather and be firm at the base. Low-set ears cause the head to appear to be too arched. The length of the natural ear should be equal or slightly less than one-half the length of the head, always straight and covered with long hair. The natural ear must not lie flat against the head and, when alert, the ears are lifted slightly, giving a square look to the top of the skull. The ears when cropped should be carried upright and parallel, emphasizing the parallel lines of the head; when alert, they should face forward, well open with long hair falling over the opening. The cropped ear should be long, broad at the base, tapering gradually to a rounded tip.

Neck: Strong and well constructed, the neck is in the shape of a truncated cone, clearing the shoulders well. It is strongly muscled and has good length.

BODY:

Chest: The chest is broad and deep with moderately curved ribs, egg-shaped in form, the ribs not too rounded. The breastbone is moderately advanced in front, descending smoothly to the level of the elbows and shaped to give good depth to the chest. The abdomen is moderately drawn up but still presents good volume.

Topline: The Briard is constructed with a very slight incline, downward from the prominent withers to the back which is straight, to the broad loin and the croup which is slightly inclined. The topline is strong, never swayed nor roached.

Proportions: The Briard is not cobby in build. In males the length of the body, measured from the point of the shoulder to the point of the buttock, is equal to or slightly more than his height at the withers. The female may be a little longer.

Tail: Uncut, well feathered, forming a crook at the extremity, carried low and not deviating to the right or to the left. In repose, the bone of the tail descends to the joint of the hock, terminating in the crook, similar in shape to the printed letter "J" when viewed from the dog's right side. In action, the tail is raised in a harmonious curve, never going above the level of the back, except for the terminal crook. *Disqualification:* Tail non-existent or cut.

Legs: The legs are powerfully muscled with strong bone. Viewed from the front or rear, the legs are straight and parallel to the median line of the body, never turned inward or outward. The distance between the front legs is equal to the distance between the rear legs. The construction of the legs is of utmost importance, determining the dog's ability to work and his resistance to fatigue. The hindquarters are powerful, providing flexible, almost tireless movement.

Forequarters: Shoulder blades are long and sloping forming a 45-degree angle with the horizontal, firmly attached by strong muscles and blending smoothly with the withers. The forelegs are vertical when viewed from the side except the pasterns are very slightly inclined.

Hindquarters: The croup is well muscled and slightly sloped to give a well-rounded finish. The pelvis slopes at a 30-degree angle from the horizontal and forms a right angle with the upper leg bone. Viewed from the side, the legs are well angulated with the metatarsus slightly inclined, the hock making an angle of 135 degrees.

Feet: Strong and rounded, being slightly oval in shape. The feet travel straight forward in the line of movement. If the rear toes turn out very slightly when the hocks and metatarsus are parallel, then the position of the feet is correct. The nails are always black and hard. The pads are well developed, compact and elastic, covered with strong tissue. The toes are strong, well arched and compact.

Dewclaws: Two dewclaws are required on each rear leg, placed low on the leg, giving a wide base to the foot. Occasionally the nail may break off completely. The dog shall not be penalized for the missing nail so long as the digit itself is present. Ideally the dewclaws form additional functioning toes. Dewclaws on the forelegs may or may not be removed. *Disqualification:* Anything less than two dewclaws on each rear leg.

Coat: The outer coat is coarse, hard and dry (making a dry rasping sound between the fingers). It lies down flat, falling naturally in long, slightly waving locks, having the sheen of good health. On the shoulders the length of hair is generally six inches or more. The undercoat is fine and tight on all the body.

Color: All uniform colors are permitted except white. The colors are black, various shades of gray and various shades of tawny. The deeper shades of each color are preferred. Combinations of two of these colors are permitted, provided there are no marked spots and the transition from one color to another takes place gradually and symmetrically. The only permissible white: white hairs scattered throughout the coat and/or a white spot on the chest not to exceed one inch in diameter at the root of the hair. *Disqualification:* White coat. Spotted coat. White spot on chest exceeding one inch in diameter.

Gait: The well-constructed Briard is a marvel of supple power. His movement has been described as "quicksilver," permitting him to make abrupt turns, springing starts and sudden stops required of the sheep-herding dog. His gait is supple and light, almost like that of a large feline. The gait gives the impression that the dog glides along without touching the ground. Strong, flexible movement is essential to the sheep dog. He is above all a trotter, single-tracking, occasionally galloping and he frequently needs to change his speed to accomplish his work. His conformation is harmoniously balanced and strong to sustain him in the long day's work. Dogs with clumsy or inelegant gait must be penalized.

Size: Males 23 to 27 inches at the withers; bitches 22 to 25½ inches at the withers. *Disqualification:* All dogs and bitches under the minimum.

DISQUALIFICATIONS

Nose any color other than black.
Yellow eyes or spotted eyes.
Tail non-existent or cut.
Less than two dewclaws on each rear leg.
White coat.
Spotted coat.
White spot on chest exceeding one inch in diameter.
All dogs or bitches under the minimum size limits.

APPROVED FEBRUARY 8, 1975

Representing the breed: Ch. Jennie Del Postre, owned by Mary Lou Tingley. Photo by John L. Ashbey.

BULLMASTIFF

The Bullmastiff is a dog of both great size and great affection, a combination that makes this breed a very satisfying pet for those who like a big dog. While the Bullmastiff is sedate in temperament they command respect and are capable of any task asked of them. They respond quickly to human companionship and are eager to dispense kindness to those that take them into their lives.

The Bullmastiff is a "man-made" breed, originating from England in the early 19th century. The breed was developed to serve as a deterrent to land and game poachers who were ravaging the territories. A careful crossbreeding of the Bulldog (with their great tenacity and ferocity) and the Mastiff (with their great size and power) resulted in the Bullmastiff of today. The breed was designed to be able to run down, catch and hold a poacher without mauling. Because of this, they were originally referred to as a "holding dog" or "gamekeeper's dog."

The first Bullmastiffs imported to America were purchased by John D. Rockefeller to patrol his huge country estate in New York. Since that time the breed's steady, dependable nature has won them a loyal following. Through many generations of careful breeding, the Bullmastiff's legendary ferocity has been made a secondary characteristic that can be evidenced only in situations that warrant it—and heaven help the midnight prowler as he has met his match in the Bullmastiff!

Buyer's guide: If you are an apartment dweller that will only settle for a large dog, consider the Bullmastiff. They are by nature somewhat lazy, and do not demand a great amount of space despite their imposing size. They should be encouraged to exercise, however, as they need to keep in good condition. The Bullmastiff tends to favor one member of the family and is sometimes possessive of them. They are gentle to everyone they know, but their placidness does not go out to strangers.

STANDARD FOR THE BULLMASTIFF

General Appearance: That of a symmetrical animal, showing great strength; powerfully built but active. The dog is fearless yet docile, has endurance and alertness. The foundation breeding was 60% Mastiff and 40% Bulldog.

Head: Skull large, with a fair amount of wrinkle when alert; broad, with cheeks well developed. Forehead flat. Muzzle broad and deep; its length, in comparison with that of the entire head, approximately as 1 is to 3. Lack of foreface with nostrils set on top of muzzle is a reversion to the Bulldog and is very undesirable. Nose black with nostrils large and broad. Flews not too pendulous, stop moderate, and the mouth (bite) preferably level or slightly undershot. Canine teeth large and set wide apart. A dark muzzle is preferable.

Eyes: Dark and of medium size.

Ears: V-shaped and carried close to the cheeks, set on wide and high, level with occiput and cheeks, giving a square appearance to the skull; darker in color than the body and medium in size.

Neck: Slightly arched, of moderate length, very muscular, and almost equal in circumference to the skull.

Body: Compact. Chest wide and deep, with ribs well sprung and well set down between the forelegs. **Forequarters:** Shoulders muscular but not loaded, and slightly sloping. Forelegs straight, well boned and set well apart; elbows square. Pasterns straight, feet of medium size, with round toes well arched. Pads thick and tough, nails black. **Back:** Short, giving the impression of a well balanced dog. **Loins:** Wide, muscular and slightly arched, with fair depth of flank. **Hindquarters:** Broad and muscular with well developed second thigh denoting power, but not cumbersome. Moderate angulation at hocks. Cowhocks and splay feet are bad faults. **Tail:** Set on high, strong at the root and tapering to the hocks. It may be straight or curved, but never carried hound fashion.

Coat: Short and dense, giving good weather protection.

Color: Red, fawn or brindle. Except for a very small white spot on the chest, white marking is considered a fault.

Size: Dogs, 25 to 27 inches at the shoulder, and 110 to 130 pounds weight. Bitches, 24 to 26 inches at the shoulder, and 100 to 120 pounds weight. Other things being equal, the heavier dog is favored.

APPROVED FEBRUARY 6, 1960

COLLIE

The life story of the Collie is the history of pastoral life, for from the first day that man herded flocks he had a dog to help him. There is a similarity in character and appearance between the sheep and cattle dogs of all countries, which points to their common origin, while the cunning and outward look of all indicate their descent from the wild dogs of nature.

The Collie is considered superior to other dogs in instinct and intelligence, and his countenance discloses sagacity, alert eagerness, and devotion to his master. There is a great difference between the Collie of the bench shows and the old working Collie of the Highlands.

The Collie of the bench shows is a fancier's creation; a more graceful and beautiful animal does not exist. He was produced from the old working type, but remote crossings and selective breedings over the years have radically changed him so that he is now almost a breed of his own.

The working qualities of the bench show Collie have been so sadly neglected that they are all but lost. Certainly they are not to be compared in this respect with the Collie of the hills, bred on purely utilitarian lines. In appearance, however, the bench show Collie is a much handsomer and more attractive type, for the working dog is on the nondescript order. The latter vary in size and color; some are smooth coated, some are rough; some have prick ears, others half-dropped or drop; while many have what is known as a watch eye.

The rough-coated Collie is a purely Scottish-bred dog, and, like all varieties of sheep and cattle dogs used in pastoral life and agricultural pursuits, is of great antiquity. Indeed, it is generally assumed that of all the varieties of the domesticated dog, the Collie is one of the oldest. This idea has doubtless arisen from the fact that the Collie resembles the wild dog, and that there is a great similarity in form and character between the sheep and cattle dogs of all countries. The little differences may be accounted for by the

ROUGH COLLIE

SMOOTH COLLIE

variations in character of the different countries which call for dogs somewhat different in build, but all are more or less of the same type and character—the Dutch, German, Belgian, French, Spanish, etc.

The smooth-coated Collie is or should be an exact replica of his rough-coated brother in every detail and particular, but with a short, dense, double coat which looks smooth to the eye, but which is harsh and weather-resisting.

The smooth Collie, as an all around utility dog, probably cannot be excelled. His short, sleek, dense coat is undoubtedly an advantage to him over his rough brother in snowy weather, and is less cumbersome to carry. He is more difficult to breed to type because of his smooth coat, which lays bare an anatomy which a rough coat covers, and without which defects of body cannot be hidden in the smooth variety. The orthodox color of the smooth is much the same as in the rough-coated variety.

The chief points to look for in the selection of Collie puppies at from two to four months old and after are: great length of head, which should be level and wedge-shaped, but should not run into coarseness or width at the base of the skull, which should be narrow. Ears small; body short and round; tail short; forelegs straight. The biggest puppies are apt to be the best if they are not coarse, but possess the desired points. The foregoing applies to both rough and smooths, the latter requiring to be very smooth in coat, short but dense. The more coat the roughs have the better.

Buyer's guide: Due to their working dog heritage, the Collie is a very active dog and requires a substantial amount of exercise and room to move about in. If you are a city dweller and are stuck on the breed, try a Shetland Sheepdog instead. Collies have kind hearts and are very good with children. Their long coat will need a lot of attention; daily brushing is recommended to keep burrs and knots from ruining the flow of the coat. The smooth coated Collie requires little or no grooming.

STANDARD FOR THE COLLIE

General Character: The Collie is a lithe, strong, responsive dog, carrying no useless timber, standing naturally straight and firm. The deep, moderately wide chest shows strength, the sloping shoulders and well-bent hocks indicate speed and grace and the face shows high intelligence. The Collie presents an impressive, proud picture of true balance, each part being in harmonious proportion to every other part and to the whole. Except for the technical description that is essential to this Standard and without which no Standard for the guidance of breeders and judges is adequate, it could be stated simply that no part of the Collie ever seems to be out of proportion to any other part. Timidity, frailness, sullenness, viciousness, lack of animation, cumbersome appearance and lack of overall balance impair the general character.

Head: The head properties are of great importance. When considered in proportion to the size of the dog the head is inclined to lightness and never appears massive. A heavy-handed dog lacks the necessary bright, alert, full-of-sense look that contributes so greatly to expression.

Both in front and profile view the head bears a general resemblance to a well blunted lean wedge, being smooth and clean in outline and nicely balanced in proportion. On the sides it tapers gradually and smoothly from the ears to the end of the black nose, without being flared out in backskull (cheeky) or pinched in muzzle (snipey). In profile view the top of the backskull and the top of the muzzle lie in two approximately parallel, straight planes of equal length, divided by a very slight but perceptible stop or break.

A midpoint between the inside corners of the eyes (which is the center of a correctly placed stop) is the center of balance in length of head.

The end of the smooth, well rounded muzzle is blunt but not square. The under-jaw is strong, cleancut and the depth of skull from the brow to the under part of the jaw is not excessive.

The teeth are of good size, meeting in a scissors bite. Overshot or undershot jaws are undesirable, the latter being more severely penalized.

There is a very slight prominence of the eyebrows. The backskull is flat, without receding either laterally or backward and the occipital bone is not highly peaked. The proper width of backskull necessarily depends upon the combined length of skull and muzzle and the width of the backskull is less than its length. Thus, the correct width varies with the individual and is dependent upon the extent to which it is supported by length of muzzle.

Because of the importance of the head characteristics, prominent head faults are severely penalized.

Eyes: Because of the combination of the flat skull, the arched eyebrows, the slight stop and the rounded muzzle, the foreface must be chiseled to form a receptacle for the eyes and they are necessarily placed obliquely to give them the required forward outlook. Except for the blue merles, they are required to be matched in color. They are almond-shaped, of medium size and never properly appear to be large or prominent. The color is dark and the eye does not show a yellow ring or a sufficiently prominent haw to affect the dog's expression.

The eyes have a clear, bright appearance, expressing intelligent inquisitiveness, particularly when the ears are drawn up and the dog is on the alert.

In blue merles, dark brown eyes are preferable, but either or both eyes may be merle or china in color without specific penalty.

A large, round, full eye seriously detracts from the desired "sweet" expression. Eye faults are heavily penalized.

Ears: The ears are in proportion to the size of the head and, if they are carried properly and unquestionably "break" naturally, are seldom too small. Large ears usually cannot be lifted correctly off the head and even if lifted they will be out of proportion to the size of the head. When in repose the ears are folded lengthwise and thrown back into the frill. On the alert they are drawn well up on the backskull and are carried about three-quarters erect, with about one-fourth of the ear tipping or "breaking" forward. A dog with prick ears or low ears cannot show true expression and is penalized accordingly.

Neck: The neck is firm, clean, muscular, sinewy, and heavily frilled. It is fairly long, is carried upright with a slight arch at the nape and imparts a proud, upstanding appearance showing off the frill.

Body: The body is firm, hard and muscular, a trifle long in proportion to the height. The ribs are well-rounded behind the well-sloped shoulders and the chest is deep, extending to the elbows. The back is strong and level, supported by powerful hips and thighs and the croup is sloped to give a well-rounded finish. The loin is powerful and slightly arched. Noticeably fat dogs or dogs in poor flesh or with skin disease or with no undercoat are out of condition and are moderately penalized accordingly. In grown males, a monorchid or cryptorchid are disqualified.

Legs: The forelegs are straight and muscular, with a fair amount of bone considering the size of the dog. A cumbersome appearance is undesirable. Both narrow and wide placement are penalized. The forearm is moderately fleshy and the pasterns are flexible, but without weakness. The hind legs are less fleshy, are muscular at the thighs, very sinewy and the hocks and stifles are well bent. A cow-hocked dog or a dog with straight stifles is penalized. The comparatively small feet are approximately oval in shape. The soles are well padded and tough and the toes are well arched and close together. When the Collie is not in motion, the legs and feet are judged by allowing the dog to come to a natural stop in a standing position so that both the forelegs and the hind legs are placed well apart, with the feet extending straight forward. Excessive "posing" is undesirable.

Gait: Gait is sound. When the dog is moved at a slow trot toward an observer its straight front legs track comparatively close together at the ground. The front legs are not out at the elbows, do not "cross over" nor does the dog move with a choppy, pacing or rolling gait. When viewed from the rear the hind legs are straight, tracking comparatively close together at the ground. At a moderate trot the hind legs are powerful and propelling. Viewed from the side the reasonably long, "reaching" stride is smooth and even, keeping the back line firm and level.

As the speed of the gait is increased the Collie single tracks, bringing the front legs inward in a straight line from the shoulder toward the center line of the body and the hind legs inward in a straight line from the hip toward the center line of the body. The gait suggests effortless speed combined with the dog's herding heritage, requiring it to be capable of changing its direction of travel almost instantaneously.

Tail: The tail is moderately long, the bone reaching to the hock or below. It is carried low when the dog is quiet, the end having an upward twist or "swirl." When gaited or when the dog is excited it is carried gaily, but not over the back.

Coat: The well-fitting, proper-textured coat is the crowning glory of the Rough Variety of Collie. It is abundant except on the head and legs. The outer coat is straight and harsh to the touch. A soft, open outer coat or a curly outer coat, regardless of quantity is penalized. The under coat, however, is soft, furry and so close together that it is difficult to see the skin when the hair is parted. The coat is very abundant on the mane and frill. The face or mask is smooth. The forelegs are smooth and well-feathered to the back of the pasterns. The hind legs are smooth below the hock joints. Any feathering below the hocks is removed for the show ring. The hair on the tail is very profuse and on the hips it is long and bushy. The texture, quantity and the extent to which the coat "fits the dog" are important points.

Color: The four recognized colors are "Sable and White," "Tri-color," "Blue Merle" and "White." There is no preference among them. The "Sable and White" is predominantly sable (a fawn sable color of varying shades from light gold to dark mahogany) with white markings usually on the chest, neck, legs, feet and the tip of the tail. A blaze may appear on the foreface or backskull or both. The "Tri-color" is predominantly black, carrying white markings as in a sable and white and has tan shadings on and about the head and legs. The "Blue Merle" is a mottled or "marbled" color, predominantly blue-grey and black with white markings as in the "Sable and White" and usually has tan shadings as in the "Tri-color." The "White" is predominantly white, with sable, tri-color or blue merle markings.

Size: Dogs are from 24 to 26 inches at the shoulder and weigh from 60 to 75 pounds. Bitches are from 22 to 24 inches at the shoulder, weighing from 50 to 65 pounds. An undersize or an oversize Collie is penalized according to the extent to which the dog appears to be undersize or oversize.

Expression: Expression is one of the most important points in considering the relative value of Collies. "Expression," like the term "Character," is difficult to define in words. It is not a fixed point as in color, weight or height and it is something the uninitiated can properly understand only by optical illustration. In general, however it may be said to be the combined product of the shape and balance of the skull and muzzle, the placement, size, shape and color of the eyes, and the position, size and carriage of the ears. An expression that shows sullenness or which is suggestive of any other breed is entirely foreign. The Collie cannot be judged properly until its expression has been carefully evaluated.

Smooth Collie: The Smooth Variety of Collie is judged by the same Standard as the Rough Variety, except that the references to the quantity and distribution of the coat are not applicable to the Smooth Variety, which has a short, hard, dense, flat coat of good texture, with an abundance of undercoat.

DOBERMAN PINSCHER

The Doberman Pinscher has come a remarkably long way in a relatively short time, having skyrocketed to the height of popularity with both the dog show fancy and the general public. The breed came about in 1880 through the efforts of Herr Louis Dobermann, the local dog pound keeper in the town of Apolda, Germany. Herr Dobermann set out to produce the ideal guard dog from the stock he had at hand. His aim was to develop a fearless watchdog that was not only good looking and well proportioned, but also affectionate and a good housepet. He based the new breed on the old German Pinscher stock, using several other breeds (presumably Rottweilers, Great Danes, Manchester Terriers and German Shepherds) to create the "ideal dog." The German Pinscher was not a handsome dog, but was unmatched in fearlessness and ferocity. Carefully selected outcrosses were made to modify these tendencies and produce a black, medium-sized dog that was good tempered and attractive in appearance, yet obviously powerful and rather massive. The final result was the Doberman Pinscher, a breed whose working dog heritage is evident at the first glance.

The Doberman type became fixed very quickly. The Dobes of today are well built and muscular, and they have fulfilled Herr Dobermann's requirements of being lively, game, good tempered, courageous and devoted. Much notoriety—both good and bad—has gone to the breed's use as a watch and police dog. Doberman Pinschers *are* the ideal guard dog that Herr Dobermann had set out to produce. They are highly intelligent and take eagerly to obedience training, and while they have the capacity to attack or defend ferociously, they are by nature friendly and alert.

The Doberman Pinscher is a sleek and shapely dog that moves with grace and agility. In the home the Doberman is very attentive to his family and does not overreact or bestow his affection on everyone he meets. He is exceptionally loyal and will assume a position of guardian for anyone in his favor, and will not become hostile to outsiders without cause. He is naturally wary of strangers, but shows the reserve and patience that makes him an outstanding pet.

Buyer's guide: Many negative words have been spoken about the alleged ferocity of the Doberman Pinscher. Dobe owners believe that a good part of a dog's personality is shaped by the treatment of the dog by the owner. Well-bred Dobermans are not prone to violent outbursts, although unstable dogs from poor breeding stock can be found in this and every breed. They do need a large amount of daily exercise, however, for they can become somewhat high-strung if kept inactive. They are strong willed, reliable and very intelligent. They should be trained from an early age to the rules of the household and treated affectionately. Those people nervous or fearful of the Doberman should, of course, steer away from this breed as it is advisable that the owner be a firm disciplinarian and have a dominant personality. Little children who may taunt the dog should not be companions for the Doberman. A good dog for adults.

STANDARD FOR THE DOBERMAN PINSCHER

General Conformation and Appearance: The appearance is that of a dog of medium size, with a body that is square; the height, measured vertically from the ground to the highest point of the withers, equalling the length measured horizontally from the forechest to the rear projection of the upper thigh.

Height: at the withers—**Dogs:** 26 to 28 inches, ideal about 27½ inches; **Bitches:** 24 to 26 inches, ideal about 25½ inches. Length of head, neck and legs in proportion to length and depth of body. Compactly built, muscular and powerful, for great endurance and speed. Elegant in appearance, of proud carriage, reflecting great nobility and temperament. Energetic, watchful, determined, alert, fearless, loyal and obedient.

The judge shall dismiss from the ring any shy or vicious Doberman.

Shyness: A dog shall be judged fundamentally shy if, refusing to stand for examination, it shrinks away from the judge; if it fears an approach from the rear; if it shies at sudden and unusual noises to a marked degree.

Viciousness: A dog that attacks or attempts to attack either the judge or its handler, is definitely vicious. An aggressive or belligerent attitude towards other dogs shall not be deemed viciousness.

Head: Long and dry, resembling a blunt wedge in both frontal and profile views. When seen from the front, the head widens gradually toward the base of the ears in a practically unbroken line. Top of skull flat, turning with slight stop to bridge of muzzle, with muzzle line extending parallel to top line of skull. Cheeks flat and muscular. Lips lying close to jaws. Jaws full and powerful, well filled under the eyes.

Eyes: Almond shaped, moderately deep set, with vigorous, energetic expression. Iris, of uniform color, ranging from medium to darkest brown in black dogs; in reds, blues, and fawns the color of the iris blends with that of the markings, the darkest shade being preferable in every case.

Teeth: Strongly developed and white. Lower incisors upright and touching inside of upper incisors—a true scissors bite. *42 correctly placed teeth,* 22 in the lower, 20 in the upper jaw. Distemper teeth shall not be penalized. **Disqualifying Faults:** Overshot more than three-sixteenths of an inch. Undershot more than one-eighth of an inch. Four or more missing teeth.

Ears: Normally cropped and carried erect. The upper attachment of the ear, when held erect, is on a level with the top of the skull.

Neck: Proudly carried, well muscled and dry. Well arched, with nape of neck widening gradually toward body. Length of neck proportioned to body and head.

Body: Back short, firm, of sufficient width, and muscular at the loins, extending in a straight line from withers to the *slightly* rounded croup. **Withers:** pronounced and forming the highest point of the body. **Brisket:** reaching deep to the elbow. **Chest:** broad with forechest well defined. **Ribs:** well sprung from the spine, but flattened in lower end to permit elbow clearance. **Belly:** well tucked up, extending in a curved line from the brisket. **Loins:** wide and muscled. **Hips:** broad and in proportion to body, breadth of hips being approximately equal to breadth of body at rib cage and shoulders.

Tail: Docked at approximately second joint, appears to be a continuation of the spine, and is carried only slightly above the horizontal when the dog is alert.

Forequarters: **Shoulder Blade:** sloping forward and downward at a 45-degree angle to the ground meets the upper arm at an angle of 90 degrees. Height from elbow to withers approximately equals height from ground to elbow. **Legs:** seen from front and side, perfectly straight and parallel to each other from elbow to pastern; muscled and sinewy, with heavy bone. In normal pose and when gaiting, the elbows lie close to the brisket. **Pasterns:** firm and almost perpendicular to the ground. **Feet:** well arched, compact, and catlike, turning neither in nor out. Dewclaws may be removed.

Hindquarters: The angulation of the hindquarters balances that of the forequarters. **Hip Bone:** falls away from spinal column at an angle of about 30 degrees, producing a slightly rounded, well-filled-out croup. **Upper Shanks:** at right angles to the hip bones, are long, wide, and well muscled on both sides of thigh, with clearly defined stifles. Upper and lower shanks are of equal length. While the dog is at rest, hock to heel is perpendicular to the ground. Viewed from the rear, the legs are straight, parallel to each other, and wide enough apart to fit in with a properly built body. **Cat Feet:** as on front legs, turning neither in nor out. Dewclaws, if any, are generally removed.

Gait: Free, balanced, and vigorous, with good reach in the forequarters and good driving power in the hindquarters. When trotting, there is strong rear-action drive. Each rear leg moves in line with the foreleg on the same side. Rear and front legs are thrown neither in nor out. Back remains strong and firm. When moving at a fast trot, a properly built dog will single-track.

Coat, Color, Markings: **Coat,** smooth-haired, short, hard, thick and close lying. Invisible gray undercoat on neck permissible. **Allowed Colors:** Black, red, blue, and fawn (Isabella). **Markings:** Rust, sharply defined, appearing above each eye and on muzzle, throat and forechest, on all legs and feet, and below tail. **Nose:** Solid black on black dogs, dark brown on red ones, dark gray on blue ones, dark tan on fawns. White patch on chest, not exceeding ½ square inch, permissible.

FAULTS

The foregoing description is that of the ideal Doberman Pinscher. Any deviation from the above described dog must be penalized to the extent of the deviation.

DISQUALIFICATIONS

Overshot more than three-sixteenths of an inch; undershot more than one-eighth of an inch. Four or more missing teeth.

APPROVED OCTOBER 14, 1969

GERMAN SHEPHERD DOG

The interest in this remarkable breed of dogs has developed so rapidly that we are gratified at being able to present this authoritative article by Jay Hall, one of the most successful exhibitors of the breed in this country:

This native German breed resembling the wolf in general appearance is known throughout the world by many different names. Commonly called the Police Dog, by reason of the large number used in night patrol duty on the police force, it is known in England as the Alsatian Wolf Dog. It is often referred to as the Belgian Police Dog and as the French Police Dog.

The breed is known in Germany as the *Deutscher Schaferhund* (or German Shepherd Dog), but when trained for police duty is designated as the *Policeihund* or police dog. It has been stated that as early as 1911 more than 400 police stations in Germany had been provided with specially-trained dogs of this species.

Primarily a herding dog descended from the long-haired dogs of

South Germany, he lends himself to training of varied character. A nose hunter, keen of scent, he makes an admirable trailer of man or game. He, by reason of his close and constant companionship with man, is generally obedient and sagacious. His physical makeup adapts him to tireless sustained effort, and the breeders responsible for the fixed type that exists wisely provided for a combination that, while it preserves a certain beauty of outline, has lost nothing in usefulness as a working dog. The German Shepherd has been found readily adapted to training both for Red Cross and police purposes, and has been used extensively in these fields.

No breed of dog has gained more favor more quickly with the public than has this breed in America. From obscurity in 1904, when the breed was first introduced into the United States, today the breed ranks third in popularity.

Perhaps the greatest misnomer on the part of the uninformed public regarding the true and natural disposition of dogs of this breed is a natural result of the commonly given name, "Police Dog." By nature the Shepherd is quick, affectionate, intelligent, faithful, of fine mind and memory, devoted to its master and zealous in his interest. It is these very attributes that constitute a fine groundwork for the training of certain of these dogs for police service.

It is well then to consider that the true dog of the breed is a shepherd by type, and that only specialized training transforms him to a police dog. As a police dog his fine basic characteristics are accentuated and developed to a point of usefulness for the particular work at hand.

The idea of using dogs for civic protection is by no means new. Louis XI, who ruled France early in the 15th century, provided the famous town of Mont St. Michel with a dog corps, and St. Malo, close by, was protected in a similar manner.

While it is generally recorded that the city of Ghent in Belgium was the first city to establish a systematic and regular school for the training of police dogs and putting them into local service after training them, it is claimed that the honor of introducing the modern police dog on the continent really belongs to Dr. Gerland, who introduced the practice at Hildesheim, Germany, early in 1896. In the training and instruction of these dogs for police duty they are taught to seize an object without seriously hurting it; to hunt for vagabonds and defend the uniforms; not to accept anything from strangers nor to be petted by them; to guard an object placed on the ground; to keep individuals at bay without biting until human help arrives, but to attack if necessary if flight is attempted; to follow through a house where dwellings or buildings require searchings; not to be afraid of firearms; to run into alleys, behind houses and outbuildings, and into many places where the human eye could not see unless provided with a light; to follow his master with or without a leash at distances ranging to a maximum of 150 feet; to bark loudly to announce a find. These dogs are finally trained to respect and protect a police uniform, and seem instinctively to know the uniform. If a man attacks its master, the dog becomes furious and savage, and often jumps at the throat of the aggressor. After their training is completed and when they are not on active duty they remain in their kennels all day, seeing only the trainers who care for them, and as they are on duty throughout the night, they have no means of becoming familiar with the public. The first essential of training this breed is to teach absolute obedience.

The following essentials are enumerated as necessary in their training for police use: A dog must be taught to give tongue when quarry is found or breaks from cover on a run, to curb its hunting instincts and stop abruptly at cry or whistle of command. Where resistance is offered it is taught to leap at the wrist or throat of the culprit, and while prowling by itself to rout from bushes or shadows all marauders.

The dog's early education for police service leads him to suspect all strangers. He cannot be intimidated, coaxed or lured. He will refuse all food when offered by strangers, even though he may be extremely hungry. A properly trained police dog is irreproachable in morals, mien and manners. He will face pistol fire unflinchingly and leap savagely to attack. A well-trained dog will easily clear a seven-foot obstacle, and can broad-jump a small stream or creek twelve to fifteen feet across. The dog's education enables him to ferret out hidden goods, to find coins that have been dropped; in fact to search out every clue of the criminal that may be of service in leading to his eventual discovery and arrest. These dogs are quick to sense the presence of criminals with whom they have had previous contact, and have been known to pick men out of a crowd under these conditions.

We would again forcefully call to the reader's attention the fact that these characteristics are peculiar to those of the breed trained for this special duty or purpose. The well-bred German Shepherd whether trained for police work or as pet, is an admirable companion, loyal, affectionate, well mannered, obedient and in no way savage or solitary.

Buyer's guide: Active people who want a large, active dog will do well to choose the German Shepherd Dog. They are a most intelligent and reliable breed, capable of defending their home and willing to do anything for their owners. Although they tend to be quite mischievous as puppies, they generally settle down at about one year of age. They are very strong and need adequate space to move and run around in, so apartment life is not recommended. German Shepherds have been known to get overexcited in play situations, so some good, thorough obedience training is advised. Although they are large eaters, they present no expense for grooming as a thorough brushing now and then should be sufficient. Not recommended around young children.

STANDARD FOR THE GERMAN SHEPHERD DOG

General Appearance: The first impression of a good German Shepherd Dog is that of a strong, agile, well-muscled animal, alert and full of life. It is well balanced, with harmonious development of the forequarter and hindquarter. The dog is longer than tall, deep-bodied, and presents an outline of smooth curves rather than angles. It looks substantial and not spindly, giving the impression, both at rest and in motion, of muscular fitness and nimbleness without any look of clumsiness or soft living. The ideal dog is stamped with a look of quality and nobility—difficult to define, but unmistakable when present. Secondary sex characteristics are strongly marked, and every animal gives a definite impression of masculinity or femininity, according to its sex.

Character: The breed has a distinct personality marked by direct and fearless, but not hostile, expression, self-confidence and a certain aloofness that does not lend itself to immediate and indiscriminate friendships. The dog must be approachable, quietly standing its ground and showing confidence and willingness to meet overtures without itself making them. It is poised, but when the occasion demands, eager and alert; both fit and willing to serve in its capacity as companion, watchdog, blind leader, herding dog, or guardian, whichever the circumstances may demand. The dog must not be timid, shrinking behind its master or handler; it should not be nervous, looking about or upward with anxious expression or showing nervous reactions, such as tucking of tail, to strange sounds or sights. Lack of confidence under any surroundings is not typical of good character. Any of the above deficiencies in character which indicate shyness must be penalized as very serious faults, and any dog exhibiting pronounced indications of these must be excused from the ring. It must be possible for the judge to observe the teeth and to determine that both testicles are descended. Any dog that attempts to bite the judge must be disqualified. The ideal dog is a working animal with an incorruptible character combined with body and gait suitable for the arduous work that constitutes its primary purpose.

Head: The head is noble, cleanly chiseled, strong without coarseness, but above all not fine, and in proportion to the body. The head of the male is distinctly masculine, and that of the bitch distinctly feminine. The muzzle is long and strong with the lips firmly fitted, and its topline is parallel to the topline of the skull. Seen from the front, the forehead is only moderately arched, and the skull slopes into the long, wedge-shaped muzzle without abrupt stop. Jaws are strongly developed. **Ears:** Ears are moderately pointed, in proportion to the skull, open toward the front, and carried erect when at attention, the ideal carriage being one in which the center lines of the ears, viewed from the front, are parallel to each other and perpendicular to the ground. A dog with cropped or hanging ears must be disqualified. **Eyes:** Of medium size, almond shaped, set a little obliquely and not protruding. The color is as dark as possible. The expression keen, intelligent and composed. **Teeth:** 42 in number—20 upper and 22 lower—are strongly developed and meet in a scissors bite in which part of the inner surface of the upper incisors meet and engage part of the outer surface of the lower incisors. An overshot jaw or a level bite is undesirable. An undershot jaw is a disqualifying fault. Complete dentition is to be preferred. Any missing teeth other than first premolars is a serious fault.

Neck: The neck is strong and muscular, clean-cut and relatively long, proportionate in size to the head and without loose folds of skin. When the dog is at attention or excited, the head is raised and the neck carried high; otherwise typical carriage of the head is forward rather than up and but little higher than the top of the shoulder, particularly in motion.

Forequarters: The shoulder blades are long and obliquely angled, laid on flat and not placed forward. The upper arm joins the shoulder blade at about a right angle. Both the upper arm and the shoulder blade are well muscled. The forelegs, viewed from all sides, are straight and the bone oval rather than round. The pasterns are strong and springy and angulated at approximately a 25-degree angle from the vertical.

Feet: The feet are short, compact, with toes well arched, pads thick and firm, nails short and dark. The dewclaws, if any, should be removed from the hind legs. Dewclaws on the forelegs may be removed, but are normally left on.

Proportion: The German Shepherd Dog is longer than tall, with the most desirable proportion as 10 to 8½. The desired height for males at the top of the highest point of the shoulder blade is 24 to 26 inches; and for bitches, 22 to 24 inches. The length is measured from the point of the prosternum or breastbone to the rear edge of the pelvis, the ischial tuberosity.

Body: The whole structure of the body gives an impression of depth and solidity without bulkiness. **Chest:** Commencing at the prosternum, it is well filled and carried well down between the legs. It is deep and capacious, never shallow, with ample room for lungs and heart, carried well forward, with the prosternum showing ahead of the shoulder in profile. **Ribs:** Well sprung and long, neither barrel-shaped nor too flat, and carried down to a sternum which reaches to the elbows. Correct ribbing allows the elbows to move back freely when the dog is at a trot. Too round causes interference and throws the elbows out; too flat or short causes pinched elbows. Ribbing is carried well back so that the loin is relatively short. **Abdomen:** Firmly held and not paunchy. The bottom line is only moderately tucked up in the loin.

Topline: **Withers:** The withers are higher than and sloping into the level back. **Back:** The back is straight, very strongly developed without sag or roach, and relatively short. The desirable long proportion is not derived from a long back, but from over-all length with relation to height, which is achieved by length of forequarter and length of withers and hindquarter, viewed from the side. **Loin:** Viewed from the top, broad and strong. Undue length between the last rib and the thigh, when viewed from the side, is undesirable. **Croup:** Long and gradually sloping.

Tail: Bushy, with the last vertebra extended at least to the hock joint. It is set smoothly into the croup and low rather than high. At rest, the tail hangs in a slight curve like a saber. A slight hook—sometimes carried to one side—is faulty only to the extent that it mars general appearance. When the dog is excited or in motion, the curve is accentuated and the tail raised, but it should never be curled forward beyond a vertical line.

Tails too short, or with clumpy ends due to ankylosis, are serious faults. A dog with a docked tail must be disqualified.

Hindquarters: The whole assembly of the thigh, viewed from the side, is broad, with both upper and lower thigh well muscled, forming as nearly as possible a right angle. The upper thigh bone parallels the shoulder blade while the lower thigh bone parallels the upper arm. The metatarsus (the unit between the hock joint and the foot) is short, strong and tightly articulated.

Gait: A German Shepherd Dog is a trotting dog, and its structure has been developed to meet the requirements of its work. **General Impression:** The gait is outreaching, elastic, seemingly without effort, smooth and rhythmic covering the maximum amount of ground with the mimimum number of steps. At a walk it covers a great deal of ground, with long stride of both hind legs and forelegs. At a trot the dog covers still more ground with even longer stride, and moves powerfully but easily, with co-ordination and balance so that the gait appears to be the steady motion of a well-lubricated machine. The feet travel close to the ground on both forward reach and backward push. In order to achieve ideal movement of this kind, there must be good muscular development and ligamentation. The hindquarters deliver, through the back, a powerful forward thrust which slightly lifts the whole animal and drives the body forward. Reaching far under, and passing the imprint left by the front foot, the hind foot takes hold of the ground; then hock, stifle and upper thigh come into play and sweep back, the stroke of the hind leg finishing with the foot still close to the ground in a smooth follow-through. The over-reach of the hindquarter usually necessitates one hind foot passing outside and the other hind foot passing inside the track of the forefeet, and such action is not faulty unless the locomotion is crabwise with the dog's body sideways out of the normal straight line.

Transmission: The typical smooth, flowing gait is maintained with great strength and firmness of back. The whole effort of the hindquarters is transmitted to the forequarter through the loin, back and withers. At full trot, the back must remain firm and level without sway, roll, whip or roach. Unlevel topline with withers lower than the hip is a fault. To compensate for the forward motion imparted by the hindquarters, the shoulder should open to its full extent. The forelegs should reach out close to the ground in a long stride in harmony with that of the hindquarters. The dog does not track on widely separated parallel lines, but brings the feet inward toward the middle line of the body when trotting in order to maintain balance. The feet track closely but do not strike or cross over. Viewed from the front, the front legs function from the shoulder joint to the pad in a straight line. Viewed from the rear, the hind legs function from the hip joint to the pad in a straight line. Faults of gait, whether from front, rear or side, are to be considered very serious faults.

Color: The German Shepherd Dog varies in color, and most colors are permissible. Strong rich colors are preferred. Nose black. Pale, washed-out colors and blues or livers are serious faults. A white dog or a dog with a nose that is not predominantly black, must be disqualified.

Coat: The ideal dog has a double coat of medium length. The outer coat should be as dense as possible, hair straight, harsh and lying close to the body. A slightly wavy outer coat, often of wiry texture, is permissible. The head, including the inner ear and foreface, and the legs and paws are covered with short hairs, and the neck with longer and thicker hair. The rear of the forelegs and hind legs has somewhat longer hair extending to the pastern and hock, respectively. Faults in coat include soft, silky, too long outer coat, woolly, curly, and open coat.

DISQUALIFICATIONS

Cropped or hanging ears.
Undershot jaw.
Docked tail.
White dogs.
Dogs with noses not predominantly black.
Any dog that attempts to bite the judge.

APPROVED APRIL 9, 1968

GIANT SCHNAUZER

As the name implies, the Giant Schnauzer is the largest of the three Schnauzer breeds. They originated in southern Bavaria, where they were called *Riesenschnauzers*. The term *schnauzer* translates to *snout*, which is the characteristic that is most emphasized in these breeds. Their prominent whiskers draw attention to their elongated yet muscular muzzle.

The Giant Schnauzer was produced from crossing the Standard Schnauzer with the larger rough-coated shepherd dogs of the region, particularly the Bouvier des Flandres and the black Great Dane. These combinations produced a dog of tremendous physical hardiness and strength whose courage and faithfulness has made him fit for even the roughest of military and police work.

Compared to the popularity of the other two Schnauzer breeds, the Giant is relatively rare in the United States. He is a high spirited animal who needs plenty of exercise to keep in top condition. The breed is not as snappy as many of the terriers in their ancestry, and Giants adapt quickly to a family. They make formidable and ferocious watchdogs, but can be trusted to be very affectionate and amiable. They do not take easily to being penned up or kept in close quarters and should be allowed to have long runs frequently to increase stamina and insure good health.

Buyer's guide: Since they are very large and active, they must be kept only by people equipped with adequate space to handle the exercising requirements of the breed. They are alert and very intelligent, but their tendency towards gameness should rule them out as companions for small children. Giant Schnauzers are high-spirited and can be years of fun for adult companions who like to be on the go.

STANDARD FOR THE GIANT SCHNAUZER

General Description: The Giant Schnauzer should resemble, as nearly as possible, in general appearance, a larger and more powerful version of the Standard Schnauzer, on the whole a bold and valiant figure of a dog. Robust, strongly built, nearly square in proportion of body length to height at withers, active, sturdy, and well muscled. Temperament which combines spirit and alertness with intelligence and reliability. Composed, watchful, courageous, easily trained, deeply loyal to family, playful, amiable in repose, and a commanding figure when aroused. The sound, reliable temperament, rugged build and dense weather-resistant wiry coat make for one of the most useful, powerful, and enduring working breeds.

Head: Strong, rectangular in appearance, and elongated; narrowing slightly from the ears to the eyes, and again from the eyes to the tip of the nose. The total length of the head is about one-half the length of the back (withers to set-on of tail). The head matches the sex and substance of the dog. The top line of the muzzle is parallel to the top line of the skull; there is a slight stop which is accentuated by the eyebrows.

Skull: (Occiput to Stop). Moderately broad between the ears; occiput not too prominent. Top of skull flat; skin unwrinkled.

Cheeks: Flat, but with well-developed chewing muscles; there is no "cheekiness" to disturb the rectangular head appearance (with beard).

Muzzle: Strong and well filled under the eyes; both parallel and equal in length to the topskull; ending in a moderately blunt wedge. The nose is large, black, and full. The lips are tight, and not overlapping, black in color.

Bite: A full complement of sound white teeth (6/6 incisors, 2/2 canines, 8/8 premolars, 4/6 molars) with a scissors bite. The upper and lower jaws are powerful and well formed. **Disqualifying Faults:** Overshot or undershot.

Ears: When cropped, identical in shape and length with pointed tips. They are in balance with the head and are not exaggerated in length. They are set high on the skull and carried perpendicularly at the inner edge with as little bell as possible along the other edges. When uncropped, the ears are V-shaped button ears of medium length and thickness, set high and carried rather high and close to the head.

Eyes: Medium size, dark brown, and deep-set. They are oval in appearance and keen in expression with lids fitting tightly. Vision is not impaired nor eyes hidden by too long eyebrows.

Neck: Strong and well arched, of moderate length, blending cleanly into the shoulders, and with the skin fitting tightly at the throat; in harmony with the dog's weight and build.

Body: Compact, substantial, short-coupled, and strong, with great power and agility. The height at the highest point of the withers equals the body length from breastbone to point of rump. The loin section is well developed, as short as possible for compact build.

Forequarters: The forequarters have flat, somewhat sloping shoulders and high withers. Forelegs are straight and vertical when viewed from all sides with strong pasterns and good bone. They are separated by a fairly deep brisket which precludes a pinched front. The elbows are set close to the body and point directly backwards.

Chest: Medium in width, ribs well sprung but with no tendency toward a barrel chest; oval in cross section; deep through the brisket. The breastbone is plainly discernible, with strong forechest; the brisket descends at least to the elbows, and ascends gradually toward the rear with the belly moderately drawn up. The ribs spread gradually from the first rib so as to allow space for the elbows to move close to the body.

Shoulders: The sloping shoulder blades (scapulae) are strongly muscled, yet flat. They are well laid back so that from the side the rounded upper ends are in a nearly vertical line above the elbows. They slope well forward to the point where they join the upper arm (humerus), forming as nearly as possible a right angle. Such an angulation permits the maximum forward extension of the forelegs without binding or effort. Both shoulder blades and upper arm are long, permitting depth of chest at the brisket.

Back: Short, straight, strong and firm.

Tail: The tail is set moderately high and carried high in excitement. It should be docked to the second or not more than the third joint (approximately one and one-half to about three inches long at maturity).

Hindquarters: The hindquarters are strongly muscled, in balance with the forequarters; upper thighs are slanting and well bent at the stifles, with the second thighs (tibiae) approximately parallel to an extension of the upper neckline. The legs from the hock joint to the feet are short, perpendicular to the ground while the dog is standing naturally, and from the rear parallel to each other. The hindquarters do not appear over-built or higher than the shoulders. Croup full and slightly rounded.

Feet: Well-arched, compact and catlike, turning neither in nor out, with thick tough pads and dark nails.

Dewclaws: Dewclaws, if any, on hind legs should be removed; on the forelegs, may be removed.

Gait: The trot is the gait at which movement is judged. Free, balanced and vigorous, with good reach in the forequarters and good driving power in the hindquarters. Rear and front legs are thrown neither in nor out. When moving at a fast trot, a properly built dog will single-track. Back remains strong, firm, and flat.

Coat: Hard, wiry, very dense; composed of a soft undercoat and a harsh outer coat which, when seen against the grain, stands slightly up off the back, lying neither smooth nor flat. Coarse hair on top of head; harsh beard and eyebrows, the Schnauzer hallmark.

Color: Solid black or pepper and salt.

Black: A truly pure black. A small white spot on the breast is permitted.

Pepper and Salt: Outer coat of a combination of banded hairs (white with black and black with white) and some black and white hairs, appearing gray from a short distance. *Ideally:* an intensely pigmented medium gray shade with "peppering" evenly distributed throughout the coat, and a gray undercoat. *Acceptable:* all shades of pepper and salt from dark iron-gray to silver-gray. Every shade of coat has a dark facial mask to emphasize the expression; the color of the mask harmonizes with the shade of the body coat. Eyebrows, whiskers, cheeks, throat, chest, legs, and under tail are lighter in color but include "peppering."

Height: The height of the withers of the male is 25½ to 27½ inches, and of the female, 23½ to 25½ inches, with the mediums being desired. Size alone should never take precedence over type, balance, soundness, and temperament. It should be noted that too small dogs generally lack the power and too large dogs, the agility and maneuverabiltiy, desired in a working dog.

FAULTS

The foregoing description is that of the ideal Giant Schnauzer. Any deviation from the above described dog must be penalized to the extent of the deviation.

The judge shall dismiss from the ring any shy or vicious Giant Schnauzer.

Shyness: A dog shall be judged fundamentally shy if, refusing to stand for examination, it repeatedly shrinks away from the judge; if it fears unduly any approach from the rear; if it shies to a marked degree at sudden and unusual noises.

Viciousness: A dog that attacks or attempts to attack either the judge or its handler, is definitely vicious. An aggressive or belligerent attitude towards other dogs shall not be deemed viciousness.

DISQUALIFICATIONS

Overshot or undershot.

APPROVED FEBRUARY 13, 1971

Representing the breed: Int. Ch. Lillemarks Kobusch, owned by Sylvia Hammarstrom.

GREAT DANE

The Great Dane, or Boarhound as it was formerly called, is of ancient type, and there are coins which were made before the Christian era that bear the impression of a large, powerful dog of the general proportions and appearance of the Great Dane.

In very early times the Dane-like dogs were used as protectors of property and person, as well as hunters. A stronger type of dog present at this time was designated the Ulmer Mastiff and no interbreeding was permitted. It wasn't until the 10th century that the Germans developed and set the conformation type of the Great Dane as we know it today. These early specimens, most likely steel-blue or gray in color, were used mainly to hunt the wild boars that were common to the German and Austrian countryside.

During the next few centuries the breed type was refined and fixed. German breeders worked hard to promote and encourage the breed's propagation upon strict guidelines set down by a national breed club. Today's beautifully proportioned Great Danes reflect the careful breeding that has gone into their making. They are remarkably well coordinated despite their imposing size and they are graceful, speedy runners.

The disposition of the Great Dane, like that of most dogs, is naturally docile, although dogs vary in their temperaments. This gentleness should be fostered when young, at which time the character of the dog is to a great extent formed.

Buyer's guide: Unless you can give your Great Dane a large space to exercise himself, don't even consider owning such a big dog. They need vigorous *daily* exercise—and there's no way around it. They are large eaters, naturally, and enjoy a spirited round of play as much as any breed. They may be a little too big and enthusiastic to be children's companions as they could end up inadvertently hurting their playmates, but their nature is to be affectionate and outgoing. Active, athletic individuals are best suited for owning the Great Dane. Do not let little children hold the leash on the Great Dane—it is dangerous simply because the dog could run off to greet a friend—and drag the child helplessly behind. Great Danes should not be owned by those who selfishly choose this breed because they think a tall, sleek dog is fashionable—proper living conditions are a *must* for these large workers.

STANDARD FOR THE GREAT DANE
STANDARD OF POINTS

1. General Conformation
    (a) General appearance..............................10
    (b) Color and markings.............................8
    (c) Size...5
    (d) Condition of coat..............................4
    (e) Substance 3 30

2. Movement
    (a) Gait 10

    (b) Rear end (croup, legs, paws)..........................10
    (c) Front end (shoulders, legs, paws)....................8 28
3. **Head**
    (a) Head conformation...................................12
    (b) Teeth..4
    (c) Eyes (nose and ears).................................4 20
4. **Torso**
    (a) Neck...6
    (b) Loin and back..6
    (c) Chest..4
    (d) Ribs and brisket.....................................4 20
5. **Tail**   2
    TOTAL..100

1. GENERAL CONFORMATION....................30 points

(a) **General Appearance (10 points):** The Great Dane combines in its distinguished appearance dignity, strength and elegance with great size and a powerful, well-formed, smoothly muscled body. He is one of the giant breeds, but is unique in that his general conformation must be so well balanced that he never appears clumsy and is always a unit—the Apollo of dogs. He must be spirited and courageous—never timid. He is friendly and dependable. This physical and mental combination is the characteristic which gives the Great Dane the majesty possessed by no other breed. It is particularly true of this breed that there is an impression of great masculinity in dogs as compared to an impression of femininity in bitches. The male should appear more massive throughout than the bitch, with larger frame and heavier bone. In the ratio between length and height, the Great Dane should appear as square as possible. In bitches, a somewhat longer body is permissible. **Faults:** Lack of unity; timidity; bitchy dogs; poor musculature; poor bone development; out of condition; rickets; doggy bitches.

(b) **Color and Markings (8 points)**

(i) Color: Brindle Danes. Base color ranging from light golden yellow to deep golden yellow always brindled with strong black cross stripes. The more intensive the base color and the more intensive the brindling, the more attractive will be the color. Small white marks at the chest and toes are not desirable. **Faults:** Brindle with too dark a base color; silver-blue and grayish-blue base color; dull (faded) brindling; white tail tip.

(ii) Fawn Danes. Golden yellow up to deep golden yellow color with a deep black mask. The golden deep-yellow color must always be given

the preference. Small white spots at the chest and toes are not desirable. **Faults:** Yellowish-gray, bluish-yellow, grayish-blue, dirty yellow color (drab color), lack of black mask.

(iii) Blue Danes. The color must be a pure steel blue, as far as possible without any tinge of yellow, black or mouse gray. **Faults:** Any deviation from a pure steel-blue coloration. Small white marks at the chest and toes are not desirable.

(iv) Black Danes. Glossy black. **Faults:** Yellow-black, brown-black or blue-black. White markings, such as stripes on the chest, speckled chest and markings on the paws are permitted but not desirable.

(v) Harlequin Danes. Base color: pure white with black torn patches irregularly and well distributed over the entire body; pure white neck preferred. The black patches should never be large enough to give the appearance of a blanket nor so small as to give a stippled or dappled effect. (Eligible, but less desirable, are a few small gray spots; also pointings where instead of a pure white base with black spots, there is a white base with single black hairs showing through which tend to give a salt and pepper or dirty effect.) **Faults:** White base color with a few large spots; bluish-gray pointed background.

(c) Size (5 points): The male should not be less than 30 inches at the shoulders, but it is preferable that he be 32 inches or more, providing he is well proportioned to his height. The female should not be less than 28 inches at the shoulders, but it is preferable that she be 30 inches or more, providing she is well proportioned to her height.

(d) Condition of Coat (4 points): The coat should be very short and thick, smooth, and glossy, **Faults:** Excessively long hair (stand-off coat); dull hair (indicating malnutrition, worms and negligent care).

Substance (3 points): Substance is that sufficiency of bone and muscle which rounds out a balance with the frame. **Faults:** Lightweight whippety Danes; coarse, ungainly proportioned Danes—always there should be balance.

2. MOVEMENT.................................28 points

(a) Gait (10 points): Long, easy, springy stride with no tossing or rolling of body. The back line should move smoothly, parallel to the ground. The gait of the Great Dane should denote strength and power. The rear legs should have drive. The forelegs should track smoothly and straight. The Dane should track in two parallel straight lines. **Faults:** Short steps. The rear quarters should not pitch. The forelegs should not have a hackney gait (forced or choppy stride). When moving rapidly the Great Dane should not pace for the reason that it causes excessive side-to-side rolling of the body and thus reduces endurance.

(b) Rear End (Croup, Legs, Paws) (10 points): The croup must be full, slightly drooping and must continue imperceptibly to the tail root. **Faults:** A croup which is too straight; a croup which slopes downward too steeply; and too narrow a croup.

Hind legs, the first thighs (from hip joint to knee) are broad and muscular. The second thighs (from knee to hock joint) are strong and long. Seen from the side, the angulation of the first thigh with the body, of the second thigh with the first thigh, and the pastern root with the second thigh should be very moderate, neither too straight nor too exaggerated. Seen from the rear, the hock joints appear to be perfectly straight, turned neither towards the inside nor towards the outside. **Faults:** Hind legs: Soft flabby, poorly muscled thighs; cowhocks which are the result of the hock joint turning inward and the hock and rear paws turning outward; barrel legs, the result of the hock joints being too far apart; steep rear. As seen from the side, a steep rear is the result of the angles of the rear legs forming almost a straight line; overangulation is the result of exaggerated angles between the first and second thighs and the hocks and is very conducive to weakness. The rear legs should never be too long in proportion to the front legs.

Paws: Round and turned neither toward the inside nor toward the outside. Toes short, highly arched and well closed. Nails short, strong and as dark as possible. **Faults:** Spreading toes (splay foot); bent, long toes (rabbit paws); toes turned toward the outside or toward the inside. Furthermore, the fifth toe on the hind legs appearing at a higher position and with wolf's claw or spur; excessively long nails; light-colored nails.

(c) Front End (Shoulders, Legs, Paws) (8 points): *Shoulders:* The shoulder blades must be strong and sloping and seen from the side, must form as nearly as possible a right angle in its articulation with the humerus (upper arm) to give a long stride. A line from the upper tip of the shoulder to the back of the elbow joint should be as nearly perpendicular as possible. Since all dogs lack a clavicle (collar bone) the ligaments and muscles holding the shoulder blade to the rib cage must be well developed, firm and secure to prevent loose shoulders. **Faults:** steep shoulders, which occur if the shoulder blade does not slope sufficiently; overangulation; loose shoulders which occur if the Dane is flabby muscled, or if the elbow is turned toward the outside; loaded shoulders.

Forelegs: The upper arm should be strong and muscular. Seen from the side or front, the strong lower arms run absolutely straight to the pastern joints. Seen from the front, the forelegs and the pastern roots should form perpendicular lines to the ground. Seen from the side, the pastern root should slope only very slightly forward. **Faults:** Elbows turned toward the inside or toward the outside, the former position caused mostly by too narrow or too shallow a chest, bringing the front legs too closely together and at the same time turning the entire lower part of the leg outward; the latter position causes the front legs to spread too far apart, with the pastern roots and paws usually turned inwards. Seen from the side, a considerable bend in the pastern toward the front indicates weakness and is in most cases connected with stretched and spread toes (splay foot); seen from the side, a forward bow in the forearm (chair leg); an excessively knotty bulge in the front of the pastern joint.

Paws: Round and turned neither toward the inside nor toward the outside. Toes short, highly arched and well closed. Nails short, strong and as dark as possible. **Faults:** Spreading toes (splay foot), bent, long toes (rabbit paws); toes turned toward the outside or toward the inside; light-colored nails.

3. HEAD..20 points

(a) Head Conformation (12 points): Long, narrow, distinguished, expressive, finely chiseled, especially the part below the eyes (which means that the skull plane under and to the inner point of the eye must slope without any bony protuberance in a pleasing line to the full square jaw), with strongly pronounced stop. The masculinity of the male is very pronounced in the expression and structure of head (this subtle difference should be evident in the dog's head through massive skull and depth of muzzle); the bitch's head may be more delicately formed. Seen from the side, the forehead must be sharply set off from the bridge of the nose. The forehead and the bridge of the nose must be straight and parallel to one another. Seen from the front, the head should appear narrow, the bridge of the nose should be as broad as possible. The cheek muscles must show slightly, but under no circumstances should they be too pronounced (cheeky). The muzzle part must have full flews and must be as blunt vertically as possible in front; the angles of the lips must be quite pronounced. The front part of the head, from the tip of the nose up to the center of the stop should be as long as the rear part of the head from the center of the stop to the only slightly developed occiput. The head should be angular from all sides and should have definite flat planes and its dimensions should be absolutely in proportion to the general appearance of the Dane. **Faults:** Any deviation from the parallel planes of skull and foreface; too small a stop; a poorly defined stop or none at all; too narrow a nose bridge; the rear of the head spreading laterally in a wedgelike manner (wedge head); an excessively round upper head (apple head); excessively pronounced cheek musculature; pointed muzzle; loose lips hanging over the lower jaw (fluttering lips) which create an illusion of a full deep muzzle. The head should be rather shorter and distinguished than long and expressionless.

(b) Teeth (4 points): Strong, well developed and clean. The incisors of the lower jaw must touch very lightly the bottoms of the inner surface of the upper incisors (scissors bite). If the front teeth of both jaws bite on top of each other, they wear down too rapidly. **Faults:** Even bite; undershot and overshot; incisors out of line; black or brown teeth; missing teeth.

(c) Eyes (4 points): Medium size, as dark as possible, with lively intelligent expression; almond-shaped eyelids, well-developed eyebrows. **Faults:** Light-colored, piercing, amber-colored, light blue to a watery blue, red or bleary eyes; eyes of different colors; eyes too far apart; Mongolian eyes; eyes with pronounced haws; eyes with excessively drooping lower eyelids. In blue and black Danes, lighter eyes are permitted but are not desirable. In harlequins, the eyes should be dark. Light-colored eyes, two eyes of different color and walleyes are permitted but not desirable.

Nose (0 points): The nose must be large and in the case of brindled and "single-colored" Danes, it must always be black. In harlequins, the nose should be black; a black spotted nose is permitted; a pink-colored nose is not desirable.

Ears (0 points): Ears should be high, set not too far apart, medium in size, of moderate thickness, drooping forward close to the cheek. Top line of folded ear should be about level with the skull. **Faults:** Hanging on the side, as on a Foxhound.

Cropped ears: high set, not set too far apart, well pointed but always in proportion to the shape of the head and carried uniformly erect.

4. TORSO..20 points

(a) Neck (6 points): The neck should be firm and clean, high-set, well arched, long, muscular and sinewy. From the chest to the head, it should be slightly tapering, beautifully formed, with well-developed nape. **Faults:** Short, heavy neck, pendulous throat folds (dewlaps).

(b) Loin and Back (6 points): The withers forms the highest part of the back which slopes downward slightly toward the loins which are imperceptibly arched and strong. The back should be short and tensely set. The belly should be well shaped and tightly muscled, and, with the rear part of the thorax, should swing in a pleasing curve (tuck-up). **Faults:** Receding back; sway back; camel or roach back; a back line which is too high at the rear; an excessively long back; poor tuck-up.

(c) Chest (4 points): Chest deals with that part of the thorax (rib cage) in front of the shoulders and front legs. The chest should be quite broad, deep and well muscled. **Faults:** A narrow and poorly muscled chest; strong protruding sternum (pigeon breast).

(d) Ribs and Brisket (4 points): Deals with that part of the thorax back of the shoulders and front legs. Should be broad, with the ribs sprung well out from the spine and flattened at the side to allow proper movement of the shoulders extending down to the elbow joint. **Faults:** Narrow (slab-sided) rib cage; round (barrel) rib cage; shallow rib cage not reaching the elbow joint.

5. TAIL . . . . *2 points*

Should start high and fairly broad, terminating slender and thin at the hock joint. At rest, the tail should fall straight. When excited or running, slightly curved (saberlike). **Faults:** A too high, or too low set tail (the tail set is governed by the slope of the croup); too long or too short a tail; tail bent too far over the back (ring tail); a tail which is curled; a twisted tail (sideways); a tail carried too high over the back (gay tail); a brush tail (hair too long on lower side). Cropping tails to desired length is forbidden.

FAULTS

Disqualification Faults: Danes under minimum height. White Danes without any black marks (albinos). Merles, a solid mouse-gray color or a mouse-gray base with black or white or both color spots or white base with mouse-gray spots. Harlequins and solid-colored Danes in which a large spot extends coatlike over the entire body so that only the legs, neck and the point of the tail are white. Brindle, fawn, blue and black Danes with white forehead line, white collars, high white stockings and white bellies. Danes with predominantly blue, gray, yellow or also brindled spots. Docked tails. Split noses.

The faults below are important according to their grouping (very serious, serious, minor) and not according to their sequence as placed in each grouping:

Very serious: Lack of unity. Poor bone development. Poor musculature. Lightweight whippety Danes. Rickets. Timidity. Bitchy dog. Swayback. Roach back. Cowhocks. Pitching gait. Short steps. Undershot teeth.

Serious: Out of condition. Coarseness. Any deviation from the standard on all coloration. Deviation from parallel planes of skull and foreface. Wedge head. Poorly defined stop. Narrow nose bridge. Snipy muzzle. Any color but dark eyes in fawns and brindles. Mongolian eyes. Missing teeth. Overshot teeth. Heavy neck. Short neck. Dewlaps. Narrow chest. Narrow rib cage. Round rib cage. Shallow rib cage. Loose shoulders. Steep shoulders. Elbows turned inward. Chair legs (front). Knotty bulge in pastern joint (adult dog). Weak pastern roots. Receding back. Too long a back. Back high in rear. In harlequins, a pink nose. Poor tuck-up (except in bitches that have been bred). Too straight croup. Too sloping croup. Too narrow croup. Overangulation. Steep rear. Too long rear legs. Poorly muscled thighs. Barrel legs. Paws turned outward. Rabbit paws. Wolf's claw. Hackney gait.

Minor: Doggy bitches. Small white marks on chest and toes—blues, blacks, brindles and fawns. Few gray spots and pointings on harlequins. In harlequins, black-spotted nose. White-tipped tail except on harlequins. Excessively long hair. Excessively dull hair. Apple head. Small stop. Fluttering lips. Eyes too far apart. Drooping lower eyelids. Haws. Any color but dark eyes in blacks, blues and harlequins. Discolored teeth. Even bite. Pigeon breast. Loaded shoulders. Elbows turned outward. Paws turned inward. Splay foot. Excessively long toenails. Light nails (except in harlequins). Low-set tail. Too long a tail. Too short a tail. Gay tail. Curled tail. Twisted tail. Brush tail.

DISQUALIFICATIONS

Danes under minimum height.

White Danes without any black masks (albinos).

Merles, a solid mouse-gray color or a mouse-gray base with black or white or both color spots or white base with mouse-gray spots.

Harlequins and solid-colored Danes in which a large spot extends coatlike over the entire body so that only the legs, neck and the point of the tail are white.

Brindle, fawn, blue and black Danes with white forehead line, white collars, high white stockings and white bellies.

Danes with predominantly blue, gray, yellow or also brindled spots.

Docked tails.

Split noses.

APPROVED NOVEMBER 14, 1944

GREAT PYRENEES

This giant white dog is a native of the Pyrenees Mountains which lie between France and Spain. Their history can be traced back to the early 16th century when they were used in great numbers to guard the large flocks of sheep that roamed the mountain slopes. Today they can still be found hard at work in a terrain that is subject to the many extremes of mountain weather. These strikingly beautiful dogs are referred to as "mat dogs" by peasant owners because they are accustomed to sleeping on the doorstep of their mountain homes.

The Great Pyrenees has not always endured the harsh winters on the slopes, but enjoyed a regal lifestyle during the 17th century when Louis XIV named the breed the official court dog. The temperament of this dignified breed endeared them to other members of royalty, such as Queen Marie Antoinette and Queen Victoria, who both owned and raised them. The Great Pyrenees walks with an aura of self-confidence and elegance and maintains an intelligent, kindly expression.

The breed is a relative newcomer to America, having arrived in 1930, but it was quickly accepted and recognized by the American Kennel Club in 1933. The majority of the breed stock was all but wiped out by the hostilities of World War II when the large kennels of France and England were devastated. Since then steady growth has continued both here and abroad, even though Great Pyrenees are an infrequent sight at the dog shows.

Any climate or environment is suitable for the adaptable Great Pyrenees. They are workmen of unmatchable stamina, but due to their calm nature and low metabolic rate they have suprisingly low requirements for food and exercise.

They are good companions, immediately assuming the job of watching over the household. Typically they position themselves against the entranceway to the home where they can keep an eye on all the business of the household. Great Pyrenees have an iron constitution which makes them very resistant to illness and tolerant of most locales. Great Pyrs make ideal companions for the winter sportsman, as they love invigorating exercise and are naturally suited for outings such as ski trips.

Buyer's guide: Considerable space and grooming are needed to keep the Great Pyrenees in prime condition. Only robust, active people should own such a dog because just walking the Pyr will require a goodly amount of strength in the owner. Their disposition is very docile and they make faithful, loving housepets. Need it be said that city living is out for these dogs? They were bred to be workers and owners should always remember and foster this in their Great Pyrenees.

STANDARD FOR THE GREAT PYRENEES

General Appearance: A dog of immense size, great majesty, keen intelligence, and kindly expression of unsurpassed beauty and a certain elegance, all white or principally white with markings of badger, gray, or varying shades of tan. In the rolling, ambling gait it shows unmistakably the purpose for which it has been bred, the strenuous work of guarding the flocks in all kinds of weather on the steep mountain slopes of the Pyrenees. Hence soundness is of the greatest importance and absolutely necessary for the proper fulfillment of his centuries' old task.

Size: The average height at the shoulders is 27 inches to 32 inches for dogs, and 25 inches to 29 inches for bitches. The average length from shoulder blades to root of tail should be the same as the height in any given specimen. The average girth is 36 inches to 42 inches for dogs and 32 inches to 36 inches for bitches. The weight for dogs runs 100 to 125 pounds and 90 to 115 pounds for bitches. A dog heavily boned; with close cupped feet; double dewclaws behind and single dewclaws in front.

Head: Large and wedge-shaped, measuring 10 inches to 11 inches from dome to point of nose, with rounding crown, furrow only slightly developed and with no apparent stop. **Cheeks:** Flat. **Ears:** V-shaped, but rounded at the tips, of medium size, set parallel with the eyes, carried low and close to the head except when raised at attention. **Eyes:** Of medium size, set slightly obliquely, dark rich brown in color with close eyelids, well pigmented. **Lips:** Close-fitting, edged with black. **Dewlaps:** Developed but little. The head is in brief that of a brown bear, but with the ears falling down. **Neck:** Short, stout and strongly muscular.

Body: Well-placed shoulders set obliquely, close to the body. **Back and Loin:** Well coupled, straight and broad. **Haunches:** Fairly prominent. **Rump:** Sloping slightly. **Ribs:** Flat-sided. **Chest:** Deep. **Tail:** Of sufficient length to hang below the hocks, well plumed, carried low in repose, and curled high over the back, "making the wheel" when alert.

Coat: Crested to withstand severe weather, with heavy fine white undercoat and long flat thick outer coat of coarser hair, straight or slightly undulating.

Qualities: In addition to his original age-old position in the scheme of pastoral life as protector of the shepherd and his flock, the Great Pyrenees has been used for centuries as a guard and watchdog on the large estates of his native France, and for this he has proven ideal. He is as serious in play as he is in work, adapting and molding himself to the moods, desires and even the very life of his human companions, through fair weather and foul, through leisure hours and hours fraught with danger, responsibility and extreme exertion; he is the exemplification of gentleness and docility with those he knows, of faithfulness and devotion for his master even to the point of self-sacrifice; and of courage in the protection of the flock placed in his care and of the ones he loves.

SCALE OF POINTS

Head
Shape of skull..........5
Ears..................5
Eyes..................5
Muzzle................5
Teeth 5 25

General Conformation
Neck 5
Chest 5

Back...................5
Loins 5
Feet 5 25
Coat.....................10
Size and Soundness..........25
*Expression and General
 Appearance* 15

TOTAL 100

APPROVED FEBRUARY 13, 1935

KOMONDOR

The Komondor must rank as the breed that garners the most *oohs* and *aahs* when exhibited at the dog shows for they are strikingly handsome and have a profuse coat that is unmatched by any other breed. In their native Hungary they have been nicknamed the "king of sheepdogs." Being one of the largest of all dogs, the Komondor makes great use of their size by developing into superlative guards over the herds of sheep in their charge. Their muscular body is even more emphasized by the thick corded coat that covers it and gives this dog their distinguished appearance.

The Komondor dog is believed to trace its ancestry to Central Asia where dogs of their type were used to defend the herds from wolf attacks. They were so adept at their job that they were imported to the prairies of Hungary by the thousands. The word

Komondor is said to have stemmed from the Hungarian word *komor*, meaning serene, which quickly sums up their temperament. They are dogs of great composure, but they work with vigor and vitality.

The cording of the Komondor's coat is quite unusual in the dog world. Because of their dense, wooly undercoat, the Komondor's wavy top hairs naturally fall into the cording pattern. When moving, the corded coat is best described as looking like the flowing of a king's robe, and their proud, majestic carriage certainly accentuates this impression. A properly corded coat is not easily achieved, however, as the coat is easily given to matting. Matted clumps of hair that must be cut out are disastrous to the appearance of the coat, which is the hallmark of the breed.

The Komondor was first recognized by the AKC in 1937 and the breed has enjoyed a growing popularity, not only based on their great beauty but also because of their gentle, intelligent nature.

Buyer's guide: Only truly dedicated dog fanciers should consider owning the Komondor. The heavily corded coat of this dog requires *extensive* care, and no short cuts can be afforded. They are quite large and must have lots of space, exercise and food. If a prospective owner can meet these imposing requirements, they will have a very fine pet. Komondorok have splendid dispositions and are natural watchdogs. Because of their size and strength, they should not be handled by children, even though they do get along well with them.

STANDARD FOR THE KOMONDOR

General Appearance: The Komondor is characterized by imposing strength, courageous demeanor and pleasing conformation. In general, it is a big muscular dog with plenty of bone and substance, covered with an unusual, heavy, white coat.

Nature and Characteristics: An excellent houseguard. It is wary of strangers. As a guardian of herds, it is, when grown, an earnest, courageous, and very faithful dog. The young dog, however, is as playful as any other puppy. It is devoted to its master and will defend him against attack by any stranger. Because of this trait, it is not used for driving the herds, but only for guarding them. The Komondor's special task is to protect the animals. It lives during the greater part of the year in the open, without protection against strange dogs and beasts of prey.

Head: The head looks somewhat short in comparison to the seemingly wide forehead. The skull is somewhat arched when viewed from the side. Stop is moderate. The muzzle somewhat shorter than the length of the skull. The top of the muzzle is straight and about parallel with the line of the top of the skull. The muzzle is powerful, bite is scissors; level bite is acceptable. Any missing teeth is a serious fault. Distinctly undershot or overshot bite is a serious fault.

Ears: Medium set, hanging and V-shaped. Erect ears or ears that move toward an erect position are faults.

Eyes: Medium-sized and almond-sized, not too deeply set. The edges of the eyelids are gray. The iris of the eyes is dark brown, light color is not desirable. Blue-white eyes are disqualifying.

Muzzle: In comparison to the length given in the head description, the muzzle is wide, coarse and not pointed. Nostrils are wide. Color of the nose is black. A dark gray or dark brown nose is not desirable but is acceptable. Flesh-colored noses are disqualifying.

Neck: Muscular, of medium length, moderately arched. The head erect. Any dewlap is a fault.

Body: Characterized chiefly by the powerful, deep chest which is muscular and proportionately wide. Shoulders are moderately sloping. The back is level. Rump is wide, muscular, slightly sloping towards the root of the tail. The body is rectangular, only slightly longer than the height at the withers. The belly is somewhat drawn up at the rear.

Tail: A straight continuation of the rumpline, and reaches down to the hocks. Slightly curved upwards at its end. When the dog is excited, the tail is raised up to the level of the back. The tail is not to be docked. A short or curly tail is a fault. Bobtails are disqualifying.

Forelegs: Straight, well boned and muscular. Viewed from any side, the legs are like vertical columns. The upper arms join the body closely, without loose elbows.

Hindquarters and Legs: The steely, strong bone structure is covered with highly developed muscles. The legs are straight as viewed from the rear. Stifles well bent. Dewclaws must be removed.

Feet: Strong, rather large and with close, well-arched toes. Nails are black or gray. Pads are hard, elastic and dark.

Movement: Light, leisurely and balanced. Takes long strides.

Coat: Characteristic of the breed is the dense, weather-resisting double coat. The puppy coat is relatively soft, but it shows a tendency to fall into cords. In the mature dog the coat consists of a dense, soft, woolly undercoat, much like the puppy coat, and a coarser outer coat that is wavy or curly. The coarser hairs of the outer coat trap the softer undercoat forming permanent strong cords that are felty to the touch. A grown dog is covered with a heavy coat of these tassel-like cords, which form themselves naturally, and once formed, require no care other than washing. Too curly a coat is not desired. Straight or silky coat is a serious fault. Short, smooth hair on the head and legs is a disqualification. Failure of the coat to cord by two years of age is a disqualification.

The coat is longest at the rump, loins and tail. It is of medium length on the back, shoulders and chest. Shorter on the cheeks, around the eyes, ears, neck, and on the extremities. It is shortest around the mouth and lower part of the legs up to the hocks.

Color: Color of the coat is white. Any color other than white is disqualifying.

In the ideal specimen the skin is gray. Pink skin is less desirable but is acceptable if no evidence of albinism. The nose, lips, outlines of eyelids and pads are dark or gray. It is good if the gums and palate are also dark.

Size: Dogs, 25½ inches and upward at the withers; bitches, 23½ inches and upward at withers. While size is important, type, character, symmetry, movement and ruggedness are of the greatest importance, and are on no account to be sacrificed for size alone.

Faults: Size below limit. Short or too curly coat. Straight or silky coat. Any missing teeth. Distinctly undershot or overshot bite. Looseness or slackness. Short or curly tail. Light-colored eyes. Erect ears or ears that move toward an erect position. Dewlaps on the neck.

DISQUALIFICATIONS

Blue-white eyes.
Color other than white.
Bobtails.
Flesh-colored nose.
Short, smooth hair on head and legs.
Failure of the coat to cord by two years of age.

APPROVED FEBRUARY 13, 1973

Representing the breed: Ch. Summithill Csontos, owned by Dorothy Stevens. Photo by Mary Bloom.

KUVASZ

This hard working Hungarian herding dog is very strong boned, sturdily built and exceptionally well proportioned in appearance. The breed is noted for their light-footedness and they seem almost tireless in their work. Their gait has been likened to that of a wolf, with a great freedom of movement, outreaching, and with a powerful elasticity and rhythmic motion. They move almost in a glide and have been known to trot 18 miles with little effort.

Theories concerning the earliest appearances of the breed are vague and unsubstantiated, but many Kuvasz fanciers believe the breed dates back to Sumerian herdsmen of 7000 years ago. Written evidences from the late 1400's have documented that the Kuvasz was the first of the Hungarian breeds to be allowed to leave the life of the prairie and assume a place in their masters' homes as domesticated pets. Their acclaim spread quickly throughout Hungary and the breed was adopted by many members of nobility who used them as guards for the palaces.

The Kuvasz is one of the loveliest of all the working breeds.

They are impressive in stature and their striking white coats have made them the vogue with the fashionable fanciers. They are most at ease when treated as one of the family and they seem to seek out the company of children. They enjoy a good frolic with their young masters, but they understand the need for gentleness and sensitivity when around them. The Kuvasz has endless energy and enjoys a good workout, whether it is in herding sheep, romping through a field or enjoying a good run with their owners. Although they are generally friendly, they are wary and suspicious of strangers and are natural watchdogs.

Buyer's guide: Even though the Kuvasz has many recommendable traits (their gentleness, fidelity, cleanliness), these dogs are just too large for most owners. If you own a large tract of land on which the Kuvasz can run, then consider this fine tempered animal. All others should not restrict these dogs by keeping them in inadequate space. They must get frequent periods of strenuous exercise and be provided with a sufficient amount of food to keep pace with their needs—which could be quite expensive. Grooming them regularly is also advisable.

STANDARD FOR THE KUVASZ

General Characteristics: A spirited dog of keen intelligence, determination, courage and curiosity. Very sensitive to praise and blame. Primarily a one-family dog. Devoted, gentle and patient without being overly demonstrative. Always ready to protect loved ones even to the point of self-sacrifice. Extremely strong instinct to protect children. Polite to accepted strangers, but rather suspicious and very discriminating in making new friends. Unexcelled guard, possessing ability to act on his own initiative at just the right moment without instruction. Bold, courageous and fearless. Untiring ability to work and cover rough terrain for long periods of time. Has good scent and has been used to hunt game.

General Appearance: A working dog of larger size, sturdily built, well balanced, neither lanky nor cobby. White in color with *no markings*. Medium boned, well muscled, without the slightest hint of bulkiness or lethargy. Impresses the eye with strength and activity combined with light-footedness, moves freely on strong legs. Trunk and limbs form a horizontal rectangle slightly deviated from the square. Slightly inclined croup. Hindquarters are particularly well developed. Any tendency to weakness or lack of substance is a decided fault.

Movement: Easy, free and elastic. Feet travel close to the ground. Hind legs reach far under, meeting or even passing the imprints of the front legs. Moving toward an observer, the front legs do not travel parallel to each other but rather close together at the ground. When viewed from the rear, the hind legs (from the hip joint down) also move close at the ground. As speed increases, the legs gradually angle more inward until the pads are almost single-tracking. Unless excited, the head is carried rather low at the level of the shoulders. Desired movement cannot be maintained without sufficient angulation and firm slimness of body.

Height: Measured at the withers: dogs, 28 to 30 inches; bitches, 26 to 28 inches.

Weight: Dogs, approximately 100 to 115 pounds; bitches, approximately 70 to 90 pounds.

Color: White.

Head: Proportions are of great importance as the head is considered to be the most beautiful part of the Kuvasz. Length of head measured from tip of nose to occiput is slightly less than half the height of the dog at the withers. Width is half the length of the head. The skull is elongated but not pointed. The stop is defined, never abrupt, raising the forehead gently above the plane of the muzzle. The longitudinal midline of the forehead is pronounced, widening as it slopes to the muzzle. Cheeks flat, bony arches above the eyes. The skin dry, no excess flews.

Muzzle: Length in proportion to the length of the head, top straight, not pointed, underjaw well developed. Inside of the mouth preferably black.

Nose: Large, black, nostrils well opened.

Lips: Black, closely covering the teeth. The upper lip covers tightly the upper jaw only. Lower lip tight and not pendulous.

Bite: Dentition full, scissors bite preferred. Level bite acceptable.

Eyes: Almond-shaped, set well apart, somewhat slanted. In profile, the eyes are set slightly below the plane of the muzzle. Lids tight, haws should not show. Dark brown, the darker the better.

Ears: V-shaped, tip is slightly rounded. Rather thick, they are well set back between the level of the eye and the top of the head. When pulled forward the tip of the ear should cover the eye. Looking at the dog face to face, the widest part of the ear is about level to the eye. The inner edge of the ear lies close to the cheek, the outer edge slightly away from the head forming a V. In the relaxed position, the ears should hold their set and are not cast backward. The ears should not protrude above the head.

Neck: Muscular, without dewlap, medium length, arched at the crest.

Forequarters: Shoulders muscular. The scapula and humerus form a right angle, are long and of equal length. Legs are medium boned, straight and well muscled. Elbows neither in nor out. When viewed from the side, the forechest protrudes slightly in front of the shoulders. The joints are dry, hard. Dewclaws on the forelegs should not be removed.

Body: Forechest is well developed, chest deep with long well-sprung ribs reaching almost to the elbows. Shoulders long with withers higher than back. Back is of medium length, straight, firm and quite broad. The loin is short, muscular and tight. The croup well muscled, slightly sloping. The brisket is deep, well developed and runs parallel to the ground. The stomach is well tucked up.

Bone: In proportion to size of body. Medium, hard. Never heavy or coarse.

Hindquarters: The portion behind the hip joint is moderately long producing wide, long and strong muscles of the upper thigh. The femur is long, creating well-bent stifles. Lower thigh is long, dry, well muscled. Metatarsus is short, broad and of great strength. Dewclaws, if any, are removed.

Tail: Carried low, natural length reaching at least to the hocks. In repose it hangs down resting on the body, the end but slightly lifted. In state of excitement, the tail may be elevated to the level of the loin, the tip slightly curved up. Ideally there should not be much difference in the carriage of the tail in state of excitement or in repose.

Feet: Well padded. Pads resilient, black. Feet are closed tight forming round "cat feet." The rear paws somewhat longer, some hair between the toes, the less the better. Dark nails are preferred.

Skin: The skin is heavily pigmented. The more slate gray or black pigmentation the better.

Coat: The Kuvasz has a double coat formed by a guard hair and fine undercoat. The texture of the coat is medium coarse. The coat ranges from quite wavy to straight. Distribution follows a definite pattern over the body regardless of coat type. The head, muzzle, ears and paws are covered with short, smooth hair. The neck has a mane that extends to and covers the chest. Coat on the front of the forelegs up to the elbows and the hind legs below the thighs is short and smooth. The backs of the forelegs are feathered to the pastern with hair 2 to 3 inches long. The body and sides of the thighs are covered with a medium length coat. The back of the thighs and the entire tail is covered with hair 4 to 6 inches long. It is natural for the Kuvasz to lose most of the long coat duiring hot weather. Full luxuriant coat comes in seasonally, depending on climate. Summer coat should not be penalized.

MASTIFF

The Mastiff is one of the oldest and most typical of British dogs. It is probable that he owes his origin to the dogs of similar type that were used by Assyrian kings for lion hunting. There is also a similarity between them and the fierce Mollosian dog of the ancient Greeks. However this may be, there is no question that the Mastiff has been cultivated in the British Isles for many centuries. It is mentioned in Roman history of the eighth year of the Christian era that the Mollosian dogs of the Greeks were pitted against the Pugnaces of Britain and that the latter overpowered them. It is also further stated by the same writer, Gratius Falliscus, that there were two kinds of British Pugnaces, a large and a small type, the latter probably being the prototype of the present Bulldog.

The word "Mastiff" is derived from the Latin *massivius*, meaning massive or large, but at different times the names Tie-dog and Ban-dog have been applied to the Mastiff. At an early date they were undoubtedly used to guard flocks and herds, as well as homes. Later they were trained to fight bulls, bears, lions, and other animals imported for that purpose. Three well-trained Mastiffs, it is recorded, were considered a fair match for a bear, four for a lion.

Fashions in dogs fluctuate. At one time the Mastiff was the pride of the British show ring and one of the most popular breeds in the country, but for some reason hard to understand—for the Mastiff is one of the most impressive of dogs—the public lost interest in the breed. Interest in this magnificent breed is now being reawakened and a resolute effort will be made to regain some of their old time popularity and glory, for as guards and companions they are unsurpassed.

In the selection of Mastiff puppies two to four months old, look for: great size; massive, short head; deep, square muzzle; big, well-chiseled skull; short, deep, round body; straight forelegs and enormous bone.

Buyer's guide: The Mastiff is a fine blend of docility and character, making them fine housepets for those who like large dogs. Despite their great size, they do not need tremendous amounts of exercise and can be kept in moderate sized households. Do not cramp them in apartments, however, as confinement can lead to a nervous tendency in Mastiffs. They are somewhat lazy if left to their own accord, so routine periods of chaperoned exercise are suggested for their good health.

STANDARD FOR THE MASTIFF

General Character and Symmetry: Large, massive, symmetrical and well-knit frame. A combination of grandeur and good nature, courage and docility.

General Description of Head: In general outline giving a massive appearance when viewed from any angle. Breadth greatly to be desired. **Skull:** Broad and somewhat rounded between the ears, forehead slightly curved, showing marked wrinkles which are particularly distinctive when at attention. Brows (superciliary ridges) moderately raised. Muscles of the temples well developed, those of the cheeks extremely powerful. Arch across the skull a flattened curve with a furrow up the center of the

forehead. This extends from between the eyes to halfway up the skull.
Ears: Small, V-shaped, rounded at the tips. Leather moderately thin, set widely apart at the highest points on the sides of the skull continuing the outline across the summit. They should lie close to the cheeks when in repose. Ears dark in color, the blacker the better, conforming to the color of the muzzle. **Eyes:** Set wide apart, medium in size, never too prominent. Expression alert but kindly. The stop between the eyes well marked but not too abrupt. Color of eyes brown, the darker the better and showing no haw.

Face and Muzzle: Short, broad under the eyes and running nearly equal in width to the end of the nose. Truncated, i.e. blunt and cut off square, thus forming a right angle with the upper line of the face. Of great depth from the point of the nose to underjaw. Underjaw broad to the end and slightly rounded. Canine teeth healthy, powerful and wide apart. Scissors bite preferred but a moderately undershot jaw permissible providing the teeth are not visible when the mouth is closed. Lips diverging at obtuse angles with the septum and sufficiently pendulous so as to show a modified square profile. Nose broad and always dark in color, the blacker the better, with spread flat nostrils (not pointed or turned up) in profile. Muzzle dark in color, the blacker the better. Muzzle should be half the length of the skull, thus dividing the head into three parts—one for the foreface and two for the skull. In other words, the distance from tip of nose to stop equal to one-half the distance between the stop and the occiput. Circumference of muzzle (measuring midway between the eyes and nose) to that of the head (measured before the ears) as 3 is to 5.

Neck: Powerful and very muscular, slightly arched, and of medium length. The neck gradually increases in circumference as it approaches the shoulder. Neck moderately "dry" (not showing an excess of loose skin).

Chest and Flanks: Wide, deep, rounded and well let down between the forelegs, extending at least to the elbow. Forechest should be deep and well defined. Ribs extremely well rounded. False ribs deep and well set back. There should be a reasonable, but not exaggerated, cut-up.

Shoulder and Arm: Slightly sloping, heavy and muscular. No tendency to looseness of shoulders.

Forelegs and Feet: Legs straight, strong and set wide apart, heavy-boned. Elbows parallel to body. Feet heavy, round and compact with well-arched toes. Pasterns strong and bent only slightly. Black nails preferred.

Hind Legs: Hindquarters broad, wide and muscular. Second thighs well developed, hocks set back, wide apart and parallel when viewed from the rear.

Back and Loins: Back muscular, powerful and straight. Loins wide and muscular, slightly rounded over the rump.

Tail: Set on moderately high and reaching to the hocks or a little below. Wide at the root, tapering to the end, hanging straight in repose, forming a slight curve but never over the back when dog is in action.

Coat: Outer coat moderately coarse. Undercoat, dense, short and close lying.

Color: Apricot, silver fawn or dark fawn-brindle. Fawn-brindle should have fawn as a background color which should be completely covered with very dark stripes. In any case muzzle, ears and nose must be dark in color, the blacker the better, with similar color tone around the orbits, extending upwards between them.

Size: Dogs, mimimum, 30 inches at the shoulder; bitches, minimum, 27 and one-half inches at the shoulder.

SCALE OF POINTS

General character and symmetry 10	Chest and ribs 10
Height and substance 10	Forelegs and feet 10
Skull 10	Back, loins and flanks 10
Face and muzzle 12	Hind legs and feet 10
Ears 5	Tail 3
Eyes 5	Coat and color 5
	TOTAL 100

APPROVED JULY 8, 1941

NEWFOUNDLAND

This magnificent breed of dog shares with the St. Bernard the honor of being a life-saving breed. The fact that a postage stamp of the island of Newfoundland bears their portrait indicates the regard in which they are held in their native lands. Abroad, they have been the subjects of painters and writers, and more than one has received the medal of the Royal Humane Society in England.

While there is no exact information as to how the breed originated, it is probable that early settlers from Europe carried with them dogs of large size. The island of Newfoundland, on account of its fishermen, has always been in close communication with other countries, and the native dogs undoubtedly were reinforced from time to time with dogs brought out by sea captains or fishermen. From this parent stock the Newfoundland was evolved.

The hazardous calling of the fishing banks naturally developed a race of men combining strength, vigor, and the coolest of courage. The same conditions that develop men also develop their dogs. In their native home the Newfoundlands share all the duties and dangers of their owners. They assist in hauling in the nets. They drag the sledges across the snow in the depths of winter, and when the men are away, as they frequently are for weeks, it is left to the dogs to guard the homes and watch over the women and children. Newfoundlands are as much at home in the water as on the land, and nature has provided them with a coat that protects them against the exigencies of their stern climate.

No dog has been the subject of more popular sentiment than the Newfoundland. The greatest portrait artists have portrayed them, and writers in all languages have related their heroic virtues. It is generally agreed that Newfoundlands are worthy of the honors and distinctions that have been heaped upon them. They are unsurpassed in strength, courage, and intelligence. Their great docility recommends them as companions and guards. The ready fortitude with which they dash to the assistance of persons in distress, particularly in danger of drowning, has gained them universal recognition as the friends of man. The Newfoundland is an aquatic dog without equal.

In choosing Newfoundland puppies at from two to four months old, look for great size; typical, moderately long head; muzzle free from lippiness, but not snipy; dark eyes; not much stop; medium ears, set close to side of head; big, short body; rather short legs with enormous bone; coat dense and almost like fur. In the white-and-blacks the color should be equally distributed.

Buyer's guide: Needless to say, a 150 pound Newfoundland is not the pet for most households. Large food bills must be expected from these dogs, and their space and exercise requirements are also very large. Grooming is at a minimum, as a good brushing should suffice. They are gentle and intelligent and can be trusted as companions for children, provided the kids are intuitive enough to know not to get under their Newf's feet or try to take them for a walk.

STANDARD FOR THE NEWFOUNDLAND

General Appearance: The Newfoundland is large, strong, and active, at home in water and on land, and has natural life-saving instincts.

He is a multipurpose dog capable of heavy work as well as of being a devoted companion for child and man. To fulfill its purposes the Newfoundland is deep bodied, well muscled, and well coordinated. A good specimen of the breed has dignity and proud head carriage. The length of the dog's body, from withers to base of tail, is approximately equal to the height of the dog at the withers. However, a bitch is not to be faulted if the length of her body is slightly greater than her height. The dog's appearance is more massive throughout than the bitch's, with larger frame and heavier bone. The Newfoundland is free moving with a loosely slung body. When he moves, a slight roll is perceptible. Complete webbing between the toes is always present. Large size is desirable but never at the expense of gait, symmetry, balance, or conformation to the Standard herein described.

Head: The head is massive with a broad skull, slightly arched crown, and strongly developed occipital bone. The slope from the top of the skull to the tip of the muzzle has a definite but not steep stop. The forehead and face is smooth and free of wrinkles; the muzzle is clean cut and covered with short, fine hair. The muzzle is square, deep, and fairly short; its length from stop to tip of nose is less than from stop to occiput. The nostrils are well developed. The bitch's head follows the same general conformation as the dog's but is feminine and less massive. A narrow head and a snipy or long muzzle are to be faulted.

The eyes are dark brown, relatively small, and deep-set; they are spaced wide apart and have no haw showing. Round, protruding, or yellow eyes are objectionable.

The ears are relatively small and triangular with rounded tips. They are set well back on the skull and lie close to the head. When the ear is brought forward it reaches to the inner corner of the eye on the same side.

The teeth meet in a scissors or level bite.

The Newfoundland's expression is soft and reflects the character of the breed; benevolent, intelligent, dignified, and of sweet disposition. The dog never looks or acts either dull or ill-tempered.

Neck: The neck is strong and well set on the shoulders. It is long enough for proud head carriage.

Body: The Newfoundland's chest is full and deep with the brisket reaching at least down to the elbows. The back is broad, and the topline is level from the withers to the croup, never roached, slack, or swayed. He is broad at the croup, is well muscled, and has very strong loins. The croup slopes at an angle of about 30 degrees. Bone structure is massive throughout but does not give a heavy, sluggish appearance.

Forequarters: When the dog is not in motion, the forelegs are perfectly straight and parallel with the elbows close to the chest. The layback of the shoulders is about 45 degrees, and the upper arm meets the shoulder blade at an angle of about 90 degrees. The shoulders are well muscled. The pasterns are slightly sloping.

Hindquarters: Because driving power for swimming, pulling loads, or covering ground efficiently is dependent on the hindquarters, the rear assembly of the Newfoundland is of prime importance. It is well muscled, the thighs are fairly long, the stifles well bent, and the hocks wide and straight. Cowhocks, barrel legs, or pigeon toes are to be seriously faulted.

Feet: The feet are proportionate to the body in size, cat-foot in type, well-rounded and tight with firm, arched toes, and with webbing present. Dewclaws on the rear legs are to be removed.

Tail: The tail of the Newfoundland acts as a rudder when he is swimming. Therefore, it is broad and strong at the base. The tail reaches down a little below the hocks. When the dog is standing the tail hangs straight down, possibly a little bent at the top; when the dog is in motion or excited, the tail is carried straight out or slightly curved, but it never curls over the back. A tail with a kink is a serious fault.

Gait: The Newfoundland in motion gives the impression of effortless power, has good reach, and strong drive. A dog may appear symmetrical and well balanced when standing, but, if he is not structurally sound, he will lose that symmetry and balance when he moves. In motion, the legs move straight forward; they do not swing in an arc nor do the hocks move in or out in relation to the line of travel. A slight roll is present. As the dog's speed increases from a walk to a trot, the feet move in under the center line of the body to maintain balance. Mincing, shuffling, crabbing, too close moving, weaving, hackney action, and pacing are all faults.

Size: The average height for dogs is 28 inches, for bitches 26 inches. The average weight for dogs is 150 pounds, for bitches 120 pounds. Large size is desirable but is not to be favored over correct gait, symmetry, and structure.

Coat: The Newfoundland has a water-resistant double coat. The outer coat is moderately long and full but not shaggy. It is straight and flat with no curl, although it may have a slight wave. The coat, when rubbed the wrong way, tends to fall back into place. The undercoat, which is soft and dense, is often less dense during summer months or in tropical climates but is always found to some extent on the rump and chest. An open coat is to be seriously faulted. The hair on the head, muzzle, and ears is short and fine, and the legs are feathered all the way down. The tail is covered with long dense hair, but it does not form a flag.

Color: **Black:** A slight tinge of bronze or a splash of white on chest and toes is not objectionable. Black dogs that have only white toes and white chest and white tip to tail should be exhibited in the classes provided for "black."

Other than black: Should in all respects follow the black except in color, which may be almost any, so long as it disqualifies for the black class, but the colors most to be encouraged are bronze or white and black (Landseer) with black head marked with narrow blaze, even marked saddle and black rump extending on to tail. Beauty in markings to be taken greatly into consideration.

DISQUALIFICATIONS
Markings other than white on a solid-colored dog.

APPROVED JUNE 9, 1970

OLD ENGLISH SHEEPDOG

The Old English Sheepdog is a highly intelligent, picturesque, affectionate, and useful member of the working group. They resemble in important particulars of conformation, appearance, and character the herd dogs of continental countries from Spain to Russia. They all undoubtedly trace their origin at some early period to a common ancestry. The continental dogs were as a rule larger and fiercer than the Sheepdogs of today, and it is probable that the early progenitors of the breed, who lived in a time when it was necessary to defend the flocks against bears and wolves, were larger, stronger and fiercer than those we have now.

The herding instincts of the Old English Sheepdog are deeply seated, and as stock dogs they are unequaled. They are also said to make capital retrievers for sportsmen, being easily controlled, soft-mouthed, good water dogs. They stay at heel by inclination. They learn readily, and are always anxious to please their masters.

There is practically no limit to what they can be taught to do, and their sphere of usefulness is a wide one.

There is a popular idea that this breed is tailless. This is a mistake. The tail is usually amputated, the custom originating with the drovers of England. According to law, dogs used for working purposes were exempt from taxation, and they adopted the docking of the tail to distinguish dogs which came under the ruling. There will be found in many litters of Sheepdogs one or two puppies without tails, while all the other puppies have them.

Buyer's guide: The Old English Sheepdog is very lovable. Their fine disposition makes them well suited for being household pets; however, their grooming requirements make them fairly hard to keep. Their long coat needs very frequent brushing to keep it from knotting up, and in hot weather they need to be bathed to prevent them from acquiring a musty smell. The coat is so thick that drying after the bath is often quite difficult.

STANDARD FOR THE OLD ENGLISH SHEEPDOG

Skull: Capacious and rather squarely formed, giving plenty of room for brain power. The parts over the eyes should be well arched and the whole well covered with hair. **Jaw:** Fairly long, strong, square and truncated. The stop should be well defined to avoid a Deerhound face. (The attention of judges is particularly called to the above properties, as a long, narrow head is a deformity.) **Eyes:** Vary according to the color of the dog. Very dark preferred, but in the glaucous or blue dogs a pearl, walleye or china eye is considered typical. (A light eye is most objectionable.) **Nose:** Always black, large and capacious. **Teeth:** Strong and large, evenly placed and level in opposition. **Ears:** Medium-sized, and carried flat to side of head, coated moderately.

Legs: The forelegs should be dead straight, with plenty of bone, removing the body a medium height from the ground, without approaching legginess, and well coated all around. **Feet:** Small, round; toes well arched, and pads thick and hard.

Tail: It is preferable that there should be none. Should never, however, exceed 1 and one-half or 2 inches in grown dogs. When not natural-born bobtails however, puppies should be docked at the first joint from the body and the operation performed when they are from three to four days old.

Neck and Shoulders: The neck should be fairly long, arched gracefully and well coated with hair. The shoulders sloping and narrow at the points, the dog standing lower at the shoulder than at the loin.

Body: Rather short and very compact, ribs well sprung and brisket deep and capacious. *Slabsidedness highly undesirable.* The loin should be very stout and gently arched, while the hindquarters should be round and muscular and with well-let-down hocks, and the hams densely coated with a thick, long jacket in excess of any other part.

Coat: Profuse, but not so excessive as to give the impression of the dog being overfat, and of a good hard texture; not straight, but shaggy and free from curl. *Quality and texture of coat to be considered above mere profuseness.* Softness or flatness of coat to be considered at fault. The undercoat should be a waterproof pile, when not removed by grooming or season.

Color: Any shade of gray, grizzle, blue or blue-merled with or without white markings or in reverse. *Any shade of brown or fawn to be considered distinctly objectionable and not to be encouraged.*

Size: Twenty-two inches and upwards for dogs and slightly less for bitches. Type, character and symmetry are of the greatest importance and are on no account to be sacrificed to size alone.

General Appearance and Characteristics: A strong, compact-looking dog of great symmetry, practically the same in measurement from shoulder to stern as in height, absolutely free from legginess or weaselness, very elastic in his gallop, but in walking or trotting he has a characteristic ambling or pacing movement, and his bark should be loud, with a peculiar "pot-casse" ring in it. Taking him all round, he is a profusely, but not *excessively* coated, thick-set, muscular, able-bodied dog with a most intelligent expression, free from all Poodle or Deerhound character. *Soundness should be considered of greatest importance.*

SCALE OF POINTS

Skull. 5	Body and loins. 10
Eyes. 5	Hindquarters. 10
Ears. 5	Legs. 10
Teeth. 5	Coat (texture, quality and condition). 15
Nose. 5	
Jaw. 5	General appearance and movement. 15
Foreface. 5	
Neck and shoulders. 5	TOTAL. 100

APPROVED OCTOBER 13, 1953

PULI

Smallest of the triumvirate of Hungarian sheepdogs comprised of the Komondor, Kuvasz and Puli, the latter is touted for his intelligence, energy and resourcefulness. In his native environment, he is especially prized for his willingness to work and his capacity to learn his sheepherding duties quickly. During the last three centuries, Hungarian shepherds were known to ride great distances with their dogs in order to keep the strain pure. Only the animals that learned most quickly and possessed the greatest endurance and reliability were designated Pulik. The others were "just dogs" and were not kept by the shepherds.

Reputed to respond to the sound of a quiet word, the Puli has always been valued for his sensitivity. In 1940 Hungarian novelist Zsolt Harsanyi reported witnessing a shepherd on the Hungarian plain give his Puli a series of commands with no particular emphasis. When the dog had finished, the author commented upon the man's "intelligent dog." "That's not a dog, mister," came the reply. "That's a Puli."

This small dog's faithfulness to master and flock is characterized in countless stories about the breed in their role as sheepherder. Dr. Sandor Palfalvy, a medical examiner, reported that a dog named Marci watched over a flock of 500 sheep alone for more than five months. According to the owner of the flock, Michael Szucs, when the sheep were found at the onset of winter in the rugged Carpathian Mountain regions near Hungary, not one was injured or missing. The skeleton of the Puli's master was found in his cabin a few miles away and Dr. Palfalvy declared the old shepherd had died some five or six months earlier.

Reputedly, a Puli has never harmed any of the animals entrusted to its care. The dog first came to the attention of Americans in the 1930's, when it was imported by the Agricultural Department to be crossbred with their own herding dogs in an attempt to breed in this quality.

The ancient history of the breed is linked with the Lhasa Apso

CORDED PULI

BRUSHED PULI

and Tibetan Terrier as they migrated westward toward Hungary with the Magyars over one thousand years ago. Some authorities claim that evidence supports the presence of Pulik dating back 8,000 years, and that this breed was domesticated before any of the four basic canine families.

This hardy, lean-muscled little dog is accustomed to being outside in all types of weather and traditionally was fed only minimally. His outer coat, like that of the Komondor, is thick and inclined to fall into heavy cords. The undercoat is softer and more fine. He adapts readily to the life of a housepet, but is most healthy when not kept in overly warm places. His protective instincts shift quickly to children and members of the family, though it has been found that once exposed to a herding situation, his instincts remain intact and respond quickly.

Buyer's guide: This medium sized working dog has great intelligence and a mild disposition. They are natural companions for children, being gentle yet assertive. To maintain a neatly corded coat for the show rings, considerable grooming time is required. The brushed out coat must also be carefully groomed because the hairs are naturally prone to matting up. Pulik are very active and like to be out of doors for considerable lengths of time. Apartment living is not suggested for this breed because they may become somewhat high-strung if not allowed proper outlets for their energy.

STANDARD FOR THE PULI

General Appearance: A dog of medium size, vigorous, alert, and extremely active. By nature affectionate, he is a devoted and home-loving companion, sensibly suspicious of strangers and therefore an excellent guard. Striking and highly characteristic is the shaggy coat which centuries ago fitted him for the strenuous work of herding the flocks on the plains of Hungary.

Head: Of medium size in proportion to the body. **The skull** is slightly domed and not too broad. **Stop:** clearly defined but not abrupt, neither dished nor downfaced, with a strong muzzle of medium length ending in a nose of good size. **Teeth** are strong and comparatively large, and the bite may be either level or scissors. Flews tight. **Ears:** Hanging and set fairly high, medium size, and V-shaped. **Eyes:** Deep-set and rather large, should be dark brown, but lighter color is not a serious fault.

Neck and Shoulders: Neck strong and muscular, of medium length, and free of throatiness. Shoulders clean-cut and sloping, with elbows close.

Body: The chest is deep and fairly broad with ribs well sprung. Back of medium length, straight and level, the rump sloping moderately. Fairly broad across the loins and well tucked up.

Tail: Occasionally born bobtail, which is acceptable, but never cut. The tail is carried curled over the back when alert, carried low with the end curled up when at rest.

Legs and Feet: Forelegs straight, strong, and well boned. Feet round and compact with thick-cushioned pads and strong nails. Hindquarters well developed, moderately broad through the stifle which is well bent and muscular. Dewclaws, if any, may be removed from both forelegs and hind legs.

Coat: Characteristic of the breed is the dense, weather-resisting double coat. The outer coat, long and of medium texture, is never silky. It may be straight, wavy, or slightly curly, the more curly coat appearing to be somewhat shorter. The undercoat is soft, woolly, and dense. The coat mats easily, the hair tending to cling together in bunches, giving a somewhat corded appearance even when groomed. The hair is profuse on the head, ears, face, stifles, and tail, and the feet are well haired between the toes. Usually shown combed, but may also be shown uncombed with the coat hanging in tight, even cords.

Color: Solid colors, black, rusty-black, various shades of gray, and white. The black usually appears weathered and rusty or slightly gray. The inter-mixture of hair of different colors is accepted and is usually present in the grays, but must be uniform throughout the coat so that the over-all appearance of a solid color is maintained. Nose, flews, and eyelids are black.

Height: Males about 17 inches, and should not exceed 19 inches. Females about 16 inches, and should not exceed 18 inches.

Serious Faults: Overshot or undershot. Lack of undercoat, short or sparse coat. White markings such as white paws or spot on chest. Flesh color on nose, flews, or eyelids. Coat with areas of two or more colors at the skin.

Representing the Corded: Am. Can. Ch. Kara's Marco, Am., Can. C.D., owned by Barbara Edwards and Constance Peterson. Photo by Jayne Langdon. Brushed: Ch. Skysyl Harvey J. Wallbanger, owned by Sylvia Owens. Photo by Gilbert.

ROTTWEILER

The first glance at a Rottweiler will impart a lasting impression of what a real working dog looks like. The Rottweiler is a large, well-muscled and proportioned dog that is every bit as compact as he is powerful. By nature they are even-tempered and intelligent, able to size up a situation and make a responsible reaction. Their ability to maintain a stable temperament in all situations has made them highly sought after as watchdogs and companions because they have an innate sense of knowing when to bark and when to bite. The Rottweiler is a wonderful family pet who not only is a great playmate for children but he naturally assumes the position of guardian and friend to all around him—provided they have been properly introduced first!

The Rottweiler heritage dates to Roman days, when they were used to control the cattle herds and guard the prisoners of war. After pushing their way through the Alps, the Romans disbanded their herds in the cattle district of Rottweil, Germany. It is from this town that the breed derived its name. When they were no longer called upon to herd cattle, Rottweilers easily adapted themselves to pulling milk carts and carrying money and messages from the town to their home. They proved themselves to be totally trustworthy and ready, willing and able to do a hard day's work.

Because their short, black coat absorbs the heat, the Rottweiler must be kept in an area complete with good shade and plenty of water in the summer. They are an active breed and must be allowed the opportunity to maintain their strength and stamina through some vigorous exercise. Just like their ancestors, the Rottweiler of today delights in pulling a cart—so load one up with a few neighborhood kids and let everyone enjoy the fun!

Buyer's guide: Robust, active people will do well to own a Rottweiler. They are large, heavily built dogs and need lots of exercise. They are not meant to be kennel dogs, however, as they expect to be treated like a member of the family. Rottweilers are loyal and trustworthy and can be counted on to watch protectively over children and property. They take easily to training, which is a necessity for any dog the size of the Rottweiler and is highly recommended. Grooming costs are negligible, but food bills may run very high.

STANDARD FOR THE ROTTWEILER

General Appearance and Character: The Rottweiler is a good-sized strongly built, active dog. He is affectionate, intelligent, easily trained to work, naturally obedient and extremely faithful. While not quarrelsome, he possesses great courage and makes a splendid guard. His demeanor is dignified and he is not excitable.

Head: Is of medium length, the skull broad between the ears. Stop well pronounced as is also the occiput. Muzzle is not very long. It should not be longer than the distance from the stop to the occiput. Nose is well developed, with relatively large nostrils and is always black. Flews which should not be too pronounced are also black. Jaws should be strong and muscular; teeth strong—incisors of lower jaw must touch the inner surface of the upper incisors. Eyes are of medium size, dark brown in color and should express faithfulness, good humor and confidence. The ears are comparatively small, set high and wide and hang over about on a level with top of head. The skin on head should not be loose. The neck should be of fair length, strong, round and very muscular, slightly arched and free from throatiness.

Forequarters: Shoulders should be well placed, long and sloping, elbows well let down, but not loose. Legs muscular and with plenty of bone and substance, pasterns straight and strong. Feet strong, round and close, with toes well arched. Soles very hard, toe nails dark, short and strong.

Body: The chest is roomy, broad and deep. Ribs well sprung. Back straight, strong and rather short. Loins strong and deep, and flanks should not be tucked up. Croup short, broad, but not sloping.

Hindquarters: Upper thigh is short, broad and very muscular. Lower thigh very muscular at top and strong and sinewy at the bottom. Stifles fairly well bent, hocks strong. The hind feet are somewhat longer than the front ones, but should be close and strong with toes well arched. There should be no dewclaws.

Tail: Should be short, placed high (on level with back) and carried horizontally. Dogs are frequently born with a short stump tail and when tail is too long it must be docked close to body.

Coat: Hair should be short, coarse and flat. The undercoat which is absolutely required on neck and thighs should not show through outer coat. The hair should be a little longer on the back of front and hind legs and on tail.

Color: Black, with clearly defined markings on cheeks, muzzle, chest and legs, as well as over both eyes. Color of markings: tan to mahogany brown. A small spot of white on chest and belly is permissible but not desirable.

Height: Shoulder height for males 23 and three-quarters to 27 inches, for females, 21 and three-quarters to 25 and three-quarters, but height should always be considered in relation to the general appearance and conformation of the dog.

FAULTS

Too lightly built or too heavily built. Swayback. Roach back. Too long body. Lack of spring of ribs. Head too long and narrow, or too short and plump. Lack of occiput, snipy muzzle, cheekiness, top line of muzzle not straight. Light or flesh-colored nose. Hanging flews. Overshot or undershot. Loose skin on head. Ears set too low, or ears too heavy. Long or narrow or rose ear, or ears uneven in size. Light, small or slanting eyes, or lack of expression. Neck too long, thin or weak, or very noticeable throatiness. Lack of bone and muscle. Short or straight shoulders. Front legs too close together, or not straight. Weak pasterns. Splay feet, light nails, weak toes. Flat ribs. Sloping croup. Too heavy or plump body. Flanks drawn up. Flat thighs. Cowhocks or weak hocks. Dewclaws. Tail set too high or too low, or that is too long or too thin. Soft, too short, too long or too open coat. Wavy coat or lack of undercoat. White markings on toes, legs, or other parts of body. Markings not too well defined or smudgy. The one-color tan Rottweiler with either black or light mask, or with black streak on back as well as other colors such as brown or blue, are not recognized and are believed to be crossbred, as is also a longhaired Rottweiler. Timid or stupid-appearing animals are to be positively rejected.

APPROVED APRIL 9, 1935

Representing the breed: Ch. Radio Ranch's Axel V. Notara, owned by Pamela Crump Weller. Photo by Fred Habit.

SAINT BERNARD

This noble breed of dogs has a strong hold on popular sentiment, as they are associated with the saving of life in Alpine snows. The breed probably originated in Switzerland, certainly the name did, but the dog that we know today is largely the product of the fanciers of other lands, England in particular.

For hundreds of years the monks of St. Bernard, a monastery in the Alps at the apex of the pass of that name, kept a kennel of large dogs, which accompanied the monks who patrolled the pass to guide and assist travelers. These dogs undoubtedly from time to time detected travelers who had fallen helpless in the snow and would have escaped the human eye. These occurrences served as a basis upon which some remarkable stories have been written of dogs patrolling the pass alone and making miraculous and thrilling rescues.

The most celebrated of the hospice dogs of the last century was

Barry, who is said to have assisted in the rescue of over forty wanderers. This dog, mounted, is now in the museum at Berne, Switzerland. He was smooth coated and bears little resemblance to the modern St. Bernard.

Just what the origin of the breed was it is impossible to say, but it is not unlikely that they sprang from the Great Pyrenees sheep dog. It is recorded that when the kennels were devastated by distemper, which occurred several times, and the dogs which were left showed signs of degenerating from inbreeding, the monks introduced the blood of the native shepherd as well as the Great Dane and the Newfoundland. Through this intermixture of blood the stamina of the breed was restored, and by careful selection the type was fixed with a reasonable degree of certainty.

The monks have never been partial to the rough-coated dogs, as they found that their heavy coat and feathering soon clogged up with snow and handicapped their movements. Consequently, they retained the smooth coats for their kennels and disposed of the rough coats to Swiss fanciers, and it was from these fanciers that most of the ancestors of the dogs with which the public is now familiar were obtained. Since then English fanciers have introduced the blood of the Mastiff and the Bloodhound, and the result of this intermixture of breeds is the St. Bernard of today, a magnificent animal that commands attention in any company for his size, beautiful coat, coloring, and majestic mien.

As a rule the St. Bernard is docile in temperament and affectionate in disposition.

The monks were not very particular about markings, and type was not so important so long as the dog was big and strong. White, orange, and black were the colors looked for, a white blaze running up the face and joining the collar of the same color that circled the neck and crossed the shoulders and chest. The body was patched with orange and the orange color gradually deepened in color as it approached the white until it became black at the fringe. Particularly desired was a spot in the center of the white on the forehead. The idea of these markings was that they represented the stole, the chasuble, and scapular of the vestments of their order. Present day fanciers do not attach so much importance to these markings.

In selecting St. Bernard puppies at from two to four months and after, look for great size and massiveness; head medium in length, with a very deep, square muzzle, decided stop, massive skull, but with the substance well distributed, not broad like a Mastiff. The puppy should show signs of growing tall, and promise enormous bone and a short, deep body. A rich red is the favorite color, with white collar, blaze, and dark shadings. The roughs show more coat as puppies than the smooths.

Buyer's guide: This huge dog adapts very well to the home, provided that they have ample room outdoors to exercise in. They have a gentle nature and an honest love of people. However, if they are not provided with enough human companionship they can quickly develop a distant, standoffish disposition. It is best to buy your St. Bernard as a puppy so that you can help shape their personality, and *be sure* to start training your dog early in life, for an unruly adult St. Bernard would be totally unacceptable. Remember, buy a St. Bernard only after much thought and consideration for both your household and the welfare of this large breed.

STANDARD FOR THE SAINT BERNARD
SHORTHAIRED

General: Powerful, proportionately tall figure, strong and muscular in every part, with powerful head and most intelligent expression. In dogs with a dark mask the expression appears more stern, but never ill-natured.

Head: Like the whole body, very powerful and imposing. The massive skull is wide, slightly arched and the sides slope in a gentle curve into the very strongly developed, high cheek bones. Occiput only moderately developed. The supra-orbital ridge is very strongly developed and forms nearly a right angle with the horizontal axis of the head. Deeply imbedded between the eyes and starting at the root of the muzzle, a furrow runs over the whole skull. It is strongly marked in the first half, gradually disappearing toward the base of the occiput. The lines at the sides of the head diverge considerably from the outer corner of the eyes toward the back of the head. The skin of the forehead, above the eyes, forms rather noticeable wrinkles, more or less pronounced, which converge toward the furrow. Especially when the dog is in action, the wrinkles are more visible without in the least giving the impression of morosity. Too strongly developed wrinkles are not desired. The slope from the skull to the muzzle is sudden and rather steep.

The muzzle is short, does not taper, and the vertical depth at the root of the muzzle must be greater than the length of the muzzle. The bridge of the muzzle is not arched, but straight; in some dogs, occasionally, slightly broken. A rather wide, well-marked, shallow furrow runs from the root of the muzzle over the entire bridge of the muzzle to the nose. The flews of the upper jaw are strongly developed, not sharply cut, but turning in a beautiful curve into the lower edge, and slightly overhanging. The flews of the lower jaw must not be deeply pendant. The teeth should be sound and strong and should meet in either a scissors or an even bite; the scissors bite being preferable. The undershot bite, although sometimes found with good specimens, is not desirable. The overshot bite is a fault. A black roof to the mouth is desirable.

Nose (Schwamm): Very substantial, broad, with wide open nostrils, and, like the lips, always black.

Ears: Of medium size, rather high set, with very strongly developed burr (Muschel) at the base. They stand slightly away from the head at the base, then drop with a sharp bend to the side and cling to the head without a turn. The flap is tender and forms a rounded triangle, slightly elongated toward the point, the front edge lying firmly to the head, whereas the back edge may stand somewhat away from the head, especially when the dog is at attention. Lightly set ears, which at the base immediately cling to the head, give it an oval and too little marked exterior, whereas a strongly developed base gives the skull a squarer, broader and much more expressive appearance.

Eyes: Set more to the front than the sides, are of medium size, dark brown, with intelligent, friendly expression, set moderately deep. The lower eyelids, as a rule, do not close completely and, if that is the case, form an angular wrinkle toward the inner corner of the eye. Eyelids which are too deeply pendant and show conspicuously the lachrymal glands, or a very red, thick haw, and eyes that are too light, are objectionable.

Neck: Set high, very strong and in action is carried erect. Otherwise horizontally or slightly downward. The junction of head and neck is distinctly marked by an indentation. The nape of the neck is very muscular and rounded at the sides which makes the neck appear rather short. The dewlap of throat and neck is well pronounced: too strong development, however, is not desirable.

Shoulders: Sloping and broad, very muscular and powerful. The withers are strongly pronounced.

Chest: Very well arched, moderately deep, not reaching below the elbows.

Back: Very broad, perfectly straight as far as the haunches, from there gently sloping to the rump, and merging imperceptibly into the root of the tail.

Hindquarters: Well-developed. Legs very muscular.

Belly: Distinctly set off from the very powerful loin section, only little drawn up.

Tail: Starting broad and powerful directly from the rump is long, very heavy, ending in a powerful tip. In repose it hangs straight down, turning gently upward in the lower third only, which is not considered a fault. In a great many specimens the tail is carried with the end slightly bent and therefore hangs down in the shape of an "*f.*" In action all dogs carry the tail more or less turned upward. However it may not be carried too erect or my any means rolled over the back. A slight curling of the tip is sooner admissible.

Forearms: Very powerful and extraordinarily muscular.

Forelegs: Straight, strong.

Hind Legs: Hocks of moderate angulation. Dewclaws are not desired; if present, they must not obstruct gait.

Feet: Broad, with strong toes, moderately closed, and with rather high knuckles. The so-called dewclaws which sometimes occur on the inside of the hind legs are imperfectly developed toes. They are of no use to the dog and are not taken into consideration in judging. They may be removed by surgery.

Coat: Very dense, short-haired (stockhaarig), lying smooth, tough, without however feeling rough to the touch. The thighs are slightly bushy. The tail at the root has longer and denser hair which gradually becomes shorter toward the tip. The tail appears bushy, not forming a flag.

Color: White with red or red with white, the red in its various shades; brindle patches with white markings. The colors red and brown-yellow are of entirely equal value. Necessary markings are: white chest, feet and tip of tail, noseband, collar or spot on the nape; the latter and blaze are very desirable. Never of one color or without white. Faulty are all other colors, except the favorite dark shadings on the head (mask) and ears. One distinguishes between mangle dogs and splash-coated dogs.

Height at Shoulder: Of the dog should be 27½ inches minimum, of the bitch 25½ inches. Female animals are of finer and more delicate build.

Considered as faults are all deviations from the Standard, as for instance a swayback and a disproportionately long back, hocks too much bent, straight hindquarters, upward growing hair in spaces between the toes, out at elbows, cowhocks and weak pasterns.

LONGHAIRED

The longhaired type completely resembles the shorthaired type except for the coat which is not shorthaired (stockhaarig) but of medium length plain to slightly wavy, never rolled or curly and not shaggy either. Usually, on the back, especially from the region of the haunches to the rump, the hair is more wavy, a condition, by the way, that is slightly indicated in the shorthaired dogs. The tail is bushy with dense hair of moderate length. Rolled or curly hair on the tail is not desirable. A tail with parted hair, or a flag tail, is faulty. Face and ears are covered with short and soft hair; longer hair at the base of the ear is permissible. Forelegs only slightly feathered; thighs very bushy.

APPROVED MAY 12, 1959

Representing the breed: Lysander's Little Bateese, owned by Barbara Anne Bessette and bred by Donald U. Bessette.

SAMOYED

It is to the writings of Arctic explorers that one must go to gather much that is enlightening concerning the various breeds of dogs which have been used for generations by the semi-nomadic people of these latitudes for traversing the barren, trackless regions of the North.

In general appearance, Samoyeds can be regarded as the most beautiful of northern breeds, their thick coats being particularly decorative. They have pointed muzzles; sharply erect ears; strong, bushy tails; and compact bodies. Their usefulness is written into their frames, and they are capable of accomplishing long journeys with tireless endurance. The Samoyed's coat is dense, harsh, and deep, especially on the neck and shoulders where it forms a ruff, and it shines with an icy sheen. They have a wooly undercoat that is capable of resisting the most penetrating snow and cold.

Samoyeds have proven themselves able to cope in even the most extreme conditions, and throughout all they have maintained a gentle, agreeable nature. One look at their "smiling" face and you can see an almost impish gleam in their eye. They are fun-loving, yet will obey completely and unhesitatingly when told to stop their games. They are instinctively loyal and homeloving, and make excellent guardians to both children and property.

The Samoyed has been bred pure for countless generations, raised as both workers and companions to the people of the North. Today they still possess an uncanny understanding of the feelings of their owners, rallying to their aid with endless affection and willing to fight to the death, if need be. Their temperament is unspoiled, and they can be as sweet as a loving child.

Buyer's guide: The friendly Samoyed makes a very reliable housepet and companion. They are not overactive or boisterous and require only a moderate amount of daily exercise and food. They can be kept in any fairly spacious home. The Samoyed's beautiful white coat is deceivingly easy to take care of since it resists dirt, sheds very little and is easily brushed out. Their extremely affectionate nature makes them a natural around children, but they are very strong and should be normally handled by adults.

STANDARD FOR THE SAMOYED

General Conformation:
(a) General Appearance: The Samoyed, being essentially a working dog, should present a picture of beauty, alertness and strength, with agility, dignity and grace. As his work lies in cold climates, his coat should be

heavy and weather-resistant, well groomed, and of good quality rather than quantity. The male carries more of a "ruff" than the female. He should not be long in the back as a weak back would make him practically useless for his legitimate work, but at the same time, a close coupled body would also place him at a great disadvantage as a draft dog. Breeders should aim for the happy medium, a body not long but muscular, allowing liberty, with a deep chest and well-sprung ribs, strong neck, straight front and especially strong loins. Males should be masculine in appearance and deportment without unwarranted aggressiveness; bitches feminine without weakness of structure or apparent softness of temperament. Bitches may be slightly longer in back than males. They should both give the appearance of being capable of great endurance but be free from coarseness. Because of the depth of chest required, the legs should be moderately long. A very short-legged dog is to be deprecated. Hindquarters should be particularly well developed, stifles well bent and any suggestion of unsound stifles or cowhocks severely penalized. General appearance should include movement and general conformation, indicating balance and good substance.

(b) Substance: Substance is that sufficiency of bone and muscle which rounds out a balance with the frame. The bone is heavier than would be expected in a dog of this size but not so massive as to prevent the speed and agility most desirable in a Samoyed. In all builds, bone should be in proportion to body size. The Samoyed should never be so heavy as to appear clumsy nor so light as to appear racy. The weight should be in proportion to the height.

(c) Height: Males—21 to 23½ inches; females—19 to 21 inches at the withers. An oversized or undersized Samoyed is to be penalized according to the extent of the deviation.

(d) Coat (Texture & Condition): The Samoyed is a double-coated dog. The body should be well covered with an undercoat of soft, short, thick, close wool with longer and harsh hair growing through it to form the outer coat, which stands straight out from the body and should be free from curl. The coat should form a ruff around the neck and shoulders, framing the head (more on males than on females). Quality of coat should be weather resistant and considered more than quantity. A droopy coat is undesirable. The coat should glisten with a silver sheen. The female does not usually carry as long a coat as most males and it is softer in texture.

(e) Color: Samoyeds should be pure white, white and biscuit, cream, or all biscuit. Any other colors disqualify.

Movement:

(a) Gait: The Samoyed should trot, not pace. He should move with a quick stride that is well timed. The gait should be free, balanced and vigorous, with good reach in the forequarters and good driving power in the hindquarters. When trotting, there should be a strong rear action drive. Moving at a slow walk or trot, they will not single-track, but as speed increases the legs gradually angle inward until the pads are finally falling on a line directly under the longitudinal center of the body. As the pad marks converge the forelegs and hind legs are carried straight forward in traveling, the stifles not turned in nor out. The back should remain strong, firm and level. A choppy or stilted gait should be penalized.

(b) **Rear End:** Upper thighs should be well developed. Stifles well bent—approximately 45 degrees to the ground. Hocks should be well developed, sharply defined and set at approximately 30 per cent of hip height. The hind legs should be parallel when viewed from the rear in a natural stance, strong, well developed, turning neither in nor out. Straight stifles are objectionable. Double-jointedness or cowhocks are a fault. Cowhocks should only be determined if the dog has had an opportunity to move properly.

(c) **Front End:** Legs should be parallel and straight to the pasterns. The pasterns should be strong, sturdy and straight, but flexible with some spring for proper let-down of feet. Because of depth of chest, legs should be moderately long. Length of dog from the ground to the elbow should be approximately 55 per cent of the total height at the withers—a very short-legged dog is to be deprecated. Shoulders should be long and sloping, with a layback of 45 degrees and be firmly set. Out at the shoulders or out at the elbows should be penalized. The withers separation should be approximately 1-1½ inches.

(d) **Feet:** Large, long, flattish—a hare-foot, slightly spread but not splayed; toes arched; pads thick and tough, with protective growth of hair between the toes. Feet should turn neither in nor out in a natural stance but may turn in slightly in the act of pulling. Turning out, pigeon-toed, round or cat-footed or splayed are faults. Feathers on feet are not too essential but are more profuse on females than on males.

Head:

(a) **Conformation:** Skull is wedge-shaped, broad, slightly crowned, not round or apple-headed, and should form an equilateral triangle on lines between the inner base of the ears and the center point of the stop. *Muzzle:* Muzzle of medium length and medium width, neither coarse nor snipy; should taper toward the nose and be in proportion to the size of the dog and the width of skull. The muzzle must have depth. *Stop:* Not too abrupt, nevertheless well defined. *Lips:* Should be black for preference and slightly curved up at the corners of the mouth, giving the "Samoyed smile." Lip lines should not have the appearance of being coarse nor should the flews drop predominately at corners of the mouth.

Ears: Strong and thick, erect, triangular and slightly rounded at the tips; should not be large or pointed, nor should they be small and "bear-eared." Ears should conform to head size and the size of the dog; they should be set well apart but be within the border of the outer edge of the head; they should be mobile and well covered inside with hair; hair full and stand-off before the ears. Length of ear should be the same measurement as the distance from inner base of ear to outer corner of eye.

Eyes: Should be dark for preference; should be placed well apart and deep-set; almond shaped with lower lid slanting toward an imaginary point approximating the base of ears. Dark eye rims for preference. Round or protruding eyes penalized. Blue eyes disqualifying.

Nose: Black for preference but brown, liver, or Dudley nose not penalized. Color of nose sometimes changes with age and weather.

Jaws and Teeth: Strong, well-set teeth, snugly overlapping with scissors bite. Undershot or overshot should be penalized.

(b) Expression: The expression, referred to as "Samoyed expression," is very important and is indicated by sparkle of the eyes, animation and lighting up of the face when alert or intent on anything. Expression is made up of a combination of eyes, ears and mouth. The ears should be erect when alert; the mouth should be slightly curved up at the corners to form the "Samoyed smile."

Torso:

(a) Neck: Strong, well muscled, carried proudly erect, set on sloping shoulders to carry head with dignity when at attention. Neck should blend into shoulders with a graceful arch.

(b) Chest: Should be deep, with ribs well sprung out from the spine and flattened at the sides to allow proper movement of the shoulders and freedom for the front legs. Should not be barrel-chested. Perfect depth of chest approximates the point of elbows, and the deepest part of the chest should be back of the forelegs—near the ninth rib. Heart and lung room are secured more by body depth than width.

(c) Loin and Back: The withers forms the highest part of the back. Loins strong and slightly arched. The back should be straight to the loin, medium in length, very muscular and neither long nor short-coupled. The dog should be "just off square"—the length being approximately 5 per cent more than the height. Females allowed to be slightly longer than males. The belly should be well shaped and tightly muscled and, with the rear of the thorax, should swing up in a pleasing curve (tuck-up). Croup must be full, slightly sloping, and must continue imperceptibly to the tail root.

Tail: The tail should be moderately long with the tail bone terminating approximately at the hock when down. It should be profusely covered with long hair and carried forward over the back or side when alert, but sometimes dropped when at rest. It should not be high or low set and should be mobile and loose—not tight over the back. A double hook is a fault. A judge should see the tail over the back once when judging.

Disposition: Intelligent, gentle, loyal, adaptable, alert, full of action, eager to serve, friendly but conservative, not distrustful or shy, not overly aggressive. Unprovoked aggressiveness to be severely penalized.

DISQUALIFICATIONS

Any color other than pure white, cream, biscuit, or white and biscuit. Blue eyes.

APPROVED APRIL 9, 1963

Representing the breed: Ch. Yurok of Whitecliff, owned by Percy Matheron and Mrs. Jean M. Blank.

SHETLAND SHEEPDOG

The Shetland Sheepdog hails from the Shetland Islands off the Scotland coast, a region which has commonly produced animals small in stature. As with the Shetland Pony, the Shetland Sheepdog is a scaled-down version of its nearest relative, in this case the Collie. The bantamizing of the breed is attributed to selective crossings of Border Collies and native breeds which had adapted to the limited space of the islands.

The Sheltie has been called the Miniature Collie or the Shetland Collie, and although they are near replicas of their Collie cousins they do have distinct traits. They breed true to type and should never be so diminutive as to resemble a toy-dog in any way, for they are a working dog by heritage and must remain so.

In their native country they are able herders, efficiently driving and gathering together the sheep that inhabit those windswept isles. Their double coat protects them from the elements and they are naturally hardy and long-lived.

In recent years they have been bred more as companions and pets than for utility, and for this purpose they are excellent as they have high intelligence and a faithful heart. Shelties have been used extensively as obedience competitors and have taken a considerable number of top honors in tough competition.

Buyer's guide: The perky, affectionate Sheltie is an excellent housedog and companion for all ages. Since they are naturally active dogs, they can obtain sufficient exercise through their normal daily routine and a brisk walk. They do well in both city and country, although the latter is preferable. Shelties are exceptionally smart and take easily to training programs, which makes them suited for guarding both children and the home. Their long coat is easily kept manageable by brushing it thoroughly with a bristle brush every few days. Although they are quite docile by nature, Shetland Sheepdogs are intelligent and quick thinking and make instinctively fine watchdogs.

STANDARD FOR THE SHETLAND SHEEPDOG

Preamble: The Shetland Sheepdog, like the Collie, traces to the Border Collie of Scotland, which, transported to the Shetland Islands and crossed with small, intelligent, longhaired breeds, was reduced to miniature proportions. Subsequently crosses were made from time to time with Collies. This breed now bears the same relationship in size and general appearance to the Rough Collie as the Shetland Pony does to some of the larger breeds of horses. Although the resemblance between the Shetland Sheepdog and the Rough Collie is marked, there are differences which may be noted.

General Description: The Shetland Sheepdog is a small, alert, rough-coated, longhaired working dog. He must be sound, agile and sturdy. The outline should be so symmetrical that no part appears out of proportion to the whole. Dogs should appear masculine; bitches, feminine.

Size: The Shetland Sheepdog should stand between 13 and 16 inches at the shoulder. Note: Height is determined by a line perpendicular to the ground from the top of the shoulder blades, the dog standing naturally, with forelegs parallel to line of measurement. **Disqualification:** Heights below or above the desired size range are to be disqualified from the show ring.

Coat: The coat should be double, the outer coat consisting of long, straight, harsh hair; the undercoat short, furry, and so dense as to give the entire coat its "stand-off" quality. The hair on face, tips of ears and feet should be smooth. Mane and frill should be abundant, and particularly impressive in males. The forlegs well feathered, the hind legs heavily so, but smooth below the hock joint. Hair on tail profuse. Note: Excess hair on ears, feet, and on hocks may be trimmed for the show ring. **Faults:** Coat short or flat, in whole or in part; wavy, curly, soft or silky. Lack of undercoat. Smooth-coated specimens.

Color: Black, blue merle, and sable (ranging from golden through mahogany); marked with varying amount of white and/or tan. **Faults:** Rustiness in a black or blue coat. Washed out or degenerate colors, such as pale sable and faded blue. Self-color in the case of blue merle, that is, without any merling or mottling and generally appearing as a faded or dilute tri-color. Conspicuous white body spots. Specimens with more than 50 per cent white shall be so severely penalized as to effectively eliminate them from competition. **Disqualification:** Brindle.

Temperament: The Shetland Sheepdog is intensely loyal, affectionate, and responsive to his owner. However, he may be reserved toward strangers but not to the point of showing fear or cringing in the ring. **Faults:** Shyness, timidity, or nervousness. Stubbornness, snappiness, or ill temper.

Head: The head should be refined and its shape, when viewed from top or side, be a long, blunt wedge tapering slightly from ears to nose, which must be black. **Skull and Muzzle:** Top of skull should be flat, showing no prominence at nuchal crest (the top of the occiput). Cheeks should be flat and should merge smoothly into a well-rounded muzzle. Skull and muzzle should be of equal length, balance point being inner corner of eye. In profile the top line of skull should parallel the top line of muzzle, but on a higher plane due to the presence of a slight but definite stop. Jaws clean and powerful. The deep, well-developed under-jaw, rounded at chin, should extend to base of nostril. Lips tight. Upper and lower lips must meet and fit smoothly together all the way around. Teeth level and evenly spaced. Scissors bite. **Faults:** Two-angled head. Too prominent stop, or no stop. Overfill below, between, or above eyes. Prominent nuchal crest. Domed skull. Prominent cheekbones. Snipy muzzle. Short, receding, or shallow under-jaw, lacking breadth and depth. Overshot or undershot, missing or crooked teeth. Teeth visible when mouth is closed.

Eyes: Medium size with dark, almond-shaped rims, set somewhat obliquely in skull. Color must be dark, with blue or merle eyes permissible in blue merles only. **Faults:** Light, round, large or too small. Prominent haws.

Ears: Small and flexible, placed high, carried three-fourths erect, with tips breaking forward. When in repose the ears fold lengthwise and are thrown back into the frill. **Faults:** Set too low. Hound, prick, bat, twisted ears. Leather too thick or too thin.

Expression: Contours and chiseling of the head, the shape, set and use of ears, the placement, shape and color of the eyes, combine to produce expression. Normally the expression should be alert, gentle, intelligent and questioning. Toward strangers the eyes should show watchfullness and reserve, but no fear.

Neck: Neck should be muscular, arched, and of sufficient length to carry the head proudly. **Faults:** Too short and thick.

Body: In over-all appearance the body should appear moderately long as measured from shoulder joint to ischium (rearmost extremity of the pelvic bone), but much of this length is actually due to the proper angulation and breadth of the shoulder and hindquarter, as the back itself should be comparatively short. Back should be level and strongly muscled. Chest should be deep, the brisket reaching to point of elbow. The ribs should be well sprung, but flattened at their lower half to allow free play of the foreleg and shoulder. Abdomen moderately tucked up. **Faults:** Back too long, too short, swayed or roached. Barrel ribs. Slabside. Chest narrow and/or too shallow.

Forequarters: From the withers the shoulder blades should slope at a 45-degree angle forward and downward to the shoulder joints. At the withers they are separated only by the vertebra, but they must slope outward sufficiently to accommodate the desired spring of rib. The upper arm should join the shoulder blade at as nearly as possible a right angle. Elbow joint should be equidistant from the ground or from the withers. Forelegs straight viewed from all angles, muscular and clean, and of strong bone. Pasterns very strong, sinewy and flexible. Dewclaws may be removed. **Faults:** Insufficient angulation between shoulder and upper arm. Upper arm too short. Lack of outward slope of shoulders. Loose shoulders. Turning in or out of elbows. Crooked legs. Light bone.

Feet (front and hind): Feet should be oval and compact with the toes well arched and fitting tightly together. Pads deep and tough, nails hard and strong. **Faults:** Feet turning in or out. Splay-feet. Hare-feet. Cat-feet.

Hindquarters: There should be a slight arch at the loins, and the croup should slope gradually to the rear. The hipbone (pelvis) should be set at a 30-degree angle to the spine. The thigh should be broad and muscular. The thighbone should be set into the pelvis at a right angle corresponding to the angle of the shoulder blade and upper arm. Stifle bones join the thighbone and should be distinctly angled at the stifle joint. The over-all length of the stifle should at least equal the length of the thighbone, and preferably should slightly exceed it. Hock joint should be clean-cut, angular, sinewy, with good bone and strong ligamentation. The hock (metatarsus) should be short and straight viewed from all angles. Dewclaws should be removed. Feet (*see* Forequarters). **Faults:** Croup higher than withers. Croup too straight or too steep. Narrow thighs. Cowhocks. Hocks turning out. Poorly defined hock joint. Feet (*see* Forequarters).

Tail: The tail should be sufficiently long so that when it is laid along the back edge of the hind legs the last vertebra will reach the hock joint. Carriage of tail at rest is straight down or in a slight upward curve. When the dog is alert the tail is normally lifted, but it should not be curved forward over the back. **Faults:** Too short. Twisted at end.

Gait: The trotting gait of the Shetland Sheepdog should denote effortless speed and smoothness. There should be no jerkiness, nor stiff, stilted, up-and-down movement. The drive should be from the rear, true and straight, dependent upon correct angulation, musculation, and ligamentation of the entire hindquarter, thus allowing the dog to reach well under his body with his hind foot and propel himself forward. Reach of stride of the foreleg is dependent upon correct angulation, musculation and ligamentation of the forequarters, together with correct width of chest and construction of rib cage. The foot should be lifted only enough to clear the ground as the leg swings forward. Viewed from the front, both forelegs and hind legs should move forward almost perpendicular to ground at the walk, slanting a little inward at a slow trot, until at a swift trot the feet are brought so far inward toward center line of body that the tracks left show two parallel lines of footprints actually touching a center line at their inner edges. *There should be no crossing of the feet nor throwing of the weight from side to side.* **Faults:** Stiff, short steps, with a choppy, jerky movement. Mincing steps, with a hopping up and down, or a balancing of weight from side to side (often erroneously admired as a "dancing gait" but permissible in young puppies). Lifting of front feet in hackney-like action, resulting in loss of speed and energy. Pacing gait.

SCALE OF POINTS

General Appearance
Symmetry 10
Temperament 10
Coat 5   25

Head
Skull and stop 5

Muzzle 5
Eyes, ears and expression
. . . . 10   20

Body
Neck and back 5

Chest, ribs and brisket	10		*Hindquarters*	
			Hip, thigh and stifle	10
Loin, croup, and tail	5	20	Hocks and feet	5 15

Forequarters
Shoulder 10
Forelegs and feet........5 15

Hindquarters
Hip, thigh and stifle....10
Hocks and feet.........5 15

Gait
Gait—smoothness and lack of waste motion when trotting..........5 5
TOTAL.............. 100

DISQUALIFICATIONS

Heights below or above the desired range, i.e. 13-16 inches. Brindle color.

APPROVED MAY 12, 1959

Representing the breed: Ch. Kismet's Centurion, owned by Mr. and Mrs. R. Bryar.

SIBERIAN HUSKY

The northern beauty of the Siberian Husky has won this breed many friends; their ability to work speedily and eagerly has won them many more. The Husky developed in a land of hard work and harsh living. They have not only survived the rigors of sled-dogging, but they have flourished and a dog of both stout heart and body has emerged.

The breed goes back nearly 2000 years in native Siberia. A group of eskimo-like people called the chuchis developed the breed and maintained the purity of their lines so that the Husky could naturally develop into a dog capable of withstanding the extremes of arctic life. The people of the North needed a dog of speed and strength that could pull light loads over long distances, while at the same time exerting little energy. The less energy they exerted on their work, the more energy they had to survive blizzard conditions and sub-zero temperatures. Siberian Huskies have a natural ability to find and follow a trail and a team in harness can pull with such speed and enthusiasm that a good brake is needed to slow them down.

The breed can adapt to most any terrain, although the heat in the summer must not be too extreme. The working dog instinct becomes apparent the instant you hitch your dog to a sled and watch him tear off down a path or covered road. The spirit of the race moves the Husky on, and whether the rider or the team gets the most delight out of the whole deal, no one really knows.

Eager to please, the Siberian Husky is a dog to be enjoyed. They are meticulously clean and make natural playmates for children of all ages. They never tire of old games, but merely make new rules to fit their scheme of things. Although sometimes very mischievous as a puppy, they are sometimes even more mischievous as an adult—they've had all the more practice at it. They are not very destructive, however, just creatively playful!

The Siberian Husky makes a great housepet because they add so much with their warm dispostion. They are loyal friends and great company, and their presence is always known and welcomed in a room. They have no trouble keeping pace with the energy and antics of young children. The Siberian Husky is more than a remarkably beautiful show and work dog, it is a great dog to have around because it is equally adept at protection and affection.

Buyer's guide: Athletic and outgoing, the Siberian Husky is a seemingly tireless dog and should therefore be owned by active people. They are enthusiastically affectionate and are sometimes given to jumping up to greet people. This is easily corrected through some type of obedience training, to which they are responsive. Siberians must be given plenty of outlet for their energy. With exercise they will be less restless in the home and less apt to continually pester their owners for attention. They are generally affectionate towards children, but may become somewhat cranky if they are exposed to too much childish abuse. They love to run (and can do so for hours), so you joggers—the Siberian is the dog for you!

STANDARD FOR THE SIBERIAN HUSKY

General Appearance: The Siberian Husky is a medium-sized working dog, quick and light on his feet and free and graceful in action. His moderately compact and well-furred body, erect ears and brush tail suggest his Northern heritage. His characteristic gait is smooth and seemingly effortless. He performs his original function in harness most capably, carrying a light load at moderate speed over great distances. His body proportions and form reflect this basic balance of power, speed and endurance. The males of the Siberian Husky breed are masculine but never coarse; the bitches are feminine but without weakness of structure. In proper condition, with muscle firm and well-developed, the Siberian Husky does not carry excess weight.

Head:

Skull: Of medium size and in proportion to the body; slightly rounded on top and tapering gradually from the widest point to the eyes. **Faults:** Head clumsy or heavy; head too finely chiseled.

Muzzle: Of medium length; that is, the distance from the tip of the nose to the stop is equal to the distance from the stop to the occiput. The stop is well-defined and the bridge of the nose is straight from the stop to the tip. The muzzle is of medium width, tapering gradually to the nose, with the tip neither pointed nor square. The lips are well-pigmented and close fitting; teeth closing in a scissors bite. **Faults:** Muzzle either too snipy or too coarse; muzzle too short or too long; insufficient stop; any bite other than scissors.

Ears: Of medium size, triangular in shape, close fitting and set high on the head. They are thick, well-furred, slightly arched at the back, and strongly erect, with slightly rounded tips pointing straight up. **Faults:** Ears too large in proportion to the head; too wide-set; not strongly erect.

Eyes: Almond shaped, moderately spaced and set a trifle obliquely. The expression is keen, but friendly; interested and even mischievous. Eyes may be brown or blue in color; one of each or parti-colored are acceptable. **Faults:** Eyes set too obliquely; set too close together.

Nose: Black in gray, tan or black dogs; liver in copper dogs; may be flesh-colored in pure white dogs. The pink-streaked "snow nose" is acceptable.

Body:

Neck: Medium in length, arched and carried proudly erect when dog is standing. When moving at a trot, the neck is extended so that the head is carried slightly forward. **Faults:** Neck too short and thick; neck too long.

Shoulders: The shoulder blade is well laid back at an approximate angle of 45 degrees to the ground. The upper arm angles slightly backward from point of shoulder to elbow, and is never perpendicular to the ground. The muscles and ligaments holding the shoulder to the rib cage are firm and well-developed. **Faults:** Straight shoulders; loose shoulders.

Chest: Deep and strong, but not too broad, with the deepest point being just behind and level with the elbows. The ribs are well-sprung from the spine but flattened on the sides to allow for freedom of action. **Faults:** Chest too broad; "barrel ribs"; ribs too flat or weak.

Back: The back is straight and strong, with a level topline from withers to croup. It is of medium length, neither cobby nor slack from excessive length. The loin is taut and lean, narrower than the rib cage, and with a slight tuck-up. The croup slopes away from the spine at an angle, but never so steeply as to restrict the rearward thrust of the hind legs. In profile, the length of the body from the point of the shoulder to the rear point of the croup is slightly longer than the height of the body from the ground to the top of the withers. **Faults:** Weak or slack back; roached back; sloping topline.

Legs and Feet:

Forelegs: When standing and viewed from the front, the legs are moderately spaced, parallel and straight, with elbows close to the body and turned neither in nor out. Viewed from the side, pasterns are slightly slanted, with pastern joint strong, but flexible. Bone is substantial but never heavy. Length of the leg from elbow to ground is slightly more than the distance from the elbow to the top of withers. Dewclaws on forelegs may be removed. **Faults:** Weak pasterns; too heavy bone; too narrow or too wide in the front; out at the elbows.

Hindquarters: When standing and viewed from the rear, the hind legs are moderately spaced and parallel. The upper thighs are well-muscled and powerful, the stifles well-bent, the hock joint well-defined and set low to the ground. Dewclaws, if any, are to be removed. **Faults:** Straight stifles, cowhocks, too narrow or too wide in the rear.

Feet: Oval in shape, but not long. The paws are medium size, compact and well-furred between the toes and pads. The pads are tough and thickly cushioned. The paws neither turn in nor out when dog is in natural stance. **Faults:** Soft or splayed toes; paws too large and clumsy; paws too small and delicate; toeing in or out.

Tail: The well-furred tail of fox-brush shape is set on just below the level of the topline, and is usually carried over the back in a graceful sickle curve when the dog is at attention. When carried up, the tail does not curl to either side of the body, nor does it snap flat against the back. A trailing tail is normal for the dog when working or in repose. Hair on the tail is of medium length and approximately the same length on top, sides and bottom, giving the appearance of a round brush. **Faults:** A snapped or tightly curled tail; highly plumed tail; tail set too low or too high.

Gait: The Siberian Husky's characteristic gait is smooth and seemingly effortless. He is quick and light on his feet, and when in the show ring should be gaited on a loose lead at a moderately fast trot, exhibiting good reach in the forequarters and good drive in the hindquarters. When viewed from the front to rear, while moving at a walk the Siberian Husky does not single-track, but as the speed increases the legs gradually angle inward until the pads are falling on a line directly under the longitudinal center of the body. As the pad marks converge, the forelegs and hind legs are carried straight forward, with neither elbows nor stifles turned in or out. Each hind leg moves in the path of the foreleg on the same side. While the dog is gaiting, the topline remains firm and level. **Faults:** Short, prancing or choppy gait, lumbering or rolling gait; crossing; crabbing.

Coat: The coat of the Siberian Husky is double and medium in length, giving a well-furred appearance, but is never so long as to obscure the clean-cut outline of the dog. The undercoat is soft and dense and of sufficient length to support the outer coat. The guard hairs of the outer coat are straight and somewhat smooth-lying, never harsh nor standing straight off from the body. It should be noted that the absence of the undercoat during the shedding season is normal. Trimming of the whiskers and fur between the toes and around the feet to present a neater appearance is permissible. Trimming of the fur on any other part of the dog is not to be condoned and should be severely penalized. **Faults:** Long, rough or shaggy coat; texture too harsh or too silky; trimming of the coat, except as permitted above.

Color: All colors from black to pure white are allowed. A variety of markings on the head is common, including many striking patterns not found in other breeds.

Temperament: The characteristic temperament of the Siberian Husky is friendly and gentle, but also alert and outgoing. He does not display the possessive qualities of the guard dog, nor is he overly suspicious of strangers or aggressive with other dogs. Some measure of reserve and dignity may be expected in the mature dog. His intelligence, tractability, and eager disposition make him an agreeable companion and willing worker.

Size: **Height:** Dogs, 21 to 23½ inches at the withers. Bitches, 20 to 22 inches at the withers. **Weight:** Dogs, 45 to 60 pounds. Bitches, 35 to 50 pounds. Weight is in proportion to height. The measurements mentioned above represent the extreme height and weight limits, with no preference given to either extreme. **Disqualification:** Dogs over 23½ inches and bitches over 22 inches.

Summary: The most important breed characteristics of the Siberian Husky are medium size, moderate bone, well-balanced proportions, ease and freedom of movement, proper coat, pleasing head and ears, correct tail, and good disposition. Any appearance of excessive bone or weight, constricted or clumsy gait, or long, rough coat should be penalized. The Siberian Husky never appears so heavy or coarse as to suggest a freighting animal; nor is he so light and fragile as to suggest a sprint-racing animal. In both sexes the Siberian Husky gives the appearance of being capable of great endurance. In addition to the faults already noted, obvious structural faults common to all breeds are as undesirable in the Siberian Husky as in any other breed, even though they are not specifically mentioned herein.

DISQUALIFICATION
Dogs over 23½ inches and bitches over 22 inches.

APPROVED NOVEMBER 9, 1971

STANDARD SCHNAUZER

The Standard Schnauzer, a medium sized working dog, was developed in the sixteenth century by German countrymen. The Standard was feisty enough to serve as a watchdog and guard, yet he exhibited an amiable and affectionate attitude when off duty. Early breeders crossed the Wolfspitz and the black German Poodle with some wirehaired Pinscher stock and arrived at today's double-coated dog. The soft, wooly undercoat serves to keep the dog warm in even the coldest weather; the hard, wiry outercoat forms the attractive, salt and pepper appearance typical of the Schnauzer.

The Standard Schnauzer's muzzle is highlighted by the wiry whiskers that accentuate the rectangular shape of the head. The breed is powerfully built, and they are agile and sound in their gait. The Schnauzer is alert to all around him and is high-spirited in temperament. While they naturally excel at rat catching and guard work, they are highly intelligent and reliable enough to trust with any task—whether babysitting or chasing wild animals away from a herd.

During the early years of the breed in the United States they were classified as terriers, but were soon moved into the working group as their usefulness as a worker and their tendency not to exhibit the temperament that is often typical of the terrier led to the change. Besides being a popular entry at dog shows, the Standard Schnauzer is also taking many top prizes in the obedience rings. They make excellent watchdogs for the home or apartments as they are keenly aware of any strange noises or people and are quick to alert their owners of any suspicions they may have.

Buyer's Guide: Although somewhat feisty in nature, the Standard Schnauzer fits well with most families. They are quite perceptive and respond to the wishes of their owners without hesitation or protest. They are a sturdy, compact dog and they place no major restrictions on their owners in regard to space, exercise requirements, etc. To keep them looking their best, they should be clipped and groomed several times a year at a professional parlor. Although they are fond of and sensitive to children, they could snap at them instinctively if taken by surprise.

STANDARD FOR THE STANDARD SCHNAUZER

General Appearance: The Standard Schnauzer is a robust, heavy-set dog, sturdily built with good muscle and plenty of bone; square-built in proportion of body length to height. His nature combines high-spirited temperament with extreme reliability. His rugged build and dense harsh coat are accentuated by the hallmark of the breed, the arched eyebrows, bristly mustache and luxuriant whiskers.

Head: Strong, rectangular, and elongated; narrowing slightly from the ears to the eyes and again to the tip of the nose. The total length of the head is about one half the length of the back measured from the withers to the set-on of the tail. The head matches the sex and substance of the dog. The top line of the muzzle is parallel with the top line of the skull. There is a slight stop which is accentuated by the wiry brows. **Skull (Occiput to Stop):** Moderately broad between the ears with the width of the skull not exceeding two thirds the length of the skull. The skull must be flat; neither domed nor bumpy; skin unwrinkled. **Cheeks:** Well-developed chewing muscles, but not so much that "cheekiness" disturbs the rectangular head form. **Muzzle:** Strong, and both parallel and equal in length to the topskull; it ends in a moderately blunt wedge with wiry whiskers accenting the rectangular shape of the head. Nose is large, black and full. The lips should be black, tight and not overlapping. **Eyes:** Medium size; dark brown; oval in shape and turned forward; neither round nor protruding. The brow is arched and wiry, but vision is not impaired nor eyes hidden by too long an eyebrow. **Bite:** A full complement of white teeth, with a strong, sound scissors bite. The canine teeth are strong and well developed with the upper incisors slightly overlapping and engaging the lower. The upper and lower jaws are powerful and neither overshot not undershot. (**Faults:** A level bite is considered undesirable but a lesser fault than an overshot or undershot mouth.) **Ears:** Evenly shaped, set high and carried erect when cropped. If uncropped, they are small, V-shaped button ears of moderate thickness and carried rather high and close to the head.

Neck: Strong, of moderate thickness and length, elegantly arched and blending cleanly into the shoulders. The skin is tight, fitting closely to the dry throat with no wrinkles or dewlaps.

Shoulders: The sloping shoulder blades are strongly muscled, yet flat and well laid back so that the rounded upper ends are in a nearly vertical line above the elbows. They slope well forward to the point where they join the upper arm, forming as nearly as possible a right angle when seen from the side. Such an angulation permits the maximum forward extension of the forelegs without binding or effort.

Chest: Of medium width with well-sprung ribs, and if it could be seen in cross-section would be oval. The breastbone is plainly discernible. The brisket must descend at least to the elbows and ascend gradually to the rear with the belly moderately drawn up.

Body: Compact, strong, short-coupled and substantial so as to permit great flexibility and agility. The height at the highest point of the withers equals the length from breastbone to point or rump. **Faults:** Too slender or shelly; too bulky or coarse; excessive tuck-up.

Back: Strong, stiff, straight and short, with a well-developed loin section; the distance from the last rib to the hips as short as possible. The top line of the back should not be absolutely horizontal, but should have a slightly descending slope from the first vertebra of the withers to the faintly curved croup and set-on of the tail.

Forelegs: Straight, vertical, and without any curvature when seen from all sides; set moderately far apart; with heavy bone; elbows set close to the body and pointing directly to the rear.

Hindquarters: Strongly muscled, in balance with the forequarters, never appearing higher than the shoulders. Croup full and slightly rounded. Thighs broad and well-bent stifles. The second thigh, from knee to hock, is approximately parallel with an extension of the upper-neck line. The legs, from the clearly defined hock joint to the feet, are short and perpendicular to the ground and when viewed from the rear are parallel to each other.

Feet: Small and compact, round with thick pads and strong black nails. The toes are well closed and arched (cat's paws) and pointing straight ahead. *Dewclaws:* Dewclaws, if any, on the hind legs are generally removed. Dewclaws on the forelegs may be removed.

Tail: Set moderately high and carried erect. It is docked to not less than 1 inch nor more than 2 inches. **Faults:** Squirrel tail.

Height: Ideal height at the highest point of the shoulder blades, 18½ to 19½ inches for males and 17½ inches to 18½ inches for females. Dogs measuring over or under these limits must be faulted in proportion to the extent of the deviation. Dogs measuring more than one half inch over or under these limits must be disqualified.

Coat: Tight, hard, wiry and as thick as possible, composed of a soft, close undercoat and a harsh outer coat which, when seen against the grain, stands up off the back, lying neither smooth nor flat. The outer coat (body coat) is trimmed (by plucking) only to accent the body outline. When in show condition, the outer coat's proper length is approximately 1½ inches, except on the ears, head, neck, chest, belly and under the tail where it may be closely trimmed to give the desired typical appearance of the breed.

On the muzzle and over the eyes the coat lengthens to form luxuriant beard and eyebrows; the hair on the legs is longer than that on the body. These "furnishings" should be of harsh texture and should not be so profuse as to detract from the neat appearance or working capabilities of the dog. **Faults:** Soft, smooth, curly, wavy or shaggy; too long or too short; too sparse or lacking undercoat; excessive furnishings; lack of furnishings.

Color: Pepper and salt or pure black.

Pepper and Salt: The typical pepper and salt color of the topcoat results from the combination of black and white hairs, and white hairs banded with black. Acceptable are all shades of pepper and salt from dark iron-gray to silver gray. Ideally, pepper and salt Standard Schnauzers have a gray undercoat, but a tan or fawn undercoat is not to be penalized. It is desirable to have a darker facial mask that harmonizes with the particular shade of coat color. Also, in pepper and salt dogs, the pepper and salt mixture may fade out to light gray or silver white in the eyebrows, whiskers, cheeks, under throat, across chest, under tail, leg furnishings, under body, and inside legs.

Black: Ideally the black Standard Schnauzer should be a true rich color, free from any fading or discoloration or any admixture of gray or tan hairs. The undercoat should also be solid black. However, increased age or continued exposure to the sun may cause a certain amount of fading and burning. A small white smudge on the chest is not a fault. Loss of color as a result of scars from cuts and bites is not a fault.

Faults: Any colors other than specified, and any shadings or mixtures thereof in the topcoat such as rust, brown, red, yellow or tan; absence of peppering; spotting or striping; a black streak down the back; or a black saddle without typical salt and pepper coloring—and gray hairs in the coat of a black; in blacks, any undercoat color other than black.

Gait: Sound, strong, quick, free, true and level gait with powerful, well-angulated hindquarters that reach out and cover ground. The forelegs reach out in a stride balancing that of the hindquarters. At a trot, the back remains firm and level, without swaying, rolling or roaching. When viewed from the rear, the feet, though they may appear to travel close when trotting, must not cross or strike. Increased speed causes feet to converge toward the center line of gravity. **Faults:** Crabbing or weaving; paddling, rolling, swaying; short, choppy, stiff, stilted rear action; front legs that throw out or in (East and West movers); hackney gait, crossing over, or striking in front or rear.

FAULTS

Any deviation from the specifications in the Standard is to be considered a fault and should be penalized in proportion to the extent of the deviation. In weighing the seriousness of a fault, greatest consideration should be given to deviation from the desired alert, highly intelligent, spirited, reliable character of the Standard Schnauzer, and secondly to any deviation that detracts from the Standard Schnauzer's desired general appearance of a robust, active, square-built, wire-coated dog. Dogs that are shy or appear to be highly nervous should be seriously faulted and dismissed from the ring. Vicious dogs shall be disqualified.

DISQUALIFICATIONS

Vicious dogs.

Males over 18 inches or over 20 inches in height. Females under 17 inches or over 19 inches in height.

APPROVED MAY 14, 1968

Representing the breed: Ch. Artula Lord Greystone, owned by Timothy L. Spurlock and bred by the owner and Eula M. Lambert. Photo by Martin Booth.

CARDIGAN WELSH CORGI

Many people liken the lively Cardigan Welsh Corgi to a large fox, citing the coloring, the bush tail and the alert stance as being similar to that of that sly predator. The similarities are superficial, however, as the Cardigan is a powerfully built, heavily boned dog that abounds with tremendous strength for its size. Being a native of Cardiganshire in Wales, the Cardigan was bred to be able to work and move cattle on the rough countryside that is typical of this area. It is a very old and well established breed, with many accounts placing the Cardigan Corgi back 3000 years to the times of the ancient Celts living in 1200 B.C. Their nearest relative, the Pembroke Welsh Corgi, (with whom they are often confused) is said to have originated about 1000 years ago.

Although similar in many ways, the Cardigan and Pembroke Corgis have been carefully and selectively bred as separate breeds throughout the ages. The very remote and hilly district that is Cardiganshire provided a seclusion in which this breed was allowed and encouraged to evolve into the hardy dog that it is today. Although one of the smallest of the working dogs, the Cardigan Corgi is as adept at his work as any of his larger counterparts. The word corgi itself translates to *dwarf dog*, but their size never hinders or inhibits them. The compact size of the Corgi is a definite advantage in escaping the legs of the cattle that they move back into the herds by nipping on their legs. Their senses are keen. Large, erect ears can hear a far-off whistle from their master telling them to recall the herd; large, widely set eyes enable them to nimbly detect and evade the kicks from the disgruntled cows in their charge. Corgis are capable workers that take pride in a job well done.

The Cardigan Welsh Corgi packs a lot of dog into a small frame. They adjust well to apartment living and won't howl or complain without reason, but they still enjoy the freedom of the hill and a spirited run.

Buyer's guide: The fine temperament of the Cardigan Corgi and their diminutive size helps them adapt to most any lifestyle. They are alert and intelligent and they get along exceptionally well with lively adults. While Corgis are very friendly, they are potentially unsuitable for households with young children simply because of their herding instincts. As herders they nip the heels of the wandering cows to move them back into place; they may snap at overly playful children in much the same manner, not meaning any harm. Lots of exercise is suggested.

STANDARD FOR THE CARDIGAN WELSH CORGI

General Appearance: Low-set, sturdily built, with heavy bone and deep chest. Over-all silhouette long in proportion to height, culminating in low tail-set and foxlike brush. Expression alert and foxy, watchful yet friendly.

General Impression: A handsome, powerful, small dog, capable of both speed and endurance, sturdy, but not coarse.

Head and Skull: Skull moderately wide and flat between the ears, with definite though moderate stop. **Muzzle** to measure about 3 inches in length, or in proportion to the skull as 3 to 5. Muzzle medium, *i.e.*

neither too pointed nor too blunt but somewhat less fine than the Pembroke. **Nose:** Black. Nostrils of moderate size. Under-jaw clean-cut and strong. **Eyes:** Medium to large, and rather widely set, with distinct corners. Color dark to dark amber but clear. Blue eyes, or one dark and one blue eye, permissible in blue merles. **Mouth:** Teeth strong and regular, neither overshot nor undershot. Pincer (level) bite permissible but scissors bite preferred, *e.g.*, the inner side of the front teeth resting closely over the front of the lower front teeth. **Ears:** Large and prominent in proportion to size of dog. Slightly rounded at the tips, moderately wide at the base, and carried erect, set well apart and well back, sloping slightly forward when erect. Flop ears a serious fault.

Neck: Muscular, well developed, especially in males, and in proportion to dog's build; fitting into strong, well-shaped shoulders.

Forequarters: Chest broad, deep, and well let down between forelegs. Forelegs short, strong, and slightly bowed around chest, and with distinct but not exaggerated crook below the carpus. Elbows close to side. A straight, terrier-like front is a fault.

Body: Long and strong, with deep brisket, well-sprung ribs with moderate tuck-up of loin. Topline level except for slight slope of spine above tail.

Hindquarters: Strong, with muscular thighs. Legs short and well boned.

Feet: Round and well padded. Hind dewclaws, if any, should be removed. Front dewclaws may be removed.

Tail: Long to moderately long, resembling a fox brush. Should be set fairly low on body line, carried low when standing or moving slowly, streaming out when at a dead run, lifted when tracking or excited, but never curled over the back. A rat tail or a whip tail are faults.

Coat: Medium length but dense. Slightly harsh texture, but neither wiry nor silky. Weather-resistant. An overly short coat or a long and silky and/or curly coat are faults. Normal grooming and trimming of whiskers is permitted. Any trimming that alters the natural length of the coat is not permitted and is a serious fault. A distinctly long coat is a disqualification.

Size: Height approximately 12 inches at the highest point of the shoulder blades. Length usually between 36 and 44 inches from nose to tip of tail. In considering the height, weight, and length of a dog, over-all balance is a prime factor.

Colors: *Accepted Colors:* All shades of red. Sables. All shades of brindle. Black with or without tan or brindle points. Blue merle (blue and gray mixed with black; marbled) with or without tan or brindle points. The above colors usually with white flashings on chest, neck, feet, face or tail tip. No preference in above colors. DISQUALIFICATION: Any merlization other than blue. Excessive (over 50%) white.

DISQUALIFICATIONS
A distinctly long coat.
Pure white.

APPROVED FEBRUARY 11, 1967

Representing the breed: Am., Mex. Ch. Aelwyd Foxglove of Dorre Don, C.D. owned by Ron and Karen Harbert.

PEMBROKE WELSH CORGI

Although the smallest of the working dogs, the Pembroke Welsh Corgi has distinguished himself as an excellent herder, being able to drive strange cattle from his fields or move his herd to market. The Pembroke is low set and built especially for maneuverability. They utilize their speed and agility in a somewhat unusual manner of herding—they dart in and out of the herd, barking and nipping on the hind legs of the cows and moving them back into position. The Pembroke also excels as a ratter and they apply their skills in a calm, workman-like manner.

Although the Pembroke is a considerably younger breed than their Cardigan Welsh Corgi cousin, their history still dates back nearly 1000 years. The breed flourished in the rolling hill country of Pembrokeshire, Wales, and is thought to have arrived during the reign of Henry I of England. The early Pembroke shows remarkable resemblance to the early Schipperkes. The Pembroke stems from the Spitz-Wolf family, which also includes the Pomeranian and Norweigian Elkhound. Although their name translates to *dwarf dog*, they are sturdily built and their small legs are little hindrance to them, as they can run swiftly and jump more ably than anyone would expect.

The Pembroke Corgi is tailless and the head is rather fox-like. They have a sweet expression that is a direct indicator of the breed's natural vivaciousness. In the home, the Pembroke is jovial, yet obedient, and they are loyal one-family dogs. They enjoy having a daily task to do, and pridefully accept the responsibility of getting the daily newspaper from the yard or retrieving fallen objects. Do not be mistaken by their affectionate nature, the Pembroke Welsh Corgi is not a lap dog for they have the instinct for work and enjoy a good work out as well as any dog.

Buyer's guide: The small size and outgoing personality of the Pembroke make them suitable for city or country life. Hardy and happy, they make the best of their surroundings and enjoy themselves in the process. Corgis are very intelligent and well behaved. They are keen learners and will be very responsive to owners who want to teach their dog tricks. Since they may instinctively snap at things that bother them, the Pembroke should not be bought primarily as a companion for children. They are easy to care for since they need little formal exercising, do not eat excessively or need much grooming.

STANDARD FOR THE PEMBROKE WELSH CORGI

General Appearance: Low-set, strong, sturdily built and active, giving an impression of substance and stamina in a small space. Should not be so low and heavy-boned as to appear coarse or overdone, nor so light-boned as to appear racy. Outlook bold, but kindly. Expression intelligent and interested. Never shy nor vicious.

Size and Proportions: Moderately long and low. The distance from the withers to base of tail should be approximately 40 per cent greater than the distance from the withers to the ground. **Height** (from ground to highest point on withers) should be 10 to 12 inches. **Weight** is in proportion to size, not exceeding 30 pounds for dogs and 28 pounds for bitches. In show condition, the preferred medium-size dog of correct bone and substance will weigh approximately 27 pounds, with bitches approximately 25 pounds. Obvious oversized specimens and diminutive toylike individuals must be very seriously penalized.

Head and Skull: Head to be foxy in shape and appearance, but not sly in expression. Skull to be fairly wide and flat between the ears. Moderate amount of stop. Very slight rounding of cheek, and not filled in below the eyes, as foreface should be nicely chiseled to give a somewhat tapered muzzle. Distance from the occiput to center of stop to be greater than the distance from stop to nose tip, the proportion being five parts of total distance for the skull and three parts for the foreface. Muzzle should be neither dish-faced nor Roman-nosed. **Nose:** Black and fully pigmented.

Eyes: Oval, medium in size, not round nor protruding, nor deep-set and piglike. Set somewaht obliquely. Variations of brown in harmony with coat color. Eye rims dark, preferably black. While dark eyes enhance the expression, true black eyes are most undesirable, as are yellow or bluish eyes.

Ears: Erect, firm, and of medium size, tapering slightly to a rounded point. Ears are mobile, and react sensitively to sounds. A line drawn from the nose tip through the eyes to the ear tips, and across, should form an approximate equilateral triangle. Bat ears, small catlike ears, overly large weak ears, hooded ears, ears carried too high or too low, are undesirable. Button, rose or drop ears are very serious faults.

Mouth: Scissors bite, the inner side of the upper incisors touching the outer side of the lower incisors. Level bite is acceptable. Lips should be tight, with little or no fullness, and black. Overshot or undershot bite is a very serious fault.

Neck: Fairly long, of sufficient length to provide over-all balance of the dog. Slightly arched, clean and blending well into the shoulders. A very short neck giving a stuffy appearance, and a long, thin or ewe neck, are faulty.

Body: Rib cage should be well sprung, slightly egg-shaped, and moderately long. Deep chest, well let down between forelegs. Exaggerated lowness interferes with the desired freedom of movement and should be penalized. Viewed from above, the body should taper slightly to end of the loin. Loin short. Firm level topline, neither riding up to nor falling away at the croup. A slight depression behind the shoulders caused by heavier neck coat meeting the shorter body coat is permissible. Round or flat rib cage, lack of brisket, extreme length or cobbiness, are undesirable.

Forequarters: Legs short; forearms turned slightly inward, with the distance between the wrists less than between the shoulder joints, so that the front does not appear absolutely straight. Ample bone carried right down into the feet. Pasterns firm and nearly straight when viewed from the side. Weak pasterns and knuckling over are serious faults. Shoulder blades long and well laid back along the rib cage. Upper arms nearly equal in length to shoulder blades. Elbows parallel to the body, not prominent, and well set back to allow a line perpendicular to the ground to be drawn from the tip of the shoulder blade through to elbow.

Hindquarters: Ample bone, strong and flexible, moderately angulated at stifle and hock. Exaggerated angulation is as faulty as too little. Thighs should be well muscled. Hocks short, parallel, and when viewed from the side are perpendicular to the ground. Barrel hocks or cowhocks are most objectionable. Slipped or double-jointed hocks are very faulty.

Tail: Docked as short as possible without being indented. Occasionally a puppy is born with a natural dock, which if sufficiently short, is acceptable. A tail up to two inches in length is allowed, but if carried high tends to spoil the contour of the topline.

Feet: Oval, with the two center toes slightly in advance of the two outer ones. Turning neither in nor out. Pads strong and feet arched. Nails short. Dewclaws on both forelegs and hind legs usually removed. Too round, long and narrow, or splayed feet are faulty.

Movement: Free and smooth. Forelegs should reach well forward, without too much lift, in unison with the driving action of hind legs. The correct shoulder assembly and well-fitted elbows allow the long, free stride in front. Viewed from the front, legs do not move in exact parallel planes, but incline slightly inward to compensate for shortness of leg and width of chest. Hind legs should drive well under the body and move on a line with the forelegs, with hocks turning neither in nor out. Feet must travel parallel to the line of motion with no tendency to swing out, cross over, or interfere with each other. Short, choppy movement, rolling or high-stepping gait, close or overly wide coming or going, are incorrect. This is a herding dog which must have agility, freedom of movement, and endurance to do the work for which he was developed.

Color: The outer coat is to be of self colors in red, sable, fawn, black and tan, with or without white markings. White is acceptable on legs, chest, neck (either in part or as a collar), muzzle, underparts, and as a narrow blaze on head.

Very Serious Faults:
Whitelies: Body color white with red or dark markings.
Mismarks: Self colors with any area of white on back between

withers and tail, on sides between elbows and back of hindquarters, or on ears. Black with white markings and no tan present.

Blues: Colored portions of the coat have a distinct bluish or smoky cast. This coloring is associated with extremely light or blue eyes and liver or gray eye rims, nose and lip pigment.

Coat: Medium length; short, thick, weather-resistant undercoat with a coarser, longer outer coat. Over-all length varies, with slightly thicker and longer ruff around neck, chest and on the shoulders. The body coat lies flat. Hair is slightly longer on back of forelegs and underparts, and somewhat fuller and longer on rear of hindquarters. The coat is preferably straight, but some waviness is permitted. This breed has a shedding coat, and seasonal lack of undercoat should not be too severely penalized, providing the hair is glossy, healthy, and well groomed. A wiry, tightly marcelled coat is very faulty, as is an overly short, smooth and thin coat.

Very Serious Fault:

Fluffies: A coat of extreme length with exaggerated feathering on ears, chest, legs and feet, underparts and hindquarters. Trimming such a coat does not make it any more acceptable.

The Corgi should be shown in its natural condition, with no trimming permitted except to tidy the feet, and, if desired, remove the whiskers.

OVER-ALL PICTURE

Correct type, including general balance and outline, attractiveness of head-piece, intelligent outlook and correct temperament, is of primary importance. Movement is especially important, particularly as viewed from the side. A dog with smooth and free gait has to be reasonably sound and must be highly regarded. A minor fault must never take precedence over the above desired qualities.

A dog must be very seriously penalized for the following faults, regardless of whatever desirable qualities the dog may present:

Whitelies, Mismarks or Blues; Fluffies; Button, Rose or Drop Ears; Overshot or Undershot Bite; Oversize or Undersize.

The judge shall dismiss from the ring any Pembroke Welsh Corgi that is vicious or excessively shy.

APPROVED JUNE 13, 1972

Representing the breed: Ch. Willets Red Jacket, owned by Mrs. William B. Long.

Group 4: Terriers

AIREDALE TERRIER

One hundred or more years ago there appeared at the dog shows in the north of England a big, useful-looking sort of a terrier whose ancestors were a cross of the old Border Terrier, the Bull Terrier and the Otter Hound. They were known sometimes as the Waterside Terrier, on account of their fondness for that element, inherited from their Otter Hound ancestors. Later they were known as the Bradford Terrier. These dogs had such appealing countenances that they attracted the attention of the public, and a club was eventually formed that promoted their interests and eventually settled upon the name of Airedale Terrier, as they were very numerous in the valley of the Airedale River.

Since that time the breed has grown very rapidly in public favor, and deservedly so, for they possess many sterling qualities. The Airedale is the largest of the terrier family, and will do anything in the way of hunting vermin but go to earth. This their size precludes. They have an excellent nose, and will hunt all sorts of game, make splendid rabbit and partridge dogs, can be trained to trail wounded deer and are used successfully in bear hunting.

The Airedale takes to water like a spaniel, and will retrieve ducks in all kinds of weather. As companions they are unexcelled, displaying the utmost devotion to their masters and an interest in all of their affairs. They are wide awake about a house, and take naturally to horses. No more useful breed exists for a country home.

In buying one of these dogs do not take one that is shy or listless. Don't accept one which is soft, scanty or long-coated. Don't take one which is weak muzzled or chiseled out below the eye. Don't choose one with a long back or heavy shoulders. Don't take one which is out at the elbows or is not perfectly straight in front or clean in bone. Don't accept one which is light-eyed. Don't pick one with weak ankles or splay feet. Don't have anything to do with one which has a poor mouth or which lacks in gameness.

Buyer's guide: Even though the Airedale is the largest of the terrier breeds, they are also one of the most docile and least excitable. They are quick thinking and obedient to their owner's wishes and they get along well with children. Airedales are not suited for city apartments because they need ample room to run. Professional clipping a few times a year will keep the Airedale's coat looking its best. If you are gone from the home a great deal of the time you should not own an Airedale because their personality may become rather harsh if they do not receive sufficient companionship.

STANDARD FOR THE AIREDALE TERRIER

Head: Should be well balanced with little apparent difference between the length of skull and foreface. **Skull** should be long and flat, not too broad between the ears and narrowing very slightly to the eyes. Scalp should be free from wrinkles, stop hardly visible and cheeks level and free from fullness. **Ears** should be V-shaped with carriage rather to the side of the head, not pointing to the eyes, small but not out of proportion to the size of the dog. The topline of the folded ear should be above the level of the skull. **Foreface** should be deep, powerful, strong and muscular. Should be well filled up before the eyes. **Eyes** should be dark, small, not prominent, full of terrier expression, keenness and intelligence. **Lips** should be tight. **Nose** should be black and not too small. **Teeth** should be strong and white, free from discoloration or defect. Bite either level or vise-like. A slightly overlapping or scissors bite is permissible without preference.

Neck: Should be of moderate length and thickness gradually widening towards the shoulders. Skin tight, not loose.

Shoulders and Chest: Shoulders long and sloping well into the back. Shoulder blades flat. From the front, chest deep but not broad. The depth of the chest should be approximately on a level with the elbows.

Body: Back should be short, strong and level. Ribs well sprung. Loins muscular and of good width. There should be but little space between the last rib and the hip joint.

Hindquarters: Should be strong and muscular with no droop.

Tail: The root of the tail should be set well up on the back. It should be carried gaily but not curled over the back. It should be of good strength and substance and of fair length.

Legs: **Forelegs** should be perfectly straight, with plenty of muscle and bone. **Elbows** should be perpendicular to the body, working free of sides. **Thighs** should be long and powerful with muscular second thigh, stifles well bent, not turned either in or out, hocks well let down parallel with each other when viewed from behind. **Feet** should be small, round and compact with a good depth of pad, well cushioned; the toes moderately arched, not turned either in or out.

Coat: Should be hard, dense and wiry, lying straight and close, covering the dog well over the body and legs. Some of the hardest are crinkling or just slightly waved. At the base of the hard very stiff hair should be a shorter growth of softer hair termed the undercoat.

Color: The head and ears should be tan, the ears being of a darker shade than the rest. Dark markings on either side of the skull are permissible. The legs up to the thighs and elbows and the under-part of the body and chest are also tan and the tan frequently runs into the shoulder. The sides and upper parts of the body should be black or dark grizzle. A red mixture is often found in the black and is not to be considered objectionable. A small white blaze on the chest is a characteristic of certain strains of the breed.

Size: Dogs should measure approximately 23 inches in height at the shoulder; bitches, slightly less. Both sexes should be sturdy, well muscled and boned.

Movement: Movement or action is the crucial test of conformation. Movement should be free. As seen from the front the forelegs should swing perpendicular from the body free from the sides, the feet the same distance apart as the elbows. As seen from the rear the hind legs should be parallel with each other, neither too close nor too far apart, but so placed as to give a strong well-balanced stance and movement. The toes should not be turned either in or out.

FAULTS

Yellow eyes, hound ears, white feet, soft coat, being much over or under the size limit, being undershot or overshot, having poor movement, are faults which should be severely penalized.

SCALE OF POINTS

Head 10	Color 5
Neck, shoulders and chest ... 10	Size 10
Body 10	Movement 10
Hindquarters and tail 10	General characteristics
Legs and feet 10	and expression 15
Coat 10	TOTAL 100

APPROVED JULY 14, 1959

Representing the breed: Ch. Turith Adonis, owned by Walter A. Troutman.

AMERICAN STAFFORDSHIRE TERRIER

The power pent up in the American Staffordshire Terrier is probably greater pound for pound than in any other breed. They are the canine embodiment of strength and capability, and because of this, their breed history centers around hard work and the once popular sport of dogfighting. They are not viscious or argumentative, however, but genuinely affectionate in nature. American Staffordshires are courageous and valiant when put to the test, and they have proven themselves capable of mastering guard, obedience and police work. In the home they are gentle, loyal companions that are sure to be live-in protection should they ever be needed.

Specimens of this type of dog have been present in England for well over 200 years, but there is often confusion over exactly which breed is which. After importations and whelpings of a sufficent number of dogs in the U.S., the American Staffordshire Terrier was registered with the American Kennel Club under the name of Staffordshire Terrier. The name was changed to its present one in 1972. They have also been called the Yankee Terrier, Pit Dog and American Bull Terrier. Quite often they are referred to as American Pit Bull Terriers, with some people distinguishing the show dogs of the breed as American Staffordshire Terriers and the working and fighting dogs as American Pit Bull Terriers. They are essentially the same breed, but the APBT fanciers put much more emphasis on producing a very game dog.

The strains in England have been developed along different guidelines and are referred to as Staffordshire Bull Terriers. They are somewhat smaller and less bulky than the American Staffordshire Terrier and are considered as a separate breed. Both breeds (and all these names) came about after some judicious crossings of the powerful Bulldog with some terrier bloodlines. The debate as to exactly which terrier was used still goes on, but the old English White Terrier, the Fox Terrier and the Black-and-Tan (or Manchester) Terrier are the likely candidates. These matings produced dogs that were as powerful as the Bulldog, while still having the speed, gameness and lightness of body of the terrier. Together they produced the forerunners of the American Staffordshire Terrier, a breed unsurpassed in courage and might.

Buyer's guide: Do not consider this breed as an inside pet unless you are a one-dog family. Although the American Staffordshire gets along very nicely with people, they generally do not tolerate other animals—particularly cats. They are not an argumentative breed, but obedience training is stressed. To maintain their strength and vigor these dogs should be able to exercise daily, but they can be successfully kept in city quarters.

STANDARD FOR THE
AMERICAN STAFFORDSHIRE TERRIER

General Impression: The American Staffordshire Terrier should give the impression of great strength for his size, a well put-together dog, muscular, but agile and graceful, keenly alive to his surroundings. He should be stocky, not long-legged or racy in outline. His courage is proverbial.

Head: Medium length, deep through, broad skull, very pronounced cheek muscles, distinct stop; and ears are set high. **Ears:** Cropped or uncropped, the latter preferred. Uncropped ears should be short and held half rose or prick. Full drop to be penalized. **Eyes:** Dark and round, low down in skull and set far apart. No pink eyelids. **Muzzle:** Medium length, rounded on upper side to fall away abruptly below eyes. Jaws well defined. Underjaw to be strong and have biting power. Lips close and even, no looseness. Upper teeth to meet tightly outside lower teeth in front. Nose definitely black.

Neck: Heavy, slightly arched, tapering from shoulders to back of skull. No looseness of skin. Medium length.

Shoulders: Strong and muscular with blades wide and sloping.

Back: Fairly short. Slight sloping from withers to rump with gentle short slope at rump to base of tail. Loins slightly tucked.

Body: Well-sprung ribs, deep in rear. All ribs close together. Forelegs set rather wide apart to permit of chest development. Chest deep and broad.

Tail: Short in comparison to size, low set, tapering to a fine point; not curled or held over back. Not docked.

Legs: The front legs should be straight, large or round bones, pastern upright. No resemblance of bend in front. Hindquarters well-muscled, led down at hocks, turning neither in nor out. Feet of moderate size, well-arched and compact. Gait must be springy but without roll or pace.

Coat: Short, close, stiff to the touch, and glossy.

Color: Any color, solid, parti, or patched is permissible, but all white, more than 80 per cent white, black and tan, and liver not to be encouraged.

Size: Height and weight should be in proportion. A height of about 18 to 19 inches at shoulders for the male and 17 to 18 inches for the female is to be considered preferable.

Faults: Faults to be penalized are: Dudley nose, light or pink eyes, tail too long or badly carried, undershot or overshot mouths.

APPROVED JUNE 10, 1936

Representing the breed: Ch. Ruffian Red Rock of Har-Wyn, owned by Mr. and Mrs. Rudolph Estevez.

AUSTRALIAN TERRIER

True to the terrier temperament, this spirited little dog matches courage and pluck with any breed and will eagerly do work usually assigned to a larger dog. They are enthusiastic in all they do and prove to be great and loyal companions to anyone who honestly returns their affection. Keenly alert, they have an instinct for sizing up most situations and responding correctly and with a self-assured air about them.

The Australian Terrier is a blend of many of the early terrier breeds, with the Dandie Dinmont, the prick-eared Skye, the Yorkshire, the Cairn and the Irish Terrier being thought to have passed on the best of their qualities to this feisty breed. The wilds of Australia were the early home of the Aussie Terrier, and their strong jaws and rough, wiry coat proved advantageous for coping with the environment. They have always earned their keep, using their acute sense of hearing and scent to track down the vermin that often invaded the land around their homes. The breed was often found guarding the mines and controlling the wandering herds of sheep.

Early Aussie specimens were referred to as Rough or Brokenhair Terriers. The breed evolution was effected from years of crossing the available stock with the dogs that arrived from abroad. Many of the original Australian settlers migrated from Great Britain and brought their favorite dogs with them to share the rugged life in the bushland. Using these dogs, a breed suited to the Australian terrain was developed. Breeders worked hard to preserve the conformation quality of the dogs they produced and expected a lot of dog in return. The Australian Terrier served them well as a guard, hunter and companion.

The first importations of Australian Terriers to other countries did not occur until the early 1900's, the breed being introduced in the United States some thirty years later. The amiable character of the Aussie won them many devoted fanciers in the coming years and the breed was officially recognized by the American Kennel Club in 1960.

The Australian Terrier is a personable dog that is long lived and a fine companion for the household. A brisk daily walk is really all that is needed to keep these dogs in top physical condition. Their harsh, wiry coat remains pliable in all weather and needs only a routine brushing to remove dead or snarled hairs.

Buyer's guide: The cheerful, active Australian Terrier is as affectionate as he is bold. They are naturally active and can be kept in any type of household, owned by people of any age. Since they have a very even disposition, there is no worry about the Aussie getting snappy with children.

STANDARD FOR THE AUSTRALIAN TERRIER

General Appearance: Small, sturdy, rough-coated terrier of spirited action and self-assured manner.

Head: Long, flat-skulled, and full between the eyes, with the stop moderate. The muzzle is no longer than the distance from the eyes to the occiput. Jaws long and powerful, teeth of good size meeting in a scissors bite, although a level bite is acceptable. **Nose:** Black. **Ears:** Set high on the skull and well apart. They are small and pricked, the leather either pointed or slightly rounded and free from long hairs. **Eyes:** Small, dark, and keen in expression; not prominent. Light-colored and protruding eyes are faulty.

Neck: Inclined to be long, and tapering into sloping shoulders; well furnished with hair which forms a protective ruff.

Body: Low-set and slightly longer from the withers to the root of the tail than from the withers to the ground. **Chest:** Medium wide, and deep, with ribs well sprung but not round. Topline level.

Tail: Set on high and carried erect but not too gay; docked leaving two fifths.

Legs and Feet: Forelegs straight and slightly feathered to the carpus or so-called knee; they are set well under the body with elbows close and pasterns strong. Hindquarters strong and well muscled but not heavy; legs moderately angulated at stifles and hocks, with hocks well let down. Bone medium in size. Feet are small, clean, and catlike, the toes arched and compact, nicely padded and free from long hair. Nails strong and black.

Coat: Outer coat harsh and straight, and about two and one half inches all over the body. Undercoat short and soft. The topknot, which covers only the top of the skull, is of finer texture and lighter color than the body coat.

Color: May be blue-black or silver-black, with rich tan markings on head and legs, sandy color or clear red. The blue-black is bluish at the roots and dark at the tips. In the silver-blacks each hair carries black and silver alternating with black at the tips. The tan is rich and deep, the richer the better. In the sandies, any suggestion of smuttiness is undesirable.

Gait: Straight and true; sprightly, indicating spirit and assurance.

Temperament: That of a hard-bitten terrier, with the aggressiveness of the natural ratter and hedge hunter, but as a companion, friendly, affectionate, and biddable.

Size: Shoulder height, about 10 inches. Average weight 12 to 14 pounds.

APPROVED OCTOBER 13, 1970

Representing the breed: Aust., Am. Ch. Tinee Town Talkbac of Pleasant Pastures Kennels, owned by Mrs. Milton Fox and bred by Pat Connor. Photo by Gilbert.

BEDLINGTON TERRIER

This breed in appearance resembles a miniature Deerhound. They originated among the sport-loving miners and gypsies in the north of England, who have bred them for many years, and have produced a useful type of dog of undeniable gameness which will cheerfully tackle anything that wears hair.

The Bedlington is named for the village of Bedlington in Northumberland, England, but the breed was originally known as the Rothbury Terrier after the gypsies of the Rothbury Forest. Early specimens of the breed were straight backed, so it seems likely that a Whippet cross was introduced in the 1870's.

Bedlingtons are not real public favorites, but as all-around workmen in a rough country for rabbit coursing, ferreting and to work to the gun, they are unequaled. They have exceptionally keen noses, take readily to the water, are devoted to their masters, but are usually suspicious of strangers. They have many good qualities which will recommend them to all those who admire a game working terrier.

In buying a Bedlington don't look at a short-legged, stumpy-built dog, as they should be active and of racy build. Don't pay any attention to one with bad teeth or a large, full eye. Don't pick one that has a thin, silky coat that would not protect its owner from water or exposure to the elements. Don't look at one with a full, rounded body and well-sprung ribs, and, last of all, don't accept one which is not game as a pebble and an energetic workman.

The chief points to look for in the selection of Bedlington puppies at from two to four months old and after, are: a long, snaky head; narrow skull; small eye; drop ears, lying close to the side of the head; short body; short sickle tail; straight forelegs, and dense lint coat.

Buyer's guide: Bedlingtons are affectionate little dogs that are basically very sedate in temperament. They need lots of exercise for a dog of their size, but this can be taken care of by two brisk walks a day. Considerable time and money will be required to keep their coat in the typical Bedlington clip. While they get along peaceably with everyone, the roughhousing of young children is not recommended for them. The Bedlington is most suitable for people with lots of time to give their dog.

STANDARD FOR THE BEDLINGTON TERRIER

General Appearance: A graceful, lithe, well-balanced dog with no sign of coarseness, weakness or shelliness. In repose the expression is mild and gentle, not shy or nervous. Aroused, the dog is particularly alert and full of immense energy and courage. Noteworthy for endurance, Bedlingtons also gallop at great speed, as their body outline clearly shows.

Head: Narrow, but deep and rounded. Shorter in skull and longer in jaw. Covered with a profuse topknot which is lighter than the color of the body, highest at the crown, and tapering gradually to just back of the nose. There must be no stop and the unbroken line from crown to nose end reveals a slender head without cheekiness or snipiness. Lips are black in the blue and tans and brown in all other solid and bi-colors. **Eyes:** Almond-shaped, small, bright and well sunk with no tendency to tear or water. Set is oblique and fairly high on the head. Blues have dark eyes; blues and tans, less dark with amber lights; sandies and tans, light hazel; liver, livers and tans, slightly darker. Eye rims are black in the blue and blue and tans, and brown in all other solid and bi-colors. **Ears:** Triangular with rounded tips. Set on low and hanging flat to the cheek in front with a slight projection at the base. Point of greatest width approximately 3 inches. Ear tips reach the corners of the mouth. Thin and velvety in texture, covered with fine hair forming a small silky tassel at the tip. **Nose:** Nostrils large and well defined. Blues and blues and tans have black noses. Livers, livers and tans, sandies, sandies and tans have brown noses. **Jaws:** Long and tapering. Strong muzzle well filled up with bone beneath the eye. Close-fitting lips, no flews. **Teeth:** Large, strong and white. Level or scissors bite. Lower canines clasp the outer surface of the upper gum just in front of the upper canines. Upper premolars and molars lie outside those of the lower jaw.

Neck and Shoulders: Long, tapering neck with no throatiness, deep at the base and rising well up from the shoulders which are flat and sloping with no excessive musculature. The head is carried high.

Body: Muscular and markedly flexible. Chest deep. Flat-ribbed and deep through the brisket, which reaches to the elbows. Back has a good natural arch over the loin, creating a definite tuck-up of the underline. Body slightly greater in length than height. Well-muscled quarters are also fine and graceful.

Legs and Feet: Lithe and muscular. The hind legs are longer than the forelegs, which are straight and wider apart at the chest than at the feet. Slight bend to pasterns which are long and sloping without weakness. Stifles well angulated. Hocks strong and well let down, turning neither in nor out. Long hare feet with thick, well-closed up, smooth pads. Dewclaws should be removed.

Coat: A very distinctive mixture of hard and soft hair standing well out from the skin. Crisp to the touch but not wiry, having a tendency to curl, especially on the head and face. When in show trim must not exceed 1 inch on body; hair on legs is slightly longer.

Tail: Set low, scimitar-shaped, thick at the root and tapering to a point which reaches the hock. Not carried over the back or tight to the underbody.

Color: Blue, sandy, liver, blue and tan, sandy and tan, liver and tan. In bi-colors the tan markings are found on the legs, chest, under the tail, inside the hindquarters and over each eye. The topknots of all adults should be lighter than the body color. Patches of darker hair from an injury are not objectionable, as these are only temporary. Darker body pigmentation of all colors is to be encouraged.

Height: The preferred Bedlington Terrier dog measures 16½ inches at the withers, the bitch 15½ inches. Under 16 inches or over 17½ inches for dogs and under 15 inches or over 16½ inches for bitches are serious faults. Only where comparative superiority of a specimen outside these ranges clearly justifies it, should greater latitude be taken.

Weight: To be proportionate to height within the range of 17 to 23 pounds.

Gait: Unique lightness of movement. Springy in the slower paces, not stilted or hackneyed. Must not cross, weave or paddle.

APPROVED SEPTEMBER 12, 1967

Representing the breed: Ch. Adona's Accent on Nikolaj, owned by Mrs. Roberta M. Held.

BORDER TERRIER

The Border Terrier is "as game as they come" and has been used as a working terrier for at least the last two centuries. The breed is thought to have evolved from the natural terrier stock that inhabited the mountainous border country between England and Scotland. Although quite small in stature, the Border Terrier is a seemingly tireless worker and excels in exterminating all types of vermin that invade the area. The Border is blessed with the true terrier spirit and many generations of breeders have adamantly strived to maintain the natural abilities and characteristics of this staunch little dog.

The conformation qualities of the Border Terrier lend themselves to working effectively in the rugged north of England. Their legs are long and sufficiently muscular for the breed to run with a horse or chase after the foxes that threaten the livestock. When confronted by a grounded fox, the Border Terrier is courageous enough to stand his ground and hold the animal at bay until relieved by his master. Their hide is loose-fitting and thick and enables them to maneuver under the ground in areas usually unreachable by other dogs. The head is quite unusual for a terrier and is said to resemble that of an otter, being wide between the ears and having a tapered muzzle. Their rather thick coat is of a hard, wiry texture and it enables the Border to withstand hours of mist or drenching rains.

The first of the Border Terrier importations arrived in the United States in 1930 and breed recognition by the American Kennel Club followed that same year. The breed has delighted many fanciers who find the good nature of these dogs an endearing characteristic. Conscientious breeders have worked hard not to alter the natural state of the breed; today Border Terriers retain the keen, alert nature that aided them in controlling the hills of their homeland. They exude a special charm that is always evident in the affectionate way they treat those they share their home with.

Buyer's guide: The spunky Border Terrier will provide animated company for his owners. Since they are rather small and naturally active, they can be comfortably raised in city apartments or on country farms where they feel most at home. Plucking away the dead hairs in their coat is all that is needed to keep them looking neat. Companionship is a necessity for the Border Terrier if you intend to keep them in the house because they are seemingly tireless and must be kept amused by taking part in the daily routine. They can be as feisty as any terrier, but can still be trusted to get along with children.

STANDARD FOR THE BORDER TERRIER

Since the Border Terrier is a working terrier of a size to go to ground and able, within reason, to follow a horse, his conformation should be such that he be ideally built to do his job. No deviations from this ideal conformation should be permitted, which would impair his usefulness in running his quarry to earth and in bolting it therefrom. For this work he must be alert, active and agile, and capable of squeezing through narrow apertures and rapidly traversing any kind of terrain. His head, "like that of an otter," is distinctive, and his temperament ideally exemplifies that of a terrier. By nature he is good-tempered, affectionate, obedient, and easily trained. In the field he is hard as nails, "game as they come" and driving in attack. It should be the aim of Border Terrier breeders to avoid such over-emphasis of any point in the Standard as might lead to unbalanced exaggeration.

General Appearance: He is an active terrier of medium bone, strongly put together, suggesting endurance and agility, but rather narrow in shoulder, body and quarter. The body is covered with a somewhat broken though close-fitting and intensely wiry jacket. The characteristic "otter" head with its keen eye, combined with a body poise which is "at the alert," give a look of fearless and implacable determination characteristic of the breed. The proportions should be that the height at the withers is slightly greater than the distance from the withers to the tail, *i.e* by possibly 1-1½ inches in a 14-pound dog.

Weight: Dogs, 13-15½ pounds, bitches, 11½-14 pounds, are appropriate weights for Border Terriers in hard-working condition.

Head: Similar to that of an otter. Moderately broad and flat in skull with plenty of width between the eyes and between the ears. A slight, moderately broad curve at the stop rather than a pronounced indentation. Cheeks slightly full. **Ears:** Small, V-shaped and of moderate thickness, dark preferred. Not set high on the head but somewhat on the side, and dropping forward close to the cheeks. They should not break above the level of the skull. **Eyes:** Dark hazel and full of fire and intelligence. Moderate in size, neither prominent nor small and beady. **Muzzle:** Short and "well filled." A dark muzzle is characteristic and desirable. A few short whiskers are natural to the breed. **Teeth:** Strong, with a scissors bite, large in proportion to size of dog. **Nose:** Black, and of good size.

Neck: Clean, muscular and only long enough to give a well-balanced appearance. It should gradually widen into the shoulder. **Shoulders:** Well laid back and of good length, the blades converging to the withers gradually from a brisket not excessively deep or narrow.

Forelegs: Straight and not too heavy in bone and placed slightly wider than in a Fox Terrier. **Feet:** Small and compact. Toes should point forward and be moderately arched with thick pads.

Body: Deep, fairly narrow and of sufficient length to avoid any suggestions of lack of range and agility. Deep ribs carried well back and not oversprung in view of the desired depth and narrowness of the body. The body should be capable of being spanned by a man's hands behind the shoulders. Back strong but laterally supple, with no suspicion of a dip behind the shoulder. Loin strong and the underline fairly straight.

Tail: Moderately short, thick at the base, then tapering. Not set on too high. Carried gaily when at the alert, but not over the back. When at ease, a Border may drop his stern.

Hindquarters: Muscular and racy, with thighs long and nicely molded. Stifles well bent and hocks well let down.

Coat: A short and dense undercoat covered with a very wiry and somewhat broken top coat which should lie closely, but it must not show any tendency to curl or wave. With such a coat a Border should be able to be exhibited almost in his natural state, nothing more in the way of trimming being needed than a tidying-up of the head, neck and feet. **Hide:** Very thick and loose fitting.

Movement: Straight and rhythmical before and behind, with good length of stride and flexing of stifle and hock. The dog should respond to his handler with a gait which is free, agile and quick.

Color: Red, grizzle and tan, blue and tan, or wheaten. A small amount of white may be allowed on the chest but white on the feet should be penalized.

SCALE OF POINTS

Head, ears, neck and teeth...20	Back and loin.............10
Legs and feet............15	Hindquarters.............10
Coat and skin............10	Tail.....................5
Shoulders and chest.......10	General appearance........10
Eyes and expression.......10	TOTAL...............100

APPROVED MARCH 14, 1950

Representing the breed: Ch. Workmore Waggoner, owned by Kate Seemann. Photo by John L. Ashbey.

WHITE BULL TERRIER

COLORED BULL TERRIER

BULL TERRIER

The Bull Terrier has been aptly described as the game cock of the canine race. He is, unquestionably, the embodiment of courage as well as the essence of docility. A good Bull Terrier is staunch and true as steel when called upon to defend his master or his home, and on other occasions is gentle, harmless and the most tractable of companions.

The clean cut, statuesque appearance of the Bull Terrier has given him a prominent position in the terrier family. His smooth, white coat is always in condition, and he is more cleanly about the house, and can be accepted on closer terms of intimacy, than the long-haired varieties.

There is no uncertainty about the origin of the Bull Terrier. When bull fighting was abolished, the gamesters took up dog fighting and badger baiting. For this purpose they wanted a dog with a longer and more punishing jaw and one that was faster on his feet than the Bulldog, but possessed all of the latter's courage and endurance. They crossed the Bulldog with the agile, alert little terrier that was used in the country and secured dogs with a punishing head of fair length, powerful jaw muscles and a strong terrier-like body and limbs. These dogs, like their ancestors, were of various colors.

There was another class of fanciers to whom we are indebted for the modern Bull Terrier. They began by refining the fighting-dog type. They bred for longer heads, straighter limbs, and a more graceful outline, and in this direction accomplished a great deal. Their dogs, however, were short-faced compared with those of today and of many colors; fawn, brindle, black-and white, etc.

About one hundred years ago, James Hinks, a clever fancier from Birmingham, England, swept the show benches with a pure white strain of Bull Terriers. His dogs were highly refined, straight on their legs, graceful and smart in appearance, with long wedge-shaped, clean-cut heads. In fact there was nothing about them that suggested the Bulldog, and it was charged that the pugnacity and courage of the old breed had been lost. To prove that his strain had not lost their fighting spirit Hinks backed his bitch, Puss, against one of the old bull-faced type for a five-pound note and a case of wine. Puss killed her opponent in thirty minutes, and her own injuries were so slight that she was able to appear at a Bench Show on the following day. It is said that Hinks used the Pointer and Dalmation in producing his strain. However that may be, they became very popular and soon drove their short-faced rivals of various colors off the Bench, and for many years the breed enjoyed great popularity.

At the present time there is a strong movement favoring the brindles and other colors which indicate strength. This has also been a good influence on checking the spread of deafness, for while white Bull Terriers are sometimes prone to deafness, this predisposition is not apparent in other colors.

Buyer's guide: The strong Bull Terrier needs a firm owner who lets him know exactly who is the boss. It is a good idea not to own any other pets besides the Bull Terrier as they can sometimes become jealous and arrogant to those vying for the affection of their master. They are not aggressive to humans, however, and make dedicated companions to children. If necessary, they would protect their charges to the death. Moderate amounts of daily exercise are all that is needed for Bull Terriers to maintain their strength and stamina. They present no real housing problems and will adapt well to city or country dwellings. If the alleged "ferocity" of the breed has made you somewhat wary of owning a Bull Terrier, consider buying a female for they have very mild dispositions.

STANDARD FOR THE BULL TERRIER
WHITE

The Bull Terrier must be strongly built, muscular, symmetrical and active, with a keen determined and intelligent expression, full of fire but of sweet disposition and amenable to discipline.

The Head should be long, strong and deep right to the end of the muzzle, but not coarse. Full face it should be oval in outline and be filled completely up giving the impression of fullness with a surface devoid of hollows or indentations, *i.e.*, egg shaped. In profile it should curve gently downwards from the top of the skull to the tip of the nose. The forehead should be flat across from ear to ear. The distance from the tip of the nose to the eyes should be perceptibly greater than that from the eyes to the top of the skull. The underjaw should be deep and well defined. **The Lips** should be clean and tight. **The Teeth** should meet in either a level or in a scissors bite. In the scissors bite the upper teeth should fit in front of and closely against the lower teeth, and they should be sound, strong and perfectly regular.

The Ears should be small, thin and placed close together. They should be capable of being held stiffly erect, when they should point upwards. **The Eyes** should be well sunken and as dark as possible, with a piercing glint and they should be small, triangular and obliquely placed; set near together and high up on the dog's head. Blue eyes are a disqualification. **The Nose** should be black, with well-developed nostrils bent downward at the tip.

The Neck should be very muscular, long, arched and clean, tapering from the shoulders to the head and it should be free from loose skin. **The Chest** should be broad when viewed from in front, and there should be great depth from withers to brisket, so that the latter is nearer the ground than the belly.

The Body should be well rounded with marked spring of rib, the back should be short and strong. The back ribs deep. Slightly arched over the loin. The shoulders should be strong and muscular but without heaviness. The shoulder blades should be wide and flat and there should be a very pronounced backward slope from the bottom edge of the blade to the top edge. Behind the shoulders there should be no slackness or dip at the withers. The underline from the brisket to the belly should form a graceful upward curve.

The Legs should be big boned but not to the point of coarseness; the forelegs should be of moderate length, perfectly straight, and the dog must stand firmly upon them. The elbows must turn neither in nor out, and the pasterns should be strong and upright. The hind legs should be parallel viewed from behind. The thighs very muscular with hocks well let down. Hind pasterns short and upright. The stifle joints should be well bent with a well-developed second thigh. **The Feet** round and compact with well-arched toes like a cat.

The Tail should be short, set on low, fine, and ideally should be carried horizontally. It should be thick where it joins the body, and should taper to a fine point.

The Coat should be short, flat, harsh to the touch and with a fine gloss. The dog's skin should fit tightly. **The Color** is white though markings on the head are permissible. Any markings elsewhere on the coat are to be severely faulted. Skin pigmentation is not to be penalized.

Movement: The dog shall move smoothly, covering the ground with free, easy strides, fore and hind legs should move parallel each to each when viewed from in front or behind. The forelegs reaching out well and the hind legs moving smoothly at the hip and flexing well at the stifle and hock. The dog should move compactly and in one piece but with a typical jaunty air that suggests agility and power.

FAULTS

Any departure from the foregoing points shall be considered a fault, and the seriousness of the fault shall be in exact proportion to its degree, *i.e.* a very crooked front is a very bad fault; a rather crooked front is a rather bad fault; and a slightly crooked front is a slight fault.

DISQUALIFICATION

Blue eyes.

COLORED

The Standard for the Colored Variety is the same as for the White except for the sub-head "Color" which reads: *Color.* Any color other than white, or any color with white markings. Other things being equal, the preferred color is brindle. A dog which is predominantly white shall be disqualified.

DISQUALIFICATIONS

Blue eyes.
Any dog which is predominantly white.

APPROVED JULY 9, 1974

Representing the White: Agates Nutcracker. Photo by Sally Anne Thompson. Colored: Ch. Willing of Upend, bred by Mrs. Butler of Staffordshire, England. Photo by B. Thurse.

CAIRN TERRIER

This fearless Highland terrier patrolled the cairns, or rock piles, of the Isle of Skye with the finesse of a highly skilled hunter. Much the terrier, the Cairn maintains attention and devotion to his task despite interruptions which could sway most other dogs. While they will be civil to anyone they are introduced to, they are not free with their affections and are rather wary of strangers. Those loved by one of these working terriers will have a friend and companion for life, as the Cairn's loyalty is unfaltering. They work hard at everything they do, putting energy and zeal in both work and play.

Cairn breeders have been steadfastly maintaining the original terrier quality of this breed, a breed that may be the oldest of all British terriers. This rugged little dog sports a long, hard coat that has insulated and protected them from the misty climate of their homeland. The breed is very long-lived and hardy enough to ward off most illnesses, and their foxy expression and pleasant personality have won many supporters who believe the Cairn to be the ideal housepet. Cairns are small and adapt to most surroundings. They are naturally active and require little formalized exercising, and they wholeheartedly defend their home from any danger that may arise. They are not highly strung and are a pleasing mixture of gentleness and cunning. Among the terriers, the number of Cairn litters produced each year is second only to those of the Miniature Schnauzer.

The Cairn's conformation is similar to many of the terriers, sharing strong hindquarters and level backs with their relatives. They are well-muscled and their sloping shoulders and broad, well-furnished head give them that special Cairn appearance. Crosses with what are now Scottish Terriers and West Highland White Terriers were inevitable in the formative years of the breed but have long since been stopped by breeders interested in retaining the qualities of these distinct breeds. However, Cairns are known to occasionally whelp a pure white puppy, the only color not permitted in this breed, as a throw-back to the early crosses.

The shaggy little Cairn is a fine tempered dog suitable for most households. They do not take to barking or carrying on to extremes, and they love to be around people and delight in the attention of their friends, especially children they can roughhouse with. They retain much of their hunting instincts, so beware—you must keep a watchful eye on your dog should he go tearing through your garden. They have been known to dig spiritedly through a prime bed of roses hot on the trail of an unlucky varmint!

Buyer's guide: The Cairn is one of the smartest terriers and they take easily to housebreaking and training. They are not destructive or mischievous in their play and would rather be in the company of their owner than do most anything else. Cairns are wonderful companions for young or old. They can keep pace with even the most active owners, but do not mind living a fairly sedate life, either. They will keep themselves fit and trim by the normal patrolling of their property. Brushing regularly and an occasional trim will keep the Cairn quite neat.

STANDARD FOR THE CAIRN TERRIER

General Appearance: That of an active, game, hardy, small working terrier of the short-legged class; very free in its movements, strongly but not heavily built, standing well forward on its forelegs, deep in the ribs, well coupled with strong hindquarters and presenting a well-proportioned build with a medium length of back, having a hard, weather-resisting coat; head shorter and wider than any other terrier and well furnished with hair giving a general foxy expression.

***Head:* Skull:** Broad in proportion to length with a decided stop and well furnished with hair on the top of the head, which may be somewhat softer than the body coat. **Muzzle:** Strong but not too long or heavy. **Teeth:** Strong but not too long or heavy. **Teeth:** Large, mouth neither overshot nor undershot. **Nose:** Black. **Eyes:** Set wide apart, rather sunken, with shaggy eyebrows, medium in size, hazel or dark hazel in color, depending on body color, with a keen terrier expression. **Ears:** Small, pointed, well carried erectly, set wide apart on the side of the head. Free from long hairs.

Tail: In proportion to head, well furnished with hair but not feathery. Carried gaily but must not curl over back. Set on at back level.

Body: Well muscled, strong, active body with well-sprung, deep ribs, coupled to strong hindquarters, with a level back of medium length, giving an impression of strength and activity without heaviness.

Shoulders, Legs and Feet: A sloping shoulder, medium length of leg, good but not too heavy bone; forelegs should not be out at elbows, and be perfectly straight, but forefeet may be slightly turned out. Forefeet larger than hind feet. Legs must be covered with hard hair. Pads should be thick and strong and dog should stand well up on its feet.

Coat: Hard and weather-resistant. Must be double-coated with profuse harsh outer coat and short, soft, close furry undercoat.

Color: May be of any color except white. Dark ears, muzzle and tail tip are desirable.

Ideal Size: Involves the weight, the height at the withers and the length of body. Weight for bitches, 13 pounds; for dogs, 14 pounds. Height at the withers—bitches, 9½ inches; dogs, 10 inches. Length of body from 14¼ to 15 inches from the front of the chest to back of hindquarters. The dog must be of balanced proportions and appear neither leggy nor too low to ground; and neither too short nor too long in body. Weight and measurements are for matured dogs at two years of age. Older dogs may weigh slightly in excess and growing dogs may be under these weights and measurements.

Condition: Dogs should be shown in good hard flesh, well muscled and neither too fat or thin. Should be in full good coat with plenty of head furnishings, be clean, combed, brushed and tidied up on ears, tail, feet and general outline. Should move freely and easily on a loose lead, should not cringe on being handled, should stand up on their toes and show with marked terrier characteristics.

FAULTS

1. **Skull:** Too narrow in skull.
2. **Muzzle:** Too long and heavy a foreface; mouth overshot or undershot.
3. **Eyes:** Too large, prominent, yellow, and ringed are all objectionable.
4. **Ears:** Too large, round at points, set too close together, set too high on the head; heavily covered with hair.
5. **Legs and Feet:** Too light or too heavy bone. Crooked forelegs or out at elbow. Thin, ferrety feet; feet let down on the heel or too open and spread. Too high or too low on the leg.
6. **Body:** Too short back and compact a body, hampering quickness of movement and turning ability. Too long, weedy and snaky a body, giving an impression of weakness. Tail set on too low. Back not level.
7. **Coat:** Open coats, blousy coats, too short or dead coats, lack of sufficient undercoat, lack of head furnishings, lack of hard hair on the legs. Silkiness or curliness. A slight wave permissible.
8. **Nose:** Flesh or light-colored nose.
9. **Color:** White on chest, feet or other parts of body.

APPROVED MAY 10, 1938

Representing the breed: Redletter McRuffie, owned by Mrs. Betty Hyslop.

DANDIE DINMONT TERRIER

Originating on the borders of Scotland, and made famous by Sir Walter Scott in his "Guy Mannering," the Dandie partakes in type and character of all of Scotland's terriers, being short on leg and long in body. His ears, however, are drooped instead of being prick. Doubtless the Dandie and the Border Terrier, which is a smaller dog with drop ears, and with which the Dandie is sometimes confused, have a common origin. The Dandie undoubtedly was a Border Terrier previous to the appearance of Sir Walter Scott's novel, being kept by such sporting personages as James Davidson, of Hindlee, a friend of Scott's, who was the original of the character of Dandie Dinmont, immortalized by the novel.

The difference in type of the three Border Terriers, the recognized Border Terrier (who may or may not be the original), the Bedlington, and the Dandie, is due to breeding by selection and to crossing. The Dandie is the one breed who retains most of his Scottish ancestry in body conformation and in head, and his fusion with the English broken-haired terriers is seen in his drop ears.

Prick ears are characteristic of all the Scottish terrier varieties; drop ears are a fixed feature of their English cousins.

Some Dandie Dinmont enthusiasts pride themselves on the purity of their strains, for which they allege they can claim direct descent through the terriers of Mr. E. Bradshaw Smith, of Ecclefechan, a great enthusiast of the breed in the early and middle part of the nineteenth century, or those of Hugh Purvis, or direct to the "Guy Mannering" dogs. Such descent in no way denotes purity, because, it is alleged, for instance, that Purvis crossed his dogs more than once with a brindled Bull Terrier in order to maintain their courage. However, the type of the Dandie has long been fixed in both color and conformation that occasional crosses have not, according to the records, in any way altered it, and today it is more sharply defined than at any other period in its history.

The great novelist Scott singularly omitted to give us a definite description of his dogs when he created the "Dandie Dinmont," but subsequently he wrote: "The race of Pepper and Mustard are in the highest estimation at the present day not only for vermin killing, but for intelligence and fidelity. Those who, like the author, possess a brace of them consider them as very desirable companions." This proves that Walter Scott kept Dandie Dinmonts, and that he gave a true definition of the dogs' splendid character and disposition. All those who have ever kept the breed since that time will bear willing testimony to the fact.

The Dandie is one of the gamest of Terriers, the most sensible of dogs, and the most devoted of canine companions. He is a hardy, handy-sized dog, makes a capital house dog, and is just as much at home in the kennel. He is a rough-and-tumble sort, to which nothing comes wrong, the tackling of fox or badger underground or one of his own species above ground, and besides his exceptional power and pluck he stands unexcelled and rarely equaled for common sense and docility.

The chief points to look for in the selection of Dandie puppies at from two to four months old and after, are: a moderately short head; strong muzzle; large, dark eye; rather strong, well-beveled skull; close-set, drop ears; strong neck; rather long body; distinct arch of loin; great bone; and short legs.

Buyer's guide: This pleasant, good natured terrier is a fine addition to the home. They are not at all snappy and they get along excellently with children. If they are to be kept in an apartment, daily walks are necessary for the Dandie to retain tone. Routine brushing and clipping of their coat will remove any untidy dead hair, and their food requirements are minimal. The charming Dandie gets along with just about anyone, and will not protest if they are not the only pet in the household. They do not take well to being confined, so if you are away from home for considerable lengths, do not own a Dandie unless you supply other companions.

STANDARD FOR THE DANDIE DINMONT TERRIER

Head: Strongly made and large, not out of proportion to the dog's size, the muscles showing extraordinary development, more especially the maxillary. **Skull** broad between the ears, getting gradually less towards the eyes, and measuring about the same from the inner corner of the eye to back of skull as it does from ear to ear. The forehead well domed. The head is *covered* with very soft silky hair, which should not be confined to a mere topknot, and the lighter in color and silkier it is the better. The **Cheeks,** starting from the ears proportionately with the skull have a gradual taper towards the muzzle, which is deep and strongly made, and measures about three inches in length, or in proportion to skull as 3 is to 5. The **Muzzle** is covered with hair of a little darker shade than the topknot, and of the same texture as the feather of the forelegs. The top of the muzzle is generally bare for about an inch from the back part of the nose, the bareness coming to a point towards the eye, and being about one inch broad at the nose. The nose and inside of **Mouth** black or dark-colored. The **Teeth** very strong, especially the canines, which are of extraordinary size for a small dog. The canines mesh well with each other, so as to give the greatest available holding and punishing power. The incisors in each jaw are evenly spaced and six in number, with the upper incisors overlapping the lower incisors in a tight, scissors bite.

Eyes: Set wide apart, large, full, round, bright, expressive of great determination, intelligence and dignity; set low and prominent in front of the head; color, a rich dark hazel. **Ears:** Pendulous, set well back, wide apart, and low on the skull, hanging close to the cheek, with a very slight projection at the base, broad at the junction of the head and tapering almost to a point, the forepart of the ear tapering very little—the tapering being mostly on the back part, the forepart of the ear coming almost straight down from its junction with the head to the tip. They should harmonize in color with the body color. In the case of a Pepper dog they are covered with a soft straight brownish hair (in some cases almost black). In the case of a Mustard dog the hair should be mustard in color, a shade darker than the body, but not black. All should have a thin feather of light hair starting about 2 inches from the tip, and of nearly the same color and texture as the topknot, which gives the ear the appearance of a *distinct point*. The animal is often 1 or 2 years old before the feather is shown. The cartilage and skin of the ear should not be thick, but rather thin. Length of ear from 3 to 4 inches.

Neck: Very muscular, well-developed and strong, showing great power of resistance, being well set into the shoulders.

Body: Long, strong and flexible; ribs well sprung and round, chest well developed and let well down between the forelegs; the back rather low at the shoulder, having a slight downward curve and a corresponding arch over the loins, with a very slight gradual drop from top of loins to root of tail; both sides of backbone well supplied with muscle.

Tail: Rather short, say from 8 to 10 inches, and covered on the upper side with wiry hair of darker color than that of the body, the hair on the under side being lighter in color and not so wiry, with nice feather about 2 inches long, getting shorter as it nears the tip; rather thick at the root, getting thicker for about 4 inches, then tapering off to a point. It should not be twisted or curled in any way, but should come up with a curve like a scimitar, the tip, when excited, being in a perpendicular line with the root of the tail. It should neither be set on too high nor too low. When not excited it is carried gaily, and a little above the level of the body.

Legs: The forelegs short, with immense muscular development and bone, set wide apart, the chest coming well down between them. The feet well formed *and not flat,* with very strong brown or dark-colored claws. Bandy legs and flat feet are objectionable. The hair on the forelegs and feet of a Pepper dog should be tan, varying according to the body color from a rich tan to a pale fawn; of a Mustard dog they are of a darker shade than its head, which is a creamy white. In both colors there is a nice feather, about 2 inches long, rather lighter in color than the hair on the forepart of the leg. The hind legs are a little longer than the forelegs, and are set rather wide apart but not spread out in an unnatural manner, while the feet are much smaller; the thighs are well developed, and the hair of the same color and texture as the forelegs, but having no feather or dewclaws; the whole claws should be dark; but the claws of all vary in shade according to the color of the dog's body.

Coat: This is a very important point; the hair should be about 2 inches long; that from the skull to root of tail, a mixture of hardish and soft hair, which gives a sort of crisp feel to the hand. The hard should not be wiry; the coat is what is termed piley or penciled. The hair on the under part of the body is lighter in color and softer than on the top. The skin on the belly accords with the color of dog.

Color: The color is pepper or mustard. The pepper ranges from a dark bluish black to a light silvery gray, the intermediate shades being preferred, the body color coming well down the shoulder and hips, gradually merging into the leg color. The mustards vary from a reddish brown to a pale fawn, the head being a creamy white, the legs and feet of a shade darker than the head. The claws are dark as in other colors. (Nearly all Dandie Dinmont Terriers have some white on the chest, and some have also white claws.)

Size: The height should be from 8 to 11 inches at the top of the shoulder. Length from top of shoulder to root of tail should not be more than twice the dog's height, but preferably 1 to 2 inches less. **Weight:** The preferred weight from 18 to 24 pounds. These weights are for dogs in good working condition.

The relative value of the several points in the standard are apportioned as follows:

SCALE OF POINTS

Head	10	Legs and feet	10
Eyes	10	Coat	15
Ears	10	Color	5
Neck	5	Size and weight	5
Body	20	General appearance	5
Tail	5	TOTAL	100

APPROVED JUNE 10, 1969

Representing the breed: Ch. Overhill Triscuit, owned by Helen D. Kirby. Photo by Steven D. Newell.

FOX TERRIER

The smart appearance, graceful conformation, and attractive coloring of the Fox Terrier has made him one of the most popular members of the terrier family.

In tracing the origin of the breed, it is impossible to go far into the past, the late 1860's apparently being the starting point of the modern Fox Terrier. Just what he sprung from is also a sealed book. Possibly it was from the white English Terrier or the Black-and-Tan Terrier crossed upon the Bull Terrier, or the Beagle, and more probably it was still more heterogeneous sources.

The modern Fox Terrier was originated by Foxhound Masters, who wanted a game little sportsman of uniform size and appearance to replace the nondescript terriers which were used to bolt the fox that had gone to earth. Before this time any dog that was plucky and whose size would permit him to go to earth was known as a Fox Terrier, no matter what his coat, color, or his general appearance might be.

There are no Fox Terrier pedigrees which date before the 1860's, and there is much doubt and question connected with some since that time. In the history of the breed there are three dogs which stand out conspicuously, and from them the Fox Terrier as a breed takes descent: Old Jock, Trap, and Tartar. Of these Old Jock was undoubtedly the best. He was exhibited as late as 1870, and was said to have been a smart, well-balanced terrier, somewhat leggy and wanting in jaw power. Tartar is said to have been much on the Bull Terrier type, while old Trap's sire is said to have been a Black-and-Tan (Manchester Terrier). It is unquestionable from these precedents that breeders have produced the modern Fox Terrier, a most impressive testimonial to their genius.

The question arises whether the Fox Terrier of today is as useful and intelligent as his predecessors. If there is anything to his name terrier, derived from *terra*, the earth, he should be able to go to ground. This is absolutely precluded by the size of some of the

WIRE FOX TERRIER

SMOOTH FOX TERRIER

dogs that are shown on the benches, and one of the greatest dangers to the breed lies in the leaning of judges toward the large size, on the grounds of the oft-repeated aphorism that a good big one is always better than a good little one. The fact should never be lost sight of that a terrier who cannot go to earth is not a terrier.

The Wirehaired Fox Terrier is identical with his smooth-coated brother, with the single exception of the character of his coat, which should be harder, more wiry, and broken. This coat should not be so long as to make his owner look shaggy, while a coat that is soft and woolly or one that has a suggestion of silky hair about the head or elsewhere cannot be tolerated. The wiry, crisp, and heavy coat is the only distinguishing trait of the breed, so too much importance cannot be attached to its character. The harder and more wiry of texture the coat is the better. It is not unusual to get both smooth and wire-coated specimens out of one litter. For a number of years the Smooth Coats had all the call, but of late the Wires have been coming to the fore rapidly, although their preparation for the ring—that is, the trimming of their coats—is an annoying proposition to many breeders. Practically all Wirehaired Fox Terriers require trimming and the line between legitimate trimming and faking—and consequent disqualification—is very faint. It is legitimate to remove dead coat or soft, superfluous hair or long, odd hair from the head, ears, limbs and body. This is done with the thumb and forefinger and a special comb made for that purpose. The use of clippers, however, to even up a coat or the application of rosin, alum, or similar agents to stiffen and harden the coat will, if detected, lead to disbarment. It is a common practice, when a dog is not to be exhibited for some time, to clip him all over, as this has a tendency to strengthen and improve the coat. No objection can be raised to this practice.

Buyer's guide: Fox Terriers are lively and not the type of dog to blend quietly into the background. They make their presence known and are delightful companions, trying to please their owners and efficiently performing any duties they may be assigned. Where other animals are concerned, the Fox Terrier is very game, but they show only the most pleasant side of their personalities when around their preferred people. Exercise enhances their lively disposition as they thrive on long, brisk walks. They can be kept in apartments, but exercise requirements *must* be met. Owners of the Wire Fox will be in for frequent trips to the grooming parlor, and the expense this entails. This active terrier should be owned by active adults, but they do get on fairly well with kids.

STANDARD FOR THE FOX TERRIER

The following shall be the standard of the Fox Terrier, amplified in part in order that a more complete description of the Fox Terrier may be presented. The standard itself is set forth in ordinary type, the amplification in italics.

Head: The skull should be flat and moderately narrow, gradually decreasing in width to the eyes. Not much stop should be apparent, but there should be more dip in the profile between the forehead and the top jaw than is seen in the case of a Greyhound. The cheeks must not be full. The ears should be V-shaped and small, of moderate thickness, and drooping forward close to the cheek, not hanging by the side of the head like a Foxhound. *The top line of the folded ear should be well above the level of the skull.* The jaws, upper and lower, should be strong and muscular and of fair punishing strength, but not so as in any way to resemble the Greyhound or modern English Terrier. There should not be much falling away below the eyes. This part of the head should, however, be moderately chiseled out, so as not to go down in a straight slope like a wedge. The nose, toward which the muzzle must gradually taper, should be black. *It should be noticed that although the foreface should gradually taper from eye to muzzle and should tip slightly at its juncture with the forehead, it should not "dish" or fall away quickly below the eyes, where it should be full and well made up, but relieved from "wedginess" by a little delicate chiseling.* The eyes and the ribs should be dark in color, *moderately* small and rather deep-set, full of fire, life and intelligence and as nearly as possible circular in shape. *Anything approaching a yellow eye is most objectionable.* The teeth should be as nearly as possible together, *i.e. the points* of the upper (*incisors*) teeth on the outside of or *slightly overlapping* the lower teeth. *There should be apparent little difference in length between the skull and foreface of a well-balanced head.*

Neck: Should be clean and muscular, without throatiness, of fair length, and gradually widening to the shoulders.

Shoulders: Should be long and sloping, well laid back, fine at the points, and clearly cut at the withers.

Chest: Deep and not broad.

Back: Should be short, straight *(i.e. level)*, and strong, with no appearance of slackness. *Brisket should be deep, yet not exaggerated.*

Loin: Should be very powerful, *muscular* and very slightly arched. The foreribs should be moderately arched, the back ribs deep *and well sprung,* and the dog should be well ribbed up.

Hindquarters: Should be strong and muscular, quite free from droop or crouch; the thighs long and powerful; *stifles well curved and turned neither in nor out;* hocks *well bent* and near the ground *should be perfectly upright and parallel with the other when viewed from behind,* the dog standing well up on them like a Foxhound, and not straight in the stifle. *The worst possible form of hindquarter consists of a short second thigh and a straight stifle.*

Stern: Should be set on rather high and carried gaily, but not over the back or curled. It should be of good strength, anything approaching a "pipe-stopper" tail being especially objectionable.

Legs: The forelegs viewed from any direction must be straight with bone strong right down to the feet, showing little or no appearance of ankle in front, and being short and straight in pasterns. Both forelegs and hind legs should be carried straight forward in traveling, the stifles not turning outward. The elbows should hang perpendicularly to the body, working free of the sides. ***Feet:*** Should be round, compact and not large; the soles hard and tough; the toes moderately arched and turned neither in nor out.

Coat: Should be smooth, flat, but hard, dense and abundant. The belly and under side of the thighs should not be bare.

Color: White should predominate; brindle, red, or liver markings are objectionable. Otherwise this point is of little or no importance.

Symmetry, Size and Character: The dog must present a generally gay, lively and active appearance; bone and strength in a small compass are essentials, but this must not be taken to mean that a Fox Terrier should be cloddy, or in any way coarse—speed and endurance must be looked to as well as power, and the symmetry of the Foxhound taken as a model. The terrier, like the hound, must on no account be leggy, nor must he be too short in the leg. He should stand like a cleverly made hunter, covering a lot of ground, yet with a short back, as before stated. He will then attain the highest degree of propelling power, together with the greatest length of stride that is compatible with the length of his body. Weight is not a certain criterion of a terrier's fitness for his work—general shape, size and contour are the main points; and if a dog can gallop and stay, and follow his fox up a drain, it matters little what his weight is to a pound or so. *According to present-day requirements, a* full-sized, well-balanced dog should not exceed 15½ inches at the withers, the bitch being proportionately lower—nor should the length of back from withers to root of tail exceed 12 inches, while, to maintain the relative proportions, the head should not exceed 7¼ inches or be less than 7 inches. A dog with these measurements should scale 18 pounds in show condition—a bitch weighing some 2 pounds less—with a margin of 1 pound either way.

Balance: *This may be defined as the correct proportions of a certain point, or points, when considered in relation to a certain other point or points. It is the keystone of the terrier's anatomy. The chief points for consideration are the relative proportions of skull and foreface; head and back; height at withers and length of body from shoulder-point to buttock—the ideal of proportion being reached when the last two measurements are the same. It should be added that, although the head measurements can be taken with absolute accuracy, the height at withers and length of back and coat are approximate, and are inserted for the information of breeders and exhibitors rather than as a hard and fast rule.*

Movement: Movement, or action, is the crucial test of conformation. The terrier's legs should be carried straight forward while traveling, the forelegs hanging perpendicular and swinging parallel with the sides, like the pendulum of a clock. The principal propulsive power is furnished by the hind legs, perfection of action being found in the terrier possessing long thighs and muscular second thighs well bent at the stifles, which admit of a strong forward thrust or "snatch" of the hocks. When approaching, the forelegs should form a continuation of the straight line of the front, the feet being the same distance apart at the elbows. When stationary, it is often difficult to determine whether a dog is slightly out at shoulder, but, directly he moves, the defect—if it exists—becomes more apparent, the forefeet having a tendency to cross, "weave" or "dish." When, on the contrary, the dog is tied at the shoulder, the tendency of the feet is to move wider apart, with a sort of paddling action. When the hocks are turned in—cowhock—the stifles and feet are turned outwards, resulting in a serious loss of propulsive power. When the hocks are turned outwards the tendency of the hind feet is to cross, resulting in an ungainly waddle.

N.B.: *Old scars or injuries, the result of work or accident, should not be allowed to prejudice a terrier's chance in the show ring, unless they interfere with its movement or with its utility for work or stud.*

WIRE

This variety of the breed should resemble the smooth sort in every respect except the coat, which should be broken. The harder and more wiry the texture of the coat is, the better. On no account should the dog look or feel woolly; and there should be no silky hair about the poll or elsewhere. The coat should not be too long, so as to give the dog a shaggy appearance, but, at the same time, it should show a marked and distinct difference all over the smooth species.

SCALE OF POINTS

Head and ears............15	Legs and feet............15
Neck....................5	Coat...................15
Shoulders and chest........10	Symmetry, size and character..............10
Back and loin............10	
Hindquarters.............15	TOTAL..............100
Stern....................5	

DISQUALIFICATIONS

Nose—White, cherry or spotted to a considerable extent with either of these colors.

Ears—Prick, tulip or rose.

Mouth—Much undershot, or much overshot.

IRISH TERRIER

Although there is the usual mystery about the exact origin of the Irish Terrier, his excitable temperament, keen intelligence, pluck and determination as well as his sociable and vivacious instinct clearly indicate that he is a worthy product of the country whose name is reflected in his own. In Ireland this breed is used for bolting foxes and for vermin and rabbit hunting. They have no superior as companions, and are game, all-around sporting propositions, ready to take an active part in anything resembling sport or pleasure. They are undoubtedly a very old breed of dog, and present-day bench show winners are not unlike those depicted in the sporting scenes of a century ago.

At the present time red is the most fashionable color. The wheaten color specimens that come out from time to time as a rule have softer coats than the red. The Irish Terrier as a breed have an expression peculiar to themselves, and a good one is sometimes referred to as having the map of Ireland on his face. The chiseling of the head is a little stronger than either the Airedale or the Fox Terrier, without being at all coarse.

In selecting Irish Terrier puppies look for a long, level head; a strong muzzle; a rather narrow skull; dark eyes; small, neat V-shaped ears; short back; narrow shoulders; straight forelegs with plenty of bone; and strong, well-knit feet. The coat should be hard to the touch and not too long. The puppies that are dark in color and have the shortest coats usually develop the best, and a little white on the chest is no real detriment.

Buyer's guide: This feisty terrier may be game to a fault. Every time they come in contact with other dogs, their instinct for the fight becomes apparent by their change in attitude. However, if the breed is always kept on a lead and obedience training is started while they are pups this tendency can be minimized. Their coat requires little more than occasional brushings to remove dead hair that may dull the coat. Exercise requirements for the Irish Terrier are quite modest and they can be kept in any size house. If they must be raised in small apartments, extra time outside and lots of personal attention will keep these dogs from becoming high-strung.

STANDARD FOR THE IRISH TERRIER

Head: Long, but in nice proportion to the rest of the body; the skull flat, rather narrow between the ears, and narrowing slightly toward the eyes; free from wrinkle, with the stop hardly noticeable except in profile. The jaws must be strong and muscular, but not too full in the cheek, and of good punishing length. The foreface must not fall away appreciably between or below the eyes; instead, the modeling should be delicate. An exaggerated foreface, or a noticeably short foreface, disturbs the proper balance of the head and is not desirable. The foreface and the skull from occiput to stop should be approximately equal in length. Excessive muscular development of the cheeks, or body development of the temples, conditions which are described by the fancier as "cheeky," or "strong in head," or "thick in skull" are objectionable. The "bumpy" head, in which the skull presents two lumps of bony structure above the eyes, is to be faulted. The hair on the upper and lower jaws should be similar in quality and texture to that on the body, and of sufficient length to present an appearance of additional strength and finish to the foreface. Either the profuse, goat-like beard, or the absence of beard, is unsightly and undesirable.

Teeth: Should be strong and even, white and sound; and neither overshot nor undershot.

Lips: Should be close and well-fitting, almost black in color.

Nose: Must be black.

Eyes: Dark brown in color; small, not prominent; full of life, fire and intelligence, showing an intense expression. The light or yellow eye is most objectionable, and is a bad fault.

Ears: Small and V-shaped; of moderate thickness; set well on the head, and dropping forward closely toward the outside corner of the eye. The top of the folded ear should be well above the level of the skull. A "dead" ear, hound-like in appearance, must be severely penalized. It is not characteristic of the Irish Terrier. The hair should be much shorter and somewhat darker in color than that on the body.

Neck: Should be of fair length and gradually widening toward the shoulders; well and proudly carried, and free from throatiness. Generally there is a slight frill in the hair at each side of the neck, extending almost to the corner of the ear.

Shoulders and Chest: Shoulders must be fine, long, and sloping well into the back. The chest should be deep and muscular, but neither full nor wide.

Body: The body should be moderately long. The short back is not characteristic of the Irish Terrier, and is extremely objectionable. The back must be strong and straight, and free from an appearance of slackness or "dip" behind the shoulders. The loin should be strong and muscular, and slightly arched, the ribs fairly sprung, deep rather than round, reaching to the level of the elbow. The bitch may be slightly longer than the dog.

Hindquarters: Should be strong and muscular; thighs powerful; hocks near the ground; stifles moderately bent.

Stern: Should be docked, taking off about one quarter. It should be set on rather high, but not curled. It should be of good strength and substance; of fair length and well covered with harsh, rough hair.

Feet and Legs: The feet should be strong, tolerably round, and moderately small; toes arched and turned neither out nor in, with dark toenails. The pads should be deep, and must be perfectly sound and free from corns. Cracks alone do not necessarily indicate unsound feet. In fact, all breeds have cracked pads occasionally, from various causes.

Legs moderately long, well set from the shoulders, perfectly straight, with plenty of bone and muscle; the elbows working clear of the sides;

pasterns short, straight, and hardly noticeable. Both fore and hind legs should move straight forward when traveling; the stifles should not turn outwards. "Cowhocks"—that is, the hocks turned in and the feet turned out—are tolerable. The legs should be free from feather and covered with hair of similar texture to that on the body to give proper finish to the dog.

Coat: Should be dense and wiry in texture, rich in quality, having a broken appearance, but still lying fairly close to the body, the hairs growing so closely and strongly together that when parted with the fingers the skin is hardly visible; free of softness or silkiness, and not so long as to alter the outline of the body, particularly in the hindquarters. On the sides of the body the coat is never as harsh as on the back and quarters, but it should be plentiful and of good texture. At the base of the stiff outer coat there should be a growth of finer and softer hair, lighter in color, termed the undercoat. Single coats, which are without any undercoat, and wavy coats are undesirable; the curly and the kinky coats are most objectionable.

Color: Should be whole-colored: bright red, golden red, red wheaten, or wheaten. A small patch of white on the chest, frequently encountered in all whole-colored breeds, is permissible but not desirable. White on any other part of the body is most objectionable. Puppies sometimes have black hair at birth, which should disappear before they are full grown.

Size: The most desirable weight in show condition is 27 pounds for the dog and 25 pounds for the bitch. The height at the shoulder should be approximately 18 inches. These figures serve as a guide to both breeder and judge. In the show ring, however, the informed judge readily identifies the oversized or undersized Irish Terrier by its conformation and general appearance. Weight is not the last word in judgment. It is of the greatest importance to select, insofar as possible, terriers of moderate and generally accepted size, possessing the other various characteristics.

General Appearance: The over-all appearance of the Irish Terrier is important. In conformation he must be more than a sum of his parts. He must be all-of-a-piece, a balanced vital picture of symmetry, proportion and harmony. Furthermore, he must convey character. This terrier must be active, lithe and wiry in movement, with great animation; sturdy and strong in substance and bone structure, but at the same time free from clumsiness, for speed, power and endurance are most essential. The Irish Terrier must be neither "cobby" nor "cloddy," but should be built on lines of speed with a graceful, racing outline.

Temperament: The temperament of the Irish Terrier reflects his early background: he was family pet, guard dog, and hunter. He is good tempered, spirited and game. It is of the utmost importance that the Irish Terrier show fire and animation. There is a heedless, reckless pluck about the Irish Terrier which is characteristic, and which, coupled with the headlong dash, blind to all consequences, with which he rushes at his adversary, has earned for the breed the proud epithet of "Daredevil." He is of good temper, most affectionate, and absolutely loyal to mankind. Tender and forebearing with those he loves, this rugged, stout-hearted terrier will guard his master, his mistress and children with utter contempt for danger or hurt. His life is one continuous and eager offering of loyal and faithful companionship and devotion. He is ever on guard, and stands between his home and all that threatens.

APPROVED DECEMBER 10, 1968

Representing the breed: Ch. Ahtram Legacy, owned by Martha J. Hall.

KERRY BLUE TERRIER

The Kerry Blue is an Irishman hailing from the County Kerry area of the isle. The beautiful blue-gray coat of the Kerry distinguishes the breed from the rest of the terrier dogs and focuses attention to how beautiful the sturdy conformation of the terrier can be. They are strong and muscularly built, having long served as hunting, guarding and herding dogs in their native terrain. Kerries are an all-around dog, fitting equally well in the home with small children or out in the wilds in search of small game. They are particularly keen retrievers and can be easily trained to master most any task.

The temperament of the Kerry Blue combines the natural feistiness of the terrier and the friendly air of a companion dog. Kerries have a great sense of humor and are not above mischief; they sense, however, where playfulness leaves off and destructiveness takes over and they can be trusted to be on their honor. Guarding the home comes naturally to the Kerry Blue. They are not prone to barking any more than is necessary, but will let out with a loud, distinctive signal should they be alerted that something is not right.

Although one of the larger terriers, the Kerry Blue is not overly demanding for space or exercise. They maintain their health and vigor with a modicum of demands on their owner and generally live to enjoy a lively old age. The Kerry Blue is enjoying a significant success in the show rings and has received considerable acclaim as an obedience contender. They have been successfully trained for farm work, but are most commonly seen as in the family watchdog, a post that they undertake gladly and with determination.

Buyer's guide: The Kerry Blue is not the dog for a city apartment. They do best when situated in the country or in a house with a good sized plot of land around it because their exercise requirements are quite large. Kerry Blues can be quite tenacious and should not be considered as full-time companions for children. Owners of this headstrong breed would do best to be assertive and firm disciplinarians, ready for a strong willed opponent. Obedience training from an early age is strongly suggested. To keep the Kerry Blue in a tidy coat, approximately six visits to the grooming parlor will be required yearly.

STANDARD FOR THE KERRY BLUE TERRIER

Head: Long, but not exaggerated and in good proportion to the rest of the body. Well-balanced, with little apparent difference between the length of the skull and foreface. *(20 points)*

Skull: Flat, with very slight stop, of but moderate breadth between the ears, and narrowing very slightly to the eyes. **Cheeks:** Clean and level, free from bumpiness. **Ears:** V-shaped, small but not out of proportion to the size of the dog, of moderate thickness, carried forward close to the cheeks with the top of the folded ear slightly above the level of the skull. A "dead" ear houndlike in appearance is very undesirable. **Foreface:** Jaws deep, strong and muscular. Foreface full and well made up, not falling away appreciably below the eyes but moderately chiseled out to relieve the foreface from wedginess. **Nose:** Black, nostrils large and wide. **Teeth:** Strong, white and either level or with the upper (incisors) teeth slightly overlapping the lower teeth. An undershot mouth should be strictly penalized. **Eyes:** Dark, small, not prominent, well placed with a keen terrier expression. Anything approaching a yellow eye is very undesirable.

Neck: Clean and moderately long, gradually widening to the shoulders upon which it should be well set and carried proudly. *(5 points)*

Shoulders and Chest: Shoulders fine, long and sloping, well laid back and well knit. Chest deep and of but moderate breadth. *(10 points)*

Legs and Feet: Legs moderately long with plenty of bone and muscle. The forelegs should be straight from both front and side view, with the elbows hanging perpendicularly to the body and working clear of the sides in movement, the pasterns short, straight and hardly noticeable. Both forelegs and hind legs should move straight forward when traveling, the stifles turning neither in nor out. *(10 points)* Feet should be strong, compact, fairly round and moderately small, with good depth of pad free from cracks, the toes arched, turned neither in nor out, with black toenails.

Body: Back short, strong and straight (*i.e.* level), with no appearance of slackness. Loin short and powerful with a slight tuck-up, the ribs fairly well sprung, deep rather than round. *(10 points)*

Hindquarters and Stern: Hindquarters strong and muscular with full freedom of action, free from droop or crouch, the thighs long and powerful, stifles well bent and turned neither in nor out, hocks near the ground and, when viewed from behind, upright and parallel with each other, the dog standing well up on them. Tail should be set on high, of moderate length and carried gaily erect, the straighter the tail the better. *(10 points)*

Color: The correct mature color is any shade of blue gray from deep slate to light blue gray, of a fairly uniform color throughout except that distinctly darker to black parts may appear on the muzzle, head, ears, tail and feet. *(10 points)* Kerry color, in its process of "clearing" from an apparent black at birth to the mature gray blue or blue gray, passes through one or more transitions—involving a very dark blue (darker than deep slate), shades or tinges of brown, and mixtures of these, together with a progressive infiltration of the correct mature color. Up to 18 months such deviations from the correct mature color are permissible without preference and without regard for uniformity. Thereafter, deviation from it to any significant extent must be severely penalized. Solid black is never permissible in the show ring. Up to 18 months any doubt as to whether a dog is black or a very dark blue should be resolved in favor of the dog, particularly in the case of a puppy. Black on the muzzle, head, ears, tail and feet is permissible at any age.

Coat: Soft, dense and wavy. A harsh, wire or bristle coat should be severely penalized. In show trim the body should be well covered but tidy, with the head (except for the whiskers) and the ears and cheeks clear. *(15 points)*

General Conformation and Characters: The typical Kerry Blue Terrier should be upstanding, well knit and in good balance, showing a well developed and muscular body with definite terrier style and character throughout. A lowslung Kerry is not typical. *(10 points)*

Height: The ideal Kerry should be 18½ inches at the withers for a dog, slightly less for a bitch. In judging Kerries, a height of 18-19½ inches for a dog, and 17½-19 inches for a bitch should be given primary preference. Only where the comparative superiority of a specimen outside of the ranges noted clearly justifies it, should greater latitude be taken. In no case should it extend to a dog over 20 inches or under 17½ inches, or to a bitch over 19½ inches or under 17 inches. The minimum limits do not apply to puppies.

Weight: The most desirable weight for a fully developed dog is from 33-40 pounds, bitches weighing proportionately less.

DISQUALIFICATIONS

Solid black.
Dewclaws on hind legs.

APPROVED SEPTEMBER 15, 1959

LAKELAND TERRIER

The Lakeland Terrier is as game and bold a dog as can be found. The breed is small but workmanlike, sturdily built and capable of enduring long hours of exhaustive hunting. The mountainous terrain of Cumberland in northwestern England presented special problems to local dog breeders who were faced with ridding the area of Westmoreland fox that preyed on their sheep. This predator was particularly large and combatant and lurked underground in deep, narrow burrows. The Lakeland Terrier was developed to squeeze into these narrow spaces, if necessary digging their way deeper into the lair in search of their prey. Once they had cornered the fox, the courage of the little Lakeland was boundless and they would efficiently subdue or flush the fox, oftentimes enduring great physical punishment. There have been numerous reports of zealous Lakelands burrowing far underground only to be trapped by the earth collapsing behind them. Remarkably, most of these hardy dogs emerged unscathed when dug up by their masters; a few, however, had burrowed too deeply to be taken out alive.

Like many other terriers, the Lakeland originated long ago from the basic terrier-type dog that inhabited the British Isles. The breed is thought to be one of the oldest working terriers and was known by numerous names throughout history: Fell Terrier, Patterdale Terrier, Westmoreland Terrier and Cumberland Terrier, to name a few. The breed's present name was selected in 1912 at the Kersurck show when the first terrier club was formed.

Through the years the Lakeland has proven himself a versatile dog. The breed was used quite extensively in scratch packs (an assembly of dogs owned by various people, primarily composed by Foxhounds and Lakelands in this case) in wide-ranging hunts aimed at destroying the foxes and other four-legged vermin that plagued the countryside. The Lakelands would follow close to the hounds, and when the prey needed flushing or took to the ground the Lakelands would take over. The breed also excelled in protecting the flocks from invading predators.

Although today's Lakeland Terrier enjoys a much more sedate existence than his ancestors, breeders of these dogs have worked hard at maintaining the breed's game, serviceable instincts. The Lakeland's tight, close-fitting jacket of hair is two-ply. Their hard, wiry outer coat and soft undercoat provide adequate protection from all types of climates, making the breed adaptable to any environment. They are exceptionally clean in their habits and their coat does not shed heavily, although routine trimming is necessary to keep it tidy.

Children and Lakeland Terriers go very well together. The breed is friendly and outgoing by nature, and seldom exhibits the sharp behavior that is regarded as typical of all terriers. If grabbed by surprise, they may snap in defense, however, and feel guilty about it later. The gay Lakeland Terrier has garnered numerous honors in the show ring in both the United States and abroad and has been showing a slow but steady rise in popularity in the last few years.

Buyer's guide: The Lakeland has a gay, stable temperament and enjoys the life of an inside dog. They are very affectionate and enjoy human companionship, but like most terriers they may instinctively snap if startled by a sudden movement. Lakelands can be raised in any size house and a daily run in the yard will keep then in fine condition. Frequent trips to the groomer are advised to retain their neat appearance. The Lakeland Terrier's coat is dense and can resist the harsh elements well.

STANDARD FOR THE LAKELAND TERRIER

General Appearance: The Lakeland Terrier is a small, workmanlike dog of square, sturdy build and gay, friendly, self-confident demeanor. He stands on his toes as if ready to go, and he moves, lithe and graceful, with a straight-ahead, free stride of good length. His head is rectangular in contour, ears V-shaped, and wiry coat finished off with fairly long furnishings on muzzle and legs.

Head: Well balanced, rectangular, the length of skull equaling the length of the muzzle when measured from occiput to stop, and from stop to nosetip. **The skull** is flat on top and moderately broad, the cheeks almost straightsided, and the stop barely perceptible. **The muzzle** is broad with straight nose bridge and good fill-in beneath the eyes. **The nose** is black, except that liver-colored noses shall be permissible on liver-coated dogs. **Jaws** are powerful. **The teeth,** which are comparatively large, may meet in either a level, edge-to-edge bite, or a slightly overlapping scissors bite. Specimens with teeth overshot or undershot are to be disqualified. **The ears** are small, V-shaped, their fold just above the top of the skull, the inner edge close to the cheeks, and the flap pointed down. **The eyes,** moderately small and somewhat oval in outline, are set squarely in the skull, fairly wide apart. Their normally dark color may be a warm brown or black. **The expression** depends upon the dog's mood of the moment; although typically alert, it may be intense and determined, or gay and even impish.

Neck: Reachy and of good length; refined but strong; clean at the throat, slightly arched, and widening gradually into the shoulders. The withers, that point at the back of the neck where neck and body meet, are noticeably higher than the level of the back.

Body: In over-all length-to-height proportion, the dog is approximately square. The moderately narrow *chest* is deep; it extends to elbows which are held close to the body. Shoulder blades are sloping, that is, well laid back, their musculature lean and almost flat in outline. **The ribs** are well sprung and moderately rounded. **The back** is short and level in topline. **Loins** are taut and short, although they may be a trifle longer in bitches than in dogs. **Quarters** are strong, broad, and muscular.

Legs and Feet: **Forelegs** are strongly boned, clean, and absolutely straight as viewed from the front or side, and devoid of appreciable bend at the pasterns. **Hind legs** too are strong and sturdy, the second thighs long and nicely angulated at the stifles and the hocks. **Hocks** are well let down, with the bone from hock to toes straight and parallel to each other. The small **feet** are round, the toes compact and well padded, the nails strong. Dewclaws, if any, are to be removed.

Tail: Set high on the body, the tail is customarily docked so that when the dog is set up in show position, the tip of the docked tail is on an approximate level with the skull. In carriage it is gay or upright, although a slight curve in the direction of the head is considered desirable. The tail curled over the back is faulty.

Coat and Color: Two-ply or double, the outer coat is hard and wiry in texture, the undercoat soft. Furnishings on muzzle and legs are plentiful as opposed to profuse. *The color* may be blue, black, liver, black and tan, blue and tan, red, red grizzle, grizzle and tan, or wheaten. Tan as desirable in the Lakeland Terrier, is a light wheaten or straw color, with rich red or mahogany tan to be penalized. Otherwise, colors, as specified, are equally acceptable. Dark-saddled specimens (whether black grizzle or blue) are nearly solid black at birth, with tan points on muzzle and feet. The black recedes and usually turns grayish or grizzle at maturity, while the tan also lightens.

Size: The ideal **height** of the mature dog is 14½ inches from the withers to the ground, with up to a ½-inch deviation either way permissible. Bitches may measure as much as one inch less than dogs. The **weight** of the well-balanced, mature specimen in hard, show condition, averages approximately 17 pounds, those of other heights proportionately more or less.

Size is to be considered of lesser importance than other qualities, that is, when judging dogs of equal merit, the one nearest the ideal size is to be preferred. Symmetry and proportion, however, are paramount in the appraisal, since all qualities together must be considered in visualizing the ideal.

Movement: Straight and free, with good length of stride. Paddling, moving close, and toeing-in are faulty.

Temperament: The typical Lakeland Terrier is bold, gay, and friendly, with a self-confident, cock-of-the-walk attitude. Shyness, especially shy-sharpness, in the mature specimen is to be heavily penalized.

SCALE OF POINTS

Head.....................15	Legs and feet.............10
Eyes, ears, expression......15	Size and symmetry.........10
Neck.....................5	Movement................10
Body....................10	Temperament.............10
Coat.....................15	TOTAL..............100

DISQUALIFICATION
The front teeth overshot or undershot

APPROVED MAY 14, 1963

MANCHESTER TERRIER

There was a Black-and-Tan Terrier in England before the days of dog shows, less graceful in outline and coarser in type to be sure, than those of today. These early dogs did not present the fancy marks of penciled toes and dotted brows that today's breed sports; their tan was smutty, but nevertheless they were sound, game, and useful dogs, the most accomplished of rat killers whether in the pit or along the water courses.

The Manchester district was a noted center for two "poor men's sports"—rat killing and rabbit coursing. A fancier by the name of John Hulme, with the idea of producing a dog that could be used at both contests, bred a Whippet bitch to a celebrated rat-killing dog, a cross bred terrier dark brown in color. The result of this cross was very satisfactory, the dogs proved useful, and other fanciers in the neighborhood took to breeding them, and the Manchester school of terriers was launched. They advanced in popularity rapidly and soon spread over the British Isles and were brought to this country in considerable numbers. Their original name of Black-and-Tan Terrier was dropped in 1923 and the name of Manchester Terrier was adopted.

As a sagacious, intelligent pet and companion and as a house dog, no breed is superior to the well-bred Manchester. There is a sleek appearance about them that no other dog presents. Their long, clean heads, keen expression, glossy coat, whip tail, and smart, wide-awake appearance always command attention. Their cleanly habits and short coats also admit them to homes that shut out their rough-haired brothers.

The Manchester Terrier, with all his refinement, has lost none of his gameness. He is still *per se* a vermin dog, unequaled and is capable of holding his own in a rough-and-tumble scrap with anything living of his weight.

The Toy Manchester Terrier is probably more popular today than its larger brother, from which it differs only in size, being nothing more or less than a vest-pocket edition. Its show points are the same. It should be simply a miniature, the smaller the better. The regulation weight is up to twelve pounds, but many specimens are under five.

Buyer's guide: The intelligent, naturally active Manchester Terrier is a devoted companion for homes with or without children. They are very clean in habits and can be comfortably raised in city apartment or rural settings. The sleek black coat of the Manchester is easily kept and needs only an occasional brushing to remove dead hairs. There is no real shedding of the coat and they do not have any odor. Manchesters should get sufficient exercise from running around the house, but time outside is recommended to keep their disposition active and alert.

STANDARD FOR THE MANCHESTER TERRIER

Head: Long, narrow, tight-skinned, almost flat, with a slight indentation up the forehead; slightly wedge-shaped, tapering to the nose, with no visible cheek muscles, and well filled up under the eyes; tight-lipped jaws, level in mouth, and functionally level teeth, or the incisors of the upper jaw may make a close, slightly overlapping contact with the incisors of the lower jaw.

Eyes: Small, bright, sparkling and as near black as possible; set moderately close together; oblong in shape, slanting upwards on the outside; they should neither protrude nor sink in the skull.

Nose: Black.

Ears (Toy Variety): Of moderate size; set well up on the skull and rather close together; thin, moderately narrow at base; with pointed tips; naturally erect carriage. Wide, flaring, blunt-tipped or "bell" ears are a serious fault; cropped or cut ears shall disqualify.

Ears (Standard Variety): Erect, or button, small and thin; smaller at the root and set as close together as possible at the top of the head. If cropped, to a point, long and carried erect.

Neck and Shoulders: The neck should be a moderate length, slim and graceful; gradually becoming larger as it approaches, and blend smoothly with the slooping shoulders; free from throatiness; slightly arched from the occiput.

Chest: Narrow between the legs; deep in the brisket.

Body: Moderately short, with robust loins; ribs well sprung out behind the shoulders; back slightly arched at the loin, and falling again to the tail to the same height as the shoulders.

Legs: Forelegs straight, of proportionate length, and well under body. Hind legs should not turn in or out as viewed from the rear; carried back; hocks well let down. **Feet:** Compact, well arched, with jet black nails; the two middle toes in the front feet rather longer than the others; the hind feet shaped like those of a cat.

Tail: Moderately short, and set on where the arch of the back ends; thick where it joins the body, tapering to a point, not carried higher than the back.

Coat: Smooth, short, thick, dense, close and glossy; not soft.

Color: Jet black and rich mahogany tan, which should not run or blend into each other but abruptly forming clear, well-defined lines of color division. A small tan spot over each eye; a very small tan spot on each cheek; the lips of the upper and lower jaws should be tanned, extending under the throat, ending in the shape of the letter V; the inside of the ears partly tanned. Tan spots, called "rosettes," on each side of the chest above the front legs, more pronounced in puppies than in adults. There should be a black "thumb mark" patch on the front of each foreleg between the pastern and the knee. There should be a distinct black "pencil mark" line running lengthwise on the top of each toe on all four feet. The remainder of the forelegs to be tan to the knee. Tan on the hind legs should continue from the penciling on the feet up the inside of the legs to a little below the stifle joint; the outside of the hind legs to be black. There should be tan under the tail, and on the vent, but only of such size as to be covered by the tail. White in any part of the coat is a serious fault, and shall disqualify whenever the white shall form a patch or stripe measuring as much as ½-inch in its longest dimension.

Weight *(Toy Variety):* Not exceeding 12 pounds. It is suggested that clubs consider dividing the American-bred and open classes by weight as follows: 7 pounds and under, over 7 pounds and not exceeding 12 pounds.

Weight *(Standard Variety):* Over 12 pounds and not exceeding 22 pounds. Dogs weighing over 22 pounds shall be disqualified. It is suggested that clubs consider dividing the American-bred and open classes by weight as follows: over 12 pounds and not exceeding 16 pounds, over 16 pounds and not exceeding 22 pounds.

DISQUALIFICATIONS

Color: White in any part of the coat, forming a patch or stripe measuring as much as ½ inch in its longest dimension.

Weight: (Standard Variety): Over 22 pounds.

Ears (Toy Variety): Cropped or cut ears.

APPROVED JUNE 12, 1962

MINIATURE SCHNAUZER

Derived from a cross between the Standard Schnauzer and the Affenpinscher, the Miniature Schnauzer is of German origin. The Schnauzer type most likely resulted from crossing a black Poodle and gray Spitz with old German Pinscher stock; the Affenpinscher cross came later to decrease size. Less aggressive in temperament than the Standard, the Miniature is hardy, active, and intelligent, good with children and an excellent ratter. This latter attribute reflects the original purpose for the breed's creation—to destroy vermin and guard the yard and stable. The Miniature was first recognized as a separate breed in 1899 when it appeared in its own classes in Germany.

The Miniature Schnauzer is classed in the Terrier Group only in the United States and Canada, though originally all three Schnauzer varieties were put in the Working Group. While in temperament the Miniature closely resembles the alert, active terriers, there is a strong element of working dog temperament in the breed. Miniature Schnauzers show none of the nervous, yappy disposition of some terriers. This "big dog" temperament is definitely an asset in obedience training and also serves the Miniature well as a homefront companion.

The breed standard calls for a robust, cobby little dog, with a fairly broad skull, sloping shoulder and a moderately broad chest. By way of explanation, it would resemble a small draft horse or Shetland Pony rather than a race horse. Its appearance should be one of solidity and strength, without those qualities being carried to the extreme. Bi-colors— solid black with silver, cream or light tannish markings—are somewhat more common than formerly and have always been recognized by the American standard. Blacks occur in the early generations of all Schnauzers if the pedigree is traced back far enough, but blacks have never been very numerous in the United States. In Germany they have their own classes and some kennels there breed blacks exclusively.

Interest in demonstrating the Miniature's prowess in obedience has increased since 1946, along with the breed's popularity. That Miniature Schnauzers lead the Terrier Group in obedience is not surprising, considering their working inheritance from the Standard Schnauzer, as well as the suspected Poodle blood in their background.

Buyer's guide: This hardy terrier is a popular pet with many households, requiring little special attention in regards to space, exercise or diet. However, to maintain a neat appearance for their coat several trips to the groomer will be required yearly. On the whole, the Miniature Schnauzer is not a fighter, but they do have a feisty side to their disposition, especially with other animals. Young children should be taught not to play roughly or tease these dogs as they may snap in defense.

STANDARD FOR THE MINIATURE SCHNAUZER

General Appearance: The Miniature Schnauzer is a robust, active dog of terrier type, resembling his larger cousin, the Standard Schnauzer, in general appearance, and of an alert, active disposition. He is sturdily built, nearly square in proportion of body length to height, with plenty of bone, and without any suggestion of toyishness.

Head: Strong and rectangular, its width diminishing slightly from ears to eyes, and again to the tip of the nose. The forehead is unwrinkled. The topskull is flat and fairly long. The foreface is parallel to the topskull, with a slight stop, and is at least as long as the topskull. The muzzle is strong in proportion to the skull; it ends in a moderately blunt manner, with thick whiskers which accentuate the rectangular shape of the head. ***Teeth:*** The teeth meet in a scissors bite. That is, the upper front teeth overlap the lower teeth in such a manner that the inner surface of the upper incisors barely touches the outer surface of the lower incisors when the mouth is closed. ***Eyes:*** Small, dark brown and deep-set. They are oval in appearance and keen in expression. ***Ears:*** When cropped the ears are identical in shape and length, with pointed tips. They are in balance with the head and not exaggerated in length. They are set high on the skull and carried perpendicularly at the inner edges, with as little bell as possible along the outer edges. When uncropped, the ears are small and V-shaped.

Neck: Strong and well arched, blending into the shoulders, and with the skin fitting tightly at the throat.

Body: Short and deep, with the brisket extending at least to the elbows. Ribs are well sprung and deep, extending well back to a short loin. The underbody does not present a tucked-up appearance at the flank. The topline is straight; it declines slightly from the withers to the base of the tail. The over-all length from chest to stern bone equals the height at the withers.

Forequarters: The forequarters have flat, somewhat sloping shoulders and high withers. Forelegs are straight and parallel when viewed from all sides. They have strong pasterns and good bone. They are separated by a fairly deep brisket which precludes a pinched front. The elbows are close, and the ribs spread gradually from the first rib so as to allow space for the elbows to move close to the body.

Hindquarters: The hindquarters have strong-muscled, slanting thighs: they are well bent at the stifles and straight from hock to so-called heel. There is sufficient angulation so that, in stance, the hocks extend beyond the tail. The hindquarters never appear overbuilt or higher than the shoulders.

Feet: Short and round (cat-feet) with thick, black pads. The toes are arched and compact.

Action: The trot is the gait at which movement is judged. The dog must gait in a straight line. Coming on, the forelegs are parallel, with the elbows close to the body. The feet turn neither inward nor outward. Going away, the hind legs are parallel from the hocks down, and travel wide. Viewed from the side, the forelegs have a good reach, while the hind legs have a strong drive with good pick-up of hocks.

Tail: Set high and carried erect. It is docked only long enough to be clearly visible over the topline of the body when the dog is in proper length of coat.

Coat: Double, with a hard, wiry outer coat and a close undercoat. The body coat should be plucked. When in show condition, the proper length is not less than three-quarters of an inch except on neck, ears and skull. Furnishings are fairly thick but not silky.

Size: From 12 to 14 inches. Ideal size 13½ inches. *(See disqualifications.)*

Color: The recognized colors are salt and pepper, black and silver, and solid black. The typical color is salt and pepper in shades of gray; tan shading is permissible. The salt and pepper mixture fades out to light gray or silver white in the eyebrows, whiskers, cheeks, under throat, across chest, under tail, leg furnishings, under body, and inside legs. The light under-body hair is not to rise higher on the sides of the body than the front elbows.

The black and silvers follow the same pattern as the salt and peppers. The entire salt-and-pepper section must be black.

Black is the only solid color allowed. It must be a true black with no gray hairs and no brown tinge except where the whiskers may have become discolored. A small white spot on the chest is permitted.

FAULTS

Type: Toyishness, raciness, or coarseness.

Structure: Head coarse and cheeky. Chest too broad or shallow in brisket. Tail set low. Sway or roach back. Bowed or cowhocked hindquarters. Loose elbows.

Action: Sidegaiting. Paddling in front, or high hackney knee action. Weak hind action.

Coat: Too soft or too smooth and slick in appearance.

Temperament: Shyness or viciousness.

Bite: Undershot or overshot jaw. Level bite.

Eyes: Light and/or large and prominent in appearance.

DISQUALIFICATIONS

Dogs or bitches under 12 inches or over 14 inches.
Color solid white or white patches on the body.

APPROVED MAY 13, 1958

Representing the breed: Knight's Happy Apache. Photo by Louise Van der Meid.

NORFOLK AND NORWICH TERRIER

Norwich Terrier breeders have always had particular ideas about which of the two accepted ear sets within the breed are the most natural and should be maintained in their breedings. Those that thought the drop-ear was best strived to produced small, neatly dropped ears that broke just about the skull line. Prick-ear enthusiasts aimed for small ears set well apart that were pointed erect. Preferences for which is best or most desirable varied from fancier to fancier. To alleviate all confusion, it has recently been decided that all the registered Norwiches with prick ears would retain the name of Norwich Terriers, while all drop ear dogs would assume the name of Norfolk Terrier and be considered as a breed unto themselves. The two breeds share a common history, but will have distinct claim to their futures.

The Norwich Terrier may be one of the smallest breeds in the group, but they are terrier through and through—as feisty and game as they come. In the home, Norwiches have a charming personality and are loyal one-man dogs. They are wary of strangers but will accept everyone that they are introduced to. Small, red terriers of the Norwich type have been known in England since the 1800's, but little was cared about their breeding until countryside farmers set out to develop a breed of dog that could effectively work the land of the area and chase out any small animals that might invade the herds or crops. They needed a dog that could go to the ground and courageously flush the animals from where they hid. To do this, they must have a protective coat, a keen spirit for the hunt and a rugged, hardy constitution. The Norwich combines all these traits.

Although an alert watchdog, the Norwich Terrier wouldn't think of attacking a person. If something arouses their attention, they raise a fuss and make their presence known, but will probably hang back and wait for their owners to take appropriate action.

NORFOLK TERRIER

NORWICH TERRIER

411

Don't confuse their self-control with cowardice, however. They are obedient dogs and can keep a stable disposition no matter what the provocation, but should a rat or small animal invade the vegetable garden, the Norwich would be right down on it. The breed has been used extensively on the hunt, and surprisingly enough their short legs do not really hinder them and they are capable of keeping up with the horses on a chase. Oftentimes the hunters have been known to carry their Norwiches with them in a satchel-type carrier that is slung over their shoulder as they ride. When the hounds have holed the prey, the Norwiches are let down to bolt the animal from where it hides. These bold terriers must be nimble to nip at the sides of the animal, taunting and confusing him until he flees.

Cantab Terrier is a name often given to the Norwich, owing to the fact that these dogs were the favorites of undergraduates of Cambridge University in the 1880's. One of the earliest fanciers, Mr. Frank Jones, did much to set the true type of today's Norwiches. Because of this, the breed was called the Jones' Terriers for a time.

Norwiches are personable dogs and seem quite intuitive in regards to the moods of those around them. They are quick thinkers and can be quite mischievous if given the chance. If left alone they will entertain themselves and not moan about it, but they prefer the company of people. Norwiches have a lively, gregarious personality that has won them many ardent fanciers. A round, well-nourished look comes natural to the breed, as does their close lying coat that keeps the dog clean and requires little or no trimming.

Great curiosity is characteristic of the Norwich, and they seem to look on everything with an inquisitive glance. They are constantly active and seem to pride themselves on knowing exactly what is going on around them. The Norwich is a top competitor on the show circuit and gait with driving yet lively movements.

Buyer's guide: The Norwich Terrier requires little or no pampering or special care and takes eagerly to an indoor life. Their coat repels most dirt and needs no extensive trimming or brushing, a fact which separates the Norwich from many other terriers. They are a lively breed capable of long, brisk runs in the country, but their exercise requirements are generally very modest and they will do well with an occasional walk. A small home is no deterrent for owning the Norwich as they adapt to whatever housing they are given. They are a game breed and should therefore be owned only by families with older children, no infants. Norwiches are good companions for older, housebound individuals.

STANDARD FOR THE NORFOLK TERRIER

Characteristics: The Norfolk Terrier is one of the smallest of the terriers, but a "demon" for its size. Of a lovable disposition, not quarrelsome, and with a hardy constitution. Temperament: Steady and fearless.

General Appearance: A small, low, keen dog, strong with good substance and bone. **Head:** Skull wide (good width between the ears) and slightly rounded. Muzzle strong; length about one-third less than a measurement from the occiput to the bottom of the stop, which should be well defined.

Eyes: Dark, intelligent, full of expression, bright and keen.

Ears: Neatly dropped, small, with break just above the skull line, carried close to the cheek, and not falling lower than the outer corner of the eye; slightly rounded at the tip.

Mouth: Tight lipped. Jaws, clean and strong, teeth strong, rather large. Scissors bite.

Neck: Medium length and strong.

Forequarters: Clean and powerful shoulders, short, powerful legs, as straight as consistently possible.

Body: Moderately short and compact, with well sprung ribs.

Hindquarters: Sound and well muscled, good turn of stifle, hocks well let down and straight when viewed from the rear, with great powers of propulsion.

Feet: Round, with thick pads.

Tail: Medium docked, carriage not excessively gay.

Coat: Hard, wiry and straight, lying close to the body. It is longer and rougher on the neck and shoulders, in full coat forming almost a mane. Hair on the head, ears and muzzle, short and smooth, except for slight eyebrows and slight whiskers.

Color: All shades of red, red wheaten, black and tan or grizzle. white marks or patches are undesirable but shall not disqualify.

Size: Ideal height 10 inches at withers. Ideal weight 10 to 12 lbs.

Faults: A mouth over- or undershot; a long narrow head. Trimming is not desirable. Honorable scars from fair wear and tear shall not count against.

STANDARD FOR THE NORWICH TERRIER

Head: Skull wide, slightly rounded with good width between the ears. Muzzle strong but not long or heavy, with slightly "foxy" appearance. Length about one-third less than the measurement from the occiput to the bottom of the stop, which should be well defined. *Faults:* A long narrow head; over square muzzle; highly rounded dome.

Ears: Prick or drop. If pricked, small, pointed, erect and set well apart. If dropped, neat, small, with break just above the skull line, front edge close to cheek, and not falling lower than the outer corner of the eye. *Faults:* Oversize; poor carriage.

Eyes: Very bright, dark and keen. Full of expression. *Faults:* Light or protruding eyes.

Jaw: Clean, strong, tight lipped, with strong, large, closely-fitted teeth; scissors bite. *Faults:* A bite over- or undershot.

Neck: Short and strong, well set on clean shoulders.

Body: Moderately short, compact and deep with level topline, ribs well sprung. *Faults:* Long weak back, loaded shoulders.

Legs: Short and powerful and as straight as is consistent with the short legs for which we aim. Sound bone, round feet, thick pads. *Faults:* Out at elbow, badly bowed, knuckled over. Too light in bone.

Quarters: Strong, rounded, with great powers of propulsion. *Faults:* Cowhocks.

Tail: Medium docked, carriage not excessively gay.

Color: All shades of red, wheaten, black and tan and grizzle. White markings on the chest, though allowable, are not desirable. *Faults:* White markings elsewhere or to any great extent on the chest.

Coat: As hard and wiry as possible, lying close to the body, with a definite undercoat. Top coat absolutely straight; in full coat longer and rougher forming almost a mane on shoulders and neck. Hair on head, ears and muzzle, except for slight eyebrows and slight whiskers, is absolutely short and smooth. These dogs should be shown with as nearly a natural coat as possible. A mimimum amount of tidying is permissible but excessive trimming, shaping and clipping shall be heavily penalized by the judge. *Faults:* Silky or curly coat.

Weight: Ideal, 11 to 12 pounds.

Height: Ideal, 10 inches at the withers.

General Appearance: A small, low rugged terrier, tremendously active. A perfect demon, yet not quarrelsome, and of a lovable disposition, and a very hardy consitutition. Honorable scars from fair wear and tear shall not count against.

DISQUALIFICATION
Cropped ears shall disqualify.

SCOTTISH TERRIER

Scotland may truly be termed the land of terriers. A half dozen or more breeds, all long and low, all rough-coated, and all prick-eared except the Dandie, hail from the land of heather. It is not extraordinary that Scotland should have so many varieties of terriers, for it is a country of cave and cleft and cavern, in which terriers have a wide sphere of usefulness. Dogs, like men, are molded by environment, and it is easy to comprehend how a rugged land would develop a rugged dog and a race of men noted world-wide for their steadfast determination, deep-seated affection, and canny intelligence. The Scots would naturally have as friends and companions a race of dogs possessing all of their master's sturdy characteristics.

Scotland's Terrier is a proud title, but the dogs that bear it are worthy of their name, for the Scottish Terrier of today is a veritable paragon of gameness, intelligence, and all-around usefulness on land or water, above or below ground; and with it all he is the most sensible and intelligent of companions.

To dive deep into the antiquity of the Scottish Terrier is simply to invite trouble, for the Scottish are a touchy race on everything pertaining to birth and pedigree. They are as loyal to their dogs as they are to their clans. To suggest or intimate that Scotland's dogs are not as old as their most cherished traditions or that their blood is not as pure as the water in their mountain lakes is sheer heresy. We venture to say, however, that these grand little dogs did not have their birth in any particular locality in Scotland. They are indigenous to all the highlands and descend from the old highland terrier, a little, long-backed, short-legged, snipy-faced, prick- or crop-eared dog, in color mostly sandy-and-black, game as a pebble, lively as a cricket, and in all a most charming companion. The crosses that were made on this parent stock many years ago were all with the best of working terriers. No breed of dog has been more carefully bred than the Scottish Terrier, and today they are extraordinarily well fixed in type and characteristics.

The enthusiasm expressed by admirers of the breed is well founded. For ratting, ferreting, rabbit-hunting, partridge-treeing, working along hedge-rows or water courses, retrieving from land or water and as all-around assistants to the gun, they are unexcelled. They are cleanly about the house, extraordinarily patient with children, the best of guards for house or bar, and distinguish intuitively between the intruder or casual observer or occasional visitor.

In selecting puppies under four months of age, look for a long, level head; a strong jaw; small dark eye; small erect ears, carried closely together; short, round, body; short sickle tail; great bone; straight forelegs and a dense, hard coat.

Buyer's guide: The Scottie is a very sensible dog that adjusts well to the rules of the house at a very young age. They are well behaved and eager for companionship. Even though their exercise requirements are minimal, the Scottie is quite active and should be owned by people who enjoy a lively walk each day. Keeping their coat in order may prove to be fairly expensive, as several trimming and stripping sessions are required to maintain the typical shape and flow of the coat. In general, they have a merry desposition and get along well with older children.

STANDARD FOR THE SCOTTISH TERRIER

Skull (5 points): Long, of medium width, slightly domed and covered with short, hard hair. It should not be quite flat, as there should be a slight stop or drop between the eyes.

Muzzle (5 points): In proportion to the length of skull, with not too much taper toward the nose. Nose should be black and of good size. The jaws should be level and square. The nose projects somewhat over the mouth, giving the impression that the upper jaw is longer than the lower. The teeth should be evenly placed, having a scissors or level bite, with the former being preferable.

Eyes (5 points): Set wide apart, small and of almond shape, not round. Color to be dark brown or nearly black. To be bright, piercing and set well under the brow.

Ears (10 points): Small, prick, set well up on the skull, rather pointed but not cut. The hair on them should be short and velvety.

Neck (5 points): Moderately short, thick and muscular, strongly set on sloping shoulders, but not so short as to appear clumsy.

Chest (5 points): Broad and very deep, well let down between the forelegs.

Body (15 points): Moderately short and well ribbed up with strong loin, deep flanks and very muscular hindquarters.

Legs and Feet (10 points): Both forelegs and hind leg should be short and very heavy in bone in proportion to the size of the dog. Forelegs straight or slightly bent with elbows close to the body. Scottish Terriers should not be out at the elbows. Stifles should be well bent and legs straight from hock to heel. Thighs very muscular. Feet round and thick with strong nails, forefeet larger than the hind feet. *Note*—The gait of the Scottish Terrier is peculiarly its own and is very characteristic of the breed. It is not the square trot or walk that is desirable in the long-legged breeds. The forelegs do not move in exact parallel planes—rather in reaching out incline slightly inward. This is due to the shortness of leg and width of chest. The action of the rear legs should be square and true and at the trot both the hocks and stifles should be flexed with a vigorous motion.

Tail (2½ points): Never cut and about 7 inches long, carried with a slight curve but not over the back.

Coat (15 points): Rather short, about 2 inches, dense undercoat with outer coat intensely hard and wiry.

Size and Weight (10 points): Equal consideration must be given to height, length of back and weight. Height at shoulder for either sex should be about 10 inches. Generally, a well-balanced Scottish Terrier dog of correct size should weigh from 19 to 22 pounds and a bitch, from

18 to 21 pounds. The principal objective must be symmetry and balance.

Color (2½ points): Steel or iron gray, brindled or grizzled, black, sandy or wheaten. White markings are objectionable and can be allowed only on the chest and that to a slight extent only.

General Appearance (10 points): The face should wear a keen, sharp and active expression. Both head and tail should be carried well up. The dog should look very compact, well muscled and powerful, giving the impression of immense power in a small size.

Penalities: Soft coat, round, or very light eye, overshot or undershot jaw, obviously oversize or undersize, shyness, timidity or failure to show with head and tail up are faults to be penalized. No judge should put to Winners or Best of Breed any Scottish Terrier not showing real terrier character in the ring.

SCALE OF POINTS

Skull	5	Legs and feet	10
Muzzle	5	Tail	2½
Eyes	5	Coat	15
Ears	10	Size	10
Neck	5	Color	2½
Chest	5	General appearance	10
Body	15	TOTAL	100

APPROVED JUNE 10, 1947

SEALYHAM TERRIER

For many years this attractive breed of terriers has been carefully bred by a small group of British sportsmen who have cherished them for their admirable working qualities and have never been interested in the fads or the mandates of the bench-show world. It may be stated without fear of contradiction that no breed is better adapted to go to earth, and that, pound for pound, they represent as much determination and dead game courage as any dog that lives.

A few years ago a number of prominent bench-show fanciers became interested in the breed and brought them to the notice of the public. Since then they have enjoyed considerable vogue on both sides of the water, for they are sporty little propositions and the most entertaining and useful of companions.

The first importations of a large number of Sealyhams to the United States began in the early 1920's. The breeders in England had put great emphasis on selective breeding and the Sealyham of this time was not only sound in appearance and conformation, but was still as game and eager as any working terrier. The breed continued to prosper in this country, going on to be a great contender for top awards at the dog shows. In the show ring their carefree movements and proud carriage have made the Sealyham a standout among the terrier breeds, as they are a great blend of beauty and breeding.

Buyer's guide: The Sealyham is recommended for only the most ardent terrier fans because they have a tendency toward a somewhat sharp personality and require substantial grooming. They are not a patient breed and will respond with a snap to anything that irritates them, and this should be sufficient reason not to consider the Sealyham if you have young children. Since they are low to the ground, their white coat may become heavily soiled and require cleaning. Routine stripping and trimming is also needed to give the Sealyham their distinctive appearance.

STANDARD FOR THE SEALYHAM TERRIER

The Sealyham should be the embodiment of power and determination, ever keen and alert, of extraordinary substance, yet free from clumsiness.

Height: At withers about 10½ inches.

Weight: 23-24 pounds for dogs; bitches slightly less. It should be borne in mind that size is more important than weight.

Head: Long, broad and powerful, without coarseness. It should, however, be in perfect balance with the body, joining neck smoothly. Length of head roughly, three-quarters height at withers, or about an inch longer than neck. Breadth between ears a little less than one-half length of head. **Skull:** Very slightly domed, with a shallow indentation running down between the brows, and joining the muzzle with a moderate stop. **Cheeks:** Smoothly formed and flat, without heavy jowls. **Jaws:** Powerful and square. Bite level or scissors. Overshot or undershot bad faults. **Teeth:** Sound, strong and white, with canines fitting closely together. **Nose:** Black, with large nostrils. White, cherry or butterfly bad faults. **Eyes:** Very dark, deeply set and fairly wide apart, of medium size, oval in shape with keen terrier expression. Light, large or protruding eye bad faults. Lack of eye rim pigmentation not a fault. **Ears:** Folded level with top of head, with forward edge close to cheek. Well rounded at tip, and of length to reach outer corner of eye. Thin, not leathery, and of sufficient thickness to avoid creases. Prick, tulip, rose or hound ears bad faults.

Neck: Length slightly less than two-thirds of height of dog at withers. Muscular without coarseness, with good reach, refinement at throat, and set firmly on shoulders.

Shoulders: Well laid back and powerful, but not over-muscled. Sufficiently wide to permit freedom of action. Upright or straight shoulder placement highly undesirable.

Legs: Forelegs strong, with good bone; and as straight as is consistent with chest being well let down between them. Down on pasterns, knuckled over, bowed, and out at elbow, bad faults. Hind legs longer than forelegs and not so heavily boned. **Feet:** Large but compact, round with thick pads, strong nails. Toes well arched and pointing straight ahead. Forefeet larger, though not quite so long as hind feet. Thin, spread or flat feet bad faults.

Body: Strong, short-coupled and substantial, so as to permit great flexibility. Brisket deep and well let down between forelegs. Ribs well sprung.

Back: Length from withers to set-on of tail should approximate height at withers, or 10½ inches. Topline level, neither roached nor swayed. Any deviations from these measurements undesirable. **Hindquarters:** Very powerful, and protruding well behind the set-on of tail. Strong second thighs, stifles well bent, and hocks well let down. Cowhocks bad fault.

Tail: Docked and carried upright. Set on far enough forward so that spine does not slope down to it.

Coat: Weather-resisting, comprised of soft, dense undercoat and hard, wiry top coat. Silky or curly coat bad fault.

Color: All white, or with lemon, tan or badger markings on head and ears. Heavy body markings and excessive ticking should be discouraged.

Action: Sound, strong, quick, free, true and level.

SCALE OF POINTS

General character, balance and size	15	Body, ribs & loin	10
Head	5	Hindquarters	10
Eyes	5	Legs and feet	10
Mouth	5	Coat	10 50
Ears	5	Tail	5
Neck	5 25	Color (body marking & ticking)	5 10
Shoulders and brisket	10	TOTAL	100

APPROVED FEBRUARY 9, 1974

SKYE TERRIER

This is one of the oldest breeds in Scotland, having its origin in the islands from which it now takes its name. The breed was originally called Scottish Terrier. In fact, all of the Scottish varieties of terriers were first so designated. Dr. Caius, one of the earliest writers on dogs, indicates the existence and type of the Skye Terrier in his work *Englishe Dogges*. He describes them as "Iseland dogges, brought out of barbarous borders from the uttermost countryes northwards," and says that "they, by reason of the length of their heare, show neither of their face or their body, and yet these curres, forsooth, because they are so strange, are greatly set by, esteemed, taken up, and made of, in room of the Spaniell gentle or comforter."

The Bishop of Ross, who wrote a little later in the sixteenth century, says: "There is also another kind of scenting dog of low height, but of bulkier body, which, creeping into subterraneous burrows, routs out foxes, badgers, martens, and wildcats from their lurking places and dens," which doubtless referred to the ancestors of our modern Skye Terriers.

Professor Low describes the dogs of the Island of Skye as follows: "The Terriers of the western islands of Scotland have long, lank hair almost trailing to the ground." This breed has been brought to perfection as a show dog, but its enormous coat and the size is a distinct disadvantage to the dog in pursuing his natural calling. Few, if any, show dogs are used for actual work, and therefore it is needless to decry the bench type which are calculated to keep intact the distinctive features and characteristics of this game, hard-bitten, and very handsome terrier. The Skye Terrier is a most companionable and faithful dog to those to whom he attaches himself, although he is not, speaking generally, as open in disposition as his cousin, the Scottie. He is one of the most snappish dogs that goes to a show, and often dangerous to handle. This surliness in the Skye is a natural characteristic, probably inherited, the outcome of nervousness created by the fact that he is buried in such long thick hair that he can scarcely see.

The chief points to look for in Skye Terrier puppies from two to four months old and after, are: a long head; strong muzzle; dark eye; long body; well-sprung ribs; deep chest; short, heavy-boned legs; and a profuse coat of good texture. In the prick-eared variety the ears should be bolt upright; and in the drop-eared, the ears should fall forward in the manner of other drop-eared terriers.

Buyer's guide: Consider carefully before selecting a Skye Terrier because they are not an ideal dog for every home. Substantial time must be devoted to brushing out the long coat of this breed since matting and cutting will all but ruin their natural appearance. They are a fairly excitable breed and will respond with a bite to anyone who is pestering them. Skyes are not recommended for households with children or other animals. They enjoy the companionship of adults but are not happy to be left alone.

STANDARD FOR THE SKYE TERRIER

General Appearance: The Skye Terrier is a dog of style, elegance, and dignity; agile and strong with sturdy bone and hard muscle. Long, low, and lank—he is twice as long as he is high—he is covered with a profuse coat that falls straight down either side of the body over oval-shaped ribs. The hair well feathered on the head veils forehead and eyes to serve as protection from brush and briar as well as amid serious encounters with other animals. He stands with head high and long tail hanging, and moves with a seemingly effortless gait. Of suitable size for his hunting work, strong in body, quarters, and jaw.

Temperament: That of the typical working terrier capable of overtaking game and going to ground, displaying stamina, courage, strength, and agility. Fearless, good-tempered, loyal and canny, he is friendly and gay with those he knows and reserved and cautious with strangers.

Head: Long and powerful, strength being deemed more important than extreme length. Moderate width at the back of the skull tapers gradually to a strong muzzle. The stop is slight. The dark muzzle is just moderately full as opposed to snipy, and the nose is always black. A Dudley, flesh-colored, or brown nose shall disqualify. Powerful and absolutely true jaws and mouth with the incisor teeth closing level, or with the upper teeth slightly overlapping the lower. **Eyes:** Brown, preferably dark brown, medium in size, close-set, and alight with life and intelligence. **Ears:** Symmetrical and gracefully feathered. They may be carried prick or drop. When prick, they are medium in size, placed high on the skull, erect at their outer edges, and slightly wider apart at the peak than at the skull. Drop ears, somewhat larger in size and set lower, hang flat against the skull.

Neck: Long and gracefully arched, carried high and proudly.

Body: Pre-eminently long and low. The backline is level, the chest deep, with oval-shaped ribs. The sides appear flattish due to the straight falling and profuse coat.

Legs and Feet: Forequarters: Legs short, muscular, and straight as possible. "Straight as possible" means straight as soundness and chest will permit; it does not mean "terrier straight." Shoulders well laid back, with tight placement of shoulder blades at the withers, and elbows should fit closely to the sides and be neither loose nor tied. Forearm should curve slightly around the chest. **Hindquarters:** Strong, full, well developed, and well angulated. Legs short, muscular, and straight when viewed from behind. **Feet:** Large harefeet preferably pointing forward, the pads thick and nails strong and preferably black.

Movement: The legs proceed straight forward when traveling. When approaching, the forelegs form a continuation of the straight line of the front, the feet being the same distance apart as the elbows. The principal propelling power is furnished by the hind legs, which travel straight forward. Forelegs should move well forward, without too much lift. The whole movement may be termed free, active, and effortless and give a more or less fluid picture.

Tail: Long and well feathered. When hanging, its upper section is pendulous, following the line of the rump, its lower section thrown back in a moderate arc without twist or curl. When raised, its height makes it appear a prolongation of the backline. Though not to be preferred, the tail is sometimes carried high when the dog is excited or angry. When such carriage arises from emotion only, it is permissible. But the tail should not be constantly carried above the length of the back nor hang limp.

Coat: Double. Undercoat short, close, soft, and woolly. Outer coat hard, straight, and flat, 5½ inches long without extra credit granted for greater length. The body coat hangs straight down each side, parting from head to tail. The head hair, which may be shorter and softer, veils forehead and eyes and forms a moderate beard and apron. The long feathering on the ears falls straight down from the tips and outer edges, surrounding the ears like a fringe and outlining their shape. The ends of the hair should mingle with the coat at the sides of the neck.

Color: The coat must be of one over-all color at the skin but may be of varying shades of the same color in the full coat, which may be black, blue, dark or light gray, silver platinum, fawn, or cream. The dog must have no distinctive markings except for the desirable black points of ears, muzzle, and tip of tail, all of which points are preferably dark even to black. The shade of head and legs should approximate that of the body. There must be no trace of pattern, design, or clear-cut color variations, with the exception of the breed's only permissible white which occasionally exists on the chest not exceeding 2 inches in diameter.

The puppy coat may be very different in color from the adult coat. As it is growing and clearing, wide variations of color may occur; consequently this is permissible in dogs under 18 months of age. However, even in puppies there must be no trace of pattern, design, or clear-cut variations with the exception of the black band of varying width frequently seen encircling the body coat of the cream-colored dog, and the only permissible white which, as in the adult dog, occasionally exists on the chest not exceeding 2 inches in diameter.

Size: Dogs: Shoulder height, 10 inches. Length, chest bone over tail at rump, 20 inches. Head, 8½ inches. Tail, 9 inches. Bitches: Shoulder height, 9½ inches. Length, chest bone over tail at rump, 19 inches.

Head, 8 inches. Tail, 8½ inches. A slightly higher or lower dog of either sex is acceptable, providing body, head, and tail dimensions are proportionately longer or shorter. The ideal ratio of body length to shoulder height is 2 to 1, which is considered the correct proportion.

Measurements are taken with the Skye standing in natural position with feet well under. A box caliper is used vertically and horizontally. For the height, the top bar should rest on the withers. The head is measured from the tip of the nose to the back of the occipital bone, and the tail from the root to tip. Dogs 8 inches or less at the withers, and bitches 7½ inches or less at the withers, are to be penalized.

DISQUALIFICATIONS

A Dudley, flesh-colored or brown nose.

APPROVED MAY 8, 1973

SOFT-COATED WHEATEN TERRIER

The farms of southern Ireland have been the home of the Soft-Coated Wheaten Terrier for more than 200 years. This long-legged terrier derives its name from the fact that their soft, wavy coat is the color of ripe wheat. Fanciers of the Wheaten believe the breed to be the oldest of the native Irish dogs, with the ancestors of the breed thought to be the progenitors of the more popular Kerry Blue Terrier. They are a sporting terrier and have been used successfully to hunt with their masters, herd sheep and cattle and rid the fields of vermin.

Soft-Coated Wheatens maintain an elegant air about them and they are not nearly as aggressive as many terriers, although they still retain a very game spirit in their pursuits. The Wheaten is a natural dog and does not require much trimming to keep him looking his best. The coat is abundant and is only a single layer, which delights most owners because the Wheaten does not shed. Noted for their good temperament, these dogs thrive on affection and make ideal guardians and playmates for children. They are quick to learn and anxious to please their owners.

The Soft-Coated Wheaten is a naturally happy, active dog that makes little demand on an owner. They normally find sufficient entertainment in their daily routine to keep them in good physical condition, although they do enjoy a good run through the countryside on occasion. Their clear wheaten coat is the hallmark of the breed and it does best when brushed and combed through daily. The texture and color of the hair does not become established until 18 or 24 months of age and the puppies are often born quite dark in color.

Although the breed has been found in the United States for several decades now, it wasn't until the last 15 years that the breed began to gain widespread popularity. In October, 1973 the Soft-Coated Wheaten was officially recognized by the American Kennel Club and they have been garnering many prestigious show ring wins in the short time they have been in competition.

Buyer's guide: The Wheaten is much less aggressive than most of their terrier relatives and is generally very good natured. They are a lively breed and will do best when owned by active people who enjoy time outside with their dogs. Do not keep a dog the size of a Wheaten penned up in an apartment as this may lead to a high-strung temperament. Wheatens thrive on affection and they are most appreciative of attention. Brushing is a must, but housekeepers will appreciate their non-shed coat.

STANDARD FOR THE SOFT-COATED WHEATEN TERRIER

General Appearance: The Soft-Coated Wheaten Terrier is a medium-sized, hardy, well-balanced sporting terrier covered abundantly with a soft, naturally wavy coat of a good clear wheaten color. The breed requires moderation in all points and any exaggerated features are to be shunned. The head is only moderately long, is well balanced and should be free of any coarseness; the back is level with tail set on high, and carried gaily; legs straight in front and muscular behind, with well-laid-back shoulders and well-bent stifles to provide a long graceful stride. The dog should present an overall appearance of a hardy, active and happy animal, strong and well-coordinated.

Head: Well balanced and moderately long, profusely covered with coat which may fall forward to shade the eyes.

Skull flat and not too wide with no suggestion of coarseness. Skull and foreface about equal length.

Cheeks clean and stop well defined.

Muzzle square, powerful and strong, with no suggestion of snipiness. Lips are tight and black.

Nose is black and large for size of the dog.

Eyes: Dark hazel or brown, medium in size and well protected under a strong brow; eye rims black.

Ears: Break level with the skull and drop slightly forward close to the cheeks rather than pointing to the eyes; small to medium in size.

Teeth: Large, clean and white with either level or scissors bite.

Neck: Medium in length, strong and muscular, well covered with protective coat.

Shoulders: Well laid back, clean and smooth.

Body: Body is compact; back strong and level. Ribs are well sprung but without roundness to provide a deep chest with relatively short coupling.

Length of back from point of withers to base of tail should measure about the same as from point of withers to ground.

Tail is docked and well set on, carried gaily but never over the back.

Legs and feet: Forelegs, straight and well boned; hind legs well developed with well bent stifles; hocks well let down, turned neither in nor out.

Feet are round and compact with good depth of pad. Nails dark.

Dewclaws on forelegs may be removed; dewclaws on hind legs should be removed.

Coat: Abundant, soft and wavy, of a good clear wheaten color; may be shaded on the ears and muzzle.

The Soft-Coated Wheaten Terrier is a natural dog and should so appear. Dogs that appear to be overly trimmed should be penalized.

Coat on ears may be left natural or relieved of the fringe to accent smallness.

Coat color and texture do not stabilize until about 18-24 months and should be given some latitude in young dogs.

For show purposes the coat may be tidied up merely to present a neat outline but may not be clipped, plucked or stylized.

Size: Dogs should measure 18-19 inches at the withers and should weigh between 35-45 pounds, bitches somewhat less.

Movement: Free; gait graceful and lively having reach in front and good drive behind; straight action fore and aft.

Temperament: Good tempered, spirited and game; exhibits less aggressiveness than is sometimes encouraged in terriers in the show ring; alert and intelligent.

Major Faults: Overshot. Undershot. Coat texture deviation. Any color save wheaten.

APPROVED JUNE 12, 1973

Representing the breed: Amaden's Katie Love, owned by Emily Holden.

STAFFORDSHIRE BULL TERRIER

This hearty dog stems from the back country of Northern England where they were originally used for bull and bear baiting. Through the years the breed developed a reputation for being fierce fighters, having the courage to fight to the death if necessary. They received much notoriety for their use in the now illegal sport of dogfighting, and much of the stigma that surrounds this gruesome sport still remains with the breed. While the Staffordshire Bull Terrier of today still retains enough innate tenacity and courage to meet any hostile enemy face to face, they are remarkably amiable and gentle by nature.

The Staffordshire Bull Terrier is said to have originated centuries ago from an infusion of early Bulldog and Bull-and-Terrier dog specimens. From these animals they retained the characteristics of tenacity, courage and unyielding strength. The breed is intelligent and exercises much control over their fighting tendencies, but once provoked they are awesome.

The Staffordshire is muscularly built and gives off a general appearance of great strength for their moderate size. Those people that assume from the Staffordshire's powerful appearance, or from hearing reports of their fighting heritage, that the breed is vicious by nature are quite mistaken and misinformed. The breed is genuinely affectionate and playful.

Buyer's guide: In the home these dogs are very sensible and they display a warm, affectionate disposition. They are not so aggressive as to pick a fight, but they will certainly take up all offers. Staffordshire Bulls are very devoted to their owners and are super protective of children. They do need a moderate amount of daily exercise and should not be confined to a very small apartment. It is advisable that the chief owner of this dog be a good disciplinarian and assertive enough to teach obedience and training to his dog. An occasional brushing with a hound glove is all that is required in regard to grooming. A good dog for the very active individual.

STANDARD FOR THE STAFFORDSHIRE BULL TERRIER

Characteristics: From the past history of the Staffordshire Bull Terrier, the modern dog draws its character of indomitable courage, high intelligence, and tenacity. This, coupled with its affection for its friends, and children in particular, its off-duty and trustworthy stability, makes it a foremost all-purpose dog.

General Appearance: The Staffordshire Bull Terrier is a smooth-coated dog. It should be of great strength for its size and, although muscular, should be active and agile.

Head and Skull: Short, deep through, broad skull, very pronounced cheek muscles, distinct stop, short foreface, black nose. Pink (Dudley) nose to be considered a serious fault.

Eyes: Dark preferable, but may bear some relation to coat color.

Round, of medium size, and set to look straight ahead. Light eyes or pink eye rims to be considered a fault, except that where the coat surrounding the eye is white the eye rim may be pink.

Ears: Rose or half-pricked and not large. Full drop or full prick to be considered a serious fault.

Mouth: A bite in which the outer side of the lower incisors touches the inner side of the upper incisors. The lips should be tight and clean. The badly undershot or overshot bite is a serious fault.

Neck: Muscular, rather short, clean in outline and gradually widening toward the shoulders.

Forequarters: Legs straight and well boned, set rather far apart, without looseness at the shoulders and showing no weakness at the pasterns, from which point the feet turn out a little.

Body: The body is close coupled, with a level topline, wide front, deep brisket and well sprung ribs being rather light in the loins.

Hindquarters: The hindquarters should be well muscled, hocks let down with stifles well bent. Legs should be parallel when viewed from behind.

Feet: The feet should be well padded, strong and of medium size. Dewclaws, if any, on the hind legs are generally removed. Dewclaws on the forelegs may be removed.

Tail: The tail is undocked, of medium length, low set, tapering to a point and carried rather low. It should not curl much and may be likened to an old-fashioned pump handle. A tail that is too long or badly curled is a fault.

Coat: Smooth, short and close to the skin, not to be trimmed or dewhiskered.

Color: Red, fawn, white, black or blue, or any of these colors with white. Any shade of brindle or any shade or brindle with white. Black-and-tan or liver color to be disqualified.

Size: Weight: Dogs, 28 to 38 pounds; bitches, 24 to 34 pounds. Height at shoulder: 14 to 16 inches, these heights being related to weights. Non-conformity with these limits is a fault.

DISQUALIFICATIONS

Black-and-tan or liver color.

Representing the breed: Eng., Am., Mex. Ch. Reetuns Lord Jim, owned by Zane Smith and bred by Albert Wood. Photo by MIKRON.

WELSH TERRIER

This handy breed is one of the smartest of guards and companions, and particularly keen on anything in the vermin line. They are indigenous to the country whose name they bear, and are undoubtedly of considerable antiquity and have been bred true to type for the many years. At one time they were exhibited as old English broken-haired terriers, and at another time certain fanciers attempted crossing them with the Wirehaired Fox Terrier, with the object of securing longer heads. The Welsh Terrier Club, however, took a very strong position against cross-bred dogs and refused to recognize any dogs whose pedigrees were not pure Welsh. Thereby they have succeeded admirably in preserving all of the older characteristics of the breed.

There is no better working terrier than the Welshman. They are not quarrelsome, show very little jealousy, can be kenneled and exercised together better than any other breed, and as a breed are dead game. They are not so easily aroused or excited as Fox or

Irish Terriers, but once you get them started they are afraid of nothing on earth and will go through to the finish. They are splendid water dogs, very affectionate companions, and no better guards nor more capable assistants to the gun will be found in the terrier family.

The Welsh Terrier in appearance is a small, beautifully proportioned, and useful dog of about twenty pounds weight, with a sporty look and a keen, intelligent, lively disposition. They should have straight forelegs and cat-like feet. Their heads are shorter than either the Fox Terrier, the Irish Terrier or Airedale, but as a rule they run truer in coat and color.

Buyer's guide: While this active terrier needs little special treatment in regard to housing or exercise, they do possess a true game terrier disposition which may deem them an unsuitable breed for a family with small children. Do not take this as meaning that they are belligerent or argumentative by nature, however. On the whole they are cheery and outgoing, but when subjected to constant teasing by overzealous children they can become short tempered and may react by snapping. Parents should be aware of this and should make their decision on which dog is best or their family by taking the best interests of both the dog and the children into consideration. The Welsh Terrier is very intelligent and responds quickly to training. They delight in sharing activities with their owners and will be excellent companions for mature, energetic people. They sport a characteristically bright and intelligent expression, which reflects their personality and wins them many devoted admirers.

STANDARD FOR THE WELSH TERRIER

Head: The skull should be flat, and rather wider between the ears than the Wirehaired Fox Terrier. The jaw should be powerful, clean-cut, rather deeper, and more punishing—giving the head a more masculine appearance than that usually seen on a Fox Terrier. Stop not too defined, fair length from stop to end of nose, the latter being of a black color.
Ears: The ear should be V-shaped, small, not too thin, set on fairly high, carried forward and close to the cheek. *Eyes:* The eye should be small, not being too deeply set in or protruding out of skull, of a dark hazel color, expressive and indicating abundant pluck.

Neck: The neck should be of moderate length and thickness, slightly arched and sloping gracefully into the shoulders.

Body: The back should be short, and well-ribbed up, the loin strong, good depth, and moderate width of chest. The shoulders should be long, sloping, and well set back. The hindquarters should be strong, thighs muscular and of good length, with the hocks moderately straight, well let down, and fair amount of bone. The stern should be set on moderately high, but not too gaily carried.

Legs and Feet: The legs should be straight and muscular, possessing fair amount of bone, with upright and powerful pasterns. The feet should be small, round and catlike.

Coat: The coat should be wiry, hard, very close and abundant.

Color: The color should be black and tan, or black grizzle and tan, free from black penciling on toes.

Size: The height at shoulder should be 15 inches for dogs, bitches proportionately less. Twenty pounds shall be considered a fair average weight in working condition, but this may vary a pound or so either way.

SCALE OF POINTS

Head and jaws	10	Legs and feet	10
Ears	5	Coat	15
Eyes	5	Color	5
Neck and shoulders	10	Stern	5
Body	10	General appearance	15
Loins and hindquarters	10	TOTAL	100

DISQUALIFICATIONS

(1) *Nose; white, cherry or spotted to a considerable extent with either of these colors.*

(2) *Ears; prick, tulip or rose.*

(3) *Undershot jaw or pig-jawed mouth.*

(4) *Black below hocks or white to an appreciable extent.*

WEST HIGHLAND WHITE TERRIER

These hardy little dogs are native to Argyleshire and the west coast of Scotland, sections of the country that are the natural home of the fox, the wildcat, the badger, and the otter.

It is a great mistake to believe that these dogs, on account of their general similarity in conformation, are an offshoot of the Scottish Terrier, produced by breeding together the albino sports, which are common in northern latitudes. On the contrary, the White Highland Terrier was of established type and ancestry years before the present Scottish Terrier had emerged from his heterogeneous ancestry.

More than three hundred years ago King James the First of England wrote to Edinburgh to have half a dozen terriers procured from Argyle and sent to France as a present, and there are records to show that as early as sixteen hundred these white terriers of Argyle and the wind-swept western coast were the best in Scotland.

The West Highland Terrier has always been a workman. His conformation permits him to work through the crevices, under the rocks, and to go to earth after his prey, and he has the pluck to do so. The small, compact bodies of these dogs encompass an unusual amount of terrier character. It is important that the jaws and teeth be strong, the feet slightly turned out, as better adapted for scrambling up rocks than a straight Fox Terrier foot.

Their color is most natural, for white has always been a favorite for working dogs since it is most easily distinguished. For a time these dogs were shown as Poltalloch Terriers, as a strain of unusual excellence was owned in that section for many years.

In summing up this breed it can be said that they are intelligent, faithful, and as persistent in pursuit of prey and as desperate fighters as any dog that lives.

Buyer's guide: The gregarious Westie will fit in with most any lifestyle—contented to be a faithful companion for the aged or infirmed, yet energetic enough to keep up with the true outdoorsman. They are very easily cared for. Brushing regularly will help keep dirt from working its way into their coat, and a light sprinkling of talcum powder will keep them looking bright and smelling sweet. Westies are small eaters, require very little space and are excellent companions for children. They have very well-rounded personalities and are not prone to becoming irritable. While a daily walk is recommended, they would get sufficient exercise by their patrolling of the indoors, hot on the trail of any unexplained noise. However, for those who can devote time to their dog, the Westie thrives on playful exercise. They will romp for hours, outlasting even the most energetic child. Frequent periods of exercise will heighten their already gay nature.

STANDARD FOR THE
WEST HIGHLAND WHITE TERRIER

General Appearance: The West Highland White Terrier is a small, game, well-balanced, hardy-looking terrier, exhibiting good showmanship, possessed with no small amount of self-esteem, strongly built, deep in chest and back ribs, straight back and powerful hindquarters on muscular legs, and exhibiting in marked degree a great combination of strength and activity. The coat should be about 2 inches long, white in color, hard, with plenty of soft undercoat. The dog should be neatly presented. Considerable hair should be left around the head to act as a frame for the face to yield a typical Westie expression.

Color and Pigmentation: Coat should be white, as defined by the breed's name. Nose should be black. Black pigmentation is most desirable on lips, eyerims, pads of feet, nails and skin. **Faults:** Any coat color other than white and nose color other than black are serious faults.

Coat: Very important and seldom seen to perfection; must be double-coated. The outer coat consists of straight hard hair, about 2 inches long, with shorter coat on neck and shoulders, properly blended. **Faults:** Any silkiness or tendency to curl is a serious fault, as is an open or single coat.

Size: Dogs should measure about 11 inches at the withers, bitches about one inch less. **Faults:** Any specimens much over or under height limits are objectionable.

Skull: Should be fairly broad, being in proportion to his powerful jaw, not too long, slightly domed, and gradually tapering to the eyes. There should be a defined stop, eyebrows heavy. **Faults:** A too long or too narrow skull.

Muzzle: Should be slightly shorter than the skull, powerful and gradually tapering to the nose, which should be large. The jaws should be level and powerful, the teeth well set and large for the size of the dog. There shall be six incisor teeth between the canines of both lower and upper jaws. A tight scissors bite with upper incisors slightly overlapping the lower incisors or level mouth are equally acceptable. **Faults:** Muzzle longer than skull. Teeth much undershot or overshot are a serious fault, as are teeth defective or missing.

Ears: Small, carried tightly erect, set wide apart and terminating in a sharp point. They must never be cropped. The hair on the ears should be short, smooth and velvety, and trimmed free of fringe at the tips. **Faults:** Round-pointed, drop, broad and large ears are very objectionable, as are mule-ears, ears set too closely together or not held tightly erect.

Eyes: Widely set apart, medium in size, dark in color, slightly sunk in the head, sharp and intelligent. Looking from under heavy eyebrows, they give a piercing look. **Faults:** Too small, too full or light-colored eyes are very objectionable.

Neck: Muscular and nicely set on sloping shoulders. **Faults:** Short neck or too long neck.

Chest: Very deep and extending at least to the elbows with breadth in proportion to size of the dog. **Faults:** Shallow chest.

Body: Compact and of good substance, level back, ribs deep and well arched in the upper half of rib, presenting a flattish side appearance, loins broad and strong, hindquarters strong, muscular, and wide across the top. **Faults:** Long or weak back; barrel ribs; high rump.

Legs and Feet: Both forelegs and hind legs should be muscular and relatively short, but with sufficient length to set the dog up so as not to be too close to the ground. The shoulder blades should be well laid back and well knit at the backbone. The chest should be relatively broad and the front legs spaced apart accordingly. The front legs should be set in under the shoulder blades with definite body overhang before them. The front legs should be reasonably straight and thickly covered with short hard hair. The hind legs should be short and sinewy; the thighs very muscular and not set wide apart, with hocks well bent. The forefeet are larger than the hind ones, are round, proportionate in size, strong, thickly padded, and covered with short hard hair; they may properly be turned out a slight amount. The hind feet are smaller and thickly padded. **Faults:** Steep shoulders, loaded shoulders, or out at the elbows. Too light bone. Cowhocks, weak hocks and lack of angulation. A "fiddle-front" is a serious fault.

Tail: Relatively short, when standing erect it should never extend above the top of the skull. It should be covered with hard hairs, no feather, as straight as possible, carried gaily but not curled over the back. The tail should be set on high enough so that the spine does not slope down to it. The tail must never be docked. **Faults:** Tail set too low; tail too long or carried at half mast or over back.

Movement: Should be free, straight and easy all around. In front, the leg should be freely extended forward by the shoulder. The hind movement should be free, strong and fairly close. The hocks should be freely flexed and drawn close under the body; so that when moving off the foot the body is thrown or pushed forward with some force. **Faults:** Stiff, stilty or too wide movement behind. Lack of reach in front, and/or drive behind.

Temperament: Must be alert, gay, courageous and self-reliant, but friendly. **Faults:** Excess timidity or excess pugnacity.

APPROVED DECEMBER 10, 1968

Group 5: Toy Dogs

AFFENPINSCHER

The small but sturdy Affenpinscher dates back to the 17th century in Germany where the breed was cultivated and used to help establish other breeds, especially the Brussels Griffon and Miniature Schnauzer. Early Affen specimens were considerably larger than those of today, averaging around 13 inches at the withers. These dogs were known as Ratting Terriers and lived in barns of the countryside farms to keep them free from destructive rodents. A breeder from Lubeck, Germany, became very interested in these dogs and began breeding them in earnest. Through careful selection he bred the Affenpinscher to their current smaller size (no more than 10½ inches tall) and introduced them as housepets and mousers.

The plucky little Affenpinscher is often referred to as the Monkey Terrier, owing to the fact that his big, round eyes, tufty facial hair, whiskers and whimsical expression are said to resemble a little monkey. The Affenpinscher does not take himself lightly, however, and delights in being a lively showman. The breed comes complete with all the pluck and spirit of the terrier and is remarkably courageous and full of stamina for a dog of its size.

The versatile Affenpinscher fits well into any household and makes the most of whatever surroundings he is in. Curious by nature, he will entertain himself if left alone, but he prefers the company of others and is remarkably perceptive to the moods of those around him. Affenpinschers possess a sensitive and gentle nature and are quick to learn. Unlike many of the toy breeds, the Affenpinscher is generally quiet and above all is obedient to the wishes of his master and friends. Do not mistake these qualities for passiveness, however, for the Affen can be fearless when provoked and will defend his home to the best of his abilities.

Buyer's guide: Apartment dwellers looking for a small, yet lively dog would do well with the Affen. The rewards of owning such a diminuitive dog are obvious: small food bills, no space problems, no extensive exercising required, no major grooming problems. Affens can be somewhat stubborn at times and can become very excited and agitated if treated too roughly or left alone for great lengths of time. They do make excellent traveling companions and enjoy even the most hectic traveling pace.

STANDARD FOR THE AFFENPINSCHER

General Appearance: Small, but rather sturdy in build and not delicate in any way. He carries himself with comical seriousness and he is generally quiet and a very devoted pal. He can get vehemently excited, however, when attacked and is fearless toward any aggressor.

Coat: A very important factor. It is short and dense in certain parts and shaggy and longer in others, but should be hard and wiry. It is longer and more loose and shaggy on the legs and around the eyes, nose and chin, giving the typical monkey-like appearance from whence comes his name. The best color is black, matching his eyes and fiery temperament. However, black with tan markings, red, gray and other mixtures are permissible. Very light colors and white markings are a fault.

Head: Should be round and not too heavy, with well-domed forehead.
Eyes: Should be round, of good size, black and very brilliant. ***Ears:*** Rather small, set high, pointed and erect, usually clipped to a point.
Muzzle: Must be short and rather pointed with a black nose. The upper jaw is a trifle shorter than the lower jaw, while the teeth should close together; a slight undershot condition is not material. The teeth, however, should not show.

Neck: Short and straight.

Body: The back should be straight with its length about equal to the height at the shoulder. Chest should be reasonably deep and the body should show only a slight tuck-up at the loin.

Legs: Front legs should be straight as possible. Hind legs without much bend at the hocks and set well under the body. ***Feet:*** Should be round, small and compact. Turned neither in nor out, with preferably black pads and nails.

Tail: Cut short, set and carried high.

Size: The smaller dog, if of characteristic type, is more valuable, and the shoulder height should not exceed 10¼ inches in any case.

APPROVED SEPTEMBER 15, 1936

Representing the breed: Ch. El Cogagi Kamehameh, owned by Jennifer D. Sharp.

BRUSSELS GRIFFON

This pert, wide-awake and amusing breed originated, as their name indicates, in the Belgian capital. It is said, however, that English dogs, the Yorkshire, the Ruby Spaniel and the Irish Terrier, were associated in the manufacture, while some authorities claim that as far back as the 1870's the miners of Yorkshire possessed a little, wiry, red-coated dog similar in appearance and disposition to the Belgian dog, that accompanied them to their work stowed away in a roomy pocket.

The Brussels Griffon gets his short, turned-up nose from the Toy Spaniel; his light-colored topknot can be attributed to the Yorkshire. His independence, the character of his coat and color must be credited to the Irish Terrier. By careful selection the type of these dogs was well fixed, and they breed remarkably true. However, breeders find themselves confronted from time to time with litters containing long faces, fluffy coats and over-sized puppies.

In Belgium there are two varieties, the rough and the smooth coated. It is, however, a misnomer to apply the term griffon to the smooths, as the word means rough. The rough coats are by far the most popular in Belgium, as well as elsewhere, and the breed has caught on rapidly wherever introduced, for they are bright, entertaining pets and companions, and their dignity in relation to their size is most amusing.

The chief points to look for in the selection of puppies at from two to four months old and after are: extreme shortness of face; short, compact bodies; crisp coats; good sound red color; and diminutiveness.

Buyer's guide: The convenient size of the Brussels Griffon is ideal for people with limited living space or for those who cannot routinely exercise their dogs. A brisk brushing is all that is needed to keep their coat in good condition and they will keep fit by just moving around the house. The Brussels Griffon cannot be expected to take part in vigorous roughhousing or long walks, so do not consider them as tiny companions for children. They do best enjoying a rather sedate, affectionate relationship with one or two devoted owners.

STANDARD FOR THE BRUSSELS GRIFFON

General Appearance: A toy dog, intelligent, alert, sturdy, with a thick-set short body, a smart carriage and set-up, attracting attention by an almost human expression.

Head: **Skull:** Large and round, with a domed forehead. **Ears:** Small and set rather high on the head. **Eyes:** Should be set well apart, very large, black, prominent, and well open. The eyelashes long and black. Eyelids edged with black. **Nose:** Very black, extremely short, its tip being set back deeply between the eyes so as to form a lay-back. The nostrils large, the stop deep. **Lips:** Edged with black, not pendulous but well brought together, giving a clean finish to the mouth. **Jaws:** Chin must be undershot, prominent, and large with an upward sweep. The incisors of the lower jaw should protrude over the upper incisors, and the lower jaw should be rather broad. Neither teeth nor tongue should show when the mouth is closed. A wry mouth is a serious fault.

Body and Legs: Brisket should be broad and deep, ribs well sprung, back level and short. **Neck:** Medium length, gracefully arched. **Tail:** Set and held high, docked to about one third. **Forelegs:** Of medium length, straight in bone, well muscled, set moderately wide apart and straight from the point of the shoulders as viewed from the front. Pasterns short and strong. **Hind legs:** Set true, thighs strong and well muscled, stifles bent, hocks well let down, turning neither in nor out. **Feet:** Round, small, and compact, turned neither in nor out. Toes well arched. Black pads and toenails preferred.

Coat: There are two distinct types of coat—rough and smooth. The rough coat should be wiry and dense, the harder and more wiry the better. On no account should the dog look or feel woolly, and there should be no silky hair anywhere. The coat should not be so long as to give a shaggy appearance, but should still be distinctly different all over from the smooth coat. The head should be covered with wiry hair slightly longer around the eyes, nose, cheeks, and chin, thus forming a fringe. The smooth coat is similar to that of the Boston Terrier or Bulldog, with no trace of wire hair.

Color: In the rough-coated type, coat is either 1. reddish brown, with a little black at the whiskers and chin allowable, or 2. black and reddish brown mixed, usually with black mask and whiskers, or 3. black with uniform reddish brown markings, usually appearing under the chin, on the legs, over the eyebrows, around the edges of the ears and around the vent, or 4. solid black. The colors of the smooth-coated type are the same as those of the rough-coated type except that solid black is not allowable. Any white hairs in either the rough or smooth coat are a serious fault, except for "frost" on the black muzzle of a mature dog, which is natural.

Weight: Usually 8 to 10 pounds, and should not exceed 12 pounds. Type and quality are of greater importance than weight, and a smaller dog that is sturdy and well proportioned should not be penalized.

SCALE OF POINTS

Head		Eyes	5
Skull	5	Chin and jaws	10
Nose and stop	10	Ears	5 35

Coat
  Color 12
  Texture 13 25

Body and General Conformation
  Body (brisket and rib)...15
  Legs 10

Feet 5
General Appearance (neck, topline, and tail carriage)
.... 10 40

TOTAL 100

DISQUALIFICATIONS
Dudley or butterfly nose, white spot or blaze anywhere on coat.
Hanging tongue.
Jaw overshot.
Solid black coat in the smooth type.

APPROVED FEBRUARY 6, 1960

CHIHUAHUA

The Chihuahuas are little known outside of this continent, as they are natives of Chihuahua, one of the largest states of Mexico, bordering on the state of Texas. They are one of the most diminutive breeds, and are believed by many to have been wild in the early days, and to have inhabited the dense forest land of northern Mexico. Some people claim that they were as expert as a squirrel in climbing trees, and were also adept at burrowing.

The Chihuahuas are remarkably game little dogs, very exclusive in their affections, and perhaps the smallest of the canine family. Some very good specimens may be so small as to stand with all-fours in the palm of one's hand, and not weigh more than twenty-three ounces, while other specimens turn the scales at four to six pounds. Their legs are very slender and their toenails very long and strong. In the wild specimens this was very serviceable to them in making their homes, as they lived in holes in the ground.

Apart from their size, the Chihuahua's most striking peculiarity and feature is the head, which is round, and from which projects a very short and pointed nose and large, standing ears. They also have a peculiar skull formation, found only in this breed. The name is pronounced Chi-wa-wa.

Buyer's guide: The diminutive Chihuahua can be an ideal companion for the home, provided that attention is paid to the somewhat limited capacities of these dogs. While they are very intelligent and affectionate by nature, they cannot take part in energetic outings with their owners or be allowed to be handled as a child's toy. Even those people on a rather limited budget will not be hard pressed by the requirements of the Chihuahua since they eat very little and require no grooming to speak of. They fit in most any type of housing and make good travelling companions. Some Chihuahuas have a fairly yappy disposition, but a well-raised dog from good breeding should not have this trait. They are quite obedient and train easily to the rules of the house.

LONG COAT CHIHUAHUA

SMOOTH CHIHUAHUA

STANDARD FOR THE CHIHUAHUA

Head: A well-rounded "apple dome" skull, with or without molera. Cheeks and jaws lean. Nose moderately short, slightly pointed (self-colored, in blond types, or black). In moles, blues, and chocolates, they are self-colored. In blond types, pink nose permissible.

Ears: Large, held erect when alert, but flaring at the sides at about an angle of 45 degrees when in repose. This gives breadth between the ears. In *Long Coats*, ears fringed. (Heavily fringed ears may be tipped slightly, never down.)

Eyes: Full, but not protruding, balanced, set well apart—dark ruby, or luminous. (Light eyes in blond types permissible.)

Teeth: Level or scissors bite. Overshot or undershot bite or any distortion of the bite should be penalized as a serious fault.

Neck and Shoulders: Slightly arched, gracefully sloping into lean shoulders, may be smooth in the very short types, or with ruff about neck preferred. In *Long Coats*, large ruff on neck desired and preferred. Shoulders lean, sloping into a slightly broadening support above straight forelegs that are set well under, giving a free play at the elbows. Shoulders should be well up, giving balance and soundness, sloping into a level back. (Never down or low.) This gives a chestiness, and strength of forequarters, yet not of the "Bulldog" chest; plenty of brisket.

Back and Body: Level back, slightly longer than height. Shorter backs desired in males. Ribs rounded (but not too much "barrel-shaped").

Hindquarters: Muscular, with hocks well apart, neither out nor in, well let down, with firm sturdy action.

Tail: Moderately long, carried sickle either up or out, or in a loop over the back, with tip just touching the back. (Never tucked under.) Hairs on tail in harmony with the coat of the body, preferred furry in *Smooth Coats*. In *Long Coats*, tail full and long (as a plume).

Feet: Small, with toes well split up but not spread, pads cushioned, with fine pasterns. (Neither the hare nor the cat-foot.) A dainty, small foot with nails moderately long.

Coat: In the *Smooth*, the coat should be soft texture, close and glossy. (Heavier coats with undercoats permissible.) Coat placed well over body with ruff on neck, and more scanty on head and ears. In *Long Coats*, the coat should be of a soft texture, either flat or slightly curled, with undercoat preferred. Ears fringed (heavily fringed ears may be tipped slightly, never down), feathering on feet and legs, and pants on hind legs. Large ruff on neck desired and preferred. Tail full and long (as a plume).

Color: Any color—solid, marked or splashed.

Weight: A well-balanced little dog not to exceed 6 pounds.

General Appearance: A graceful, alert, swift-moving little dog with saucy expression. Compact, and with terrierlike qualities.

SCALE OF POINTS

Head, including ears.......20
Body, including tail........20
Coat....................20
Legs....................20
General Appearance and action
.....................20
TOTAL..............100

DISQUALIFICATIONS

Cropped tail, bobtail.
Broken down or cropped ears.
Any dog over 6 pounds in weight.
In Long Coats, too thin coat that resembles bareness.

APPROVED NOVEMBER 14, 1972

Representing the Long Coat: Ch. Tiny Mite's El Pepita, owned by Robert L. DeJonge. Smooth: Ch. Pittore's Miz Mini Mouse, owned by Patricia Kirms.

ENGLISH TOY SPANIEL
KING CHARLES, PRINCE CHARLES, BLENHEIM AND RUBY

The four spaniels classified as toys were all formerly known as King Charles Spaniels. The division into four varieties is governed entirely by their color, as they are alike in other respects. In fact, it is not an unusual occurrence for the four varieties to be present in one litter.

The King Charles is a glossy black with rich mahogany markings, tan spots over the eyes, on the cheeks, the lining of the ear, and the lower parts of the legs and under part of the tail. White is not permissible in the variety, although at one time black-and-white was accepted as a desirable color.

The Prince Charles was produced by the interbreeding of the black-and-white and black-and-tan King Charles Spaniels. They are a pearly white, with evenly distributed glossy black markings covering the body in patches, tan over the eyes and on the cheeks; ears lined with tan, and with tan under the tail.

The Blenheim is red and white in color. They should be pearly white, with patches of rich red chestnut or ruby red, evenly distributed over the body. The ears and cheeks must be red and a white blaze should extend from the nose to the forehead and then curve between the ears. Much importance is attached to the presence in the middle of the blaze of a spot of red the size of a dime. This mark is called the Blenheim spot, and in connection with a profuse mane, is considered as adding much to the beauty of the breed.

The Ruby is, as its name indicates, a rich, unbroken ruby red, the nose, of course, being black. The Ruby is the latest member of this family, but one already very popular, and many good specimens are being shown.

There is no question about the long descent and aristocratic associations of the Toy Spaniels, for they have been the favorites of royalty for many years. They are frequently mentioned in history and occupy prominent positions in the portraiture of various periods. They were popular with royalty in the days of Henry the Eighth and Queen Elizabeth. Charles the Second was devoted to them, and during his reign they were said to have overrun Hampton Court and other palaces. The unhappy Queen of Scots went to the scaffold accompanied by her spaniel, and the Marlborough family, dating from the first duke, had a red-and-white spaniel at their country place, Blenheim, that was known by that name.

It is generally believed that the Toy Spaniels came from Spain in much their present form, or were bred from Cocker Spaniels in England. They resemble the Cocker in disposition, have the same colors and markings, and the Blenheim spot previously referred to is frequently present on the forehead of Cockers.

The portraits of Van Dyke, Boucher and Greuze, in which spaniels are frequently introduced, show that the toy spaniel of the past had a longer nose and smaller head than those of the present day, and that their ears were longer and often dragged on the ground. The Blenheims of Marlborough were also used for working the coverts for pheasant and woodcock shooting, and were said to have had splendid noses, which many still possess.

The fact that the dogs in the old portraits differed but little from the authentic portraits of Cockers in the beginning of the last century confirms the belief in their relationship.

The contention that the Toy Spaniel is descended from the Japanese Chin is contradicted by differences in character, as the Jap has more of the disposition of the Pug.

The chief points to look for in the selection of all English Toy Spaniel puppies at from two to four months old are the same, except, of course, color, to which some weight should be given according to the standard laid down. They are: diminutiveness compatible with soundness and robustness, extreme shortness of face, large eyes, lofty skull, short body, nicely proportioned all around, low-set and rather long ears.

Buyer's guide: English Toy Spaniels, oftentimes referred to as Charlies, are extremely devoted by nature and are fine companion dogs. Whether they enjoy the life of a lap dog or a more energetic regimen, they can be relied upon to be cheerful and amusing housepets. Like any dog of their size, they do not pose any problem about the space of the living quarters. These spaniels have a long coat that is very easily kept manageable by scheduled brushings and combings. Their food needs are low. English Toy Spaniels are well suited for people who enjoy owning an outgoing, active dog but cannot tend properly to the needs of a larger dog. Older people are exceptionally fond of them as they are faithful, simple to tend to and natural watchdogs.

STANDARD FOR THE ENGLISH TOY SPANIEL
King Charles, Prince Charles, Ruby and Blenheim

Head: Should be well domed, and in good specimens is absolutely semi-globular, sometimes even extending beyond the half-circle, and absolutely projecting over the eyes, so as nearly to meet the upturned nose. **Eyes:** The eyes are set wide apart, with the eyelids square to the line of the face—not oblique or foxlike. The eyes themselves are large and dark as possible, so as to be generally considered black, their enormous pupils, which are absolutely of that color, increasing the description. **Stop:** The stop, or hollow between the eyes, is well marked, as in the Bulldog, or even more so; some good specimens exhibit a hollow deep enough to bury a small marble in it. **Nose:** The nose must be short and well turned up between the eyes, and without any indication of artificial displacement afforded by a deviation to either side. The color of the end should be black, and it should be both deep and wide with open nostrils. A light-colored nose is objectionable, but shall not disqualify. **Jaw:** The muzzle must be square and deep, and the lower jaw wide between the branches, leaving plenty of space for the tongue, and for the attachment of the lower lips, which should completely conceal the teeth. It should also be turned up or "finished," so as to allow of its meeting the end of the upper jaw, turned up in a similar way as above described. A protruding tongue is objectionable, but does not disqualify. **Ears:** The ears must be long, so as to approach the ground. In an average-sized dog they measure 20 inches from tip to tip, and some reach 22 inches or even a trifle more. They should be set low down on the head and hang flat to the sides of the cheeks, and be heavy-feathered.

Size: The most desirable size is from 9 pounds to 12 pounds. **Shape:** In compactness of shape these Spaniels almost rival the Pug, but the length of coat adds greatly to the apparent bulk, as the body, when the coat is wetted, looks small in comparison with that dog. Still, it ought to be decidedly "cobby," with strong, stout legs, short broad back and wide chest.

Coat: The coat should be long, silky, soft and wavy, but not curly. There should be a profuse mane, extending well down in the front of the chest. The feather should be well displayed on the ears and feet, and in the latter case so thickly as to give the appearance of being webbed. It is also carried well up the backs of the legs. In the Black and Tan the feather on the ears is very long and profuse, exceeding that of the Blenheim by an inch or more. The feather on the tail (which is cut to the length of about 1½ inches) should be silky, and from 3 to 4 inches in length, constituting a marked "flag" of a square shape, and not carried above the level of the back.

COLORS OF THE TWO VARIETIES

King Charles and Ruby: The King Charles and Ruby types which comprise one show variety are solid-colored dogs. The King Charles are black and tan (considered a solid color), the black rich and glossy with deep mahogany tan markings over the eyes and on the muzzle, chest and legs. The presence of a few white hairs intermixed with the black on the chest is to be faulted, but a white patch on the chest or white appearing elsewhere disqualifies. The Ruby is a rich chestnut red and is whole-colored. The presence of a few white hairs intermixed with the red on the chest is to be faulted, but a white patch on the chest or white appearing elsewhere disqualifies.

Blenheim and Prince Charles: The Blenheim and Prince Charles types which comprise the other show variety are broken-colored dogs. The Blenheim is red and white. The ground color is a pearly white which has bright red chestnut or ruby red markings evenly distributed in large patches. The ears and cheeks should be red, with a blaze of white extending from the nose up the forehead and ending between the ears in a crescentic curve. In the center of the blaze at the top of the forehead, there should be a clear "spot" of red, the size of a dime. The Prince Charles, a tri-colored dog, is white, black and tan. The ground color is a pearly white. The black consists of markings which should be evenly distributed in large patches. The tan appears as spots over the eyes, on the muzzle, chest and legs; the ears and vent should also be lined with tan. The Prince Charles has no "spot," that being a particular feature of the Blenheim.

SCALE OF POINTS

King Charles, or Black and Tan.
Prince Charles, White, with Black and Tan Markings.
Ruby, or Red.

Symmetry, condition, size and soundness of limb........20	Eyes....................10
Head....................15	Ears....................15
Stop.....................5	Coat and feathering........15
Muzzle..................10	Color...................10
	TOTAL...............100

Blenheim, or White with Red Markings

Symmetry, condition, size and soundness of limb........15	Ears....................10
Head....................15	Coat and feathering........15
Stop.....................5	Color and markings........15
Muzzle..................10	Spot.....................5
Eyes....................10	TOTAL...............100

DISQUALIFICATIONS

King Charles and Ruby: A white patch on the chest, or white or any other part.

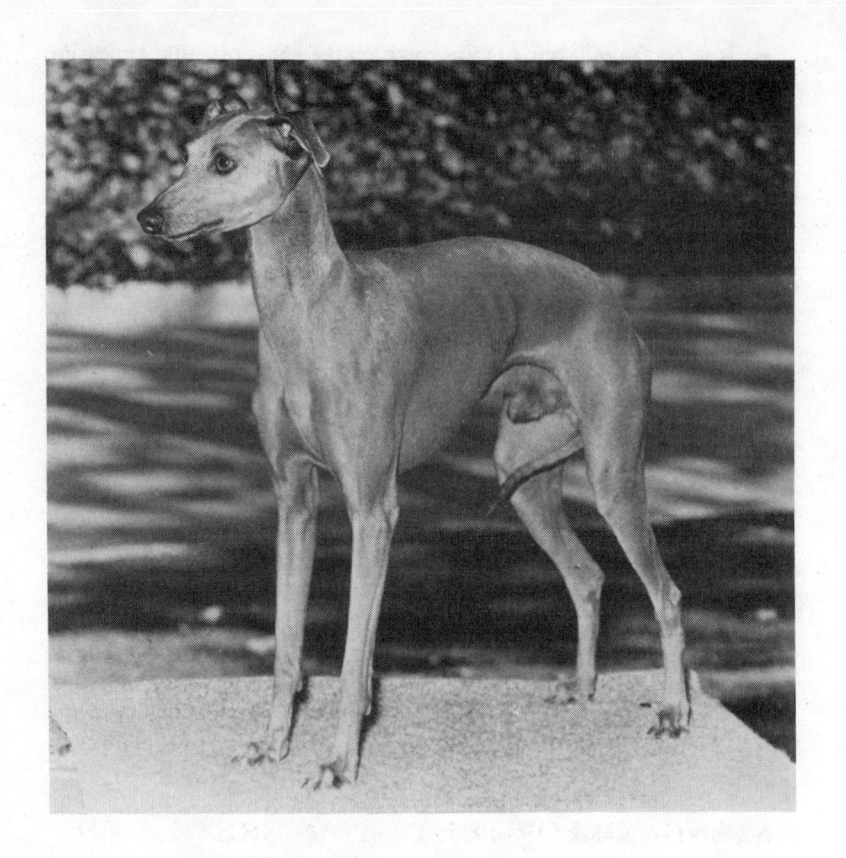

ITALIAN GREYHOUND

The Italian Greyhound is a very old breed, descended from the dwarfed Greyhounds that were kept as domestic pets. For delicacy, refinement, grace and gentleness they have no equals. There is little of the aggressive spirit about them, their most striking trait being their universal docility. They are too light for work of any kind and have no inclination in that direction, and many will play with a rat or rabbit without a thought of animosity.

The delicate lines of the Italian Greyhound, their soft, pleading eyes, gentle natures and cleanly habits commend them to the public. It may be mentioned, however, that they are not as fragile as they appear. They have much stronger constitutions than is generally supposed. Naturally they are not able to endure much cold or dampness, but other than that they require no pampering. Many are extremely long lived.

One of the peculiarities of the breed lies in their action, as they have a spirited, high-stepping walk much like the highly schooled horses of a circus ring.

The chief points to select for in puppies at from two to four months are diminutiveness, slightness, and apparent fragility, with a distinct arch of loin.

Buyer's guide: Although Italian Greyhounds are rather timid dogs, those that own them have nothing but superlatives to say about their disposition. They are quite affectionate and are quick learners, provided the training is done with patience and kindness. Italian Greyhounds cannot tolerate roughhousing, and are not recommended for houses with young children. Their food, exercise and housing requirements are minimal, and they are fastidiously clean by nature. Do not let the Italian Greyhounds overextend themself in exercising since they have a rather delicate physique.

STANDARD FOR THE ITALIAN GREYHOUND

Description: The Italian Greyhound is very similar to the Greyhound, but much smaller and more slender in all proportions and of ideal elegance and grace.

Head: Narrow and long, tapering to nose, with a slight suggestion of stop.

Skull: Rather long, almost flat.

Muzzle: Long and fine.

Nose: Dark. It may be black or brown or in keeping with the color of the dog. A light or partly pigmented nose is a fault.

Teeth: Scissors bite. A badly undershot or overshot mouth is a fault.

Eyes: Dark, bright, intelligent, medium in size. Very light eyes are a fault.

Ears: Small, fine in texture; thrown back and folded except when alerted, then carried folded at right angles to the head. Erect or button ears severely penalized.

Neck: Long, slender and gracefully arched.

Body: Of medium length, short coupled; high at withers, back curved and drooping at hindquarters, the highest point of curve at start of loin, creating a definite tuck-up at flanks.

Shoulders: Long and sloping.

Chest: Deep and narrow.

Forelegs: Long, straight, set well under shoulder; strong pasterns, fine bone.

Hindquarters: Long, well-muscled thigh; hind legs parallel when viewed from behind, hocks well let down, well-bent stifle.

Feet: Harefoot with well-arched toes. Removal of dewclaws optional.

Tail: Slender and tapering to a curved end, long enough to reach the hock; set low, carried low. Ring tail a serious fault, gay tail a fault.

Coat: Skin fine and supple, hair short, glossy like satin and soft to the touch.

Color: Any color and markings are acceptable except that a dog with brindle markings and a dog with the tan markings normally found on black-and-tan dogs of other breeds must be disqualified.

Action: High stepping and free, front and hind legs to move forward in a straight line.

Size: Height at withers, ideally 13 inches to 15 inches.

DISQUALIFICATION

Dogs with the tan markings normally found on black and tan dogs of other breeds.

JAPANESE CHIN

These diminutive Orientals have for a number of years enjoyed a remarkable vogue in both this country and in Europe. They are not as popular today as they were many years ago, but a good specimen never fails to command admiration and a handsome price.

The Japanese Chin is a native of Nippon. In general appearance, they resemble the Toy Spaniel species, but are in no ways related. Like them, they are short-faced toys quite similar in shape and alike in coat, except that black-and-white is the prevailing color.

The Jap differs from the Toy Spaniel in the shape of the head, which is less domed, and the placement of the eye, which is more to the side. The ears are placed higher on the head, the nostrils are smaller, the foreface is wider and not so deep.

The first Japs imported were on the large order, many of them scaling over ten pounds. Later it was learned that in Japan only the diminutive species weighing in the vicinity of five pounds were in demand, and that these dogs were carried in the sleeves of the ladies of rank and fashion. There was an immediate slump in the values of the larger Japs and a craze for the smallest obtainable. Many were imported and English and American breeders also devoted themselves to bantamizing the Jap. They succeeded admirably, and now there are many small-sized Japs of splendid quality in this country.

The Japanese Chin, particularly the dwarfed specimens, are delicate and hard to raise, as they are susceptible to many diseases.

The Jap has, above all things, the appearance of an aristocrat, with a finished dignity and self-satisfied air of importance that is an amusing contrast to his diminutive size. They make interesting companions and affectionate pets.

Buyer's guide: Chins are sweet natured and alert companions. They are not yappy or given to extremes of bad temperament, but they are exuberant. When a Chin is happy to greet you, he gives out a little snort of welcome and his joy is evident. They are always good company. Chins need little grooming or food and are equally happy in a large house or small apartment. They are self-assured and don't shirk away from strangers, yet they aren't the least bit pesty. Chins are good with children, but no roughhousing can be allowed as the Chin is not a big enough dog for heavy exercising or zealous playing.

STANDARD FOR THE JAPANESE CHIN

General Appearance: That of a lively, high-bred little dog with dainty appearance, smart, compact carriage and profuse coat. These dogs should be essentially stylish in movement, lifting the feet high when in action, carrying the tail (which is heavily feathered, proudly curved or plumed) over the back. In size they vary considerably, but the smaller they are the better, provided type and quality are not sacrificed. When divided by weight, classes should be under and over 7 pounds.

Head: Should be large for the size of the dog, with broad skull, rounded in front.

Eyes: Large, dark, lustrous, rather prominent and set wide apart.

Ears: Small and V-shaped, nicely feathered, set wide apart and high on the head and carried slightly forward.

Nose: Very short in the muzzle part. The end or nose proper should be wide, with open nostrils, and must be the color of the dog's markings, *i.e.* black in black-marked dogs, and red or deep flesh color in red or lemon-marked dogs. It shall be a disqualification for a black and white Japanese Chin to have a nose any other color than black.

Neck: Should be short and moderately thick.

Body: Should be squarely and compactly built, wide in chest, "cobby" in shape. The length of the dog's body should be about its height.

Tail: Must be well twisted to either right or left from root and carried up over back and flow on opposite side; it should be profusely covered with long hair (ring tails not desirable).

Legs: The bones of the legs should be small, giving them a slender appearance, and they should be well feathered.

Feet: Small and shaped somewhat long; the dog stands up on its toes somewhat. If feathered, the tufts should never increase in width of the foot, but only its length a trifle.

Coat: Profuse, long, straight, rather silky. It should be absolutely free from wave or curl, and not lie too flat, but have a tendency to stand out, especially at the neck, so as to give a thick mane or ruff, which with profuse feathering on thighs and tail gives a very showy appearance.

Color: The dogs should be either black and white or red and white, *i.e.* parti-colored. The term red includes all shades of sable, brindle, lemon and orange, but the brighter and clearer the red the better. The white should be clear white, and the color, whether black or red, should be evenly distributed patches over the body, cheek and ears.

SCALE OF POINTS

Head and neck............10	Tail 10
Eyes....................10	Feet and legs.............5
Ears....................5	Coat and markings.........15
Muzzle..................10	Action 5
Nose....................5	Size....................10
Body....................15	TOTAL 100

DISQUALIFICATION

In black and whites, a nose any other color than black.

APPROVED AUGUST 9, 1977

MALTESE

These diminutive specimens of the canine race, as their name indicates, are descended from native dogs on the Island of Malta or Melita, in the Mediterranean Sea. They are among the oldest of breeds, for they are mentioned three hundred years before the Christian era. The principal thing about them that attracts the interest of the public is their soft, silky, snowy-white coat. They were more popular seventy-five years ago than at the present time although their popularity is once more on the rise.

The Maltese does not thrive well except in a moist climate. Even in England, where the climate is damp, the most expert fanciers have their hands full in keeping them in condition.

The Maltese as a rule breeds very true to type. They are an ornament to a parlor or a carriage, and despite their diminutive size, they are quite courageous and can be relied on to be faithful and affectionate companions.

The points to be considered in Maltese Terriers are: size—the smaller the better, if sound; luxurious coat; and short body.

In selecting Maltese puppies at from two to four months old, those are likely to make the best dogs which are the smallest (not weaklings), possess most coat, shortest bodies, and shortest legs.

Buyer's guide: Maltese are lovely to look at, but a tough dog to own. They have a wonderfully friendly personality and a sweet disposition, but their long, white coat requires considerable care to keep it looking the way it should. Potential owners must be willing to take care that the coat is not exposed to too much sun or dirt, and daily brushing is a *must*. If you cannot dedicate yourself to taking proper care of the lovely long coat that is the pride of this breed, choose another breed. Maltese are naturally active and fit well in any type of home. They need little formal exercising and just about one half pound of food a day to stay in top shape, but their coat needs tending and cannot be neglected.

STANDARD FOR THE MALTESE

General Appearance: The Maltese is a toy dog covered from head to foot with a mantle of long, silky, white hair. He is gentle-mannered and affectionate, eager and sprightly in action, and, despite his size, possessed of the vigor needed for the satisfactory companion.

Head: Of medium length and in proportion to the size of the dog. **The skull** is slightly rounded on top, the stop moderate. **The drop ears** are rather low set and heavily feathered with long hair that hangs close to the head. **Eyes** are set not too far apart; they are very dark and round, their black rims enhancing the gentle yet alert expression. **The muzzle** is of medium length, fine and tapered but not snipy. **The nose** is black. **The teeth** meet in an even, edge-to-edge bite, or in a scissors bite.

Neck: Sufficient length of neck is desirable as promoting a high carriage of the head.

The Body: Compact, the height from the withers to the ground equaling the length from the withers to the root of the tail. Shoulder blades are sloping, the elbows well knit and held close to the body. The back is level in topline, the ribs well sprung. The chest is fairly deep, the loins taut, strong, and just slightly tucked up underneath.

Tail: A long-haired plume carried gracefully over the back, its tip lying to the side over the quarter.

Legs and Feet: Legs are fine-boned and nicely feathered. Forelegs are straight, their pastern joints well knit and devoid of appreciable bend. Hind legs are strong and moderately angulated at stifles and hocks. The feet are small and round, with toe pads black. Scraggly hairs on the feet may be trimmed to give a neater appearance.

Coat and color: The coat is single, that is, without undercoat. It hangs long, flat, and silky over the sides of the body almost, if not quite, to the ground. The long head-hair may be tied up in a topknot or it may be left hanging. Any suggestion of kinkiness, curliness, or woolly texture is objectionable. Color, pure white. Light tan or lemon on the ears is permissible, but not desirable.

Size: Weight under 7 pounds, with from 4 to 6 pounds preferred. Over-all quality is to be favored over size.

Gait: The Maltese moves with a jaunty, smooth, flowing gait. Viewed from the side, he gives an impression of rapid movement, size considered. In the stride, the forelegs reach straight and free from the shoulders, with elbows close. Hind legs to move in a straight line. Cowhocks or any suggestion of hind leg toeing in or out are faults.

Temperament: For all his diminutive size, the Maltese seems to be without fear. His trust and affectionate responsiveness are very appealing. He is among the gentlest mannered of all little dogs, yet he is lively and playful as well as vigorous.

APPROVED MARCH 10, 1964

Representing the breed: Ch. Joanne Chen's Mino Maya Dancer, owned by Blanche M. Tenerowicz.

TOY MANCHESTER TERRIER

The Toy Manchester Terrier is distinguished from the larger version of the breed, the standard Manchester, strictly on the basis of size. The breed is one of the oldest to stem from England, where it was originally referred to as the Black-and-Tan Terrier. The Toy Manchester is also often referred to as the English Toy Terrier.

Despite their diminutive size, the Toy Manchester Terrier is a compact and sturdy dog. Their coat is short and sleek and trimmed with rich red/brown highlights that set off their natural jet black coloring. Manchesters are fastidiously clean and require only a minimum of grooming to keep them in top shape. They have a sturdy constitution and are resistant toward most respiratory and digestive diseases that plague many of the toy breeds.

The Toy Manchester Terrier is as game a dog as can be found. They are intelligent and will courageously defend their property and home from any intruder. Although naturally wary of strangers, once properly introduced the Toy Manchester will be both friendly and courteous to all visitors and will welcome the company as a chance to strut and show their finest aristocratic nature.

The standard for the Toy Manchester Terrier is the same as that of the Manchester Terrier except in regard to weight and ears. Please refer to the discussion of the Manchester in the Terrier Group, for the official standard.

Buyer's guide: The Toy Manchester Terrier is clean and easy to care for, besides having a bright personality. As housepets go, the Toy Manchester is one of the most devoted and they are well suited for the indoor life. Exercise requirements are minimal, but an occasional walk will do wonders for their tone and disposition. They are not frail, as are many toy breeds, but they should not be subjected to overexertion or the roughhousing of children. They are a good dog for the person living alone who enjoys the company of a smart, vibrant dog.

STANDARD FOR THE MANCHESTER TERRIER (TOY)

The Standard for the Manchester Terrier (Toy variety) is the same as for the Manchester Terrier except as regards weight and ears. See standard in section on Terrier Breeds.

MINIATURE PINSCHER

Miniature Pinschers may be small in stature, but they make up in liveliness and spunk what they lack in size. They are an alert, intelligent breed with confidence enough to approach dogs many times their size without any hint of fear or submissiveness. The high regard with which they hold themselves makes them valuable watchdogs as they have keen hearing and will readily give tongue to any intruders and, if needed, will attack to protect their house and home.

The Miniature Pinscher and the Doberman Pinscher both originated in Germany, but unlike popular belief, they are two distinct breeds—not just differentiated by size. Historians of the breed believe that the Min Pin came about well over 200 years ago as a result of some crossings of Dachshunds and Italian Greyhounds. In their original homeland they were originally referred to as *Reh Pinschers* because they were said to resemble the small red deer that inhabited the forests of Germany. Since the formation of the parent club in 1929, the breed has made great gains in popularity and their proud and regal attitude has won them the nickname of King of Toys.

The Miniature Pinscher makes an ardent show dog. They move with a flashy, hackney gait and are among the keenest of competitors for the ribbons, loving the chance to strut around the show ring and show off for the crowds. In the home they are lovable and loyal, usually preferring to be a one-person dog. When they decide on who is their favorite, they generally show distinct preferences for that sex over the other. However, all people are treated amicably. Min Pins are exceptionally long-lived and are among the most hardy of all breeds in regard to resistance to diseases.

Buyer's guide: The Min Pin is self-assured and does not back away from anything. They are affectionate and well mannered, suitable for any size home. Timidity and yappiness are not traits common to the Min Pin, and you will have to look far to find a nicer all-around small dog. Older, less active people will enjoy the unending antics of this breed, and they are well suited for people living alone. They are devoted to their owners and will live happily in any surrounding, providing they are not left alone for long. Grooming and exercise requirements are minimal. They can be kept by families with children, but they must not be subjected to any harsh treatment.

STANDARD FOR THE MINIATURE PINSCHER

General Appearance: The Miniature Pinscher was originated in Germany and named the "Reh Pinscher" due to his resemblance in structure and animation to a very small specie of deer found in the forests. This breed is structurally a well-balanced, sturdy, compact, short-coupled, smooth-coated toy dog. He is naturally well groomed, proud, vigorous and alert. The natural characteristic traits which identify him from other toy dogs are his precise Hackney gait, his fearless animation, complete self-possession, and his spirited presence.

Faults: Structurally lacking in balance, too long- or short-coupled, too coarse or too refined (lacking in bone development causing poor feet and legs), too large or too small, lethargic, timid or dull, shy or vicious, low in tail placement and poor in action (action not typical of the breed requirements). Knotty over-developed muscles.

Head: In correct proportion with the body. **From Top:** Tapering, narrow with well-fitted but not too prominent foreface which should balance with the skull. No indication of coarseness. **From Front:** Skull appears flat, tapering forward toward the muzzle. Muzzle itself strong rather than fine and delicate, and in proportion to the head as a whole; cheeks and lips small, taut and closely adherent to each other. Teeth in perfect alignment and apposition, **From Side:** Well-balanced with only a slight drop to the muzzle, which should be parallel to the top of the skull. **Eyes:** Full, slightly oval, almost round, clear, bright and dark even to a true black; set wide apart and fitted well into the sockets. **Ears:** Well-set and firmly placed, upstanding (when cropped, pointed and carried erect in balance with the head). **Nose:** Black only (with the exception of chocolates, which may have a self-colored nose).

Faults: Too large or too small for the body, too coarse or too refined, pinched and weak in foreface, domed in skull, too flat and lacking in chiseling, giving a vapid expression. **Jaws and Teeth** overshot or undershot. **Eyes** too round and full, too large, bulging, too deep-set or set too far apart; or too small, set too close (pig eyes). Light-colored eyes not desirable. **Ears** poorly placed, low-set hanging ears (lacking in cartilage) which detract from head conformation. (Poorly cropped ears if set on the head properly and having sufficient cartilage should not detract from head points, as this would be a man-made fault and automatically would detract from general appearance.) **Nose** any color other than black (with the exception of chocolates which may have a self-colored nose).

Neck: Proportioned to head and body. Slightly arched, gracefully curved, clean and firm, blending into shoulders, length well-balanced, muscular and free from a suggestion of dewlap or throatiness. **Faults:** Too straight or too curved; too thick or too thin; too long or short; knotty muscles; loose, flabby or wrinkled skin.

Body: **From Top:** Compact, slightly wedge-shaped, muscular with well-sprung ribs. **From Side:** Depth of brisket, the base line of which is level with the points of the elbows; short and strong in loin with belly moderately tucked up to denote grace in structural form. Back level or slightly sloping toward the rear. Length of males equals height at withers. Females may be slightly longer. **From Rear:** High tail-set; strong, sturdy upper shanks, with croup slope at about 30 degrees; vent opening not barreled. **Forequarters:** Forechest well-developed and full, moderately broad, shoulders clean, sloping with moderate angulation, co-ordinated to permit the true action of the Hackney pony. **Hindquarters:** Well-knit muscular quarters set wide enough apart to fit into a properly balanced body.

Faults: From top: Too long, too short, too barreled, lacking in body development. **From side:** Too long, too short, too thin or too fat, hips higher or considerably lower than the withers, lacking depth of chest, too full in loin, sway back, roach back or wry back. **From rear:** Quarters too wide or too close to each other, overdeveloped, barreled vent, underdeveloped vent, too sloping croup, tail set low. **Forequarters:** Forechest and spring of rib too narrow (or too shallow and underdeveloped), shoulders too straight, too loose, or too short and overloaded with muscles. **Hindquarters:** Too narrow, undermuscled or overmuscled, too steep in croup.

Legs and Feet: Strong bone development and small clean joints; feet catlike, toes strong, well-arched and closely knit with deep pads and thick blunt nails. **Forelegs and Feet:** As viewed from the front straight and upstanding, elbows close to body, well-knit, flexible yet strong with perpendicular pasterns. **Hind Legs:** All adjacent bones should appear well-angulated with well-muscled thighs or upper shanks, with clearly well-defined stifles, hocks short, set well apart turning neither in nor out, while at rest should stand perpendicular to the ground and upper shanks, lower shanks and hocks parallel to each other.

Faults: Too thick or thin bone development, large joints, spreading flat feet. *Forelegs and Feet:* Bowed or crooked, weak pasterns, feet turning in or out, loose elbows. **Hind legs:** Thin undeveloped stifles, large or crooked hocks, loose stifle joints.

Tail: Set high, held erect, docked to ½ to 1 inch. **Faults:** Set too low, too thin, drooping, hanging or poorly docked.

Coat: Smooth, hard and short, straight and lustrous, closely adhering to and uniformly covering the body. **Faults:** Thin, too long, dull; upstanding; curly; dry; area of various thickness or bald spots.

Color: 1. Solid red or stag red. 2. Lustrous black with sharply defined tan, rust-red markings on cheeks, lips, lower jaw, throat, twin spots above eyes and chest, lower half of forelegs, inside of hind legs and vent region, lower portion of hocks and feet. Black pencil stripes on toes. 3. Solid brown or chocolate with rust or yellow markings. **Faults:** Any color other than listed; very dark or sooty spots. **Disqualifications:** Thumb marks or any area of white on feet or forechest exceeding one-half (½) inch in its longest dimension.

Size: Desired height 11 inches to 11½ inches at the withers. A dog of either sex measuring 10 inches or over 12½ inches shall be disqualified.

Faults: Oversize; undersize; too fat; too lean.

SCALE OF POINTS

General appearance and movement—(*very important*) ... 30	Body ... 15
Skull ... 5	Feet ... 5
Muzzle ... 5	Legs ... 5
Eyes ... 5	Color ... 5
Ears ... 5	Coat ... 5
Neck ... 5	Tail ... 5
	TOTAL ... 100

DISQUALIFICATIONS

Color: Thumb marks or any area of white on feet or forechest exceeding one-half (½) inch in its longest dimension.

Size: A dog of either sex measuring under 10 or over 12½ inches.

APPROVED MAY 13, 1958

Representing the breed: Int., Am., Can., Bda., Mex. Ch. Repeage's Toma, owned by Rose and Edward Radel.

PAPILLON

This breed is sometimes referred to as the Squirrel Spaniel. It is not, however, any more of a spaniel than is the Pekingese, and one of the countless stories in regard to its descent is that its ancestors were tiny, silky-haired lap dogs which the Spaniards brought over from Mexico in the 16th century. It is undoubtedly a very old breed, as dogs of similar type are seen in portraits in Spanish galleries as well as in paintings by Watteau, Fragonard and Boucher.

The Papillon's name is evidently derived from its ears, which stand erect like the wings of the butterfly, *papillon*. There is also a variety with drop ears. The tail is long and bushy and carried over the back like a squirrel, which is why the name Squirrel Spaniel is sometimes applied to the Papillon.

The Papillon is a lively little dog, with an abundant coat of long, silky hair. The head is small, the skull slightly domed, the muzzle rather snipy. About the face and on the front of the legs the coat is short; the eyes are dark, round, set somewhat low; the expression is alert and intelligent; the back is straight and rather short, but not so cobby as that of the Blenheim or the Pomeranian. The legs are short, straight, and rather fine. In color they are ruby, red mahogany, reddish chestnut, dark yellow or white with patches.

Buyer's guide: Papillons are happy dogs and make likeable companions for the home. They are not argumentative or yappy, and do not sport a pompous or spoiled air (no matter how much you pamper them.) A routine of brushing and combing will keep their long coat in fine order, and they adapt well to any size house. Papillons enjoy attention and are quite good with children, but they should only be allowed around children who know how to be gentle with small dogs.

STANDARD FOR THE PAPILLON

General Appearance: The Papillon is a small, friendly, elegant toy dog of fine-boned structure, light, dainty and of lively action; distinguished from other breeds by its beautiful butterfly-like ears.

Head: Small. The skull of medium width, and slightly rounded between the muzzle is fine, abruptly thinner than the head, tapering to the nose. The length of the muzzle from the tip of nose to stop is approximately one third the length of the head from tip of nose to occiput.

Nose: Black, small, rounded and slightly flat on top.

Eyes: Dark, round, not bulging, of medium size and alert in expression. The inner corner of the eyes is on a line with the stop. Eye rims black.

Mouth: Lips are tight, thin and black. Teeth meet in a scissors bite. Tongue must not be visible when jaws are closed. *Fault:* Overshot or undershot.

Ears: The ears of either the erect or drop type should be large with rounded tips and set on the sides and toward the back of head.

1) Ears of the erect type are carried obliquely and move like the spread wings of a butterfly. When alert, each ear forms an angle of approximately 45 degrees to the head. The leather should be of sufficient strength to maintain the erect position.
2) Ears of the drop type, known as Phalene, are similar to the erect type, but are carried drooping and must be completely down.

Faults: Ears small, pointed, set too high, one ear up or ears partly down.

Neck: Of medium length.

Body: Must be slightly longer than the height at withers. It is not a cobby dog. Topline straight and level. The chest is of medium depth with well-sprung ribs. The belly is tucked up.

Forequarters: Shoulders well developed and laid back to allow freedom of movement. Forelegs slender, fine-boned and must be straight. Removal of dewclaws on forelegs optional.

Hindquarters: Well developed and well angulated. Hocks inclined neither in nor out. The hind legs are slender, fine-boned, and parallel when viewed from behind. Dewclaws, if any, must be removed from hind legs.

Feet: Thin and elongated (harelike), pointing neither in nor out.

Tail: Long, set high and carried well arched over the body. The plume may hang to either side of the body. *Fault:* Low-set tail, one arched over back or too short.

Coat: Abundant, long, fine, silky, flowing, straight with resilient quality, flat on back and sides of body. A profuse frill on chest. There is no undercoat. Hair short and close on skull, muzzle, front of forelegs and from hind feet to hocks. Ears well fringed with the inside covered with silken hair of medium length. Backs of the forelegs are covered with feathers diminishing to the pasterns. Hind legs are covered to the hocks with abundant breeches (culottes). Tail is covered with a long flowing plume. Hair on feet is short but fine tufts may appear over toes and grow beyond them forming a point.

Size: Height at highest point of shoulder blades, 8 to 11 inches. Weight is in proportion to height. *Fault:* Over 11 inches. Over 12 inches disqualifies.

Gait: Free, quick, easy, graceful, not paddle-footed, or stiff in hip movements.

Color: Always parti-color, white with patches of any color. On the head color other than white must cover both ears, back and front, and extend without interruption from the ears over both eyes. A clearly defined white blaze and noseband are preferred to a solidly marked head. Symmetry of facial markings is desirable. The size, shape, placement or absence of patches on the body are without importance. Papillons may be any parti-color, provided nose, eye rims and lips are well-pigmented black. Among the colors there is not preference.

The following faults shall be severely penalized:
1) Nose not black.
2) Color other than white not covering both ears, back and front, or not extending from the ears over both eyes. A slight extension of the white collar onto the base of the ears or a few white hairs interspersed among the color, shall not be penalized provided the butterfly appearance is not sacrificed.

Disqualification: An all white dog or a dog with no white.

DISQUALIFICATIONS

Height: Over 12 inches.
An all white dog or a dog with no white.

APPROVED FEBRUARY 8, 1975

Representing the breed: Ch. Windsongs Copyright, owned by Mrs. Vida Wayne.

PEKINGESE

This breed has enjoyed many years on the tide of popularity. Just how long they will continue in that envied position it is impossible to say, as fashions in the pet-dog world fluctuate rapidly, but it is safe to say that their interesting personality will always command a strong following.

The Pekingese shares with the Chow Chow the honor of being the national dogs of China. That they are a very old breed is indicated by some bronze statues of these dogs that have been proved to be two thousand years old. It is further claimed that the first dogs brought to England in 1860 were taken from within the walls of the sacred city, and that since then few from the Royal Kennels have found their way into the outer world. There is, however, no difficulty in procuring them from other sources, as they are bred extensively.

The Pekingese has been classified among the spaniels by some authorities, which is a mistake, as they are not of spaniel descent and have no spaniel instincts or characteristics. On the contrary, they are very much like the Pugs in disposition and temperament, and undoubtedly there is a relationship between them.

The Pekingese is a much hardier dog than the Jap Chin, easier bred and raised, and able to adapt themselves readily to most climates.

The admirers of the breed are very enthusiastic over their dispositions. They are said to be the most affectionate and faithful companions, and lend themselves to domesticity with cat-like love of comfort. They accept gracefully all the luxuries of civilization. They display much of the independence and pugnacity of the Pug and a most amusing self-pride and conscious dignity in the presence of other dogs or strangers.

In the selection of Pekingese puppies at from two to four months old, look for: diminutiveness compatible with soundness and robustness; shortness and width of foreface; large eyes; deep stop; well-wrinkled forehead; moderately short and compact body; shortness of leg and great bone; with an abundant and dense fur-like coat; tail well feathered, and showing an indication to curl well over body.

Buyer's guide: The Pekingese is a good dog for those people that like an aloof, unobtrusive dog who is totally loyal to those he loves. They do well in most any type of housing, but do not navigate stairs very well. Today's Pekes are not structured for heavy exercise and should not be expected to be companions to active children or athletes. Pekes are very moderate eaters and are exceptionally hardy. Their coat needs a lot of care if it is to grow to its potential, and a prospective owner should be willing to devote considerable time to it. They may seem quite aloof, but when at ease in their home they are quite affectionate. They are natural watchdogs.

STANDARD FOR THE PEKINGESE

Expression: Must suggest the Chinese origin of the Pekingese in its quaintness and individuality, resemblance to the lion in directions and independence and should imply courage, boldness, self-esteem and combativeness rather than prettiness, daintiness or delicacy.

Skull: Massive, broad, wide and flat between the ears (not dome-shaped), wide between the eyes. **Nose:** Black, broad, very short and flat. **Eyes:** Large, dark, prominent, round, lustrous. **Stop:** Deep. **Ears:**

Heart-shaped, not set too high, leather never long enough to come below the muzzle, nor carried erect, but rather drooping, long feather. **Muzzle:** Wrinkled, very short and broad, not overshot nor pointed. Strong, broad underjaw, teeth not to show.

Shape of Body: Heavy in front, well-sprung ribs, broad chest, falling away lighter behind, lionlike. Back level. Not too long in body; allowance made for longer body in bitch. **Legs:** Short forelegs, bones of forearm bowed, firm at shoulder; hind legs lighter but firm and well shaped. **Feet:** Flat, toes turned out, not round, should stand well up on feet, not on ankles.

Action: Fearless, free and strong, with slight roll.

Coat, Feather and Condition: Long, with thick undercoat, straight and flat, not curly nor wavy, rather coarse, but soft; feather on thighs, legs, tail and toes long and profuse. **Mane:** Profuse, extending beyond the shoulder blades, forming ruff or frill round the neck.

Color: All colors are allowable. Red, fawn, black, black and tan, sable, brindle, white and parti-color well defined; black masks and spectacles around the eyes, with lines to ears are desirable. **Definition of a Parti-Color Pekingese:** The coloring of a parti-colored dog must be broken on the body. No large portion of any one color should exist. White should be shown on the saddle. A dog of any solid color with white feet and chest is not a parti-color.

Tail: Set high; lying well over back to either side; long, profuse, straight feather.

Size: Being a toy dog, medium size preferred, providing type and points are not sacrificed; extreme limit 14 pounds.

SCALE OF POINTS

Expression 5	Shape of body 15
Skull 10	Legs and feet 15
Nose 5	Coat, feather and condition
Eyes 5	 15
Stop 5	Tail 5
Ears 5	Action 10
Muzzle 5	TOTAL 100

FAULTS

Protruding tongue, badly blemished eye, overshot, wry mouth.

DISQUALIFICATIONS

Weight: over 14 pounds.
Dudley nose.

APPROVED APRIL 10, 1956

POMERANIAN

This vivacious and interesting breed that has strongly caught the fancy of the country is nothing more or less than a pocket edition of the old-fashioned Spitz, a dog always popular with the Germans.

The Pomeranian derives its name from the province of Pomerania, in the north of Germany. Here these dogs are very numerous, being, in fact, the house dog of that country, and are bred there to a state of perfection. The ancestors of the Pomeranians are undoubtedly related to the Samoyed and the Eskimo Dog. They both present a foxy head, prick ears, curled tail and a marked similarity in coats. What the Germans did was to take the material at hand and reduce it in size by careful selection and in-breeding, so as to make them more acceptable as house pets. This has been done slowly. The old-fashioned Wolf Spitz or Wolf Sable, a direct descendant of the Eskimo Dog, weighed from 25 to 50 pounds. Eighty years ago the Pomeranian of the show bench weighed from fifteen to twenty-five pounds. Today dozens of them are benched weighing well below five pounds, and all have the beauty, the vivacity and the marked characteristics of their early ancestors, the same foxy head and ears, the short back and the enormous coat of their 75 pound Arctic brethren.

The old-fashioned 20 pound Pom or Spitz dog was usually white or sable in color. Today they range in color from all shades of black to black-and-tan, orange and tri-color.

The Pom is one of the most popular pet dogs. They are very intelligent and faithful, as well as more active than most toys, and their diminutive size, vivacious manner and wonderful coat and coloring are always sure to attract attention.

The Pomeranian inherits from his rugged northern ancestors a very sturdy constitution. They are more easily raised than most breeds. During the period that breeders were devoting themselves to bantamizing the Pomeranian, little attention was paid to color. Sires were selected for their size alone. Beautifully colored puppies, however, appeared from time to time, and this prompted many breeders to turn their attention to color breeding. A point has been reached whereby some colors can be produced at will. Orange sires and black or chocolate bitches produce usually chocolate puppies. Chocolate sires and orange or sable bitches produce pure orange puppies. The blues are descendants of the blacks, but blue parents seldom have blue puppies unless there is more blue behind them. Orange and sable parents do not produce blue puppies. After birth puppies frequently change their colors, black puppies becoming blue, and blues frequently turning into blacks and beautiful shades of sable.

In selecting puppies, look for small size, light bone, prick ears, short backs, and thick, heavy coats.

Buyer's guide: The tiny Pom should not be treated as a play toy, or pampered so that it becomes nervous and yappy. They have been bred strictly as housepets and have a nice, friendly nature. The amount of required food and exercise for this breed should be proportionate to their size. Too much physical exertion should not be encouraged, and playing with overzealous children should be avoided. The profuse coat must be brushed regularly, but not too often since this may tear out too much hair. Poms are quite intelligent and will learn whatever you set out to teach them if you are patient and rewarding. They can become quite overactive and nervous if continually spoiled and treated like a real toy.

STANDARD FOR THE POMERANIAN

Appearance: The Pomeranian in build and appearance is a cobby, balanced, short-coupled dog. He exhibits great intelligence in his expression, and is alert in character and deportment.

Head: Well-proportioned to the body, wedge-shaped but not domed in outline, with a foxlike expression. There is a pronounced stop with a rather fine but not snipy muzzle, with no lippiness. The pigmentation around the eyes, lips, and on the nose must be black, except self-colored in brown and blue.

Teeth: The teeth meet in a scissors bite, in which part of the inner surface of the upper teeth meets and engages part of the outer surface of the lower teeth. One tooth out of line does not mean an undershot or overshot mouth.

Eyes: Bright, dark in color, and medium in size, almond-shaped and not set too wide apart nor too close together.

Ears: Small, carried erect and mounted high on the head, and placed not too far apart.

Neck and Shoulders: The neck is rather short, its base set well back on the shoulders. The Pom is not straight-in-shoulder, but has sufficient layback of shoulders to carry the neck proudly and high.

Body: The back must be short and the topline level. The body is cobby, being well ribbed and rounded. The brisket is fairly deep and not too wide.

Legs: The forelegs are straight and parallel, of medium length in proportion to a well balanced frame. The hocks are perpendicular to the ground, parallel to each other from hock to heel, and turning neither in nor out. The Pomeranian stands well-up on toes.

Tail: The tail is characteristic of the breed. It turns over the back and is carried flat, set high. It is profusely covered with hair.

Coat: Double-coated; a short, soft, thick undercoat, with longer, coarse, glistening outer coat consisting of guard hairs which must be harsh to the touch in order to give the proper texture for the coat to form a frill of profuse, standing-off straight hair. The front legs are well feathered and the hindquarters are clad with long hair or feathering from the top of the rump to the hocks.

Color: Acceptable colors to be judged on an equal basis; any solid color, any solid color with lighter or darker shadings of the same color, any solid color with sable or black shadings, parti-color, sable and black & tan. Black & tan is black with tan or rust, sharply defined, appearing above each eye and on muzzle, throat, and forechest, on all legs and feet and below the tail. Parti-color is white with any other color distributed in even patches on the body and a white blaze on head.

Movement: The Pomeranian moves with a smooth, free, but not loose action. He does not elbow out in front nor move excessively wide nor cowhocked behind. He is sound in action.

Size: The weight of a Pomeranian for exhibition is 3 to 7 pounds. The ideal size for show specimens is from 4 to 5 pounds.

Trimming and Dewclaws: Trimming for neatness is permissible around the feet and up the back of the legs to the first joint; trimming of unruly hairs on the edges of the ears and around the anus is also permitted. Dewclaws, if any, on the hind legs are generally removed. Dewclaws on the forelegs may be removed.

Classifications: The Open Classes at Specialty shows may be divided by color as follows: Open Red, Orange, Cream & Sable; Open Black, Brown & Blue; Open Any Other Allowed Color.

APPROVED MARCH 9, 1971

TOY POODLE

The Toy Poodle is a tiny replica of the Standard and Miniature Poodle, and, like them, one of the most intelligent, affectionate, and interesting of canine pets.

Please refer to the standard and discussion of the Poodle in the Non-Sporting section of this book.

Buyer's guide: The most popular of housepets, the Poodle is a superb companion for both active and sedate individuals. Toys are very easily managed, require little in the way of exercise and food, and can be kept just about anywhere. Considerable time and money will be required to keep their coat neatly trimmed as it grows very quickly. Toys have a tendency toward nervousness and yappiness, so over pampering should be avoided.

PUG

There exists a popular opinion that this interesting breed of toy dog had its origin through a cross of the Bulldog on some smaller breed. This supposition is incorrect. The Pug is a very old breed, and shares with the Greyhound the honors of long descent. It is probable that the Pug originated in China, a land whose dogs are characterized by short noses and curled tails.

The Dutch, through their East Indian Trading Company, brought these dogs to Holland, and later they came to England, where they were known for a time as Dutch Pugs. About the middle of the last century two enthusiasts, Lady de Willoughby and Mr. Morrison, established kennels in England, and both succeeded in creating an extraordinary vogue. The stock from their respective kennels presented distinct characteristics and were known accordingly. The Willoughby Pugs were silver fawn, with very black marks and distinct tracings. The Morrisons were of a brighter golden fawn. The two strains have since been crossed so many times that these characteristics have been lost.

The Black Pug is a more recent production, appearing about 1886. The blacks have since divided popularity with the fawns. They are alike in everything but color.

For many years the Pug was the most fashionable of pet dogs. Pugs are not lacking in intelligence, as was sometimes supposed, but are, on the contrary, highly intelligent, wide awake and alert, prompt to give warnings of the approach of strangers. They make the most interesting of companions. Their natural cleanliness, freedom from smell, and the slight care necessary to keep them in perfect condition go far to recommend them as house pets.

The chief points to look for in the selection of puppies at from two to four months old, are: short, square faces, great wrinkle, short backs, great bone.

Buyer's guide: The Pug is a very friendly dog, probably the toy most suitable for a house with children. They are very intelligent and take training easily and eagerly. Pugs are very moderate eaters and require little outside exercise to keep in good physical tone. They can be raised in either city or country locations, and make good companions wherever they are. Because of their very short muzzle, they do have a tendency to snore, which some people find objectionable. They are naturally clean and have no doggy odor. Untrained Pugs sometimes become somewhat yappy, so discipline them and do not let them become too overactive.

STANDARD FOR THE PUG

Symmetry: Symmetry and general appearance, decidedly square and cobby. A lean, leggy Pug and a dog with short legs and a long body are equally objectionable.

Size and Condition: The Pug should be *multum in parvo*, but this condensation (if the word may be used) should be shown by compactness of form, well-knit proportions, and hardness of developed muscle. Weight from 14 to 18 pounds (dog or bitch) desirable.

Body: Short and cobby, wide in chest and well ribbed up.

Legs: Very strong, straight, of moderate length and well under.

Feet: Neither so long as the foot of the hare, nor so round as that of the cat; well-split-up toes, and the nails black.

Muzzle: Short, blunt, square, but not up-faced.

Head: Large, massive, round—not apple-headed, with no indentation of the skull.

Eyes: Dark in color, very large, bold and prominent, globular in shape, soft and solicitous in expression, very lustrous, and, when excited, full of fire.

Ears: Thin, small, soft, like black velvet. There are two kinds—the "rose" and "button." Preference is given to the latter.

Markings: Clearly defined. The muzzle or mask, ears, moles on cheeks, thumb mark or diamond on forehead, back-trace should be as black as possible.

Mask: The mask should be black. The more intense and well defined it is the better.

Trace: A black line extending from the occiput to the tail.

Wrinkles: Large and deep.

Tail: Curled tightly as possible over the hip. The double curl is perfection.

Coat: Fine, smooth, soft, short and glossy, neither hard nor woolly.

Color: Silver or apricot-fawn. Each should be decided, to make the contrast complete between the color and the trace and the mask. Black.

SCALE OF POINTS

	Fawn	Black		Fawn	Black
Symmetry	10	10	Eyes	10	10
Size	5	10	Mask	5	—
Condition	5	5	Wrinkles	5	5
Body	10	10	Tail	10	10
Legs and feet	5	5	Trace	5	—
Head	5	5	Coat	5	5
Muzzle	10	10	Color	5	5
Ears	5	5	TOTAL	100	100

SHIH TZU

The eye-catching Shih Tzu has enjoyed a royal heritage and was the favored dog bred in the Imperial Palace in China. The breed is thought to date back over 1000 years to a time when the breeding of fine Shih Tzu was entrusted to court eunuchs who strived to develop specimens that would please the emperors. The Shih Tzu, whose name translates to Lion Dog in Chinese, is believed by many people to have evolved from the interbreeding of native Pekingese and Lhasa Apso, the Lhasa stock coming as presents from the Dalai Lama of Tibet.

The Shih Tzu was always a well protected breed, and very few specimens of the breed were offered for exportation. A few dogs did find their way to Europe, however, and the breed found a foothold, especially in Scandinavia. Soldiers returning from the hostilities of World War II in Europe are credited for introducing the Shih Tzu to the United States. More than twenty years later the breed was officially recognized by the American Kennel Club and permitted to compete in the Toy Group. Today they are quickly becoming one of the most popular of the toy dogs; doubtless their regal bearing and elegant appearance are winning them many admirers.

The coat of the Shih Tzu is luxurious and flowing and is best described as a wealth of hair. Shih Tzu possess an exotic beauty and the dogs have a proud and regal carriage. They have a most charming personality that seems to command affection from all that surround them. Affectionate yet serene, Shih Tzu make excellent companions for people who enjoy and appreciate the qualities of a beautiful canine.

Buyer's guide: The Shih Tzu has an endearing personality and serves strictly as a companion for the home. No special arrangements are needed in regard to housing, exercise or food, but potential owners must be willing to take the time to groom and brush the coat of the Shih Tzu every day. Without this attention the coat will mat up and require cutting and trimming—which is to be avoided at all costs. Shih Tzu may appear quite aloof, but underneath they are warm, affectionate dogs that get along very well with children and adults alike, and they are commonly favored by women.

STANDARD FOR THE SHIH TZU

General Appearance: Very active, lively and alert, with a distinctly arrogant carriage. The Shih Tzu is proud of bearing as befits his noble ancestry, and walks with head well up and tail carried gaily over the back.

Head: Broad and round, wide between the eyes. Muzzle square and short, but not wrinkled, about one inch from tip of nose to stop. *Definite Stop.* **Eyes:** Large, dark and round but not prominent, placed well apart. Eyes should show warm expression. **Ears:** Large, with long leathers, and carried drooping; set slightly below the crown of the skull; so heavily coated that they appear to blend with the hair of the neck. **Teeth:** Level or slightly undershot bite.

Forequarters: Legs short, straight, well boned, muscular, and heavily coated. Legs and feet look massive on account of the wealth of hair.

Body: Body between the withers and the root of the tail is somewhat longer than the height at the withers; well coupled and sturdy. Chest broad and deep, shoulders firm, back level.

Hindquarters: Legs short, well boned and muscular, are straight when viewed from the rear. Thighs well rounded and muscular. Legs look massive on account of wealth of hair.

Feet: Of good size, firm, well padded, with hair between the pads. Dewclaws, if any, on the hind legs are generally removed. Dewclaws on the forelegs may be removed.

Tail: Heavily plumed and curved well over the back; carried gaily, set on high.

Coat: A luxurious, long, dense coat. May be slightly wavy but *not* curly. Good woolly undercoat. The hair on top of the head may be tied up.

Color: All colors permissible. Nose and eye rims black, except the dogs with liver markings may have liver nose and slightly lighter eyes.

Gait: Slightly rolling, smooth and flowing, with strong rear action.

Size: Height at withers—9 to 10½ inches—should be no more than 11 inches nor less than 8 inches. Weight of mature dogs—12 to 15 pounds—should be no more than 18 pounds nor less than 9 pounds. However, type and breed characteristics are of the greatest importance.

FAULTS

Narrow head; overshot bite; snipiness; pink on nose or eye rims; small or light eyes; legginess; sparse coat; lack of definite stop.

APPROVED MAY 13, 1969

Representing the breed: Ch. Chumulari Ying Ying, owned by the Rev. and Mrs. D. Allan Easton.

SILKY TERRIER

The Sydney Silky was the first name assigned to this charming terrier, reflecting the name of the town in Australia where the breed first flourished. Silkies were developed from two main strains, the Australian and the Yorkshire Terrier, with some elements of the Skye and Dandie Dinmont Terriers undoubtedly figuring in the early specimens of the breed.

They are a small, attractive dog that presents an active, alert appearance. Referred to abroad as the Australian Silky Terrier, they are indeed fortunate enough to sport a soft silky coat that shines with a natural gloss. The breed is not content to be treated like a toy or lap dog and could easily fit into the terrier group. They have had a heritage of usefulness and are easily trained. In Australia they have been successfully used to rid the fields of mice and rats.

At home the Silky makes no great demands on an owner. They are quite adaptable and fit well into the most active lifestyle, yet they are content to live quietly in small apartments. They are an agile, naturally active breed and not typically yappy or temperamental. Lovable by temperament, the Silky Terrier is obedient and bright and makes a suitable pet for the inside life.

Buyer's guide: The Silky is a very friendly dog, and they may be a little *too* friendly at times. They tend to get overexcited if allowed and will run around the house and jump up to greet visitors. Silkies are very successful as companions for elderly or infirmed individuals and children. Their exercise requirements are fairly low, but an occasional walk will be appreciated. They can be raised in any size house and should be obedience trained from an early age to curb their tendency towards overreacting.

STANDARD FOR THE SILKY TERRIER

The Silky Terrier is a lightly built, moderately low-set toy dog of pronounced terrier character and spirited action.

Head: The head is strong, wedge-shaped, and moderately long. The skull is a trifle longer than the muzzle, in proportion about three-fifths for the skull, two-fifths for the muzzle. **Skull:** Flat, and not too wide between the ears. **Stop:** Shallow. **Ears:** Small, V-shaped and pricked. They are set high and carried erect without any tendency obliquely off the skull.

Eyes: Small, dark in color, and piercingly keen in expression. Light eyes are a fault. **Teeth:** Strong and well aligned, scissors bite. A bite markedly undershot or overshot is a serious fault. **Nose:** The nose is black.

Neck and Shoulders: The neck fits gracefully into sloping shoulders. It is medium long, fine and to some degree crested along its topline.

Body: Low-set, about one fifth longer than the dog's height at the withers. A too short body is a fault. The back line is straight, with a just perceptible rounding over the loins. Brisket medium wide, and deep enough to extend down to the elbows.

Tail: The tail is set high and carried erect or semi-erect but not overgay. It is docked and well coated but devoid of plume.

Forequarters: Well laid back shoulders, together with good angulation at the upper arm, set the forelegs nicely under the body. Forelegs are strong, straight and rather fine-boned.

Hindquarters: Thighs well muscled and strong, but not so developed as to appear heavy. Legs moderately angulated at stifles and hocks, with the hocks low and equidistant from the hock joints to the ground.

Feet: Small, cat-like, round, compact. Pads are thick and springy while the nails are strong and dark colored. White or flesh-colored nails are a fault. The feet point straight ahead, with no turning in or out. Dewclaws, if any, are removed.

Coat: Flat, in texture fine, glossy, silky; on matured specimens the desired length of coat from behind the ears to the set-on of the tail is from five to six inches. On the top of the head the hair is so profuse as to form a topknot, but long hair on face and ears is objectionable. Legs from knee and hock joints to feet should be free from long hair. The hair is parted on the head and down over the back to the root of the tail.

Color: Blue and tan. The blue may be silver blue, pigeon blue or slate blue, the tan deep and rich. The blue extends from the base of the skull to the tip of the tail, down the forelegs to the pasterns, and down the thighs to the hocks. On the tail the blue should be very dark. Tan appears on muzzle and cheeks, around the base of the ears, below the pasterns and hocks, and around the vent. There is a tan spot over each eye. The topknot should be silver or fawn.

Temperament: The keenly alert air of the terrier is characteristic, with shyness or excessive nervousness to be faulted. The manner is quick, friendly, responsive.

Movement: Should be free, light-footed, lively, and straightforward. Hindquarters should have strong propelling power. Toeing in or out is to be faulted.

Size: Weight ranges from eight to ten pounds. Shoulder height from nine to ten inches. Pronounced diminutiveness (such as a height of less than 8 inches) is not desired; it accentuates the quality of toyishness as opposed to the breed's definite terrier character.

APPROVED APRIL 14, 1959

YORKSHIRE TERRIER

This elegant breed makes most interesting pets and companions, for they are keen, active and intelligent, and on the show bench never fail to attract attention on account of the length, color, quantity and quality of their coat.

The finest specimens of this breed are found not only in the homes of the rich, but they are almost invariably in the homes of all classes, typically in the hands of some working man whose wife and family are devoted to dogs and are quite ready to convert their home into a kennel and give their pets the constant attention which they require, not only to grow these wonderful coats, but also to preserve them. It may also be mentioned that considerable skill is also essential. The feet of even the puppies are stockinged to prevent scratching of the hair on any part of their bodies. They are combed and brushed every day, periodically bathed, and the skin carefully watched and kept in a healthy condition by a careful selection of diet and the application of various preparations.

At birth all Yorkshire Terriers are black. When three to six months of age a blue shade begins to develop at the roots of the hair. This gradually changes until they are from 12 to 18 months, at which age the coat should be a real golden tan, deepening at the head, with the ears and legs almost mahogany.

In selecting Yorkshire Terrier puppies, diminutiveness, shortness of back and lightness of bone should be looked for, as well as anything that indicates the long, straight coat, with the dark tan on head and legs.

Buyer's guide: Only devoted lovers of toy dogs should consider owning the Yorkie. Their coat is the pride of the breed and requires substantial grooming and protecting. They are lively by nature and will keep themselves fit through their normal movements around the house. Protecting the coat must be stressed, as even going for a walk would require wrapping the coat to keep it from tearing and other damage. Yorkshire owners typically carry their dog, grooming them habitually. This breed is really suited for the person who wants to dedicate himself to caring for the dog. They, in return, give years of companionship and attention.

STANDARD FOR THE YORKSHIRE TERRIER

General Appearance: That of a long-haired toy terrier whose blue and tan coat is parted on the face and from the base of the skull to the end of the tail and hangs evenly and quite straight down each side of body. The body is neat, compact and well proportioned. The dog's high head carriage and confident manner should give the appearance of vigor and self-importance.

Head: Small and rather flat on top, **the skull** not too prominent or round, **the muzzle** not too long, with **the bite** neither undershot nor overshot and teeth sound. Either scissors bite or level bite is acceptable. **The nose** is black. **Eyes** are medium in size and not too prominent; dark in color and sparkling with a sharp, intelligent expression. Eye rims are dark. **Ears** are small, V-shaped, carried erect and set not too far apart.

Body: Well proportioned and very compact. The back is rather short, the back line level, with height at shoulder the same as at the rump.

Legs and Feet: **Forelegs** should be straight, elbows neither in nor out. **Hind legs** straight when viewed from behind, but stifles are moderately bent when viewed from the sides. **Feet** are round with black toenails. Dewclaws, if any, are generally removed from the hind legs. Dewclaws on the forelegs may be removed.

Tail: Docked to a medium length and carried slightly higher than the level of the back.

Coat: Quality, texture and quantity of coat are of prime importance. Hair is glossy, fine and silky in texture. Coat on the body is moderately long and perfectly straight (not wavy). It may be trimmed to floor length to give ease of movement and a neater appearance, if desired. The fall on the head is long, tied with one bow in center of head or parted in the middle and tied with two bows. Hair on muzzle is very long. Hair should be trimmed short on tips of ears and may be trimmed on feet to give them a neat appearance.

Colors: Puppies are born black and tan and are normally darker in body color, showing an intermingling of black hair in the tan until they are matured. Color of hair on body and richness of tan on head and legs are of prime importance in *adult dogs*, to which the following color requirements apply:

BLUE: Is a dark steel-blue, not a silver-blue and not mingled with fawn, bronzy or black hairs.

TAN: All tan hair is darker at the roots than in the middle, shading to still lighter tan at the tips. There should be no sooty or black hair intermingled with any of the tan.

Color on Body: The blue extends over the body from back of neck to root of tail. Hair on tail is a darker blue, especially at end of tail.

Headfall: A rich golden tan, deeper in color at sides of head, at ear roots and on the muzzle, with ears a deep rich tan. Tan color should not extend down on back of neck.

Chest and Legs: A bright, rich tan, not extending above the elbow on the forelegs nor above the stifle on the hind legs.

Weight: Must not exceed seven pounds.

APPROVED APRIL 12, 1966

Group 6: Non-Sporting Dogs

BICHON FRISE

The Bichon Frise is a relatively new addition to the American dog show scene, but the breed dates back many hundreds of years in the Mediterranean region. Bichons are thought to have descended from the Barbet, an early breed of water spaniel which played a key role in the formation of four types of Barbichon dogs: the Bichon Bolognese, the Bichon Maltaise, the Bichon Ravenese and our Bichon Teneriffe. Today's Bichon Frise was known as the Bichon Teneriffe for many years, the latter name being given because the breed was kept in great abundance on Teneriffe Island in the Canary Islands. Nevertheless, Spain is regarded as the original homeland of the Bichon Frise. The breed is said to have found its way to these other lands through the travels of Spanish sailors who used these dogs for sale and barter in foreign ports. In this way the Bichons spread from continent to continent, taking hold in many countries.

The Bichon Teneriffe was quite the vogue in Italy during the Renaissance, especially with the upper class and nobility. It was popular during this time to keep the Bichons groomed and trimmed in lion-like patterns. The lovely little Teneriffe were considered fashionable and can be frequently found in the works of the great Spanish painters of the time, Goya being the most notable. Henry III of France was also an ardent fancier of the Teneriffe and kept a large number of dogs, all perfumed and pampered. The breed enjoyed years of being the darlings of the court, but through a fickle turn of fashion, the Teneriffe suddenly went out of style. Their people-loving nature saved them from impending doom, however, as the Teneriffe warmed the hearts of the common people and was soon adopted as a popular housepet.

It was not until the late 1950's that considerable numbers of Bichons Frises made their way to the United States, most coming as imports from the fine kennels of France. Recognition was almost twenty years in coming, but in April, 1973 the Bichon Frise was officially admitted to the Non-Sporting Group by the American Kennel Club. The eye-catching Bichons have been garnering many top awards at the dog shows since that time and their popularity has skyrocketed, making the breed one of the fastest growing.

These charming "powder puffs" are amiable dogs for even the most busy households. Bichons Frises retain today an air of dignity and confidence that befits their noble heritage. Their glorious white coat is silky in texture and sheds only slightly once the dog has received his adult coat. To keep the Bichon ready for the show ring requires considerable attention to trimming and a constant routine of brushing and bathing, but those dogs not actively involved in conformation competition can have their coat cut slightly shorter and thus avoid matting problems. Bichons Frises are relatively hardy dogs and make little demand as for space, food or activity. The breed is lively by nature and usually acquires sufficient exercise through the normal course of their day to keep them fit, but they love the chance to get out and investigate their neighborhood in daily walks with their owners. The Bichon Frise has a quick mind and a keen memory, so don't try to pull something over on them too often. Once you've set up a routine of a walk at a certain time, don't be surprised if you find your dog sitting at the door waiting rather impatiently for his tardy master!

Buyer's guide: A disposition friendlier than the Bichon's would be hard to find, for they are a fun-loving and good natured breed. Grooming and trimming the hair to stand out in typical Bichon fashion is quite a job and a daily brushing is highly recommended. They are a very adaptable breed and do fine in city or country provided they are not cooped up and are allowed to exercise themselves. Bichons are alert and smart and can be easily trained to the rules of the house. Children are especially fond of them and they return all attention and affection. Keeping their coat white and undamaged is the trick with this breed, but aside from this they are easily managed dogs.

STANDARD FOR THE BICHON FRISE

General Appearance: A sturdy, lively dog of stable temperament, with a stylish gait and an air of dignity and intelligence.

Color: Solid white, or white with cream, apricot, or gray on the ears and/or body.

Head: Proportionate to the size of the dog. Skull broad and somewhat round, but not coarse; covered with a topknot of hair.

Muzzle: Of medium length, not heavy or snipy. Slightly accentuated stop.

Ears: Dropped, covered with long flowing hair. The leather should reach approximately halfway the length of the muzzle.

Eyes: Black or dark brown, with black rims. Large, round, expressive, and alert.

Lips: Black, fine, never drooping.

Nose: Black, round, pronounced.

Bite: Scissors.

Neck: Rather long, and gracefully and proudly carried behind an erect head.

Shoulders: Well laid back. Elbows held close to the body.

Body: Slightly longer than tall. Well developed with good spring of ribs. The back inclines gradually from the withers to a slight rise over the loin. The loin is large and muscular. The brisket, well let down.

Tail: Covered with long flowing hair, carried gaily and curved to lie on the back.

Size: The height at the withers should not exceed 12 inches nor be under 8 inches.

Legs and Feet: Strong boned; forelegs appearing straight, with well-knit pasterns. Hindquarters well angulated. Feet, resembling cat's paws, are tight and round.

Coat: Profuse, silky and loosely curled. There is an undercoat.

Grooming: Scissored to show the eyes and give a full rounded appearance to the head and body. Feet should have hair trimmed to give a rounded appearance. When properly brushed, there is an overall "powder puff" appearance. Puppies may be shown in short coat, but the minimum show coat for an adult is two inches.

Faults: Cowhocks, snipy muzzle, poor pigmentation, protruding eyes, yellow eyes, undershot or overshot bite.

Serious Faults: Corkscrew tail, black hair in the coat.

APPROVED NOVEMBER 14, 1972

Representing the breed: Ch. Miracle's Freudian Slip, owned by Don Thie.

BOSTON TERRIER

The Boston Terrier is one of the few breeds that is distinctly of American origin. Their name indicates their nativity, and all that can be learned of their ancestry points to their having been of a pit bull terrier origin. Pit bulls are usually the result of a cross between bulldogs and terriers, and vary in form. Some have the long, clean head of a terrier, others, the round, almost puggish head of the bulldog. The round-headed, short faced brindle dogs that were a result of these crosses could not win against the terrier types in their own classes, and as they were crowded out their admirers succeeded in having classes organized for them, and these classes were eventually recognized by the American Kennel Club.

In the early history of the breed there was no established type, some favoring the bulldogs, while others were partial to those that were on the terrier order. As late as 1894, the American Kennel Club canceled a Boston Terrier pedigree because the sire was a Bulldog. The registrar of the Boston Terrier Club, when called upon for an explanation, stated that it was necessary to resort to the bulldog cross to retain certain characteristics of the bulldog, namely, the rose ears, flat skull, and short, tapering tail, and further asserted that the Boston Terrier at that time was becoming too strongly terrier. At the present time the best opinion on this subject is that the Boston should be neither bulldog nor terrier in type, but a happy medium.

The Boston Terrier has proven to be the great commercial success of this country, and no other breed ever attained such great popularity in so short a time. For a time in the early part of this century they were the most commonly owned purebred housepet. The tendency from year to year has been to reduce them in size, and as a result of careful selection they have become well fixed in type and much of their early irregularity has disappeared.

Buyer's guide: Bostons are well mannered and even tempered, excellent pets for older children and adults. They are a compact, lively dog and will do well in most environments, provided they receive a moderate amount of exercise. Their short coat is easily kept neat and is naturally odor free. Bostons are quite smart and will train quite easily. They are an excellent all-around dog that gets along with most everyone and lives anywhere.

STANDARD FOR THE BOSTON TERRIER

General Appearance: The general appearance of the Boston Terrier should be that of a lively, highly intelligent, smooth-coated, short-headed, compactly built, short-tailed, well-balanced dog of medium station, of brindle color and evenly marked with white. The head should indicate a high degree of intelligence, and should be in proportion to the size of the dog; the body rather short and well knit, the limbs strong and neatly turned; tail short; and no feature be so prominent that the dog appears badly proportioned. The dog should convey an impression of determination, strength and activity, with style of a high order; carriage easy and graceful. A proportionate combination of "color" and "ideal markings" is a particularly distinctive feature of a representative specimen, and a dog with a preponderance of white on body, or without the proper proportion of brindle and white on head, should possess sufficient merit otherwise to counteract its deficiencies in these respects. The ideal "Boston Terrier expression" as indicating "a high degree of intelligence," is also an important characteristic of the breed. "Color and markings" and "expression" should be given particular consideration in determining the relative value of "general appearance" to other points.

Skull: Square, flat on top, free from wrinkles; cheeks flat; brow abrupt, stop well defined. **Eyes:** Wide apart, large and round, dark in color, expression alert, but kind and intelligent. The eyes should set square in the skull, and the outside corners should be on a line with the cheeks as viewed from the front. **Muzzle:** Short, square, wide and deep, and in proportion to skull; free from wrinkles; shorter in length than in width and depth, not exceeding in length approximately one third of length of skull; width and depth carried out well to end; the muzzle from stop to end of nose on a line parallel to the top of the skull; nose black and wide, with well defined line between nostrils. The jaws broad and square, with short regular teeth. Bite even or sufficiently undershot to square muzzle. The chops of good depth but not pendulous, completely covering the teeth when mouth is closed. **Ears:** Carried erect, either cropped to conform to the shape of head, or natural bat, situated as near the corners of skull as possible.

Head Faults: Skull "domed" or inclined; furrowed by a medial line; skull too long for breath, or *vice versa;* stop too shallow; brow and skull too slanting. Eyes small or sunken; too prominent; light color or walleye; showing too much white or haw. Muzzle wedge-shaped or lacking depth; down-faced; too much cut out below the eyes; pinched or wide nostrils; butterfly nose; protruding teeth; weak lower jaw; showing turn-up, layback, or wrinkled. Ears poorly carried or in size out of proportion to head.

Neck: Of fair length, slightly arched and carrying the head gracefully; setting neatly into shoulders. **Neck Faults:** Ewe-necked; throatiness; short and thick.

Body: Deep with good width of chest; shoulders sloping; back short; ribs deep and well sprung, carried well back to loins; loins short and muscular; rump curving slightly to set-on of tail; flank very slightly cut up. The body should appear short but not chunky. **Body Faults:** Flat sides; narrow chest; long or slack loins; roach back; swayback; too much cut up in flank.

Elbows: Standing neither in nor out. **Forelegs:** Set moderately wide apart and on a line with the point of the shoulders; straight in bone and well muscled; pasterns short and strong. **Hind Legs:** Set true; bent at stifles; short from hocks to feet; hocks turning neither in nor out; thighs strong and well muscled. **Feet;** Round, small and compact and turned neither in nor out; toes well arched. **Legs and Feet Faults:** Loose shoulders or elbows; hind legs too straight at stifles; hocks too prominent; long or weak pasterns; splay feet.

Gait: The gait of the Boston Terrier is that of a sure-footed, straight-gaited dog, forelegs and hind legs moving straight ahead in line with perfect rhythm, each step indicating grace with power. **Gait Faults:** There shall be no rolling, paddling or weaving when gaited and any crossing movement, either front or rear, is a serious fault.

Tail: Set-on low; short, fine and tapering; straight; or screw; devoid of fringe or coarse hair, and not carried above horizontal. **Tail Faults:** A long or gaily carried tail; extremely gnarled or curled against body. (Note—The preferred tail should not exceed in length approximately half the distance from set-on to hock.)

Ideal Color: Brindle with white markings. The brindle to be evenly distributed and distinct. Black with white markings permissible but brindle with white markings preferred. **Ideal Markings:** White muzzle, even white blaze over head, collar, breast, part or whole of forelegs, and hind legs below hocks. **Color and Markings Faults:** All white; absence of white marking; preponderance of white on body; without the proper proportion of brindle and white on head; or any variations detracting from the general appearance.

Coat: Short, smooth, bright and fine in texture. **Coat Faults:** Long or coarse; lacking luster.

Weight: Not exceeding 25 pounds, divided by classes as follows: lightweight, under 15 pounds; middleweight, 15 and under 20 pounds; heavyweight, 20 and not exceeding 25 pounds.

SCALE OF POINTS

General appearance	10	Hind legs	5
Skull	10	Gait	10
Eyes	5	Feet	5
Muzzle	10	Tail	5
Ears	2	Color	4
Neck	3	Ideal markings	5
Body	15	Coat	2
Elbows	4		
Forelegs	5	TOTAL	100

BULLDOG

The origin of the Bulldog is closely associated with the Mastiff; in fact, he was originally a smaller variety that was used for bull baiting, the larger variety being used in battles with the bear.

The first mention of a Bulldog occurs in 1631 or 1632 in a letter written by Prestwich Eaton, of St. Sebastian, to George Wellingham, London, asking for a good Mastiff and two good Bulldogs. The sport of bull baiting was initiated with the disappearance of the wild oxen from the woods in the reign of King John, toward the close of the 12th or beginning of the 13th century. We read that: "William, Earl Warren, Lord of Stamford, standing upon the castle walls of this town, saw two bulls fighting for a cow in the meadow. The butcher's dog pursued one of the bulls, which, maddened with the noise and the multitude, galloped through the town. This sight so pleased the Earl that he gave the meadows, called the Castle Meadows, where first the duel began, for a common to the butchers of the town, on condition that they find a mad bull six weeks before Christmas for the continuance of the sport every year."

"Bull baiting," writes Marples, "became a very fashionable British sport, and was at one time patronized by persons of the very highest rank, from the King and Queen of England down, just as bull fighting in Spain is a leading and most fashionable sport, in which matadors take the place of Bulldogs. As the sport developed and became popular, naturally the breedings of dogs best adapted for bringing down the bull followed, and in this way originals of our present-day Bulldogs were evolved, but of course not so pronounced in type nor so perfectly fitted structurally and anatomically for their specific avocation. It was no doubt found that a less heavy and more agile dog than a Mastiff would be better for the purpose, and either smaller specimens would be used or the Mastiff became dwarfed by crossing, probably with a terrier. As the bull always attacks his canine foes head down so as to catch them up with his horns, the dogs would be taught to seize him by the nose, which indeed would be the natural mode of attack of the dog in such circumstances. The type of dog that would be suggested to careful students of the sport, even in the old days, would be a low-set, powerfully fronted and jawed dog, with light quarters, and whose nose receded from his lower jaw to enable him to breathe while hanging on his quarry, his light hindquarters further assisting him in hanging on the bull, whose habit in such circumstances invariably is to whirl the dog in the air in his frantic endeavor to shake him off."

Theoretically, the Bulldog may be anatomically adapted to holding bulls, but the present show dogs could neither catch nor hold a bull or escape his feet and horns. They have lost, however, none of their old-time courage and tenacity, and will go to their death as cheerfully as their ancestors did 300 years ago. Bulldogs are not fierce in disposition; in fact, they are among the kindest of the canine race, free from treachery and the most faithful of companions, all of which in a great measure accounts for their popularity.

The chief points to look for in the selection of Bulldog puppies at from two to four months old and after are: a massive head, with long, sweeping underjaw, well turned up, but not necessarily short nose, but must be retrousse—laid well back, massive, broad foreface, big skull, little ears, short back and tail, short legs, with enormous bone.

Buyer's guide: Looks are deceiving in the case of the Bulldog. Beneath that gruff exterior is a warm, gentle dog. They are powerfully built and quite strong, but need relatively little exercise to stay in top health. In fact, overexertion and obesity are the main causes for heart attacks and early death in Bulldogs. If good nutrition and proper exercise is stressed throughout their life, they can be expected to live 8 to 12 years. Despite their size, they will fit in most anywhere and can be kept in apartments if daily walks are scheduled. They have a good appetite and eat as much as would be expected of a dog of their size. Grooming is minimal. Bulldogs are good with children and welcome companions in the home.

STANDARD FOR THE BULLDOG

General Appearance, Attitude, Expression, etc.: The perfect Bulldog must be of medium size and smooth coat; with heavy, thick-set, low-swung body, massive, short-faced head, wide shoulders and sturdy limbs. The general appearance and attitude should suggest great stability, vigor and strength. The disposition should be equable and kind, resolute and courageous (not vicious or aggressive), and demeanor should be pacific and dignified. These attributes should be countenanced by the expression and behavior.

Gait: The style and carriage are peculiar, his gait being a loose-jointed, shuffling, sidewise motion, giving the characteristic "roll." The action must, however, be unrestrained, free and vigorous.

Proportion and Symmetry: The "points" should be well distributed and bear good relation one to the other, no feature being in such prominence from either excess or lack of quality that the animal appears deformed or ill-proportioned. **Influence of Sex:** In comparison of specimens of different sex, due allowance should be made in favor of the bitches, which do not bear the characteristics of the breed to the same degree of perfection and grandeur as do the dogs.

Size: The size for mature dogs is about 50 pounds; for mature bitches about 40 pounds.

Coat: The coat should be straight, short, flat, close, of fine texture, smooth and glossy. (No fringe, feather or curl.)

Color of Coat: The color of coat should be uniform, pure of its kind and brilliant. The various colors found in the breed are to be preferred in the following order: (1) red brindle, (2) all other brindles, (3) solid white, (4) solid red, fawn or fallow, (5) piebald, (6) inferior qualities of all the foregoing. *Note:* A perfect piebald is preferable to a muddy brindle or defective solid color. Solid black is very undesirable, but not so objectionable if occurring to a moderate degree in piebald patches. The brindles to be perfect should have a fine, even and equal distribution of the composite color. In brindles and solid colors a small white patch on the chest is not considered detrimental. In piebalds the color patches should be well defined, of pure color and symmetrically distributed.

Skin: The skin should be soft and loose, especially at the head, neck and shoulders. **Wrinkles and Dewlaps:** The head and face should be covered with heavy wrinkles, and at the throat, from jaw to chest, there should be two loose pendulous folds, forming the dewlap.

Skull: The skull should be very large, and in circumference, in front of the ears, should measure at least the height of the dog at the shoulders. Viewed from the front, it should appear very high from the corner of the lower jaw to the apex of the skull, and also very broad and square. Viewed at the side, the head should appear very high, and very short from the point of the nose to occiput. The forehead should be flat (not rounded or domed), neither too prominent nor overhanging the face. **Cheeks:** The cheeks should be well rounded, protruding sideways and outward beyond the eyes. **Stop:** The temples or frontal bones should be very well defined, broad, square and high, causing a hollow or groove between the eyes. This indentation, or stop, should be both broad and deep and extend up the middle of the forehead, dividing the head vertically, being traceable to the top of the skull. **Eyes and Eyelids:** The eyes, seen from the front, should be situated low down in the skull, as far from the ears as possible, and their corners should be in a straight line at right angles with the stop. They should be quite in front of the head, as wide apart as possible, provided their outer corners are within the outline of the cheeks when viewed from the front. They should be quite round in form, of moderate size, neither sunken nor bulging, and in color should be very dark. The lids should cover the white of the eyeball, when the dog is looking directly forward, and the lid should show no "haw." **Ears:** The ears should be set high in the head, the front inner edge of each ear joining the outline of the skull at the top back corner of skull, so as to place them as wide apart, and as high, and as far from the eyes as possible. In size they should be small and thin. The shape termed "rose ear" is most desirable. The rose ear folds inward at its back lower edge, the upper front edge curving over, outward and backward, showing part of the inside of the burr. (The ears should not be carried erect or prick-eared or buttoned and should never be cropped.)

Face: The face, measured from the front of the cheekbone to the tip of the nose, should be extremely short, the muzzle being very short, broad, turned upward and very deep from the corner of the eye to the corner of the mouth. **Nose:** The nose should be large, broad and black, its tip being set back deeply between the eyes. The distance from bottom of stop, between the eyes, to the tip of nose should be as short as possible and not exceed the length from the tip of nose to the edge of under lip. The nostrils should be wide, large and black, with a well-defined line between them. Any nose other than black is objectionable, and a brown or liver colored nose shall disqualify. **Chops:** The chops or "flews" should be thick, broad, pendant and very deep, completely overhanging the lower jaw at each side. They join the under lip in front and almost or quite cover the teeth, which should be scarcely noticeable when the mouth is closed. **Jaws:** The jaws should be massive, very broad, square and "undershot," the lower jaw projecting considerably in front of the upper jaw and turning up. **Teeth:** The teeth should be large and strong, with the canine teeth in front, between the canines, in an even, level row.

Neck: The neck should be short, very thick, deep and strong and well arched at the back.

Shoulders: The shoulders should be muscular, very heavy, widespread and slanting outward, giving stability and great power.

Chest: The chest should be very broad, deep and full.

Brisket and Body: The brisket and body should be very capacious, with full sides, well-rounded ribs and very deep from the shoulders down to its lowest part, where it joins the chest. It should be well let down between the shoulders and forelegs, giving the dog a broad, low, short-legged appearance. The body should be well ribbed up behind with the belly tucked up and not rotund.

Back: The back should be short and strong, very broad at the shoulders and comparatively narrow at the loins. There should be a slight fall in the back, close behind the shoulders (its lowest part), whence the spine should rise to the loins (the top of which should be higher than the top of the shoulders), thence curving again more suddenly to the tail, forming an arch (a very distinctive feature of the breed), termed "roach back" or, more correctly, "wheel-back."

Legs and Feet: **Forelegs:** The forelegs should be short, very stout, straight and muscular, set wide apart, with well developed calves, presenting a bowed outline, but the bones of the legs should not be curved or bandy, nor the feet brought too close together. **Elbows:** The elbows should be low and stand well out and loose from the body. **Hind Legs:** The hind legs should be strong and muscular and longer than the forelegs, so as to elevate the loins above the shoulders. Hocks should be slightly bent and well let down, so as to give length and strength from loins to hock. The lower leg should be short, straight and strong, with the stifles turned slightly outward and away from the body. The hocks are thereby made to approach each other, and the hind feet to turn outward. **Feet:** The feet should be moderate in size, compact and firmly set. Toes compact, well split up, with high knuckles and with short stubby nails. The front feet may be straight or slightly out-turned, but the hind feet should be pointed well outward.

Tail: The tail may be either straight or "screwed" (but never curved or curly), and in any case must be short, hung low, with decided downward carriage, thick root and fine tip. If straight, the tail should be cylindrical and of uniform taper. If "screwed" the bends or kinks should be well defined, and they may be abrupt and even knotty, but no portion of the member should be elevated above the base or root.

SCALE OF POINTS

General Properties
Proportion and symmetry 5
Attitude 3
Expression 2
Gait 3
Size 3
Coat 2
Color of coat..........4 22

Head
Skull 5
Cheeks 2
Stop 4
Eyes and eyelids......3
Ears 5
Wrinkle 5
Nose 6
Chops 2

Jaws 5
Teeth 2 39

Body, Legs, etc.
Neck 3
Dewlap 2
Shoulders.............5
Chest 3
Ribs 3
Brisket 2
Belly 2
Back..................5
Forelegs and elbows...4
Hind legs.............3
Feet 3
Tail 4 39
TOTAL 100

DISQUALIFICATIONS
Dudley or flesh-colored nose.

CHOW CHOW

This breed is undoubtedly descended from the arctic dog. They come from the north of China, where they are used to draw sledges and also for hunting. Their head and ears and general expression, as well as their fur-like coat and curled tail, all indicate their relationship to the Eskimo Dog.

They are sometimes referred to as the Edible Dog of China, from the fact that the Chinese at one time bred them for food, puppies eight to ten months old being selected for that purpose. Although Chows have been brought to this and other countries for more than one hundred years, it is only within the last half century that they have been received with much favor. At the present time they are very popular.

There is a good deal of character to the Chow. No dog has a braver spirit or is more devoted to his master. They are not, however, what may be called sociable, and do not make up with strangers. They hold themselves aloof even from their own species. Chows are not quarrelsome, but will not evade a combat, and in a mix-up can hold their own with any dog of their size. Their homing instinct is remarkable and it is almost impossible to lose them. They will find their way for miles through country entirely new to them, and if they become separated from their masters in a crowd will thread their way through with the utmost confidence in their own ability until they find him. All of these are traits inherited from their arctic ancestors.

Dogs weighing from 40 to 50 pounds are considered by judges as the most typical of the breed. The most popular color is the red, with black next.

The chief points to look for in the selection of puppies of from two to four months old, are: short faces, short backs, dense coats, great bone, short feet, and well-twisted tails.

Buyer's guide: The Chow Chow is a very devoted breed and prefers to be a one-man's dog. They may exhibit signs of jealousy where their master is concerned, and can be quite irritable to other people that come on too strongly for them. Chows are not recommended for families with children as they are quick to bite when they are displeased. They also do not take well to being kennelled or left alone for great lengths of time, as they will grieve for their owner's return. Grooming is no problem as long as routine brushing is carried out faithfully. Chows should be encouraged to exercise as they can become quite lazy if left to their own choice. Start training early for the best adult disposition.

STANDARD FOR THE CHOW CHOW

General Appearance: A massive, cobby, powerful dog, active and alert, with strong, muscular development, and perfect balance. Body squares with height of leg at shoulder; head, broad and flat, with short, broad, and deep muzzle, accentuated by a ruff; the whole supported by straight, strong legs. Clothed in a shining, offstanding coat, the Chow is a masterpiece of beauty, dignity, and untouched naturalness.

Head: Large and massive in proportion to size of dog, with broad, flat skull; well filled under the eyes; moderate stop; and moderately carried.

Expression: Essentially dignified, lordly, scowling, discerning, sober, and snobbish—one of independence. **Muzzle:** Short in comparison to length of skull; broad from eyes to end of nose, and of equal depth. The lips somewhat full and overhanging. **Teeth:** Strong and level, with a scissors bite; should neither be overshot, nor undershot. **Nose:** Large, broad, and black in color. (Disqualification—Nose spotted or distinctly other color than black, except in blue Chows, which may have solid blue or slate noses.) **Tongue:** A blue-black. The tissues of the mouth should approximate black. (Disqualification—Tongue red, pink, or obviously spotted with red or pink.) **Eyes:** Dark, deep-set, of moderate size, and almond-shaped. **Ears:** Small, slightly rounded at tip, stiffly carried. They should be placed wide apart, on top of the skull, and set with a slight, forward tilt. (Disqualification—Drop ear or ears. A drop ear is one which is not stiffly carried or stiffly erect, but which breaks over at any point from its base to its tip.)

Body: Short, compact, with well-sprung ribs, and let down in the flank.

Neck: Strong, full, set well on the shoulders.

Shoulders: Muscular, slightly sloping.

Chest: Broad, deep, and muscular. A narrow chest is a serious fault.

Back: Short, straight, and strong.

Loins: Broad, deep, and powerful.

Tail: Set well up and carried closely to the back, following line of spine at start.

Forelegs: Perfectly straight, with heavy bone and upright pasterns.

Hind Legs: Straight-hocked, muscular, and heavy boned. *Feet:* Compact, round, catlike, with thick pads.

Gait: Completely individual. Short and stilted because of straight hocks.

Coat: Abundant, dense, straight, and off-standing; rather coarse in texture with a soft, woolly undercoat. It may be any clear color, solid throughout, with lighter shadings on ruff, tail, and breechings.

DISQUALIFICATIONS

Nose spotted or distinctly other color than black, except in blue Chows, which may have solid blue or slate noses.

Tongue red, pink or obviously spotted with red or pink.

Drop ear or ears.

APPROVED MARCH 11, 1941

DALMATIAN

This attractive breed of dogs comes from Dalmatia, Yugoslavia, and the countryside adjacent to the Gulf of Venice. In their native land they serve the purpose of the Pointer and resemble them closely in conformation and appearance.

In this country their sporting proclivities have never been developed, but they display such marked fondness for the stable and the companionship of horses that they are known as coach dogs. The well-bred coach dog's devotion to horses is really second nature or an instinct. He will assume the duties of guard about a stable, follow the horses at exercise, and take up a position between the wheels of a carriage on the road, all without any particular training. He is peculiarly adapted for the purpose, as he is of a size and build that will enable him to keep easy pace with the horses for a long distance.

The Dalmatian is big enough and plucky enough to command

the respect and caution of intruders. His smooth, short coat is always clean, and his symmetrical proportions, intelligent features and clean, white body, evenly spotted with black, make him an attractive addition to any household. By reason of his markings, he is also easier seen at night than most any other breed.

The coach dog is usually of friendly disposition, though inclined to be distrustful of those who take liberties with his master's property.

In selecting puppies, it is well to remember that they are born pure white, the spots developing with age. Puppies curl their tails, which often become straight with age. After that general symmetry, soundness, clean Pointer-like heads, and distinctness of spots are the points to be looked for.

Buyer's guide: Dalmatians can be quite gregarious pets. They are very sensible around the house and make superlative companions for growing kids, as they love to play yet instinctively know the right thing to do in most situations. They make natural guardians. Because they are quite active, Dalmatians need a goodly amount of exercise and cannot be kept strictly within a house. They do best in rural or spacious settings and should be owned by energetic owners. Dalmatians are affectionate dogs and respond to the moods of their owners, so they should be given lots of personal attention.

STANDARD FOR THE DALMATIAN

The Dalmatian should represent a strong, muscular, and active dog; poised and alert; free of shyness; intelligent in expression; symmetrical in outline; and free from coarseness and lumber. He should be capable of great endurance, combined with a fair amount of speed.

Head: Should be of a fair length, the skull flat, proportionately broad between the ears, and moderately well defined at the temples, and not in one straight line from the nose to the occiput bone as required in a Bull Terrier. It should be entirely free from wrinkle. **Muzzle:** Should be long and powerful—the lips clean. The mouth should have a scissors bite. Never undershot or overshot. It is permissible to trim whiskers. **Eyes:** Should be set moderately well apart, and of medium size, round, bright, and sparkling, with an intelligent expression; their color greatly depending on the markings of the dog. In the black-spotted variety the eyes should be dark (black or brown or blue). In the liver-spotted variety they should be lighter than in the black-spotted variety (golden or light brown or blue). The rim around the eyes in the black-spotted variety should be black; in the liver-spotted variety, brown. Never flesh-colored in either. Lack of pigment a major fault.

Ears: Should be set rather high, of moderate size, rather wide at the base, and gradually tapering to a rounded point. They should be carried close to the head, be thin and fine in texture, and preferably spotted.
Nose: In the black-spotted variety should always be black; in the liver-spotted variety, always brown. A butterfly or flesh-colored nose is a major fault.

Neck and Shoulders: The neck should be fairly long, nicely arched, light and tapering, and entirely free from throatiness. The shoulders should be oblique, clean and muscular, denoting speed.

Body, Back, Chest and Loins: The chest should not be too wide, but very deep and capacious, ribs well sprung but never rounded like barrel hoops (which would indicate want of speed). Back powerful; loin strong, muscular and slightly arched.

Legs and Feet: Of great importance. The forelegs should be straight, strong, and heavy in bone; elbows close to the body; feet compact, well-arched toes, and tough, elastic pads. In the hind legs the muscles should be clean, though well defined; the hocks well let down. Dewclaws may be removed from legs. **Nails:** In the black-spotted variety, black or white; or a nail may be both black and white. In the liver-spotted variety, brown or white; or a nail may be both brown and white.

Gait: Length of stride should be in proportion to the size of the dog, steady in rhythm of 1, 2, 3, 4 as in the cadence count in military drill. Front legs should not paddle, nor should there be a straddling appearance. Hind legs should neither cross nor weave; judges should be able to see each leg move with no interference of another leg. Drive and reach are most desirable. Cowhocks are a major fault.

Tail: Should ideally reach the hock joint, strong at the insertion, and tapering toward the end, free from coarseness. It should not be inserted too low down, but carried with a slight curve upwards, and never curled.

Coat: Should be short, hard, dense, and fine, sleek and glossy in appearance, but neither woolly nor silky.

Color and Markings: Are most important points. The ground color in both varieties should be pure white, very decided, and not intermixed. The color of the spots in the black-spotted variety should be dense black; in the liver-spotted variety they should be liver brown. The spots should not intermingle, but be as round and well defined as possible, the more distinct the better. In size they should be from that of a dime to a half-dollar. The spots on the face, head, ears, legs, and tail to be smaller than those on the body. Patches, tri-colors, and any color markings other than black or liver constitute a disqualification. A true patch is a solid, sharply defined mass of black or liver that is appreciably larger than any of the markings on the dog. Several spots that are so adjacent that they actually touch one another at their edges do not constitute a patch.

Size: The desirable height of dogs and bitches is between 19 and 23 inches at the withers, and any dog or bitch over 24 inches at the withers is to be disqualified.

MAJOR FAULTS

Butterfly or flesh-colored nose. Cowhocks. Flat feet. Lack of pigment in eye rims. Shyness. Trichiasis (abnormal position or direction of the eyelashes).

FAULTS

Ring or low-set tail. Undersize or oversize.

SCALE OF POINTS

Body, back, chest and loins 10	Head and eyes 10
Coat 5	Legs and feet 10
Color and markings 25	Neck and shoulders 10
Ears 5	Size, symmetry, etc. 10
Gait 10	Tail 5
	TOTAL 100

Representing the breed: Ch. Fobette's Fanfare, C.D.X., owned by Mr. and Mrs. Alfred E. Treen.

FRENCH BULLDOG

Authorities are of the opinion that the French Bulldog is strictly of French origin, yet they are willing to admit that in earlier years importations from England had been used as a cross with the native dog, and that this cross has led to a nearer approximation to the British type.

The chief difference between English and French Bulldogs is in the foreface, ears and front; in most other points the two breeds are very nearly identical. The body of the Frenchman should be short and rotund, with a distinct roach and light but sound quarters. His shoulders should be strong, and he should stand on short, fairly stout limbs for his size. He should be extremely agile, and indeed almost terrier-like in action and movement. The fundamental difference is seen in the foreface, which in the French should show some slight protrusion of the underjaw and some turn-up but no lay-back, which, through Bulldog optics, give the dog the appearance of being frogfaced. The eyes should be set far apart and a good distance shown between the eye and the ear, and the skull should be flat. The ears, of course, should be on the lines of the ears of a bat. The tail again, like that of the English variety, should be short, low set, and tapering to a point.

Buyer's guide: The French Bulldog has a fine temperament and will do well in any size housing. They retain their physical tone very easily, but should be allowed daily outings to keep them content in the home. They are quite personable and will get along with just about everyone—including young children and other animals. They tend to be very even tempered around children and enjoy watching over and entertaining them. Frenchies are small eaters and require very little in regard to grooming. They have nice, pleasant dispositions, and thrive on companionship.

STANDARD FOR THE FRENCH BULLDOG

General Appearance: The French Bulldog should have the appearance of an active, intelligent, muscular dog, of heavy bone, smooth coat, compactly built, and of medium or small structure. **Proportion and Symmetry:** The points should be well distributed and bear good relation one to the other, no feature being in such prominence from either excess or lack of quality that the animal appears deformed or poorly proportioned. **Influence of Sex:** In comparison of specimens of different sex, due allowance should be made in favor of the bitches, which do not bear the characteristics of the breed to the same marked degree as do the dogs.

Weight: A lightweight class under 22 pounds; heavyweight class, 22 pounds, and not over 28 pounds.

Head: The head should be large and square. The top of the skull should be flat between the ears; the forehead should not be flat but slightly rounded. The stop should be well defined, causing a hollow or groove between the eyes. The muzzle should be broad, deep and well laid back;

the muscles of the cheeks well developed. The nose should be extremely short; nostrils broad with well defined line between them. The nose and flews should be black, except in the case of the lighter-colored dogs, where a lighter color nose is acceptable. The flews should be thick and broad, hanging over the jaw at the sides, meeting the underlip in front and covering the teeth which should not be seen when the mouth is closed. The underjaw should be deep, square, broad, undershot and well turned up. **Eyes:** The eyes should be wide apart, set low down in the skull, as far from the ears as possible, round in form, of moderate size, neither sunken nor bulging, and in color dark. No haw and no white of the eye showing when looking forward.

Ears: The ears shall hereafter be known as the bat ear, broad at the base, elongated, with round top, set high on the head, but not too close together, and carried erect with the orifice to the front. The leather of the ear, fine and soft.

Neck: The neck should be thick and well arched, with loose skin at throat.

Body: The body should be short and well rounded. The chest, broad, deep and full, well ribbed with the belly tucked up. The back should be a roach back, with a slight fall close behind the shoulders. It should be strong and short, broad at the shoulders and narrowing at the loins.

Legs: The forelegs should be short, stout, straight and muscular, set wide apart. The hind leg should be strong and muscular, longer than the forelegs, so as to elevate the loins above the shoulders. Hocks well let down. **Feet:** The feet should be moderate in size, compact and firmly set. Toes compact, well split up, with high knuckles and short, stubby nails; hind feet slightly longer than forefeet.

Tail: The tail should be either straight or screwed (but not curly), short, hung low, thick root and fine tip; carried low in repose.

Color, Skin and Coat: Acceptable colors are: All brindle, fawn, white, brindle and white, and any color except those which constitute disqualification. The skin should be soft and loose, especially at head and shoulders, forming wrinkles. Coat moderately fine, brilliant, short and smooth.

SCALE OF POINTS

General Properties

Proportion and symmetry 5

Expression 5
Gait 4
Color 4
Coat 2 20

Head
Skull 6
Cheeks and chops 2
Stop 5
Ears 8
Eyes 4
Wrinkles 4
Nose 3
Jaws 6
Teeth 2 40

Body, Legs, etc.
Shoulders 5

Back 5
Neck 4
Chest 3
Ribs 4
Brisket 3
Belly 2
Forelegs 4
Hind legs 3
Feet 3
Tail 4 40

TOTAL 100

DISQUALIFICATIONS

Other than bat ears.

Black and white, black and tan, liver, mouse or solid black (black means black without any trace of brindle).

Eyes of different color.

Nose other than black, except in the case of the lighter-colored dogs, where a lighter color nose is acceptable.

Hare lip.

Any mutilation.

Over 28 pounds in weight.

APPROVED FEBRUARY 11, 1947

Representing the breed: Ch. Smith's Petit Maitre, owned by Abe and Suzi Segal.

KEESHOND

The Keeshond is an endearing breed that has flourished for several centuries primarily as loyal housepets and companions. They have been raised as members of the family and their gentle attitude and unmatched devotion to children are products of years of being "people dogs." The breed is descended from the same arctic strains that produced the Samoyed, Spitz and the Norwegian Elkhound, and the Keeshond is thought to have figured heavily in the ancestry of the tiny Pomeranian.

The breed was originally known as the Dutch Barge Dog, owing to the fact that the breed was used in Holland to guide the barges through the fog. Another common nickname for the Keeshond is "the smiling Dutchman," which stems from the alert expression and ever-present smile that seems to fill their face.

The breed's profuse gray and black coat stands away from the body and seems to impart the impression of great bulk. They are double-coated, with a soft, light colored undercoat and a dense, harsh outercoat that not only protects them from the extremes of weather but also repels dirt and resists matting. Despite their long hair, Keeshonden require relatively little grooming and an occasional brushing will keep the coat in fine condition.

The Keeshond will be most happy living wherever he can be around people. They make the most out of the amount of space they are given and naturally assume the role of watchdog for the area. A fenced in yard to romp and play in is ideal. They are acceptable and outgoing by nature and will readily accept anyone that their owners accept, but they will regard any intruder with force. Keeshonden have a travelling instinct and go willingly and enthusiastically on any journey or adventure, just as long as there is someone there to share the experience with!

Buyer's guide: The Keeshond is a dog that expects to be treated like one of the family, and is loyal and dependable in return. They take affectionately to children and will good-naturedly tolerate some childish abuse. They generally appear slightly larger than they actually are, owing to their lovely full coat, and do not need extensive exercising or large amounts of food. A daily brushing is advised to keep the coat tangle-free.

STANDARD FOR THE KEESHOND

General Appearance and Conformation: The Keeshond is a handsome dog, of a well-balanced, short-coupled body, attracting attention not only by his alert carriage and intelligent expression, but also by his luxurious coat, his richly plumed tail, well curled over his back, and by his foxlike face and head with small pointed ears. His coat is very thick round the neck, fore part of the shoulders and chest, forming a lionlike mane. His rump and hind legs, down to the hocks, are also thickly coated forming the characteristic "trousers." His head, ears and lower legs are covered with thick short hair.

The ideal height of fully matured dogs (over 2 years old), measured from top of withers to the ground, is: for males, 18 inches; bitches, 17 inches. However, size consideration should not outweigh that of type. When dogs are judged equal in type, the dog nearest the ideal height is to be preferred. Length of back from withers to rump should equal height as measured above.

Head: Expression: Expression is largely dependent on the distinctive characteristic called "spectacles"—a delicately penciled line slanting slightly upward from the outer corner of each eye to the lower corner of the ear, coupled with distinct markings and shadings forming short but expressive eyebrows. Markings (or shadings) on face and head must present a pleasing appearance, imparting to the dog an alert and intelligent expression. **Fault:** Absence of "spectacles."

Skull: The head should be well proportioned to the body, wedge-shaped when viewed from above. Not only in muzzle, but the whole head should give this impression when the ears are drawn back by covering the nape of the neck and the ears with one hand. Head in profile should exhibit a definite stop. **Fault:** Apple head, or absence of stop.

Muzzle: The muzzle should be dark in color and of medium length, neither coarse nor snipy, and well proportioned to the skull.

Mouth: The mouth should be neither overshot nor undershot. Lips should be black and closely meeting, not thick, coarse or sagging; and with no wrinkle at the corner of the mouth. **Faults:** Overshot or undershot.

Teeth: The teeth should be white, sound and strong (but discoloration from distemper not to penalize severely); upper teeth should just overlap the lower teeth.

Eyes: Eyes should be dark brown in color, of medium size, rather oblique in shape and not set too wide apart. **Fault:** Protruding round eyes or eyes light of color.

Ears: Ears should be small, triangular in shape, mounted high on head and carried erect; dark in color and covered with thick, velvety short hair. Size should be proportionate to the head—length approximating the distance from outer corner of the eye to the nearest edge of the ear. **Fault:** Ears not carried erect when at attention.

Body: Neck and Shoulders: The neck should be moderately long, well shaped and well set on shoulders; covered with a profuse mane, sweeping from under the jaw and covering the whole of the front part of the shoulders and chest, as well as the top part of the shoulders. **Chest, Back and Loin:** The body should be compact with a short straight back sloping slightly downward toward the hindquarters; well ribbed, barrel well rounded, belly moderately tucked up, deep and strong of chest.

Legs: Forelegs should be straight seen from any angle and well feathered. Hind legs should be perfectly feathered down to the hocks—not below, with hocks only slightly bent. Legs must be of good bone and cream in color. **Fault:** Black markings below the knee, penciling expected.

Feet: The feet should be compact, well rounded, catlike, and cream in color. Toes are nicely arched, with black nails. *Fault:* White foot or feet.

Tail: The tail should be set on high, moderately long, and well feathered, tightly curled over back. It should lie flat and close to the body with a very light gray plume on top where curled, but the tip of the tail should be black. The tail should form a part of the "silhouette" of the dog's body, rather than give the appearance of an appendage. *Fault:* Tail not lying close to the back.

Action: Dogs should show boldly and keep tails curled over the back. They should move cleanly and briskly; and the movement should be straight and sharp (not lope like a German Shepherd). *Fault:* Tail not carried over back when moving.

Coat: The body should be abundantly covered with long, straight, harsh hair; standing well out from a thick, downy undercoat. The hair on the legs should be smooth and short, except for a feathering on the front legs and "trousers," as previously described, on the hind legs. The hair on the tail should be profuse, forming a rich plume. Head, including muzzle, skull and ears, should be covered with smooth, soft, short hair—velvety in texture on the ears. Coat must not part down the back. *Fault:* Silky, wavy or curly coats. Part in coat down the back.

Color and Markings: A mixture of gray and black. The undercoat should be very pale gray or cream (not tawny). The hair of the outer coat is black tipped, the length of the black tips producing the characteristic shading of color. The color may vary from light to dark, but any pronounced deviation from the gray color is not permissible. The plume of the tail should be very light gray when curled on back, and the tip of the tail should be black. Legs and feet should be cream. Ears should be very dark—almost black. Shoulder line markings (light gray) should be well defined. The color of the ruff and "trousers" is generally lighter than that of the body. "Spectacles" and shadings, as previously described, are characteristic of the breed and must be present to some degree. There should be no pronounced white markings. *Very Serious Faults:* Entirely black or white or any other solid color; any pronounced deviation from the gray color.

SCALE OF POINTS

General conformation and appearance 20
Head

Shape 6
Eyes 5
Ears 5
Teeth 4   20

Body
Chest, back and loin
.....................10
Tail 10
Neck and shoulders
.....................8

Legs 4
Feet 3 35
Coat 15
Color and markings 10
TOTAL 100

APPROVED JULY 12, 1949

Representing the breed: Eng., Am., Can. Ch. Wrocky of Wistonia, owned by Mr. and Mrs. Porter Washington and bred by Fred and Nan Greenwood.

LHASA APSO

In earliest times, Lhasa Apsos lived within the palaces of the Dalai Lama as the chosen pets of Tibetan nobility. Anyone acquainted with the breed today will surely attest that time has only served to enhance the affectionate, congenial nature of this most revered "little lion dog." *Apso Seng Kye*, (translated to Bark Sentinel Lion Dog in English), is the title by which the breed is known in their homeland. These hardy little dogs date back to 800 B.C. and have been revered as bringers of good luck by all who were fortunate enough to come in contact with them. Raised in monasteries by religious leaders, the Lhasa Apso was guarded and nurtured; although dogs would sometimes be presented to visiting dignitaries as honored guests or symbols of good will and thanks, the little lion dogs were never sold or widely bred. The mountainous and isolated land of Tibet provided a haven for this breed to mature and develop the aristocratic temperament that is so much a characteristic of the breed today.

The Lhasa Apso's most distinctive physical trait is their flowing, profuse coat which if properly cared for will fall straight to the ground without wave or curl. The hair around the head and eyes adds to the oriental look of the breed, the moustache and goatee being especially attractive. This heavy coat greatly aids the Lhasa Apso in surviving the extremes of weather that are common to the high, mountainous altitudes of their homeland.

Lhasa Apsos are extremely personable animals, who, if given their way, will sleep alongside their masters each night to watch for any signs of danger. They make excellent housedogs and are healthy and energetic. Happy by nature, the Lhasa Apso can be quite aloof to strangers, but once the wariness wears off they are entertaining and hospitable. Lhasa Apsos are obedient and quick to learn what is expected of them and will fit well in both city and country environments.

Buyer's guide: The aloof air of the Lhasa Apso just enhances their charm. While generally stand-offish to strangers, they are very affectionate and joyful with the ones they love. Daily brushing is a must, as their coat must be taken good care of in order for it to look up to its full potential. Lhasas are full of life and make the most out of whatever household they are in, adapting their daily routine to the space they are alloted. They should not need any supplementary exercise to retain tone. Lhasas are recommended for adults who like to lavish attention on their dogs.

STANDARD FOR THE LHASA APSO

Character: Gay and assertive, but chary of strangers.

Size: Variable, but about 10 inches or 11 inches at shoulder for dogs, bitches slightly smaller.

Color: All colors equally acceptable with or without dark tips to ears and beard.

Body: The length from point of shoulders to point of buttocks longer than height at withers, well ribbed up, strong loin, well-developed quarters and thighs.

Coat: Heavy, straight, hard, not woolly nor silky, of good length, and very dense.

Mouth and Muzzle: The preferred bite is either level or slightly undershot. Muzzle of medium length; a square muzzle is objectionable.

Head: Heavy head furnishings with good fall over eyes, good whiskers and beard; skull narrow, falling away behind the eyes in a marked degree, not quite flat, but not domed or apple-shaped; straight foreface of fair length. Heavy head furnishings with good fall over eyes, good whiskers and beard; skull narrow, falling away behind eyes in a marked degree, not quite flat, but not domed or apple-shaped; straight foreface of fair length. Nose black, the length from tip of nose to eye to be roughly about one-third of the total length from nose to back of skull.

Eyes: Dark brown, neither very large and full, nor very small and sunk.

Ears: Pedant, heavily feathered.

Legs: Forelegs straight; both forelegs and hind legs heavily furnished with hair.

Feet: Well feathered, should be round and catlike, with good pads.

Tail and Carriage: Well feathered, should be carried well over back in a screw; there may be a kink at the end. A low carriage of stern is a serious fault.

APPROVED APRIL 9, 1935

POODLE

The Poodle is naturally a sporting dog, and was formally used for that purpose. No dog surpasses him as a retriever from the water, and he is still used for that purpose in Europe. The breed is well distributed the world over, and there are Russian and German Poodles, as well as those of France, which is generally considered their native home. There are three recognized varieties, separated by size.

No dog surpasses the Poodle in intelligence; in fact, no dog is his equal, and he is best known to the public as a cherished pet or the star artist in companies of performing dogs. He has a quality of

MINIATURE POODLE

STANDARD POODLE

mind that borders on the human; his reasoning powers are evident to all with whom he is associated, and there is apparently no limit to his aptitude for learning. Although considerable attention is needed to keep their coat in show condition, in all other respects they require no more attention than other dogs. All who are familiar with the breed are firm in their belief that no dog is so interesting a companion.

The Poodle is usually seen clipped, the pattern varying with the tastes of the owner and the age of the dog. It is the rule to shave the face, legs and loins, with the exception of tufts of hair here and there, and foster a lion-like mane and body covering. If the Poodle is active in show competition, either the Puppy, English or Continental clip must be worn.

Buyer's guide: Poodles are extremely intelligent and responsive to their owners. They are happiest when they have plenty of human companionship and are quite loyal to those they love. Standards are quite large and need plenty of space and exercise to keep them happy and healthy; miniatures require much less in regards to space and outside exercise. All varieties will need considerable grooming, with a 10 minute per day brushing as a minimum and at least six trips to the grooming parlor a year. On the whole, Poodles do not take very kindly to small children and much prefer the company of the mature adult. They are quick learners and do very well in obedience competition, besides being an inherently clean dog. They do not shed. Do not own a Poodle unless you can give them plenty of attention, as they tend to get nervous and yappy if left alone for too long a time.

STANDARD FOR THE POODLE

General Appearance, Carriage and Condition: That of a very active, intelligent and elegant-appearing dog, squarely built, well proportioned, moving soundly and carrying himself proudly. Properly clipped in the traditional fashion and carefully groomed, the Poodle has about him an air of distinction and dignity peculiar to himself.

Head and Expression: **(a) Skull:** Moderately rounded, with a slight but definite stop. Cheekbones and muscles flat. Length from occiput to stop about the same as length of muzzle. **(b) Muzzle:** Long, straight and fine, with slight chiseling under the eyes. Strong without lippiness. The chin definite enough to preclude snipiness. Teeth white, strong, and with a scissors bite. **(c) Eyes:** Very dark, oval in shape and set far enough apart and positioned to create an alert intelligent expression. **(d) Ears:** Hanging close to the head, set at or slightly below eye level. The ear leather is long, wide, and thickly feathered; however, the ear fringe should not be of excessive length.

Neck and Shoulders: Neck well proportioned, strong and long enough to permit the head to be carried high and with dignity. Skin snug at throat. The neck rises from strong, smoothly muscled shoulders. The shoulder blade is well laid back and approximately the same length as the upper foreleg.

Body: To insure the desirable squarely-built appearance, the length of body measured from the breastbone to the point of the rump approximates the height from the highest point of the shoulders to the ground. **(a) Chest:** Deep and moderately wide with well sprung ribs. **(b) Back:** The topline is level, neither sloping nor roached, from the highest point of the shoulder blade to the base of the tail, with the exception of a slight hollow just behind the shoulder. The loin is short, broad, and muscular.

Tail: Straight, set on high and carried up, docked of sufficient length to insure a balanced outline.

Legs: (a) Forelegs: Straight and parallel when viewed from the front. When viewed from the side the elbow is directly below the highest point of the shoulder. The pasterns are strong. Bone and muscle of both forelegs and hindlegs are in proportion to size of dog. **(b) Hindlegs:** Straight and parallel when viewed from the rear. Muscular with width in the region of the stifles which are well bent; femur and tibia are about equal in length; hock to heel short and perpendicular to the ground. When standing, the rear toes are only slightly behind the point of rump. The angulation of the hindquarters balances that of the forequarters.

Feet: The feet are rather small, oval in shape with toes well arched and cushioned on thick firm pads. Nails short but not excessively shortened. The feet turn neither in nor out. Dewclaws may be removed.

Coat: (a) Quality: (1) curly: of naturally harsh texture, dense throughout. (2) corded: hanging in tight even cords. **(b) Clip:** A Poodle under 12 months may be shown in the "Puppy" clip. In all regular classes, Poodles 12 months or over must be shown in the "English Saddle" or "Continental" clip. In the Stud Dog and Brood Bitch classes and in a non-competitive Parade of Champions, Poodles may be shown in the "Sporting" clip. A Poodle shown in any other type of clip shall be disqualified. (1) "Puppy": A Poodle under a year old may be shown in the "Puppy" clip with the coat long. The face, throat, feet and base of the tail are shaved. The entire shaven foot is visible. There is a pompon on the end of the tail. In order to give a neat appearance and a smooth unbroken line, shaping of the coat is permissible. (2) "English Saddle": In the "English Saddle" clip, the face, throat, feet, forelegs and base of the tail are shaved, leaving puffs on the forelegs and a pompon on the end of the tail. The hindquarters are covered with a short blanket of hair except for a curved shaved area on each flank and two shaved bands on each hindleg. The entire shaven foot and a portion of the shaven leg above the puff are visible. The rest of the body is left in full coat but may be shaped in order to insure overall balance. (3) "Continental": In the "Continental" clip the face, throat, feet, and base of the tail are shaved. The hindquarters are shaved with pompons (optional) on the hips. The legs are shaved, leaving bracelets on the hindlegs and puffs on the forelegs. There is a pompon on the end of the tail. The entire shaven foot and a portion of the shaven foreleg above the puff are visible. The rest of the body is left in full coat but may be shaped in order to insure overall balance. (4) "Sporting": In the "Sporting" clip a Poodle shall be shown with face, feet, throat, and base of tail shaved, leaving a scissored cap on the top of the head and a pompon on the end of the tail. The rest of the body and legs are clipped or scissored to follow the outline of the dog leaving a short blanket of coat no longer than one inch in length. The hair on the legs may be slightly longer than that on the body.

In all clips the hair of the topknot may be left free or held in place by no more than three elastic bands. The hair is only of sufficient length to present a smooth outline. **Color:** The coat is an even and solid color at the skin. In blues, grays, silvers, browns, cafe-au-laits, apricots and creams the coat may show varying shades of the same color. This is frequently present in the somewhat darker feathering of the ears and in the tipping of the ruff. While clear colors are definitely preferred, such natural variation in the shading of the coat is not to be considered a fault. Brown and cafe-au-lait Poodles have liver-colored noses, eye-rims and lips, dark toenails and dark amber eyes. Black, blue, gray, silver, cream and white Poodles have black noses, eye-rims and lips, black or self colored toenails and very dark eyes. In the apricots while the foregoing coloring is preferred, liver-colored noses, eye-rims and lips, and amber eyes are permitted but are not desirable.

Parti-colored dogs shall be disqualified. The coat of a parti-colored dog is not an even solid color at the skin but is of two or more colors.

Gait: A straightforward trot with light springy action and strong hindquarters drive. Head and tail carried up. Sound effortless movement is essential.

Size: The Standard Poodle is over 15 inches at the highest point of the shoulders. Any Poodle which is 15 inches or less in height shall be disqualified from competition as a Standard Poodle.

The Miniature Poodle is 15 inches or under at the highest point of the shoulders, with a minimum height in excess of 10 inches. Any Poodle which is over 15 inches or is 10 inches or less at the highest point of the shoulders shall be disqualified from competition as a Miniature Poodle.

The Toy Poodle is 10 inches or under at the highest point of the shoulders. Any Poodle which is more than 10 inches at the highest point of the shoulders shall be disqualified from competition as a Toy Poodle.

VALUE OF POINTS

General appearance, temperament, carriage and condition 30
Head, expression, ears, eyes and teeth 20
Body, neck, legs, feet and tail 20
Gait 20
Coat, color and texture 10

Major Faults

Any distinct deviation from the desired characteristics described in the Breed Standard with particular attention to the following:

Temperament: Shyness or sharpness.
Muzzle: Undershot, overshot, wry mouth, lack of chin.
Eyes: Round, protruding, large, or very light.
Pigment: Color of nose, lips and eye rims incomplete, or of wrong color for color of dog.
Neck and Shoulders: Ewe neck, steep shoulders.
Tail: Set low, curled, or carried over the back.
Hindquarters: Cow hocks.
Feet: Paper or splayfoot.

Disqualifications

Clip: *A dog in any type of clip other than those listed shall be disqualified.*
Parti-colors: *The coat of a parti-colored dog is not an even solid color at the skin but is of two or more colors. Parti-colored dogs shall be disqualified.*
Size: *A dog over or under the height limits specified shall be disqualified.*

Representing the Standard: Ch. Alekai Aphrodite, owned by Mr. and Mrs. Terrence Levy. Miniature: Ch. Puttencove Gay Valentino, owned by the Puttencove Kennels.

SCHIPPERKE

The Schipperke comes from Belgium, where he is the popular watch dog of the barges used on Flemish canals. There is a ledge one foot wide that runs about the canal boats a short distance from the top. Here the Schipperke (pronounced Skip-per-ke, the Flemish for little skipper) spends his time. He is trained to race around this ledge, acting as guard and sentinel, an office for which he is particularly well fitted, as he is the most wide awake, liveliest, and inquisitive of canines. The slightest noise attracts his attention, and he never neglects to investigate the cause.

The Schipperke is always shown tailless. It was decreed on the canal boat many years ago that the presence of the tail prevented the Schipperke from turning on the narrow ledge as rapidly as he could without it. Occasionally, it was said, his tail precipitated him into the water, and as a result a systematic docking was decreed. Continued for years, docking has had its influence upon the caudal appendage, for some are now born tailless and others have only a stump. Those born with normal tails are docked. This operation should be performed by a skillful veterinarian, as the whole tail is removed, a much more delicate operation than the case in the docking of terriers.

The Schipperke is a very good water dog and does not mind a dunking in the least. He is also a first-class ratter.

There is no limit to his prying liveliness. They are bright, smart, and very affectionate, so much as to be usually intensely jealous. While they constitute themselves guardians of the household, they usually select one member of the family as their particular property, and to them devote the greater part of their attention.

Buyer's guide: The lively Schipperke is a good dog for those people who appreciate an active dog but prefer the convenience of a compact size. They are good companions for adults and children alike and they delight in a spirited round of play. Grooming, exercise and feed requirements are quite minimal and they will do well in any size housing, provided that they have plenty of room to move about in. They have very nice personalities and temperaments.

STANDARD FOR THE SCHIPPERKE

Appearance and General Characteristics: Excellent and faithful little watchdog, suspicious of strangers. Active, agile, indefatigable, continually occupied with what is going on around him, careful of things that are given him to guard, very kind with children, knows the ways of the household; always curious to know what is going on behind closed doors or about any object that has been moved, betraying his impressions by his sharp bark and upstanding ruff, seeking the company of horses, a hunter of moles and other vermin; can be used to hunt, a good rabbit dog.

Color: Solid black.

Head: Foxlike, fairly wide, narrowing at the eyes, seen in profile slightly rounded, tapering muzzle not too elongated nor too blunt, not too much stop.

Nose: Small and black. *Eyes:* Dark brown, small, oval rather than round, neither sunken nor prominent. *Expression:* Should have a questioning expression: sharp and lively, not mean or wild. *Ears:* Very erect, small, triangular, placed high, strong enough not to be capable of being lowered except in line with the body. *Teeth:* Meeting evenly. A tight scissors bite is acceptable.

Neck: Strong and full, slightly arched, rather short.
Shoulders: Muscular and sloping.
Chest: Broad and deep in brisket.
Body: Short, thick-set and cobby. Broad behind the shoulders, seeming higher in front because of ruff. Back strong, short, straight and level or slightly sloping down toward rump. Ribs well sprung. **Loins:** Muscular and well drawn up from the brisket but not to such an extent as to cause a weak and leggy appearance of the hindquarters. **Forelegs:** Straight under body, with bone in proportion, but not coarse. **Hindquarters:** Somewhat lighter than the fore-parts, but muscular, powerful, with rump well rounded, tail docked to no more than 1 inch in length. **Feet:** Small, round and tight (not splayed), nails straight, strong and short.
Coat: Abundant and slightly harsh to the touch, short on the ears and on the front of legs and on the hocks, fairly short on the body, but longer around neck beginning back of the ears, and forming a ruff and cape; a jabot extending down between the front legs, also longer on rear where it forms a culotte, the points turning inward. Undercoat dense and short on body, very dense around neck making ruff stand out. Culotte should be as long as the ruff.
Weight: Up to 18 pounds.

FAULTS

Light eyes; large round prominent eyes; ears too long or too rounded; narrow head and elongated muzzle; too blunt muzzle; domed skull; smooth short coat with short ruff and culotte; lack of undercoat; curly or silky coat; body coat more than three (3) inches long; slightly overshot or undershot; swayback; Bull Terrier shaped head; straight hocks. Straight stifles and shoulders; cowhocks; feet turning in or out; legs not straight when viewed from front. Lack of distinction between length of coat, ruff and culotte.

DISQUALIFICATIONS

Any color other than solid black.
Drop or semi-erect ears.
Badly overshot or undershot.

APPROVED MAY 12, 1959

Representing the breed: Ch. Jetstar's Command Performance, owned by William H. Raines, Jr.

TIBETAN TERRIER

Few breeds enjoy as romantic a history as the Tibetan Terrier. These dogs can be traced back over 2000 years to the Lost Valley of Tibet, an area of the country to which all access was destroyed by an earthquake 600 years ago. Tibetan Terriers were raised solely by the Dalai Lamas that lived in the monasteries of the area, and were seldom seen by outsiders. The dogs were closely guarded but were sometimes presented to visiting dignitaries or to people of the area that were about to embark on a hazardous journey through the Tibetan mountainsides. Tibetan Terriers have been called the Holy Dog of Tibet, Luck Bringers and Little People; all these names attest to the high esteem the dogs were regarded with.

Tibetan Terriers have been bred true throughout their history because people that were honored enough to own these dogs would not chance a mismating. Such a deed was considered as a bad omen, breaking the luck that they had been privileged enough to own. The dogs were never sold, as the owner would be selling away his own good fortune.

The first export of Tibetan Terriers was in the early 1920's when a grateful Tibetan gave a pair of dogs to a physician from England who had cared for his family. With this the first kennel of Tibetan Terriers outside of their native land was established. It wasn't until 1956 that these dogs reached the United States, and their rise in popularity continued steadily until the breed was officially admitted to the Non-Sporting group by the American Kennel Club in 1973. Although their name includes the title *terrier*, this name was given to them in regard to their body size, not for an ability to go to the ground or because they have the feisty temperament of a terrier.

The profusely coated Tibetan Terrier has often been likened to a miniature Old English Sheepdog. The Tibetan, however, has a tail which they carry curled over their back. They are square in proportion, the body being the same distance from the withers to the root of the tail as it is from the withers to the ground. They have a small beard on their chin and their hair covers the entire face. Despite outward appearances, the Tibetan Terrier's long eyelashes help hold the hair away from the eyes, thus enabling the dog to see. Their coat is double with a fine layer of wooly hair and a long, protective outer coat. The breed is exceptionally hardy, able to withstand the extremes of any climate, and they are very long-lived.

The Tibetan Terrier is a pleasure to have around the house and has enjoyed a history of being a treasured companion and friend. He is an alert and jolly fellow whose faithfulness has won him many devoted fanciers. If given a choice, Tibetans prefer to remain around their home, close to the people dearest to them. They do not take quickly to strangers and are natural watchdogs. This breed has been unspoiled by time and owners today are indeed to be considered fortunate to own one of these lovely "little people."

Buyer's guide: Tibetans make good companion pets—trustworthy enough to play with children and dignified and placid enough to live peaceably in the home. They are very affectionate and are most happy when included in all family activities. Tibetans need routine combing and brushing to keep their coat from snarling, but unlike many breeds, they thoroughly enjoy this grooming process. Although they can be quite headstrong when puppies, patiently applied obedience training will be readily accepted and practiced by the Tibetan. They are fundamentally housedogs, but should be allowed to exercise properly. Confinement may tend to make their disposition sharp, so if you are away from home for considerable lengths of time, the Tibetan Terrier is not the dog for you.

STANDARD FOR THE TIBETAN TERRIER

Skull and Head: Skull of medium length, not broad or coarse, narrowing slightly from ear to eye, not domed but not absolutely flat between the ears. The malar bones are curved, but should not be overdeveloped so as to bulge. There should be a marked stop in front of the eyes, but this must not be exaggerated. The head should be well furnished with long hair, falling forward over the eyes. The lower jaws should carry a small but not over-exaggerated amount of beard. Jaws between the canines should form a distinct curve. The length from the eye to tip of nose should be equal to that from eye to base of skull, not broad or massive.

Nose: Black. Any color other than black shall disqualify.

Eyes: Large, dark, neither prominent nor sunken; should be set fairly wide apart. Eyelids dark.

Ears: Pendant, not too close to the head, "V" shaped, not too large; heavily feathered.

Mouth: Level by preference but a slight undershot should not be penalized.

Forequarters: Legs straight, heavily furnished.

Body: Compact and powerful. Length from point of shoulder to root of tail equal to height at withers. Well ribbed up. Loin slightly arched.

Hindquarters: Heavily furnished, hocks well let down.

Feet: The feet should be large, round, and heavily furnished with hair between the toes and pads. The dog should stand well down on its pads.

Tail: Medium length, set on fairly high and carried in a gay curl over the back. Very well feathered. There is often a kink near the tip.

Coat: Double-coated. The undercoat fine wool, the top coat profuse, fine, but not silky or woolly; long; either straight or waved.

Color: Any color or colors including white.

Weight and Size: Average weight 22 to 23 pounds, but may be 18 to 30 pounds. Height from 14 to 16 inches.

Faults: Poor coat; mouth very undershot or overshot; a weak snipy foreface.

DISQUALIFICATION
Nose any color other than black.

APPROVED JUNE 12, 1973

Representing the breed: Ch. Legs-Pa Changthang, C.D., owned by Dr. and Mrs. F.H. Corcoran and bred by L.Y. Postman.

DOG CARE

A guide to health care, training, breeding and showing

THE NEW PUPPY

PREPARING FOR THE PUPPY'S ARRIVAL

In choosing a puppy, be certain beforehand that each member of the family is truly enthusiastic about having this particular breed of dog as an addition to their circle. Dogs are much too intelligent not to sense whether or not they are liked. If your puppy feels unwanted, you may find an unhappy dog on your hands that could easily turn into a "problem child." Before buying, research the breed and make sure it is the one for you. Besides reading, a good way to learn about your prospective pet is to observe one of the same breed in its permanent home surroundings. Most owners will be only too happy to show off their furry friend.

One of the most important factors to consider when selecting a dog, whether it is to be a pet or show dog, is its temperament. When looking at a litter of puppies for a prospective purchase, spend time just quietly observing them. Usually the most outgoing or aggressive puppy is your best bet. However, do not overlook the more reserved puppy. Most dogs are wary of strangers, so reserve may indicate caution, not timidity. He may calmly accept your presence when he senses that all is well. In any event, never force yourself on a puppy—let him come to you. Beware of the puppy that hides in the corner and won't emerge until you have left. Chances are he will always be high-strung and may develop more undesirable habits as a result of his nervousness.

Because at least three out of four prospective purchasers of dogs want to buy a young rather than an adult or almost adult dog, the problem of preparing for the arrival of a permanent canine house guest almost always means preparing for the arrival of a puppy. This is not to say that there is anything wrong with purchasing an adult dog; on the contrary, such a purchase has definite advantages in that it often allows freedom from housebreaking chores and rigorous feeding schedules, and these are a definite benefit to prospective purchasers who have little time to spare. Since the great majority of dog buyers, however, prefer to watch their pet grow from sprawlingly playful puppyhood to dignified maturity, buying a dog, practically speaking, means buying a puppy. Before you get a puppy be sure that you are willing to take the responsibility of training him and caring for his physical needs. His early training is most important, as an adult dog that is a well-behaved member of the family is the end product of your early training. Remember that your new puppy knows only a life of romping with his littermates and the security of being with his mother, and that coming into your home is a new and sometimes frightening experience for him. He will adjust quickly if you are patient with him and show him what you expect of him. If there are small children in the family be sure that they do not abuse him or play roughly with him. A puppy plays hard, but he also requires frequent periods of rest. Before he comes, decide where he is to sleep and where he is to eat. If your puppy does not have a collar, find out the size he requires and buy an inexpensive one, as he will soon outgrow it. Have the proper grooming equipment on hand. Consult the person from whom you bought the puppy as to the proper food for your puppy, and learn the feeding time and amount that he eats a day. Buy him some toys—usually the breeder will give you some particular toy or toys which he has cherished as a puppy to add to his new ones and to make him less homesick. Get everything you need from your pet shop before you bring the puppy home.

MALE OR FEMALE?

Before buying your puppy you should have made a decision as to whether you want a male or female. Unless you want to breed your pet and raise a litter of puppies, your preference as to the sex of your puppy is strictly a personal choice. On the whole both sexes are pretty much the same in disposition and character, and both make equally good pets.

SHOW DOG OR PET?

It is well to define in your own mind the purpose for which you want a dog, and to convey this to the breeder. A great deal of disappointment and dissatisfaction can be avoided by a meeting of the minds between seller and buyer.

Although every well-bred healthy member of the breed makes an ideal companion and pet, actual pet stock is usually the least expensive of the purebred registered stock. The person who asks for a pet, pays a pet-geared price for the animal. Pet stock is least expensive because these dogs are deemed unsuitable for breeding or exhibition in comparison to the standard of perfection for the breed. Generally only skilled breeders and judges can point out the structural differences between a pet and show quality dog.

If you are planning to show your dog, make this clear to the breeder and he will aid you in selecting the best possible specimen of the breed. A show quality dog may be more expensive than one meant for a pet, but it will be able to stand up to show ring competition.

WHERE TO BUY YOUR PUPPY

Once you have decided on the particular breed that you want for your pet, your task is to find that one special dog from among several outlets. Buying a well-bred, healthy dog is your foremost concern. By doing a little research in the various dog magazines and newspapers you can locate the names and addresses of breeders and kennels in your area that are known for breeding quality animals. The American Kennel Club will also furnish you with addresses of people to contact that are knowledgeable about your chosen breed.

Your local pet shop, although necessarily restricted from carrying all breeds in stock, may sometimes be able to supply quality puppies on demand. Due to the exorbitant amount of space and time needed to properly rear puppies, pet shops generally prefer to assist owners by supplying all the tools and equipment needed in the raising and training of the puppies. The pet shop proprietor, if unable to obtain a dog for you, can often refer you to a reputable kennel with which he has done business before.

SIGNS OF GOOD HEALTH

Picking out a healthy, attractive little fellow to join the family circle is a different matter from picking a show dog: it is also a great deal less complicated. Often the puppy will pick you. If he does, and it is mutual admiration at first sight, he is the best puppy for you. Trust your eyes and hands to tell if the puppy is sound in body and temperament. Ears and eyes should not have suspicious discharges. Legs should have strong bones; bodies should have solid muscles. Coats should be clean. Lift the hair to see that the skin is free of scales and parasites.

Reliable breeders and pet shops will urge you to take your puppy to the veterinarian of your choice to have the puppy's health checked, and will allow you at least two days to have it done. It should be clearly understood whether rejection by a veterinarian for health reasons means that you have the choice of another puppy from that litter or that you get your money back.

PAPERS

When you buy a purebred dog you should receive his American Kennel Club registration certificate (or an application form to fill out), a pedigree and a health certificate made out by the breeder's veterinarian. The registration certificate is the official A.K.C. paper. If the puppy was named and registered by his breeder you will want to complete the transfer and send it, with the appropriate fee, to the American Kennel Club. They will transfer the dog to your ownership in their records and send you a new certificate. If you receive, instead, an application for registration, you should fill it out choosing a name for your dog, and mail it, with the fee, to the A.K.C.

The pedigree is a chart showing your puppy's ancestry and is not a part of his official papers. The health certificate will tell what shots have been given and when the next ones are due. Your veterinarian will be appreciative of this information, and will continue with the same series of shots, if they have not been completed. The health certificate will also give the date on which the puppy has been wormed.

REGISTERING YOUR PUPPY

For information on how to register a new litter of pedigreed dogs owners may write to the following:

American Kennel Club
51 Madison Ave.
New York, N.Y. 10010

Canadian Kennel Club
111 Eglinton Avenue East
Toronto 12, Ontario
Canada

Australian Kennel Club
Royal Show Grounds
Ascot Vale, Victoria
Australia

British Kennel Club
1 Clarges Street
Picadilly, London W.1
England

THE PUPPY'S FIRST NIGHT WITH YOU

The puppy's first night at home is likely to be disturbing to the family. Keep in mind that suddenly being away from his mother, brothers and sisters is a new experience for him; he may be confused and frightened. If you have a special room in which you have his bed, be sure that there is nothing there with which he can harm himself. Be sure that all lamp cords are out of his reach and that there is nothing that he can tip or pull over. Check furniture that he might get stuck under or behind and objects that he might chew. If you want him to sleep in your room he probably will be quiet all night, reassured by your presence. If left in a room by himself he will cry and howl, and you will have to steel yourself to be impervious to his whining. After a few nights alone he should adjust. The first night that he is alone it is wise to put a loud-ticking alarm clock, as well as his toys, in the room with him. The alarm clock will make a comforting noise, and he will not feel that he is alone.

YOUR PUPPY'S BED

Every dog likes to have a place that is his alone. He holds nothing more sacred than his own bed whether it be a rug, dog crate, or dog bed. If you get your puppy a bed be sure to get one which discourages chewing. Also be sure that the bed is large enough to be comfortable for him when he is full grown. Locate it away from drafts and radiators. A word might be said here in defense of the crate, which many pet owners think is cruel and confining. Given a choice, a young dog instinctively selects a secure place in which to lounge, rest or sleep. The walls and ceiling of a crate, even a wire one, answer that need. Once he regards his crate as a safe and reassuring place to stay, you will be able to leave him alone in the house.

FEEDING YOUR PUPPY

At the time of purchase, most breeders will give you food for a few days, along with instructions for feeding so that your puppy will have the same diet he is accustomed to until you can buy a supply at your pet shop.

As a general rule, a puppy from weaning time (six weeks) to three months of age should be fed four meals a day; from three months to six months, three meals; from six months to one year, two meals. After a year, a dog does well on one meal daily. There are as many feeding schedules as there are breeders, and puppies do fine on all of them, so it is best for the new owner to follow the one given him by the breeder of his puppy. Remember that all dogs are individuals. The amount that will keep your dog in good health is right for him, not the "rule book" amount. A feeding schedule to give you some idea of what the average puppy will eat is as follows:

Morning meal: Puppy meal with milk.
Afternoon meal: Meat mixed with puppy meal, plus a vitamin-mineral supplement.
Evening meal: Same as afternoon meal, but without a vitamin-mineral supplement.

Do not change the amounts in your puppy's diet too rapidly. If he gets diarrhea it may be that he is eating too much, so cut back on his food and when he is normal again increase his food more slowly.

There is a canned food made especially for puppies which you can buy with a veterinarian's prescription, and several commercially prepared products. Some breeders use this method very successfully from weaning to three months.

TRANSITIONAL DIET

Changing over to an adult program of feeding is not difficult. Very often the puppy will change himself: that is, he will refuse to eat some of his meals. He'll adjust to his one meal (or two meals) a day without any trouble at all.

BREAKING TO COLLAR AND LEASH

Puppies are usually broken to a collar before you bring them home, but even if yours has never worn one it is a simple matter to get him used to it. Put a loose collar on him for a few hours. At first he may scratch at it and try to get it off, but gradually he will take it as a matter of course. To break him to a lead, attach his leash to his collar and let him drag it around. When he becomes used to it pick it up and gently pull him in the direction you want him to go. He will think it is a game, and with a bit of patience on your part he will allow himself to be led.

DISCIPLINING YOUR PUPPY

The way to have a well-mannered adult dog is to give him firm basic training while he is a puppy. When you say "No" you must mean "No." Your dog will respect you only if you are firm. A six-to eight-week-old puppy is old enough to understand what "No" means. The first time you see your puppy doing something he shouldn't be doing, chewing something he shouldn't chew or wandering in a forbidden area, it's time to teach him. Say "No" firmly. Usually a firm "No" in a disapproving tone of voice is enough to correct your dog, but occasionally you get a puppy that requires a firmer hand, especially as he grows older. In this case hold your puppy firmly and slap him gently across the hindquarters. If this seems cruel, you should realize that no dog resents being disciplined if he is caught in the act of doing something wrong, and your puppy will be intelligent enough to know what the slap was for.

After you have slapped him and you can see that he has learned his lesson, call him to you and talk to him in a pleasant tone of voice—praise him for coming to you. This sounds contradictory, but it works with a puppy. He immediately forgives you, practically tells you that it was his fault and that he deserved his punishment, and promises that it will not happen again. This form of discipline works best and may be used for all misbehaviors.

Never punish your puppy by chasing him around, making occasional swipes with a rolled-up newspaper: punish him only when you have a firm hold on him. Above all, never punish you dog after having called him to you. He must learn to associate coming to you with something pleasant.

HOUSEBREAKING

While housebreaking your puppy, do not let him have the run of the house. If you do you will find that he will pick out his own bathroom, which may be in your bedroom or in the middle of the living room rug. Keep him confined to a small area where you can watch him, and you will be able to train him much more easily and speedily. A puppy does not want to dirty his bed, but he does need to be taught where he should go. Spread papers over his living quarters, then watch him carefully. When you notice him starting to whimper, sniff the floor or run agitatedly in little circles, rush him to the place that you want to serve as his relief area and gently hold him there until he relieves himself. Then praise him lavishly. When you remove the soiled papers, leave a small damp piece so that the puppy's sense of smell will lead him back there next time. If he makes a mistake, wash the area at once with warm water, followed by a rinse with water and vinegar or sudsy ammonia. This will kill the odor and prevent discoloration. It shouldn't take more than a few days for him to get the idea of using newspapers. When he becomes fairly consistent, reduce the area of paper to a few sheets in a corner. As soon as you think he has the idea fixed in his mind, you can let him roam around the house a bit, but keep an eye on him. It might be best to keep him on a leash the first few days so that you can rush him back to his paper at any signs of an approaching accident.

The normal healthy puppy will want to relieve himself when he wakes up in the morning, after each feeding and after strenuous exercise. During early puppyhood any excitement, such as the return home of a member of the family or the approach of a visitor, may result in floor-wetting, but that phase should pass in a few weeks. Keep in mind that you can't expect too much from your puppy until he is about five months old. Before that, his muscles and digestive system just aren't under his control.

OUTDOOR HOUSEBREAKING

You can begin outdoor training on a leash even while you are paper-training your puppy. First thing in the morning take him outdoors (to the curb, if you are in the city) and walk him back and forth in a small area until he relieves himself. He will probably make a puddle and then walk around, uncertain of what is expected of him. You can try standing him over a newspaper, which may give him the idea. Praise your dog every time taking him outside brings results, and he will get the idea. You'll find, when you begin the outdoor training, that the male puppy usually requires a longer walk than the female. Both male and female puppies will squat. It isn't until he is older that the male dog will begin to lift his leg. If you hate to give up your sleep, you can train your puppy to go outdoors during the day and use the paper at night.

ALL DOGS NEED TO CHEW

Puppies and young dogs need something with resistance to chew on while their teeth and jaws are developing—for cutting the puppy teeth, to induce growth of the permanent teeth under the puppy teeth, to assist in getting rid of the puppy teeth at the proper time, to help the permanent teeth through the gums, to assure normal jaw development and to settle the permanent teeth solidly in the jaws.

The adult dog's desire to chew stems from the instinct for tooth cleaning, gum massage and jaw exercise—plus the need for an outlet for periodic doggie tensions.

Dental caries as it affects the teeth of humans is virtually unknown in dogs—but tartar accumulates on the teeth of dogs, particularly at the gum line, more rapidly than on the teeth of humans. These accumulations, if not removed, bring irritation, and then infection which erodes the tooth enamel and ultimately destroys the teeth at the roots. Most chewing by adult dogs is an effort to do something about this problem for themselves.

Tooth and jaw development will normally continue until the dog is more than a year old—but sometimes much longer, depending upon the breed, chewing exercise, the rate at which calcium can be utilized and many other factors, known and unknown, which affect the development of individual dogs. Diseases, like distemper for example, may sometimes arrest development of the teeth and jaws, which may resume months, or even years later.

Saving your possessions from destruction, assuring proper development of teeth and jaws, providing for 'interim' tooth cleaning and gum massage, and channeling doggie tensions into a non-destructive outlet are, therefore, all dependent upon the dog having something suitable for chewing readily available when his instinct tells him to chew. If your purposes, and those of your dog, are to be accomplished, what you provide for chewing must be desirable from the doggie viewpoint, have the necessary functional qualities, and above all, be safe for your dog.

It is very important that dogs not be permitted to chew on anything they can break, or indigestible things from which they can bite sizeable chunks. Sharp pieces, such as from a bone which can be broken by a dog, may pierce the intestine wall and kill. Indigestible things which can be bitten off in chunks, such as toys made of rubber compound or cheap plastic, may cause an intestinal stoppage, if not regurgitated—to bring painful death, unless surgery is promptly performed.

Strong natural bones, such as 4 to 8 inch lengths of round shin bone from mature beef—either the kind you can get from your butcher or one of the variety available commercially in pet stores—may serve your dog's teething needs, if his mouth is large enough to handle them effectively.

You may be tempted to give your puppy a smaller bone and he may not be able to break it when you do—but puppies grow rapidly and the power of their jaws constantly increases until maturity. This means that a growing dog may break one of the smaller bones at any time, swallow the

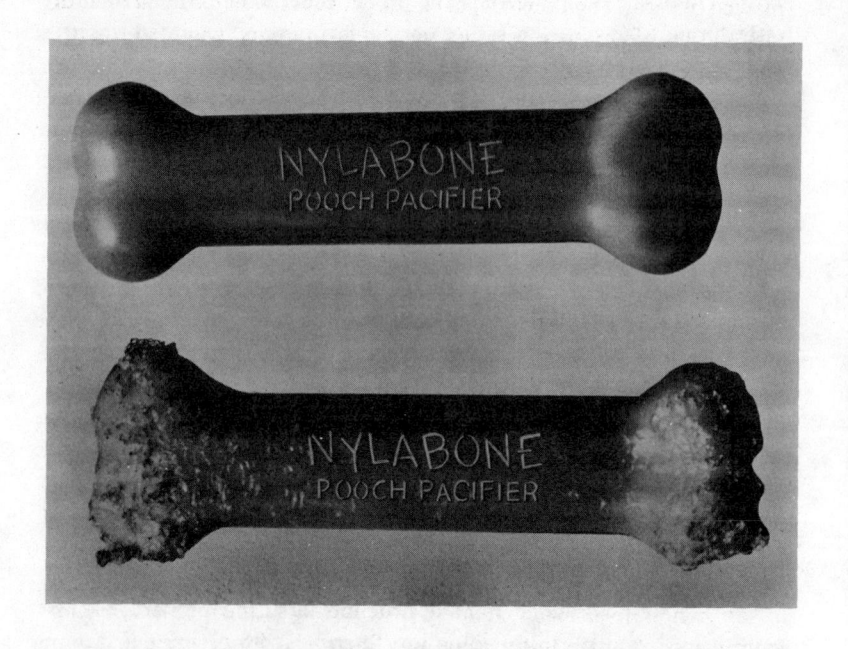

Nylabone® is the best bet for a safe, healthy chew product for your dog. It can't splinter or chip; instead, it is frizzled by the dog's chewing action, creating a toothbrush-like surface that cleanses the teeth and massages the gums. Nylabone® is also excellent for the teething puppy.

pieces and die painfully before you realize what is wrong.

All hard natural bones are highly abrasive. If your dog is an avid chewer, natural bones may wear away his teeth prematurely; hence, they then should be taken away from your dog when the teething purposes have been served. The badly worn, and usually painful, teeth of many mature dogs can be traced to excessive chewing on natural bones.

Contrary to popular belief, knuckle bones which can be chewed up and swallowed by the dog provide little, if any, useable calcium or other nutriment. They do, however, disturb the digestion of most dogs and cause them to vomit the nourishing food they need.

An old leather shoe is another popular answer to the chewing need—but be very sure that the rubber heel, all nails, and other metal parts such as lace grommets, metal arches, etc., have been removed. Be especially careful to get all of the nails. A chunk of rubber heel can cause an intestinal stoppage. If it has a nail in it, the intestine wall may be pierced or torn. Then there is, of course, always the hazard that your dog may fail to differentiate between his shoe and yours, and eat up a good pair while you're not looking.

Dried rawhide products of various types, shapes, sizes and prices have come on the market during the past few years. They don't serve the primary chewing functions very well, they are a bit messy when wet from mouthing, and most dogs chew them up rather rapidly—but they have been considered safe for dogs until recently. During the past few months, however, a number of cases of death, and near death, by strangulation have been reported to be the result of partially swallowed chunks of rawhide swelling in the throat. More recently, some veterinarians have been attributing cases of acute constipation to large pieces of incompletely digested rawhide in the intestine.

The nylon bones, especially those with natural meat and bone fractions added, are probably the most complete, safe and economical answer to the chewing need. Dogs cannot break them or bite off sizeable chunks; hence, they are completely safe—and being longer lasting than other things offered for the purpose, they are economical.

Hard chewing raises little bristle-like projections on the surface of the nylon bones—to provide effective interim tooth cleaning and vigorous gum massage, much in the same way your tooth brush does it for you. The little projections are raked off and swallowed in the form of thin shavings—but the chemistry of the nylon is such that they break down in the stomach fluids and pass through without effect.

The toughness of the nylon provides the strong chewing resistance needed for important jaw exercise and effective help for the teething functions—but there is no tooth wear because nylon is non-abrasive. Being inert, nylon does not support the growth of microorganisms—and it can be washed in soap and water, or it can be sterilized by boiling or in an autoclave.

Nylabone® is highly recommended by veterinarians as a safe, healthy nylon bone that can't splinter or chip. Instead, Nylabone is frizzled by the dog's chewing action, creating a toothbrush-like surface that cleanses the teeth and massages the gums. Nylabone® and Nylaball®, the only chew products made of flavor-impregnated solid nylon, are available in your local pet shop.

Nothing, however, substitutes for periodic professional attention to your dog's teeth and gums, not any more than your toothbrush can do that for you. Have your dog's teeth cleaned by your veterinarian at least once a year, twice a year is better—and he will be healthier, happier and far more pleasant to live with.

TRAINING

WHEN TO START TRAINING

You should never begin *serious* obedience training before your dog is seven or eight months old. (Some animal psychologists state that puppies can begin training when seven weeks old, if certain techniques are followed. These techniques, however, are still experimental and should be left to the professional trainer.) While your dog is still in his early puppyhood, concentrate on winning his confidence so he will love and admire you. Basic training can be started at the age of three or four months. He should be taught to walk nicely on a leash, sit and lie down on command, and come when he is called.

YOUR PART IN TRAINING

You must patiently demonstrate to your dog what each word of command means. Guide him with your hands and the training leash, reassuring him with your voice, through whatever routine you are teaching him. Repeat the word associated with the act. Demonstrate again and again to give the dog a chance to make the connection in his mind.

Once he begins to get the idea, use the word of command without any physical guidance. Drill him. When he makes mistakes, correct him, kindly at first, more severely as his training progresses. Try not to lose your patience or become irritated, and never slap him with your hand or the leash during the training session. Withholding praise or rebuking him will make him feel bad enough.

When he does what you want, praise him lavishly with words and with pats. Don't continually reward with dog candy or treats in training. The dog that gets into the habit of performing for a treat will seldom be fully dependable when he can't smell or see one in the offing. When he carries out a command, even though his performance is slow or sloppy, praise him and he will perform more readily the next time.

THE TRAINING VOICE

When you start training your dog, use your training voice, giving commands in a firm, clear tone. Once you give a command, persist until it is obeyed, even if you have to pull the dog to obey you. He must learn that training is different from playing, that a command once given must be obeyed no matter what distractions are present. Remember that the tone and pitch of your voice, not loudness, are the qualities that will influence your dog most.

Be consistent in the use of words during training. Confine your commands to as few words as possible and never change them. It is best for only one person to carry on the dog's training, because different people will use different words and tactics that will confuse your dog. The dog who hears "come," "get over here," "hurry up," "here, Rex," and other commands when he is wanted will become totally confused.

TRAINING LESSONS

Training is hard on the dog and the trainer. A young dog just cannot take more than ten minutes of training at a stretch, so limit the length of your first lessons. Then you can gradually increase the length of time to about thirty minutes. You'll find that you too will tend to become impatient when you stretch out a training lesson. If you find yourself losing your temper, stop and resume the lesson at another time. Before and after each lesson have a play period, but don't play during a training session. Even the youngest dog soon learns that schooling is a serious matter; fun comes afterward.

Don't spend too much time on one phase of training, or the dog will become bored. Always try to end a lesson on a pleasant note. Actually, in nine cases out of ten, if your dog isn't doing what you want it's because you're not getting the idea over to him properly.

YOUR TRAINING EQUIPMENT AND ITS USE

The leash is more properly called the lead, so we'll use that term here. The best leads for training are the six-foot webbed-cloth leads, usually olive-drab in color, and the six-foot leather lead. Fancier leads are available and may be used if desired.

You'll need a metal-link collar, called a choke chain, consisting of a metal chain with rings on each end. Even though the name may sound frightening, it won't hurt your dog, and it is an absolute MUST in training. There is a right and a wrong way to put the training collar on. It should go around the dog's neck so that you can attach the lead to the ring at the end of the chain which passes over, not under the neck. It is most important that the collar is put on properly so it will tighten when the lead is pulled and ease when you relax your grip.

The correct way to hold the lead is also very important, as the collar should have some slack in it at all times, except when correcting. Holding the loop in your right hand, extend your arm out to the side, even with your shoulder. With your left hand, grasp the lead as close as possible to the collar, without making it tight. The remaining portion of the lead can be made into a loop which is held in the right hand. Keep this arm close to your body. Most corrections will be made with the left hand by giving the lead a jerk in the direction you want the dog to go.

HEELING

"Heeling" in dog language means having your dog walk alongside you on your left side, close to your leg, on lead or off. With patience and effort you can train your dog to walk with you even on a crowded street or in the presence of other dogs.

Now that you have learned the correct way to put on your dog's collar and how to hold the lead, you are ready to start with his first lesson in heeling. Make the dog sit at your left side. Using the dog's name and the command "Heel," start forward on your LEFT foot, giving a tug on the lead to get the dog started. Always use the dog's name first, followed by the command, such as "Rex, heel." Saying his name will help get his attention and will let him know that you are about to give a command.

Walk briskly, with even steps, going around in a large circle, square or straight line. While walking, make sure that your dog stays on the left side and close to your leg. If he lags behind, snap gently on the lead to get him up to you, then praise him lavishly for doing well. If he forges ahead or swings wide, stop and jerk the lead sharply and bring him back to the proper position. Always praise him when he returns to the correct place. As soon as you have snapped the lead to correct your dog, let it go slack again at the desired length. Don't drag the dog or keep the lead taut as this will develop into a tug of war which is ineffective.

To keep your dog's attention, talk to him as you keep him in place. You can also do a series of fast about-turns, giving the lead a jerk as you turn. He will gradually learn that he must pay attention or be jerked to your side. You can vary the routine by changing speeds, doing turns, figure-eights, and by zig-zagging across the training area.

"HEEL" MEANS "SIT," TOO

To the dog, the command "Heel" will also mean that he has to sit in the heel position at your left side when you stop walking with no additional command from you. As you practice heeling, make him sit whenever you stop, at first using the word "Sit," then with no command at all. He'll soon get the idea and sit down when you stop and wait for the command "Heel" to start walking again.

TRAINING TO SIT

Training your dog to sit should be fairly easy. Stand him on your left side, holding the lead fairly short, and command him to "Sit." As you give the verbal command, pull up slightly with the lead and push his hindquarters down. Do not let him lie down or stand up. If he does lie down, snap up on the lead until he rises to a sitting position again. If he is slow to respond, tug more sharply until he has done what you want him to. Keep him in a sitting position for a moment, then release the pressure on the lead and praise him. Constantly repeat the command as you hold him in a sitting position, thus fitting the word to the action in his mind. If he moves at all, immediately repeat the command and press him into a sitting position. After a time he will begin to get the idea and will sit without having to push his hindquarters down. When he reaches that stage, insist that he sit on command.

THE "LIE DOWN" OR "DOWN"

The object of this is to get the dog to lie down either on the verbal command "Down" or when you give the hand signal, your hand raised in front of you, palm down. However, until the dog is really sure of the meaning of the command, and will do it by himself with no forcible action from you, the hand signal should only be used to accompany the verbal command. This command may be more difficult at first because it places the dog in a defenseless position, which may cause him to bolt away. Be lavish with your praise and affection when he has assumed the correct position and he will soon learn that nothing bad happens to him, and on the contrary will associate the "Down" position with pleasing his master or mistress.

Don't start training to lie down until the dog is almost letter-perfect in sitting on command. Place the dog in a sit, and kneel before him. With both hands, reach forward to his legs and take one front leg in each hand, thumbs up, holding just above the elbows. Lift his legs slightly off the ground and pull them somewhat out in front of him. Simultaneously, give the command "Down" and lower his front legs to the ground.

Hold the dog down and stroke him to let him know that staying down is what you want him to do. This method is far better than forcing a young dog down. Using force can cause him to become very frightened and he will begin to dislike any training. Always talk to your dog and let him know that you are very pleased with him, and soon you will find that you have a happy working dog.

After he begins to get the idea, slide the lead under your left foot and give the command "Down." At the same time, pull the lead. This will help get the dog down. Meanwhile, raise your hand in the down signal. Don't expect to accomplish all this in one session. Be patient and work with the dog. He'll cooperate if you show him just what you expect him to do.

THE "STAY"

The next step is to train your dog to stay either in a "Sit" or "Down" position. As before, use the lead to teach this command until your dog is responding perfectly to your instruction, then you may try it off the lead. To begin with the Sit-Stay, place your dog in a sitting position beside you in the automatic heel-sit position. Holding the leash in one hand (most trainers prefer the left), take a long step forward and turn to face him holding your free hand open, palm toward him, fingers pointing downward, in front of his nose and speak the command "Stay." If he offers to follow you, as it would be natural for him to do since this has been his ready position for heel, snap up on the lead to return him to the sit, put your hand in front of his face and repeat the command firmly once more. Allow him to remain sitting for a few seconds before going through the procedure again. Each time he successfully performs, praise him profusely and show him you are pleased with him.

Repeat this procedure until your dog behaves as if he understands what is expected of him. When he has mastered this procedure, step away to the right of him, then behind, then a few steps forward, a few steps to the side, and so on, until you have gone the full length of the leash. Anytime your dog offers to follow you, snap upward on the leash, extending your arm palm forward to him and repeat the command sharply. When he has demonstrated a willingness to remain in the correct position while you walk the full extent of the lead, you are ready to train him to remain in position using a longer length of cord, about 25 or 30 feet, and finally the Sit-Stay off the lead.

Once the Sit-Stay is learned, you can teach the Down-Stay by beginning with the Down command, then apply approximately the same methods as in the Sit-Stay.

THE COME ON COMMAND

You can train your dog to come when you call him if you begin when he is young. At first, work with him on lead. Sit the dog, then back away the length of the lead and call him, putting into your voice as much coaxing affection as possible. Give an easy tug on the lead to get him started. When he does come, make a big fuss over him—it might help at this point to give him a small piece of dog candy or food as a reward. He should get the idea soon. You can also move away from him the full length of the lead and call to him something like "Rex, come," then run backward a few steps and stop, making him sit directly in front of you.

Don't be too eager to practice coming on command off lead. Wait until you are certain that you have the dog under perfect control before you try calling him when he's free. Once he gets the idea that he can disobey a command and get away with it, your training program will suffer a serious setback. Keep in mind that your dog's life may depend on his immediate response to a command to come when he is called. If he disobeys off lead, put the lead back on and correct him severely with jerks of the lead.

TEACHING TO COME TO HEEL

The object of this is for you to stand still, say "Heel," and have your dog come right over to you and sit by your left knee in the heel position. If your dog has been trained to sit without command every time you stop, he's ready for this step.

Sit him in front of and facing you and step back one step. Moving only your left foot, pull the dog behind you, then step forward and pull him around until he is in a heel position. You can also have the dog go around by passing the lead behind your back. Use your left heel to straighten him out if he begins to sit behind you or crookedly. This may take a little work, but he will get the idea if you show him just what you want.

THE STAND

Your dog should be trained to stand in one spot without moving his feet, and he should allow a stranger to run his hand over his body and legs without showing any resentment or fear. Employ the same method you used in training him to stay on the sit and down. While walking, place your left hand out, palm toward his nose, and command him to stay. His first impulse will be to sit, so be prepared to stop him by placing your hand under his body, near his hindquarters, and holding him until he gets the idea that this is different from the command to sit. Praise him for standing, then walk to the end of the lead. Correct him strongly if he starts to move. Have a stranger approach him and run his hands over the dog's back and down his legs. Keep him standing until you come back to him. Walk around him from his left side, come to the heel position, and make sure that he does not sit until you command him to. This is a very valuable exercise. If you plan to show your dog he will have to learn to stand in a show pose and allow the judge to examine him. The judge will run his hands along the dog's back and down the legs, so it is important that the dog stands calmly and steadfastly.

TRAINING SCHOOLS AND CLASSES

There are dog training schools in all parts of the country, some sponsored by the local humane society.

If you feel that you lack the time or the skill to train your dog yourself, there are professional dog trainers who will do it for you, but basically dog training is a matter of training YOU and your dog to work together as a team, and if you don't do it yourself you will miss a lot of fun. Don't give up after trying unsuccessfully for a short time. Try a little harder and you and your dog will be able to work things out.

ADVANCED TRAINING AND OBEDIENCE TRIALS

Once you begin training your dog and you see how well he does, you'll probably be bitten by the "obedience bug"—the desire to enter him in obedience trials held under American Kennel Club auspices.

The A.K.C. obedience trials are divided into three classes: Novice, Open and Utility.

In the Novice Class the dog will be judged on the following basis:

TEST MAXIMUM SCORE

Test	Maximum Score
Heel on lead	40
Stand for examination	30
Heel free—off lead	40
Recall (come on command)	30
One-minute sit (handler in ring)	30
Three-minute down (handler in ring)	30
Maximum total score	200

If the dog "qualifies" in three shows by earning at least 50% of the points for each test, with a total of at least 170 for the trial, he has earned the Companion Dog degree and the letters C.D. (Companion Dog) are entered after his name in the American Kennel Club records.

After the dog has earned his Companion Dog title, he is eligible to enter the Open Class competition and compete for his next degree. He will be judged on this basis:

TEST MAXIMUM SCORE

Test	Maximum Score
Heel free	40
Drop on recall	30
Retrieve (wooden dumbbell) on flat	20
Retrieve over obstacle (hurdle)	30
Broad jump	20
Three-minute sit (handler out of ring)	30
Five-minute down (handler out of ring)	30
Maximum total score	200

Again he must qualify in three shows for the C.D.X. (Companion Dog Excellent) title, earning at least 50% of the points for each test, with a total of at least 170 for the trial. He is then eligible to compete in the Utility Class, where he can earn the Utility Dog (U.D.) degree in these rugged tests:

TEST	MAXIMUM SCORE
Scent discrimination (picking up article handled by master from group) Article 1	30
Scent discrimination Article 2	30
Directed Retrieve	30
Signal exercise (heeling, etc., on hand signal)	40
Directed jumping (over hurdle and bar jump)	40
Group examination	30
Maximum total score	200

For more complete information about these obedience trials, write for the American Kennel Club's *Regulations and Standards for Obedience Trials*. Dogs that are disqualified from breed shows because of neutering or physical defects are eligible to compete in these trials. Besides the formal A.K.C. obedience trials, there are informal "match" trials in which dogs compete for ribbons and inexpensive trophies. These shows are run by many local fanciers' clubs and by all-breed obedience clubs. In many localities the humane society and other groups conduct their own obedience shows. Your local newspaper, pet shop proprietor or kennel club can keep you informed about such shows in your vicinity, and you will find them listed in the different dog magazines or in the pet column of your paper.

BREEDING

THE QUESTION OF SPAYING

If you feel that you will never want to raise a litter of purebred puppies, and if you do not wish to risk the possibility of an undesirable mating and surplus mongrel puppies inevitably destined for euthanasia at the local pound, you may want to have your female spayed. Spaying is generally best performed after the female has passed her first heat and before her first birthday; this allows the female to attain the normal female characteristics, while still being young enough to avoid the possible complications encountered when an older female is spayed. A spayed female will remain a healthy, lively pet. You often hear that an altered female will become very fat. However, if you cut down on her food intake, she will not gain weight.

On the other hand, if you wish to show your dog in American Kennel Club competition (altered females are disqualified) or enjoy the excitement and feeling of accomplishment of breeding and raising a litter of quality puppies, particularly in your breed and from your pet, then do not spay your dog until a more appropriate time.

Male dogs are almost never altered (castrated) unless they exhibit excessive sexual tendencies.

SEXUAL PHYSIOLOGY

Females usually reach sexual maturity (indicated by the first heat cycle, or season) at eight or nine months of age, but sexual maturity may occur as early as six months or as late as thirteen months of age. Generally, the larger the breed is the longer it takes to reach full maturity.

The average heat cycle (estrus period) lasts for twenty or twenty-one days, and occurs approximately every six months. For about five days immediately preceeding the heat period, the female generally displays restlessness and an increased appetite. The vulva, or external genitals, begins to swell. The discharge, which is bright red at the onset and gradually becomes pale pink to straw in color, increases in quantity for several days and then slowly subsides, finally ceasing altogether. The vaginal discharge is subject to much variation; in some bitches it is quite heavy, in others it may never appear, and in some it may be so slight as to go unnoticed.

About eight or nine days after the first appearance of the discharge, the female becomes very playful with other dogs, but will not allow a mating

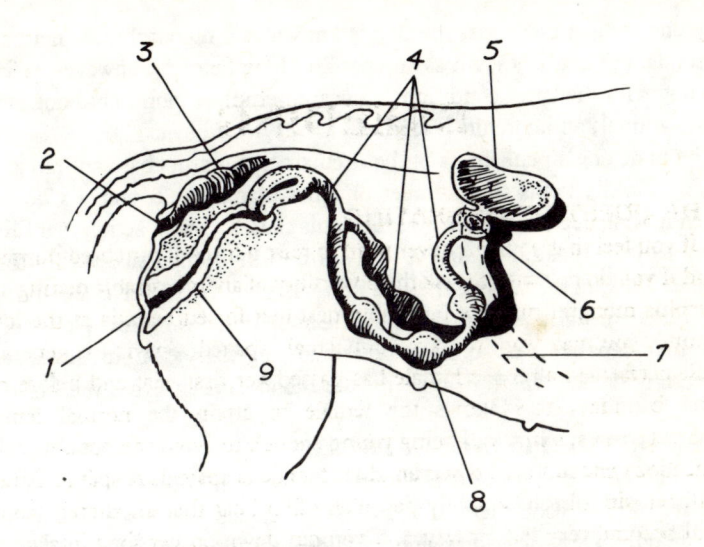

REPRODUCTIVE SYSTEM OF BITCH
1. Vulva 2. Anus 3. Rectum 4. Uterus 5. Kidney 6. Ovary 7. Ribs (indicated by broken lines) 8. Developing embryo 9. Vagina.

to take place. Anywhere from the tenth or eleventh day to the seventeenth or eighteenth day, the female will accept males and be able to conceive. Many biologists apply the term "heat" only to this receptive phase rather than to the whole estrus period, as is commonly done by dog fanciers.

The ova (egg cells) from the female's ovaries are discharged into the oviduct toward the close of the acceptance phase, usually the sixteenth to eighteenth day. From the eighteenth day until the end of the cycle, the female is still attractive to males, but she will repulse their advances. The entire estrus, however, may be quite variable; in some females vaginal bleeding ends and mating begins on the fourth day; in others the discharge may continue throughout the entire cycle and the female will not accept males until the seventeenth day or even later.

The male dog—simply referred to by fanciers as the "dog" or "stud," in contrast to the female, which is referred to as the "bitch"—upon reaching sexual maturity, usually at about six to eight months, is able, like other domesticated mammals, to breed at any time throughout the year.

The testes, the sperm-producing organs of the male, descend from the body cavity into the scrotum at birth. The condition of cryptorchidism refers to the retention of one or both testes within the body cavity. A testicle retained within the body cavity is in an environment too hot for it to function normally. A retained testicle may also become cancerous. If only one testicle descends, the dog is known as a monorchid; if neither descends, the dog is known as an anorchid (dog fanciers, however, refer to a dog with the latter condition as a cryptorchid). A monorchid dog is a fertile animal; an anorchid is sterile.

The male dog's penis has a bulbous enlargement at its base and, in addition, like the penis of a number of other mammals, contains a bone. When mating occurs, pressure on the penis causes a reflex action that fills the bulb with blood, swelling it to five times its normal size within the female. This locks, or ties, the two animals together. After ejaculation, the animals usually remain tied for fifteen to thirty minutes. However, they may separate very quickly or remain together an hour or more, depending on the length of time for the blood to drain from the bulb.

CARE OF THE FEMALE IN ESTRUS

If you have a dog-proof run within your yard, it will be safe to leave your female in season there; if you don't have such a run, she should be shut indoors. Don't leave her alone outside even for a minute; she should be exercised only on lead. If you want to prevent the neighborhood dogs from congregating around your doorstep, as they inevitably will as soon

REPRODUCTIVE SYSTEM OF THE MALE DOG
1. Prostate 2. Rectum 3. Anus 4. Pelvis 5. Testicle 6. Scrotum 7. Bulb 8. Penis 9. Sheath 10. Vas deferens 11. Bladder.

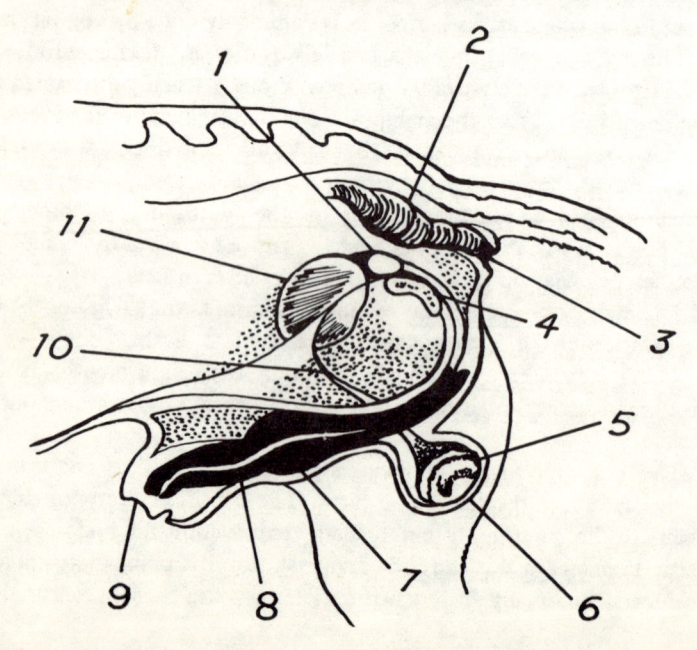

as they discover that your female is in season, take her some distance from the house before you let her relieve herself. Take her in your car to a park or field for a chance to "stretch" her legs (always on lead, of course). Keep watch for male dogs, and if one approaches take the female back to the car. After the three weeks are up you can let her out as before with no worry that she can have puppies until her next season.

Some owners find it simpler to board their female at a kennel until her season is over. However, it really is not difficult to watch your female at home. There are various products on the market which are useful at this time. Although the female in season keeps herself quite clean, sometimes she unavoidably stains furniture or rugs. You can buy sanitary belts made expecially for dogs at your pet shop. Consult your veterinarian for information on pills to be taken to check odor during this period. There also is a pill that prevents the female from coming in season for extended periods, and there are many different types of liquids, powders and sprays of varying efficiency used to keep male dogs away. However, the one safe rule (whatever products you use) is: keep your bitch away from dogs that could mount her.

SHOULD YOU BREED YOUR MALE?

When questioning whether or not to use a male dog as a stud, there are several points to consider. Arguments for and against are often exaggerated. For example, a classic example would be the tale that once you use a dog as a stud he will lose his value as a show dog or any one of the other functions a dog may have. A sound rule may well be: if you have a stud who has proven his worth at the shows, place his services out for hire, if only for the betterment of the breed; if your dog is not of show quality, do not use him as a stud.

Top champion studs can bring their owners many dollars in breeding revenue. If the stud is as good as you feel he is, his services will soon be in great demand. Using a dog as a stud will not lower his value in other functions in any way. Many breeders will permit a male dog to breed an experienced female once, when about a year old, and then they begin to show their stud until he has gained his conformation championship. He is then placed out for hire through advertising in the various bulletins, journals and show catalogues, and through the stud registers maintained by many pet shops and kennel clubs.

SHOULD YOU BREED YOUR FEMALE?

If you are an amateur and decide to breed your female it would be wise to talk with a breeder and find out all that breeding and caring for puppies entails. You must be prepared to assume the responsibility of caring

NORMAL BITCH MATING CYCLE

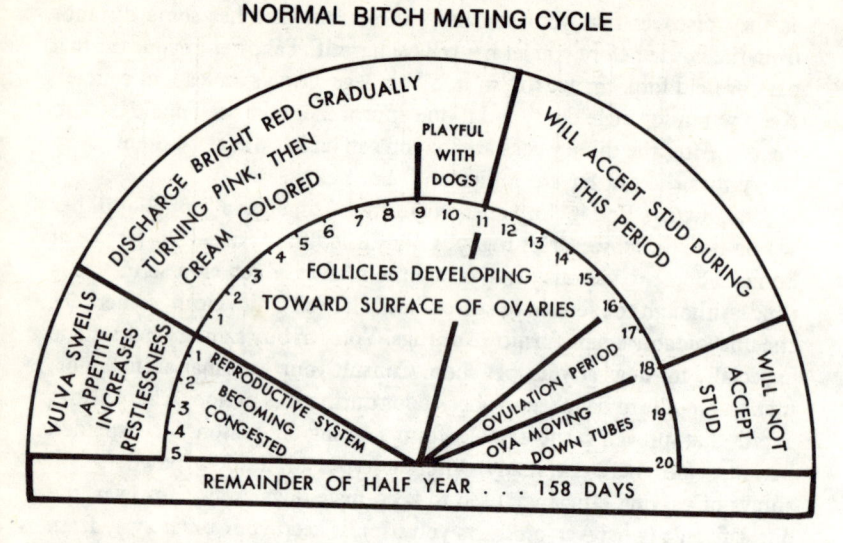

Diagram showing a semicircular chart of the bitch mating cycle with the following labels:

- VULVA SWELLS, APPETITE INCREASES, RESTLESSNESS (days 1-5)
- REPRODUCTIVE SYSTEM BECOMING CONGESTED (days 1-5)
- DISCHARGE BRIGHT RED, GRADUALLY TURNING PINK, THEN CREAM COLORED (days 3-9)
- FOLLICLES DEVELOPING TOWARD SURFACE OF OVARIES (days 1-11)
- PLAYFUL WITH DOGS (days 9-11)
- WILL ACCEPT STUD DURING THIS PERIOD (days 11-16)
- OVULATION PERIOD, OVA MOVING DOWN TUBES (days 16-20)
- WILL NOT ACCEPT STUD (days 18-20)
- REMAINDER OF HALF YEAR ... 158 DAYS

for the mother through her pregnancy and for the puppies until they are of saleable age. Raising a litter of puppies can be a rewarding experience, but it means work as well as fun, and there is no guarantee of financial profit. As the puppies grow older and require more room and care, the amateur breeder, in desperation, often sells the puppies for much less than they are worth; sometimes he has to give them away. If the cost of keeping the puppies will drain your finances, think twice.

If you have given careful consideration to all these things and still want to breed your female, remember that there is some preparation necessary before taking this step.

WHEN TO BREED

It is usually best to breed in the second or third season of your bitch. Consider when the puppies will be born and whether their birth and later care will interfere with your work or vacation plans. Gestation period is approximately fifty-eight to sixty-five days. Allow enough time to select the right stud for her. Don't be in a position of having to settle for any available stud if she comes into season sooner than expected. Your female will probably be ready to breed twelve days after the first colored discharge. You can usually make arrangements to board her with the owner of the male for a few days to insure her being there at the proper time, or you can take her to be mated and bring her home the same day. If she still appears receptive she may be bred again a day or two later. Some females never show signs of willingness, so it helps to have the experience of a breeder. The second day after the discharge changes color is the pro-

Perpetual Whelping Chart

Bred—Jan.	1	2	3	4	5	6	7	8	9	10	11	12	13	14	15	16	17	18	19	20	21	22	23	24	25	26	27	28	29	30	31	
Due—March	5	6	7	8	9	10	11	12	13	14	15	16	17	18	19	20	21	22	23	24	25	26	27	28	29	30	31	April 1	2	3	4	
Bred—Feb.	1	2	3	4	5	6	7	8	9	10	11	12	13	14	15	16	17	18	19	20	21	22	23	24	25	26	27	28				
Due—April	5	6	7	8	9	10	11	12	13	14	15	16	17	18	19	20	21	22	23	24	25	26	27	28	29	30	May 1	2				
Bred—Mar.	1	2	3	4	5	6	7	8	9	10	11	12	13	14	15	16	17	18	19	20	21	22	23	24	25	26	27	28	29	30	31	
Due—May	3	4	5	6	7	8	9	10	11	12	13	14	15	16	17	18	19	20	21	22	23	24	25	26	27	28	29	30	31	June 1	2	
Bred—Apr.	1	2	3	4	5	6	7	8	9	10	11	12	13	14	15	16	17	18	19	20	21	22	23	24	25	26	27	28	29	30		
Due—June	3	4	5	6	7	8	9	10	11	12	13	14	15	16	17	18	19	20	21	22	23	24	25	26	27	28	29	30	July 1	2		
Bred—May	1	2	3	4	5	6	7	8	9	10	11	12	13	14	15	16	17	18	19	20	21	22	23	24	25	26	27	28	29	30	31	
Due—July	3	4	5	6	7	8	9	10	11	12	13	14	15	16	17	18	19	20	21	22	23	24	25	26	27	28	29	30	31	August 1		
Bred—June	1	2	3	4	5	6	7	8	9	10	11	12	13	14	15	16	17	18	19	20	21	22	23	24	25	26	27	28	29	30		
Due—August	3	4	5	6	7	8	9	10	11	12	13	14	15	16	17	18	19	20	21	22	23	24	25	26	27	28	29	30	31	Sept. 1		
Bred—July	1	2	3	4	5	6	7	8	9	10	11	12	13	14	15	16	17	18	19	20	21	22	23	24	25	26	27	28	29	30	31	
Due—September	2	3	4	5	6	7	8	9	10	11	12	13	14	15	16	17	18	19	20	21	22	23	24	25	26	27	28	29	30	Oct. 1	2	
Bred—Aug.	1	2	3	4	5	6	7	8	9	10	11	12	13	14	15	16	17	18	19	20	21	22	23	24	25	26	27	28	29	30	31	
Due—October	3	4	5	6	7	8	9	10	11	12	13	14	15	16	17	18	19	20	21	22	23	24	25	26	27	28	29	30	31	Nov. 1	2	
Bred—Sept.	1	2	3	4	5	6	7	8	9	10	11	12	13	14	15	16	17	18	19	20	21	22	23	24	25	26	27	28	29	30		
Due—November	3	4	5	6	7	8	9	10	11	12	13	14	15	16	17	18	19	20	21	22	23	24	25	26	27	28	29	30	Dec. 1	2		
Bred—Oct.	1	2	3	4	5	6	7	8	9	10	11	12	13	14	15	16	17	18	19	20	21	22	23	24	25	26	27	28	29	30	31	
Due—December	3	4	5	6	7	8	9	10	11	12	13	14	15	16	17	18	19	20	21	22	23	24	25	26	27	28	29	30	31	Jan. 1	2	
Bred—Nov.	1	2	3	4	5	6	7	8	9	10	11	12	13	14	15	16	17	18	19	20	21	22	23	24	25	26	27	28	29	30		
Due—January	3	4	5	6	7	8	9	10	11	12	13	14	15	16	17	18	19	20	21	22	23	24	25	26	27	28	29	30	31	Feb. 1		
Bred—Dec.	1	2	3	4	5	6	7	8	9	10	11	12	13	14	15	16	17	18	19	20	21	22	23	24	25	26	27	28	29	30	31	
Due—February	2	3	4	5	6	7	8	9	10	11	12	13	14	15	16	17	18	19	20	21	22	23	24	25	26	27	28	March 1	2	3	4	

per time; she may be bred for about three days following. For an additional week or so she may have some discharge and attract other dogs by her odor, but she can seldom be bred at this time.

HOW TO SELECT A STUD

Choose a mate for your female with an eye to countering her deficiencies. If possible, both male and female should have several ancestors in common within the last two or three generations, as such combinations generally "click" best. The male should have a good show record himself or be the sire of champions. The owner of the stud usually charges a fee for the use of the dog. The fee varies. Payment of a fee does not guarantee a litter, but it does generally confer the right to breed your female again to the stud if she does not have puppies the first time. In some cases the owner of the stud will agree to take a choice puppy in place of the stud fee. You and the owner of the stud should settle all details beforehand, including such questions as what age the puppies should reach before the stud's owner can make his choice, what disposition is made of the single surviving puppy under an agreement by which the stud owner has the pick of the litter, and so on. In all cases, it is best that all agreements entered into by bitch owner and stud owner be in the form of a written contract.

It is customary for the female to be sent to the male. If the stud dog of your choice lives any distance from you, you will have to make arrangements to have your female shipped to him. The quickest way is by air, and if you call your nearest airport the airline people will give you information as to the best and fastest flight. Some airlines furnish their own crates for shipping, whereas others require that you furnish your own. The owner of the stud will make the arrangements for shipping the female back to you. You have to pay all shipping charges.

PREPARATION FOR BREEDING

Before you breed your female, make sure she is in good health. She should be neither too thin nor too fat. Skin diseases must be cured before breeding; a bitch with skin diseases can pass them on to her puppies. If she has worms she should be wormed before being bred, or within three weeks afterward. It is a good idea to have your veterinarian give her a booster shot for distemper and hepatitis before the puppies are born. This will increase the immunity the puppies receive during their early, most vulnerable period. Choose a dependable veterinarian and rely on him if there is an emergency when your female whelps.

Do not breed your bitch after she reaches six years of age. If you wish to breed her several times while she is young, it is wise to breed her only once a year. In other words, breed her, skip at least one season, and then breed her again. This will allow her to gain back her full strength between whelpings.

THE IMPORTANCE AND APPLICATION OF GENETICS

Any person attempting to breed dogs should have a basic understanding of the transmission of traits, or characteristics, from the parents to the offspring and some familiarity with the more widely used genetic terms that he will probably encounter. A knowledge of the fundamental mechanics of genetics enables a breeder to better comprehend the passing on of good traits and bad from generation to generation and how a stud and bitch either complement or detract from each other's traits. It enables him to make a more judicial and scientific decision in selecting potential mates.

Inheritance, fundamentally, is due to the existence of microscopic units, known as *GENES*, present in the cells of all individuals. Genes somehow control the biochemical reactions that occur within the embryo or adult organism. This control results in changing or guiding the development of the organism's characteristics. A "string" of attached genes is known as a *CHROMOSOME*. With a few important exceptions, every chromosome has a partner chromosome carrying a duplicate or equivalent set of genes. Each gene, therefore, has a partner gene, known as an *ALLELE*. The number of different pairs of chromosomes present in the cells of the organism varies with the type of organism; a certain parasitic worm has only one pair, a certain fruit fly has four different pairs, man has 23 different pairs and your dog has 39 different pairs per cell. Because each chromosome may have many hundreds of genes, a single cell of the body may contain a total of several thousand genes. Heredity is obviously a very complex matter.

In the simplest form of genetic inheritance, one particular gene and its duplicate, or allele, on the partner chromosome control a single characteristic. The presence of freckles in the human skin, for example, is believed to be due to the influence of a single pair of genes.

Each cell of the body contains the specific number of paired chromosomes characteristic of the organism. Because each type of gene is present on both chromosomes of a chromosome pair, each type of gene is therefore present in duplicate. The fusion of a sperm cell from the male with an egg cell from the female, as occurs in fertilization, should therefore result in offspring having a quadruplicate number (4) of each type of gene. Mating of these individuals would then produce progeny having an octuplicate number (8) of each type of gene, and so on. This, however, is normally prevented by a special process. When ordinary

MENDELIAN EXPECTATION CHART

The six possible ways in which a pair of determiners can unite. Ratios apply to expectancy over larger numbers, except in lines number 1, 2, and 6, where expectancy is realized definitely in every litter (the exception due to mutation).

body cells prepare to divide to form more tissue, each pair of chromosomes duplicates itself so that there are four partner chromosomes of each kind instead of only two. When the cell divides, two of the four partners, or one pair, go into each new cell. This process, known as *MITOSIS*, insures that each new body cell contains the proper number of chromosomes. Reproductive cells (sperm and egg cells), however, undergo a special kind of division known as *MEIOSIS*. In meiosis, the chromosome pairs do not duplicate themselves, and thus when the reproductive cells reach the final dividing stage only one chromosome, or one-half of the pair, goes into each new reproductive cell. Each reproductive cell, therefore, has only half the normal number of chromosomes. These are referred to as *HAPLOID* cells, in contrast to *DIPLOID* cells, which have the full number of chromosomes. When the haploid sperm cell fuses with the haploid egg cell in fertilization, the resulting offspring has the normal diploid number of chromosomes.

If both partner genes, or alleles, affect the trait in an identical manner, the genes are said to be *HOMOZYGOUS*, but if one affects the character in a manner different from the other gene, or allele, the genes are said to be *HETEROZYGOUS*. For example, in the pair of genes affecting eye color in humans, if each gene of the pair produces blue eyes, while the other gene, or allele, produces brown eyes, they are said to be heterozygous. The presence of heterozygous genes raises the question, "Will the offspring have blue eyes or brown eyes?" which in turn introduces another genetic principle.

DOMINANCE and RECESSIVENESS

If one gene of a pair can block the action of its partner, or allele, while still producing its own effect, that gene is said to be dominant over its allele. Its allele, on the other hand, is said to be recessive. In the case of heterozygous genes for eye color, the brown eye gene is dominant over the recessive blue eye gene, and the offspring therefore will have brown eyes. Much less common is the occurrence of gene pairs in which neither gene is completely dominant over the other. This, known as INCOMPLETE or PARTIAL DOMINANCE, results in a blending of the opposing influences. In cattle, if a homozygous (pure) red bull is mated with a homozygous (pure) white cow, the calf will be roan, a blending of red and white hairs in its coat, rather than either all red or all white.

During meiosis, or division of the reproductive (sperm and egg) cells, each pair of chromosomes splits, and one-half of each pair goes into one of the two new cells. Thus, in the case of eye color genes, one new reproductive cell will get the chromosome carrying the blue eye gene, while the other new reproductive cell will get the chromosome carrying the brown eye gene, and so on for each pair of chromosomes. If an organism has only one pair of chromosomes—called pair A, made up of chromosomes A_1 and A_2, and pair B, made up of chromosomes B_1 and B_2—each new reproductive cell will get one chromosome from each pair, and four different combinations are possible: A_1 and B_1; A_1 and B_2; A_2 and B_1; or A_2 and B_2. If the blue eye gene is on A_1, the brown eye gene on A_2, and the gene for curly hair on B_1, and the gene for straight hair on B_2, each of the above combinations will exert a different genetic effect on the offspring. This different grouping of chromosomes in the new reproductive cell as a result of meiotic cell division is known as *INDEPENDENT ASSORTMENT* and is one reason why variation occurs in the offspring. In the dog, with 39 pairs of chromosomes, the possibilites of variation through independent assortment are tremendous.

But variation does not end here. For example, if two dominant genes, such as the genes for brown eyes and dark hair, were on the same chromosome, all brown-eyed people would have dark hair. Yet in instances where such joined or *LINKED* genes do occur, the two characteristics do not always appear together in the same offspring. This is due to a process known as a *CROSS-OVER* or *RECOMBINATION*.

Recombination is the mutual exchange of corresponding blocks of genes between the two chromosomes in a pair. That is, during cell division, the two chromosomes may exchange their tip sections or other corresponding segments. If the segments exchanged contain the eye color genes, the brown eye gene will be transferred from the chromosome carrying the dark hair gene to the chromosome carrying the light hair gene, and then brown eyes will occur with light hair, provided that the individual is homozygous for the recessive light hair gene.

Another important source of variation is *MUTATION*. In mutation, a gene becomes altered, such as by exposure to irradiation, and exerts a different effect than it did before. Most mutations are harmful to the organism, and some may result in death. Offspring carrying mutated genes and showing the effects of these mutations are known as *MUTANTS* or *SPORTS*. Mutation also means that instead of only two alleles for eye color, such as brown and blue, there may now be three or more (gray, black, etc.) creating a much larger source for possible variation in the offspring.

Further complications in the transmission and appearance of genetic traits are the phenomena known as *EPISTATIS* and *PLEIOTROPY*. Epistatis refers to a gene exerting influence on genes other than its own allele. In all-white red-eyed (albino) guinea pigs, for example, the gene controlling intensity of color is epistatic to any other color gene and prevents that gene from producing its effect. Thus, even if a gene for red spots were present in the cells of the guinea pig, the color intensity gene would prevent the red spots from appearing in the guinea pig's white coat. *Pleiotropy* refers to the fact that a single gene may control a number of characteristics. In the fruit fly, for example, the gene that controls eye color may also affect the structure of certain body parts and even the lifespan of the insect.

One special pair of chromosomes is known as the sex chromosomes. In man, dog, and other mammals, these chromosomes are of two types, designated as X and Y. Under normal conditions, a mammal carrying one X-type and one Y-type is a male. Females have two X chromosomes and can only contribute X chromosomes to the offspring, but the male can contribute either an X or a Y.

If the male's sperm carrying an X chromosome fertilizes the female's egg cell (X), the offspring (XX) will be a female; if a sperm carrying a Y chromosome fertilizes the egg (X), the offspring (XY) will be male. It is the male, therefore, that determines the sex of the offspring in mammals.

Traits controlled by genes present on the sex chromosome, and which appear in only one sex, are said to be *SEX LINKED*. If, for example, a rare recessive gene occurs on the X chromosome, it cannot exert its effect

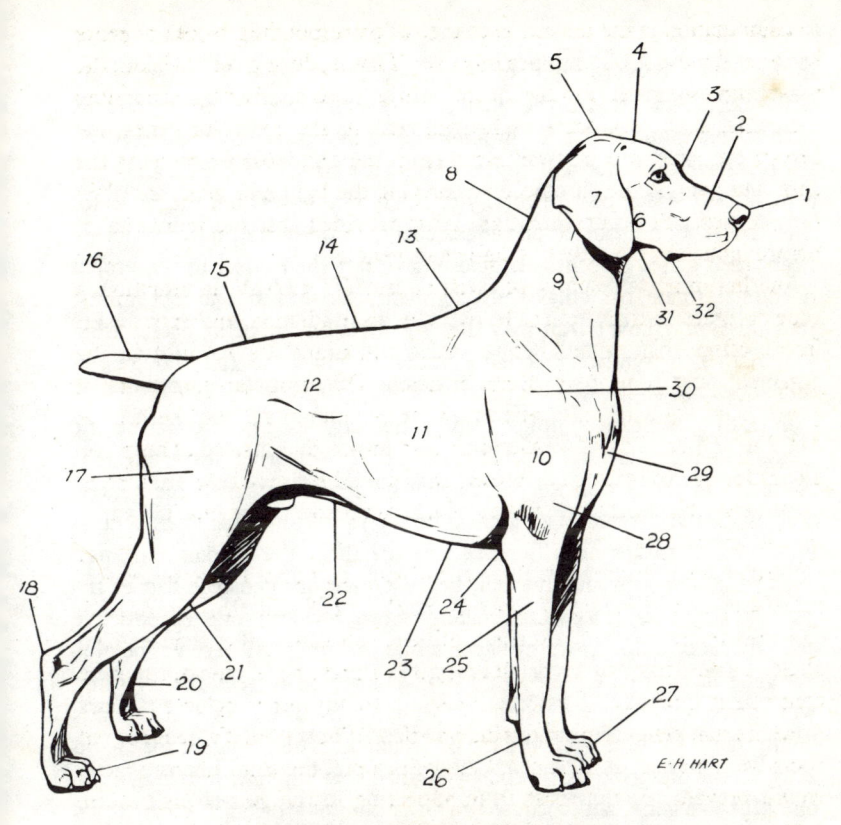

EXTERNAL PARTS OF THE DOG

All dogs under consideration for a mating must be evaluated against the points of the standard for their breed. A breeder needs a thorough understanding of what sound structure is and how each part of the dog interacts in the overall structure of the animal. Without a basic understanding of the physical make-up of the dog, serious evaluations of breeding stock cannot be made and little progress in strengthening the breed can be expected. The points of conformation that breeders must familiarize themselves with are: 1. Nose 2. Muzzle 3. Stop 4. Skull 5. Occiput 6. Cheek 7. Ear 8. Crest of neck 9. Neck 10. Shoulder 11. Ribs 12. Loin 13. Withers 14. Back 15. Croup 16. Tail or stern 17. Thigh 18. Hock joint 19. Rear feet 20. Metatarsus 21. Stifle 22. Abdomen 23. Chest 24. Elbow 25. Foreleg 26. Pastern 27. Front feet 28. Upper Arm 29. Forechest 30. Shoulder blade 31. Throat latch 32. Lip Corner.

in the female because the dominant allele on the other X chromosomes will counteract it. In the male, however, there is no second X chromosome, and if the Y chromosome cannot offer any countereffect, the recessive character will appear. There are also *SEX-LIMITED* characteristics: these appear primarily or solely in one sex, but the genes for these traits are not carried on the sex chromosomes. Sex-limited traits appear when genes on other chromosomes exert their effect in the proper hormonal (male or female) environment. Sex-linked and sex-limited transmission is how a trait may skip a generation, by being passed from grandfather to grandson through a mother in which the trait, though present, does not show.

In dealing with the simplest form of heredity—one gene effecting one character—there is an expected ratio of the offspring displaying the character to those who do not display it, depending upon the genetic makeup of the parents. If a parent is homozygous for a character, such as blue eyes, it makes no difference which half of the chromosome pair enters the new reproductive cell, because each chromosome carries the gene for blue eyes. If a parent is heterozygous, however, one reproductive cell will receive the brown eye gene while the other will receive the blue eye gene. If both parents are homozygous for blue eyes, all the offspring will receive two blue eye genes, and all will have blue eyes. If a parent is homozygous for blue eyes, and the other parent is homozygous for brown eyes, all the offspring will be heterozygous, receiving one brown eye and one blue eye gene, and because brown is dominant, all will have brown eyes. If both parents are heterozygous, both the blue eye gene and the brown eye gene from one parent have an equal likelihood of ending up with either the blue eye or the brown eye gene from the other parent. This results in a ratio of two heterozygous offspring to the one homozygous for brown eyes and one homozygous for blue eyes, giving a total genetic, or genotypic, ratio of 2:1:1 or, as it is more commonly arranged, 1:2:1. As the two heterozygous as well as the homozygous brown eye offspring will have brown eyes, the ratio of brown eyes to blue eyes (or phenotypic ratio) will be 3:1.

If one parent is heterozygous and the other parent is homozygous for the recessive gene for blue eyes, but the other half of the offspring will be heterozygous and have brown eyes. (Here both the genotypic and phenotypic ratio is 1:1.)

If the homozygous parent, however, has the dominant gene (brown eyes), half of the offspring will be heterozygous and half will be homozygous, as before, but all will have brown eyes. By repeated determinations of these ratios in the offspring, geneticists are able to analyze the genetic makeup of the parents.

Before leaving heredity, it might be well to explain the difference between inbreeding, outcrossing, line breeding, and similar terms. Basically, there are only inbreeding and outbreeding. Inbreeding, however, according to its intensity, is usually divided into interbreeding proper and line breeding. Inbreeding proper is considered to be the mating of very closely related individuals, generally within the immediate family, but this is sometimes extended to include matings to first cousins and grandparents. Line breeding is the mating of more distantly related animals, that is, animals not immediately related to each other but having a common ancestor, such as the same grandsire or great-grandsire. Outbreeding is divided into outcrossing, which is the mating of dogs from different families within the same breed, and cross-breeding, which is mating purebred dogs from different breeds.

From the foregoing discussion of genetics, it should be realized that the theory of telegony, which states that the sire of one litter can influence future litters sired by other studs, is simply not true; it is possible, however, if several males mate with a female during a single estrus cycle, that the various puppies in the litter may have different sires (but not two sires for any one puppy). It should also be realized that blood does not really enter into the transmission of inheritance, although people commonly speak of "bloodlines," "pure-blooded," etc.

CARE OF THE MOTHER AND FAMILY

PRENATAL CARE OF THE FEMALE

You can expect the puppies nine weeks from the day of breeding, although 58 days is as common as 63. During this time the female should receive normal care and exercise. If she is overweight, don't increase her food at first; excess weight at whelping time is not good. If she is on the thin side, build her up, giving her a morning meal of cereal and egg yolk. Consult your veterinarian as to increasing her vitamins and mineral supplement. During the last weeks the puppies grow enormously, and the mother will have little room for food and less appetite. Divide her meals into smaller portions and feed her more often. If she loses her appetite, tempt her with meat, liver, chicken, etc.

As she grows heavier, eliminate violent exercise and jumping. Do not eliminate exercise entirely, as walking is beneficial to the female in whelp, and mild exercise will maintain her muscle tone in preparation for the birth. Weigh your female after breeding and keep a record of her weight each week thereafter. Groom your bitch daily—some females have a slight discharge during gestation, more prevalent during the last two weeks, so wash the vulva with warm water daily. Usually, by the end of the fifth week you can notice a broadening across her loins, and her breasts become firmer. By the end of the sixth week your veterinarian can tell you whether or not she is pregnant.

PREPARATION OF WHELPING QUARTERS

Prepare a whelping box a few days before the puppies are due, and allow the mother to sleep there overnight or to spend some time in it during the day to become accustomed to it. Then she is less likely to try to have her pups under the front porch or in the middle of your bed. The box should have a wooden floor. Sides about a foot high will keep the puppies in but enable the mother to get out after she has fed them. If the weather is cold, the box should be raised about an inch off the floor.

You should place a guard rail in the whelping box to prevent the mother from rolling over onto the pups and smothering them. This guard is a strip of wood which will project out and above the floor of the box, keeping the bitch from pressing up against the sides of the box.

Layers of newspaper spread over the whole area will make excellent bedding and be absorbent enough to keep the surface warm and dry. They should be removed daily and replaced with another thick layer. An old quilt or washable blanket makes better footing for the nursing puppies than slippery newspaper during the first week, and is softer for the mother. The quilt should be secured firmly.

SUPPLIES TO HAVE ON HAND

As soon as you have the whelping box prepared, set up the nursery by collecting the various supplies you will need when the puppies arrive. You should have the following items on hand: a box lined with towels for the puppies, a heating pad or hot water bottle to keep the puppy box warm, a pile of clean terrycloth towels or washcloths to remove membranes and to dry puppies, a stack of folded newspapers, a roll of paper towels, vaseline, rubber gloves, soap, iodine, muzzle, cotton balls, a small pair of blunt scissors to cut umbilical cords (place scissors into an open bottle of alcohol so they keep freshly sterilized), a rectal thermometer, white thread, a flashlight in case the electricity goes off, a waste container, and a scale for weighing each puppy at birth.

It is necessary that the whelping room be warm and free from drafts, because puppies are delivered wet from the mother. Keep a little notebook and pencil handy so you can record the duration of the first labor and the time between the arrival of each puppy. If there is trouble in whelping, this is the information that the veterinarian will want. Keep his telephone number handy in case you have to call him in an emergency, and warn him to be prepared for an emergency, should you need him.

WHELPING

Be prepared for the actual whelping several days in advance. Usually the female will tear up papers, try to dig nests, refuse food, and generally act restless and nervous. These may be false alarms; the real test is her temperature, which will drop to below 100°F about twelve hours before whelping. Take her temperature rectally at a set time each day, starting about a week before she is due to whelp. After her temperature goes down, keep her constantly with you or put her in the whelping box and stay in the room with her. She will seem anxious and look to you for reassurance. During the birth, if necessary, be prepared to remove the membranes covering the puppy's head if the mother fails to do this, for the puppy could smother otherwise.

The mother should start licking the puppy as soon as it is out of the sac, thus drying and stimulating it, but if she does not perform this task you can do it with a rough towel, instead. The afterbirth should follow

WHELPING BOX

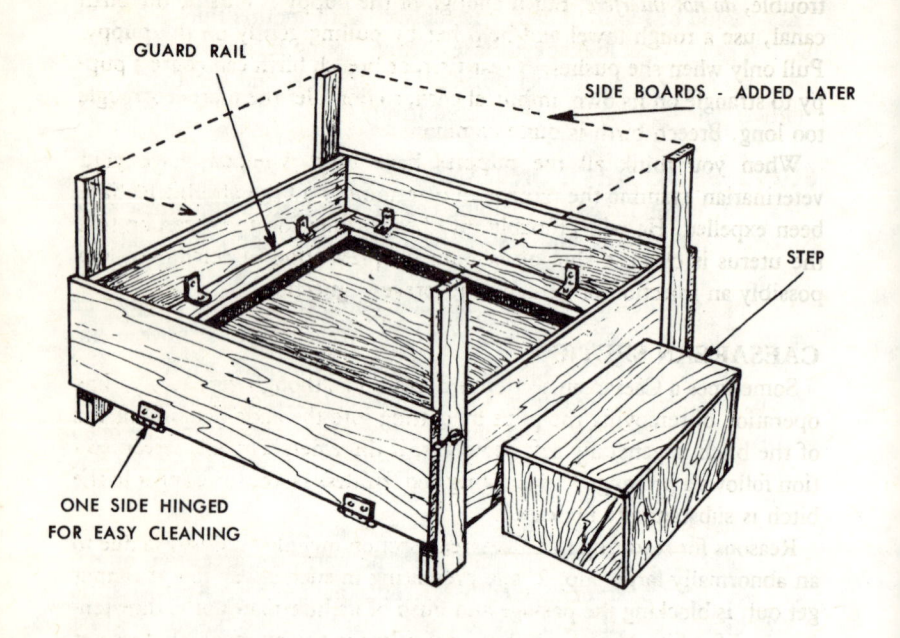

Labels on figure: GUARD RAIL; SIDE BOARDS – ADDED LATER; STEP; ONE SIDE HINGED FOR EASY CLEANING

the birth of each puppy, attached to the puppy by the umbilical cord. Watch to make sure that each is expelled, for retaining this material can cause infection. The mother probably will eat the afterbirth after biting the cord. One or two will not hurt her; they stimulate milk supply as well as labor for remaining puppies. Too many, however, can make her lose her appetite for the food she needs to feed her puppies and regain her strength, so remove the rest of them along with the soiled newspaper, and keep the box dry and clean to relieve her anxiety.

If a puppy does not start breathing, wrap him in a towel, hold him upside down with his head toward the ground, and shake him vigorously. If he still does not breathe, rub his ribs briskly; if this also fails, administer artificial respiration by compressing his ribs about twenty times per minute.

If the mother does not bite the cord, or bites it too close to the body, you should take over the job to prevent an umbilical hernia. Cut the cord a short distance from the body with your blunt scissors. Put a drop of iodine on the end of the cord; it will dry up and fall off in a few days.

The puppies should follow each other at regular intervals, but deliveries can be as short as five minutes or as long as two hours apart. A puppy may be presented backwards; if the mother does not seem to be in trouble, *do not interfere*. But if enough of the puppy is outside the birth canal, use a rough towel and help her by pulling gently on the puppy. Pull only when she pushes. A rear-first, or breech birth can cause a puppy to strangle on its own umbilical cord, so don't let the mother struggle too long. Breech birth is quite common.

When you think all the puppies have been whelped, have your veterinarian examine the mother to determine if all the afterbirths have been expelled. He will probably give her an injection to be certain that the uterus is clean, a shot of calcium for prevention of eclampsia, and possibly an injection of penicillin to prevent infection.

CAESAREAN SECTION

Sometimes a Caesarean section is necessary, although very rarely. The operation of removing the pups by cutting into the abdomen and uterus of the bitch is generally safe; however, if the emergency Caesarean section follows a prolonged, exhausting and fruitless labor, the danger to the bitch is substantially increased.

Reasons for resorting to a Caesarean section include: 1. dystocia due to an abnormally large pup, 2. one presenting in such a way that it cannot get out, is blocking the passage and birth of its littermates or is threatening the life of its dam, 3. an abnormal pelvis in the bitch which does not allow passage of the pups (such as a previous pelvic fracture), 4. inertia, 5. long and arduous labor which exhausts the bitch to the point where weakness causes the uterine and abdominal contractions to stop.

Your bitch can be operated on without losing consciousness if your veterinarian selects to operate with a hypnotic and local anesthesia. The local anesthesia is injected, the incision made, and the pups taken from the semi-conscious bitch.

Gas anesthesia is the safest type of general anesthetic for delivering pups; if barbiturate anesthetics are used intravenously, the puppies may be quite affected by these drugs as they pass through the placental barrier.

Regardless of which method is used for the Caesarean section, the patient should be kept in a warm, clean bed after surgery until she recovers from the anesthesia. The pups should not be placed with the dam until she is once again alert. If the pups are also depressed from the anesthetic, artificial respiration may be required. It is imperative that the pups be kept dry and warm following the delivery.

Offer the puppies to their mother one at a time. After she licks a pup, help it to get settled on a teat and observe them carefully. Rarely, the bitch may not accept her puppies, but this may only be a temporary situation. Watch the mother when she goes out to do her duties; her sutures (stitches) should not be subjected to any undue strain. A binder may interfere with emptying several breasts, but aside from this she will behave in a normal manner. The stitches will be removed in about two weeks and she will be as good as new.

In the cases of both normal and Caesarean delivery the female's temperature should be checked twice daily for one week after delivery. A temperature of over 102°F should be reported to your veterinarian and his directions followed to the letter.

ECLAMPSIA

Eclampsia, or "milk fever," is caused by a lowered calcium content of the blood, due to the bitch's depleting her body's calcium reserves for the production of milk. It is a word that has been fearsome in the dog-breeding world for many years. If it occurs after whelping, the puppies and the mother are in severe danger. Help must be given immediately. The female stiffens her legs, has pale gums, and is likely to have minor convulsions. Puppies must be taken from her and calcium and dextrose administered to her intravenously. However, this is a rare thing and the symptoms so obvious, that assuredly the owner's first thought is that something is wrong and that the veterinarian is needed at once. With proper nutrition during gestation and lactation, a lack of calcium is not to be expected. The best preventive medicine is to see that the female is parasite free, in good condition, and properly cared for from the day she is mated.

HOW TO TAKE CARE OF A LARGE LITTER

The size of a litter varies greatly. If your bitch has a large litter she may have trouble feeding all of the puppies. You can help her by preparing an extra puppy box. Leave half the litter with the mother and the other half in a warm place, changing their places at two-hour intervals at first. Later you may change them less frequently, leaving them all together except during the day. Try supplementary feeding, too, as soon as their eyes are open, since at about two weeks they will lap from a dish.

RAISING THE PUPPIES

Hold each puppy to a breast as soon as he is dry, for a good meal without competition. Then he may join his littermates in the basket, out of his mother's way, while she is whelping. Keep a supply of evaporated milk on hand for emergencies, or later weaning. A formula of evaporated milk, corn syrup and a little water with egg yolk should be warmed and fed in a doll or baby bottle if necessary. A supplementary feeding often helps weak pups over the hump. Keep track of birth weights and take weekly readings so you will have an accurate record of the pups' growth and health.

After the puppies have arrived, take the mother outside for a walk and drink, and then leave her to take care of them. She will probably not want to stay away more than a minute or two for the first few weeks. Be sure to keep water available at all times, and feed her milk or broth frequently, as she needs liquids to produce milk. To encourage her to eat, offer her the foods she likes best, until she asks to be fed without your tempting her. She will soon develop a ravenous appetite and should have at least two large meals a day, with dry food available in addition.

Prepare a warm place to put the puppies after they are born to keep them dry and help them to a good start in life. Cover an electric heating pad or hot-water bottle with flannel and put it in the bottom of a cardboard box. Set the box near the mother so that she can see her puppies. She will usually allow you to help, but don't take the puppies out of sight, and let her handle things if your interference seems to make her nervous.

Be sure that all of the puppies are getting enough to eat. If the mother sits or stands, instead of lying still to nurse, the probable cause is scratching from the puppies's nails. You can remedy this by clipping them, as you do hers. Manicure scissors will do for these tiny claws.

The puppies should normally be completely weaned at six weeks, although you start to feed them at three weeks. They will find it easier to lap semi-solid food. At four weeks they will eat four meals a day, and soon do without their mother entirely. Start them on mixed dog food, or leave it with them in a dish for self-feeding. Don't leave water with them all the time; at this age everything is to play with and they will use it as a wading pool. They can drink all they need if it is offered several times a day, after meals.

As the puppies grow up the mother will go into the pen only to nurse them, first sitting up and then standing. To dry her up completely, keep the mother away for longer periods, and then completely.

AIRING THE PUPPIES

The puppies may be put outside, unless it is too cold, as soon as their eyes are open. They will benefit from the sunlight and the vitamin D it provides. A rubber mat or newspapers underneath will protect them from cold or damp.

WORMING

You can expect a litter of pups to need at least one worming before they are ready to go to new homes, so take a stool sample to your veterinarian at about six weeks of age. Also, the litter should receive their first temporary shots, which are usually distemper-hepatitis-leptospirosis globulin. Today many kennels are advised by veterinarians to administer these preventative shots even earlier than six weeks, and in special cases they may begin right after birth. The puppy derives immunity from his mother's milk during the first twenty-four hours of his life; this immunity lasts for a varying length of time. Some mothers do not offer any immunity to their young at all. Therefore, in a kennel where the exposure rate is high, and many dogs come and go to shows, and disease may easily be brought to the premises, prophylactic treatment must start early. In the average home, where there is one female and one litter, six weeks is the proper time to start this treatment, and it must be repeated every one to two weeks until the puppies are old enough to have their permanent shots.

PUPPY SOCIALIZATION

Animal psychologists, research scientists and people who train dogs to work closely with people, such as trainers of seeing-eye dogs, have found that the first few weeks of a puppy's life is a critical time. The treatment a puppy receives during this stage determines whether he will become a mentally stable, trustworthy dog that likes people and is able to fit into their particular lifestyle. In general, the dog that is to be a reliable show dog or loving pet must be cuddled often, and experience pleasurable associations with people from a very early age. It is the duty of every creditable breeder to be willing to commit the amount of time necessary to socialize his puppies before he decides to breed his bitch. The behavior of his puppies, whether they are show prospects or pets, reflects on the breed and on his kennel name, two very good reasons for giving the puppies the kind of exposure to human companionship that will turn them into desirable adult dogs. This is not to deny heredity, but to stress the importance of human association in the early weeks of a puppy's life.

Some experts feel that the first three weeks of a puppy's life are completely taken up with nursing, sleeping and keeping warm snuggling with his littermates and dam, and that people-geared socialization should begin after these first three weeks. Others feel that it should begin right away, but that the form varies with the age. During the first weeks while the puppy is still gaining strength and weight and until his eyes are open, socialization should consist of simply holding the tiny pup, stroking its back and tummy for a few minutes and then putting it back with its mother. This should take place with each puppy, every day. As the puppy grows older, the time can be lengthened.

When the puppies are old enough to start eating solid foods, you can reinforce the pleasure contact by feeding them by hand. Basic training and developing receptivity to further training when they are older takes place at this point, so when you call them to you for the hand-held food, always use the same catch phrase. When the puppies are about a month old it's time to reinforce their sense of self-sufficiency and ease in new surroundings. This will also ease the transition to a new home. Remove the pups from their whelping box, which until now has circumscribed nearly their entire world, and take them to a different scene. The pup with the most adaptable nature is the one who will immediately move about and begin to explore this new setting. Puppies that are frightened and do not relax after a short time in this new environment should be put back with their mates until next time.

When they are six weeks old, puppies can be further disposed to training by putting a collar on them so they will get used to the feeling of it. Then put on the leash, not to take them for a walk, but just to let them run around in it so they get used to the idea. Later, more serious training can take place by the new owner with the puppy that is taking his place as a temperamentally sound, self-assured, friendly youngster in the world of his human companions.

HEALTH

WATCHING YOUR PUPPY'S HEALTH

First, don't be frightened by the number of diseases a dog can contract. The majority of dogs never get any of them. Don't become a dog-hypochondriac. All dogs have days when they feel lazy and want to lie around doing nothing. For the few diseases that you might be concerned about, remember that your veterinarian is your dog's best friend. When you first get your puppy, select a veterinarian whom you have faith in. He will get to know your dog and will be glad to have you consult him for advice. A dog needs little medical care, but that little is essential to his good health and well-being. He needs:

1. Proper diet at regular hours
2. Clean, roomy housing
3. Daily exercise
4. Companionship and love
5. Frequent grooming
6. Regular check-ups by your veterinarian

THE USEFUL THERMOMETER

Almost every serious ailment shows itself by an increase in the dog's body temperature. If your dog acts lifeless, looks dull-eyed, and gives the impression of illness, check his temperature by using a rectal thermometer. A stubby end rectal thermometer of either plastic or glass is best suited for this procedure. Although uncommon, there is always the hazard of possible breakage should he become excited during insertion. However, he is easily calmed if you soothe him when the routine is taking place. Hold the dog securely, and insert the thermometer, which you have lubricated with vaseline, and take a reading. The average normal temperature for your dog will be 101.5°F. Excitement may raise the temperature slightly, but any rise of more than a few points is cause for alarm, and your vet should be consulted.

EMERGENCY FIRST AID

In general, a dog will heal his wounds by licking them. If he swallows anything harmful, chances are that he will throw it up. But it will probably make you feel better to help him if he is hurt, so treat his wounds as you would your own. Wash out the dirt and apply an antiseptic.

If you fear that your dog has swallowed poison, get him to the veterinarian's *at once*. In the meantime, try and locate the source of poisoning; if he has swallowed, for example, a cleaning fluid kept in your house, check the bottle label to see if inducing the dog to vomit is necessary. In some cases, inducing the dog to vomit can be very harmful, depending upon the type of poison swallowed. Amateur diagnosis is very dangerous, when you consider that time is so extremely important. Make no delay in getting your dog emergency veterinary treatment.

Accidents

Accidents, unfortunately, will happen so it is best to be prepared. If your dog gets hit by a car, keep him absolutely quiet, move him as little as possible and get veterinary treatment as soon as possible. It is unwise to give any stimulants such as brandy or other alcoholic liquids where there is visible external hemorrhage or the possibility of internal hemorrhaging. If your dog has cut his foot or leg badly, on glass or otherwise, bandage the wound as tightly as possible to stop the bleeding. A wad of cotton may serve as a pressure bandage, which will ordinarily stop the flow of blood. Gauze wrapped around the cotton will hold it in place. Usually, applying such pressure to a wound will sufficiently stop the blood flow; however, for severe bleeding, such as when an artery is cut, a tourniquet may be necessary. Apply a tourniquet between the injury and the heart if the bleeding is severe. To tighten the tourniquet, push a pencil through the bandage and twist it. Take your dog to a veterinarian immediately since a tourniquet should not be left in place any longer than fifteen minutes.

Blood coming from an artery is bright red in color and will spurt in unison with the heart beat. From a vein, it is dark red and continuous in flow.

Burns and Scalds

Any dog kept in the home runs the risk of being burned or scalded at one time or another. If your pet sustains a serious burn, call the vet immediately as shock quickly follows such a burn. The dog should be kept warm and quiet, wrapped in a blanket. If he still shows signs of being chilled, use a hot water bottle. Clean the burn gently, removing any foreign matter such as bits of lint, hair, grass or dirt. Act as quickly as possible. Prevent exposure to air by applying olive oil or another similar substance and cover with gauze, cotton and a loose bandage. To prevent the dog from interfering with the dressing, muzzle him and have someone stay with him until veterinary treatment is at hand.

If the burn or scald is a minor one clip hair away from the affected area and apply a paste of bicarbonate of soda and water. Apply it thickly to the burned area and try to keep the dog from licking it off.

Snake Bite

If your dog is bitten by a poisonous snake, open up the wound with any available instrument that is sharp and clean. Squeeze the wound to cause a fair amount of blood to flow. This will wash the poison from the wound as much as possible. The dog should be taken to the veterinarian immediately so antitoxins can be administered. If the bite has been sustained on the leg, it is advisable to apply a tourniquet if at all possible to keep the poison from flowing further. Under no circumstances should snake bite from a poisonous snake, or its treatment, be taken lightly.

Stings

Many dogs enjoy trying to catch wasps and bees. When these insects are prevalent it is difficult to stop your pet from snapping at them. A sting frequently follows a successful catch and it often occurs inside the mouth, which can be very serious. The best remedy is to get him to a veterinarian as soon as possible, but there are some precautionary measures to follow in the meantime. If the dog has been lucky enough to only be caught on the outside of the face, try to extricate the stinger, then swab the point of entry with a solution of bicarbonate of soda. In the case of a wasp sting, use vinegar or some other acidic food stuff. A useful remedy for wasp stings is to rub the part with moistened tobacco, i.e., an unsmoked cigarette end that has been moistened.

IMPORTANCE OF INOCULATIONS

With the proper series of inoculations, your dog will be almost completely protected against disease. However, it occasionally happens that the shot does not take, and sometimes a different form of the virus appears against which your dog may not be protected.

Distemper

Probably the most virulent of all dog diseases is distemper. Young dogs are most susceptible to it, although it may affect dogs of all ages. The dog will lose his appetite, seem depressed, chilled, and run a fever. Often he will have a watery discharge from his eyes and nose. Unless treated promptly, the disease goes into advanced stages with infections of the lungs, intestines, and nervous system, and dogs that recover may be left with some impairment such as paralysis, convulsions, a twitch, or some other defect, usually spastic in nature. The best protection against this is very early inoculation with a series of permanent shots and a booster shot each year thereafter.

Hepatitis

Veterinarians report an increase in the spread of this viral disease in recent years, usually with younger dogs as the victims. The initial symptoms—drowsiness, vomiting, great thirst, loss of appetite, and a high temperature—closely resemble those of distemper. These symptoms are often accompanied by swellings of the head, neck, and abdomen. The disease strikes quickly; death may occur in just a few hours. Protection is afforded by injection with a vaccine recently developed.

Leptospirosis

This disease is carried by bacteria that live in stagnant or slow-moving water. It is carried by rats and dogs; infection is begun by the dog's licking substances contaminated by the urine or feces of infected animals. The symptoms are diarrhea and a yellowish-brownish discoloration of the jaws, tongue, and teeth, caused by an inflammation of the kidneys. This disease can be cured if caught in time, but it is best to ward it off with a vaccine which your veterinarian can administer along with the distemper shots.

Rabies

This is an acute disease of the dog's central nervous system. It is spread by infectious saliva transmitted by the bite of an infected animal. Rabies is generally manifested in one of two classes of symptoms. The first is "furious rabies," in which the dog shows a period of melancholy or depression, then irritation, and finally paralysis. The first period lasts from a few hours to several days. During this time the dog is cross and will change his position often. He loses his appetite for food and begins to lick, bite and swallow foreign objects. During the irritative phase the dog is spasmodically wild and has impulses to run away. He acts in a fearless manner and runs at and bites everything in sight. If he is caged or confined he will fight at the bars, often breaking teeth or fracturing his jaw. His bark becomes a peculiar howl. In the final, or paralytic, stage, the animal's lower jaw becomes paralyzed and hangs down; he walks with a stagger and saliva drips from his mouth. Within four to eight days after the onset of paralysis, the dog dies.

The second class of symptoms is referred to as "dumb rabies" and is characterized by the dog's walking in a bearlike manner, head down. The lower jaw is paralyzed and the dog is unable to bite. Outwardly, it may seem as though he had a bone caught in his throat.

Even if your pet should be bitten by a rabid dog or other animal, he probably can be saved if you get him to the veterinarian in time for a series of injections. However, after the symptoms have appeared no cure is possible. But remember that an annual rabies inoculation is almost certain protection against rabies. If you suspect that your dog has rabies, notify your local Health Department. A rabid dog is a danger to all who come near him.

HIP DYSPLASIA

This often crippling condition is more prevalent in large breeds than in small, but has occurred in almost every breed. The cause is not absolutely known though it is believed to be hereditary and as yet there is no known cure. The condition exists in varying degrees of severity. In general, hip dysplasia can be described as a poor fit between the two bones of the hip joint—the femur and the acetabulum—and is caused by a malformation of one or the other. Either the head of the femur is flattened causing it to slip out of the socket, or a shallowness of the acetabulum causes the femur to slip out. HD is usually graded according to severity and poorness of fit between the ball and socket, with the lowest grades being the best fit and the higher end of the scale denoting the worst cases.

HD causes stiffness in the hindlegs, considerable pain in the more severe cases and difficulty of movement. It generally manifests itself in puppyhood and can be noticed by the time the young dog is two months old. Severity can usually be determined by the age of six months. If HD is suspected, the dog should be x-rayed, and if afflicted it should not be used for breeding. Cases vary greatly, but severe pain may be more or less continuous in advanced cases. When this is true euthanasia is occasionally recommended, though medication is available to control the pain and allow the dog to move with more ease. Rigorous exercise is not recommended since it only increases the rate at which the bone surfaces wear away.

COUGHS AND COLDS

Respiratory diseases may affect the dog because he is forced to live under man-made conditions rather than in his natural environment. Being subjected to cold or a draft after a bath, sleeping near an air conditioner or in the path of a fan or near a radiator can cause respiratory ailments. The symptoms are similar to those in humans. The germs of these diseases, however, are different and do not affect both dogs and humans, so they cannot be infected by each other. Treatment is much the same as for a child with the same type of illness. Keep the dog warm, quiet, and well fed. Your veterinarian has antibiotics and other remedies to help the dog recover.

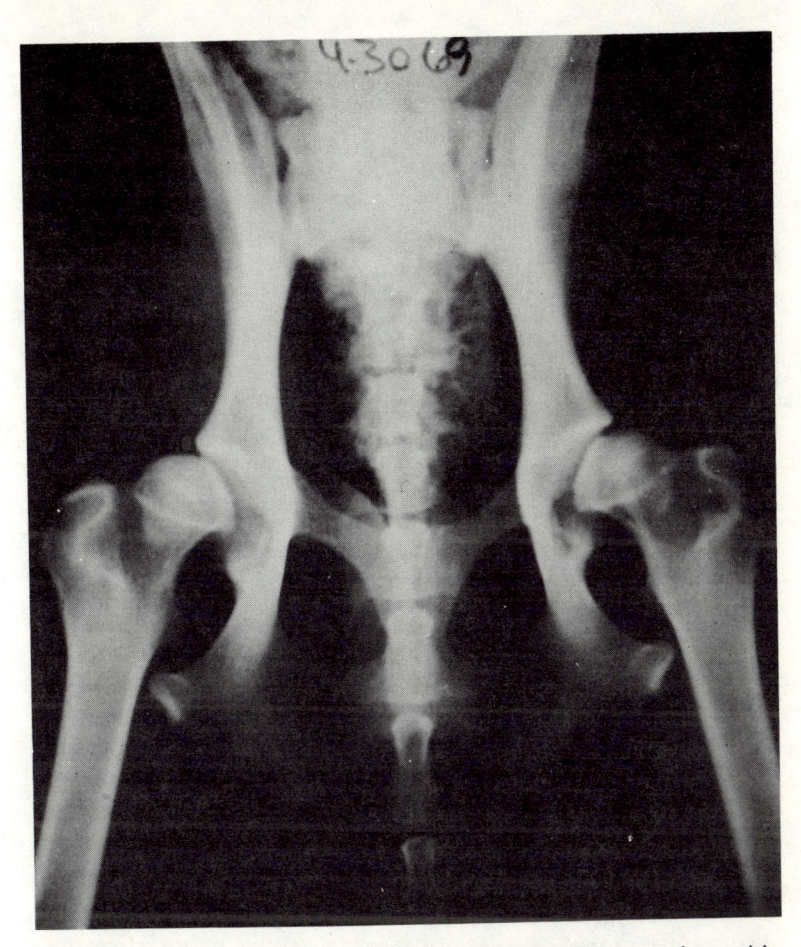

Severely dysplastic hips, such as those pictured here, are incurable and hereditary. It is generally agreed that newborn puppies do not phenotypically exhibit the hip dysplasia trait and they begin life with properly fitted hips. The first signs of hip dysplasia become noticeable as unsteady movement in puppies at several months of age. Sometimes the gait of the puppy appears normal, but he tires very easily. The length of the stride is usually limited. The condition worsens with age, as the rim of the hip socket slowly wears down until there is no longer a proper fit between the femoral head of the hip bone and the hip socket. Since a predisposition for the disease is passed from parent to offspring, it is imperative that no dog exhibiting signs of hip dysplasia be used for breeding.

DIABETES MELLITUS (Sugar Diabetes)

This is a disease wherein the sugar balance of the body is disturbed because of insufficient production of the hormone insulin. The pancreas secretes insulin which regulates carbohydrate/sugar usage. When the insulin-producing cells are damaged, the condition arises. It is marked by an increase in the blood sugar level and an excessive amount of sugar is excreted in the urine.

Symptoms of the condition are great thirst, increased urination and loss of weight while the appetite and food consumption increases. The signs vary in severity. If overlooked, emaciation and collapse rapidly occur. The dog can go into a diabetic coma and die.

Treatment is the same as for human diabetes, utilizing dietary regulation and insulin injections if necessary. The diet should be one of very low fat, with a low percentage of carbohydrate and a higher pecentage of protein. The insulin dose must be adjusted as indicated by urine tests which your veterinarian can teach you to administer at home. The test makes use of chemically treated sticks, pale yellow in color, which turn to various shades of green when dipped in urine. The darker the shade, the more serious the condition.

INTERNAL PARASITES

There are four common internal parasites that may infect your dog. These are roundworms, hookworms, whipworms, and tapeworms. The first three can be diagnosed by laboratory examination; the presence of tapeworms is determined by seeing segments in the stool or attached to the hair around the tail. Do not under any circumstances attempt to worm your dog without the advice of your veterinarian. After first determining what type of worm or worms are present, he will advise you of the best method of treatment.

A dog or puppy in good physical condition is less susceptible to worm infestation than a weak dog. Proper sanitation and a nutritious diet help in preventing worms. One of the best preventative measures is to always have clean, dry bedding for your dog. This will diminish the possibility of reinfection due to flea or tick bites.

Heartworms

Heartworm infestation in dogs is passed by mosquitoes and can be a life threatening problem. Dogs with the disease tire easily, have difficulty breathing, cough and may lose weight despite a hearty appetite. If caught in the early stages, the disease can be effectively treated; however, the administration of daily preventative medicine throughout the spring, summer and fall months is strongly advised. Your veterinarian must first take a blood sample from your dog to test for the presence of the disease, and if the dog is heartworm-free, pills or liquid medicine can be prescribed that will protect against any infestation.

It was formerly believed that heartworms occured only in warmer climates, but it is now known that they may occur anywhere that they can be carried by any of several species of mosquitoes.

Adult worms are found in the right side of the heart, the vena cavae and the pulmonary artery. There the eggs develop and are released as microfilariae. The microfilariae circulate in the blood of the dog until a mosquito ingests them, starting the larval growth cycle. Being carried by the various mosquito species induces the third-stage larval development. The third-stage larvae are re-deposited during a subsequent feeding by the mosquito and proceed to grow into mature heartworms.

Microfilariae remain inactive while in the blood of the dog in which they were originally deposited by the female. It is only after they have been ingested by a subsequent mosquito and redeposited in another host that they begin to develop. These larvae lodge in subcutaneous tissue or muscle where they stay about three months, when at between three and four months they migrate to the heart. Three to four months later the adult worm begins producing microfilariae.

Adult worms are creamy white in color. The female grows to 11 or 12 inches in length, the male, to six or seven inches. The sexes are distinquished by length since both are about the diameter of the lead in a mechanical pencil. Each mature female worm is capable of producing 30,000 microfilariae each day. A hundred adult females can account for about two billion microfilariae in the body of a dog since microfilariae live up to two years.

Apparently canines of all ages are susceptible to heartworm infestation, but they must have been exposed to mosquitoes in order to have acquired the third-stage infective larvae. Heartworm infection increases markedly as the dog matures. If left undetected, it will erode the heart.

A microscopic search for microfilariae is necessary to prove that adult worms are present. Because of the large number and size of the worms, treatment must be careful and slow to minimize damage to the circulatory system.

SKIN AILMENTS

Any persistent scratching may indicate an irritation. Whenever you groom your dog, look for the reddish spots that may indicate eczema, mange, or fungal infection. Rather than treating your dog yourself, take him to the veterinarian, as some of the conditions may be difficult to eradicate and can cause permanent damage to his coat.

External Parasites

The dog that is groomed regularly and provided with clean sleeping quarters should not be troubled by fleas, ticks, or lice. If the dog should become infested with any of these parasites, he should be treated with medicated dip bath or the new oral medications that are presently available.

Mange

There are two types of mange, sarcoptic and follicular, both of which are caused by a parasite. The former is by far the more common, and results in an intense irritation, causing violent scratching. Close examination will reveal small red spots which become filled with pus. This is a highly contagious condition, and any dog showing signs of the disease should be isolated. Consult your veterinarian for the proper treatment procedures. Follicular mange is very much harder to cure, but fortunately, it is much rarer and less contagious. This disease will manifest itself as bare patches appearing on the skin, which becomes thickened and leathery. A complete cure from this condition is only rarely effected.

Eczema

This disease occurs most often in the summer months and affects the dog down the back, especially just above the root of the tail. It should not be confused with mange, as it is not caused by a parasite. One of the principle causes of eczema is improper nutrition, which makes the dog susceptible to disease. Hot, humid weather predisposes the growth of bacteria, which can invade a susceptible dog and thereby cause skin irritations and lesions. It is imperative that the dog gets relief from the itching that is symptomatic of the disease as this self-mutilation by scratching will only help to spread the inflammation. Antibiotics may be necessary if a bacterial infection is, indeed, present. The dog must be thoroughly ridded of fleas to avoid any recurrance of the scratching that can spread the disease.

Moist eczema, commonly referred to as "hot spots," is a rapidly appearing skin disease that produces a moist infection. Spots appear very suddenly and may spread rapidly in a few hours, infecting several parts of the body. These lesions are generally bacterially infected and are extremely itchy, which will cause the dog to scratch frantically and further damage the afflicted areas. Vomiting, fever and an enlargement of the lymph nodes may occur. The infected areas must be clipped to the skin and thoroughly cleaned. Your veterinarian will prescribe an anti-inflammatory drug and antibiotics, as well as a soothing emollient to relieve itching.

EYES, EARS, TEETH AND NAILS

If your dog is to remain in good health, you must be aware of the need for periodic "examinations" in which you routinely inspect him for unusual signs of irritation or infection. In most cases, the tell-tale warning signals are any unusual swelling, discharge or redness that may appear, especially after an injury.

The eyes, because of their sensitivity, are prone to injury and infection. Dogs that spend a great deal of time outdoors in heavily wooded areas may return from an exercise excursion with watery eyes, the result of brambles and high weeds scratching them. The eyes may also be irritated by dirt and other foreign matter.

Should your dog's eyes appear red and watery, a mild solution can be mixed at home for a soothing washing. Your veterinarian will be able to tell you what percentage of boric acid, salt, or other medicinal compound to mix with water.

You must monitor your dog's eyes after such a solution is administered; if the irritation persists, or if there is a significant discharge, immediate veterinary attention is warranted.

Your dog's ears, like his eyes, are extremely sensitive and can also be prone to infection, should wax and/or dirt be allowed to build up. Ear irritants may be present in the form of mites, soap or water, or foreign particles which the dog has come into contact with while romping through a wooded area. If your dog's ears are bothering him, you will know it—he will scratch and paw them, shake his head, and the ears will show a foul-smelling dark secretion. This pasty secretion usually signals the onset of *otorrhea*, or ear canker, and at this stage proper veterinary care is essential if the dog's hearing is not to be permanently impaired. In the advanced stages of ear canker, tissue builds up within the ear, and the ear canal becomes blocked off, thus eliminating the hearing abilities of that ear.

If this is to be prevented, you should wash your dog's ears as they require it, with a very dilute solution of hydrogen peroxide and water, or an antibacterial ointment, as your vet suggests. In any case, the ears, because of their delicacy, are to be washed gently, with a soft cloth or cotton.

The good health of your pet's teeth can be maintained by his regular use of a chew product such as Nylabone® or Nylaball®, which serves to clean the teeth of tartar accumulation and massage and stimulate the gums. With puppies, a chew product helps to relieve the discomfort of the teething stage, and of course prevents the pup's chewing of your furniture and slippers!

A periodic inspection of your dog's mouth will alert you to any problem he might have that would require a trip to the veterinarian's office. Any signs of tooth or gum sensitivity, redness or swelling, signal the need for professional treatment. Also, it is best to have your pet's teeth scraped once or twice a year, at the time that he goes to the vet's for his general physical check-up. This simple procedure removes any excess tartar that has accumulated on his teeth that could cause degeneration of tooth enamel, if left to build up.

If you live in a city and walk your dog regularly on pavement, chances are that his nails are kept trimmed from the "wear and tear" they receive from the sidewalks. However, if your dog gets all of his exercise in your yard, or if his nails simply grow rather quickly, it will occasionally be necessary for you to clip his nails. It is best for you to have your veterinarian show you the proper way to perform the nail clipping at first. Special care must always be taken to avoid cutting too far and reaching the "quick." If you cut into the quick of the nail, it will bleed, so it is easy to see why an expert must show you the proper procedure. A nail clipper designed especially for dogs can be purchased at any pet shop.

CARE OF THE AGED DOG

With the increased knowledge and care available, there is no reason why your dog should not live to a good old age. As the years go by he may need a little additional care. Remember that an excessively fat dog is not healthy, particularly as he grows older, so limit the older dog's food accordingly. He needs exercise as much as ever, although his heart cannot bear the strain of sudden and violent exertion. Failing eyesight or hearing means lessened awareness of dangers, so you must protect him more than ever.

Should you decide at this time to get a puppy, to avoid being without a dog when your old friend is no longer with you, be very careful how you introduce the puppy. He naturally will be playful and will expect the older dog to respond to his advances. Sometimes the old dog will get a new lease on life from a new puppy, but he may be consumed with jealousy. Do not give the newcomer the attention that formerly was exclusively the older dog's. Feed them apart, and show your old friend that you still love him the most; the puppy, not being accustomed to individual attention, will not mind sharing your love.

TATTOOING

Tattooing is an increasing popular method of identifying your dog that has met with growing success in assuring the safe return of lost or stolen dogs. Several registries exist that will record a dog's tattoo number along with his owner's name, address and telephone number. Two types of tattoo numbers can be assigned. In the case of mixed breed dogs, the owner's social security number is generally used; in the case of pedigreed dogs, the dog's AKC registration number is used. These two numbers are the most common means of identification. The groin or inside of the ear is the usual spot for the tattoo mark, though cases have been cited in which a dog's ear was cut off to eliminate the possibility of catching the dognappers.

For a minor fee, your veterinarian can do the simple, painless job that may insure the return of a beloved pet or show dog. Such return would be reward enough for the few minutes it takes to have this simple procedure done. Since a puppy grows very rapidly, it is best not to have him tattooed until he is at least four months old to avoid any possible smearing of the tattoo ink. There is almost no danger of infection if the job is done properly and exhibitors run no risk of having the show dog's career impaired by the tattoo mark since the AKC has ruled that no judge may disqualify or penalize a dog because of a tattoo.

Your local kennel club will be able to supply the name of a registry in your area.

SHOWING

There is no greater pleasure for the owner than showing a beautiful dog perfectly groomed and trained for the show ring. Whether he wins or not, it is gratifying to show a dog in superb condition, one that is a credit to your training and care. A great deal of preparation, both for you and your dog, is needed before the day that you do any serious winning. Showing is not as easy as it looks, even if you have a magnificent dog. He must be presented to the judge so that all of his good points are shown to advantage. This requires practice in gaiting, daily grooming from puppyhood, and the proper diet to make him sound in body.

When you buy your puppy you probably will think he is the best in the country and possibly in the world, but before you enter the highly competitive world of dog shows, get an unbiased expert opinion. Visit a few dog shows as a spectator and make mental notes of what is required of the handlers and dogs. Watch how the experienced handlers manage their dogs to bring out their best points.

HOW TO SELECT A SHOW DOG

If you are planning to show your dog, it is best not to buy a puppy any younger than four or six months of age. Since it is difficult at best to predict what a puppy will look like at maturity, you cannot rely wholly on its appearance while it is only six or eight weeks old. By doing a certain amount of homework before purchasing your show dog, you can be assured to an extent that you will end up with a show quality dog that will hold its own in the show rings. Before going out to buy, read some good books on your breed. Consult a reputable book of standards for the breed to get an idea of what the dog should look like as an adult. Remember that no individual dog ever completely achieves the standard, but knowing the important conformational points of the breed will help to illustrate what you are aiming for in your show dog. Attending dog shows and talking with veterans who have been in the dog game for a while will give you valuable information to use when choosing your own show prospect.

One of the best assurances you can get in a field where there are no real guarantees is to search out well-known breeders who are known to have successfully bred show winners through several generations. Ask to look at the pedigree of any puppy you are considering buying, noting whether there are numerous top-quality dogs in the ancestry. Have the sire and dam of the litter you are interested in been bred before, and if so, what was the overall quality of their previous offspring? If they have produced consistently good dogs through several of the same pairings, your chances of getting a good specimen are fairly high. If the stud or bitch, or both, are unproven in previous litters, the probability of attaining top quality in the puppies is less likely.

In general, the rule of thumb to follow is to go by the expertise of the breeder. A reputable breeder will sell you the best dog possible if you make it clear to him that the dog will definitely be used for a show career. The show contender you purchase not only represents you as its owner, but also reflects the quality of the kennel of the breeder. The reputation of both exhibitor and breeder is made by the quality of the dogs they present, so careful selection of a show dog is essential to all involved.

TYPES OF DOG SHOWS

There are various types of dog shows. The American Kennel Club sanctioned matches are shows at which purebred dogs may compete, but not for championship points. These are excellent for you to enter to accustom you and your dog to showing. If your dog places in a few match shows, then you might seriously consider entering the big-time shows. An American Kennel Club all-breed show is one at which purebred dogs compete for championship points. An American Kennel Club specialty show is for one breed only. It may be held in conjunction with an all-breed show (by designating the classes at that show as its specialty show) or it may be held entirely apart. Obedience trials are different in that in them the dog is judged according to his obedience and ability to perform, not by his conformation to the breed standard.

There are two types of championship conformation shows: *benched* and *unbenched*. At a benched show your dog must be on his appointed bench during the advertised hours of the show's duration. He may be removed from the bench only to be taken to the exercise pen or to be groomed (an hour before the showing) in an area designated for handlers to set up their crates and grooming tables. At an unbenched show your car may serve as a bench for your dog.

To become a champion your dog must win fifteen points in competition with other dogs; a portion of the fifteen points must be awarded as major point wins (three to five points) under different judges.

HOW TO ENTER

If your dog is purebred and registered with the AKC—or eligible for registration—you may enter him in the appropriate show class for which his age, sex, and previous show record qualify him. You will find coming shows listed in the different dog magazines or at your petshop. Write to the secretary of the show, asking for the premium list. When you receive the entry form, fill it in carefully and send it back with the required entry fee. Then, before the show, you should receive your exhibitor's pass, which will admit you and your dog to the show. Here are the five official show classes:

PUPPY CLASS: Open to dogs at least six months and not more than twelve months of age. Limited to dogs whelped in the United States and Canada.

NOVICE CLASS: Open to dogs six months of age or older that have never won a first prize in any class other than puppy class, and less than three first prizes in the novice class itself. Limited to dogs whelped in the United States or Canada.

BRED BY EXHIBITOR CLASS: Open to all dogs, except champions, six months of age or over which are exhibited by the same person, or his immediate family, or kennel that was the recognized breeder on the records of the American Kennel Club.

AMERICAN-BRED CLASS: Open to dogs that are not champions, six months of age or over, whelped in the United states after a mating which took place in the United States.

OPEN CLASS: Open to dogs six months of age or over, with no exceptions.

In addition there are local classes, the Specials Only class, and brace and team entries.

For full information on dog shows, read the book *How to Show Your Own Dog,* by Virginia Tuck Nichols. (T.F.H.)

JUNIOR SHOWMANSHIP

If you have decided that you and your dog are going to go the show route, you might consider having your youngster show the dog in the ring. If your child has an especially good relationship with his pet, or if he has trained the dog himself, as many children do, then Junior Showmanship might be a good learning experience.

Junior Showmanship is competition among children of different age groups, handling dogs owned by their immediate families. The age divisions are: Novice A, for 10 to 12 year olds; Novice B, for those boys and girls from 13 to 16 (entrants in these two classes must have one or no prior Junior Showmanship wins); Open A for those 10 to 12 years of age; Open B for those 13 to 16 (these entrants must have earned two or more Junior Showmanship awards).

Children involved in JS have the wonderful opportunity to feel a sense of achievement and victory, should they walk away with the ribbons after a show. Even still, winning is not the most important factor here: the pride and responsibility the youngster feels at having reached the ring is surely worth the effort and discipline required to enter showmanship competition.

For more information on JS, and to obtain a rules and regulations booklet, you can contact the American Kennel Club in New York.

ADVANCED PREPARATION

Before you go to a show your dog should be trained to gait at a trot beside you, with head up and in a straight line. In the ring you will have to gait your dog around the edge with other dogs and then individually up and down the center runner. In addition the dog must stand for examination by the judge, who will look at him closely and feel his head and body structure. He should be taught to stand squarely, hind feet slightly back, head up on the alert. Showing requires practice training sessions in advance. Get a friend to act as judge and set the dog up and "show" him a few minutes every day.

THE DAY OF THE SHOW

Don't feed your dog the morning of the show, or give him at most a light meal. He will be more comfortable in the car on the way, and will show more enthusiastically. When you arrive at the show grounds, find out where he is to be benched and settle him there. Your bench or stall number is on your identification ticket, and the breed name will be on placards fastened to the ends of the row of benches. Once you have your dog securely fastened to his stall by a bench chain (use a bench crate instead of a chain if you prefer), locate the ring where your dog will be judged (the number and time of showing will be on the program of judging which came with your ticket). After this you may want to take your dog to the exercise ring to relieve himself, and give him a small drink of water. Your dog will have been groomed before the show, but give him a final brushing just before going into the show ring. When your breed judging is called, it is your responsibility to be at the ringside ready to go in. The steward will give you an armband which has on it the number of your dog.

Then, as you step into the ring, try to keep your knees from knocking! Concentrate on your dog and before you realize it you'll be out again, perhaps back with the winners of each class for more judging and finally, with luck, it will be over and you'll have a ribbon and trophy—and, of course, the most wonderful dog in the world!

Index

A

Affenpinscher, 442-444
Afghan Hound, 114-118
African Lion Hound, 177
Aged dog, care of, 596
Airedale Terrier, 348-351
Akita, 191-194
Alsatian Wolf Dog, 256
Alaskan Malamute, 195-199
American Foxhound, 151-156
American Kennel Club, 549
American Staffordshire Terrier, 352-354
American Water Spaniel, 63-65
Apso Seng Kye, 528
Australian Kennel Club, 549
Australian Silky Terrier, 492
Australian Terrier, 355

B

Barbet, 498
Barbichon dogs, 498
Barkless dog, 119
Basenji, 119-121
Basset Hound, 122-126
Beagle, 127-131
Bearded Collie, 200-204
Bedlington Terrier, 358-361
Belgian Malinois, 205-208
Belgian Sheepdog, 209-213
Belgian Tervuren, 214-219
Berger de Brie, 236
Bernese Mountain Dog, 220-222
Bichon Bolognese, 498
Bichon Frise, 498-501

Bichon Maltaise, 498
Bichon Ravenese, 498
Bichon Teneriffe, 498-499
Black and Tan Coonhound, 132-134
Blenheim Toy Spaniel, 453-457
Bloodhound, 135-138
Border Terrier, 362-365
Borzoi, 139-142
Boston Terrier, 502-505
Bouvier des Flandres, 223-227
Boxer, 228-234
Breeding, preparation for, 570-571
Briard, 235-240
Briard Club of America, 236
British Kennel Club, 549
Brittany Spaniel, 66-70
Brussels Griffon, 445-448
Bulldog, 506-511
Bullenbeissers, 229
Bullmastiff, 241-243
Bull Terrier, 367-370
Burns and scalds, 587-588

C

Ca Eivissenc, 162
Caesarean section, 581-582
Cairn Terrier, 371- 374
Caius, Dr., 423
Canadian Kennel Club, 549
Cantab Terrier, 412
Cardigan Welsh Corgi, 339-342
Chesapeake Bay Retriever, 28-32
Chewing, 552-555

603

Chien de Berger Belge, 205, 214
Chihuahua, 449-452
Chow Chow, 512-514
Clumber Spaniel, 71-73
Cocker Spaniel, 74-78
Collie, rough and smooth, 244-250
Coughs and colds, 590
Cumberland Terrier, 397
Curly-Coated Retriever, 33-35

D

Dachshund, smooth, wire-haired and longhaired, 143-150
Dalmatian, 515-518
Dandie Dinmont Terrier, 375-379
Darwin, Charles, 10
Deutscher Schaferhund, 256
deWilloughby, Lady, 486
Diabetes mellitus, 592
Disciplining, 551
Distemper, 588
Dobermann, Herr Louis, 251-252
Doberman Pinscher, 251-255
Dodge, Geraldine, 80
Dog Shows, 599-601
  advanced preparation, 601
  entering, 599-600
  types, 599
Dominance, 573
Drahthaar, 25
Dukes of Gordon, 51
Dutch barge dog, 523
Dwarf dog, 340, 344

E

Ears, care of, 595
Ecclefechan, 376
Eclampsia, 582
Eczema, 594

Emergency first aid, 586-588
English Cocker Spaniel, 79-83
Englishe Dogges, 423
English Foxhound, 151-156
English Setter, 47-50
English Springer Spaniel, 84-90
English Toy Spaniel, 453-457
Epagneul Breton, 66
Epistatis, 574
External parts of dog, chart, 575
Eyes, care of, 595

F

Falliscus, Gratius, 290
Fell Terrier, 397
Field Spaniel, 91-93
Flat-Coated Retriever, 36-38
Forest and Stream, 16, 28, 112
Foxhound, 151-156
  American, 151-154
  English, 151, 155-156
Fox Terrier, smooth and wire, 380-386
French Bulldog, 519-522

G

Genealogy of the dog, 12
Genetics, application of, 571-577
Gerland, Dr. 257
German Shepherd Dog, 256-263
German Shorthaired Pointer, 19-23
German Wirehaired Pointer, 24-27
Giant Schnauzer, 264-268
Golden Retriever, 39-42
Gordon Setter, 51-56
Great Dane, 269-277
Great Pyrenees, 278-281
Greyhound, 157-159
Groenendael, 209, 210, 214
Guy Mannering, 375

H
Hall, Jay, 256
Harrier, 160-161
Harsanyi, Zsolt, 302
Heartworms, 592
Heim, Professor Albert, 220-221
Hepatitis, 589
Highland Collie, 201
Hinks, James, 367-368
Hip dysplasia, 590
Hounds, 114-190
Housebreaking, 551-552
　outdoors, 552
Hulme, John, 401
Hungarian Pointer, 105

I
Ibizan Hound, 162-165
Inoculations, importance of, 588-90
Irish Setter, 57-60
Irish Terrier, 387-391
Irish Water Spaniel, 94-97
Irish Wolfhound, 166-169
Italian Greyhound, 458-460

J
Japanese Chin, 461-463
Junior Showmanship, 600-601
Jones, Frank, 412

K
Keeshond, 523-527
Kerry Blue Terrier, 392-395
King Charles Toy Spaniel, 453-457
"King of Dogs," 115
Komondor, 282-285
Komor, 283
Kuvasz, 286-289

L
Labrador Retriever, 43-46
Lakeland Terrier, 396-400
Large litter, care of, 582
Laverack, Edward, 48
Leptospirosis, 589
Les Amis du Briard, 236
Lhasa Apso, 528-530

M
Magyars, 304
Maltese, 464-466
Manchester Terrier, 401-404
Mange, 594
Massivius, 290
Mastiff, 290-293
Mating cycle, 568
McCarthy, Justin, 94
Mendelian expectation chart, 572
Miacis, 10
Miniature Pinscher, 469-473
Miniature Poodle, 531-536
Miniature Schnauzer, 405-409
Mollosian dog, 290
Monkey Terrier, 443
Morrison, Mr., 486
Mountain Collie, 201
Mutants, 574
Mutation, 574

N
Nails, care of, 596
Newfoundland, 294-298
Non-Sporting Dogs, 498-543
Norfolk Terrier, 410-415
Norwegian Elkhound, 170-173
Norwich Terrier, 410-415

O
Obedience trials, 562-563
　classes, 562

605

Old English Sheepdog, 299-301
Origin of Species, 10
Otter Hound, 174-176

P

Palfalvy, Dr. Sandor, 302
Papers, registration, 548
Papillon, 474-477
Parasites, external, 594
Parasites, internal, 592-593
Patterdale Terrier, 397
Pekingese, 478-480
Pembroke Welsh Corgi, 343-347
Pleiotropy, 574
Poltalloch Terriers, 439
Pointer, 15-18
Policeihund, 256
Pomeranian, 481-484
Poodle, 485, 531-536
   Miniature, 531-536
   Standard, 531-536
Prince Charles Toy Spaniel, 453-457
Psovoi, 139
Pug, 486-488
Pugnaces, 290
Puli, 302-305
Puppies, airing, 583
   care of, 547-555
   raising, 582-583
   socialization of, 584-585
Purvis, Hugh, 376

R

Rabies, 589-590
Recessiveness, 573
Recombination, 573-574
Registration of puppies, 548-549
Reh Pinschers, 470
Rhodesian Ridgeback, 177-179

Riesenschnauzers, 264
Rosseau, Percival L., 111
Rothbury Terrier, 358
Rottweiler, 306-309
Royal dog of Egypt, 180
Royal Humane Society, 294
Ruby Toy Spaniel, 453-457

S

Saint Bernard, 310-315
Saluki, 180-182
Samoyed, 316-321
Schipperke, 537-539
Scottish Deerhound, 183-186
Scottish Terrier, 416-419
Scott, Sir Walter, 375-376
Sealyham Terrier, 420-422
Sex-limited, 576
Sex-linked, 574
Shetland Sheepdog, 322-327
Shih Tzu, 489-491
Show dog, selection of, 547, 598-599
Siberian Husky, 328-333
Silky Terrier, 492-494
Skin ailments, 593-594
Skye Terrier, 423-427
Smith, E. Bradshaw, 376
Snake bite, 588
Socialization of puppy, 584-585
Soft-Coated Wheaten Terrier, 423-431
Spaniel family, 61-62
Spaying, 564
Sporting Dogs, 15-113
Sports, 574
Staffordshire Bull Terrier, 432-434
Standard Poodle, 531-536
Standard Schnauzer, 334-338
Stings, 588
Stud, selection of, 570

Sugar Diabetes, 592
Sussex Spaniel, 98-100
Sydney Silky, 492

T
Tattooing, 596
Teeth, care of, 595-596
Terriers, 348-441
Thermometer, use of, 586
Tibetan Terrier, 540-543
Tomarctus, 11
Toy Dogs, 442-497
Toy Manchester Terrier, 467-468
Toy Poodle, 485
Training equipment, 557-558
   lessons, 557
   schools, 561-562

U
Ulmer Mastiff, 269

V
Vizsla, 104-106

W
Weimaraner, 107-110
Welsh Springer Spaniel, 101-103
West Highland White Terrier, 438-441
Welsh Terrier, 435-437
Westmoreland Terrier, 397
Whelping, 597-581
   chart, 569
Whippet, 187-190
Wirehaired Pointing Griffon, 111-113
Working dogs, 191-347
World War II, 279
Whelping quarters, preparation of, 578-579
   supplies, 579
Worming, 583-584

Y
Yorkshire Terrier, 495-497

SUGGESTED BIBLIOGRAPHY

H-969 DOG BREEDING FOR PROFESSIONALS, by Dr. Herbert Richards. Here is the most complete and authoritative book on breeding ever published, covering in great detail the entire breeding process. Step-by-step photos of actual matings and whelpings, which some readers may find objectionable, are included.
ISBN 0-87666-659-4
224 pages, 105 black & white photos, 62 color photos

H-976 DOG GENETICS, by Dr. Carmelo Battaglia. This informative guide clarifies the principles of genetics as they apply to the breeding of dogs and focuses on easy-to-understand plans for producing quality puppies. Structural color charts aid the breeder in working out on paper the prospects for their own breeding plans and the potential quality of their litters.
ISBN 0-87666-662-4
192 pages, 68 black & white photos, 10 color photos, 6 color charts.

H-934 DOG OWNER'S ENCYCLOPEDIA OF VETERINARY MEDICINE, by Dr. Allan Hart. Here is a book that will become, next to his pet itself, the truest friend a dog-owner has. Page after page and chapter after chapter of valuable, pertinent information that allows an owner to make sure that his pet is given the best of care at all times.
ISBN 0-87666-287-4
186 pages, 61 black & white photos, 25 line illustrations

PS-607 HOW TO SHOW YOUR OWN DOG, by Virginia Tuck Nichols, paves the highroad to success in the fascinating and steadily growing avocation of exhibiting dogs. All of the intricacies of the show ring are explained in detail, coupled with explicit treatments of the basics of dog shows; terms and definitions, how a champion is made, getting ready for the show, AKC rules and regulations, etc. Plus a bonus chapter on the tricks of the trade.
ISBN 0-87666-390-0
254 pages, 136 black & white photos, 10 line illustrations

H-972 DOG TRAINING, by Lew Burke. With the help of this book, any owner can do a first class job of training his dog. Fully and completely illustrated, the author discusses vital, new concepts of training which, if carefully followed, are guaranteed to have long-lasting results.
ISBN 0-87666-651-9
255 pages, 64 black and white photos, 23 color photos